I SPEAK OF THE CITY

MAURICIO TENORIO-TRILLO

The
University of
Chicago Press
Chicago and
London

I Speak of the City

MEXICO
CITY
AT THE
TURN
OF THE
TWENTIETH
CENTURY

MAURICIO TENORIO-TRILLO

is professor of history at the University of Chicago, and *profesor asociado* at the Centro de Investigación y Docencia Económicas, Mexico City. He is the author, among others, of *Mexico at the World's Fairs, Argucias de la historia, De cómo ignorar*, and *Historia y celebración*.

The University of Chicago Press, Chicago 60637
The University of Chicago Press, Ltd., London
© 2012 by The University of Chicago
All rights reserved. Published 2012.
Printed in the United States of America
21 20 19 18 17 16 15 14 13 12   1 2 3 4 5
ISBN-13: 978-0-226-79271-2 (cloth)
ISBN-10: 0-226-79271-4 (cloth)

Library of Congress Cataloging-in-Publication Data
Tenorio-Trillo, Mauricio, 1962–
    I speak of the city : Mexico City at the turn of the twentieth
century / Mauricio Tenorio-Trillo.
        pages. cm.
    Includes bibliographical references and index.
    ISBN-13: 978-0-226-79271-2 (cloth : alkaline paper)
    ISBN-10: 0-226-79271-4 (cloth : alkaline paper) 1. Mexico
City (Mexico)—History. 2. Mexico City (Mexico)—Social
conditions. I. Title.
F1386.3.T465 2012
972'.530816—dc23   2011052768

A Beatriz, César, Fernando, Fausto, Gerardo, Helena y Jean . . .
A la Xaparreu.

hablo de la ciudad inmensa, realidad diaria hecha de dos palabras:
los otros,
y en cada uno de ellos hay un yo cercenado de un nosotros,
un yo a la deriva,
hablo de la ciudad construida por los muertos, habitada por sus tercos
fantasmas, regida por su despótica memoria,

I speak of the immense city, that daily reality composed of two words:
the others
and in every one of them there is an I clipped from a we,
an I adrift
I speak of the city built by the dead, inhabited by the stern ghosts, ruled
by their despotic memory

— Octavio Paz, "Hablo de la ciudad" [fragment] Vuelta,
no. 118 (September 1986), 8. Poem dedicated to, and
translated by, Eliot Weinberger

CONTENTS

ACKNOWLEDGMENTS

Friends and institutions made these essays possible. My life-long friends Gerardo Laveaga, César Fonseca, Alfredo Hidalgo, Salvador Cañez, and Eduardo Padilla walked through the city with me at an age when oblivion was an impossible mental exercise. Moreover, I could have not imagined this or any other book or essay without the people I have lost: Juan Tenorio Carmona, Leonor González, Arcelia Trillo Aviña, Melchor Solis, Fredrick Bowser, Luis Cadena, Carlos Ávila, and Charles A. Hale. My actual or virtual teachers, Raúl Valadés, Ernesto Azuela, José Luis Piñeyro, the late Cathy Nelson, the late Richard Morse, Jean Meyer, Beatriz Rojas, Fernando Escalante, William Tobin, David Brading, James Sidbury, Judith Coffin, Neal Kamil, William Forbath, Charles R. Hale, Enrique Fierro, Ida Vitale, Emilio Kourí, Dain Borges, Apen Ruiz, and Helena Bomeny, assisted me in indescribable fashions. The intellectual companionship of the *Chilakapalukulu* editorial board, Sanjay Subrahmanyam, Wang Hui, David Shulman, Muzaffar Alam, Navid Kermani, Partha Chatterjee, Philippe Burrin, and N. V. Rao, reached me in important stages of this project.

Three institutions have been kind and generous over the last years. I express my profound gratitude to the Centro de Investigación y Docencia Económicas in Mexico City, to the Department of History, the University of Texas at Austin, and to the Wissenschaftskolleg zu Berlin, which granted me the time and ambiance to complete these essays. I also thank the project "Art and National Identity in India, Japan, and Mexico," coordinated by Partha Mitter, Toshio Watanabe, and Oriana Baddeley. These scholars, in addition to Bert Winther-Tamaki, Gayatri Sinha, Naazish Ata-Ullah, and Toshiharu Omuka, helped me in particular sections. Also, I dwelled among the stacks of the Nattie Lee Benson Latin American Collection of the University of Texas at Austin for too long. I found the warmest of homes among its books and, especially, among its devoted and notable librarians. Anything I write is somehow a gesture of gratitude to them: Margo Gutiérrez, Ann Hartness, Michael Hironymous, Carmen Sacomani, Craig Schroer, and D. Gibbs. I extend my gratitude to the Institut de Historia Jaume Vicens Vives in Barcelona, whose library kindly housed me as a faithful, albeit anonymous, tenant. Fabiola Martínez, Antonio Saborit, Víctor Macías-González, Patrick Iber, Teresa Davis, Carlos Bravo, Adrian Anagnost, Ernesto Capello, Daniel Haworth, and Jessica Locke assisted me with ideas, editing, and translations. The History Department at the University of Chicago offered invaluable intellectual and economic support in the time-consuming last stages of the production of this book.

Finally, I thank my students in various Mexican and U.S. institutions. At last they will be able to perceive their impact on their teacher and to reconfirm that so much talking about walks, stories, histories, and views of cities was only their teacher's way to cope with his puzzling relationship to Mexico City.

Lucía, as always, was very much part of these essays, as we both belonged to our happy years spent between Austin, Mexico City, Chicago, and Barcelona. *Moltes gràcies Xaparreu.*

NOTE ON TRANSLATIONS

The texture of language is an important part of these stories. I would have liked to include the original version of all quotations, so that readers could fully appreciate the nature of the cultural interactions I examine. But editorial concerns prevailed, and I provide translated versions for most quotations without the original text, except for those pieces whose richness can be rendered in English only very inexactly, in which case I provide both the original and an approximate translation.

INTRODUCTION

A minute island, in a lake, where "fishes fly" and eagles eat serpents: "There we will rule . . . That [place] will become our endless city of Mexico-Tenochtitlán!"[1] According to legend, these are the origins of Mexico-Tenochtitlán, the city upon the Texcoco Lake that the people of mythical Aztlán founded in the early fourteenth century, and where their city-state would prosper endlessly. And thrive Mexico-Tenochtitlán did, before and after the Spanish Conquest, and as the capital city of a nineteenth-century nation-state (Mexico). Hence Mexico City could be described by Eça de Queiros's comments on Lisbon—"nem cria, nem inicia; vai"—that it neither raises, nor begins; it just goes.[2] For the city has no real discernible beginning. It just *vai*. I *Speak of the City* is formed by stories related, I confess, to my own experience of the *vai* of Mexico City, disguised as things that can actually secure a history: walks, urban voices, the experience of monuments, the nostalgia of past styles, and the estrangement of realities that once did not need to be named—they just were.

I focus on the years between circa 1880 and 1930 for these were the decisive decades in which Mexico City started upon the route toward what it is today, namely, a megalopolis, an ecological disaster, and the enchanting monstrous capital of a modern nation. In so being, Mexico City is not something peripheral and unintentional that should never have occurred. In fact, it has been the fulfillment of many modern promises—either rapid economic and demographic growth or cosmopolitanism. Far from being the exotic town described by foreign travelers or the mere involuntary consequence of cultural atavisms, Mexico City has been so much a part of the making of the modern that examining it is but another way to inhabit what is known as the modern world.[3]

The book, however, is not a monograph, a chronological narrative of a chunk of the city's time. Rather, it is formed by ways of essaying the history of the modern urban experience. Thus, these essays are ways of capturing different aspects of the modern urban experience: the city as a walking history textbook; the city as a global expression of the modern state; the city as an ephemeral modernist capital of the world's utopias; the city as an orientalist object; the city as an orientalist subject fascinated with Japan and India; the city as a scientific laboratory; and, finally, the city as language. By essaying modern history through an assumed marginal mirror (Mexico City), I simply depart from the uncanny conviction that Mexico City has not been the mime, but rather the unfolding of such modern phenomena as history writing, nationalism, revolutions, science, and language.

Urban Experience

The urban experience is not a cinematic one, but rather a collection of overlapping vistas that can dilate the historian's perception of the borders between past, present, and future. Entire libraries have been written on the notion of "experience" as a philosophical, historiographical, and even an urban-centered occurrence. The notion of urban experience that propels my essaying, however, appeals only marginally to the philosophical controversies about *Erlebnis*. Experience here is a concept closer to the *simultaneous* occurrence of *vivencias* (lived moments) and *ensimismamientos* (literally, one-in-one-self-ness: wondering about being conscious of consciousness). To be sure these terms do not entail a French-like conceptual repute, nor do they echo the acceptable tropical sonority of *siesta* or *sombrero*, to be incorporated easily into the English language. But for me they do the job marvelously. For *vivencias* and *ensimismamientos* are common occurrences for urban ramblers everywhere. Thus understood, experience becomes first, if not a fixed object of study for the historian, at least a well-demarcated set of historical evidences; and second, experience becomes thus the historian's guiding hope—to try to render vivid images of past urban occurrence. Hence by history of urban experience I mean the attempt to grasp a past of simultaneous and chaotic mixtures of feelings, knowledges, and wonderings (in sum, *ensimismamientos*) produced by an urban walk, a building, a monument, a street, a scientific discovery, an urban poem, or a corner (that is, *vivencias*).

This is thus a kind of history of *vivencias citadinas*, of the very experiencing of cities whose separation between past and present, alas clearly distinguishable in terms of chronology, is less conspicuous. The urban experience of the past, without my present urban experience, becomes unintelligible. Past evidence ought to be dwelled in with the familiarity of that one who has walked and seen enough streets in the present. This might be because cities produce what Georg Simmel called in 1903 the "intensification of nervous stimulation," which makes the "metropolitan man" "develop an organ protecting him against the threatening currents and discrepancies of his external environment which would uproot him . . . Intellectuality is thus seen to preserve subjective life against the overwhelming power of metropolitan life." Or perhaps cities unite *vicencias* and *ensimismamientos* because speaking of cities is to speak about, according to Octavio Paz, "that daily reality composed of two words: the others," . . . "and in every one of them there is an I clipped from a we, an I adrift."[4] Be that as it may, to write history of modern urban experiences calls for a blend of empirical research, imagination nurtured by urban life, and literary intuitions; it is, in a way, essaying the consciousness of urban *vivencias* that is also an essaying of the city-like shape of the modern consciousness.

Essaying

The essay is the narrative genre intrinsically linked to accounts of the urban experience in the past and the present. Understood as a modern genre, it is characterized by persuasion and the necessary incompleteness derived from the many realms and broad topics that any essay explores; a stylistic union of form and content through the freedom to establish empirical and conceptual connections often with irony; an esteem of what the young Georg Lukács called the joy of conceptual logic; and, finally, the need to provoke further thinking. I do not claim, however, that the essays in the book are akin to classics of the genre. My essaying is much more modest because it is above all painstaking historical research; and yet, it is also part of the important—if devalued in the English language—expansion and transmission of historical knowledge through essays.

Often I have wondered why I wrote these essays in English. There are the demands of a U.S. academic life, but quite honestly, these imperatives played a minor role in my decision. For better or for worse, one day I started these essays in my alien English and continued over the years, aware of my limitations and of the difficulties I would face in trying to publish such bizarre products. I continued in English even when anonymous reviewers of bits and pieces of the project—reviewers for a "Latin American Studies" journal at that—responded with: "the problem with Tenorio is that he thinks he writes English." Sure, but for a nonnative, writing in English becomes a mandatory challenge and an inevitable hope. It is a challenge because it is one thing to write an academic report competently in academic English, and quite another to mess up with the difficult art of essaying. And it is a hope, perhaps self-defeating, that having been in dialogue with the experience of many past and present cities thanks to the intermediation of today's lingua franca, one hopes to enter into broader dialogues through the same language. A hope also because while I talk about Mexico City, the topic is not solely, or mainly, Mexico City, and thus the optimism of reaching a wider readership gets inevitably activated.

These essays build on the insightful contributions of urban history, which have naturally nurtured the approach of an academic historian trained in the late 1980s.[5] But I originally arrived at the subject of cities by a different route—that of my own urban experience filtered through essays about the city, its intellectual life, its experience. In the early 1980s, my ignorance of various languages hindered my realization that such nineteenth-century essayists as

M. J. de Larra, João do Rio, and Manuel Gutiérrez Nájera, and twentieth-century writers such as Fernando Pessoa, Octavio Paz, Angel Rama, and Beatriz Sarlo, were already part of a larger essayist tradition that included Georg Simmel, R. Müsil, Franz Hessel, Karl Kraus, Walter Benjamin, Siegfried Kracauer, Osip Mandelstam, and Adam Zagajewski, among many others in various languages. Unconsciously, I started to smuggle my urban experience and the essayist tradition into my academic work, but as something different from the theory that historians at times use as a template to make sense of historical evidence. Essayism and the city allowed me precisely to escape the chronological accounting as well as the formalism of academic theories. An essay, writes Gabriel Zaid, a master of the genre in Spanish, "no es un informe de investigación realizado en el laboratorio: es el laboratorio mismo."—it is not a research report made in the laboratory, it is the laboratory itself.[6]

The City as Subject

How could a place be an alive historical actor? For throughout these essays the city is a subject, often a woman. In Mexico City, space acquired significant agency due to the weight of history, especially when that space turned into a repository for the infrastructure of Nation and State and the raison d'être of science and culture. This centrality explains many of the architectural, political, and urban-planning decisions of the city. But it also explains why, for instance, despite the hatred that the city produced in all the revolutionary factions that arrived in the city from the exterior world, the appeal of the city was overwhelming.

Centrality, moreover, is intrinsic to greed. Between 1880 and 1910, Mexico City acquired such political, economic, and cultural centrality—drawn from the city's long history—, that it acted as an autonomous pole of economic attraction for speculation, opportunities, and investment. The city was already the center of human capital, of a railroad network, and of many economic activities; the profit incentives and opportunities of war and revolution were added to these preexisting factors. Economically, then, it should not be very controversial to depict the city as a historical subject.

But there is a third attribute, along with their centrality and the greed they awakened, that made cities, especially Mexico City, historical characters for the historian. This is simply Mexico City's long history of being cast as a person, more specifically as a woman and, in the words of the early twentieth-century novelist Julio Sesto, a courtesan, one whose detractors, nevertheless, "could not extract a single kiss from her lips. ¡Ciudad al fin!"[7] Indeed, since colonial times, but especially during the second part of the nineteenth century, when the city regained its centrality, Mexico City had been depicted as a woman by poets, novelists, cartoonists, political speechwriters, and all sorts of scientific literature that made of the city a body, with organs and a heart. In the sanitary crises of the nineteenth century, the city was depicted in political cartoons as a sick woman. In 1901, Mexico City's most prominent illustrator, Julio Ruelas, depicted the city as a woman: a mixture of republican and modernist symbols of freedom and sovereignty.[8] Likewise, revolutionary generals, including Álvaro Obregón, identified the city as a cowardly, antirevolutionary, and licentious woman. Popular ballads identified the city as a woman. This was a trend in popular lyrics that would continue into the 1970s, with the woman remaining the most prominent allegories in writing about the city: "My city . . . washes her brown skin in the afternoon rain and when she unbraids her hair, her sad eyes close," says a tune that almost has reached the status of the city's anthem.[9]

Of course, these many characterizations could be seen as mere literary allegories, nothing more than the construction of a wooden doll manipulated in the hands of politicians, intellectuals, popular voices . . . and the historian. But whenever in Spanish I visualize the female-image of the city, its past and present become less a matter of fact and more a matter of *ensimismamiento*. This was the metaphor of the city as a subject, which was at the core of the major urban commentators of the late nineteenth and early twentieth centuries, from Dickens to Walter Benjamin, from Simmel to Salvador Novo, from Lewis Mumford to contemporary accounts such as that of Marshall Berman. Moreover, if we bear in mind while reading these essays the allure of economic, political, and cultural centrality inspired by this wooden doll, then the rigid figure acquires the agency of a historical subject that is difficult for the historian to miss. Then again, I can be accused of being simply another manipulator of the wooden doll. I hope not, but if so, please bear in mind Karl Kraus's dictum: "When I can interpret a woman as I arbitrarily wish, it is the woman's merit."[10]

On Echoes and Voices

Echoes are not voices. Yet in the midst of the noise and mess of modern urban history, what voice is not an echo and what echo is not a voice? These essays deal with a long-lasting global flow of concerns and ideas. In a way, in English my essays may sound like a de-Mexicanizing of Mexican history through Mexico City. Maybe. I, however, advance no alternative definition of Mexico or the city. I would want to return the idea of "Mexico" to the larger experimental impulses where it belongs. It is time for the word "Mexico" to mean what its people, ideas, and circumstances are: the flow. This simple proposal, I hope, would in the long run change the understanding of Mexico, and, more importantly, it would alter the global flow.[11]

Therefore, these essays undertake various "odd" parallelisms, too many crossings of assumed barriers among civilizations—the same Mexico or the U.S. or France or Japan. In terms of these barriers, nonetheless, my aim is neither to deny nor to affirm the existence of so-called "civilizational" differences between Mexico and the U.S., for example. My goal is simply to show that, in the case of the region we now call Mexico City, cultural phenomena are not about the relationships of spiritual Ariels vs. materialist and powerful Calibans. I aim, rather, to show that these matters are about the Island and the chaotic interactions of all its modern castaways.

On Limits

More than well-articulated theories, personal preoccupations, as it were, drive my essaying. On one hand, I am concerned with history and freedom; on the other, with words. History, thought Benedetto Croce, would liberate individuals and societies from all sorts of atavism. In its Enlightenment origins, history was, as historian Constantin Fasolt maintains, a powerful and dangerous form of knowledge. It therefore has been, some believe, the acid that dissolves all absolutes, even history itself. Whether seen as a historicist acid, or as the path of power or/and freedom—as Richard McKean submitted—, history, I believe, still ought to assist collective reinventions.[12] In my own career as a historian I have seen many academic fashions come and go, and I have benefited from a growing historiography on all sorts of aspects of Mexico and France and the U.S. and India. And yet, despite so much historicizing, the category "Mexico" seems to me caged in a set of inevitable and robust cultural assumptions. These essays are my attempt to analytically capture and question these assumptions.

On the other hand, words and language have concerned me in more than just a utilitarian manner. Every word to me brings stories alive, and thus due to an inexcusable fixation for the early twentieth-century urban language of Mexico, I have learned old and *cursi* (gaudy) utterances of composers, scientists, artists, writers, and urban dwellers in general. I have command of this dead language, and thus I have been fascinated by the pervasiveness of some rather dense words. But it seems that Mexico has been a global idea to be spoken of in a language of simple, if well-established, terms: from *siesta* to *guerrilla*, from *pistola* to *tequila*, from *machismo* to *mestizaje*, from *sombrero* to *cojones* (the last a recent Spanish addition to the English language). It is as if the complex, immense, and dynamic universe of words produced or consumed in Mexico City was not a part of the city's meaning. As it will be clear throughout the book, I treasure words and the human realms they encompass.

Finally, my approach is also driven by the simple fact that I do have interesting, colorful, emblematic, and ill-known stories to tell. Why does the historian need to tell the story, say, of lice or of the fascination with Tagore's poetry in Mexico City? I do not know. Marc Bloch, as an anti-Nazi French officer in a Normandy garden, answering to why history had betrayed France, still found that the simple pleasure of telling stories was one of history's main leitmotifs.[13] He did not know why either. I simply wanted to tell all these stories, to show these images, to dialogue with all these words.

My "theories," thus, are too many and none. My footnotes, though, are as succinct as possible.

Communicating Vessels

As whimsical as I Speak of the City could seem as a mere compilation of essays, the book as a whole has three basic concerns that make the various parts essential counterparts of each other. First, there is the need to comprehend the universal through the particular and vice versa; that is, the inevitable strategy of reading Mexico City as an essentially local and yet inevitably global historical phenomenon. Second, there is language. These essays are simply the effort to understand past circumstances through the reality of past words and styles, analyzed as objectively as possible. Finally, there is the craving to experiment with different essay-like forms of storytelling.

As a result, the book is made up of six parts that blend these basic concerns through different recipes that often return to the same dates, events, streets, buildings, actors, and objects. Part I deals with 1910 as a year of weighty historical connotations that reached well beyond Mexico. Thus, the essay on 1910 begins with a momentary exercise in historical amnesia, useful for rethinking our selective equilibrium of memory and oblivion: taking 1910 as one of the last years of the nineteenth century, a year in an era of profound and accelerated transformations, in which the self-consciousness of achieved progress interacted with the insecurity of the world's political, social, and economic circumstances. That is, I see 1910 in Mexico City less as the year of the Revolution and more as the year of the *Centenario*—the centennial celebration of the beginning of Mexico's independence, which had an extraordinary impact on the city's shape. The city can be read as the central allegory of a nation and a memory, but this was nothing particularly Mexican. Thus, a second essay in part I launches the oddest possible contrast of cities in 1910: Mexico City and Washington, D.C. By contrasting these two cities around 1910, the essay seeks to demarcate the true parameters, and the common grounds, of two historical exceptionalisms—that of Mexico and that of the U.S. Finally, whereas the essay on the *Centenario* is by and large based on the city's public exteriors, a third essay in part I inhabits the interiors of the city around 1910. By looking at bourgeois and popular interiors, I seek to essay the forms of intimacy that emerged at the moment of the launching of the city on its path toward megalopolis.

In turn, various vistas of Mexico City in and around 1919 make up part II, which attempts to imagine the life of the city as the capital of twenty years of the world's radical hopes: revolution, avant-garde art, exoticism, love, and betrayal. Around 1919 Mexico City became for many foreigners a summer resort of the sort sought by such modernist poets as Wallace Stevens, who spoke of an essence of summer needed to rejuvenate and recapture peace, permanence, and intellectual conformity; a summer to "fill the foliage with arrested peace, / Joy of such permanence, right ignorance / Of change still possible. Exile desire / For what is not. This is the barrenness / Of the fertile thing that can attain no more." Mexico City was this modernist summer: a shared epic for a generation of world intellectuals, activists, and artists. The city housed the hopes of many of the world's radicals, and part II, through sequential stories, tries to capture the simultaneity of the city as a moment of the world's radical hopes. Rather than trying to test a hypothesis, this series of stories aims to make the reader experience this world capital in all its contradictions and creativity. The stories focus on specific groups, events, and individuals, all of them as supporting characters in a plot in which the main role is played, if quietly, by the city itself.

Part III is the necessary complement to the vistas of the cosmopolitan Mexico City of 1919. The city was the center of the intellectual radical milieu, thus becoming the odd center of what I call the search for "a Brown Atlantis": Mexico as the world's imaginary space made of modernist dreams of racial, cultural, and social authenticity and disenchantment. The city thus became a seemingly passive site of fakeness where foreign and local literati merely happened to be located in order to envisage the "real" Mexico of Indigenous people faithful to their racial purity and untouched by four centuries of massive demographic, cultural, and political transformations. Whereas the goal in writing part II is to zoom in for narrative close-ups of the lives of different kinds of cosmopolitans in the city, part III zooms out for a wide view of the disdain of the city—often enforced by the same cosmopolitans. And it does so by examining the variegated clichés in foreign and local views—and nonviews—of the city, which were indispensable in conceiving Mexico as a mythical place, a Brown Atlantis that was everything Mexico City was not. By doing this I seek to display the contours of the Brown Atlantis and how such confines have led to a relatively fixed and lasting idea of "Mexico" in the world: *fiesta, siesta, sombrero, pistola,* and *Frida Kahlo.*

In a way, part III is an analysis of Mexico as the object of the world's exoticist needs—as well as of Mexico's self-exoticism. Part IV therefore completes this exploration by examining an uncanny exoticism, one that was part and parcel of that which maintained the search of a Brown Atlantis but was of a different polarity. That is, an excursion into Mexico City as the center of what I call Mexican odalisque-mania: a momentary but deep urban fascination with Japan and India. Many echoes clashed and blended in this bizarre Mexican orientalism: those of the 1910 capital of a local expression of republican nationhood and memory, those of revolutionary global hopes, and those of the Brown Atlantis excitedly sought by the world's luminaries. All these echoes acquired different connotations when the city's intelligentsia eagerly sought oriental ecstasies in Japan and India—through great experiments in language and the arts—at the same time that it nourished local and global similes of what Mexico meant for the world. At the risk of its own invisibility, modernist Mexico City tried out and produced the ingredients necessary to maintain the global search for a Brown Atlantis. But such a trial could not stop in the many efforts at self-exoticism; it simultaneously involved the imaging of Mexico City's own private Oriental Atlantis through, say, Japanese haikus, Hindu thought, or Rabindranath Tagore's poetry. As a fake local West, as a second-class East, the city participated in the global circulation of various Easts and Wests for, after all, Mexico City was a world capital of this obsession with defining the East and the West.

Part V deals with these local and global connections but uses science as the lens, a realm that remains seemingly unsuitable to observe anything Mexican. That is why, I think, it is so revealing. The essays on science and the city thus tramp the Mexico City of the decades from 1890 to 1930—the period in which the city was finally and definitively "scientized"—to tell the joint story of local and global knowledge, experience, and city life, and not the conventional account of the city's progressive modernization, which at times historians have absurdly called Westernization. By using variegated foci of analysis—from the import of history in the science of the city to rats, lice, and typhus—part V aims to provide views on how an old city urbanized modern science, on how modern science scrutinized the city, and on how this scientism and urbanism were part of a larger modernist matrix including literature, journalism, and the arts.

To conclude, part VI stops to examine in detail the language of the city, which is at the core of all of this book's essays. Language is the most fleeting but most present realm; all of the book's essays in one way or another attempt to hear languages of the past, but it is impossible to listen to or comprehend all, in the same way that it would be hard to decipher all the words one hears in a single day in a city. Language in the past, as fashionable as it is to study it, is an undecipherable riddle that we can only partially, and only after a long immersion into past languages, discern. Part VI examines the city's words, inviting the reader to sharpen her ear for sounds that are colors and styles. Though Mexico City was not a Buenos Aires or a New York of the turn of the century, in those decades it was a major linguistic laboratory that produced the unique *chilango* (belonging to Mexico City) tongue. More than examining this tongue, part VI dialogues with it in order to enact in the present the vividness of past urban experiences. But the sounds I examine have so many subtleties and differences across social, temporal, and spatial contexts that one ought not to maintain any great interpretative pretensions. One is better served by doubting like Antonio Machado, who *en las bóvedas del alma* (in the soul's vaults) never knew whether the whispers were voices or echoes of his own voice.

In sum, these essays are about Mexico City from the 1880s to the 1930s. That is why I *Speak of the City* is useless in speaking merely of Mexico City, incapable of talking only about those decades. It is as if in essaying, the evocation of the city's name would free an uncontrollable naming of other eras, of other places.

PART I RIGHT AROUND 1910 . . .

Con un poco de método y laboriosidad se es erudito. Con
otro poco de cuidado, se es castizo. Lo que no se puede
ser ni con método, ni con laboriosidad, ni con cuidado, es
pensador . . . ten talento y escribe lo que te plazca, cuando
ya no tengas talento métete a erudito.

With a little method and industriousness one can be an
erudite person. With a little more care, one becomes *castizo*
[a purist in the use of language]. What one cannot be with
either method or labor, not even with care, is a thinker . . .
be talented and write whatever you want, when you run out
of talent become an erudite scholar.
— Amado Nervo, "Algo sobre la erudición y el estilo,"
   Obras completas, vol. 23 (Madrid: Biblioteca Nueva, 1949),
   278

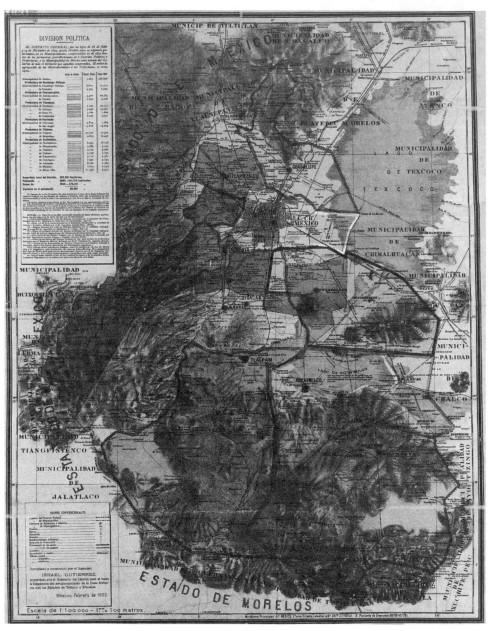

Map, Federal District, Mexico (1902),
courtesy Archivo General de la Nación, Mexico.

ON 1910 AND THE CITY
OF THE CENTENNIAL

On 1910 and the city of the centennial or on how Mexico City was lastly transformed by the utopia of an ideal city conceived for the 1910 celebration of Mexico's independence. Thus, after short introductory remarks, the essay provides a postcard of the entire celebration for the reader to grasp what the Centenario was about. Then follows a brief explanation of the three main utopias epitomized by the centennial city—modernization, nationhood, and cosmopolitanism. The essay then walks the reader through three imaginary tours to the centennial city: the first walks the streets, avenues, and monuments; the second through the history, and the third over the styles epitomized by those stones and pavements. In concluding, the essay briefly contrasts the centennial city—a supposed paradise of, as it were, old-regime-ness—with the first vista of the new revolutionary city that emerged out of the 1910 Revolution, namely, the 1921 celebration of the consummation of Mexico's independence (1821) in the city.

1910 is for us, twentieth-first-century observers, not just another year. It is a year with weighty historical connotations. It is the year around which "human character changed,"[1] and it is also, of course, the year of the first massive popular revolution of the twentieth century: the Mexican Revolution. The end of an era, we now know, was then nearer than ever before. Mexico's 1910 was not solely the year of the Revolution but, more clearly, the peak of an era, that of *Centenarios*.

The centennial celebration of Mexico's independence in 1910 materialized in Mexico City in an extraordinary fashion, producing vistas of the ideals within which the *Centenario* was conceived. These ideals, though never fully brought to fruition, defined the parameters within which many realities were discussed. It would be an act of faith to declare "real" or "correct" or "popular" those ideals. But to map this celebration in order to simply confront the fake vs. the true cultural geographies of 1910 Mexico City would be an act of faith of a different kind, one resting on the belief of a "genuine" cartography of the city of the *Centenario*. I simply map the celebration in order to demarcate the parameters of the politically and culturally possible around 1910 and around Mexico City.

El Centenario: A Postcard

1910 was consciously planned to be the apotheosis of a nationalist consciousness; it was meant to be the climax of an era. In many ways, it was.[2] It constituted a testimony to the political and economic success of a regime. The *Centenario* also documented Mexico's achievement of supreme ideals: its economic and scientific progress as well as its cultural modernism. After all, centenaries, since 1876, were meant to be the sort of "mission accomplished" for national histories in Europe and the Americas.[3]

As early as 1907, the Porfirian government established the Comisión Nacional del Centenario, which was in charge of staging the luxurious and extravagant commemoration. From 1907 to 1910 this commission received thousands of proposals by all classes and regions for different ways to honor the national past: changes in the names of streets, mountains, and avenues; air shows; new monuments and parks; changes in the national flag, anthem, and other symbols; freedom for political prisoners; and a project for young daughters of the high classes to educate their *criadas* (maids).[4] The Comisión Nacional appointed sub-commissions to evaluate proposals; those made by distinguished members of the political or intellectual classes were often accepted. Accordingly September, the month in which a local revolt in 1810 began what eventually would result in Mexico's independence, became thirty days of inaugurations for monuments, official buildings, institutions, and streets; thirty days of countless speeches, parties, cocktails, receptions, and dancing fiestas. A national fund was created to collect the contributions of businessmen, financiers, professional organizations, and mutualist societies. By September 1910, Mexico City had acquired the visible and lasting marks of the notions of nation, progress, and modernization that the *Centenario* intermingled and made visible.

From September 1 through 13, Mexico City saw the inaugurations of a new modern mental hospital, a popular hygiene exhibition, an exhibition of Spanish art and industry, exhibitions of Japanese products and avant-garde Mexican art, a monument to Alexander von Humboldt at the National Library, a seismological station, a new theater in the Escuela Nacional Preparatoria, primary schools, new buildings for the ministries, and new large schools for teachers. All this was in addition to other events, like laying the cornerstones of the planned National Penitentiary. In addition there were opening sessions of many and varied congresses, such as the 17th International Congress of Americanists, the 4th National Medical Congress, and the Congreso Pedagógico de Instrucción Primaria. And all this was only the first thirteen days of September.

On September 16, 1810, Father Miguel Hidalgo began the rebellion that eventually and chaotically led to independence. Consequently, days fourteen, fifteen, and sixteen were, of course, the apotheosis of the entire celebration. The fourteenth, the "Gran Procesión Cívica formada por todos los elementos de la sociedad mexicana" (great civic procession of all sectors of Mexican society) paraded from the Alameda park to the Cathedral, depositing flowers at the graves of national heroes and then marching to the National Palace. On the fifteenth, as in a good dramatic play, the theatrical tension rose with the "Gran Desfile Histórico" (great historical parade): the entire history of the nation on foot, episode after episode; this was a march of the stages of Mexico's patriotic history as understood by the Porfirian liberal reconstruction of the past. In effect, these were walking chapters of an official history that marched over the chapters of yet another history recorded in the city itself. The new civic parades walked over the routes of all of the city's well-established religious processions. Accordingly, the parade traversed the chapters of the city as a history textbook—it went from the Plaza de la Reforma, along the Avenida Juárez, and finally to the Plaza de la Constitución.[5]

On September 15 a number of parties and receptions took place. Fireworks illuminated the city skies and at eleven o'clock that night at the Zócalo, President Porfirio Díaz, in the midst of a popular gathering, rang the bell that Miguel Hidalgo had rung a hundred years earlier. For aristocratic observers la noche del grito was a quasi-tourist portrait of Mexico's popular fiestas and joy. This was the exotic Mexico that intrigued the world, a version that, rather than compromising Mexico's cosmopolitanism, made it distinctive: guitars, fiesta, enchiladas, pulque, sombreros. But the night also saw undesired and unplanned popular discontent. Mexican writer and diplomat Federico Gamboa, for instance, described the protests of the followers of Francisco I. Madero, the leader that ignited the Revolution. Gamboa himself accepted the task of concealing those expressions of opposition from foreign observers. In turn, F. Starr—by 1910 an established U.S. anthropologist of Mexico—in the violent year of 1914 recalled the celebrations as bombastic self-delusions, as was to be expected from anyone writing about the Mexico of 1910 in 1914. But the *Centenario* was far from a Leviathan imposition by a rather weak state; it was chaotic and contested in every detail, but under a great consensual myth: peace.[6]

September 16, in turn, was the official day of commemoration of Independence. The long-planned monument El Ángel de la Independencia was inaugurated in the Paseo de la Reforma. A military parade went from the Paseo de la Reforma to the National Palace, and at night luxurious dancing parties took place in various official buildings. The celebrations continued until the end of the month. During this time, public parks and grand monuments—such as one for former president Benito Juárez in the Alameda—were inaugurated. In addition a gunpowder factory in Santa Fe, the hydraulic works of Mexico City, the National University, a livestock exhibition at Coyoacán, the Gran Canal del Desagüe, and an extension of the National Penitentiary were all also inaugurated. There were ceremonies to honor the beginning construction of the planned enormous new Palacio Legislativo (Parliament), and of a monument to Pasteur. Extravagant celebrations commemorated Spain's and France's diplomatic courtesies: the former returned the personal belongings of the national hero José María Morelos; in turn, France returned Mexico City's key that was, presumably, stolen by the French invaders in 1862, though, as Federico Gamboa pointed out, Mexico City never had an entrance let alone a key. Finally there was the great Apotheosis of the Caudillos and Soldiers of the War of Independence: a giant altar constructed on the main patio of the National Palace to revere the heroes, to which the entire government, foreign missions, and the elite as a whole paid respects.

The centenary was a fleeting show, but never before had the city been so radically and profusely embellished and transformed in such a short span of time. The remains of the centennial city are still essential components of the city; they still produce the same respectful and consensual effect that, according to the Porfirian lawyer and writer Emilio Rabasa, Porfirio Díaz aroused as the embodiment of the nation. During the *Centenario*, said Rabasa, "when cheering him [Díaz] in the streets, the people saw not the man full of personal prestige, but instead, recognizing the national flag crossed over the chest of the arrogant old man, they acclaimed the ruler only as the symbol of the enhanced nation."[7] For indeed, the *Centenario* celebrated a hitherto unknown link between the imagery of the dictator, the idea and experience of peace, the image of the nation, and that of the state. It is impossible to know how different urban dwellers experienced the celebration, but one thing is certain: for good or bad, it was then hard to distinguish between Díaz, peace, nation, and state. This was not because the quartet embodied the "real" Mexico, but because it was the first powerful modern articulation of what Mexico meant. "The only national and patriotic program," said Porfirio Díaz in 1904, "that the government meant to undertake . . . has been to reinforce peace, to reinforce the links that before only war had the privilege to join, thus making more solid and more permanent the ideals and aspirations expressed—sadly with intermittencies—by the various factions of what is a single and indisputable nationality."[8] In this sense, the celebration is historically telling not as evidence of a "fake" and "elitist" nation (as many historians and commentators have elaborated a posteriori), but especially because it was then the most comprehensive and articulated view of the nation ever conceived. That is why it had a central theme, peace, which then meant of course Porfirio Díaz but much more. That is why the ruins of that fake city were able to become the foundations of new articulations of the nation over the twentieth century.

Mapping the Celebration

In 1910 various ideals of the city overlapped in a limited space and time. One was the ideal of modernization, understood as harmonious economic and scientific development, as well as progress. The best embodiment of this ideal was the modern capital city, whereby Mexico City or any other capital could contain the proofs of a nation's pedigree: economic prosperity and cultural greatness encompassing sanitation, comfort, and beauty. Second, there was the ideal of a long-sought coherent and unified concept of nation; that is, the need for consolidating in chorus as a nation and as a state. The particular epitome of such an ideal was the capital city understood as a textbook of civic religion; a story-telling city that through streets and avenues, monuments, and planning of public and private spaces narrated to the city dweller the nation and the state as a unique local tale, but also as an echo of a larger historical process. Third, there was the modern ideal, inseparable from the other two, of a cosmopolitan style. By the last part of the nineteenth century the quintessential incarnation of the cosmopolitan ideal was a Paris- or Vienna-like city. In the early twentieth century it was impossible for the capital of both a modern nation and a modern state to remain oblivious of its reflection of major late nineteenth-century capital cities—then in constant construction and reconstruction—such as Berlin, Vienna, Washington, Buenos Aires, and Madrid.

Finally, there was in the centennial city the supreme ideal and central theme: peace. It was embodied in everything: in the monuments, in the urban planning, in the parades and parties, in the gigantic effort to celebrate the *Centenario* as the final proof of Mexico's productive peace. Mexico City was then made into a grand monument to peace, though ironically the *Centenario* marked the beginning of a major and violent revolution. The city thus was indeed fake and ephemeral (as all cities at all times are), but not because it was unfaithful to the notion of peace it praised. The Revolution did not erase what the city celebrated: the first three decades of relative peace for a nation that violently emerged from the ruins of the Spanish empire. Moreover, the city of the *Centenario* celebrated peace so pompously because its planners knew the peace they celebrated was not a paradise-like absence of violence. What the city celebrated was the triumph of the state (as in the monopoly of the legitimate use of violence) and the achievement of an economically profitable peace. It also paradoxically celebrated the fear of breaking with the miracle of having achieved peace. The spark of the Revolution, in a way, soon (by 1913) showed how hard it was to live without the link between state, peace, and nation that the city of the *Centenario* celebrated.

To examine these ideals I undertake tours around the city of the *Centenario*.

Tour 1

Since the 1880s, the economic, symbolic, and political interests that supported urban transformation were associated with the centennial celebration in two respects: on the one hand, through the long-standing idea of staging a world's fair in Mexico City in order to celebrate the centennial; on the other, by using the *Centenario* to accelerate the development of an ideal city within the actual city.

As in the U.S. when celebrating the centennial of American Independence, or in Paris to commemorate the centenary of the French Revolution, in Mexico the idea took root of celebrating the *Centenario* with a world's fair staged in Mexico City. This was but a natural conclusion for all good modern nations and cities; the project was debated throughout the Porfirian period, though it never materialized. World's fairs were expensive, and furthermore it was one thing to create an imagined picture of Mexico for exhibition at fairs attended by the entire world, and another thing to make the world come to an old city full of problems. Nonetheless, these projects that never materialized involved ideas about how the city ought to be transformed to favor modern urban planning, sanitation reforms, nationalist symbolism, and, of course, private economic interests.

As early as 1889 Antonio A. de Medina y Ormaechea, founder of the Sociedad Mexicana de Consumo (Mexican Consumers Society), conceived the idea of a universal exhibition in Mexico for the year 1910. What de Medina y Ormaechea proposed was a version of a then well-established economic view: the undeveloped internal market was due not to low wages but to "wrong" cultural patterns of consumption—a view very much rejected by early twentieth-century Mexican economic thinker Andrés Molina Enríquez.[9] Inspired by the 1889 Paris exhibition, de Medina y Ormaechea claimed that, like France,

Mexico ought to celebrate the centennial anniversary of its major historical event with the first Mexican universal exhibition.[10] He argued that a Mexican world's fair would help to educate and modernize Indians, who "are content with a simple shirt and trousers [*camisa y un calzón de manta*] to cover their flesh, with a pair of *guaraches* to wear on their feet . . . with a pot of chiles, beans, and tortillas, and with a pint of *pulque*." A Mexico City world's fair would also serve to show that Mexico had achieved international standards of comfort, sanitation, and general progress. Armed with these arguments de Medina y Ormaechea persisted in advocating his project for the rest of the century, but it was never realized.

From the 1890s to the 1910s the idea of a universal exposition in Mexico City to celebrate Mexico's centennial of independence reemerged with various sponsorships. The first such occasions occurred in the early 1890s. Then companies that specialized in the management and organization of world's fairs—often funded by U.S. capital—came together with Mexican private interests involved in Mexico City's profitable urban development to envision a Mexican fair. A specialist at organizing European exhibitions, René de Cornely, interested a group of Mexican politicians and industrialists in staging an international exhibition from September 1895 to April 1896 in Mexico City. This exhibition was publicized and indeed arranged almost to the last detail.[11] The former *rancho* of Anzures near the Paseo de la Reforma and Chapultepec Park, owned by the wealthy speculator Salvador Malo, was the proposed location for the fair. Malo was in fact one of the most important urban developers of the time. He had developed the Hacienda de la Teja, the rancho de Anzures, and the Hacienda de la Castañeda. He was a member of the Mexico City Improvement Company. In fact, Malo had advanced a Barcelona-like *eixample* (enlargement) for Mexico City, in order to gentrify the grounds surrounding the Paseo de la Reforma.[12] He embodied the successful urban speculator—a friend of Presidents Manuel González and Díaz—, who was actually constantly losing money, and yet until his death he kept obtaining credit.[13]

John R. Dos Passos, the U.S. son of Portuguese immigrants and stepfather of the not yet famous writer, was one of the head investors in this exposition aimed at developing the Anzures rancho. A Mexican, Ignacio Bejarano, served as the front for an international concern involved with Mexico City real estate.[14] Friction developed between the company and the Mexican government.[15] In July 1897 Cornely wrote to Mexico's finance minister, José Yves Limantour, requesting that the government reenact the Exposition Company, but Limantour considered the matter *cosa parada* (stagnated).[16] In 1899 Malo wrote Limantour asking him to lobby for the Anzures business in his recommendations to President Díaz: "Otherwise I am afraid that Dos Passos will take advantage and later set such a price that it will be impossible to acquire the lots."[17] In that year Malo wanted to be saved "from misery" by asking the government to acquire 58 percent of the company's stocks by buying them from Dos Passos (the rest of the stocks were owned, according to Malo, by their—Malo's and Limantour's—"friends" in Mexico). The potential expo and the entire real estate of the city were indeed a question of friends. There the matter rested, yet another project for a Mexican world's fair that never materialized. The same occurred with the proposal by Fernando Pimentel y Fagoaga of the Banco Central Mexicano in 1908. In the *Mexican Financier*, Pimentel y Fagoaga offered to collect two to three million pesos among the Mexican financiers by coining 50-centavo commemorative coins. With this he proposed to organize a major world's fair around the Castillo de Chapultepec and on the grounds on both sides of the Paseo de la Reforma. The commission for the centenary responded negatively, arguing lack of time to organize such a fair.[18]

Another attempt to organize an exhibition led to the construction of a Mexican version of the London Crystal Palace. In 1895, the Compañía Mexicana de Exposiciones constructed a steel-and-crystal structure in Germany to serve as the Mexican palace for permanent exhibitions in Mexico City. However, by 1903 the company was dissolved, and one of its wealthiest investors, José Landero y Cos, became the owner of the building. In 1910, the government decided to acquire the building and assembled it at the site known as El Chopo at Santa María la Ribera. The Mexican Crystal Palace was then used to house the Japanese exhibition during the centennial celebration, and afterwards became the National Museum of Natural History (see chapter 7). In this way, after the many attempts to celebrate the centennial anniversary of independence with a world's fair, at last a Crystal Palace *à la mexicain* became part of the celebration.

It could be said that in 1910 a universal exhibition in Mexico City was an unachievable dream of cosmopolitanism and international recognition. Ironically, the only successful attempt at cosmopolitanism and international acceptance took place in Mexico City not just before but soon after a social revolt: 1968. Mexico City's Olympic Games and Cultural *Olimpiada* in 1968 were postrevolutionary Mexico's celebration of its own achieved peace, progress, and modernization. And this time around was indeed a triumphant cosmopolitanism as never before for Mexico City or any other "third-world" city. A true cosmopolitan city that received the world and was projected to the world as never before or after. As fleeting and ephemeral as the event was, it was what the centennial city sought but never achieved.[19]

Nevertheless, to go back to 1910, what all the planned fairs included around the *Centenario* was the notion of developing the ideal city along the spinal column of the Paseo de la Reforma. Every plan involved the grounds surrounding the Paseo de la Reforma (whether at Chapultepec or at Anzures). This was but an echo of the process of urbanization that Mexico City underwent beginning in 1890. The old colonial city was abandoned by the elite, who moved to the growing suburbs west of the city. In fact, the entire *Centenario* was an episode in the development of this ideal city.

One can clearly distinguish the borders of the ideal city—from the inside out—by mapping the celebration. Or, alternatively, one could delimit the ideal city from the outside in: for instance, by following the geographical limits established by the Consejo Superior de Salubridad (the city's sanitary board) for the distribution and consumption of *pulque* in Mexico City.[20] The ideal city was, as any city, a messy model derived from the ancient colonial Spanish urban tradition combined with the influence of nineteenth-century U.S. and European urban planning.[21] Hence the ancient (political, cultural, and geographical) center was extended through main avenues that linked the comfortable modern suburbs with the old city. During the centennial celebration all the monuments, events, and parades appeared within (and were part of the making of) this ideal city.

Beginning in the 1860s Mexico City experienced a selective and pragmatic urban transformation that was in part inspired by many versions of modern capitals and garden cities. Thus the Paseo de la Reforma was developed on the model of Champs Élysées, and suburbs that combined urban comfort with the beauty and health of gardens grew to the west of the city. There residences at the edges of the Paseo de la Reforma were required to keep eight meters of garden on the front façade.[22]

Buenos Aires, which also organized a grand centennial celebration in 1910, is a good parallel. Together with New York, in 1910 Buenos Aires was the most important city in the American continent, and it underwent a major transformation and, like Mexico City, experienced its first radical reshaping from the 1880s to 1910s. In both cities the elites moved out from their traditional setting to the "Casa Quinta" (Buenos Aires) or to new elegant *colonias* (Mexico City).[23] Public space was reshaped and resegregated in order to accommodate the growing population of foreign immigrants in Buenos Aires, and of workers and internal immigrants in Mexico City. In addition, public space was reshaped according to new cosmopolitan fashions—required formats for all modern capital cities.[24] Therefore in Buenos Aires "the old city is abandoned and Paris is reenacted,"[25] and in Mexico "the city multiplies prodigiously the number of their modern *barrios* . . . at the western front the wealthy classes have constructed a true city full of attractive chalets and sumptuous residences."[26]

In Mexico, most of the planned workers' *barrios* and wealthy neighborhoods were developed in the 1900s. To the northeast such *barrios* as Santa María and

Guerrero housed middle-class workers and artisans, while the newly developed *colonias* Morelos, La Bolsa, Díaz de León, Rastro, and Maza y Valle Gómez were Mexican versions of proletarian quarters. Indian communities remained at the edges of the city (sometimes prospering through their commerce with the city, and sometimes disappearing due to the expansion and attraction of the city).[27] In contrast, the west was developed with two huge projects for the growing urban middle class, the *colonias* San Rafael and Limantour. Finally, during the 1900s the southwest became the city of wealth, style, and power with such *colonias* as Juárez, Cuauhtémoc, Roma, and Condesa. These last *colonias* were connected to the traditional city through the Paseo de la Reforma, Avenida Juárez, and such fashionable streets as San Francisco. In turn, Cinco de Mayo Street linked the old city to the not so new but still elegant San Cosme. Electrification and modern street planning accompanied these new urban developments. These transformations followed the pace of consolidation of a relatively authoritarian and centralist national administration, which has proven to be a necessary component of this type of urban change in the Americas and Europe.[28] There was nothing particularly Mexican about it.

The *Centenario* could be seen as the final touch in the demarcation of the ideal city conceived by the Porfirian elite. This ideal encompassed the Zócalo and its surroundings, ran west to the Alameda park and then along the Paseo de la Reforma as far as Chapultepec. On the south side of the Paseo de la Reforma the ideal city ended at the Río de la Piedad, where the border went to Niño Perdido and back to downtown. On the north side the city limit blurred into haciendas and countryside (especially Anzures and Los Morales). See figure 1.1.[29]

During the *Centenario* the streets and avenues around the Paseo de la Reforma were embellished with commemorative posters, electric lights, flowers, medallions, and the national colors.[30] The decoration constantly reiterated the Latin word *Pax*, not as a mockery of Porfirian peace through the reference to Pax Romana, but *Pax* as republican peace (that is the conquest of the legitimate monopoly of violence). In addition the ideal city, as historian John Lear has shown, included the project of "ridding the center of the poor [. . .] the Government wished to eliminate the presence of the poor so close to the corridors of power and wealth and feared the problems of health and morality."[31] In truth the ideal city was developed apart from the rest of the city. By 1906 an architect clearly distinguished the existence of two cities within the city:

Between the city's east and west parts there exists a very conspicuous difference; the former is old, sad, narrow, often of rough terrain, and always filthy, with meager and insignificant streets, abandoned and antiquated pla-

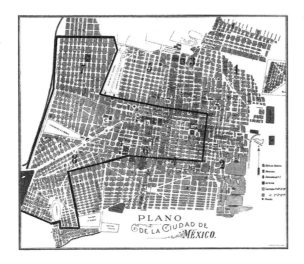

1.1. Map of the "ideal city" (ca. 1910).

zas, ruinous bridges, deposits of swamp-like water, and insignificant adobe houses, in which live miserable people. For its part, the west is modern, joyful, wide, carefully designed, clean, with carefully paved streets, lush parks, gardens and *alamedas*, passages in good conditions, and comfortable and elegant residences.[32]

Mexico's Haussmanns laid out avenues and boulevards but, unlike their European counterparts, they did not have to destroy urban sectors or relocate large inhabited zones. Instead, they displaced campesinos and Indian communities from the nearby haciendas. Indeed, compared to Europe, where urban reform was considered a matter of social reform and internal security, or the product of "catastrophic change," in Mexico it was a manner of frontier expansion. The ideal city, therefore, was conceived as a conquest not only over tradition, chaos, and backwardness, but also over nature. What the Porfirian elite did was to blend, on one hand, ancient urban planning, architecture, and old symbols and forms of domination with, on the other, a new planned urban landscape and social stratification. Therefore, the Zócalo remained the central point of departure but the Paseo de la Reforma became the path of power, the representation of the course of the nation toward supreme order and progress: from the Plaza de la Reforma (with the statue of Carlos IV, El Caballito) to Columbus's monument, past Cuauhtémoc and the monument of Independence, arriving, finally, at the Castillo de Chapultepec (the presidential residence).[33] At the entrance of the Paseo de la Reforma, near Bucareli, there were already two statues: *Los Indios Verdes*, two of the examples of Porfirian indigenist art, both designed by Alejandro Casarín and inaugurated in 1889. The statues represented the Aztec kings Itzcóatl and Ahuízotl in bronze (figure 1.2). According to an organic conception of the city, other parts of the city were developed to serve as providers, storage areas, or working complements for the ideal city.

As in Paris, Madrid, and Buenos Aires, parks were developed within the ideal city.[34] Since the time of Maximilian, Chapultepec had been the prime example of Mexico's modern urban gardens. The new luxurious suburbs were proof of the modern combination of urban comfort and green beauty. The development of parks in zones outside the limits of the ideal city was a matter of debate concerning the sanitary, moral, and regenerating aspects of nature, especially in regard to their effects on the lower classes. Throughout the 1890s and 1900s defenders of the ecological conservation of the city spoke out, but their opinions were ignored. In fact a workers' park at Balbuena, constructed for the *Centenario*, was one of the very few parks developed outside the ideal city.[35]

As part of the events of the *Centenario*, the city's main environmentalist, Miguel Ángel de Quevedo, delivered a report, "Free Spaces in the City's Interior, Their Adaptation into Monumental Plazas, Gardens, Tree Squares, and Sports Camps." Quevedo explained how, as director of Mexico City's public works, he sought to shift the official preference for luxurious French-style gardens in favor of simple "squares" that could accommodate trees and provide healthy recreation for the lower classes. He therefore presented a project for a garden in the populous Calzada de la Viga. No grounds were available at La Viga, but an alternative location were the ninety-six hectares at Balbuena and, as a result, the workers' park of Balbuena was created in order to make "nuestra querida capital como el París de América" (our dear capital city like the Paris of America).[36]

Although to us current victims of Mexico City, a bucolic Mexico City seems part of a mythical past, there were in fact many forests near the city, as Quevedo explained. However, deforestation meant that ample deserts extended between, for example, Mexico City and Tacubaya, Santa Fe, and Santa Lucía. These broad tracts caused terrible dust storms and pollution. In fact the civic ideal that the *Centenario* epitomized lacked grand "bucolic" content; it was simply a defense of the modern urban tree. Historically, Mexican elites had an urban attachment, though their fortunes could have had rural origins. Since colonial times prestige and status were either urban or nothing. But by the early twentieth century the model of the garden city, and the planning of parks and gardens, were cosmopolitan ideals that the Porfirian elite aimed to pursue. Unlike American Jeffersonians or those American urbanizers who sought a balance between city and countryside, Mexicans from different classes and regions regarded the city as the only form of true civilization.

In this sense, the ideal city consolidated by the Porfirians should be seen as a civilizing process, as a frontier expansion. The civilizing conquest began the slow physical blurring of the firm distinction between city and countryside. In an 1870s landscape canvas of the Valley of Mexico, by the great nineteenth-century landscape painter José María Velasco, we can clearly point out where the city ended, where the countryside began, and where small towns were located. By the 1910s, the Porfirian ideal city had reshaped the old city, but had also colonized (through what were revealingly called *colonias*) what was believed to be the uncivilized "emptiness" of the countryside. Thereafter, the city gradually lost its firm physical borders. Nonetheless, both socially and massively, as historian Alan Knight has observed, it was the Revolution that began the merging of city and countryside.[37] By the 1940s, with the onset of rapid industrialization, the pristine countryside could not be found in Mexico City in reality but could be seen in many popular nostalgic films of *charros* and haciendas. Those mules, chickens, cows, and *milpas* that indeed could be found in the 1940s were closer to the telling urban depictions of Spanish-exile director Luis Buñuel's film, *Los Olvidados* (1950), than to the bucolic dreams of unpolluted nonurban realities.

As in Europe and the rest of America, in Mexico there was a belief in the evil and degenerating characteristics of cities. Agglomeration, pollution, lack of nature, and industrialization led to corruption, laziness, and degeneration of races, as Federico Gamboa's popular myth of Santa crystallized.[38] But as good inhabitants of the Roman and Iberian urban tradition, Mexicans were confident that upon achieving a modern city—and not a bucolic return to nature—those evil by-products of urban development would be overcome. In this sense, the achieved ideal city of the *Centenario* was both the climax of the city of wealth and the main therapeutic measure for the poor. The return to the "village" as an intellectual and cultural ideal emerged in Mexico in the 1920s, fostered both by Mexican nationalists and by foreign travelers and anthropologists. At that point intellectuals and artists found in the small town and the countryside the soul of the nation, though this was a turn taken from and for the city (see chapters 5 and 6).

All in all the *Centenario* furnished and rearranged the main spaces of symbolic importance for the nation. The monument to Independence was placed along the Paseo de la Reforma. The old project of having monuments of distinguished citizens from every single state of the nation along the Paseo de la Reforma reemerged.[39] In the Alameda park, on Benito Juárez Avenue, the elaborate monument to Juárez was constructed.[40]

The monument to Independence, designed by the architect Antonio Rivas Mercado, echoed the theme epitomized by the entire Paseo de la Reforma.

Rivas Mercado feared that the column would be overshadowed by the nearby trees and houses, so he built a thirty-five-meter column from which the entire city could be viewed: on one side, the Castillo de Chapultepec; on the other, the Alameda park and the Zócalo. Between these two points along the Paseo de la Reforma there were luxurious modern urban developments. The ancient, aristocratic old Mexico and the new ideal city were thus united in a single panorama from the standpoint of a towering monument to a great historical moment.[41]

Other monuments were inaugurated, several of them gifts from foreign missions. In the sumptuous Colonia Roma, a statute of Giuseppe Garibaldi was donated by Italy. Thus the elegant Colonia Roma acquired the complicated image of a flamboyant guerrilla fighter, one who fought for the independence of the failed republic of Rio Grande do Sul in Brazil yet also defeated Italian monarchies on behalf of King Victor Emmanuel II. All in all, the avalanche of monuments occurred within the parameters of the ideal city. The same was true of all centennial parades that traversed the planned geography of the ideal city, whose avenues synthesized Mexican modernism and cosmopolitanism as well as national history. A parade of allegorical chariots rolled from the Plaza de la Reforma to the Plaza de la Constitución (Zócalo, which honored not the 1857 constitution followed by the Porfirian regime, but rather the liberal 1812 Cádiz constitution). A Gran Procesión Cívica went from the Glorieta de Colón to the Alameda park. In turn the military parade went from the monument of Independence to Avenida Juárez, and then along Calle San Francisco to the Palacio Nacional. By traversing these streets and avenues the parades occupied public space that was simultaneously an urban utopia and a conceptualization of the nation's history.

In addition, the *Centenario*, as part of the world's cycle of centennial celebrations, counted on a number of diplomatic missions.[42] The ideal city within Mexico City hosted these envoys of the world. That could be easily observed in the way most of the diplomats were accommodated. Although there were comfortable and luxurious hotels in Mexico City, as well as many large diplomatic residences, the Ministry of Foreign Relations had since 1909 compiled a list of houses that could be used to host the foreign.[43] Thus the ideal city welcomed the world, literally at home, at the various houses of the small and tightly interrelated Porfirian elite. Most of the houses that were identified as potential accommodations were located along the Paseo de la Reforma and Avenida Juárez, and the environs of these avenues. (See chapter 3.)

Both the inaugurated and planned new buildings, depending on their function, were located either within or outside the ideal city of the centenary. There were buildings to house undesirables, which were of course located outside the limits of the ideal city, as was the national mental hospital (at the Hacienda de la Castañeda) and the penitentiaries (San Lázaro and San Jacinto). By contrast, it was projected that the great new Palacio Legislativo would be an inherent part of the ideal city, a prolongation of Avenida Juárez. The same was true of the planned new Mexican Opera House, which was to be placed between the Alameda park and the new luxurious Post Office building, facing the replanned Avenida Cinco de Mayo. When the old National Theatre, which stood at the end of Cinco de Mayo, was demolished, the avenues of the new ideal city were embellished. Therefore, when Cinco de Mayo became the direct link between the Zócalo, the Alameda, and the new Opera House, a contest was held to select the most beautiful of the many new buildings that lined the street.[44]

These buildings and streets formed the desired core of the ideal city: instead of antiquated colonial buildings, the National Palace would form a straight line with the huge neoclassic republican parliamentary palace designed by a distinguished French engineer, Émile Bénard. This straight path included the luxurious San Francisco Street and the Avenida Juárez, and along them the modern monument of Juárez, the Alameda park, and the new art-nouveau white marble Opera House. This was indeed a cosmopolitan urban mirage.

The ideal city was also demarcated by a sort of cordon sanitaire. A city free of miasma and illness was a difficult achievement in the valley of Mexico, with its long history of floods and epidemics. Nonetheless, the city of the Centenario saw the conclusion of the desagüe works.[45] It also hosted the first large popular hygienic exhibition, built a national penitentiary, opened a new modern mental hospital, and forced communers to shower and dress in pants.

The organizers of the Centenario were convinced that the city needed to be whitened racially and culturally. During the centennial this goal reached extreme standards. As John Lear shows, there were various efforts to eradicate the presence of Indians and lower classes from the ideal city. But the very functional needs of the ideal city required the presence of Indians as well as all kinds of servants and workers. To solve this dilemma during the Centenario a solution was found: if we cannot get rid of them, at least let us camouflage them.

Indians habitually wandered throughout the city in calzón de manta (trousers) and guaraches (sandals). Therefore, during the Centenario influential Mexican diplomats proposed either prohibiting Indians from circulating in the city during the celebration, or dressing them properly: "Vistámosla [a la población indígena] y obligémosla a que use pantalones y blusa y calzado" (let us dress them, let us force them to wear real trousers and shirts and shoes).[46] Not only because "que dirán los extranjeros" (what are foreigners going to say?), but because it was important to make the Indian population tener necesidades (have needs) so that para vivir tenga que trabajar (in order to live it ought to work). For Indians, it was argued in this kind of proposal, "in order to obtain affection there is almost a physiological need to please others. Yet our *pelado* (urban pauper) instead attempts enchantment with his bristly hair and bare feet. Even among savage tribes a man wears his most showy collar when he pursues a female."[47]

These proposals were part of the hygienic needs of the ideal city. Since the 1880s Mexican hygienists had been dealing with urban-planning theories and practices of the hygienic city. By the 1900s this maneuvering was linked both to urban developers' interests and to the growing influence of sanitary ideas. Consequently, to a certain extent the sanitary city was made possible within the limits of the ideal city. The team of doctors and engineers that had been in charge of Mexico's sanitation since the 1880s were all actively involved in the centennial celebration.[48]

A Hygienic Exhibition and a National Congress of Medicine completed the picture of a hygienic city. The Hygienic Exhibition was organized by the Consejo Superior de Salubridad, meaning Eduardo Liceaga, who for decades had been in charge of Mexico's hygiene as eternal director of the Consejo.[49] In fact, the exhibition was a copy of the many kinds that had been organized at world's fairs during the late nineteenth century. The goal of these exhibitions was not only to display advances in hygiene but, more importantly, to popularize basic notions of hygiene. The greatest advance of hygienic theory was to make hygiene a concern of the state, beyond the common distinction between the public and private realms. The Hygienic Exhibition was placed at a special site constructed on the avenue of Los Hombres Ilustres. The paraphernalia of Mexican hygienists, which had been exhibited around the world to produce Mexico's modern image, were at last displayed in Mexico City for the benefit of Mexicans.[50]

The sanitary exhibitions were joined by many scientific (if less propagandistic) endeavors that included an international competition to find the cause and cure of typhus fever, which periodically attacked the city. These scientific endeavors were of course part of the *Centenario* but also belonged to the development of science in Mexico, and as such merit a special treatment (see chapter 10). All hygienic and scientific exhibits, congresses, and debates were, to be sure, part of the self-congratulatory official propaganda of the regime, but were also proof that the state had conquered its role as both educator of the masses and as promoter of useful science.

With this our first tour finishes. The shadow of the ideal city was there, and as such it was an idealized spectrum always in the making, always on the verge of extinction. And yet it was somehow real, for Mexico City's physical shape was significantly and lastly marked by the ideal city conceived in the era of the *Centenario*.

Tour 2

The city of the *Centenario* was the city of written and rewritten history, a story erected in monuments and piled over and over again in the same places. In order to examine this history, let us limit our tour to two main series of vistas. First, let us examine the two principal monuments that were inaugurated in 1910 and the exercise of historical reconstruction represented by the Desfile Histórico. Second, let us review the rewriting of history made by the city on and around the *Centenario*.

Given that the Paseo de la Reforma was the spine of the ideal city, it was natural that the city as a textbook of national history be written along this avenue and its surroundings. In the 1880s the Porfirian government pondered a plan to make the Paseo de la Reforma an exact chronological reconstruction of the nation's history, from its origins to its modern peace and progress. The Emperor Maximilian and his architect Louis Bolland originally designed the Paseo de la Reforma as a modern way to link the Castillo de Chapultepec with the Zócalo (1865).[51] In 1852 the monument of Carlos IV (known as El Caballito) was placed at the Plaza de la Reforma, marking the beginning of the Paseo de la Reforma, which was also the location of the monument to Columbus, designed by the French sculptor Carlos Cordier, erected in the 1860s by Antonio Escandón, and placed at the next circle in the Paseo de la Reforma on the way from Juárez to Chapultepec.[52] Next came Cuauhtémoc, one of the most important products of Porfirian *indigenismo*, whose statue was inaugurated in 1886; it was the glorification of Mexico's great Indian past.[53] Following this sequence it was thought that the Paseo de la Reforma could present a precise narration of Mexico's history: Spanish past (El Caballito), discovery (Columbus), Indian past (Cuauhtémoc), and the logical conclusion in the great monument of Independence. Thus in 1910 the "Ángel" of Independence was placed in the circle after Cuauhtémoc (figure 1.3).

Plans existed to construct another monument at the last circle before Chapultepec: an Arc de Triomphe that would celebrate the achievement of peace through its main architect and embodiment, Porfirio Díaz.[54] The debate was intense, financial problems limited the plans, and it seems that Díaz himself hesitated to accept a monument. There is no way to know for certain but it seems that Díaz was quite aware of the fact that his persona embodied not only his regime, but also lasting peace, the nation, and the state. At the very least there is some durable evidence: unlike many dictators in the nineteenth

1.2. Beginning of El Paseo de la Reforma (1900s),
courtesy A. Briquet Collection, Archivo General de la Nación, Mexico.

and twentieth centuries, both big and small, Díaz never allowed a monument to himself anywhere in the country. But there were plans—made by Italian architect Adamo Boari, the same architect who designed the Opera House and the Post Office building—for a fancy monument to Díaz.[55] In it Díaz would be represented as an eighteenth-century king standing on a neoclassic and art-nouveau pedestal. But it was never erected. The *Centenario* therefore limited the "monumental fever" to two important pieces of history set in stone: the monument to Independence, and that to Juárez.

The Independence monument has endured as Mexico City's landmark, and indeed was conceived as the universal symbol of Mexico's modernism and sovereignty. The designer, Antonio Rivas Mercado, was one of the few Mexican architects favored with contracts for major national construction projects. But he was a French-trained architect, a follower of the Paris beaux-arts style, who had lived in London and Paris for many years.[56] After winning the contract for the monument of Independence in 1906, he was sent to France and Italy to study sculptural works.[57] Rivas Mercado decided to place a Winged Victory standing on a column rooted to a vast base that encompassed even more symbols and extended the column's height (figure 1.3).[58] The Winged Victory, a half-naked Greek-like woman carrying laurels, was the quintessential representation of republican liberty throughout the nineteenth century. In 1910, for the first time, Mexico obtained its own version of this universal symbol.

A bronze composition of an enormous lion guided by a little boy was at the center of the base, and in the corners of the lower base there were representations of Law, Justice, War, and Peace. The lion and the boy, according to Rivas Mercado, was a representation of "el pueblo, fuerte en la guerra y dócil en la paz" (the people, strong in war, docile in peace). The statue of Miguel Hidalgo was placed on the upper base, facing the city and "recibiendo el homenaje de la Patria y de la Historia" (receiving the homage from *la Patria* and History). Also on the upper base, on either side of Hidalgo, were statues of heroes of the wars of Independence: José María Morelos, Vicente Guerrero, Francisco Javier Mina, and Nicolás Bravo. All the marble statues were designed by the sculptor Enrique Alciati and made in Carrara; the bronze statues were made in Florence, and the decorations for the monument in Paris. The ashes of the founding fathers of the nation were housed in the interior of the monument.

Inside the column and hidden from the public sight, between the two "Gloria" doors, a monument of a peculiar character guarded the heroes' ashes. This was the monument of Guillerme de Lampart, a rather obscure personality who nevertheless found a spot in Porfirian patriotic history. He was a seventeenth-century Irishman who, through a bizarre reading of the Bible, concluded that Spain did not have sovereign rights over New Spain, and thus plotted an inde-

1.3. Independence monument (1900), El Ángel, courtesy H. Duhart Collection,
Archivo General de la Nación, Mexico.

pendence movement. His story is worth a novel. After years of multiple perse-
cutions and several dispensations he was finally burned by the Inquisition in
1650.[59] This monument seemed to honor a precursor to Independence, but in
fact Lampart was a controversial figure in the late nineteenth-century reconstruction of the national past. In the first modern synthesis of the national
history (*México a través de los siglos*, edited by Vicente Riva Palacio), Lampart was

seen as an independence plotter but also one whose only goal was to distribute "a perpetuidad los naturales entre los encomenderos" (the Indians to *encomenderos* forever).[60] Alberto Lombardo was the first to conceive the idea to include a Lampart statue in the Independence monument.[61] For Lombardo, Lampart was not just a hero à la Carlyle, but also a martyr.[62] However, the influential liberal thinker and historian of the city, Luis González Obregón, strongly opposed the idea of including a statue of Lampart in the Independence monument. For him, Lampart was neither a hero "ni actor en aventuras ciertas o soñadas en su locura de grandeza" (nor an actor in true adventure or in adventures dreamt in his greatness madness).[63] Vicente Riva Palacio himself, in the last of his historical novels, portrayed Lampart as ambitious and intelligent, but not as a heroic character.[64]

In fact, Lampart represented a troublesome chapter for the Porfirian approach to the national past because his story distressed the balance of the reconciliation. For Jacobin, anti-Church liberals, Lampart was an opportunity to include in the Independence monument a heroic victim of the Church's darkness and cruelty. For more moderate, and often Catholic, liberals Lampart was not a hero, and the inclusion of a statue of him in the monument would weaken the national reconciliation. In the end the Lampart statue itself was made part of the reconciliation: it was erected, and included in the monument, but in its hidden location, showing that the Porfirian intelligentsia and bureaucracy were not willing to reopen hostilities with the Church. Undoubtedly, to place such a monument in the publicly visible portion of the Monumento de la Independencia would have generated a huge political, religious, and historiographical debate. Nonetheless Lampart is still there, in a quasi-secret cavern, guarding the heroes (or the madmen) he preceded.

The entire composition of the monument formed a mélange of republican neoclassic symbolism. There was nothing particularly Mexican about it, nor should there have been: republicanism and nationalism were universal values.[65] And, El *Ángel*, as it is known, still performs the function it was meant to play: to this day the reactionary and Porfirian icon par excellence is the site seized by people of all classes after either Mexican victories in an international soccer match or contested presidential elections. El *Ángel* is the nation, apparently accepted by all, though revered in different ways. Was this made possible despite or thanks to its original Porfirian amalgamation of peace-nation-state?

The Juárez monument, in turn, was located in the Alameda along the avenue that shared its name. The monument was a fundamental icon of the Porfirian pantheon: Benito Juárez was the epitome of the nineteenth-century liberalism that Porfirio Díaz constantly invoked regardless of his own ideological transformations. Juárez was considered the provider of justice for the

1.4. Avenida Juárez, Mexico City (circa 1922), showing axis Reforma-Juárez and the structure of the Legislative Palace then under construction.
Courtesy C. I. F. Collection, Mexico, Archivo General de la Nación, Mexico.

nation during what was then called the second independence (La Reforma). He was the architect of modernizing liberal reforms and the commander against the French invasion. What Juárez represented was the political and military background of Díaz's generation, which by 1910 was almost obsolete. But the monument was so important for the regime's symbolic purposes that originally its intended location was just in front of the National Palace, in the Zócalo. The influential and "modern" urban-planning view of Limantour encouraged a change of plans, and thus the monument was located on Avenida Juárez on one side of the Alameda, even though this meant dismantling and relocating the Mexican Alhambra, Mexico's pavilion at the 1884 New Orleans world's fair (figure 1.4).[66]

In the 1890s a national commission for the construction of the Juárez monument was created.[67] A contest for the model was organized, with Guillermo Heredia's design the winner. His was a grand project for a marble monument weighing 1,625 tons and occupying 510 square meters. The monument represented Juárez seated in a regal throne with two allegoric women surrounding him and a gardenia on his head. As the then Mexican diplomat Francisco León de la Barra described it, the monument had a "pure Hellenistic style, a divine blend of sweetness and strength, majesty and grace. To see it evokes Hegel's beautiful thought: 'beauty is the identity of thought and form.'"[68] Such style suited Juárez as a hero because, it was argued during the inauguration, he was "firme ante el huracán desbordante de las pasiones" (firm before the hurricane of unbounded passions). Two bronze lions, designed by the Mexican sculptor Guillermo Cárdenas, concluded the monument. All the marble and bronze works were contracted in Paris.

Unlike the monument of Cuauhtémoc that was meant to honor a mythical Indian past, the monument of Juárez was dedicated to an Indian who sought to honor the present. Here was an Indian who responded to contemporary universal values: republicanism, liberty, and justice—although Juárez's Jacobinism was not mentioned in this selective Porfirian reappropriation of the Benemérito de las Américas. Juárez carried a message, as orator Carlos Robles eloquently argued during the inauguration of the monument, for Mexicans and foreigners alike: "Here is the flesh of my flesh!, the blood of my blood! Juárez is mine, but he is also yours; he belongs to humankind."[69] An Indian who belonged to humanity had to be represented with Hellenic fashion and white marble. There was a design for a Juárez monument in Zapoteco style (Zapotec was Juárez's mother tongue); nevertheless, the Juárez centennial commission judged it as a "brave" but improper project.[70]

With both the Juárez and Independence monuments the ideal city acquired a coherent set of icons that made the idea of the nation discursively, ideologically, and physically real. This was a national history built on a specific conception of a liberal and republican consensus that made the nation possible and durable. Whether read from the Zócalo to Chapultepec or from Chapultepec to the Zócalo, the Paseo de la Reforma told the same story, fulfilling the ideal of an objective patriotic history: to make history a perfect unmistakable palindrome, with no conflicts or contradictions.

In turn, the Desfile Histórico was the momentary reshaping of the public space to make it into a perfect simulacrum of the official past. Like the Paseo de la Reforma itself, the desfile was divided into three great eras: Conquest, Spanish Rule, and Independence. Conquest was allegorized by a specific historical event that belonged to the chapter "Conquest." The selected event was acted out and turned into history-in-motion. This historical event was Moctezuma's meeting with Cortés outside Mexico City. The composition was formed by one thousand people, largely Indians, divided into warriors, priests, captains, virgins, and kings. The Spanish part of the scene was constituted by a troop of men on horseback, by Cortés and Doña Marina, as well as by a company of Tlaxcatecan Indians. The procession marched from La Plaza de la Reforma toward the Zócalo.

The scene selected to represent Spanish domination was "El Paseo del Pendón"—the colonial ceremony organized in Mexico City to commemorate the anniversary of Conquest every August 13. That scene was formed by 800 persons dressed in colonial style and aligned according to colonial hierarchy (headed by the Viceroy and the members of the Ayuntamiento). The parade went from San Hipólito toward Calle San Diego, and from San Francisco toward the Zócalo.

Finally the era of Independence was originally planned to include more than ten different scenes.[71] But at the end Independence was represented only by the entrance into Mexico City of the Ejército Trigarante—the army of the three guaranties, religion, unity, and national independence—, headed by its commander Agustín de Iturbide. The procession was followed by many allegorical carriages, equipped by the various states, representing scenes of the War of Independence that took place in their particular territories. It went from La Plaza de la Reforma (in El Caballito) toward the National Palace at the Zócalo.

It was estimated that more than fifty thousand people witnessed the entire Desfile Histórico. This was the first time that such a secular public civics lesson had taken place in Mexico City. Indeed, the Desfile Histórico was from the outset thought to be a conscious pedagogic and visual nationalistic lecture specifically meant to target the special needs of illiterate Mexicans, but in an allegorical language understandable to the world at large. Such influential personalities as Guillermo de Landa y Escandón and José Casarín were the original choreographers of the desfile.[72] And they aimed to make it a nationalistic lesson, but one that could be pedagogic (magnificent), historically accurate (scientific), and multicomprehensive. But in creating civic walks in the city, the civic discourse had to necessarily rewalk the many religious routes that were written in the city's streets over three centuries. The parade was not an original route but a rerouting of the ruins of paths left in the city by centuries of all sorts of parades and walks.[73]

The designers of the project emphasized the importance of authenticity and historical accuracy. All clothing "will rigorously match historical truth." Casarín sent envoys to Oaxaca, San Luis Potosí, Tlaxcala, Morelos, and Chiapas, as well as to the National Penitentiary in search of Indians. He wrote to the governor of Tlaxcala, Próspero Cahuantzi, himself an Indian, requesting 110 Tlaxcalan Indians to join the representation of Cortés meeting Moctezuma. From the governor of San Luis Potosí, Manuel Sánchez Rivero, he requested 250 Indians and, "if it were possible," 20 Indian women "de las más hermosas."[74] The search for *indias bonitas* would eventually return in 1921, in the centennial of the final completion of Independence, when a beauty contest titled La India Bonita took place. In the same way, Spanish organizations were asked for "native" or native-looking Spaniards to represent *gachupines* in the various scenes of the Desfile Histórico. The emphasis on historical accuracy was but one of the echoes of a scientific era.

This emphasis was expressed not only in the historical accuracy of the *desfile* but also, more importantly, in the many scientific events dealing with Mexico's past. In these congresses the themes of science, nation, and race were discussed. The relationship between science and nation had a pivotal topic: the intricate interrelation between the conceptualization of modern nation, cosmopolitan city, and race. In the last analysis, what this interrelation showed (at least in its materialization in the ideal city) was the insurmountable ambivalence of Porfirian scientists and thinkers in regard to race. While fostering the universal acceptance of a mestizo nation they had to manipulate international and national sciences and prejudices that were applied to Indians in order to produce both modern science and a cosmopolitan nation.

As part of the *Centenario* (and, for the second time, hosted by Mexico) the prestigious scientific Congress of Americanists was organized in Mexico City.[75] The 17th Congress of Americanists had great significance for the history of Mexican anthropology and archaeology. The reconstruction of Teotihuacán was concluded and the celebration was a good excuse to publicize Mexico as the Egypt of America. In addition, as a result of the 17th Congress of Americanists, the International School of Anthropology was created in Mexico City, headed by Franz Boas and sponsored by the Porfirian regime.[76] Simultaneously, the first *Indianista* congress took place, as well as the Pedagogical Congress.

Together these congresses displayed several ambivalent approaches to Mexico's Indian reality. An ancient Las Casas-type of paternalism combined with late nineteenth-century scientific racism, innovative forms of culturalist anthropology, and new avant-garde views in politics and the arts. By and large there existed a consensus on the perfectibility of Indians through education. Moreover, by 1910 the celebration of a mestizo nation had already acquired an importance that produced a scientific and ideological infrastructure that survived for the rest of the century. In both the *Indianista* and the Americanists congresses the glorification of *mestizaje*—often considered a postrevolutionary accomplishment—was a fundamental ingredient. No one better embodied the particularly ambivalent *indigenismo* and pro-*mestizaje* of the Porfiriato than the Minister of Justice and Education (as well as writer and poet) Justo Sierra. He stated at the inauguration of the 17th Congress of Americanists that "all the pre-Cortés world . . . belongs to us, it is our past, we have incorporated into ourselves . . . into our true national history, that which goes back to the union of conquered and conquerors in order to found a mestizo people that—allow me this display of patriotic pride—is gaining the right to be grand."[77]

The view of Indians expressed by the congress of Indianistas differed slightly from that of the Americanists.[78] Following Catholic and quasi-Lascasian approaches as well as nineteenth-century biological thought, this congress promoted the education and welfare of Indians in order to foster the achievement of a real and homogeneous nation. Jesús Díaz de León, a member of the Sociedad Indianista Mexicana, observed that surviving Indigenous kingdoms constituted Mexico. One of these kingdoms dominated the rest, "los convirtió en elementos de nutrición para su desarrollo" (it converted Indigenous cultures into nutritious elements for national development). In this sense, for Díaz de León, Mexico's war of Independence was a sort of "incomplete" physiological revolution. This movement was rooted not in an Indigenous utopia but rather in a biological and evolutionary trend that would select the best Indian attributes and project them toward a progressive future. These emerging ideas about the worth of Indigenous Mexicans contrasted with the many scientific evaluations of Indians as an inherently inferior, degenerative, and—for the purposes of national development—obstructive race.

Yet there was also a strong sense of solidarity with Spain during the Centenario, a kind of pan-Hispanism that acknowledged Spain at its head. Since 1876 Spain and Mexico seemed to live "parallel lives." After decades of instability defined by liberals fighting against conservatives, religious wars, and the imposition of Bourbon and other foreign monarchs, Mexico and Spain reached an era of stability that, from the perspective of 1910, appeared clearly demarcated. The stability started in 1876 with the ascension of Porfirio Díaz in Mexico and la restauración of the Bourbon monarchy, commanded by the young and popular Alfonso XII with an Iberian Machiavelli, Antonio Cánovas del Castillo, in Spain. By 1910 the Porfiriato and la restauración had gone through many ups and downs, but both regimes were epochal symbols of reaching peace, overcoming the weight of history, and achieving economic progress after their difficult nineteenth centuries. Thus in the 1890s it was common to find phrases such as Cánovas, "the Bismarck of Spain"; Díaz, "the Bismarck of Mexico"; and Cánovas and Díaz, "tamers of lions." And of course there were the events of 1898, which caused the Spain of la restauración to rediscover its own pan-Hispanism and its links with Mexico. Thus the official pan-Hispanism of the Centenario was also a Spanish rediscovery of Mexico through both Spain's own discovery of oligarchic peace and progress and its nostalgic imperial pan-Hispanism—which, translated as anti-Americanism, could be either Mexican or Spanish.

That is why it was none other than Camilo García de Polavieja y del Castillo, Marqués de Polavieja, who became the Spanish envoy to Mexico City in 1910. He was a successful officer who had defeated Cuban and Philippine revolts, had been a main exponent of Spanish *regeneración* (scientific, political, and cultural renewal of Spain) after 1898, served as minister of war, and by 1910 was a very close adviser to King Alfonso XIII. The man embodied the spirit of Spain during *la restauración*: a military guardian of oligarchic peace, a nostalgic imperialist (a biographer and admirer of none other than Cortés), and thus a deep anti-American (U.S.), and also a great promoter of the Spanish spirit he still found alive in the old daughters of Spain. Therefore, he brought symbolic presents with him—Morelos's possessions, for one—but also promoted a very important exhibit of Spanish art housed in a special building located in the corner of Avenida Juárez and Balderas. There the inhabitants of the city experienced in the same location new Mexican art—with artists such as Saturnino Herrán, Diego de Rivera (as Diego Rivera was then known), and José Clemente Orozco—, Japanese products in the Japanese exhibition, and great new Spanish paintings from Benlliure, Nogales, García Rodríguez, Lucena, Huerta, Serra, Zubiaurre, Placencia, Zuloaga, Sorolla, and Chicharro.[79]

This pan-Hispanic switch was a result both of a generational change in the political elite (the old Jacobin anti-Spanish liberals had been supplanted by the *científicos*), and of a deliberate attempt to display reconciliation in the context of the hundredth anniversary of the nation's birth. The new generation was strongly marked by a modernist vocabulary (as, for instance, articulated by Rubén Darío after 1898) in which a quasi-racist pan-Hispanism—mostly directed against the U.S. "lion"—was a fundamental component. In addition, within a scheme of organic cultural growth, reconciliation was considered a sign of physical and cultural maturity. As Pimentel y Fagoaga, president of the *ayuntamiento* of Mexico City, stated at the dedication of the Isabel la Católica Street: "We might as well say it. Today the growing culture of the Mexican people has erased, with the clean water of a well-understood and better-practiced cosmopolitanism, the prejudices, the hatreds, and the resentments that until recently hindered the recognition of the cultural merits that produce this ceremony."[80]

However strong this renewed pan-Hispanism was, it had to be constantly adapted and accommodated to *indigenismo*, *indianismo*, and pro-*mestizaje*. Nonetheless, the fact that in 1910 this sort of pan-Hispanism was so apparent helps to explain why the generation that was coming of age at this precise moment pushed these tendencies further. (Consider, for instance, the case of José Vasconcelos and the Ateneo de la Juventud.) It also helps to explain why the 1930s indigenist reaction was so powerful.

These tendencies were part of the continual rewriting of national history. Monuments, parades, streets, and even modern moving pictures were the pens with which the *Centenario* wrote national history.[81] Either new heroes were created or new virtues were found in the eternal heroes, all according to the context of the 1900s. With one last revealing example of implicit historical revisionism, we conclude our visits to the centennial city. In 1910 Mexican sociologist and writer Porfirio Parra accepted a proposal to alter stanzas of the national anthem. Accordingly, the fourth stanza was totally expunged and the seventh was modified significantly. The fourth, a glorification of Antonio López de Santa Anna, had previously gone unnoticed by official historians. The seventh stanza alluded to the problematic figure of the conservative emperor, Agustín de Iturbide. The historiographical ambivalence toward the role of Iturbide in the war of Independence was one thing, but it was a quite different matter to glorify him in the national anthem. Parra did not hesitate to change a verse so that, instead of saying "de Iturbide la sacra bandera" (from Iturbide the sacred flag), it said "de la patria la sacra bandera" (from *la patria* the sacred flag).[82]

This is the end of our tour: we have seen how the stone lines of the city make a complicated history textbook, one that is physically fixed yet has a fluid meaning.

Tour 3

This tour of the centennial city can be arranged only at a historical distance. It is an excursion into the experience of style and its historical metamorphosis. By rewalking the centennial city, one can grasp how a particular notion of cosmopolitanism was generalized and became the common style, first, of an elite. But I also want to show how easily such a style became no-style, i.e., *cursilismo*: a garish, frustrated attempt to achieve a universal canon. That was the nature of modern cosmopolitanism: ephemeral, trendy, homogenizing, and yet compulsory.[83]

The ideal city did not present a harmonious and homogeneous unique style. Rather, it contained the marks of decades of cultural and aesthetic experimentation, the marks of a long trial-and-error pursuit of cosmopolitan fashions. The well-known building of the La Perla jewelry near La Profesa temple, for example, or the particular baroqueism of the new Post Office building contrasted with the modern steel-and-concrete buildings of Cinco de Mayo, as well as with the expensive residences in all sorts of modern European and American styles in the *colonias* Juárez and Cuauhtémoc.[84] These modern constructs shared the space with old colonial buildings and monuments. The ideal city was already an architectural collage of different chronological and conceptual understandings of a cosmopolitan style. The ideal city promoted by the *Centenario* was yet another important layer in these attempts at collage.

To be sure, in 1910 there was a more or less clear style that was officially pursued. However, artistic forms follow a capricious global development that bureaucrats cannot easily manage. A sort of officially sponsored style could be perceived, with slight differences, in the monument to Independence, the Juárez monument and, very importantly, in the two most extensively planned buildings of the early twentieth century (the Mexican Opera House and the Palacio Legislativo). But artists at the Mexican art exhibit showed a complex combination of styles, as well as social and artistic preoccupations. At the Mexican artist display in the Academia de San Carlos, traditional nineteenth-century trends merged with impressionist, indigenist, figurative, and modernist influences. They ranged from the rather conservative sculptures by Fidencio Nava to Saturnino Herrán's and José Clemente Orozco's first innovative paintings. Moreover a young Mexican painter, then known as Diego de Rivera, returned from his European studies sponsored by the Porfirian governor of Veracruz in order to exhibit for the fist time in his own country, only to return to Europe soon after the *Centenario*.[85] This exhibit was indeed artistically revolutionary, and it showed how Porfirian support for the arts lay at the roots of well-known postrevolutionary Mexican art.

The *Centenario* was also an unparalleled occasion to inaugurate the largest architectural projects of the Porfirian government. Even though economic and technical difficulties delayed the conclusion of the two largest projects, cornerstones were still laid and by the time of the centennial celebration both projects were fully on their way. Many Mexican architects participated in the design contest for both buildings, but, after much controversy, both contracts were granted to foreigners: an Italian, Adamo Boari, for the National Opera House, and a Frenchman, Émile Bénard, for the Palacio Legislativo.[86] Boari had worked in Burnham's architectural office in Chicago during the 1893 World's Fair.

The discussion and planning of these two buildings is a long story.[87] Suffice it to say that both were meant primarily as proof of Mexico's cosmopolitanism: an Opera House constructed in the avant-garde art-nouveau style with marble from Carrara; and a Palacio Legislativo in the colossal neoclassic style of French public buildings. However, both buildings were designed according to modern steel-and-concrete construction techniques rather than the customary construction methods of the early nineteenth-century neoclassic buildings.[88] Both French and Italian sculptors and architects were hired for the many marble and granite columns, caryatides, frontons, bronze lions, and eagles.[89]

Given that these buildings were the main examples of Porfirian cosmopolitanism, it is small wonder that they underwent more transformations during the postrevolutionary regimes than any other civic building. The art-nouveau Opera House was finished in 1934 as a grotesque mixture of art-nouveau, functionalist-deco, and indigenist motifs. The Palacio Legislativo, after many failed attempts, became a 1930s type of quasi-fascist immense monument to revolution, though its cornerstone still held coins and newspapers from September 23, 1910, and a crystal sphere containing the poems and speeches delivered that day. Indeed, underneath architect Carlos Obregón Santacilia's 1930s revolutionary adaptation of the Palacio Legislativo lay, enclosed within the crystal sphere, Alejandro Nuñez's Porfirian rhetorical piece, garish by the 1930s: "Que en el alcazar marmóreo se agigante/de ardoroso civismo el sentimiento/y entre bregas patrióticas levante/los himnos de concordia el parlamento."[90]

How cosmopolitan was that language in 1910, and how modern were the great buildings of the ideal city that it figuratively and literally embodied? By and large, the designed new urban landscape constituted an unquestionable cosmopolitan experience: rather than antiquated colonial buildings, the National Palace formed a straight line with the giant neoclassical republican parliamentary palace, a line formed in turn by luxurious San Francisco Street and Juárez Avenue, where the modern monument to Juárez, the garden of the Alameda, and the marble white art-nouveau Opera House could be found. The Paseo de la Reforma intersected this line with an elegant design that told the history of the nation. This was a dream that very few contemporaries would have repudiated. However, when taken building by building and decision by decision, there were many conflicting and contradictory views of cosmopolitanism. Mexican architects strongly criticized the various designs of official and private buildings, especially because very few nationals won contracts for major buildings. In addition, Mexican architects (especially professors at the national school of architecture) profoundly disapproved of rapid steel-and-concrete constructions.[91] Since colonial times, there had been conflict between architects and engineers, i.e., between classic views of architecture as art against technological improvements and functionalism in architecture. Manuel Torres Torrija, an architect and engineer, in commenting on the development of architecture in the early 1900s, observed: "We have had in Mexico pre-Columbian architectures, vivid colonial architectures, and conspicuous influences from French styles . . . as well as the more and more frequent imitation of American buildings. [All this] has led to the prostitution of architectural tastes supported by the evangelization of incredible absurdities."

What Torres Torrija criticized was precisely what the ideal city stood for: rapid, speculative, and commercialized architecture. Urban developers and foreign architects were accumulating great fortunes and thus, Torres Torrija believed, beauty was sacrificed. Other influential architects, such as the Mariscal brothers, articulated similar complaints.[92] In the 1900s prominent Mexican architects believed that Mexican cosmopolitanism was under attack from commercialism and from the north through U.S. influence and money.[93]

In 1898, when discussing different proposals for the Palacio Legislativo, a jury of the most distinguished Mexican architects hesitantly favored a neoclassic project that included steel construction.[94] The approved project was subsequently criticized as one of those buildings that "came into existence when buildings became steel cages covered with stone, the latter having no other use save to hide the beams, girders and trusses of steel."[95] Within the jury a bitter controversy took place regarding the project submitted as "Majestas." Apparently this project presented a novel functional use of space and several engineering innovations. The project was strongly supported by some juries. Nonetheless, the jury reluctantly decided to favor the neoclassical project arguing, as the secretary of the jury wrote, that "the builder shall not forget that he must also be an artist if he wants to earn the name of architect; let the outrageous idea that buildings can be separated from beauty not be propagated." Thus Majestas was "decadent architecture, an industrial construction rather than an artistic building."[96] Eventually none of the projects discussed in 1898 was accepted. Instead the French architect Émile Bénard was hired to make the *palacio* even more classic and "artistic." A similarly neoclassical and grandiose project, by the German architect P. J. Weber, was awarded the second prize. This project exemplifies the chaotic Porfirian craft of their own cosmopolitism: architect Manuel Francisco Álvarez discovered afterwards that Weber's project was a copy of the design Friedrich von Thiersch submitted for the 1882 contest for the new Reichstag in Berlin. For diplomatic reasons the monetary prize was granted nevertheless.[97]

Émile Bénard had worked under architect Charles Garnier in the construction of the Paris Opera. In 1867 he won a Gran Prix de Rome for an art exposition building, which later seemed to have been copied by the architects for the 1893 Chicago World's Fair. His great success was marked by his winning design for the Berkeley campus of the University of California, a bizarre mixture of neoclassic architecture and the city beautiful movement. His California project, however, was never fully completed because Phoebe Apperson Hearst, the wealthy donor for the project, engaged in various mêlées with Bénard and ended up hiring an American architect to replace him in 1901. Bénard's U.S. exposure is vital for understanding Mexico's selection. He was the perfect synthesis of modern aesthetics, technical skill, and classical taste. Díaz himself invited Bénard. The French architect designed an immense building that was seriously criticized by a Mexican commission made up of, among others, distinguished architects Antonio Rivas Mercado, Guillermo Heredia, and Nicolás Mariscal. The commission argued that the building was excessive in size, style, and cost. Despite these protests Bénard's final project was approved in 1905, observing that the building was to remain a *Templo de la Ley* (Temple of Law) in which the *sacerdotes* (priests) would be the *diputados* (congressmen).[98]

Bénard was joined by a French architect who had experience in China, M. Rosin, and a group of sculptors (André Joseph Allar, Paul Gasq, Laurent Marqueste, and George Gardet). The technological challenges were significant since the building, like the Reichstag in Berlin, was heavy and the soil watery. The Parliament would have to combine the republican classicism of the U.S. capitol and the grand style of Roman statuary. This was in fact one of the greatest undertakings of the Porfiriato. But Bénard's destiny was to never complete his great projects. "He was," said one of his students in 1939, "an 1820 man lost in our days. Practical considerations were nothing to him." The Mexico City of 1910 echoed this anachronism. The Revolution stopped not just the construction, but also the spirit that inspired the original Palacio Legislativo.[99]

The expensive building, however, was meant to house a republican parliament. Why devote so many resources to a simple façade for an undemocratic regime? Façades are as important in architecture as they are in politics, not only for an undemocratic regime but for any kind of regime. In the 1900s our contemporary understanding of a representative parliament did not exist in any of the world's parliaments, not even in Washington (where a large percentage of the population remained shut out of democratic institutions) or London (where only about 6 percent of the population could vote). The undemocratic Bismarck built a Reichstag that survived all sorts of revolutions and regimes save the openly undemocratic National Socialists, which could easily afford to burn it soon after the election of Adolf Hitler. The Porfirian parliament was thus an indispensable structure: indeed a façade, but one without which the city, the nation, and the state could not be established. It was worth any expense.

The official buildings were seen by foreigners as too classical and imitative (the Opera House and the Palacio Legislativo), and the private architecture of the ideal city was considered too commercialized, nonclassical, and American. For some French architects who supported the revival of neoclassicism, Mexicans were too Americanized, and thus Mexico's architecture was less beautiful than functional, and by and large uneven. A French architect argued that "the Mexican sense of style is formed," but the final style was as yet unclear and imitative. This was not an atavist defect of Mexicans but rather a natural consequence of Mexico's accelerated economic development. Mexico could only have a transitional style, which was but a Spanish style "modifié."[100] If the doggedly argued *afrancesamiento* of Mexico meant modernism and cosmopolitanism, Mexico City had an ungrateful response from its model: for the French, Mexico was not sufficiently French. American architects, in turn, admired Mexico's colonial architecture more than the many buildings and houses designed by Americans in Mexico City. In fact avant-garde American architects were imitating Spanish-colonial style, for instance in Californian architecture that became fashionable in the 1910s. In the 1900s American companies constructing buildings within the ideal city outnumbered both Mexican and European contractors. When the *ayuntamiento* of Mexico City decided to organize a contest to honor the most beautiful building on the reshaped Cinco de Mayo Avenue in 1903, most of the contractors were Americans, and steel construction covered by plaster and concrete prevailed. Rapidly constructed tall buildings were amusing for the people but a real headache for promoters of the ideal city à la française. So much was this the case that in 1904 Adamo Boari, designer of both the Opera House and the Palacio de Correos, complained about the altitude of the new buildings on Cinco de Mayo that eclipsed his Palacio de Correos.

The architectural collage of the 1910 ideal city can be considered according to two historical viewpoints. On one hand, from a panoramic historical perspective, it was yet another frustrated experiment in cosmopolitanism. On the other, from a historical close-up that highlights the specificity of the moment in view of what followed, the collage created by the centennial ideal city was indisputable proof of genuine cosmopolitanism and modernism. In other words, architecturally the ideal city was a failed style, even for contemporaries, because it was absurdly imitative and unfaithful to universal canons. (And, of course, the ideal city would have produced a sharp contrast if compared with the deterioration and sanitary problems in the rest of the city.) But the ideal city was truly cosmopolitan precisely because of its imitative trends. It was cosmopolitan and modern because it was mimetic, and because it was already a realm of capital speculation, trendy and ephemeral aesthetics, and technological advancement. In this sense the ideal city was as modern and cosmopolitan as Paris, while beginning to experiment with new cosmopolitan models in Chicago and New York.

In sum, the desire for style was a fundamental component of the culture of the centennial city. However passé it could appear to contemporary eyes, that style was a collage of tendencies old and new, national and international; a collage that was dictated, first, by the intrinsic ephemeralness and globality of modern styles. But the collage also responded to efforts at achieving cosmopolitanism on the margins. In the final analysis the ideal city contained within Mexico City fell short of a total belle époque city not because it lacked energy, mimetic abilities, or a powerful elite, but simply because Mexico City was not Paris. Even the New York of *The American Scene* was not Paris. Yet by the 1900s the ideal city was an experiment that already included inventive and hypermodern styles; it was a city already making the switch to new poles of cultural attraction, towards all that which was often known, both by Mexicans and foreigners, as "American."

And Then . . .

Mexico City stacked various cities within itself. There were many sanitary, social, urban, and cultural anti-ideals running against the elites. After all, the ideal views epitomized by the *Centenario* were only a simulacrum; "reality" did not match these ideals, yet that fact neither hindered the celebration nor terminated the ideals. If anything it made them more alluring. Nevertheless, only a month after the great celebration, the cultural fabric I have surveyed here was contested. The democratic movement headed by the wealthy landowner Francisco I. Madero unlocked violence. But even by 1912 no one knew they were living a revolution. By 1914 the Porfirian city was taken over by *campesinos*, and gradually violence acquired the name "Revolution." By 1921 the city once again celebrated, in a conscious revolutionary fashion, a *centenario*: the centennial of the end of Mexico's war of Independence in 1821.

The postrevolutionary city eventually redirected the essentials of the Porfirian ideal city, in time radically departing from the Porfirian style. For the culture epitomized by the 1910 centennial city was over by 1940 not only because of Mexico's Revolution. The Revolution was a part of a wider demise: the nineteenth century itself had come to an end. But it was a gradual decline. In 1912 President Madero consulted with Bénard about the continuation of the great building; the city represented by the Palacio Legislativo could possibly be rehabilitated in a way that would not contradict the democratic opening Madero had epitomized. As late as 1922 Alberto J. Pani and Émile Bénard's son signed a contract to reconstruct the main dome of the building as a Pantheon for Mexico's heroes, who were the same characters of the story written over the Porfirian decades. Bénard presented the designs; but the project, though signed, was never completed.[101] The Pantheon was conceived with a strong nineteenth-century sense of grandeur. It was supposed to be a sort of Napoleonic grave for all the nation's heroes.

By contrast, 1921 meant for the city a sort of déjà vu: the revolutionary celebration reiterated, as unintended parody, what the pompous Porfirian celebration had been. For what 1921 celebrated was not 1821, but the assumed triumph over what the 1910 celebration meant.[102] In fact, the Mexico City of 1921 culturally meant not a break but the expansion of what the Porfirian *Kulturkämpfe* and contradictions had advanced. In trying to be so different, and yet in being so much as the 1910 celebratory city, the Mexico City of 1921 inaugurated the revolutionary city as the appropriation of the Porfirian city—its symbolic styles, its speculative nature, its urban plan, its tackiness, and its power. And yet, the 1921 celebration announced the vast economic and cultural success that was to come over the twentieth century, the one that altered the city's destiny, transforming it into one of the world's first megalopolises.

Revolutionary general and President Álvaro Obregón appointed a commission in charge of the celebration, headed by lawyer and former Maderista chief of Mexico City's police Emiliano López Figueroa. The goal of the celebration was to be popular, not the commemoration of the privileged class, but the "triumph of the people."[103] In fact, many intellectuals and media entrepreneurs, who had in common their link to the growing newspaper industry, were incorporated into the revolutionary coalition. Thus the entire celebration was marked by press propaganda skills. But to be sure, the regime had no time, no money, to plan a great celebration, and thus it ended up being a collage of the interests and dreams of the old and new political and intellectual classes.

The person, however, who truly controlled the celebration was the same character who had become extremely influential in controlling the urban, cultural, and political development of Mexico City, namely, Alberto J. Pani—in 1921 the minister of foreign affairs. Pani received numerous proposals, from citizens, from governors, from newspapers, and from diplomats: a proposal to bring to the capital three Indigenous men, according to their level of civilization, or another one from California, suggesting the use of the celebration to pay U.S. journalists to write favorable pieces about Mexico in order to ease the discrimination against Mexicans in the United States. Curiously, as in 1910, there were proposals to change the national anthem, once again related to Emperor Iturbide's role in Mexican history: Bernando Beltrán wrote to Pani asking to reinclude Catholics and Iturbide in its lyrics. There were proposals for an international exhibition, and old Porfirian goal and objects were recycled, like the four Pegasus by French sculptor Querol—originally part of the Porfirian Opera House—, which were used to crown parades and official celebrations.

From banquets to archaeology, the revolutionary celebration was a total Porfirian reenactment. There was a major banquet in the main patio of the National Palace converted into a garden, which followed *avant la lettre* the script of 1910. Regardless of the organizers' "populist" rhetoric, the banquet's menu was as French as in Porfirian times—consommé Rachel, darnes de saumon Chambord, asperges sauce mousseline. On behalf of the diplomatic delegations, the Brazilian ambassador responded to General Obregón's toast, which talked about the cultural revolution that was to come after the violent part of the Revolution. Another banquet took place in the Congress, again with French menu, and in it Congressman Miguel Alonso Romero—with no sense of irony whatsoever, with champagne and with glasses and plates from the Habsburg emperor Maximilian—toasted: "this Mexico that now is aware that the endless hope of men and peoples is not in the furniture of perfumed halls . . . but in the busy apiary of factories and in the sublime pray of the plow." And thus they toasted in the rhetoric of 1921 that sounded like that of 1910, the same literary heroes now recycled as heroes of the social revolution headed by Obregón:

> And you all [vosotros], brothers in Cervantes, in Darío, in Rodó, in Juan Montalvo, go tell the legitimate representatives of you peoples, to those proletarians like us who do not see themselves in Rigaud's aroma but in libertarians themselves, tell them that one evening Mexico hugs them tightly with the unique and sincere embrace of its one-armed hero of Celaya [Obregón].[104]

Like in 1910, the 1921 celebration included a visit to Teotihuacán archaeological ruins for all the foreign envoys, guided by the new luminary of Mexican anthropology and archaeology, Manuel Gamio—who was then writing his Columbia doctoral dissertation about the population of Teotihuacán. The Porfirian chief of archeological works, Leopoldo Batres, was exiled, and Gamio was in 1921 the star student of the great Porfirian intellectuals of the National Museum—Batres, Andrés Molina Enríquez, Pablo González Casanova—, and had become an important cultural promoter of the revolutionary regime. The emphasis on the mestizo as the national character, the effort to make Teotihuacán the Egypt of America, and the culturalist twisting of global evolutionary anthropology—all these went back to Porfirian times. But regardless of Gamio's intellectual trajectory, the 1921 visit to Teotihuacán was but the repetition of an old nationalist ritual, and in it Gamio consciously played the role of the translator of his Porfirian lessons to the emerging revolutionary vocabulary.[105] That is why in the 1921 visit to Teotihuacán, the minister of agriculture, Antonio I. Villarreal, explained to the audience that the Obregón regime was set on making the "antigua Roma de las razas aborígenes de México" (ancient Rome of Mexico's aboriginal races) the most interesting archaeological city of the world, which is exactly what the Porfirian archaeologists did. After the visit followed a banquet at nearby caves, all as 1910 had done.

Due to the celebration's link with the booming newspaper industry in the capital—especially stimulated by the growing importance of print media for national and international political and commercial propaganda, sponsored by generals, intellectuals, and private interests—, the event was replete with "civic" commemorations assembled by newspapers and civic organizations. According to the official chronicler, these commemorations, regardless of their actual leitmotifs, were remarkably democratic—they were undertaken by those who conceived them. Thus there were kermises in an elegant social club and restaurant planned by the French community of Mexico City, and also distribution of clothing in prisons and in orphanages planned and undertaken by President Obregón's wife. There were ceremonies honoring the Indigenous warriors of Sonora and Sinaloa, organized by the army—in view of their participation in Obregón's armies from 1914 to 1917. The city's Commercial and Industrial Chamber organized flower battles, and, together with the city's government, private companies of all sorts, and various newspapers, organized a parade of allegorical carriages, which once again circulated through Reforma, Juárez, Madero, and Zócalo. Of special notice was the carriage of El Universal— the newspaper closest to the government and owned by the influential politician and cultural entrepreneur F. J. Palavicini. The carriage carried the winner of the concurso racial (racial competition), as it was characterized by the newspaper, "La India Bonita" (the beautiful Indian woman), who sat in a moving stage full with Aztec motifs, reproductions of Cuauhtémoc, pyramids, and Aztec stones.[106] Maria Bibiana Uribe was "la india bonita," and rival newspapers contested her crowning—for being not really Indian, but mestiza—, but there were poems, popular plays, and experts' opinions about her. The contest, however, was only one of many that followed the 1920s international beauty contests in the world—in Mexico City in 1921 there were also contests for the best female worker and the best maid.

The carriages, far from being a more democratic expression, were a blend of new and old nationalistic motifs and the luminaries of the leftovers of Mexican aristocracy. Thus: "driving a carriage alike to a huge tray from Michoacán, were the Pani, Osorio, and Braniff children." The judges in charge of selecting the best allegoric carriage were prominent ladies of Porfirian and the new revolutionary elites, such as Esther Alva de Pani, María G. Braniff, and Concepción Rincón Gallardo. These family names sharply contrasted with the popular spirit of the celebration.

The arts were also part of the celebration, though instead of exhibits of Spanish and Japanese art the organizers sponsored an exhibit of popular arts— conceived by revolutionary publicist and painter Gerardo Murillo, Dr. Atl. The exhibit was akin to the many collections of pots, textiles, and crafts assembled by the Porfirian regime to exhibit in many world's fairs. What was different was the justification and the context of the exhibit. The exhibit was not meant as a simple picturesque sample of Mexico's popular arts, but as the roots of the emerging real, truly Mexican new art. That is why more important than the objects exhibited was the appropriation of the event, and of the motifs and styles, by a the group of artists who soon were put to work for the Revolution by Education Minister José Vasconcelos: Dr. Atl, Roberto Montenegro, and the Parisian artist who came back to Mexico in 1921, not as Diego de Rivera but simply as Diego Rivera.

In sum, the 1921 celebration followed the script of 1910 almost *avant la lettre*, and yet added several tones that significantly marked the future of the city. First, while the 1910 celebration was, as it were, elitist, the 1921 was not only elitist but consciously organized as the party of the good families of Mexico, as a sign of a new harmony among old Porfirian and new revolutionary elites. As such it was the party of the enchantment of the city by the new revolutionary provincial elites. But, second, this display of the *gente decente* was nevertheless rhetorically supported not in abstract liberal notions of "the people," but in more concrete ideas of the peasant, the Indian, the worker, the urban poor, the maid. Whereas the 1910 celebration included the debates about race and nation, the 1921 celebration expanded the Porfirian racial debates toward contradictory notions: racial improvement, miscegenation, *indigenismo*, and a sort of folklorist mania for authenticity. Whether Porfirian debates would have led to these contradictory goals without the 1910 Revolution is a counterfactual exercise that is hard to solve. But that all the scientific, moral, and political elements that sustained the 1921 debates were part of the Porfirian milieu is undeniable. What is true is that Porfirian *indigenismo* was made into a more commercial nationalism and a more scientifically racial welfare state. Finally, the 1921 celebration, in its conscious search for local authenticity, started the articulation of a nation, of a capital city, militantly designed to embody a more socially comprehensive and, in a word, more modern state and culture.

End

By the 1940s, the 1910 ideal city was uncovered, almost in an archaeological fashion, by Carlos Obregón Santacilia. The official postrevolutionary architect transformed the ruins of the Porfirian Palacio Legislativo into an enormous fascist-like monument of Revolution. The cornerstone that Porfirio Díaz had laid during the 1910 celebration was unearthed and its cargo of newspapers, coins, and documents was stolen. With the disappearance of these objects, Obregón Santacilia observed, "Even the last vestige of the Porfirian building has disappeared, as it ought to in yielding to another epoch that builds on these ruins."[107]

Indeed, Obregón Santacilia's final use of the *palacio*'s ruins meant a grave for Porfirian Mexico City. The metropolis began to pile on a new "modern" city over the remains of the Porfirian ideal city, not only because of the Revolution but also because of the emergence of twentieth-century massive politics and avant-garde cultural trends. Yet, as in Italo Calvino's imaginary Berenice city, what I wanted to convey was not only that "the real Berenice is a temporal succession of different cities, alternatively just and unjust," but also to warn about "something else: all the future Berenices are already present in this instant, wrapped one within the other, confined, crammed, inextricable."[108] The essential ideals—conclusive nationalism, cosmopolitanism, and modernization—that inspired the centennial city are still today's goals. Whatever the twenty-first-century megalopolis does with those ideals now will be an unavoidable lesson, however devastating and heartless, for a world that for so long has asserted them.

ON 1910 CONTRASTS
WASHINGTON AND MEXICO CITY

True: Mexico City, Buenos Aires, Madrid, and Barcelona, despite their dissimilarities, share unmistakable historical echoes. Or so we assumed. Washington, D.C., on the other hand, appears as a city of a very different kind—no two cities, no two national histories, could seem less alike. But to historically gaze at both cities around 1910 furnishes, I believe, a unique picture of the contrasts involved in global urban planning, nationalism, state-building, citizenship, and the beginnings of megalopolises at the end of the nineteenth century. Brief vistas to these contrasts—to paraphrase George de Santayana who, as Spaniard, claimed to conceive un-English things in English—result in un-Mexican ways of Mexican history, and in un-American forms of American history.

I

Between 1900 and 1925 both Mexico City and Washington underwent radical modern transformations. Like the group formed for the centennial celebration in Mexico City around 1910, in 1901 the McMillan Commission was organized in Washington, D.C.—a group of artists, engineers, and architects that undertook the studies that eventually resurrected the blueprint of the original design of the city by the French architect Pierre Charles L'Enfant. Thus began the final construction of the ideal modern capital within Washington.[1] By the 1910s the new capital was emerging to incarnate a renewed nationalism, one that was post-Reconstruction, post-1898, post-depression, progressive, cosmopolitan, and imperial. The nationalism of the 1890s was epitomized by the European travels of the McMillan Commission in search of grandiose designs for the capital, in the comprehensive plan for a beautiful city, or in the decision to build an immense memorial monument to Lincoln. By 1900 this new nationalism was indeed symbolized by the cultural triumph of a national capital that had finally overcome its inferiority complex and its love and hate vis-à-vis European standards. Such a triumph was achieved, ironically, by European-izing the capital, while the world was Americanizing architecture and urban planning.[2]

Late nineteenth-century ideal cities—either in Mexico City or Washing-ton—were the main offspring of their respective state-sponsored national-isms, conceived according to common cosmopolitan models. Washington and Mexico City were thus together, at times looking at each other face to face, but most of the time through a cosmopolitan mirror made by global industrial change, technological innovation, and trendy aesthetic and scientific ideas. These ideal cities, like those of the Renaissance, were never fully realized, al-though they kept a conspicuous resemblance to military order.[3]

Washington became a capital depicting a nation erected on universal, mod-ern axes (freedom, democracy, individualism, industriousness); a nation, like Mexico, that had as much history as it had a need to teach it, to exhibit it, to impose it, and to express it materially. The Washington Mall finally material-ized this version of the new nation. Two monuments can help understand the likeness in the 1910s of these apparently dissimilar capital cities: the Lincoln Memorial (planned in 1900 and finally finished in 1922) and the Juárez monu-ment (inaugurated in 1910).[4] Both followed a similar neoclassic marble style. Both were at the core of the geographical axes planned by their respective ideal cities as epitomes of their respective civil religions and national histories. Moreover, there was a Plutarch-like parallel between the lives of Teddy Roose-velt's Lincoln and Porfirio Díaz's Juárez. The Lincoln of early radical Recon-struction was unacceptable not only to defeated Southern states, but also to the more moderate, but alas imperialist, Republicanism sponsored by Roosevelt as historian, military officer, and president. Yet Roosevelt and the McMillan Plan sanitized Lincoln in order to make it into the most unified myth of the Progressive Era. Finally, Lincoln was canonized as the savior of the union, not as an emancipator of slaves. His monument, as well as the engraving of his image on the penny coin, was the final enthronement of such a hero in the na-tional history. A similar path followed Juárez: a liberal president of Indigenous origins who had commanded the defeat of the French-sponsored Maximilian empire in Mexico. But he was also a controversial Jacobin who caused enor-mous antipathy among Catholics and moderate liberals. More importantly, by the late 1860s Juárez was Porfirio Díaz's main enemy. Once dead (1872), Juárez was canonized by the Díaz regime, pasteurized from his Jacobin conno-tations, and made into a unified myth of liberal law (separation of Church and state, sovereignty of the state, and equal citizenship). Finally, it was dogma: Juárez's heroism did not come from defeating conservatives, the Church, and the French, but from "justicia," that is, from establishing the secular and liberal rule of law for the country. Juárez and Lincoln monuments in Mexico City and Washington not only embodied the same style, the same need for national consensus, but actually the same contentious hero-making process.

Between Washington and Mexico City, however, lies a gulf not only of historical differences, but also of mutually exclusive nationalist mythologies. The former was a new capital, a city created ex nihilo to be the head of a new nation, a city (if arguably un-American) from the family of the "city upon hill." Hence, Washington was far from Mexico City's old "microcosms of the imperial and ecclesiastical order," from the chaotic city upon a lake.[5] Mexico City was the capital (of an even newer nation) that was, arguably, the result of the most un-American (U.S.) things: a centralized state, a hierarchical and authoritarian Church, an aristocratic society, a city-oriented and genteel intelligentsia, and a general cultural and political disdain for the countryside. In turn, Washington was the corollary of a nationalism defined in opposition to both Europe and the Spanish frontier. A nationalism that was as explicitly, if ambivalently, anti-European as it was implicitly and unashamedly anti-Mexican; thus, by the 1860s the greatest moments of nationalistic sociability had been two wars: a defeat against England and its American allies (1812–14), and a victory over Mexico (1846–48). From the former, the U.S. gained its national anthem, whereas the latter would conclusively mark U.S. nationalism as well as the destiny of the nation and its political class up to the final consequence of that triumph over Mexico—a bloody civil war.

By contrast, Mexico City was the anti-Yankee capital that in 1847 had seen the American flag crowning the National Palace and the resulting popular riot. Unknowingly, the old city of Mexico then housed both the worst fears of Mexico's nationalism—the end of the nation—and the uncontrollable contradictions of U.S. nationalism—which explained the withdrawal of General Winfield Scott from Mexico City, but which in due time would also put that same general in command of the armies that had to save the U.S. from its own contradictions. "Mexico will poison us," so wrote Ralph Waldo Emerson in his journals, but Mexico was no fatal venom; it just produced "genetic" variations in the assumed historical DNA of the U.S. Ever since that "will poison us," whether it is recognized or not, there has been no U.S. history without those odd components: Mexico and Mexicans.[6] Washington and Mexico City were thus capitals of mutually exclusive, but inevitably consubstantial, national projects.

Despite its difficult beginnings—when Jeffersonian anti-urbanism and the states' distrust of a centralized state made the city an "exceptional" chaos—, in the long run Washington was not an exceptional capital city; it had a lot in common with Mexico City and other capital cities. It was an undeniable, if conflictive, product of a growing state power. By the 1900s unfinished Washington was material proof of the mythical contours of the idea of a weak state in U.S. historiography. Therefore, its history is full of ideological antagonisms and, of course, corruption. Washington became "the testing ground of radical Republicanism," as well as, at the end of the self-ruling experiment in 1847 after the Mexican war, a rather authoritarian and corrupt city of political and economic speculation, "a monument to the Civil War legacy of strengthened American nationalism," similar in its national context to Mexico City, Madrid, Berlin, and Buenos Aires.[7]

Indeed, Washington was a product and embodiment of the state from its L'Enfant origins and neither—as recent historians would have it—one of the greatest urban plans of the world, nor an exceptional depiction of the democratic spirit of America expressed in vast green public spaces and squares.[8] In fact, L'Enfant and the later reincarnation of his plans were necessarily inspired by baroque models derived not only from Versailles or Roman ancient plans, as historian J. L. Sibley Jennings showed, but also, as L'Enfant explicitly expressed, from Madrid and southern Mediterranean cities. In the late eighteenth century, Madrid was an excellent example of imperial urban transformation whose new squares and parks were copied by L'Enfant.[9] The aristocratic Spain that created Mexico City also thus marked the plans for the U.S. capital. The influence of the garden city movement expanded the green spaces and the already large public squares by the late nineteenth century. More than an expression of democratic values, this was, as many visitors commented, a terrible decision in a Southern city whose summers are as unbearably warm as its winters are cold. That such public spaces achieved democratic use throughout the twentieth century is not a matter of design but a matter of fact; the same democratic uses occurred in such supposedly undemocratic designs as Mexico City's Zócalo or Buenos Aires's Plaza de Mayo.

But Washington was uncommonly green. This surprisingly green character—which indeed was mesmerizing and unexpected to many visitors—had less to do with any spirit of democratic design than with the fact that, unlike Mexico City, Paris, or Barcelona, Washington did not have to deal with the weight of history in space; that is, it was constructed, as were Canberra and Brasília in the twentieth century, over nature and not over old cities. Thus, unlike Mexico City or Istanbul, over the nineteenth century Washington's green spaces had to gain the symbolic centrality that history did not grant them.

II

The will of a president made the Potomac basin the political nucleus of the U.S. These were lands previously inhabited by the Susquehannock and Powhatan peoples (as well as by a failed colony of Spanish Jesuits). The decision to locate the capital there was taken only after long debates and contestation. Following the agreement between various states (1790–91), the national government was moved from Philadelphia to the new city in 1800.[10] A city of 14,000 inhabitants, Washington became the almost capricious capital of the first independent nation of the Americas, a nation believed born modern, republican, and democratic.[11] In 1800, however, the city had yet to be finished according to L'Enfant's grand design—a conventional grid crossed by boulevards that formed individual neighborhoods with public spaces. The avenues, streets, and parcels sustained a well-orchestrated naming of states and characters that together told the American epic.[12]

This intended city, despite its unmistaken baroque contour, in the long run aimed to be as far from the authoritarian grandiosity of Paris, Madrid, or Vienna as from the eclectic and baroque majesty of such Ibero-American capitals as Rio de Janeiro and Mexico City. In fact, in comparison to the aristocratic order of the cities of the Iberian part of the new continent, Washington seemed simply meager. Its 14,000 inhabitants in 1800 matched only the number of aristocrats who joined the Portuguese king in his exile in Rio de Janeiro in 1808. Rio boasted 43,000 souls by 1799.[13] And, needless to say, the size, urban planning, and architecture of Washington in the 1800s paled before the grandeur of Mexico City, the core of the kingdom of New Spain, which was a *ciudad* indeed, an urban center of more than 150,000 inhabitants in 1800.[14]

But by 1910 Washington and Mexico City were both consolidated federal districts, capitals whose nineteenth-century histories were marked by their federalization. On one hand, Washington was built over nature by the government of a de facto federal nation. On the other, old Mexico City, as the former capital of New Spain, was converted into a federal district by a government that fluctuated between centralism and federalism within a de facto regionalist power structure—a structure that nevertheless functioned through a complex centralizing cultural and institutional tradition. In a way, Washington's history went from centralism and state control—reinforced during the Civil War and Reconstruction—to more or less unsuccessful efforts to gain independence and self-government. By contrast, Mexico City's nineteenth-century history went from the autonomy gained by the revolutionary *juntas* and granted by the 1812 Cádiz Constitution to the gradual consolidation of centralism and state control as a historical solution to political instability.[15]

These dissimilar routes are echoes of two different historical ways whereby city and nation interacted in the Americas. By the early twentieth century all capitals of the Americas had established a contrasting collage. On December 12, 1900, while numerous official acts commemorated the hundredth anniversary of Washington, U.S. architects debated solutions for the disappointing economic, aesthetic, and urban shape of Washington, a city "not worthy of the nation."[16] In sharp contrast, Mexico City and Buenos Aires (cities that by 1910 had more than 300,000 and 800,000 inhabitants respectively) began an impressive urban transformation in the 1880s that could not match the general state of their respective nations. They seemed nations not worthy of their capitals.[17] In a way, the history of Tocquevillian *Amérique* was an idealization of the nation that barely included Washington. By contrast, the history of Domingo Faustino Sarmiento's Argentina was indeed the idealization of Buenos Aires. And José Vasconcelo's 1922 *raza cósmica* was not made to germinate in nations, but in cities: Mexico City, Rio de Janeiro, São Paulo, Montevideo, Buenos Aires, and "Universópolis"—the city that, he thought, would rise in the midst of the Amazon as the core of the Cosmic Race.

In 1910, despite their different urban traditions, Washington and Mexico City had constructed their own ideal capital cities that seemed profoundly national and totally cosmopolitan. Their urban cosmopolitanism depended on a common cultural reference. By the early twentieth-century, however, Mexico City and Washington, together with many other cities, were jointly promoting the emergence of a new cosmopolitan canon. With their promiscuous cosmopolitanism, their scientific racism and antidemocratism, and their urban speculation, Washington and Mexico City were entering into a new era in which they acquired mutual references without European intermediaries. This was a shift that had long been in the making in the Americas, but which finally came to be accepted with the Americanization of Western architecture and art. While the McMillan Commission searched in France for an urban model for Washington, Paris looked to America fascinated by the functional use of space, the skyscrapers, the technological innovation, and the massive real-estate speculation. As the Austrian critic Robert Scheu put it in 1909, America is "a bright beauty, a unique crash of the greatest technological economy with green and wild lands, in a word: Style."[18] This was a transformation especially visible in the private architecture of the suburbs, banks, factories, and shops in Mexico City, Washington, and many other cities. Rapid industrial growth, suburbanization of elites, steel construction, tall buildings, speculation, the machine beauty: these were the characteristics of the new paradigm to which both Mexico City and Washington were contributing beside their official neoclassical ideal cities.

But when the Lincoln Memorial was inaugurated in 1922, the entire Washington Mall, as well as the remains of Mexico City's ideal city, were aesthetically and culturally passé if compared, for instance, to Le Corbusier's La ville contemporaine de trois millions d'habitants, presented in 1922, or to the avant-garde Paulicéa desvairada embodied in the 1922 week of modern art in São

Paulo.[19] The Lincoln Memorial was, as Robert Harbison characterized it, an "uncommunicative monumentality" typical of Washington, "the largest conglomerate on the earth which has any hope of achieving the dream of being pure commemoration, an enormous living cemetery."[20] Already by the 1920s the victorious Americanism in art and architecture blamed the architecture of Chicago's White City and of the Washington Mall for the delay in the emergence of the real modern American style.[21] Postrevolutionary Mexicans, for their part, saw in the Porfirian "afrancesada" (French-like) city a fake city that did not incarnate the "real" Mexico. They recycled all plans and monuments and made them more indigenist, more revolutionary, less obsolete, more according to a time of social concerns, avant-garde art, and revolutions.[22]

III

The U.S. was a persistent economic and constitutional archetype for the rest of the Americas throughout the nineteenth century. But not Washington, D.C. Its perennial incompleteness, its vast distances, its great and tasteless pretensions, and above all its large African-American population made Washington the mockery of the inhabitants of the other America, the so-called Latin. In fact, during the nineteenth century mocking Washington became commonplace in the Americas. For the problem was that late nineteenth-century Washington was an important capital for Afro-America.

In the 1890s nearly 76,000 of the 230,000 inhabitants of the District of Columbia were African Americans. Washington was the city with the largest percentage of African Americans in the U.S., and the city was strictly segregated on racial lines.[23] In aiming to be a bureaucratic centralized city, or the site of white entrepreneurship, many fortunes were made and indeed gradually the capital prospered, but not the entire city. An African-American "aristocracy" also prospered, but in segregation. This pastiche of plebeian and patrician cities was ridiculed by world observers. Domingo Faustino Sarmiento, an Argentinean Tocqueville, visited the unfinished Washington of the 1840s. He saw a "villa," not a society, that, on one hand, was "the center of nothing, not of the country, nor of the intelligentsia, nor of wealth, nor of commercial venues." On the other hand, he praised the "modern Ithaca" that was not the city of Washington, but the nation, the U.S., which was so great as not to need the capital.[24] But Sarmiento hardly mentioned segregation, swamps, and the very presence of blacks in the city, though Washington was in fact one of the most important sites for the slave trade. Fifty years later the prominent Mexican writer and educator Justo Sierra scorned post-Reconstruction Washington's ideal city as a silent majesty that bordered with death: "[a city] almost empty, pleasant, polite, ample shapes formed by endless streets lined with trees, pale and whispering like those of cemeteries." It was, he believed, a capital for the country of "hyperbolic dimensions": "Oh! What a city so quaint, so sad." This melancholic perfection was ruined, in Sierra's sarcastic eyes, by the black presence. Despite all the sanitary measures, Washington, he argued, was sick, it suffered from "black smallpox": "Washington is one of the capitals of the black nation, and this burdens it with dark shade," because "liberty has not made them [blacks] free, but rather, insolent." For Mexican liberals, such as Justo Sierra, a nondemocratic and segregated city like Washington was not a surprise. In fact, what the city showed was the undesired excesses of an egalitarian dogma that freed blacks only to then segregate them.[25] As late as the 1970s, Jorge Ibargüengoitia, one of the most sarcastic Mexican literary voices of the twentieth century, shared the same views about Washington: a city capable of producing the ugliest people, where racism existed but only because whites were treated as "trapo de frejar," and where blacks were not "a sector of the population but a constant affront."[26] Mexicans, like many other foreign travelers in Washington, expressed a cunning sense of nationalist superiority when observing the incomplete grandeur of Washington (vis-à-vis the magnificence of other capitals in the Americas). But this sense of supremacy was especially nurtured by the conviction of not having the "black problem."

Washington, however, produced in many travelers from the Americas a very favorable ecological impression. In Washington the tree was king; green was the color that guarded both power and wealth. In the early twentieth century Carlos González Peña, a Mexican philologist and writer, saw the greenness of Washington as a unique form of urbanism. "Washington is not a city," he argued, "it is an immense garden . . . in cities everything becomes walls, houses and more houses. Here, the trees are everything and it could be said that in foliages all houses and walls are expressed." However, with this beauty Washington marked its unimportance: González Peña thought it would never be like Paris for France or Mexico City for Mexico. It was a garden. Mexico City, by sharp contrast, was the city of old and thick walls, narrow streets and green spaces only slowly being opened within the city in the last part of the nineteenth century. In 1904, nonetheless, Mexico's most prominent environmentalist, Miguel Ángel de Quevedo, in a study of gardens for Mexico City, imaged a map of the city clearly inspired by Washington's garden-city, multiplazas approach (figure 2.1). The project never materialized. Pavement ruled and continues to rule in Mexico City.[27]

IV

As in Mexico City, the cultural modernization of Washington was often carried out by an amalgam of enlightened despotism. In Mexico City the urban

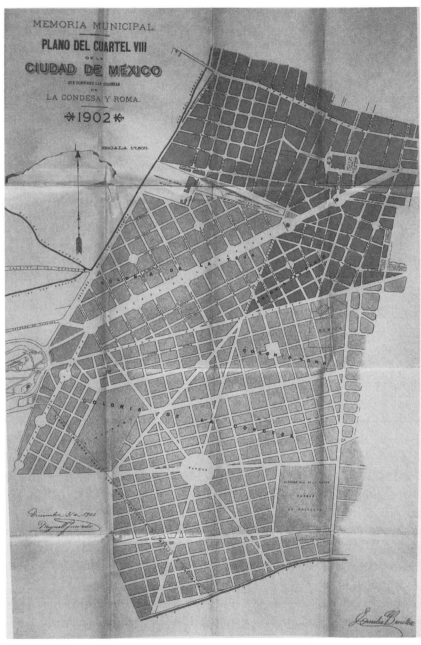

2.1. M. A. de Quevedo's project inspired by Washington, D.C.
M. A. de Quevedo, *Espacios libres y reservas forestales de las ciudades*
(Mexico City: Gomar y Busson, 1911).

reform was done by a small and tightly linked group of assorted interests: politicians, new and old fortunes, influential middle-class professionals, and foreign bankers and constructors—all were co-investors in the greatest and safest business of late nineteenth-century Mexico: Mexico City itself.[28] The physical and cultural modernization of Washington was commanded, for instance, by an authoritarian Fine Art Commission that, until World War I, was the "arbiter of public taste" (an agency that, according to historian Howard Gillette, enlarged the distance between the capital and the city).[29] Of course, the high centralism and explicit bonds between artists, intellectuals, investors, and the state that prevailed in Mexico were far from Washington's contested political arena. As capitals, both cities were subjected to this culturally centralized and undemocratic modernization. In both cities, there were surely important controversies within the centralized agencies over the selection of heroes, historical moments, symbols, and the best adaptations of cosmopolitan forms. But in both cities, history was set in stone undemocratically.[30]

By 1910, through cosmopolitan science (racial theories, hygiene, sanitation) and politics (liberal antidemocratism) the social segregation of Washington and Mexico City, as well as the differences in the uses of green space, seemed to be reflections of the same mirror. For science was the great consensus not only of the new American history of the 1900s that supported the script of the Mall, but also of other countries' histories. What scientific historians did with their narratives was echoed by the new predominance of engineers over architects, a phenomenon that took place, with ups and downs, in many Western cities. Scientific history was echoed by the emergence of scientific planning, scientific management of cities, and a scientific—anthropological, sociological, hygienic, and criminological—handling of race. It would be beyond the scope of this essay to detail this vast cultural shift. Suffice to say that the cosmopolitan sciences and arts that supported segregation—the epic past, the national myths, the manifest destiny of America, as well as the Washington Mall—were the same ones that allowed the reconstruction of Mexico's preHispanic past, the treatment of "the Indian problem," the very idea of ending politics itself in the name of política científica, and, of course, the conceptualization of Mexico City's ideal city.

Nationalism, science, and wealth, fused in space, loaded the sites of cities with historico-symbolical weight. The sites of Washington and Mexico City were filled with this heavy load. For many years an incomplete and unattractive capital was in itself a nationalist statement for the U.S. In the 1800s the site with no discernable history except as part of George Washington's soil seemed to make Washington both geographically central and politically and culturally neutral—just what the U.S., then a divided set of towns and states and hardly a nation-state, needed. By the 1900s this geographical and neutral centrality had been reimposed through a military victory and reinvigorated by reconstructing the capital as the symbolic, consensual, and physical expression of the nation.[31] The old assumed mythical neutrality became a decree.

For its part, Mexico City was geographically and strategically located at the center of a pre-Hispanic network of domination. (Just recall the importance of centrality in the foundational legend of the city: "*un islote*, a small island, in the middle of a lake, which was at the center of a valley"). This was the historical centrality that Hernán Cortés seized on in order to establish a new center in accordance with a long-established Iberian urban tradition. The early independent period brought about deurbanization, atomization, *caudillismo*, and regionalism. The new Mexico City, the modern capital of an independent nation, resulted from a decision of the same historical kind as George Washington's agreement to locate the capital at the edges of the Potomac River, or Philip II's proclamation of Madrid as the capital of united Spain.[32] It was in October 1824 that the newly created Mexican constitution made old Mexico City into the Federal District. Of course there was controversy (as in the U.S. and Spain); Querétaro and Aguascalientes were Mexico City's main rivals.[33] But the cultural and historical weight of the site of Mexico City was never lost. Throughout Mexican history the capital has kept its historical heaviness, and thus to conquer it has meant to be victorious. Mexico City has been a reserve of mythical neutrality that makes us often see it as a passive historical actor always being invaded. In fact, the city has been like the *krater*, the silver bowl given to triumphant Greek warriors, which was not only valued for its beauty but "had also a complex history of elite ownership."[34]

Thus, the abundance or lack of history grants valuable neutrality and centrality to space. Commenting on the parallels between post-1820s Athens and Washington, historian Yannis Tsiomis stated that both cities needed to set the central power of the state in a neutral place: "In the case of Washington, D.C., neutral due to the total absence of history. In the case of Athens, neutral because of the overwhelming presence of history."[35] The great Greek past, as the great Aztec past, served to make Athens, as Mexico City, neutral. Similarly Madrid, a Moorish fortress that was conquered by Castile and made into a frontier fortress against the Moorish armies, became the capital of unified Spain in 1607. But it was consciously rebuilt in order to symbolize the nation under Charles III (1759–88), and was made by decree the center of the nation despite cultural and economic fragmentations and disparities. Its centrality was geographically evident; its neutrality has long been a matter of contestation.[36]

V

Washington, it is often maintained, is an exception: it is the most un-American city.[37] By contrast Mexico City is believed to be, like Paris or Buenos Aires, the state entirely, the nation *tout court*—except of course for foreign orientalists, for whom Mexico City had never been really Mexico. In fact, as I have said, both Mexico City and Washington were the result of state intervention and sponsorship, as well as of private investment and speculation. In both cases undemocratic policies prevailed. Between 1871 and 1874, Alexander Shepherd, regularly referred to as the Boss, was appointed by the federal government as chief of the agency in charge of Washington's public works. He undertook the massive transformation of the city. When corruption scandals and political opposition removed him from control of public works, he went to Chihuahua to make more money in a silver mine. He left a mark in Washington's urban shape, just as he left a sample of American nineteenth-century Gothic revival architecture in a castle constructed in a small town in Chihuahua.[38] In the 1880s he admitted that "the District of Columbia is really a big government reservation," in which democratic rules were, he believed, an absurdity.[39] By 1900 the federally appointed McMillan Commission and the Fine Art Commission played the role of an early twentieth-century Haussmann in an apparently benign and philanthropic fashion, although state-centered and undemocratic.

In Mexico City the 1860s liberal reforms incorporated Church property (the main rural and urban real-estate holder) as well as Indian communal lands into the market. This started a cycle of speculation and urban transformation. Convents and houses were destroyed, and great fortunes were made.[40] In the 1880s, a closely linked team of influential characters undemocratically directed the Porfirian plans for Mexico City. Indeed, in Shepherd's Washington or in Díaz's Mexico City, what took place was urban modernization and beautification combined with corruption and real-estate speculation. To argue that Washington was an exception because it was not exceptional (in the sense of American exceptional democratic, societal, and antistatist tradition) is a logical absurdity. Perhaps Washington is just physical proof that the U.S. was not so exceptional after all.

Washington and Mexico City, nonetheless, embody two different ways of constructing state and society in the late nineteenth century. These differences are especially illustrated by their distinct conceptions of citizenship and race, since the two cities enacted two apparently antithetical conceptions of citizenship and representation. Cities in American history had often been seen as "excrescences, [as] necessary evils."[41] The growing scale of urban problems in late nineteenth-century America produced a fear of civic and moral decay, expressed in urban utopias (such as Edward Bellamy's) and conscious progressive attempts to create a civic awakening for maintaining social control.[42] Even though 1900s Washington did not embody American republican citizenship and antistatism, it became a national model of beautification that marked the beginning of widespread city planning as a form of social control, urban reform, and economic efficiency.

The capital throughout the nineteenth century was a terrain of experimentation and confrontation with different conceptions of state and society. By the mid-nineteenth century, Washington was, if a city at all, a southern city. Radical Republicanism made it (and not without hesitation) into a showcase of universal enfranchisement and civic rights. This spirit did not last, due in part to the general disregard of the city by Congress, as well as by corruption, pressure from Washingtonians themselves, and, not least, the shared underlying fear of the "darkening" of politics. Then came another experiment: the territorial period, which conceived the city government in a sort of corporatist, federal, ruling of the wise men—a *caudillismo à la américain* with Boss Shepherd as commander. Later, self-government was finally abolished, leaving the city not as a *polis* but as an administrative agency of the state. Washington was considered economically, politically, and intellectually expensive, corrupt, and nonproductive. How does an undemocratic capital reconcile with a democratic nation? Who ought to pay for the capital? Or, what to do with the large African-American population of Washington—the undesired consequence of a war of national unity? There were no easy answers, either in terms of policies or intellectual explanations.

Mexico City, in turn, had been since colonial times an organic corporativist body of interests represented in a peculiar undemocratic fashion based on old rules that were not always in written form. As historian Andrés Lira has shown, these rules remained more or less undefined until they were defied.[43] Unlike the African-American communities in postbellum Washington, Indian *parcialidades* (the term for their spatial and legal autonomy) were defined—and defined themselves—"in opposition to the city." In Washington, African Americans owed their civil existence to a southern city that was made into a Northern abolitionist urban center by state decree. A growing African-American intelligentsia actively fought for political participation, appealing to quasi-mythical categories of democratic inclusion. By contrast, Mexico City's Indian communities appealed more to old rules of corporativist representation and identity; their appeals for corporative autonomous representation were often successful, at least until the city's imperative of expansion prevailed.

In Mexico City the notion of *ayuntamiento* (city council) was a constitutional arrangement with old legal roots that acquired a new sense of practicality in 1808, the year of the Napoleonic invasion of Spain. In the absence of a king, the corporativist entities exercised the autonomy that they possessed, de facto, as indirect mediators between a king and his subjects. As historian Ariel Rodríguez has shown, the nineteenth-century history of Mexico City's *ayuntamiento* is that of a gradual loss of power in favor of the authority of the federal state. But for a long period the city council was the institutional space in which the idea of "bien común" ("common good") acquired political tangibility. Although this was a not fully democratic body, it represented the rights of individuals against the state, or of local authorities against the national government. Needless to say, this buffer was rife with corruption and personal interests, especially after a powerful economic elite took control of the city council and made the city one of its most profitable businesses. Yet, because of its role as guardian of the public good, the city council was the institution that undertook social scientific research and consultation in order to deal with the city's problems. Importantly, the city council was also in charge of electoral registration.[44] However, it gradually became an agency of a central state, a Leviathan in the making whose main concrete being was realized through the city itself. When the Díaz regime formally ended self-rule in the city, the model apparently was Washington, D.C.: a federal capital unashamedly run by the federal state.[45] By 1910 there was a consolidated state structure, perhaps for the first time in Mexico's history, with liberal democratic institutions but effective semi-authoritarian ruling. The state, in this time, had become inseparable from the city. Mexico City was the nation-state in the same sense that Paris was the French state. The city grew like the Mexican state: chaotically and uncontrolled.[46] The power of the city, however, grew vaster than that of the state itself.

Thus, in Mexico City and in Washington, citizenship oscillated between city-citizenship and nation-citizenship. In Washington it was easier to be a citizen vis-à-vis the nation than vis-à-vis the city, providing that one had the right characteristics of race, gender, and class. In Mexico City, however, it was equally difficult, and equally simple, depending on the circumstances, to become a full citizen of the city as of the nation. Becoming part of the city's "gente decente" (respectable peoples), which by the 1890s included the lower middle classes, the skilled working class, and bureaucrats, was the way to acquire Mexico's version of national citizenship. And it was easier to become *gente decente* in Mexico City than in the countryside, in small towns, and in provincial capitals. For Mexico City offered, like no other cities, possibilities of personal and collective reinvention, but rejecting the notion of Indian communities.

This created an ironic historical picture of countertradition: in the U.S., an anti-urban national culture was disputed by an urban (and even urbane) African-American tradition. Increasingly throughout U.S. history, the city became a more desirable location for African-Americans than the country-side, even though the pastoral dream remained ascendant for white Americans.[47] In Mexico, on the other hand, a profoundly urban national tradition was ambivalently either sought by popular sectors in view of Mexico City's appeal as a mestizo space of reinvention, or questioned by the appreciation of small rural, Indigenous communities. Late nineteenth-century Mexico City absorbed—not without difficulties and conflicts—the Indian towns that not merely surrounded the city, but had also formed it since the colonial project of two separated republics ("la república de indios, la república de españoles"). By 1910 old Indian towns and barrios in and near Mexico City had acquired a distinct urban contour—they were the city and the city constituted them.[48] In Washington the promise of freedom, the search for economic opportunities, and a well-established African-American urban "community" served as poles of attraction for former slaves well into the 1900s. In Mexico, Indian towns of the large valley for such a long time had resisted, adapted, and taken advantage of the city as an economic and cultural opportunity, that gradually they became one with the city. By 1921, 19 percent of the city's population was identified as "Indian" and 55 percent as "mestizos."[49] Some nearby towns prospered com-mercially from the city, without being absorbed by it. But gradually these towns succumbed to the attraction and growth of the city.

Both the mestizo city and a color-divided city attempted for all entails seg-regation by class and race. But while cities like Washington clearly and strictly segregated the entire city's space, in Mexico City every piece of space was so-cially divided in variegated ways every single day. Nearly all streets in the cen-tral part of the city were popular public spaces (for both women and men) or gentrified avenues depending on the hour of day. Every large new residence in the new suburbs was a miniature of the social universe of the entire city. Even miserable tenement houses made up cities in themselves in which race was not only an issue but above all a moving target used and abused by different sectors in various ways. Washington was, for its part, clearly, strictly, and insurmount-ably divided by a race line.

In the countryside, as Andrés Lira has shown, Indians were viewed as part of a bucolic and exotic Mexican landscape.[50] But in Mexico City Indians could be Indians or mestizos, but above all they were "pueblo" (commoners). At the turn of the century, Mexico City was an expanding urban center of landless Indians and mestizos who had been made into an urban proletariat and who had lost old forms of representation (not necessarily democratic) and had gained an "imaginary citizenship" (to borrow Fernando Escalante's term). An imaginary citizenship that nevertheless offered them certain possibilities of upper social mobility beyond the race line—as the urban meant above all the sanctioning of all forms, not only sexual, of miscegenation.[51]

Race thus had a less fixed cartographic and biological materialization in Mexico City. The ideal city of Mexico both hated and loved "racialized" Mexicans. The 1910 ideal city included monuments of Indian heroes from the great pre-Hispanic past of the nation. The monument of Cuauhtémoc, last of the Aztec leaders, in Mexico's Champs Élysées (Paseo de la Reforma) could seem to be the product of a meager and romanticized indigenism. But could one even imagine a monument to a Native American or an African-American warrior on the Washington Mall at the turn of the century? By the 1920s a popular Revolution, and the global cultural transformation that began around 1910, had opened new spaces of political participation and cultural expression for all sorts of people under the universal cult of *mestizaje*. These were spaces that the large African-American communities of Washington could not find outside their segregated sites until well into the 1960s.

Successful Indian males could overcome racial distinctions in Mexico City, especially through *mestizaje*—which was not necessarily sexual but above all urban: to live the city was to become a mestizo. But segregated Washington never tolerated such traversing, especially not miscegenation. The prominent black aristocracy of Washington (which, according to historian Willard B. Gatewood, numbered no more than a hundred people) prospered within segregation.[52] They had very little to do with the growing white intellectual community and aristocracy of Washington (from the Cosmos Club to the Washington Academy of Science).[53] There was no parallel for this black intelligentsia in Mexico City's population. Education and intellectual prominence were, in fact, a difficult but real way of breaking the race line in Mexico City. For instance, Francisco Manual Altamirano, a Nahuatl speaker, was the boss of the city's literati during the 1870s and 1880s; whether he was an "Indian" or not was secondary to the fact that he was the national writer par excellence.

With its large African-American population, Washington became an intellectual and physical ground for experimentation with different political, scientific, and intellectual conceptions of race and citizenship.[54] Not since Reconstruction had northern ideas of social reform faced the resistance of a de facto southern city. Radical Republicans forced Washington to accept electoral and social reforms, and thus Washington became a city in a constant state of exception (or in Mexican historical terms, a perpetual "parcialidad"). For a brief period of time federal intervention in the city brought about physical improvements and social reforms. The capital was put in the hands of all sorts of experts (engineers, managers, social scientists) who undertook the long-overdue electrification of the city, the paving of streets, the "pasteurization" of the capital, and the scientific legitimization of racial segregation. The reformist conviction that a good environment would create good citizens was not much of a concession for either the black intelligentsia, who still did not have access to national politics and culture, or for the many impoverished Washingtonian African-Americans.[55] When Jacob Riis was hired to see how the other half of Washington lived, scientific sociology and politics justified the rampant destruction of African-American settlements within the city in the name of hygiene.[56] Indeed, neither political rights won after the Civil War nor scientific management of society and race expanded the possibilities of citizenship for blacks in Washington. The legacy of slavery, the imprint of the old essential Western distinction of humanness vs. nonhumanness, subsisted, most especially in Washington, D.C.

In brief, Washington's white ideal city, as an architect observed in the 1930s, was an architectural "program of isolation" that left the greater bulk of Washington to "welter in its chaos."[57] This is not to say that Mexican elites did not attempt similar projects of isolation. However, their own historical ambivalence toward Indians, as well as the porous borders of Mexico City's ideal city and of Mexico's historical racial distinctions, made total segregation difficult. Miscegenation prevailed in social relations, but above all it became culturally and legally acceptable. Thus the 1910s' contrast between Mexico City and Washington discloses a historical paradox: the insurmountable fate and the uneven advantage of being either "imaginary" (Mexicans) or "unimaginable" (African-Americans) citizens.

VI

By around 1910, Washington and Mexico City were modern cities with a place among the many modern capitals. They were also "fallen cities," cities of sin, misery, mystery, miasma, exploitation, philanthropy, civilization, and barbarie. Henry Adams's portrait of Washington as a center of political intrigue and careerism (Democracy, 1880) could have been written for Mexico City. But two images could fully comprehend both Mexico's City's cultural transformation from the 1900s to the 1930s, and the different perceptions of such a transformation. Diego Rivera's "Dream of a Sunday Afternoon in the Alameda Park" is the total history of Mexico formatted according to the quotidian culture of Mexico City around 1910, with its spontaneity, dynamism, and social distinctions (figure 2.2). The mural depicted the stereotypical historical narrative that supported the 1910 reconstruction of the city but also, ironically, the postrevolutionary nacionalismo revolucionario. Thus the heroes of the ancient regime, Cuauhtémoc, Juárez, and Hidalgo, are joined in the mural by

2.2. Diego Rivera, *Sueño de una noche de verano en la Alameda.*
© 2011 Banco de México, Diego Rivera Frida Kahlo Museums Trust,
Instituto Nacional de Bellas Artes, Mexico. Reproducción autorizada
por el Instituto Nacional de Bellas Artes y Literatura, 2011.

the revolutionary hero Francisco I. Madero and the representation of death, La
Catrina—an elegantly dressed female skull—, popularized by Mexico City's
1900s printer José Guadalupe Posadas. All of them in a typical Sunday in the
Alameda around 1910: balloons, all sorts of social classes and personalities
interacting in the park, the crazy old man wearing lots of medals who dwelled
in the Alameda in Porfirian times, and a child: Diego Rivera, who in the mural
appears at the side of his then former wife Frida Kahlo. The mural, however,
was painted in 1947 by a well-established Rivera mocking the old Porfirian
times he had lived in, and according to the official postrevolutionary caricature
of Mexico's Porfirian past. The mural was located in the interior walls of a
new building, the Hotel del Prado, owned by the bosses of postrevolutionary
Mexico City and designed by the architect of the postrevolutionary regime,
Carlos Obregón Santacilia. Rivera's mockery of Mexico City in 1910, for all
its sarcasm, was full of nostalgia for a city where good and evil were clear, a
city with well-defined parks and buildings, with Rivera's childhood remem-
brances; a city far different from the chaotic city Rivera was living in in the
1940s. As divine irony would have it, the 1985 earthquake destroyed the Hotel
del Prado, as well as many other buildings from the city's postrevolutionary
speculation. Rivera's mural survived to rest in a special compound near Alameda park, flanked by colonial, Porfirian, and newer buildings that guard
the Alameda park of Rivera's memory, as a relic of two eras: that of Rivera's
nostalgia and that of *nacionalismo revolucionario.*

By contrast, Juan O'Gorman's canvas of a Mexico City map in the late 1940s
shows, with all its indescribable nuances, an industrial yet Mexican city always
under construction (figure 2.3). O'Gorman was a unique artist: his Mexico
City canvas was clearly a take on the old depiction of cities and their maps as
palimpsest, a style epitomized by *Vista y Plano de Toledo* (1600s) by El Greco—

2.3. Juan O'Gorman's Mexico City (1947), courtesy Instituto Nacional de Bellas Artes, Museo de Arte Moderno, Mexico. Reproducción autorizada por el Instituto Nacional de Bellas Artes y Literatura, 2011.

O'Gorman's canvas was indeed a modernist version of that old painting. But he was also the architect who introduced functionalism to Mexico in the 1920s, and he depicted a rising modern city from the perspective of a monument to the Revolution: the old structure of the Porfirian parliament transformed into a massive concrete arch in the 1930s (also by Carlos Obregón Santacilia). That is, the city as seen from the new revolutionary present of Mexico, with its surrounding volcanoes, its embodiment of the state and the nation, its streets and cars, and the mestizo myth of the nation flying in the skies with a banner (VIVA MEXICO) carried by two females, one brown and the other white. A construction worker in overalls, the proletariat, the Mexican par excellence, with his tools and blueprint in hand, seems to introduce the city to the viewer. At the side of the worker O'Gorman's hands support the original colonial map of the city, moving from a royal Catholic city on a small island in a lake to a workers' city upon a vast desiccated lake, the par excellence capital city of that which was taboo for such cities as Washington—human, aesthetic, social, and historical miscegenation.

There might be an analogous depiction of Washington, but I am convinced by the irony of the lucid Brazilian writer Érico Veríssimo, who, in the 1930s, captured with Mexican eyes the radical transformation of Washington, into a twentieth-century imperial capital. "If I were to paint," he explained, "a Diego Rivera–like mural that could give an idea of Washington, D.C., I would use caricature terms." Right center the Lincoln Memorial, with "his Greek-Doric serenity," then a portion of Constitution Avenue, with its classical buildings, and an old judge descending the stairs of the Supreme Court building ("surrounded by an aura made of glory and infallibility"): "Numerous typewriters and bureaucrats could be seen through the windows of the many official buildings and across from the great avenue, a solid wall of prejudices (but how to furnish prejudices with a pictorial expression?), a miserable urban swamp where black boys play baseball in the mud, mud that sprinkles the fat bourgeois black who passes by [*salpica o gordo burguês prêto que passa*]. Also tourists and bureaucrats in countless shops, and army personnel, veterans, unemployed men and women, and the 'daughters of the revolution' who 'knit sweaters for the child victims' of natural tragedies in Mississippi or China. Perched on the dome of the Capitol, a senator with a cowboy hat makes a political speech, while a zeppelin pours scraps of paper with ads for Coca-Cola over the Hellenic serenity of the city." At one corner of the mural, Veríssimo concluded, a scientist with a microscope and, at the other, a journalist with a microphone transmitting news of Washington to the world.[58] This was, in a Rivera-like fashion, the new Washington, D.C.

INTERIORS

¿*Qué de'óndi amigo vengo?* (Would you like to know, my friend, where I come from?): so went *La casita* (the little house), a popular 1920s Mexico City tune, composed by poet Rafael Rubio and still sung today by some démodés like myself. In answering the question, the lyrics become a detailed evocation of lost domestic rural interiors: [I come from] "una casita que tengo/más abajo del trigal" (a little house I own/there, down below the wheat field), and then follows a description of every single room and interior design, all featured in interesting poetic images that consciously seek naïve intimacy. The house, despite its claimed unpretentiousness, possesses all the ingredients of domestic intimacy: a canary, a dog, a bed, a cabinet, a mirror, and, of course: "bajo un ramo que la tupe/la Virgen de Guadalupe/está en la puerta de entrar" (under a bouquet that wraps her/the Virgin of Guadalupe/is located at the entrance).[1] The bucolic song, however, was composed in the city, sung in the city with nostalgia over many decades, in that huge city where the *casita* very likely had suffered the metamorphosis into a one-room dwelling in a *vecindad* (poor tenement house); dwellings that by 1930 became the subject of sociological scrutiny. By the 1970s, both the song and *vecindades* were used to talk of new forms of intimacy: the song was parodied by a Mexican songwriter (Óscar Chávez) in order to unveil the fatuous and tacky domestic interiors of Mexican corrupt politicians, and *vecindades* became the embodiment, in the influential anthropological account by U.S. anthropologist Oscar Lewis, of the culture of poverty. The same urban interiors, thus, have been experienced differently as the 1910 Mexico City embarked on its twentieth-century path toward the megalopolis.

Who could add something interesting to debates on the *Öffentlichkeit*? Rather, I offer an essay on the experience of the intimacies of the changing meanings of *adentros*—which were simultaneously public and private—of the city around 1910. And I examine these *adentros* on the opposite sides of the social scale, for the extremes are revealing. I deal, on one side, with *vecindades* as paradises of the promiscuous inside; on the other, with the apparently inviolable private intimacy of Mexican bourgeois interiors around 1910 and over the early revolutionary years.

Vecindades

Like any modern city government, that of Mexico City sought to control "dangerous" interiors out of fear of diseases and revolts. Rapid change in the city's life and traditions brought about nostalgia of seemingly pristine, innocent, and authentic forms of intimacy. Hence, social science as urban reportage or the mere sense of modern *urbanidad* emerged in Mexico City through the observation and handling, in Salvador Novo's words, of "huecos en la carne de los edificios"—"recesses in the buildings' flesh"; that is, passing views of urban poor interiors that commonly assault the urban transient in Mexico City.[2]

Indeed, views of those "recesses" in crowded tenement houses have become par excellence symbols of the evils of urbanization. In New York City there were tenements inhabited by recently arrived immigrants and urban poor. In Buenos Aires they were called *conventillos*, also inhabited by immigrants. In Mexico City there were *vecindades*: a peculiar Mexican version of urban tenements that went back to colonial times but grew significantly during Porfirian times, booming in the decades after 1910. Throughout the nineteenth century colonial buildings at the center of the city were converted into *vecindades* for low-income workers and artisans. Starting in the 1870s, in old and new areas of the city, this kind of habitation was the response to the growing demand for housing. But some new proletarian quarters emerged: Colonia de la Teja (1882), Colonia Violante, a refractioning of Tepito (1882), Morelos (1899), Colonia Hidalgo (1899), Peralvillo (1910), Buenos Aires (1911), Portales (1914), and Argentina (1915), as well as such unauthorized proletarian quarters as La Viga and Colonia de la Bolsa.

Only a decade after the 1910 centennial celebration, the victorious revolutionary city grew at a very rapid pace, creating a serious housing problem, which led to urgent measures and a fever of legal and illegal construction, as well as to popular mobilization against high rents and expulsions. In 1922, popular *barrios* such as Guerrero, Morelos, and Peralvillo mobilized against high rents. Rapid urban speculation soon followed the model of growth and the social map of the Porfirian city. Political and economic personalities of both the Porfirian and the revolutionary regimes were personally invested in the real-estate development of the capital. José and Julio Limantour developed the Colonia Limantour in 1888, and by 1900 they owned *vecindades* and commercial buildings in old and new parts of the city. And such postrevolutionary personalities as Alberto J. Pani became important investors in new buildings and developments, including poor housing, a very profitable business.

The 1910 census estimated that nearly 80,000 people lived in *vecindades*, and some believed that more than 100,000 people lived in these tenements. By 1920, a survey by the Departamento del Trabajo studied 116 tenements of different sizes in Mexico City, and it was estimated that a quarter of the population lived in tenements.[3] The *vecindad* thus was an old phenomenon intrinsically linked to the city as the greatest postrevolutionary business opportunity.[4]

From the 1880s to the 1950s, the peculiarities of modern *vecindades* made them the target of scientific research, urban reportage, legends, and sanitary concerns, especially, first, in view of their spatial and architectonical characteristics, which blended old habits and trends with the post-1880s urban transformation; and second, in view of the *vecindades'* odd cultural profile: a source of myths, fear, and mass culture.

Spatially, *vecindades* followed global trends: they were mostly large colonial buildings at the center of the city that, with both the gradual move of elites toward suburbs and the growing internal migration to Mexico City, became a collection of crowded tenements. Over the turn of the century, there was a rush of refurnishing old colonial buildings to make them into clusters of one-room apartments. The growing demand also stimulated the construction of many new *vecindades*. But what is striking is the emergence of what can be called the *vecindad* architectonical style. Wealthy Porfirian entrepreneurs invested in tenements, following the architectonical styles of old downtown *vecindades* as a sort of insurmountable paradigm: rows of one- or two-story one-room apartments around consecutive patios. This pattern would eventually create the characteristic social profile of the *vencidad* whose cultural and scientific appeal endures to the present. For *vecindades* meant, first, human agglomeration, not only in one single *vecindad*—which could house 900 inhabitants—, but within each single room—the average number of tenants per room was five. Second, *vecindades* inevitably came to mean their patios and their surrounding sidewalks, rather than the intimacy of small rooms. Patios were the center of all social and human activities (communal latrines or toilets, common laundry and fountains); in patios children played, and in the patios seduction and crime took place. This peculiar situation explains typhus experts' concerns with *vecindades*, or the obsession of journalists with *vecindades* as foci of crime and degeneration, or the quasi-erotic fixation by anthropologists with the promiscuity of small rooms and patios where men, women, and children coexisted, or the concern of journalists and travelers with a life so much lived outside, never in interiors. Thus, passing views of the *vecindades'* patios and their life became an essential part of the city's *imaginario*. *La Guacamaya*, an urban workers' periodi-

Un Baño de Vecindad.

Estas cuatro muchachonas
de belleza escultural,
han decidido bañarse
en la misma vecindad.

No temen á las miradas
de algún curioso galán,
y lucen sus desnudeces
por delante y por detrás.

3.1. *Vecindad.*
La Guacamaya
(July 4, 1906).

cal, in 1906 kept a joke running: a sexual curiosity with the *vencindad*'s patio, with its open spaces and the promiscuity of bodies and gazes. Thus a drawing showed women showering unconcerned by the gazes that could observe "their front and their behind" (figure 3.1).

The image likely was a take on what must have been common views about women's lack of coyness in *vecindades*' patios. A traveler in 1909 considered *vecindades* pigpens, in which people passed most of the time outside, degenerating into near animals.[5] "And it was then that the *vecindad*," said a writer in the late 1910s, "came to be a society in and for itself, like another true city, with its hierarchy and its social demands."[6] But as if talking about the entrance into an unexplored cave, commentators rarely talked of the actual interior of rooms—not until urban reportage and anthropology started to reach the insides of *vecindades*.

Of course textual scenes from *vecindades* could be found in literature before 1920. In 1915, novelist Julio Sesto described the interior of a *vecindad*'s room perhaps as a collection of personal memories but more than anything as a summary of what must have been common quasi-mythical flashes of what the Mexican urban interior was like, a mirror-like existence between things and persons:

> Poco había que ver en la misérrima vivienda, poco. A la entrada, para lim-
> piar los pies, un deshilado fragmento de tapete; a la izquierda, en el rincón,
> un despegado estípite que sostenía un busto roto, bajo el que había una
> cubierta de hilo, tejida de gancho por la señora; falta a la cuadrada rinco-
> nera uno de los pies torneados de la base, y en lugar del pie mutilado por el
> tiempo, había un pedacito de ladrillo; junto al muro, del lado izquierdo, un

arcaico sofá de tallado respaldo, sostenido por la pared, porque los torni-
llos y las espigas que armaban el mueble, ya no tenían fuerzas para sostener
el respaldo, que se quejaba de viejo cuando se recostaban en él; en torno
del sofá, dando vuelta al ángulo, hasta la mitad de la pared de enfrente, los
sillones, las sillas compañeras de aquel sofá, todo desvencijado, todo ello
clavado y vuelto a clavar cada cinco años, por ir tirando, como los flácidos
músculos de la consumida dueña.[7]

La musa bohemia (1908), by Carlos González Peña, described common family interiors as full of cachibaches, that is, all sorts of ruins of everything: tools,
furniture, decorations, appliances, and construction material.[8] The prominent
Mexican writer Guillermo Prieto described the same mixture of poverty, possession, and tackiness: "un santo con su lamparilla ardiendo . . . estampas de
colores chillantes representando escenas de Atila y Guillermo Tell; soldados
recortados a tijeras, pegados a la pared con engrudo . . ."[9]

In the twentieth century, artists started to depict these scenarios. One of the
first photographers to venture a photographic shot of vecindades' traditional
large foyers and patios was German photographer Hugo Brehme in 1925.
The photo captures the common passing view of the patio from the sidewalk,
and only shows children, furnishing thus a sense of misery and desolation
(figure 3.2).

In the 1910s, José Clemente Orozco for a while moved to Cuauhtemotzin
Street—the prostitutes street—and painted scenes of the vecindades' surroundings, as H. Cartier-Bresson later did with the camera. Also, Francisco Goitia,
between 1928 and 1930, painted "Patio de vecindad" and "Cilindrero," where
all the melancholy and colors of vecindades' patios were captured—not only the
desolated patios, but the rich human landscape (figure 3.3).

In the 1920s, it became fashionable for the new revolutionary intelligentsia
to visit vecindades and pulquerías. Edward Weston sought the fascination of the
vecindad in the few urban photos he shot in Mexico—he did so advised by
Goitia himself (figure 3.4). These were photos taken from flat roofs, vistas
aloof and safe from the chaos of vecindades. They seem ethnographic vistas
from a safari to a wild urban jungle. In 1914, Arte y Letras devoted a report to
"La Colonia de la Bolsa," known then as one of the most dangerous barrios of
the city (figure 3.5). The journalist found vecindades whose entrance "is everything: family room, boudoir, dining room . . ." A picture showed people drinking and resting at the entrance of an adobe construction. Later photographic
depictions of vecindades can be seen in a quasi-scientific official account (1934;
figure 3.6) and an urban journalistic report (1944). In these images, we obtain
glimpses of the life lived outside (in the streets), of the famous beds—scenar-

3.2. Hugo Brehme, *vecindad* (1926). Courtesy H. Brehme Collection, Archivo General de la Nación, Mexico.

3.3. Francisco Goitia, *Patio de vecindad* (1920s). Courtesy Museo Francisco Goitia, Zacatecas; Instituto Nacional de Bellas Artes, Mexico. Reproducción autorizada por el Instituto Nacional de Bellas Artes y Literatura, 2011.

ios of promiscuity—in small rooms, the prominent *saguanes* (forays), children and the outside life. In both reports, the narratives condemned the *vecindades* as foci of infection and crime, and the 1944 report ridiculed the national and foreign fascination with the "tradition" of *casas de vecindad*.[10]

The scientific gaze applied to the *vecindad* began of course with sanitary concerns. Starting in the 1890s, sanitary agents periodically visited *vecindades* in order to look for cases of typhus, smallpox, and tuberculosis. In 1901, for instance, the inspector of *cuartel* 6, having visited 272 *vecindades*, reported many typhus cases, recommending the construction of real toilets in the patios, and a campaign to wash the garments of sick people separately from the rest. This *cuartel*, which included such poor *barrios* as Hidalgo and Indianilla, housed

3.4. *Vecindad*, patio, photograph by Edward Weston (1921).
Collection Center for Creative Photography, ©1981 Arizona Board of Regents.

many *vecindades*, which the inspector described as unobservant of sanitary rules, recommending their destruction.[11] The inhabitants of *vecindades* seemed to be willing to take advantage of modern sanitation, and thus many of them became vaccination agents, though always suspicious of the authority. In 1901, the inspector of *cuartel 7*, where the popular Colonia Guerrero, Tepito, was located, reported difficulties in following up on sanitary conditions: vaccinated people "do not come back after a week in order to check the result of the vaccine and, maybe due to their twisted minds, many of them register their names [in the sanitary records] with fake addresses."[12] This distrust was based, perhaps, on the *vecindades'* own self-achieved sovereignty as *zonas francas* (free zones), where authority could act only with difficulty and after many negotiations. An outspoken sanitary agent reported in 1901 that due to the lack of drinking water, *vecindades* were returning to latrines, contradicting official instructions, but since the city could not provide enough water, the use

3.5. "Una excursión a la Colonia de la Bolsa,"
Arte y Letras (September 12, 1914).

3.6. View of *vecindad*. From *Informe y memoria del Departamento del Distrito Federal que rinde el C. Jefe del mismo Lic. Aarón Sáenz por el periodo administrativo comprendido entre el 1 de julio de 1933 y el 30 de junio de 1934* (Mexico City: Departmento del Distrito Federal, 1934).

of latrines was welcomed. But he also reported that some servants of wealthy people were sent to live in *vecindades* the moment they got infected with typhus or tuberculosis. In such a way, diseases were not only produced in *vecindades* but also sent to live in them.

The scientific intervention into *vecindades* bit by bit constituted an urban science of sanitation, sociology, and *reconocimiento* (surveying). To fully experience the city's streets and public spaces became a symptom. In the 1890s, Mexican criminologist Julio Guerrero, researching the origins and life of prisoners, classified the city's population according not simply to class but to a bizarre mixture of private vs. public existence and sexuality: the closer to the streets, to the outside, the lower and more promiscuous people were. For, said Guerrero, Mexico City did not have to prove Denis Jourdanet's theory about degeneration in view of the city's high altitude and racial mixture. The degeneration of people truly experiencing the city was all too evident. Thus, from low to high, Guerrero identified as the first group the total homeless people who lived in the streets basically like animals; then there were the "leftovers of the Aztecs"— Indigenous people who daily came in and out of the city's streets; then people with salaries: soldiers, workers in the 248 (1896) factories and shops—among them many urban women. These low-salary people were for Guerrero the men and women between street life and private existence; they were the people of the *vecindades*, the core of the city's population, characterized by excessive freedom for women, machismo, adultery, and too much street and patio life. He also added a different group: maids and servants, often from the provinces, who lived among the city's *gente decente*, an outpost of barbarism residing within civilized residences, street life parasitically living within decent domestic life. So much so that for Guerrero, maids introduced "the good families' kids to the secrets of love; [maids] inspire the first students' novel and they are zealously chased by the sanitary police." Then came what we can call the inside people: *gente de casa* (home people) and the "professionals and decent women," not forgetting "thin and stretched out *beatas*," who of course lived confined in houses and convents, but as *beatas* who were thin and ugly they were out of the streets' sexual market.[13]

In 1913 a sociological study considered the racial and urban profile of *vecindades*, and stated that no more than 8 or 10 percent of the residents were Caucasian, and they included lots of migration from the countryside: "city of the palaces, city of the contrasts," rich people with cars and Indians as the pavement's leper, a "fantastic court of miracles." Ergo, the study concluded, tenements ought to be destroyed. But the city's economic success offered no housing solutions for the increasing labor force it required. Similar sociological studies and categories were continued after the Revolution, including sanitary visits and surveys of people's origins, conditions, and crime in *vecindades*. In 1932, a sociological survey of the *vecindades* concluded that "the Revolution has not arrived at the core of the city." Thus the city's government organized a contest for a new kind of popular interior, the "minimum house," which aimed to be everything that the single-room apartments in *vecindades* were not. These houses were constructed experimentally in Balvuena: two bedrooms— to separate boys and girls—, one master bedroom with space for a cradle, a bathroom, and fifty-four square meters containing kitchen and dining room.[14] Ideally, the revolutionary urban poor would thus overcome the *vecindad* paradigm of promiscuous intimacy.

But the most influential "scientific" depiction of the *vecindades* started with anthropologists in the 1940s. Of course since the late nineteenth century the par excellence anthropological subject of study was the Indian community. With Manuel Gamio's study of Teotihuacán (1921), Franz Boas's studies of folklore in the areas around Mexico City (1910s), and Robert Redfield's studies of Tepoztlán (1931), the anthropology of Mexico had started its modern momentum. The goal was both to find and to examine *Gemeinschaft*, traditional and authentic communities; nothing could be further from the city's *vecindades*. The Chicago school of urban sociology, however, was an intrinsic part of these community studies. Redfield originally meant to study, as his father-in-law Robert Park demanded, Mexican immigrants in Chicago, and he did—though he never published the study. He explained to his Chicago mentors that he needed to study the original setting that Mexicans came from, and thus went to Mexico. Instead of studying Jalisco or Michoacán—where Mexicans in Chicago came from—he undertook the study of Tepoztlán, a Nahuatl-speaking town, very near Mexico City, through which he constructed the until then most complete and lasting version of the unique Mexican, Indian, community. Of course Redfield left the city aside—though he lived by and large in Mexico City over his field research.

In the 1940s, however, Oscar Lewis, a Columbia-trained anthropologist, after studying Tepoztlán—very much demystifying Redfield's harmonious view of Indian communities—, started to work on the personality of the Mexican Indian, a University of Chicago project. This eventually led him to his notion of the "culture of poverty" and his famous studies of families in Mexico City in the late 1940s. The main foci of his early studies were two families: the Gómez family from what he called *casa grande*—a vecindad in Tepito with 157 families living in single-room apartments, housing more than 700 people—, and the Gutiérrez family from the *vecindad* in Panaderos Street, downtown Mexico

City—a newer, poorer, and smaller *vecindad* (housing 13 families) than the *casa grande*. Of course, he also studied the Sánchez family, which by the late 1940s had constructed a little house at the outskirts of the city, but whose family networks reached the *casa grande vecindad*. To this family he later devoted a lengthy best seller, *The Children of Sánchez*.[15]

Lewis's approach to the *vecindad* was advanced as a new kind of anthropology, one that finally studied urban people and thus found "culture" or "subculture" in such modern peripheral settings. In fact, in the continuum between love and hate that the *vecindades* had inspired, Lewis merely reformatted the old views in a new "scientific" approach that incorporated participant observation, biographies, and development studies. First, he lived with the families, trying to observe them not as in a neutral Gessel-window kind of perspective, but in a participant-observer fashion. With the help of his wife and some Mexican assistants, he extensively interviewed and tested the tenants, and thus claimed that his findings had a minimum deviation from data in the original. He even titled his book on the Sánchez family an "autobiography," as if there had been no interventions in his writing, in English, of their lives. Moreover, his narrative strategy was novelistic, consciously and militantly literary, narrating the life of each family in a single day as short stories made of random scenes collected and put together by the anthropologist. In the stories, each character spoke in his or her own language—though this is only visible in the Spanish translation of *Five Families*, which transcribed the original recordings.[16]

Vecindades hence became best sellers, for Lewis's depictions included several traits of the lasting fascination with *vecindades*. Indeed, he narrated misery and moral decay—describing fetid odors, ignorance, ugliness, betrayal, and crime—but with empathy for both the people's survival skills and people who resisted "Americanization" and urbanization. Also, he fed the lasting voyeuristic obsession with urban promiscuity, enjoying the descriptions of the families' sexual mores—boys, girls, mother, and father sleeping together; sexually powerful women with different partners; adultery; and polygamy. Therefore, at the time of publication, Lewis's studies provoked the negative reaction of the Mexican government, precisely for so much emphasis on a sort of *chilango* Sodom and Gomorrah.[17]

Finally, Lewis produced in a scientific format the antimodern fixation with change from rural (traditional, non-Western) to modern intimacy. Of course he lamented the transformation but also showed the lasting survival of unique Mexican values, which turned out to be the stereotypes often assigned to the patios of *vecindades*—sense of community, family closeness, inventiveness, machismo, religious traditions, and capability of adaptation to change. The 1978 film *The Children of Sánchez*—starring Anthony Quinn and Dolores del Río—brought this view of *vecindades* to Hollywood.[18]

In the 1980s, a Mexican anthropologist, Guillermo Bonfil Batalla, continued the saga: once more returning to the *vecindad*; once more filtering out the positive communal interiors from undesired facts coming out of mere misery. Thus he claimed that the new housing projects of the 1950s and 1960s—massive blocks of small, low-income, and subsidized apartments—were Western and thus individualistic forms of living, while the *vecindades* represented, with their communal patios, the authentic community that went back to the "profound Mexico," the real one, i.e., the pre-Hispanic Mexico.[19]

From the fascination with urban interiors while walking the sidewalk we have come to this literary and scientific appropriation of *vecindades*. From there to mass culture there was only one step: films and radio. The 1947 film *Nosotros los pobres* (We the Poor), one of Mexico's most popular and enduring classics, put in motion the many appropriations of *vecindades*—starring the twentieth-century Mexican icon Pedro Infante, not as rural *charro* but as an urban carpenter, not as a womanizer but as a responsible family man. Of course, the movie did not make any reference to a pre-Hispanic paradise, but instead constructed an urban form of acceptable proletarian interiors for massive consumption by all classes. After all, most famous Mexican comedians, boxers, and wrestlers had come from *vecindades*—from Cantinflas to El Santo and Ratón Macías. The film depicted love, community, and life in a *vecindad*, with extensive close-ups of the patios and interiors, in a sort of romantic ethnography of how the other half lives. The characters, without cursing, spoke with an exaggerated version of the urban slang, which through the film became the stereotype in the entire Spanish-speaking world. This idealization was crowned by the popular 1940s tune (composed by Luis Arcaráz) "Quinto patio": love in the last of the patios, the less visible, of *vecindades* where it was true that "el dinero no es la vida/es tan solo vanidad" (money is not life/it's only vanity), for

El amor cuando es sincero
se encuentra lo mismo
en las torres de un castillo
que en humilde vecindad.

When sincere, love
can be found the same
in the towers of a castle
as in a humble *vecindad*.

But one ought not to forget that *vecindades* were and are not about tradition or community but about misery and survival. After the 1985 earthquake, many of Tepito's *vecindades* had to be destroyed or reconstructed. Among them was Lewis's *casa grande*, which was demolished in 1986 in order to construct a block of affordable apartments. In the aftermath of the earthquake, the organization of the *vecindades*' inhabitants was indeed an example of communal spontaneous social action. Years of officially frozen rents had led to landowners' total disinterest in even minimal structural maintenance of the old buildings. The earthquake hit them hard. The reconstruction of some *vecindades* according to their inhabitants' stylistic desires—with their labor force, official funding, and the help of architecture students—resulted in a memorable exercise of popular kitsch. But in 2007, after a series of police actions against drug trafficking in Tepito, the city's government appropriated one of these reconstructed kitsch *vecindades* (between Tenochtitlán and Jesús Carranza streets). And thus the post-1985 interiors of the so-called *fortaleza* (fortress) of crime were made visible by the media: there were ornate baroque altars to Guadalupe, as well as colorful and realistic murals in walls and ceilings depicting the heroes of Tepito: film stars Cantinflas and Pedro Infante, boxers and wrestlers El Santo, Ratón Macías, and Púas Olivares together with Zapata, Cuauhtémoc, and Frida Kahlo. This was the intimate space of families who had left misery through crime and drugs, and who have learned their heroes in their patios and in the lasting literary, scientific, and media fascination with *la vecindad*.

Interiors

It is safe to say that the late nineteenth century was kitsch everywhere. Then there were, as Mario Praz listed, such things as "the Victorian train stations imitating either Gothic castles or Greek temples, trains' chimneys disguised as Doric columns, Dickens's false sentimentalism in his lachrymal scenes, Whistler's false orientalism, D'Annunzio's pseudo Nietzsche and pseudo Swinburne, and a lot of nineteenth-century painting."[20] The Mexican bourgeois interiors were not an exception but, to the contrary, an unintended overacted performance of the kitsch. An exaggeration that resulted from both the eagerness to isolate selective intimacy from the overall city's promiscuity and the need to display—even more than a bourgeois interior in the middle of Paris—wealth, possessiveness, cosmopolitanism, and modern intimacy. That is why, for all their tackiness, Porfirian interiors—par excellence examples of the belief in having at last reached peace and stability—were proof of the epochal wisdom that Ramón Gómez de la Serna found in nineteenth-century *cursilismo* (tackiness): "If the nineteenth century had a defense, it is because it accepted lo cursi as a vital ingredient, as the essential keeper of peace, as a safe anchor of its own time."[21]

In the 1920s, Salvador Novo put this interior kitsch quite simply: Porfirian bourgeois interiors were to blame for Mexican bad taste; Porfirian elites had made an industry of tackiness.[22] In fact, what Porfirian bourgeois interiors did was to infer a modern Mexican bourgeois style out of the British arts and crafts school, French and Belgian art nouveau, European Jugendstil, all sorts of modern orientalisms, and U.S. mass production of all the above. In a way, Porfirian elites attempted their own version of Gesamtkunstwerk, a total work of art publicly admired and recognized and yet privately lived as bourgeois intimacy precisely due to its public notoriety. Whether they were gaudy in their endeavors is not primarily a matter of the interiors they created, but of their location: Mexico City.[23]

Though invisible to the pedestrian, wealthy Mexico City's inhabitants boasted elaborated interiors. Large mansions included interior design in Gothic, Chinese, Japanese, or English Imperial styles. Even the National Palace hosted foreign personalities in an elaborated Chinese-style hall, which British sculptor Clare Sheridan in 1922 found ridiculously gaudy—as a result not only of a poor selection of Chinese forms, but also of the very fact of staging a Chinese hall in the middle of Mexico City.[24] No doubt, 1900s bourgeois Mexican interiors were gaudy—failed attempts at reaching high styles, fake replicas of late nineteenth-century historicist interior design. But they were so not solely due to what they displayed, but especially due to where they were. The kitsch is a matter of location.

Writer Angel del Campo, also known as "Micrós," mastered the art of inhabiting nostalgically the Porfirian middle-class interior through words that were as gaudy as the interiors they described: "los muebles viejos eran una ironía bajo el cielo raso, donde fingían las pinturas una guirnalda de extravagantes hiedras de bulto" (old furniture formed an irony under the cloth ceiling where a painting imitated a garland made of an extravagant wreath of ivy in a bumpy shape). He described intimate scenarios with gaudy porcelain dolls, plum plaster angels at the corners of the ceilings, convoluted round shape legs of tables and chairs . . . all yet in a daily-existence matter-of-fact way, with no high pretensions. In the common unpretentious interiors rested a sense of intimacy and the weight of the past in the city.[25] But the bourgeois Mexican interiors were different precisely because they sought to obliterate simultaneously the Micrós-like familiar intimacy and the very weight of the city's past and present.

Thanks to some magazines that published the interiors of fancy mansions,

and thanks to the photographic records left by the hosting of foreign delegations over the *Centenario* celebration, I have a sample of the *vecindades*' opposite
extreme on the social scale.[26] But before briefly dwelling on these interiors,
allow me two notes of caution. First, today it would be rather easy to laugh at
bourgeois Porfirian interiors. A quotation from Walter Benjamin's deep views
of the bourgeois Parisian interior, though certainly apropos, would be considered too much profundity applied to so much peripheral pretentiousness.
For today tourists queue to enter into the well-staged "authentic" interiors
of Frida Kahlo's house or Diego Rivera's studio, today Californian mansions
flaunt canonized fancy Mexican interior design, and today thus the Porfirian
high-class interior seems a total exercise of fakery vis-à-vis the "real" Mexican
interior.[27] Though it would be hard to date with certainty when this became a
canonized Mexican style, maybe the first and most important samples of this
new trend were Rivera's houses, U.S. ambassador D. W. Morrow's house in
Cuernavaca, and Miguel and Rosa Covarrubias's house (all from the 1930s and
1940s).

The crafting of such a style involved many experiments, like the Maya-
inspired furniture exhibited by a Mexican designer at the 1929 Seville World's
Fair: a gaudy archaeological approach to modern comfort. Rivera's and Morrow's houses included pre-Hispanic motifs and statuary, their quota of popular
arts and crafts, and a selective appropriation of regional furniture traditions;
this kind of modern kitsch rendered pre-Hispanic motifs in modern furniture.
Like the bombastic Porfirian interiors, these new Mexican interiors in due time
became a matter of possession, of exquisite collectors and fancy craftsman-
ship. Of course, before and after fancy nouveau-riche Porfirian interiors and
postrevolutionary canonized Mexican interiors, there were "local" forms of
elegant intimacy. These forms were by and large combinations of Spanish baroque, romantic, and neoclassical styles that locally already included a heavy
input of pre-Hispanic, Moorish, Chinese, German, English, Japanese, and Indian (from India) styles in furniture, architecture, textiles, paintings, and uses
of space. Late nineteenth-century commoditized orientalism, romanticism,
and art nouveau in interior design apparently made old forms of elegance in
interiors obsolete. I have found no record of the interiors of the old aristocratic houses of Mexico City in the nineteenth century, which very likely were
museum-like collections of scarce colonial furniture and objects. But after all,
the late nineteenth-century bourgeois interior design, as expensive as it could
be, was massively produced and accessible for people of means. Old forms
of Mexican elegance were not that easily accessible and, for a while, until the
1920s when a serious colonial revival started in Mexico and the world, they
were not much desired.

Second, Porfirian bourgeois interiors closely followed international trends. With certain nuances, one could say with Benjamin that to live in Porfirian interiors was "to have woven a dense fabric about oneself, to have scheduled oneself with a spider's web, in whose tales world events hang [history] loosely suspended like so many insects' bodies sucked dry." It would be more accurate to say of the Porfirian interiors what Praz said of the tacky Roman bourgeois interiors that included huge collections of classic Roman and Greek art: "These Roman drawing rooms, to tell the truth, are no more civilized than an Izba in the steppes; worse, for in such rooms civilized forms have decayed into threadbare formulas intended only to impress the vulgar and the superficial. Of the many pleasures that furnishings can give their owners, such rooms can give only the ugliest: the pleasure of possession."[28] But for all their echoes of world's bourgeois interiors, the Porfirian ones had their own unique characteristics.

Like all late nineteenth-century interiors, whether in Paris, New York, Buenos Aires, or Mexico City, the Porfirian were imitative and could not be otherwise. Not because they were about, à la Benjamin, "the individual [overcoming] technology on the basis of his own inwardness [leading] him to ruin." But instead because they were not really about individual intimacy; rather, they were an indispensable performance of staged intimacy for a class to see, to experience, to copy, and to be jealous about. And as such the Porfirian interiors were halls of multifarious passions that staged the wealth of rich people who nevertheless were peripheral to the world's circulation of styles and objects. Thus the need to overdo the already exaggerated bourgeois necessity to collect and to stage.

On the other hand, an army of servants and maids, as well as the travels of dealers and elites, made possible the Porfirian or postrevolutionary bourgeois interiors. Thus, like all bourgeois interiors, the Mexican ones were carefully staged scenarios put together by an army of people belonging to a radical outside, for sharp inequality dictated that the many servants, maids, nannies, carpenters, and masons they needed not only worked for them but lived in those interiors more than the elites themselves. When we see in the photo of a studio's desk opened books, conspicuous skulls, carefully distributed pens and antiques, laying over the desk as if the *señor de la casa* had just worked there, in fact we are witnessing a staged vista thoroughly put together by plebs residing in the residences with detailed instructions on how to do it. In part that is how, even before radio, television, massive literacy, and films, the imitative nature of bourgeois style reached even working-class cheap styles. In turn, dealers and the elites' own travels determined their interiors, which had nothing to do with intimacy but on the contrary with the need to show an openness beyond the confines of the city in which they were located. In such a show of openness resided their own real bourgeois selves.

Late nineteenth-century interior design everywhere was historicist and eclectic, but as peripheral forms of bourgeois interiors, the Porfirian ones—perhaps more than their counterparts in Paris or Vienna—were even more omnivorous. At times, this happened in the same hall; other times, a mansion included one room in generic Arabic styles, one in all Oriental motifs, one in French Louis XV style, and one in Imperial English style. For the idea was not to satisfy the individual's sense of self but to cover all fronts of potential styles; the goal was to show off. For the modern self lay in consumption, not in one or another commodity.

The Porfirian interior implied by its very existence a sense of security that was not often visible by merely looking at pictures or descriptions. The interiors were like Russian dolls: they were an inside within an enormous mansion that in turn was a massive inside with heavy, tall, thick brick and stone walls—far, for instance, from the wooden houses of American elites—, surrounded by gardens with tall, fixed, secure fences. The mansion's location, moreover, was at times already another inside, outside the city's miasmas; other times, mansions were hermetic fortresses within the city's core. This sense of security was meant not only to prevent the outside to enter—as the outside was already residing inside in the form of maids and servants—but also to ensure that the inside not be exposed to the outside: especially women and children, who themselves embody the meaning of real intimacy and privacy.

Curiously, I have found little evidence of fancy bourgeois kitchens, for kitchens were a special case in Porfirian interiors: they were by and large the domain of maids and servants. It seems that new technological appliances were only slowly introduced. After all, it was assumed that maids and cooks did all the work; why bother with comfort? Besides, maids could not handle new technology. Moreover, despite their wealth and afrancesamiento, the culinary needs of elites demanded the time-consuming preparation of local food: tortillas, salsas, and complex mixtures that required molcajetes, metates, cooper and ceramic pots and pans. Or so it seems in the few available views of the urban Mexican kitchens. Middle-class housing was different. Kitchens and bathrooms were the core of transformation of the new middle-class housing in the early twentieth century. Prominent cigarette entrepreneur Ernesto Pugibet constructed a housing project for middle-class managers and workers (on Bucareli Street), and the media reported on his houses for not very wealthy people who, nevertheless, deserved "comfort and hygiene." Instead of fancy halls, a kitchen and a bathroom were photographed, showing modern appliances (1900s).

Magazines started to report on the interiors of the homes of the wealthy in

3.7. Salones de México, *La Revista Moderna* (1901).

the 1900s. In *La Revista Moderna* a series on "Mexican halls" reported on one designed by Salvador Echegaray at a fancy mansion at 304 Calzada Reforma: a Louis XV hall with high elaborated ceilings, curvilinear tables, and a piano; in sum, a perfect mimicking of the French Second Empire style (figure 3.7). Nevertheless, it is an interior with no sense of human existence, as if it were a theatrical stage to perform receptions. Another interior of the same house reproduced in the reporting was an art-nouveau lobby—carefully designed for all the walls and doors, all the furniture and figurines, to match a conservative version of art-nouveau trends. Like the halls of seventeenth-century kings, the elites' halls that were exhibited by the media were not the corners where families actually lived. One could imagine that within those mansions, there were rooms where women and children carried on their daily life, interiors that were likely not professionally designed, or if so, were changed on a daily basis by the hanging of a daughter's school drawing, the little shoes of the last baby in

3.8. Part of the collection of clandestine high-class brothels
collected by Ava Vargas—*La casa de citas: en el barrio Galante*
(Mexico City: Grijalbo, CONACULTA, 1991).

the family, the lasting ink stain on the family table . . . In the 1890s, the great
examiner of Viennese modern interiors, Adolf Loos, mocked the historicist
obsession of "designing" interiors in perfect imitation of medieval Imperial
French or English styles; spaces that any kind of use would immediately spoil,
while the real family spaces were randomly transformed by use; family interiors that were like violins: one could learn to play the violin, one could grow
familiar in those spaces. We have no record of those interiors, only those of
the Louis XV halls used by elites to socialize, to show up a designed intimacy.

More astounding was the clandestine image of a sort of porno interior
made in the early twentieth century that must have circulated among wealthy
men (figure 3.8). In it we see a Rubens-like naked woman over a marble Versailles table at the center of a room carpeted with the skins of a bear and a deer.
Elaborated figurines and statues completed the scene, with a very French and
very Mexican utensil behind the main table: a spittoon. Though the whole inte-

3.9. Arabesque interior (1910), James Braniff's mansion.
Courtesy Genaro García Collection, Nettie Lee Benson Latin American Collection, the University of Texas, Austin.

rior is designed as some sort of tacky revival, the presence of the naked woman makes the scene profoundly art-nouveauish, only missing here or there that unmistakably Gothic mark, a skull, and some Oriental and pre-Hispanic artifact to be a completely modernist Mexican scenario.[29]

The pictures of the elegant interiors that hosted the foreign delegations over the 1910 Centennial celebration offer an apropos sample of bourgeois interiors. The French military delegation stayed in the ornate mansion of the wealthy entrepreneur James Braniff on San Cosme Avenue. One of the chambers of the house presented a Moorish interior complete with arabesque arches, lamps, furniture, and carpets (figure 3.9). There is no room in such a space for an additional decorative object. The wooden furniture included encrusted metal and stone motifs. Again, in this interior there is no sense of life, no feeling that this was the shell without which a snail cannot live; these interiors were mere orientalist performances. Even as late as 1921, Thomás [sic] Braniff's mansion, despite the Revolution, still was visited by journalists "amazed" by the incredible Arabic bath it contained—a exact replica of La Alhambra. It was reported that he read Rabindranath Tagore, and his library treasure was a handsome illustrated twenty-volume English copy of *The Arabian Nights*.[30] This repertoire of all possessable things is what made possible an orientalized Mexico (in many world interiors full of Mexican things), and a Mexican orientalism. Regardless of whether or not cultural producers or wealthy collectors worked for one or the other, what they aspired to was to count on such a private repertoire of possibilities in their homes.

In turn, the library of James Braniff's house displayed a different style: wooden walls and bookcases, leather couches, animal skins as carpets, as in an English country house mansion. On the central tables, books carefully open, and a chair located as if some devoted reader had just left his or her reading. The bookshelves display no untidiness of sizes and colors, but rows and rows of equally bound books of the same size. We have another view from a library, that of Guillermo de Anda y Escandón, one of the wealthiest men in Mexico and a longtime member of the city's council. The Spanish delegation stayed in his house, and the library showed no books, but rather a central table and a desk in dark wood with encrusted metal (perhaps gold or bronze). This interior is less dense in furniture and decorations than other Porfirian interiors, but only to highlight the conspicuous presence of a large pipe organ (figure 3.10). On top of the side cabinet, the family pictures—mostly women—produce the effect of domesticity and real life. The desk is full of objects: from a sword-like letter opener, to a highly crafted cigar box, all sorts of figurines, candelabras, and stylish electric lamps. The papered wall, with circular and square motifs, frames the curtained entrance that looks into a hall where we can see chairs designed in a different style from the library, namely the late nineteenth-century medieval revival. The main living room of de Anda y Escandón's mansion impresses the viewer with a square internal gallery, and the entrance to stairs leading to a main window before dividing into two. The furniture style differs from the one found in the library; it is more ornate and pretentious, with heavy porcelains and carpets. To be sure, this must have been one of the fanciest interiors of the time, ironically maybe because of its "austerity," as it was less rococo than many of the interiors of surrounding mansions.

The Japanese delegation stayed at the house of another member of the Braniff family, Lorenza R. viuda de Braniff, on Reforma Avenue (figure 3.11).

3.10. Guillermo de Anda y Escandón's library (1910).
Courtesy Genaro García Collection, Nettie Lee Benson Latin American Collection,
the University of Texas, Austin.

The architecture of the extravagant villa could belong to Grünewald in Berlin
or to the new suburbs in Buenos Aires. The backyard garden and the hall of the
house were a monument to possession and gaudy nouveau-riche *mexicaine*. The
garden appears warded by tall fences and adorned by a Versailles-like fountain.
The picture of viuda de Braniff's living room shows a succession of halls in an
eighteenth-century French palace way; all the halls are heavily furnished and
adorned with busts, mirrors, gigantic jars, and canopies hanging everywhere.
This pretentiousness must have been difficult to inhabit on a daily basis, and
very likely the only daily dwellers in these interiors were maids and servants.

As interiors were meant to be glimpses into their owners' inner selves, they
displayed the great appeal of the exotic as a form of the bourgeoisie's intimacy (spirituality), thus references to India, China, Japan, and Arabia. Matilde
Martínez de la Horfa's mansion on Indio Triste Street in Mexico City had an
Arabic corner, perfectly staged, maybe never actually lived but experienced as
a personal ownership of the exotic.[31]

3.11. Viuda de Braniff's living room (1910). Courtesy Genaro García Collection, Nettie Lee Benson Latin American Collection, the University of Texas, Austin.

The Italian delegation was housed at one of the best located mansions in the city: that of Ignacio de la Torre y Mier in the Plaza de Reforma, the beginning of the most important Porfirian avenue, crowned with the eighteenth-century neoclassical statue of Charles IV. De la Torre y Mier was the wealthy inheritor of sugar fortunes and also Porfirio Díaz's son-in-law—as well as the protagonist of a legendary homosexual scandal in 1901 Mexico City. The mansion included an art room crowded with chairs and sofas, the ceiling heavily adorned with Second Empire deco. The furniture was already indicative of the art-nouveau trend to come, and the walls showed several canvases that are difficult to clearly distinguish in the picture. This was one of the fanciest houses in the city; it was experienced by Emiliano Zapata, who worked as de la Torre's horseman for some months. The bedroom of the house adds rococo to the eclectic kitsch of the art room. The bedroom was a simulacrum of flowers, secretarie, dense wallpapers, and canopies, where the man of the house performed both his wealth and his manhood. Wealth he had, manhood . . . (figure 3.12).

3.12. I. de la Torre y Mier's bedroom (1910). Courtesy Genaro García Collection, Nettie Lee Benson Latin American Collection, the University of Texas, Austin.

Historian Víctor González-Macías has documented the Porfirian use of aristocratic protocols in the political rituals of the regime, as well as the aristocratic interiors of official buildings. But a unique view is a good way to complement the examining of official interiors: Porfirio Díaz's private *sala de armas* in his home on Cadena Street (figure 3.13). A Catalan artist, Antonio Fabrés, designed it. He was hired in 1902 as art professor at Mexico's Academia de San Carlos. He was a devoted orientalist and a convert to art nouveau via Catalan *noucentisme*. His design for Díaz's *sala de armas* was decisively experimental art nouveau, utilizing metal (bronze and iron) in a ductile fashion. The magazine *Savia Moderna* described the main desk: "The desktop is made of copper covered in Russian maroon fur, and is full of golden hinges. Out of the desktop emerges a monster, representing war, spreading its wings in antique bronze-like green. The monster's glossy gold craws lean on two big steel guns; a stack of bullets is visible at the bottom of the monster's open mouth."[32] The monster's gigantic ears rhymed with the many peafowl's tail-like metal deco-

3.13. Porfirio Díaz's *sala de armas. Savia Moderna* (April 1906).

rations, and *noucentista* tables, full of metal curves. The rooms housed the dictator's collections of armors, swords, guns, and rifles. Though Díaz was not an aristocrat or a friend of the arts, his *sala de armas* was undoubtedly one of the most harmonious, least historicist, and almost vanguard interiors of the times.

Curiously, two decades later, in 1930, while traveling and witnessing the decline in vanguard *noucentista* architecture in Barcelona, Marte R. Gómez—one of the most accomplished members of the new postrevolutionary intelligentsia—wrote to revolutionary chief Plutarco Elías Calles: it used to be that Catalans followed "dislocated customs (*costumbres descoyuntadas*) with no other goal than to kill geometric shapes and edges. Today once more they bet for that which has the flavor of tradition and thus they will make gothic contributions that are positive achievements."[33] Gómez, as revolutionary, hated the old-regime styles both because they were Porfirian and because they were, by 1930, tacky. And of course during the Revolution many of the above-mentioned mansions were looted and destroyed. For the revolutionary aesthetics hated both the bourgeois eclecticism and the vanguard Porfirian experiments. In due time, however, the Revolution's *indigenista* style, its socialist realism, its bizarre functionalism, would become also *cursi*.

"The surroundings are the resonance chamber," wrote Mario Praz, and in the variegated ways of inhabiting the kitsch, *chilangos* found their ways of vibrating their moody selves as unstoppable reconstructions—*Wiederaufbau*: once more to build, to inhabit, to be. All the misery, all the tacky proletarization of high-class styles, and all the gentrification of local styles, all the experimentations, all were but intrinsic to any urban life around 1910. It would be hard to point out a real urban Mexican style of interior, but somehow to be, to inhabit, for many generations of Mexico City's inhabitants, has been to feel at home in the kitsch. When evoking memories of our own interiors, wrote Gaston Bachelard, "we are never true historians, we are always somehow poets and our emotions perhaps only render lost poetry."[34] I grew up in unpretentious interiors, comfortable cheap furniture manufactured in mass, imitating Mexican colonial styles, and lots of modern 1960s Formica and plastic. But as in past *vecindades* or bourgeois interiors, I lived in baroque, dense interiors. Minimalism and empty spaces were sins. In the family provincial home, in La Piedad Michoacán, my grandmother—the unschooled daughter of a prostitute—accustomed us to the unpretentious but useful kitchen where over an old simple chair tortillas were made with a little rustic wooden machine. The house had patios and its main dining room was a pretentious imitation of nineteenth-century medieval tables, chairs, and cabinets (full of cheap Chinese tea sets), all reserved for guests. The living room, banned to us children, had a cheap goblin depicting the Last Supper, and Louis XVI sofas whose red velvet was covered in thick transparent plastic. Pure kitsch. Today I would never re-create those interiors in my house. I now belong to IKEA interior. But in my *ensimismamientos*, whenever I feel a deep sense of self, I found myself comfortably and safely surrounded by those kitsch interiors. Perhaps because, as Gómez de la Serna thought, "No se descansa sino en lo cursi y todos sentimos el deseo de esa regresión hacia el pasado y hacia el futuro, pues lo más grato del porvenir es que tendrá sus formas nuevas de cursilería" (One cannot have a rest but in lo *cursi*, and we all feel the desire for that regression into the past and into the future, for the more pleasing aspect of the future is that surely it will come with its new forms of *cursilería*).[35]

PART II 1919

What my eyes beheld was simultaneous,
what I shall now write down will be successive for so is
language.
— Jorge Luis Borges, *Aleph* (1945)

IN AND AROUND 1919 MEXICO CITY

The year 1919 saw the world adrift. It seemed that never before had the world known the clash of mighty historical forces: nationalisms, imperialism, and the Revolution, which then meant something more than an intellectual lucubration—it was the all too tangible inevitability of radical social change. Revolution was a fate that gained both a founding moment, in the Russian Revolution, and a driving force: the workers' struggle throughout the world. Yet 1919 was the year of peace after World War I; it was also the year when world peace meant starvation in Germany, Russia, Hungary, and Poland; when Wilsonian dreams of global stability contrasted with U.S. and Allied forces' hesitations and interventions in the bloody Russian civil war. This was the year when, while soldiers returned home from the battlefront, unions everywhere revolted, cities were paralyzed by strikes and by anarchist and socialist terrorist acts; it was the same in Philadelphia as in Buenos Aires, in Mexico City as in Barcelona, in Berlin as in Delhi. Nationalisms prevailed, whether through an intransigent Georges Clemenceau, eager to humiliate Germany, or in all sorts of regionalisms blended with revolutionary impulses—in Bavaria, Catalonia, or Bengal, wherefrom such characters as B. Traven, Felipe Teixidor, and M. N. Roy, respectively, would reach Mexico City. This was one of those years when either revolutionary or reactionary factions profited politically from xenophobia, anti-Semitism, and racism. Furthermore, 1919 was a terrible year for the demographic balance of the world: countrysides were abandoned, infrastructure in Europe was destroyed, and the frightful consequences of the Spanish influenza were felt all over the world. It was a cold, very cold winter, and an unusually warm summer. It was nightmarish, or so it seemed then.

The concentric waves of this world in disarray reached Mexico City, which, however, was both too far away and too close to what 1919 meant in the world. After all, Mexico had been an integral part of the social and cultural change that had started "right around 1910"—it had furnished the era of modern revolutions with the first massive popular revolution. But the city was far from either the famine in Europe or the red scare à la américaine. That is why Mexico City became both a refuge for the world's radicals and a battlefield for world radicalism. La ciudad was not Moscow or Paris and yet it was full of interests, agents, and intellectuals from all over the world. It was not peaceful, as it had just come out of a bloody and messy revolution, yet it surely knew less violence in 1919 than Berlin, Barcelona, Philadelphia, or Chicago. It was not a decadent European city whose cultural life would have gone, as it were, from Spencerean or Nietzschean surmenages to German-like expressionism and disenchanted radical vanguardism. It was, however, the laboratory where, in 1919, such notions as "the nation," "the people," "the Revolution," as well as "authenticity," "race," and "avant-garde" were being experimented with in a Mexican and in a more than Mexican fashion.[1]

That is why the city became so important around 1919. To a world in despair, whose leitmotifs were revolution, vanguardism, disillusionment, and the collapse of the West, Mexico City offered a unique site in which to safely try out all sorts of enchantments and disenchantments. The multifarious evidence left by contemporaries is clear—Mexico City was great, it was a modern and relatively secure city, close to the U.S., never too cold, never too warm. It was comfortable, yet had the advantage of the exotic and authentic without the 1900s disgrace of the West; ironically, it was what the West was exactly about in 1919: revolution, experimentation, poverty, aesthetic and social innovation, and search for lost innocence.

The life of a city, any city, is simultaneity; historical narratives are succes-sive by necessity. It would be impossible to recover the simultaneity of ideas and events of Mexico City as a center of global cultural encounters. A string of consecutive interconnected stories is a way to compensate for the fleeting concurrence of urban life. I seek merely to immerse the reader in one of the poorly known capitals of the modernist world around 1919. Hence, the follow-ing stories show what was at stake in terms of intellectual experimentations and political trial and error. That is, in a culturally promiscuous revolution-ary capital, a city of bizarre discoveries and inventions, of love and betrayal, not only the meaning of Mexico was at stake, but also the new connotations of paramount modernist concepts—revolution, the popular, avant-garde, au-thenticity, race, and desire. Thus these consecutive stories go from an array of cultural options that seemed possible (some became lost futures, some others became cultural canon by the 1930s) to moments of radical performances and plottings in which the city itself was the most meaningful. From the stories of artists and intellectuals who reached the city to partake in the devising of mod-ernist enchantment and disenchantment, to urban perdición: the real bohemia, that which is not mere fashion but vice and poverty converted into cultural and moral mutiny.

For most foreigners, however, the city was a scenario, by and large a disappointing one, that betrayed their exoticist dreams. For its inhabitants, on the other hand, the city was simply them. In 1919, for instance, Charles Phillips, one of the many U.S. radicals who were enchanted by the city, disappointingly found that "Mexican cities mean nothing without/Oliver, Singer, and Libby." Realizing this, he, like many others, wondered about the utopia of revolution and untouched genuine cultures that had brought him and many others to Mexico City in the first place: "Where are the soldiers of the Revolution?" In the urban masses? In the "syphilitic hand stretched out" in the midst of the streets? "Which one of these is you?"

Despite the poverty—or perhaps because of it—the city must have been, for all the intellectuals and activists who discovered it, a sensual, exotic delight, filled with those revolutionary moments and the desire for strange bodies. The world started to become fascinated with Mexico, and the city transformed that fascination into its own might as a modernist world capital.

For their part, in 1919 the city's inhabitants felt part of a changing world, as frightened about the future and as happy about the end of massacres as the inhabitants of European cities were. The future of the country and of the Revolution was still uncertain, but so was the future of the world. The benign global fascination with violence, revolution, and race that Mexico City represented had a different meaning for the city's own intelligentsia. It was as if the city were lost in its own chaotic essaying. The world search for fixed racial and cultural hopes in a tropical land was just another sound lost in the midst of varied urban noises. As Mexico City's young poet Julio Torri wrote around 1919, evoking the goddess Circe, "Since I was set on losing myself, the sirens didn't sing for me." In 1919 the city's cultural possibilities called for perdición (getting lost) and also for perspective: experimentation joined by the realization that, in view of what the world was going through, Mexico City was a paradise for that—namely, perdición, trial and error.[2]

1

On the night of December 31, 1919, an earthquake shook Mexico City; this was a goodbye to a shaky decade, for in 1919 it was clear that Mexico City not only had survived the Revolution but was also taming the strong antiurban spirit of most revolutionary factions. A popular novel, La ciudad de los palacios by Spanish writer and longtime Mexico City resident Julio Sesto, then fictionalized the horrors suffered by the city in 1914 and 1915, when the city was invaded by various revolutionary troops. In the story the heroine returns to the city to look at and hear "colonial moles that flaunted their secular potency . . . songs of metropolitan life, jovial, crazed, overwhelming and rhythmic; fumes of the hot pavement . . . scrubbed marble . . . smiles of hopefulness; glances of longing; rumors of life and living . . . Oh! The city of palaces." The city indeed had returned to its natural and creative chaos, its streets and corners echoed what they were: "songs of metropolitan life."

That year, 1919, Emiliano Zapata, the "Attila of the south" who once terrorized the city, was assassinated in Chinameca, not very far from the city. The news was received in a relatively peaceful Mexico City with a blend of indifference and relief. When alive, Zapata was seen as a potential threat to the city—unlike Francisco Villa's troops, the social base of Zapata's movement was just too close to the city. Once dead, the Attila could easily be made into the hero of progressive urbanites. No open combat had occurred in the city since 1914; and the city would not be a major battlefield for the rest of the twentieth century.

The city then had around 600,000 inhabitants. That year about 14,000 died—the lowest death rate (22 per 1000 inhabitants) in the city's history. Nevertheless, scientists debated the official figures and the effects of war, altitude, weather, and race on the still-too-high mortality rate. But in 1919 about twenty-seven persons committed suicide, not much to match post–World War I depressed Berlin, but enough to keep alive the modernist epic of suicidal poets such as Manuel Acuña. This was also enough to show that the supposed Mexican *Gemeinschaft* was indeed a complex *Gesellschaft*. The Spanish influenza that affected the city very likely came from the U.S., though the city's most prestigious environmentalist, Miguel Ángel de Quevedo, believed it came from Barcelona. Don Miguel Ángel lost his wife to the influenza epidemic. Like Guillaume Apollinaire, who died in 1918 during the epidemic in Paris, his brother residing in Mexico City, the financier Albert Kostrowitzky, died a year later from either influenza or the city's periodic typhus outbreaks. Young U.S. writer Katherine Anne Porter survived the influenza and moved to Mexico City, rather than to Paris, to craft her modernist profile as a writer.

In 1919, Mexico City was still living out of its former Porfirian *belle-époque* grandeur, alas with close memories of the worst revolutionary years; a new era seemed to be starting, but the city lived with nostalgia of what was known. Architects and poets lamented the destruction of the colonial past that had started in the Porfirian time. But in 1919, as engineer Domingo Díez stated in a meeting of the prestigious Sociedad Científica Antonio Alzate, the new architecture led to the loss of "the references of childhood." Felipe Teixidor—

a Catalan intellectual who came to the city around 1919 and never left, becoming a prominent art collector, publicist, and narrator of the city—recalled that the city in 1919 was extremely dark at night, and the shadow of Don Porfirio could still be felt. The Revolution in 1919 was "re-codifying" the city and itself, losing what Teixidor recalled in the 1970s as the appeal of both the Revolution and the city: "Napoleon codified the French Revolution. Well, here the Revolution is codified and thus what was lost was not only the picturesque, which is something important, but also the flame."

By 1919 the city must have lost the stink of blood and violence and returned to its natural aromas—horse manure, cilantro, onion, gasoline, flowers, and human excrement. Walking in the city meant seeing new automobiles and buses, and lots of horses and mules, an open sewer system and dust storms. In 1923 Miguel Ángel de Quevedo explained that the city would be buried neither by the Revolution nor by lava from the nearby Popocatepetl volcano (known as El Popo), but would instead be buried in excrement (*popó* in prudish Mexican Spanish). All in all the new postrevolutionary buildings and street plans started to emerge. The city was like a stylish and wicked femme fatale just awakening from a long spree of revolutions and abuses, gazing at her disheveled and hungover self: everything to be redone. The city of nineteenth-century-like ennui coexisted with the city of twentieth-century avant-garde bohemia; old cosmopolitan forms of agrarianism and radicalism coexisted with the new radical cosmopolitanism marked by the 1917 Soviet revolution.[3]

While in 1910 the city's German, American, Spanish, and French colonies were formed by longtime residents dedicated to commerce and finance, in 1919 many new foreigners started to arrive in the city, escaping persecution in Europe and the U.S. or in search of the revolutionary appeal. Whereas in 1914 Apollinaire, informed by his brother's letters, announced in *La vie anecdotique* that French, German, and British citizens were preparing in Mexico City their armed defense from the revolutionary chaos, in 1919 U.S. slackers—young radicals (pacifists, socialists, and communists) who in the context of World War I escaped the draft and persecution—had taken over the Genova Hotel in downtown Mexico City, organizing from there the escape of many other U.S. socialists and pacifists.

One of the dead of 1919 was the most distinguished poet in Mexican letters of three decades, Amado Nervo. His death in Montevideo, Uruguay, produced a plethora of reactions in the entire Spanish-speaking world. Nervo had been the greatest expression of Mexican *modernismo*—understood within the literary history of the Spanish language, that is, as a peculiar blend of decadentism, spiritualism, symbolism, and rhetorical innovation. But by 1919 Nervo's style, even if still praised, was considered the target, the passé style that the city's avant-garde writers were trying to surpass. In 1919, with Nervo, an entire era came to an end. As Alfonso Reyes wrote in his "Epitafio" to Nervo:

Pero es tanta la malicia
de morirse de una vez,
que ya parece mentira
lo que nos faltas después.

But so vast is the malice
to die at once,
that already it seems a lie
how much we'll miss you.

Another important death around 1919 was that of the city's poet who had done the most to innovate locally, namely Ramón López Velarde. "Had I never left my little town," López Velarde wrote in Mexico City around 1919, "a saintly wife would have been my sole comfort/from only having known the world from a single hemisphere" (Si yo jamás hubiera salido de mi villa/con una santa esposa tendría el refrigerio/de conocer el mundo por un solo hemisferio). The provincial poet from Jerez, Zacatecas, had reached Mexico City in the early twentieth century, blending his melancholy for a lost provincial world with the urban bohemia and cosmopolitanism that he both loved and despised. By 1919 he had distanced himself from Catholic circles, experimenting with political and aesthetic ideas. He and the poet laureate of Mexico City, Enrique González Martínez, were the most prominent inhabitants of the lettered republic that Mexico City was around 1919. In 1918 and 1919 some of the well-established intellectuals disapproved of López Velarde's bizarre metaphors as well as his Catholic provincialism. But he was sought eagerly by young vanguard poets such as Xavier Villaurrutia and Salvador Novo—dandies who soon formed a prominent intellectual cohort, a sort of Mexico City's Bloomsbury, around the literary periodical Contemporáneos.

By 1919 López Velarde was a conspicuous presence in the city's periodicals and literary gatherings, displaying his unusual metaphors, full of provincial as well as technical references and an uncanny melancholy. The city's cultural life revealed nostalgia for the social structure and order of the Porfirian city, but its intellectuals were engaged in vivid debates, deciding the educational, artistic, and political course of postrevolutionary Mexico; debates that blended scientific, political, social, and aesthetic rhetorical devices. "The city has become a carnival, with prostitutes everywhere," read a 1916 article in the prestigious literary journal *Vida Moderna*, "in which it would be difficult to tell wheat from darnel" (en el que difícilmente podría distinguirse el trigo de la cizaña). And the author, full of nostalgia, recalled: "remember the shining San Francisco Avenue [Madero Street by 1919], that our modest boulevard, that our humble Puerta del Sol, where all of our elegances paraded on those glorious afternoons and voluptuous dusks . . . with such a satisfaction and safety could you take your wife, sister, or daughter to revel in the innocence of such honest amusement!" Now, the author concluded, the Revolution had made the city a place of sin. In the same issue of *Vida Moderna*, however, López Velarde—a Catholic poet who both feared and loved urban sensuality—published a story that would have been unacceptable in the language of the Porfirian city: the story of three worms that in very graphic terms eat a woman's corpse as if devouring women's "natural" fear, indifference, and hate. In effect, as critic José Emilio Pacheco writes, López Velarde had made from trendy late nineteenth-century Mexican literary modernism simple modernity: "he is no longer a victim of *Weltschmerz*, the illness of the century: he is his own tyrant so overwhelmed by himself that he distances from his own self and ironically contemplates himself from the outside."

Also around 1919 Manuel Gamio, a future father of Mexican revolutionary archaeology and anthropology and a great ideologue of postrevolutionary mestizo ideology, was in Mexico City finishing his Columbia Ph.D. under Franz Boas's supervision, seeking political positions and writing stories full of both nostalgia about the old Mexico and fear and excitement about the emerging one. In one of those stories, "La zahurda" (The Pigpen), written around 1919, he collapsed all his concerns: the destruction of provincial communities, the city's appeal and its immorality, the massive migration of Mexicans to the U.S. during the Mexican Revolution, and the emergence of a common nationality based on the survival skills derived from misery. The tale told the story of a pauperized woman who migrated from the provinces to Mexico City, where she married an urban proletarian who left her and their two children in order to follow the revolutionary troops north. Alone, the woman faced the city with despair, experiencing hunger, prostitution, and abandonment in one of the many rooms of the city's *vencidades*. But she found help in one of the city's most marginal dwellers: a crippled *mandadero* (errand-man) who helped her and fathered another baby, only to die from malnutrition and the city's mistreatment. Her first husband returns from the U.S., where he had sought work following the dismantling of Villa's army and disillusion with the Revolution—"¡Qué ideales ni qué ojo de hacha!" (who cares about ideals!) he is told by a former revolutionary officer in the U.S. On his return he finds his wife burying her new man, with a new baby in arms. He tries to hit her, only to succumb to

4.1. Illustration, Julio Sesto's *La ciudad de los palacios*, illustrated by
Duhart, Gutiérrez, and Zaldivar (Mexico City: El Libro Español, 1917).

those arms, for "she, like he, was a victim of life; crushed to a pulp by the cruel
machinations of misery." The city was the center of these contradictions and
new syntheses that frightened and fascinated both López Velarde and Gamio.[4]

Julio Sesto's popular novels—not only *La ciudad de los palacios* but also *La tórtola del Ajusco*—had previously shown a revolutionary city where, for instance,
bread was scarce but there was plenty of Bergson and Nietzsche. The symbolist
illustrations of Sesto's novel (by Duhart, Gutiérrez, and Zaldivar—first names
are unavailable) depicted the omnipresence of the city and the vanguard impulses of its artists. One image showed the entire symbolist city quietly sleeping through its sins and dangers, while a wizard surrounded by naked women,
representing the temptation of the city, guards the sleep of the city's humble
inhabitants (figure 4.1).

The few novels with the city as leitmotif since the 1880s had presented, like
Gamio or Sesto, this ambivalence about the dangers of the city and nostalgia
for a lost past. "How does one not feel nostalgic about the countryside?" wrote
lawyer and novelist Emilio Rabasa in the 1880s about one of his urban characters who is forced by an urban thunderstorm to recall his *querencia* (longing)
for the bucolic past. The same was argued by such Mexican artists as Roberto
Montenegro and Francisco Goitia, who in the 1910s were in Europe painting

sad urban landscapes, devoid of people and full of melancholy, like the good symbolists they had become. The city was thus turned into a well-demarcated subject involved in the intellectual, spiritual, and moral life of its inhabitants.

But the city's poetic and plastic landscapes were composed by struggles against the old, finding solace both by rhetorical innovation and by the nostalgia intrinsic to any modern city. There was the excitement of urban sin, the possibility of anonymity, and the inevitable gatherings and intrigues. For in those years, writes poet and critic Gabriel Zaid, there was "a certain complacency in one's own sadness." The city was thrilling, as López Velarde wrote before his premature death:

Sobre tu Capital, cada hora vuela
ojerosa y pintada, en carretela;
y en tu provincia, del reloj en vela
que rondan los palomos colipavos,
las campanadas caen como centavos

Above your Capital the hours soar,
hollow-eyed and rouged, in a coach-and-four,
while in your provinces the hours
roll like *centavos* from insomniac
clocks with fan-tail dove patrols.

Urban hours passed away rapidly, as women passed by in the night, covered with makeup, with dark circles under their eyes. The provinces, by contrast, meant the calm sound of temple's bells. The *patria's* secret of happiness, López Velarde wrote, was this: "Patria, I give you the key to your good fortune: always be the same, true to your daily mirror" (Patria, te doy de tu dicha la clave: sé siempre igual, fiel a tu espejo diario). The clue was for the nation not to be like its capital city. But the city was neither always the same, nor a mirror that could reflect any national essence. However, the city made possible the intellectual conception of the nation; its intellectual promiscuity and dynamism both produced and made necessary the idea of being always truthful to the nation's "daily mirror."

For López Velarde, as for the many inhabitants of the "Brown Atlantis"— the mythical capital of radical, exoticist, racial, and primitivist dreams of a generation of the world's activists and intellectuals (see chapter 5)—the real and eternal nation was in the small town. But unlike, say, Diego Rivera's nationalism or Stuart Chase's Mexican ideal *Gemeinschaft* (Mexico: A Study of Two Americas, 1930, illustrated by Rivera), López Velarde's provincialism did not dream of atavist racial or cultural mandates. His urbane melancholy constituted a longing for a lost innocence, a frequent feeling resulting from cities. For López Velarde, wariness was indispensable in order to build the new *patria* and to face the city. He was, he wrote around 1919, "then a seminarian," without urban taste, "with no Baudelaire, neither rhyme nor instinct," who faced urban temptations but wanted above all the return to innocence, for him, for the nation, for the city:

Yo quisiera acogerme a la mesura,
a la estricta conciencia y al recato
de aquellas cosas que me hicieron bien . . .

I'd wish to welcome restraint
to welcome the strict awareness and the prudence
of those things that did me good . . .

For after all, lost innocence is what the world's radicals and writers sought in 1920s Mexico City, albeit Mexican innocence had, for them, to be somehow racial. The mythical provinces granted a modernist *in illo tempore*, a golden age of peace and harmony: the community that Mexico City at once disallowed and made more vivid and alluring in the consciousness of poets and observers. Even the most urban of the city's poets around 1919, Manuel Maple Arce—a sort of Mexican futurist poet—seemed caught by the city's nostalgia in the midst of reference to electric cables, cars, and airplanes: "Suadade/Estoy solo en el último tramo de la ausencia/y el dolor hace horizonte en mi demencia" (Nostalgia/I'm lonely in desertion's last stride/and pain bends a horizon in my madness).

Soon, very soon, in 1921, López Velarde died: a disappearance that can serve to mark the potential futures that the city's cultural encounters were pointing to. López Velarde's poetic blend of newness and traditionalism became an emblem. The city woke up—wrote Honduran poet, longtime resident in Mexico City, Rafael Heliodoro Valle—, and its poet was dead. And another Mexico City poet—this one from Colombia—then Rafael Arenas, soon to become Porfirio Barba Jacob, and the friend whom the pious López Velarde used to visit with terror in Arenas's urban and sinful hiding places—mourned the disappearance of the poet, of a way of seeing things, and did it with López Velarde–like bizarre images ("Canción de la noche diamantina"):

Musa solar con nardos irreales
El cielo niño del abril decora

Y éste era el huerto de una Reina mora
Y un lirio que la aurora aljofaró
Pero mi corazón balbucea ante la aurora:
—¡No! ¡No! ¡No! ¡No!

Muse of the sun with dreamlike spikes
Adorn the infant sky of April
And once upon a time there was the orchard of a Moorish queen
And there was an iris, set ablaze by glorious light
But my heart stammers before the lights:
No! No! No! No!

Thus Amado Nervo's apparently solid Mexico was gone; gone also was López Velarde's experimentalism. The struggle continued. At the beginning of the 1920s, the city was the site of a brawl between a militant nationalism (*indigenista*, nativist, and revolutionary) and an even more activist cosmopolitanism—both trends urban, both melancholic about the loss of mythic and innocent origins. It seemed adamant: the national was local, unsophisticated, real, popular, non-Western; cosmopolitanism was foreign, fancy, sissy, elitist, un-Mexican, and simply an impersonation of the West. "We are neither Spanish nor aboriginals," López Velarde had written in 1917, "consequently, the nationalist cries should embrace neither the bronzed nor the blonde, rather this shade of coffee with milk that tinges us." Of course the city showed at every moment and everywhere that such antagonism was a mirage created by different ideological interests (all cosmopolitan, all national). Members of both trends were admirers of French, German, English, and Spanish literatures. All were fascinated by science and history and by the city's life; and both factions, in one way or another, were tempted by the allure of romantic ecstasies—in the form of Oriental or Aztec motifs. The literary periodicals that circulated in 1919 included translations of prose and poetry by Paul Valéry, Rabindranath Tagore, André Gide, and Oscar Wilde, and of Japanese, Chinese, Aztec, and Mixteco poetry, as well as news about archaeological discoveries, the Russian Revolution, scientific advances. Mexican haikus coincided with translations from Nahuatl and Mixteco poetry; the intellectuals' fascination with Sarah Bernhardt coincided with that for Tagore. If Yeats had found refuge in spiritualism and Celtic mythology, some Mexican poets found renewal in their invention of a local poetic tradition and in many forms of Oriental ecstasies. López Velarde's legacy was an affirmation of how to live, intellectually, in the in-betweens of nineteenth-century rhetorical devices, science, urban bohemia, revolutionary nationalism, Catholic values, the weight of history, and changing cosmopolitan canons. He can be read as a lost direction in the history of the city's culture, one that ended with his death. Or he can also be read as a condensation of the possibilities that the city offered to all those who dared to see it and leave it around 1919.[5]

For there was another significant loss in 1918, again a provincial immigrant (from Aguascalientes) to the city—the painter Saturnino Herrán. He lived in the former well-to-do *barrio* of Santa María la Ribera. Herrán, like López Velarde, never left the city. Unlike the new American and European visitors in the city, Herrán never attempted to escape the city. He was an innovator, a student of Mexican and Spanish professors in the city's art school, a painter who, like many others—such as Diego Rivera—had the opportunity to go to Europe on a Porfirian government scholarship. But like López Velarde, Herrán stayed, becoming the master of domesticity and thus reaching a cultural blend that was very Mexican and thus more than local. That localness turned out to be inevitably *citadino* (belonging to the city): a locally brewed form of universalism that the intellectuals and artists who eventually reached the city only footnoted, if not unconsciously then out of necessity. Because the city ruled, it made innovation and mixture possible, and purity and essences even less feasible. And Herrán was what the city had produced visually. While the young José Clemente Orozco, as he recalled, began to depict the worst *barrios* of the city, Herrán started to paint "criollas que él conocía, en lugar de manolas a la Zuloaga" (*criollas* he had met, instead of Zuloaga-like *manolas*—Andalusian-looking women). Herrán painted scenes of Mexican history out of real, if stylized, Mexican urban characters. He was respected by the city's intelligentsia, but he seemed to be ahead of his time, or so his friend Julio Sesto thought when he imagined Herrán departing with the phrase: "you do not deserve to have painters or artists of any kind: you are all brutal [*bellacos*]: I am leaving." And depart he did.[6]

Whereas López Velarde innovated with metaphors in the discovery of the local in the midst of cosmopolitan urban bohemia and melancholy, Herrán depicted local colors and characters in insightful renditions of urban people in stylized yet sensual and trendy fashions. Art historian Fausto Ramírez considers Herrán the first and more accomplished depicter of the mestizo as the national character. But Herrán's mestizos were that not because they were the right genetic blend but because they were what mestizo meant and means: urban. Herrán, together with illustrator and painter Julio Ruelas, became the painter of the city par excellence, not only because of his masterful urban characters—beggars, children—, but above all because he was the illustrator of many of the city's literary publications. As López Velarde said in his eulogy to Herrán in 1919:

If only passion is fruitful, then it is appropriate to proclaim the name of Herran's lover. He loved his country but using a most sincere allegory, I can attest that Herran's lover was the city of Mexico, rich in pain and pleasure; he caressed her stone by stone, resident by resident, cloud by cloud.[7]

Herrán: the lover of la ciudad—a female name and reality in Spanish—, the artist who was never in Montparnasse and yet had to find a way to depict his lover in universal terms. These two extremes, López Velarde and Herrán, one in poetry, the other in painting, encompassed the huge domestic transformation toward a cosmopolitan, conflicted, urban discovery of the local, that is, the city: very local and yet never solely native. Before Diego Rivera, before the international discovery of the Brown Atlantis, these extremes demarcated what was happening intellectually in the city.

Locally, artists and intellectuals started to create the porous cultural borders of the city that extended its reach to Paris, Barcelona, New York. Hence the years from 1919 to 1921 were of returns—of Mexicans in Europe and the U.S. to the city, of Mexicans in the city back to New York, the new international Mecca of arts, in order to display the new discoveries of a Brown Atlantis in Mexico City. Herrán was at the center of the milieu that Rivera's Mexico later overwhelmed.

In 1918 two important Mexican artists returned, one from New York, the other from Barcelona: cartoonist Ernesto García Cabral and painter Francisco Goitia. The former became a success in Mexico City's growing magazine industry, creating a Mexico City style of cartoons that was influential for many decades to come. Goitia started to exhibit in the city in 1918 and worked with Manuel Gamio, illustrating archaeological discoveries. But Goitia soon left the city to live as an anchorite in Xochimilco, starting the myth of abandoning the city that many others soon followed—for instance, B. Traven, Antonin Artaud, and Hart Crane on countless occasions. Goitia painted landscapes and events of the Revolution, and captured popular scenes in a Goya-like expression of faces.[8] He brought back the lessons of postimpressionist nationalist primitivism from Catalonia and inserted those trends into the thick flow of Mexico City's experimental possibilities.

Many others followed this double return to Mexico and to Mexican topics: Roberto Montenegro, Carlos Mérida, Adolfo Best Maugard, and finally, in July 1921, Diego Rivera. He left Paris and all its experiments except one: he opted to go native and revolutionary; he decided to become the Mexican painter. Some left Mexico City to promote their findings (like Best Maugard, who went to New York). All of them experimented with European vanguards and debated the return to authenticity and primitivism. Carlos Mérida, a Guatemalan, is an emblematic case: he was in Europe up to 1914, then in Guatemala and then in Mexico in 1918. He became, together with Gamio, a leading advocate of one kind of indigenism, a militantly cosmopolitan and urban depiction that did not support a Brown Atlantis kind of destiny for Mexico, but simply a sophisticated study of the Indigenous past and arts in order to transform them into modern and innovative cultural forms.

All in all, the literary circles in the streets and cafes of Mexico City were, as contemporary critic Castro Leal put it, about the "vogue of the primitive," and that is why Carlos Mérida "enters the picture through the well-known path of the primitive." Indeed, they were all orientalist in more than one sense. By 1922 many of these artists were involved in the most ironic of gestures: painting stylish art nouveau or social realist or Italian fresco-like images of Indians, countrysides, bucolic motifs, and idealized harmonious views of the pre-Hispanic past on the very urban walls of the official buildings of a massive city that hosted them, fostered them, taught them: made them. These were tattoos in the very urban flesh of the city.[9]

2

In September 1919, Mexican musician Manuel M. Ponce—another exile from Zacatecas and Aguascalientes to Mexico City—wrote that Mexico was in need of its own Grieg. And to this end, musicians and folklorists needed to collect more popular tunes and lyrics (a task that Porfirian folklorists had already started). He sought the synthesis that López Velarde and Herrán were already doing. But what Ponce, Gamio, and Mérida overlooked is that cultural syntheses are unstable; they never really end.

Ponce had also returned to Mexico City from Europe in 1909, and thereafter dedicated himself to the teaching and incorporation of traditional tunes into a form of Mexican classical music. In 1919 he headed the *Revista Musical de México*, in which he advocated the return to popular tunes at the same time that he welcomed Arthur Rubenstein, for instance, to the city. In the same journal, Mexico's leading folklorist, Rubén M. Campos, reviewed Anna Pavlova's performance in Mexico City, in a highbrow rhetorical style that only he, one of the few intellectuals who could truly speak the city's slang, could feel free to exaggerate—impossible to translate:

Semejante a Siringa, la cefirosa ninfa de los pies ligeros, rondadora del rondo de la alegría. Anna Pavlova ha tenido al tiempo maravilloso ante la gracia ebúrnea de su fragilidad tanagrina. . . . presta a desprenderse en vuelo voluble para errar como una hora o una musa de pubis de Chavannes de flor en flor, sobre las mieles doradas y las aguas pluviales.[10]

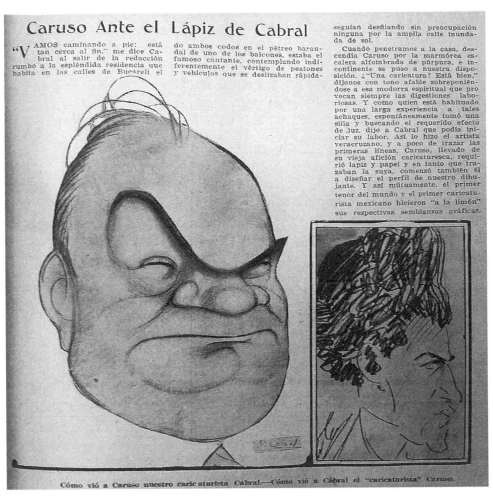

Caruso Ante el Lápiz de Cabral

"VAMOS caminando a pie: está tan cerca al fin." me dice Cabral al salir de la redacción rumbo a la espléndida residencia que habita en las calles de Bucareli el do ambos codos en el pétreo barandal de uno de los balcones, estaba el famoso cantante, contemplando indiferentemente el vértigo de peatones y vehículos que se deslizaban rápida-

seguían desfilando sin preocupación ninguna por la amplia calle inundada de sol.

Cuando penetramos a la casa, descendía Caruso por la marmórea escalera alfombrada de púrpura, e incontinente se puso a nuestra disposición. ¿"Una caricatura? Está bien," díjonos con tono afable sobreponiéndose a esa modorra espiritual que provocan siempre las digestiones laboriosas. Y como quien está habituado por una larga experiencia a tales achaques, espontáneamente tomó una silla y buscando el requerido efecto de luz, dijo a Cabral que podía iniciar su labor. Así lo hizo el artista veracruzano, y a poco de trazar las primeras líneas, Caruso, llevado de su vieja afición caricaturesca, requirió lápiz y papel y en tanto que trazaban la suya, comenzó también él a diseñar el perfil de nuestro dibujante. Y así mútuamente, el primer tenor del mundo y el primer caricaturista mexicano hicieron "a la limón" sus respectivas semblanzas gráficas.

Cómo vió a Caruso nuestro caricaturista Cabral.—Cómo vió a Cabral el "caricaturista" Caruso.

4.2. Caruso, García Cabral, *El Heraldo* (September 28, 1919).

Ponce lamented, in turn, that not many people saw Pavlova or heard Rubenstein because the city was hosting a unique guest: Enrico Caruso, who sang, among other things, pieces from *El Elixir del Amor* and *Carmen*. He gave a public popular concert at El Toreo, where U.S. boxer Jack Johnson also fought the same year. Europe's chaos had made it possible for opera premieres to be performed in America, not only in Buenos Aires and New York—consecrated Meccas of opera—but also in Mexico City. "As Sappho said about Aphrodite" wrote Ponce, commenting on Caruso's visit, "I would not have wanted to die before hearing that singing"[11] (figure 4.2).

In this way the capital city meant the eternal return to innocence and native authenticity but was nevertheless at the peak of its cosmopolitanism. Caruso was in Mexico City, where he and García Cabral echoed the encounters of the world with the city, of the city with the world, in mutual cartoons of each other. This was the humor of the lack of civilizational barriers. Caruso was, in turn, photographed in Xochimilco, where Goitia escaped to—and where Edward Weston would soon arrive to photograph *vecindades*—drinking *pulque* with an Italian soprano dressed in a *charro* outfit. Soon Mexican musicians would start the same antagonism between those in favor of a militant indigenism (Carlos Chávez) and those in favor of a more cosmopolitan music (Julián Carrillo). Ponce, like López Velarde, Herrán, and Goitia, seemed caught in inhabiting the options that the city then offered.

But while the city's intelligentsia was still digesting the departure of López Velarde and Herrán, and while the newspapers still commented on Caruso's and Johnson's visits, a new dancing hall was inaugurated in April 1920 on the old site of the panadería Los Gallos on Pensador Mexicano Street. This was the Salón México, where for more than a decade the urban proletariat would dance *danzones*—a mixture of Cuban tunes, Spanish counter-dance, and Vera-cruz musical traditions. This was the place where great Mexican *orquestras* (for instance, Dimas) played, and where eventually Aaron Copland would hear the tunes that inspired him to create *Salón México* (1936).

It comes as no wonder then that in 1920 the Mexican artistic copyright agency registered a bizarre blend of creative products: the fox-trot, "Blues oh Helen," and "I Wonder If the Same Moon Shines"; a *Sanduga Oaxaqueña* by the famous María Conesa; and a manuscript "El triunfo de la raza." And in 1918 Mexico City saw a Porfirian novel—*Santa* (1903) by Federico Gamboa—made into a modern public display of technology and sentimentality, a successful silent film about a young girl from the nearby town of Chimalistac who was se-duced by a military man and then corrupted by the city, becoming a prostitute. The plot would have many cinematic renditions, among them one that would eventually have a soundtrack and lyrics by Agustín Lara (1931). The rural girl converted into an urban prostitute became, in Lara's lyric, the city's form of redemption: "In the eternal night/of my sorrow/you [Santa] have been the star that lit up my sky" (En la eterna noche/de mi desconsulo/tú [Santa] has sido la estrella que alumbró mi cielo).

Sometime in the early 1920s, Lara, a very young son of a pauperized Por-firian bourgeois family, having been expelled from home by his father due to his vices (drugs, alcohol, women), started to work as the pianist in the Salambó cabaret (and brothel) in Mexico City. He composed many songs dedicated to women, prostitutes, and love betrayals, which would eventually become part of Mexican urban popular culture. A writer who shared the same *barrio* with

Lara recalled: "Since those days [circa 1920], since those nights, he made up [atisbaba] what we could call the inverse of our sentimental tradition." By 1929 Lara had become a radio star. In the sinful life of early 1920s Mexico City, a legend of Mexican culture, Agustín Lara, was in the making.[12]

By 1919 popular tunes were experiencing an incredible distribution and consumption in the city, though most recordings were made in the U.S. Never had the city danced, as it did then, to the same tunes. In 1920 El Teatro Lírico had great success with Mi querido capitán, a late nineteenth-century-style musical. But soon recordings of such famous revolutionary tunes as "Adelita" and other songs like "A la orilla de un palmar" arrived from the U.S. for by then the popular rural lyrics had become urban common sense. By 1919 "Perjura"—a piece composed in 1901 by musician Miguel Lerdo de Tejada and poet Fernando Luna y Drusina—had been sung by so many popular singers that its original "sinful" nature seemed to be forgotten: "When my lips, on your fair neck/with mad fever, you possess them" (Cuando mis labios en tu albo cuello/con fiebre loca mi bien posee). In the city, Lerdo de Tejada recalled in the 1930s, people received the song "without reservations, it spoke to them in the language of things that had already been said in La Traviata." In 1919, too, popular composer Armando Villarreal Lozano wrote "Morenita mía" (My Little Brown Girl), and by 1921 it was, and remained for decades, an everyday understanding in Mexico City. In 1922, in addition, Mexican popular composer Alfonso Esparza Oteo released his "Mi viejo amor" (lyrics by poet Adolfo Fernández Bustamante), a romantic take on the nostalgia of old love, which contrasted that year with the popularity in the city of a Cuban tune by Manuel Corona, "Falsaria," an ode to urban love and to what economists would call rational choice:

Cuan falso fue tu amor, me has engañado
el juramento aquél era fingido.
Sólo siento, mujer, haber creido
Que eras el ángel que yo había soñado.
Con que te vendes, ieh!, noticia grata,
no por eso te odio y te desprecio;
aunque tengo poco oro y poca plata
en materia de compras soy un necio.
Espero a que te pongas más barata
sé que algún día bajarás de precio.

Your love was so fake, you betrayed me,
that commitment, the one I got from you, was mere pretending.

I only regret, woman, to have believed
you were the angel I had dreamt.
So, you're for sale, ah!, good news,
that makes me neither love nor hate you,
though I have neither gold nor silver,
I'm stubborn businesswise.
I wait for you to get cheaper
I'm sure sooner or later your price'll go down.

Poems and lyrics from all over the Spanish-speaking world were made into the everyday understanding of the urban masses. The poem "Flor de Mayo," by the most prominent Porfirian poet, Amado Nervo, was set to music by Mario Talavera. Popular singers and composers from Veracruz, Mérida, and Monterrey arrived in the city, and it became a musical capital. In 1925 one of the most popular tunes was "Ella," an edited version of the poem "Pequeño nocturno" by Osvaldo Bazil, a modernist and bohemian poet from the Dominican Republic. The poem was set to music by Domingo Casanova Heredia and made popular by Guty Cárdenas's voice and guitar playing in a Yucatan rhythm known as *bambuco*. Its popular appropriation involved, curiously, editing the gaudy decadentism of the original piece in order to emphasize the everyday beauty of the images. For instance, the original included such lines as "[Ella] la que el más blando susurrar de égloga/derramó en el azul de mis mañanas" (She, the one a soft whisper of eclogue/spilled over the blue of my mornings), but the musical version eliminated such dated language and left the lyrics to fly in a sonorous blend of feelings and metaphors:

Ella, la que hubiera amado tanto,
la que echizó de música mi alma,
me pide, con ternura, que la olvide,
que la olvide sin odio y sin llanto

Yo que llevo enterrados tantos sueños,
yo que guardo tantas tumbas en el alma,
no sé por qué sollozo y tiemblo
al cavar, al cavar, una más en mis entrañas.

She, the one I would have loved so much,
the one who enchanted with music my soul,
tenderly asks me to forget her,
to forget her with no hate and no tears

I, who go by with so many buried dreams,
I, who guard so many graves in my soul,
I don't know why I cry and tremble
digging just one more grave in my heart.

In 1923 two new radio stations started to broadcast music and by 1929 there were twenty-five stations in the city. By 1930 station XEW—"The voice of Latin America from Mexico," the station's slogan—opened, marking the start of the globalization of the city's music in the entire Spanish-speaking world.[13] In this way, Mexico City was at the center of the closest thing to twentieth-century Mexican cultural imperialism in the Spanish-speaking world.

When foreign intellectuals and activists began to arrive in the city, they could not resist being enchanted by its music. In 1914 Guillaume Apollinaire's brother, Albert, responded to Guillaume's request for folk music from Mexico with: "There is no popular literature or song belonging to the streets of Mexico. The Indians cannot read and they sleep in slums on the ground, on dirt very often . . . The entertainment for the people does not exist, other than military music and films, being predominantly French and Italian films." Nothing exotic. But many new radical visitors to the city were fascinated by its musical landscape. Journalist Timothy G. Turner, who had covered the Revolution, annotated the tunes he encountered. In 1925 Anita Brenner copied the first lines of the popular Mexican tune "Morenita mía" in her diary: "I knew a lovely little brown girl, and I loved her so much" [Conocí una linda morenita, y la quise mucho)—considered the first Mexican bolero. Most visitors compared their own stories of love and betrayal with the ballads they heard in the city's bars and from street singers. Bertram Wolfe collected songs, poet Witter Bynner translated them, editors Francis Toor and Idella Purnell published them in *Mexican Folkways* and *The Palm*. Wolfe took courses at the School for Foreigners at the National University, where he studied with the great philologist Pedro Henríquez Ureña and wrote a paper on Mexican romances; Bynner translated the old Mexican tune "Mi Viejo Amor":

My older love
Though the world has come between us,
We can never say good-bye
My older love.

And of course a great moment in the city's musical enchantment was the Yucateco tune "Peregrina" by poet Luis Rosado Vega and popular composer Ricardo Palmerín, requested by the radical governor of Yucatan, Felipe Carrillo

Puerto, for his lover the U.S. journalist Alma Reed (1922). "I could easily have wept," wrote Reed, recalling the first time she heard the song, "when I grasped the resignation in the words of unfulfillment, stressed in the closing lines with Felipe's reiterated appeal: 'do not forget, do not forget my land, do not forget, do not forget, my love.'" The song became part of the voices of the city, though the love affair between a young U.S. journalist and a socialist governor (soon to be assassinated) was somehow lost. In due time Aaron Copland would internationalize the tunes that were already, in 1919 Mexico City, the closest thing to the first citywide collective sentimentality.[14] To be sure, not everybody in the city felt the same; different classes, different people, felt every song in varied and indescribable ways. But by 1930, the reader can be sure, almost any inhabitant of the city could, as I can, sing the next stanza of Lara's first bolero (1920), which began: "I know it's impossible for you to love me, I know that my love for you was transient, and that you trade your kisses for money, thus poisoning my heart . . ." (Yo sé que es imposible que me quieras/que mi amor para ti fue pasajero/y que cambias tus besos por dinero/envenenando así mi corazón . . .).

3

In 1919, the Mexico City of Aaron Copland or Agustín Lara was yet to come. But, as if it were being visited and seen for the very first time, 1919 Mexico City became a capital for runaways of all sorts. Jack Johnson, the black heavyweight boxer, arrived from Spain with his white wife Lucille. In Barcelona he had defeated Arthur Cravan—nephew of Oscar Wilde, poet, boxer, and photographer—, and during 1918 had been in touch with Cravan in order to reenact the fight in El Toreo, on the outskirts of Mexico City. Johnson had been on the run for a while, escaping ostracism and racism due to his flamboyant lifestyle and his breaking of the race code. He stayed on Donceles Street in downtown Mexico City for some months, traveling to different parts of the country, performing staged exhibitions. Two U.S. socialists and slackers, Charles Phillips and Mike Gold, sought out Johnson in his Mexico City flat, requesting money to publish Bolshevik propaganda. Johnson gave them ten dollars, as he could not remember having anything against Bolsheviks. Johnson's most impressive performance in the capital took place in September in El Toreo, where he fought not Cravan but another white U.S. boxer, Marty Cutler. Mexico City's newspapers were full of reports about the flashy black giant. He was like no one else in the city. But people wanted blood: the newspapers reported the popular discontent because the huge black boxer did not fully destroy his white opponent.

Unknowingly, the fighter spurred the continued breakup of the city's social map that had started in 1914: a black man in a fancy apartment in the old Porfirian ideal city. In 1919 Johnson visited Sanborns in downtown Mexico City, the same stylish restaurant that was taken over by Zapatista and Villista troops five years earlier, and the same restaurant that in 1926 would be considered by John Dos Passos the center of Mexico City's Yanquilandia. He took a table there with his wife and asked to be served. Unknown to him, M. N. Roy was also present—the handsome Indian Brahman who had arrived from California, also with his U.S. wife Evelyn Trent, a radical Stanford student. Roy's memoirs describe how Johnson was denied service. Roy and Trent had also used the city to break rules: he was a Bengali nationalist, married to a socialist U.S. woman whose father had accused Roy of abducting her daughter when she followed him from San Francisco to New York. But at Sanborns the American owner of the restaurant apparently reasserted the social map of the city. Johnson, Roy tells us, was denied service and left Sanborns, only to come back later with Mexican police authorities who forced Sanborns's owner to serve the boxer and his wife himself.

Yes—Mexico City was the revolutionary capital that would not allow such racial discrimination. Later that same year, 1919, young Langston Hughes came to Mexico City believing that there was no race problem in the city—his father was a lawyer in Mexico City and Toluca. Unfortunately, facing the race line was not part of the agenda of the utopian city of socialists or slackers. In 1919 the police probably helped Johnson more out of anti-American feelings—against the owner of Sanborns—than from notions of racial equality. The city was fascinated with the size and power of the boxer, and with Caruso's voice, but it totally ignored the young Hughes. Nonetheless, in the early 1930s Hughes, as in a good novel, came back to conquer and be conquered by the city.[15]

When not at Sanborns, Roy could be found in a Chinese restaurant on Dolores Street—the city's small Chinatown—where he met many U.S. radicals, people who had been introduced to him by Evelyn. The Roys arrived during the summer of 1918 at the Genova Hotel, where young U.S. Americans avoided the draft, and pacifists or socialists fled from the witch hunts in New York or Chicago following the Sedition Act. There were also several German guests, who sat apart from the cadre of gringos. The hotel was situated at the heart of the city, a few steps from the immense central square (Zócalo) just around the corner from the Alameda park, a favorite rendezvous for all foreigners. The same streets and parks were patronized, in 1919, by such young Mexican dandies as Xavier Villaurrutia and Salvador Novo or the bohemian Barba Jacob, and soon after by three Spaniards who would become friends of the radical circles Roy left in Mexico after his departure for Berlin and Moscow in

1922—Monna and Felipe Teixidor and León Felipe. U.S. slacker Charles Phillips was there too, planning the revolution with other U.S. radicals, Mike Gold and Eleonora Parker, whom Phillips had married (but who was then having an affair with the radical U.S. cartoonist Henry Glintenkamp). Carleton Beals was part of the circle in the restaurant and in the Genova Hotel, where all the U.S. slackers first touched base in the city. Alameda park, Donceles, Dolores, Madero, Cinco de Mayo, and Colonia Roma were the typical settings of their discussions and encounters.

For all these characters the city had specific geographical contours. Their city did not include the entire city: it encompassed the two main historico-geographical interpretations of the city and its centers of power; that is, the colonial center as reinterpreted and beautified by Porfirian architects and planners, and the new city constructed by Porfirians, especially in the first decade of the twentieth century. So in the narrow streets of the colonial greed, from Zócalo to Alameda, and in the extensions around El Paseo de la Reforma, the confines of the Porfirian ideal city, lived those who dreamt of a Brown Atlantis and a socialist revolution.

In 1919, Mexico City had not yet been totally reconstructed after the events of 1914 and 1915. But the streets of the old colonial city and the Porfirian ideal city had returned to a vivid urban life. Rampant crime had declined, and political violence had become selective. By 1926 a U.S. military attaché in Mexico informed authorities in the U.S. that city security had improved greatly, that criminals were apprehended and killed, and that General Roberto Cruz, chief of police, was truly cleaning up the city. Joseph Retinger, a powerful Polish adviser to Mexican union leader Luis N. Morones, recalled, however, that in the early 1920s political violence was still part of daily life. But the streets were relatively safe, at least for men; women were expected not to be in the streets. Arthur Cravan's wife, Mina Loy, was free to circulate with her tall, strong man, but Evelyn Trent and, after 1921, Ella Wolfe were breaking the city's code when they rambled alone in Alameda or in Colonia Roma. But the Roys and their many visitors never had a problem; however, they had money.[16]

M. N. Roy's circle was formed by radicals, always conflicted and crossed by ideological and personal passions. From 1918 to 1925 this group included such people as Charles Phillips, Linn A. Gale, Bertram Wolfe, Ella Wolfe, Maurice Baker, Mike Gold, Henry Glintenkamp, Joseph Retinger, Roberto Haberman, Tina Modotti, Julio Antonio Mella, and the Soviet envoys Michael Borodin, Sen Katayana, and Louis Fraina. Almost all of them meant to be elsewhere, but ended up in Mexico City, living near each other. Mexican radicals joined them: Dr. Atl, Diego Rivera (after 1921), Xavier Guerrero, José Valadés, Elena Torres, José Allen, and Santibañez. Before Rivera, the center of interactions was José Vasconcelos, a bilingual intellectual who knew the U.S. very well, who gave them jobs and talked to them about books and ideas.

The outcome of these interactions could have been easily predicted: in 1919 Mexican and foreign communists founded the Mexican Communist Party, and appointed M. N. Roy, along with Evelyn Trent and Charles Phillips, to be Mexican envoys at the 1921 meeting of the Comintern. Another U.S. slacker, Linn A. Gale, had introduced a mixture of socialism and New Thought into Mexico, and had struggled with Roy for the leadership of the new party and for the availability of international communist funds. Gale allied himself with union leader Morones, whose party line was closer to that of U.S. labor leader Samuel Gompers and the American Labor Federation (a more evolutionary than revolutionary organization). Also close to Morones were two inhabitants of the city who exemplified its status as a revolutionary capital: Roberto Haberman and Joseph Retinger. Thus by 1920 the Mexican Communist Party was already divided. In turn, the Indian radicals divided too and in Berlin and Moscow Virendranath Chattopadhyaya (Chatto) and his U.S. lover Agnes Smedley were defeated by the intrigues of the Roys. M. N. Roy and Smedley had developed a mutual dislike, born of Roy's sexual advances and of Smedley's protagonism in Indian affairs and her sense of lack of class—she came from working-class origins—vis-à-vis the bourgeois origins of Evelyn Trent, Roy's U.S. wife. By the end of the 1920s, Roy had lost the support of Moscow; Trent had been accused of being a British spy, and had been abandoned by Roy; Smedley had left Chatto, and had gone to China—as Roy did—and both enemies, Chatto and Roy, had traded their U.S. partners for German radical lovers—Lucie Hecht and Louise Geissler respectively.[17] International communism was an erotic mess whose scenarios were Berlin, Moscow, and, of course, Mexico City.

Because of the language barriers and the cult of secrecy, the urban lives of all these radicals appear in the historical record as totally apart from the rest of urban bohemia and cultural life. But in fact these visitors were known not only by the Mexican and U.S. secret services but also by José Vasconcelos (who helped many of them) and by Spanish expatriates who were often intermediaries between Mexicans and other foreigners (for instance, Felipe Camino—aka Léon Felipe—and Felipe Teixidor). By the late 1920s Diego Rivera became the center of all cultural and political actions and thus various cities that seemed disconnected became a single city.

4

Long before the 1939 exile, Spaniards in Mexico City formed one city cluster close to other foreigners and Mexican radicals in 1919. By 1920 poet León Felipe and painter Rafael Sala and his wife Monna were in Mexico, interacting with Americans and Mexicans. León Felipe had arrived sometime in 1919 or 1920, escaping prosecution for an incident in a bar in Spain. He had met Mexican writer Alfonso Reyes in Madrid, and with this introduction he decided to migrate to Mexico. In 1921 two U.S. radicals, Ella and Bertram Wolfe, shared the same patio with León Felipe and his sister, and thereafter, until the 1950s, León Felipe interacted with many of the U.S. intellectuals and radicals who came to Mexico City. For three decades León Felipe was a common reference for Mexicans and Americans alike. In 1939 he recalled:

> I am not a refugee that today calls upon the doors of Mexico asking for hospice. Mexico gave me its hospitality sixteen years ago when I came here for the first time, alone and poor with nothing more than a letter of introduction that Alfonso Reyes gave me in Madrid.

León Felipe eventually became a popular poet; but in 1920s Mexico City he found, in the many personalities attracted by the city, not only friends but also intellectual and social crusades. He befriended the Wolfes, and as Ella Wolfe recalled, became particularly interested in the worldwide Jewish question. After 1945 he dedicated many poems to Jewish suffering and later to the state of Israel. But before that, perhaps as a result of his interaction with various U.S. Jewish radicals, he wrote in Mexico City the "First Epistle to the Jews" (Primera epistola a los judíos) as a way to temper his friends' radicalism with their own Jewishness:

> Los profetas [Judíos] no tenían sabiduría,
> apenas sabían leer,
> pero del "comunismo sicialista",
> de ese fraternal socialismo
> que estáis buscando tan heróicamente vosotros . . .
> Sabían mucho . . . tal vez más que Marx.

> The [Jewish] prophets had no wisdom,
> they barely knew how to read,
> but about the 'socialist communism,'
> about that fraternal socialism,
> that you search for so heroically,
> they knew much . . . maybe more than Marx.

Rafael Sala, in turn, was a Catalan painter close to the Italian futurists in Florence just before the start of World War I and later close to Joan Miró's circle. Like Felipe Teixidor, Sala was from Vilanova i la Geltrú, near Barcelona.

He left Catalonia for New York together with Teixidor. In Mexico City he became one of the adherents of the idea of the Brown Atlantis, searching for official favors from the revolutionary government, and open to exotic ideas about Mexico. "If not for the nine million Indians in Mexico," he wrote to a Catalan friend, "I would have never had come; if Mexico is interesting it is due to these nine million Indians and not due to all these Spanish merchants, these *indianos* who you know very well, as they are an abundant race along the entire Catalan coast" (wealthy Catalans who made their fortunes in the Americas were often called *indianos* in Catalonia). How was Sala able to see so many millions of Indians in Mexico City? This was the mystery of exoticism that the city offered to all its visitors. Nevertheless, he and his friend Teixidor found jobs writing texts sponsored by the revolutionary government. Sala circulated freely among U.S. expatriates in Mexico—Edward Weston, Tina Modotti, Ella and Bertram Wolfe, Anita Brenner—and Mexican intellectuals and officials, as well as his fellow Catalan Teixidor, who married Monna Sala in 1927 after Sala's death.

Felipe Teixidor also arrived in Mexico in 1919, and he too became an acquaintance of Weston and other U.S. radicals. He became editor of literary journals such as *Contemporáneos*, collector of Mexican urban motifs, and publicist. He lived for a while on Coahuila Street. He and Monna became English teachers for various Mexicans, among them the prominent Mexican economist Jesús Silva Herzog. Monna was an important link between Barcelona, Mexico City, and New York, as she had, as she put it, no fatherland. Her family had migrated to the U.S., and thus she was perfectly bilingual—her brother Felipe Alfau managed to write a novel in English in the 1930s, which was resurrected in the 1990s and greatly admired. In New York, Monna was close to the Spanish Hispanicist and Columbia University professor Federico de Onís and to the Nicaraguan intellectual and later resident of Mexico City, Salomón de la Selva. De Onís's knowledge of Spanish and Spanish-American literature, as well as his concern with popular literature in Spanish, influenced not only Monna, but also Ella and Bertram Wolfe and many others.

Soon after Monna met Rafael Sala in the U.S., they moved to Veracruz and arrived in Mexico City in 1923.[18] Monna was an intriguing female resident of 1920s Mexico City. When Sala developed a fatal illness, the couple left Mexico City with Edward Weston's assistance to find professional help in the U.S. He died in Los Angeles. Monna returned to Mexico City, where she became Monna Teixidor, friend of José Vasconcelos, Anita Brenner, the Wolfes, Rivera . . . For Monna the city was a cosmopolitan site, an extraordinary Mexico—as she recalled in the 1970s—with no inhibitions and no inferiority complex.[19]

Also around 1919 a famous Spanish writer, Vicente Blasco Ibáñez, visited

Mexico and wrote what seemed to be mandatory in those days: an opinion on the Mexican Revolution, El militarismo mejicano, published in 1921. In 1919, he claimed, U.S. journalists, especially women (so he explicitly claimed), demanded his opinion about Mexico, since he had been in Mexico City. He therefore wrote several articles for U.S. newspapers that later became El militarismo: a view of Mexico as a land of savages written by an incredibly self-aggrandizing gachupín.

In 1921 an old Spanish friend of the city, Ramón del Valle Inclán, returned as a celebrity. He had been a bohemian in Porfirian Mexico City; but when invited and subsidized by the Mexican revolutionary government—in view of his desperate economic situation in Spain—he returned and published Tirano Banderas (1927). The product of Valle Inclán's life in Mexico City in the 1890s and in 1921 and 1922, the book is an icon in the Spanish-speaking world of the sort of conventional racial and cultural aspects assigned to such tropical places as Mexico.[20] This was the first in the saga of world-acclaimed Mexico-centered novels—but not one with Mexico City as the center of action. This Spanish novel was soon followed by B. Traven's Der Schatz der Sierra Madre (1927) and Malcolm Lowry's Under the Volcano (1947)—very different novels and yet with a similar fixation on racial atavism and similar indifference to the city.

Valle Inclán went to Mexico in 1921 as a special guest at the Centenario. He was an outspoken critic of the Spanish monarchy, which had in turn expressed reservations about the Jacobin and anti-Spanish rhetoric of the Mexican revolutionary government. Thus, Valle Inclán's anti-Spanish statements in many magazines and periodicals were widely celebrated by various Mexican intellectuals and officials. But for Valle Inclán, the return to Mexico City was a return to a lost innocence: to his own youth of excesses in Mexico City. In 1921, Mexico City offered more of the same, all contained in the exotic valley of Anáhuac. His wizard-like figure was captured by the caricaturist García Cabral: a Spanish Wise Man, the emblem of wit, blasphemy, and love for Mexico. Valle Inclán's romantic encounters with Lupe Marín—later wife of both Diego Rivera and writer Jorge Cuesta—and his enchantment with the city's language became matters of legend. In 1922, in a stereotypical fashion, he said goodbye to the city with a poem: "With your wan sad gesture, I say goodbye to you, Mexican Indian,/I say farewell, hand in hand!"[21]

The streets of the city also knew an influential group of people from Central and South America: Carlos Mérida (Guatemala), Salomón de la Selva (Nicaragua), Porfirio Barba Jacob (Colombia and Guatemala), Rafael Heliodoro Valle (Honduras), and Aquiles Vela (Guatemala)—and a unique intellectual from the Dominican Republic, Pedro Henríquez Ureña, the only truly universal person among the inhabitants of or visitors to modernist Mexico City, including

Henry Adams (either a very American European or vice versa), Blasco Ibáñez (too much of a *gachupín* in Mexico), André Breton (an extremely French poet), or Stuart Chase (a parochial exoticist). Don Pedro deserves an entire book and not a simple stamp in this collection of stories.

5

There was still space on the streets for another unconnected group of less radical foreigners—Bob Brown, Mina Loy, and Arthur Cravan. In 1916 modernist poet Mina Loy met Arthur Cravan in New York. He had come to the U.S. escaping World War I in the Montserrat steamboat that left Barcelona with him and Leon Trotsky—Cravan, said Trotsky, "preferred to go and smash the jaws of Yankee gentlemen than being stabbed by any unknown German soldier." In December 1917 Cravan escaped again, from the draft, by going to Mexico City. Mina followed him, leaving New York bohemian life and her children in Europe in order to live with Cravan in Mexico City, where they later married. No traces are left of their life there, other than Mina's departure, pregnant, to Buenos Aires in late 1918. Cravan was supposed to meet her but suddenly disappeared, becoming a legend. Cravan might have drowned trying to escape Mexico, though some argued that The Colossus, as Loy called him, survived for many decades with a new identity. For Mexico City in those days offered the possibility of escape and reinvention. That was what the city was about for its foreign conquerors, though not for Mexicans who were expected by foreigners to maintain their racial composition and remain eternally the same.

Arthur Cravan might have died, but B. Traven, who arrived in the early 1920s, died in 1969 without really revealing who he was. Traven very likely was the radical actor and writer Ret Marut, sentenced to death in Munich in 1919 for his participation in the Congress of Workers', Peasants' and Soldiers' Councils in Bavaria. In the last piece he wrote in Munich for an anarchist periodical, the protagonist, Khundar, invites his followers to go and search for "the unknown tracks where we should find truth, wisdom, salvation, and life." And thus, the story goes, Khundar, like Traven, left to faraway exotic lands. In Mexico, Traven hated the city and went to live in Chiapas and then near Acapulco; but by the 1930s he had succumbed to the attraction of the city, where he lived until his death, without ever revealing his real name and life. M. N. Roy reinvented himself as a communist in Mexico City; Linn A. Gale went through several metamorphoses—socialist, communist, New Age spiritualist; Charles Phillips was in Mexico City first as Frank Seaman, then as Manuel Gómez; and Diego Rivera reinvented himself as the real Mexican.[22]

Bob Brown, a journalist and novelist, also joined this group of vanguard women and men. "Where was Buttery J during the Great War?," Brown's autobiographical novel of those years in Mexico City began. Buttery J was the alter ego of Brown. He was "in romantic old Mexico whose sun-cured, fly-blown corpses, desecrated human herrings, hung by their gills cured still out from straight, tamed, gaunt-armed telegraph crosses," was the answer. Brown counted sixty slackers in his group in Mexico City. Rex (Cravan) and Rita (Mina Loy) were part of the novel, as well as Henry Glintenkamp—who seems to be the character who seduced many Mexican maids and servants. "Here she comes [Rita]," he wrote remembering the interactions of these slackers in Mexico City, "Lady Godiva! Galloping after me with her icicle dagger. *Generalissimussus* Joan D'Arc of the Queen's own slackers, riding at the head of her hussars with her blood-red icicle dagger drawn. The succubus come with her deadly might shard kiss."[23]

Mina Loy left Mexico City, and Fabienne (Mina and Cravan's daughter) was born in England in 1919. Loy tried to find Cravan for many years, and her poem "Mexican Desert" (1921) became a modernist emblem of loss and endless mourning: a female locomotive entering into Mexico's landscape, total isolation, and constant restarting of pain:

The mountains in a row
set pinnacles of ferocious isolation
under the alien hot heaven.

Her metaphors were no less odd or modernist than those of López Velarde ("belching ghost-wail of the locomotive," "into the jazz-band sunset").

So much bohemian life, and yet up until the late 1930s, almost none of these characters lived outside the comfortable confines of the city, except, and for a brief period of time, Langston Hughes, who shared a place with Henri Cartier-Bresson and Andrés Henestrosa in the 1930s in La Merced—a poor commercial part of the city. Antonin Artaud and Porfirio Barba Jacob were two other exceptions in the late 1930s and early 1940s.

Langston Hughes, López Velarde, and—say—M. N. Roy never met, yet the intellectual village they had constructed within Mexico City was the same—each belonged to his own private Mexico City, offering each the same possibilities. I am sure López Velarde or Salvador Novo was aware of the existence in the city of, for instance, Roy and his friend H. Gupta, who translated Bengali literature into Spanish, but the opposite path was possible only by living wholly the cultural life of the city—not just the city as temporary site for international radical networking. Foreigners often hated the city's intellectuals, except for José Vasconcelos, whom they befriended as a politician. Mexican intellectuals were too urban, too Westernized, and too frivolous for the many visitors of Mexico City.

6

In 1919 the most powerful and prominent Mexican financier of Porfirian times, José Y. Limantour, wrote to a friend and partner from his exile in depressed Paris: "Our Bolsheviks have not shown to be as bad as their successors in other countries . . . we should attempt to put innovation back on track and on the path toward evolution, the only means to prevent revolution." But the cult of Bolshevik Revolution was booming in Mexico City in 1919. Let us return to the intriguing M. N. Roy. He filled the radical circles of the city with money and inspiration. Herrán's beautiful native bodies were paralleled by Roy's figure as an emblem of ethnic beauty and wisdom—characteristics that helped him to quickly become the center of communist intrigues. M. N. Roy was being followed by the English and American secret services because of his association with German spies and arms traders. He had initially arrived in the United States in search of German arms shipments to send over the Pacific back to India. The Germans proved amenable to the illusions of the young Indian. He soon left New York for Stanford, California, were he met Evelyn Trent. They left for Mexico City, then a dangerous and appealing city of hope.[24]

Roy recalled in his memoirs, he fell in love with the city's nearby volcanoes, especially that of the Sleeping Lady. He and Evelyn lived in a comfortable abode on the outskirts of Colonia Roma, at 33 Córdoba Street. From the window, with its vista of maize seedlings, the city seemed to end just beyond the house. On one side lay the countryside and the Sleeping Lady; on the other were the streets and nooks of the urban revolutionary paradise. They lived austerely as good socialists or even as Hindu ascetics, despite their wealth, but they boasted Louis XIV furniture, a Mexican servant named María, and a muchacho (boy) who performed odd jobs around the house. The city's inequality had conquered them. Many would follow the same route of employing a Mexican criada or a male servant, who was an intrinsic part of the sensual, exotic, and comfortable experience of the city.

International characters visited Roy: Louis Fraina, Charles Phillips, Bertram Wolfe, and Sen Katayama. Louis Fraina was eventually accused of spying and, disillusioned with Leninism, he escaped to the U.S.—apparently with Comintern money—in search of his Russian wife and a new beginning, becoming Lewis Corey in 1926. Fraina's perspective on the Revolution, like Roy's, came into conflict with his views on human loneliness and love—which were unrevolutionary, and even reactionary, issues: "A man is," Fraina wrote, "and then thinks; he feels, and therefore acts. Man has tried to make intellect the ruler, but it has been a marionette ruler with instinct and feeling pulling the strings."

Indeed, there was a high price to pay in the personal lives of all these radicals for fully embracing the universal hopes and the exotic allure of the city, where political and personal betrayals were common. That is why, in 1958, Joseph Freeman, one of the radicals living in Mexico in the early 1930s, wrote to Bertram Wolfe, in the way he had learned in the city, in a *corrido* (popular storytelling lyric): "Was it all a dream?" he wrote. "Did we really want"

An end to murder, theft and cant
Hunger and war? Did we really hope . . .
To make men freer wherever they are?
When we two parted in polemics and jeers,
Completely unheated to argue for years,
Pale was your hate and cold, colder your hiss.[25]

Inescapable destiny: José Vasconcelos, in his later years, ended up asking the same question and becoming a retrograde Catholic, resentful of his own patronage of all those radicals and slackers; and M. N. Roy became a disillusioned nationalist trying to invent the new conservative universalism of what he coined Radical Humanism.

In 1925 Roy left Evelyn Trent, as I have said, and went away with a German radical—Louise Geissler—who had enchanted many radicals in Berlin and Moscow. The Indian and German comrades accused Evelyn of being an English spy, or at least, an enemy of Lenin. Roy died without giving his version of the intrigues that ended not only their relationship, but also his role as a protagonist on the stage of world communism. Toward the end of his life he turned to Radical Humanism, a desperate call for access to the central role already played by figures like Nehru and Gandhi. Ironically, he then suffered, as Evelyn once had, from rumors that he was a spy: there was the story that the CIA had lent its support to the Radical Humanists. He abandoned his Hindu spiritualism, becoming pro-Western in the process. Evelyn must have read the publications of Roy's group, hoping to see her name in Roy's pages, but she probably lost track of them eventually.[26] Roy had become a true subject of Her British Majesty, lambasting and admonishing his former allies, saying it was useless "to sling mud at the moon for its blemishes when you are angry at it." He ended up as a caricature of himself.

In 1919, of course, it was not easy for Evelyn—a young, well-educated, and refined American woman—to leave everything in order to be with a foreigner—and a "colored" one at that. But she shared Roy's antimaterialism and his passion for the one "true" cause—the Bengali nationalism and opposition to colonialism. Imagine, in the 1910s, the allure of this man in a Western suit—a black Quixote preaching about the evils of British and Yankee imperialism. Those were years in which, physically, intellectually, and politically, love and surrender were one and the same. They lived for their love, and their love was a social cause, which was a political but also an aesthetic hope, one that rejected bourgeois taste for the exotic, and yet reproduced it in the form of messianic revolutions in India and Mexico (see chapter 7).[27]

This was a kind of love that was demanded by revolutionary Mexico City. Urban domestic life occurred as business as usual in the Roy house. Every day a new radical would visit from the corners of the globe, looking for wisdom, contacts, plans, money . . . Everyone ate and drank for free. María cooked. The men would lock themselves up with the black Quixote to discuss matters not suitable for women's ears. Evelyn served tea over the latest news from Moscow or the newest Marxist analysis of the troubles of colonialism. Once the guest was a Russian aristocrat with English like any gringo and features so delicate they were almost effeminate. It turned out to be Michael Borodin, the Russian Revolution's envoy to the Latin American republics. He stayed with the Roys for months, searching for some jewels of the czar that he had misplaced at some point during a lark. He had left his wife and son in Chicago, which gave him license to flirt with both María and Roy, who viewed this physical and intellectual proximity as a simple revolutionary necessity. Borodin would eventually take them—Roy, Evelyn, and Charles Phillips—to Berlin and Moscow for the 1921 Comintern Congress.

But Roy loved Mexico City. He later wrote that he would like to return to live there when he was old. He spent hours in correspondence and working on documents, forever gazing out the window to the transparent city, contained in its valley, yet far away from the Sleeping Lady. For Evelyn Trent and Ella Wolfe things should have been different. Evelyn, as the gringa, as Roy's wife, and as a communist, had a sort of diplomatic passport and immunity in the city. She, like Ella Wolfe, strolled through the city at night—a time no decent woman would show her face. Roy bought an enormous dog to protect the house—a beast that soon captivated him. The city, on the other hand, was secure—at least for those with President Carranza's friendship. Nothing ever happened to them, while the dog died of a rare disease. Later, the animal, not Evelyn, would be the one with a special place in Roy's memoirs.[28]

In effect, love and betrayal were everywhere in the capital of the world's utopias. Charles Phillips would spend hours walking on the Paseo de la Reforma and Dolores Street speaking of his wife, Eleonora Parker, who had left him for Henry Glintenkamp. Mina Loy left the city pregnant and without having befriended the bizarre circles of M. N. Roy and Linn A. Gale; and Arthur Cravan had disappeared. Another important couple would arrive by the early 1920s and also bring their revolt against the city's morals: Edward Weston (and his young son) and Tina Modotti—a couple who have been written about many times, but were only one of many similar cases.

7

Love and betrayal were everywhere in the city. The intellectuals and activists enchanted with Mexico enacted them. Ella Wolfe recalled how she was visited and sought after when Bertram was not around, and Ella herself invited her "friend" Joseph Lovestone to come to Mexico. Lovestone, in turn, became involved in Moscow with Louise Geissler, the same woman for whom M. N. Roy left Evelyn Trent. Katherine Anne Porter also reached Mexico around 1920 and soon had an affair, followed by disillusion and an abortion, with the Nicaraguan poet and bon-vivant Salomón de la Selva. By 1923 Anita Brenner was in Mexico, not only writing and researching for Ernest Gruening's project, *Mexico and Its Heritage* (1928), and for her own *Idols behind Altars* (1929), but also madly in love with a young French painter, Jean Charlot, who was in Mexico City with his mother.

Anita Brenner was a Jew, and Jean Charlot and his mother were very Catholic. Love and attraction were intense, as Brenner's diary shows, but they were also torture. Charlot was an acute observer of the city and an illustrator of some of the first poetry by Mexicans that took the city as its leitmotif—such as Germán List Arzubide's *Esquina: Poemas* (1923) and Manuel Maples Arce's *Urbe: Super-poema bolchevique en 5 cantos* (1924). "At six o'clock in the morning," wrote Charlot in 1922, commenting on the city, "I was in the streets. Automobiles and ladies were still asleep, and the true features of the town emerged. Beautiful beings people the street like Ladies of Guadalupe innumerable. They move noiselessly, feet flat to the ground, antique beauty come to life. The wealthier quarters are as empty and soiled as a music hall at noon, but everywhere else, among those low-lying houses, cubic and freshly daubed, processions are staged. At first glance the crowd is the color of dust. Flesh and cloth, both worn out with use, melt into this grey that is the very livery of humbleness. Eye and mind soon learn to focus, and this race, its confidence won, attests to its beauty through fabrics, its straw, its flesh." The city enchanted them while they enchanted each other thanks to their youth and the city.

Anita Brenner did not marry Charlot. He later married Dorothy Zohmah Day, who was visiting the young U.S. painter, Rivera's student Ione Robinson, in Mexico City in 1931. Anita, however, had affairs with Mexican officials and intellectuals and later went on to marry a Jewish physician from New York.

Leaving the city of love and betrayal, she reported in her diary on January 12, 1926, in the language of the city as only she, more than any foreigner in the city, could do (she was truly bicultural); "Looking for statistics [for Gruening], discussing art . . . what the hell do I care! Nothing comes to me and when it does it's not worth it." And in the city of betrayals and seduction she wrote the poem (diary June 9, 1926):

I am a lover of love
not knowing
what love to love.
I am a maker of tales
not knowing
what tale to make.

Mexico City, like any city, was a sensual temptation, but the revolutionary situation made desire difficult to distinguish from intellectual deduction. "What makes revolutionists," Brenner wrote after a conversation with Peter Panter in Mexico City, "is either self-pity, or indignation for the sake of others (*vidas*) or a sympathetic perception of the dominant undercurrent of progress in things (Siqueiros). . . . That truthfulness of temper, that receptivity, which professors often strive in vain to form, is engendered here less by wisdom than by innocence."[29] The specter of López Velarde seemed to return.

There were those who did manage to love and marry in the city. Jean Charlot was one. Ione Robinson saved herself from Diego Rivera's large hands and belly, but was enchanted by the U.S. socialist Rodolfo Valentino: Joseph Freeman, whom she married in 1929. He would not allow her to paint *bodegones* (bourgeois art). The marriage was a disaster when they returned to New York, as they could not reproduce there the bohemia and innocence they believed to be real in Mexico City. Ione had to attend long meetings in the houses of the comrades in Mexico City. And in New York, she had to face the rejection of Freeman's family—a wealthy New York Jewish family that could not weather the Depression or abide a non-Jewish twenty-year-old girl who asked for butter on the Sabbath table.[30]

Romanian and U.S. radical Roberto Haberman also managed to find love in the city. According to FBI files, in 1914 he had married a Swede, Thorberg Brundin, a radical woman who fought for women rights and lived a vanguard bohemian life. After working for the governor of Yucatán, Carrillo Puerto, and labor leader Luis N. Morones, Haberman offered his services as a propagandist and spy to Plutarco Elías Calles. In August 1921, he contacted the FBI and informed them on Mexican radical affairs, denouncing his fellow radicals Linn

A. Gale and Charles Phillips as communists. In those days, as the Mexican saying goes, "nadie sabe para quién trabaja" (nobody knows who they really work for). Many U.S. radicals worked for José Vasconcelos; Mexican communist José Allen was a spy for U.S. military intelligence, and Haberman, it seems, worked for both the Mexican and U.S. intelligence services.

In the early 1920s Haberman left Thorberg and married Esperanza Domínguez, moving to New York in order to work for Calles (now the strongman of the Revolution) in radical union circles. In June 1926 Esperanza began to write to Calles's secretary, Soledad González (Cholita), revealing not the New York of free and communitarian men and women, but a city in which, it seems, she was there only to do the laundry and ironing. She asked Cholita for a job so she could return to Mexico City, and by September 1927 she wrote in pure Mexico City ironic language: Haberman had two intentions, revolution and to "do with my poor bones to the grave from so much affection" (dar con mi pobre esqueleto en el joyo [sic] de tanto cariño). Her husband was having an affair, she wrote, with a wealthy, intelligent, and beautiful woman, and "naturally I'm terrible, I've seen all the devils with their respective tails" (naturalmente estoy viendo a toditos los diablos con sus respectivas colas). Domínguez was, by then, not revolutionary enough for Haberman and they divorced, though, according to FBI informants, he was particularly concerned with the status of women in Mexico—lessons very likely learned from Thorberg—, and without a hint of irony in view of his own personal life, he stated in 1924: "I am convinced that the salvation of Mexico rests entirely with women. . . . The Mexican home is reactionary par excellence." He married a wealthy New Yorker, and by 1933 was a counselor at Mexican law with an office in New York.[31]

In those days, circa 1919, not a soul among the radicals believed that a lovers' quarrel was even thinkable, much less important, while the international revolution continued to march forward. So if the city meant so much love, why was it so invisible? This silence would be equivalent to García Lorca going to New York and writing about Granada.

8

Ella and Bertram Wolfe can serve to tell the story of the kind of domestic life that was being explored in the 1919 revolutionary city. Bertram was a first-generation Jewish immigrant from New York City, leader of the faction of the U.S. Communist Party led by Jay Lovestone, and one of the founders of the New York Workers School. In Mexico he became a member of the M. N. Roy faction of the Mexican Communist Party. Through Roberto Haberman he was on good terms with Plutarco Elías Calles, but he soon broke with the official labor movement and was expelled from Mexico, accused of sedition. Thanks to his connections with Pedro Henríquez Ureña and León Felipe, he became a scholar of Mexican literature and a writer, especially of biographies—of Lenin, Trotsky, and Stalin (*Three Who Made a Revolution*, 1948). He was friend and twice biographer of Diego Rivera. In his reincarnation as a disenchanted Stalinist, he became an adviser on Russian and Latin American issues to the U.S. State Department, as well as a recalcitrant anticommunist and senior fellow at the Hoover Institution.

In Mexico and for his entire life Bertram Wolfe was joined by his wife, Ella, a unique personality who paralleled so many other women of that cosmopolitan Mexico City—Evelyn Trent, Tina Modotti, Anita Brenner, Frances Toor, Katherine Anne Porter, among many others. Bertram had a long life, but not as long as Ella, who died in 2000 at the age of 103. Throughout his life Bertram reinvented himself, while Ella kept many secrets and was in charge of preserving Bertram's memory according to how he wanted it remembered. The records of their lives, as kept by Ella, who was in charge of their archive at the Hoover Institution at Stanford for more than two decades, talk of an invisible aspect of Mexico City as a radical capital city.

For Ella and Bertram Wolfe life in early 1920s Mexico City was an uncertain thing, full of economic depression and social unrest. But those were also days of colossal hopes and doctrinaire certainties and, above all, total engagement. In the city they became inhabitants of the beginning and the end of what they believed to be history, and when destiny caught up with them, guilt emerged in the form of militant oblivion. They made the city out of the ruins of their memories, and over the ruins of the world Mexico City represented, they had to reconstruct new lives.

In their memories and in the historical records, however, the city that made their hopes possible appears as a passive actor, unaware of its own enchantment, as if its *barrios*, coffee houses, sins, and cultural life were there only for the mere possibility of becoming the personal experience of all those men and women who dreamt of revolutions. But passive actors cities are not, especially that Mexico City around 1919—a global cultural capital.

It is hard to find evidence in the city about the life of Ella Wolfe—or for that matter Evelyn Trent or Esperanza Domínguez. Even such prolific writers as Katherine Anne Porter, Anita Brenner, and Frances Toor left little written record of their lives and feelings during their years in Mexico City. But to be sure the "old gringas" of that Mexico City reveal a very different city from that of the "old gringos." No man left a record of urban hostility, only of the ambivalent—and passive—appeal of the beauty of servants, the stink of people, women's gazes, and disconcerting beggars. It was different for women. Katherine Anne Porter, like Ella Wolfe, grew tired of the harassment by Mexicans and foreigners, socialist or not, straight or homosexual; for behind the revolutionary facades, the dwellers of the revolutionary capital seemed to have been incontinent Don Juans or homosexuals who found liberation in a city whose bodies, apparently, were there just for them in a way that bodies in New York were not. Bohemian writer Carmen Mondragón affirmed, according to Edward Weston, that "every other man in Mexico is a homosexual," an exaggeration no doubt made out of revenge. The same city becomes a different one depending on the angle of passions through which one looks.[32]

In 1919, the city was not yet that of Diego Rivera's virile and revolutionary character. Eventually the city would welcome the passions of someone like Hart Crane, but also that model of asceticism, John Dewey. Crane's adventures in Mexico City, Tepoztlán, and other places in the early 1930s could fill an entire book. His passion for Mexican male bodies and alcohol led him to problems with the police, with his own U.S. friends, and finally to his death while returning to the U.S. in 1932 (see chapter 8). Dewey, in turn, came back to Mexico in 1937. He had been there in the mid-1920s, witnessing the application of his pedagogical theories in the schools that his follower Moisés Sáenz—then a high official of the Ministry of Education—had started. In 1937 he was invited to Mexico City by the American Committee for the Defense of Leon Trotsky, which included, among others, Franz Boas, Anita Brenner, John Dos Passos, Meyer Shapiro, and Lionel Trilling. There Dewey had a moral authority based not only on the fame of an honest intellectual, but also on a subtle conclusion in that dynamic city: at seventy-eight, Dewey was not a man, but an elder; he could juzgar (judge) passions because he could not jugar (play) them. In thanking Dewey for his presence in the city, Trotsky at sixty expressed the opinion that in Mexico City—the refuge of an era—an indisputable moral authority did not belong to men of action, but to those of idealism (Dewey, "the personification of great American idealism") and of old age: "in the fact that at its head [of the commission], is a man of unshakeable moral authority, a man who by virtue of his age should have the right to remain outside the skirmishes in the political arena . . . I see a new and truly magnificent reinforcement of the revolutionary optimism which constitutes the fundamental element of my life."[33]

Of course Trotsky's house in Coyoacán was itself a zoo of political and human intrigues. Trotsky's secretary, Jean Van Heijenoort, told the story of a house of betrayals: Trotsky's escapes to the woman in the neighboring house, Trotsky's abuse of his wife, Trotsky's affair with Frida Kahlo, Frida's affair with himself, Heijenoort . . . The end of the story is well known: Trotsky was killed by the Catalan boyfriend of his female assistant, and later Heijenoort was killed in Mexico City in 1986 by his fourth wife, a wealthy Mexican he met there. In the early 1930s Heijenoort noted that Mexico for him was "what Abyssinia was for Rimbaud, a country that was outside the civilized, industrialized, western world." It was not, however; it was very much part of the violent, traidor (traitor), and bloody twentieth-century Western world.[34]

But before that, Bertram Wolfe's city was, like that of M. N. Roy, a city of action. Wolfe would eventually count on the complicity of the great revolutionary and artistic god of the city, Diego Rivera. In 1929 Wolfe published a biography of Rivera: what he considered to be the first biography of revolutionary art that he nevertheless wanted to be a best seller published by Knopf in New York; later he sought support from the Guggenheim Foundation. Rivera disliked the book, and accused Wolfe not only of antirevolutionary tendencies, but worse, of female influence: "The list of illustrations shows that you were more influenced by Freud than by Marx, or that you have tried to help the sales of your book among members of the women's clubs of the States by showing more of my sex life."

In 1963 Bertram Wolfe decided to edit and republish his Rivera biography, this time with a more aesthetic emphasis, and highlighting the contrast between Rivera's artistic genius and his lies. Rivera was, indeed, a Pantagruelian liar. The new version erased the memories of the Mexico City where Rivera and Wolfe had lived at the same time, leaving no trace of the causes and beliefs they shared. This new version reestablished the Brown Atlantis with its civilizational differences: the U.S. observer looking aloofly at the Brown Atlantis. "The life of the Mexican folk," wrote Wolfe in his revised biography, "is a civilization more passionate and aesthetic than rational in its quality." Wolfe was reason; Mexico was passion: what is new? In 1963 the real Mexico was not Rivera's Mexico City, but this was less transcendental than the fact that Mexico became lastingly what it was for Wolfe, a succession of Riveras.

When I corresponded with Ella Wolfe about the Mexico City of and around 1919, she wrote, in perfect Spanish, referring to many mythmakers (Rivera, Freeman, Gale), and to an exciting city. Whereas around 1919 they believed themselves to be engaged in an escape from the draft, capitalism, and oppression, by the early 1930s, say, Freeman, Wolfe, and Waldo Frank believed themselves truly to be in the revolutionary vanguard (far from modernist disenchantment). Then they also claimed to be experts on Mexico, and all of them endlessly repeated that the real Mexico was of course not Mexico City. They did not know that the city had already left its mark on them. If U.S. socialist and populist trends influenced U.S. views of the Mexican Revolution and Mexico as a whole, the cultural life of 1920s and 1930s Mexico City left a mark on U.S. radicalism. U.S. and Mexican ideas traveled back and forth from Mexico City to New York, from Tepoztlán to Middletown, from Coyoacán to Los Angeles.

In 1919 a national labor strike was declared in the U.S. steel industry. Mexicans who had migrated to Texas and Arizona were brought to Chicago to serve as strike breakers. By 1930 there were nearly 20,000 Mexicans in Chicago. U.S. sociologists and anthropologists quickly started to study these Mexican immigrants, and thus, secretly, the Mexico City of the early 1920s started to mark the views of Mexico and Mexicans in the U.S. and the world. For the cohort of bohemians, radicals, and intellectuals of 1920s Mexico City soon produced books and studies that turned into scientific "knowledge" the idea of Mexicans and their environment as the expression of either pristine *Gemeinschaft* or, when degenerated by modernity, ugly and hybrid *Gesellschaft*. Carleton Beals produced a series of books setting out a primitivist and revolutionary view of a nation of rifles and Indians. Manuel Gamio, trained in Porfirian Mexico City and at Columbia University, advised his friend, Chicago anthropologist Robert Redfield—who studied Mexican immigrants in Chicago in 1925—to study Tepoztlán. The town was the perfect compromise for antiurban anthropologists and travelers: it was close to the comfort and security of the city, yet Nahuatl-speaking people inhabited it. By the 1930s Tepoztlán had become the archetype of real Mexico, which was of course everything Mexico City, Chicago, and New York were not. Thus Stuart Chase published *Mexico: A Study of Two Americas* (1931)—a contrast between Tepoztlán and Middletown, Indiana: genuine pristine community vs. fake industrial society. In this way the intellectual milieu of Mexico City in the early 1920s formed the basis of all these interconnected stories.

But before long the Mexico City they all lived in, both Mexicans and foreigners, seemed like a bad dream. By the 1950s, all of them had, in effect, killed the Mexico City they had created together. They abandoned the common cause—either social revolution, social engineering, or aesthetic innovation—and saved the essence, what was there before, namely, the belief in race and civilizational differences. Thus, with the arguments of disenchanted revolutionaries, they reinforced the belief in the exotic Mexico of racially fixed Indians.

One need only think of the futures of Ella Wolfe and her friends: Ella safe and comfortable in Palo Alto, Evelyn Trent back in the U.S. remarried in a "normal" American life, Katherine Anne Porter living in New York always feeling unappreciated. The world they invented together in 1920s and 1930s Mexico City was like a messy shocking film turned into a fixed and clean portrait, frozen by intentional oblivion and exoticization. Ella Wolfe would not talk about struggles and betrayals, nor of the memory of passion and betrayal with Lovestone. Evelyn Trent died without telling her story; her papers that reached the Hoover Institution offered very little information about her. By the 1950s Katherine Anne Porter was not only happy with a picturesque memory of her

Mexico City but was also willing to betray the past: she became an informant for the House Un-American Activities Committee, accusing her old friend in New York and Mexico City, Josephine Herbst.

Of the foreign women who participated in the Mexico City of the 1920s, Katherine Anne Porter is, without doubt, one of the best known. As her biographer Thomas F. Walsh tells us, Porter did not share the origins, social status, or education of the New York intellectuals. But like Ella Wolfe, Thorberg Haberman, Alma Reed, and Anita Brenner, she fluctuated from the left to the right. The old city and its hope died in them. Mexico, says Walsh, was for Porter "like a lover who always betrayed her trust, but on some unconscious level she welcomed the betrayal because it always revealed tragic truths that became the subject of her art." Truly, Mexico City was a painful, indispensable, return to creativity.

Anita Brenner was not from New York but from Aguascalientes, though she moved to San Antonio, Texas, as a teenager. Together with Salomón de la Selva, Monna Teixidor, and perhaps José Vasconcelos, Brenner was one of the few who were able to circulate easily from the language, habits, and styles of Mexico City to those of New York or San Antonio. Thus she became a true cultural broker between Mexico and the U.S. She was, like Ella Wolfe, a Jewish woman who fought to establish her own voice, but also one who helped various men speak in English (Brenner translated many of the writings of Manuel Gamio, Carlos Mérida, and Jean Charlot). Brenner knew how to present and sell Mexico; she taught Mexican intellectuals and scholars to understand their own marketing possibilities in the arts, academia, and intellectual life of the U.S. Her polymorphism was made possible only by Mexico City around 1919, the capital of an intellectual and revolutionary pact in which differences and distance were impossible.

Ella Wolfe, like Edward Weston and Brenner, remembered the early 1920s city of parties, always with very little female presence. Ella worked at the TASS agency in the Russian Embassy together with Carleton Beals. She translated and handled daily life in the city, as Trotsky's wife or Anita Brenner did—going to markets, hiring servants, cooking, etc. We will never know what Ella was actually doing at the Russian Embassy, or what Evelyn Trent was doing in Moscow or Berlin; but that they controlled domesticity in the city is a fact. Ella recommended servants to Tina Modotti, Evelyn cooked for Roy's guests . . .

"I have great feelings of affection for Mexican roofs," wrote Spanish exile Juan Rejano in 1945, "and I constantly go up to them in order to dive into that original and incessant spectacle. From their invisible battlements I feel closer to my city, and I trust that some of its shyest and more impenetrable angles lay bare before me."[35] On the flat roofs—the *azoteas*—is, in effect, where one con-

4.3. Bertram and Ella Wolfe (upper right and lower right),
Russian Embassy, early 1920s. Courtesy, Bertram and Ella Wolfe Papers,
Hoover Institution, Stanford University.

sciously becomes the city. It was on one of those flat roofs in La Condesa that
Tina Modotti and Edward Weston fell under the spell of a menage à trois (Tina,
Edward, and Mexico City). It was on a 1920s *azotea* in Colonia Cuauhtémoc that
Frances (Paca) Toor edited her magazine *Mexican Folkways*, devoted precisely
to the non-city. There she could, as it were, direct the city, but in fact the flat
roof was where the city dictated the lessons of revolution, *Volk*, and idealized
countryside. Indeed, for a city that knows neither entry nor exit, the real saluta-
tion is on the *azoteas*. Thus the picture of Ella, Bertram, and others at the roof
of the Russian Embassy is emblematic: a collection of revolutionaries, spies,
and families, in a Porfirian house in Colonia Condesa, the urban trees visible
in the backdrop (figure 4.3). They could see and feel the city of their work and
hope surrounding them.

In order to reach that Mexico City, women like Ella Wolfe and Anita Brenner
had to overcome many obstacles. And, as for Evelyn Trent and Thorberg
Haberman, we will never know the entire story. Many were left quietly in the
back of the synagogue, or silenced by the revolutionary self-censorship that
established that everything feminine was petit bourgeois and thus antirevolutionary. Everything had to be neutral, that is, virile. As was the case with López

Velarde, for all these radicals la ciudad was a corrupted and corrupting woman. From their position of disadvantage some women came out even wiser, only to face the 1950s American dream in the era of the "largest Cadillac." By the time of the emergence of the New Left and feminism, many of those old gringas and gringos were emerging from their self-exploration and from McCarthyism, simply trying to survive.

The story of these commitments and disappointments can be finally explored through the relationship of Ella Wolfe and Frida Kahlo. For two decades Ella was linked to Frida, her Coyoacán and the different lefts. Mexico City and its surroundings formed the capital of a generation that grew in fear, seeing solid certitudes collapse. Mexico City provided antidotes to those times: a social revolution, authenticity, innocence, brotherhood, pure race . . . and a safe and cosmopolitan refuge in which to hide from persecution and from bourgeois morality. That is why Ella and Evelyn and Katherine Anne were there . . . and that is why this was also the city where new forms of Mexican womanhood—Carmen Mondragón, Lupe Marín, Frida Kahlo, Elena Torres, and many unknown others—flourished.

After they left Mexico City in 1921, and over many years, Ella and Bertram Wolfe were constantly worried by the political and personal problems of the Riveras. Especially worrisome was Frida's fondness for alcohol. They asked her to exchange cognac for milk ("life is just one bottle after another in any case," Bertram wrote her). Frida answered that she had reduced alcohol consumption to "dos copi..osas lágrimas by day" [sic] (two glasses a day). On every visit by Bertram to Mexico Frida asked him to bring with him "that girl that both you and I love exhaustively named Ella" (esa muchachita que tú y yo queremos y harto y se llama Ella). Ella Wolfe wrote to me in the 1980s in a discussion of the affection Frida had for Diego, that "the only thing that interested him, really, was his art, and due to his remarkable imagination, he could create fantasies, that is why his politics—full of fantasy—were of no significance. One could not accept the crazy things he explained." He was a quasi animal, Ella told me, who made love like anyone else urinates. Though Ella came from a family of socialist convictions—she was the one who introduced Bertram to socialism—she had very little patience for a man like Diego, for whom, as Frida wrote to her in 1934, "faithfulness was a bourgeois virtue . . . that only exists to exploit and to procure economic gain" (fidelidad [era] una virtud burguesa . . . que no existe más que para explotar y sacar ventaja económica). Ella offered all of her solidarity as an activist and as a woman to Frida, who heartbreakingly wrote her "with my bourgeois prejudices of faithfulness I shall take my music elsewhere" (con mis prejuicios burgueses de fidelidad me iré con mi música a otra parte). Of course, as we have seen, the city they lived in was helping them to reinvent themselves and their sexualities, but to ask then and there for faithfulness was something Frida could do but not deliver.

Ella Wolfe knew a lot more about the Mexico City of around 1919 but she never talked about it. For the historian, her silence is as eloquent as her stories. In early twentieth-century New York, she was a Jew who was seen, as she recalled, as a "dirty foreigner." She wanted to be *American*, and just as she was starting to be, the U.S. entered into a period of social instability. She freely talked to me about Mexican machismo, but was not as ready to talk about the U.S. version, though she mentioned it anyway when referring to Edmund Wilson and many of the New York intellectuals. In the late 1980s she did not want to badmouth her new refuge, America, and that old Mexico City was left truly unconfessed, and despite the many years she never reached total imprudence in memory. Thus Mexico City as experienced by the women of the radical milieu died with their memories. What survived was the refuge in the belief in an exotic, pristine, and inexistent Atlantis.[36]

9

Around 1919, Mexico City furnished all its radical visitors with the surrender to ideological and personal doubts, as if one could wonder about one's own authenticity and rightness when surrounded by vivid authenticity and pureness. The city, however, was full of contradictions that they saw but did not want to see. The only collective record the U.S. radicals left about 1919 and 1920 Mexico City was the English section of El *Heraldo*. Apart from the section run by the U.S. radicals, however, El *Heraldo* was very much a part of the city's life. It printed a poem by López Velarde that was no less escapist, yet more innovative, than poems by Michael Gold or Henry Glintenkamp published in its English pages. In the same way that people from different groups walked the same streets unknown to each other, López Velarde's poem existed in the same pages where U.S. radicals in Mexico used to think aloud about their ideas and dreams. But around 1919 U.S. radicals thought very little about the city they lived in and they soon called those years the golden era of the city. One of Phillips's poems said this—though actually attaching memories to something other than Mexico City—in a piece written as a result of a trip to the mountains around Guadalajara:

Guadalajara, memories of my love!
Of gold and his golden Mexican days
The golden Mexican days have been mine
. . .

Mexican days my treasure sure and strong
That in the death-like north when all is old
And dutiful and grim, shall be my gold
To give me hope that life is brave and fine
Mexican days warming my veins like wine.[37]

How did the sinful city come to furnish them with so much pureness? In the pages of El Heraldo, probably unknown to the U.S. editors of the English section, another golden age was in the making, namely urban bohemia, both as a desired modern nonidentity for many and as self-destructive destiny for some. In the summer of 1919, El Heraldo published a series of articles by "Califas." "The Lady with the Burning Hair drains the life out of her lovers" (La dama de los cabellos ardientes se bebe la vida de sus amantes) was the title of the first installment on July 26, 1919. It dealt with marijuana, its consumption by street people, even by conductors of trams and buses. A drawing illustrated the article: a man consumed by the fumes of the drug represented by a snake, while in the background the fumes form a ghost that destroys the towers of a Catholic temple. The article gave a doctor's opinion on the effects of marijuana consumption. It described the lives of the grifos (addicts). The poetic phrasing of the effects of drugs warned people of the dangers: "the initiated in the cult of the Green Goddess perishes with the three classic puffs of the reeking smoke." Califas was indeed Ricardo Arenales, who soon became Porfirio Barba Jacob and was a great devotee of the Diosa Verde (Green Goddess). He was a poet, a journalist, and a writer who, from the 1900s to the early 1940s, lived in and embodied Mexico City's dark bohemia—a bohemia composed of hunger, misery, drugs, alcohol, and sex, but also of intellectual creativity (figure 4.4).

Of course, not radical Jews in the U.S., but other Jews, the poor immigrants, not in English, not in Spanish, but in Yiddish saw the Mexico City that Barba Jacob inhabited and thus produced what cities often produce: revealing poems, such as this one by Isaac Berliner:

The road is so muddy—
There is a man shuffling along
His lazy steps tread on the damp earth
As though his feet were heavy weights—
And eyes, that gleam like candles,
Spreading the flames that fall
On female bodies and hips
On the tender faces of girls[38]

4.4. "La dama de los cabellos ardientes se bebe la vida de sus amantes."
El Heraldo (July 26, 1919).

The man in the poem smokes marijuana and feels no hunger. The foreigners who reached the city around 1919 saw what Berliner described, and by
the late 1930s bohemian life of the ugly city had become fashionable. It had
become a rite of passage to visit *pulquerías* and even to paint their walls. But
bohemia is a difficult area for the historian to approach, that is, as more than
an urban lifestyle impersonated by many, lived by few. Many claimed to be bohemians, from Diego Rivera to José Clemente Orozco, from Anita Brenner to
Frances Toor, from Dr. Atl to Joseph Freeman . . . Rivera told Bertram Wolfe
great stories about experiments with drugs and bohemian life, but who could
believe Rivera? In fact, Mexico City, like any city, offered a vivid bohemian life.

But real bohemia is the creative and destructive might of a city unbounded, in which one cannot easily dwell: it walks all over you.

For the many who claimed to live in the great bohemia of the city starting in 1920, very few really knew it. Some were anonymous, such as Leonardo R. Pardo, whose life was told by Julio Sesto. Pardo was a journalist and poet, an inhabitant of the city, a friend of beggars, and a great chatterer in coffee shops and bars. He was "quintessential socialism" (el socialismo quintaesencial) for his great generosity with the inhabitants of the streets. He died in 1914. But there were very few bohemians whose names we know, and they were not the Riveras, the Kahlos, the Glintenkamps, and, of course, not López Velarde. I can mention very few: perhaps Dr. Atl and Antoniota Rivas Mercano—a patron of bohemians—, surely Antonin Artaud, Silvestre Revueltas, Nahui Ollin (Carmen Mondragón), and of course Porfirio Barba Jacob and Hart Crane. Let us focus on Barba Jacob.

Ricardo Arenales, originally from Colombia, reinvented himself—like many others—several times, in Mexico City, in Monterrey, in Guatemala, in Bogotá, in Barranquilla. He had been a journalist on Porfirian newspapers (El Imparcial), a supporter of Porfirio Díaz, and a well-known bohemian in the city. In 1918 he edited the satiric publication Fierabrás. His articles, his poems, and his anecdotes were repeated by different sectors of Mexico's intelligentsia; his homosexual orgies became urban legends.

While U.S. radical men and women were betraying each other erotically and politically while living comfortably in Colonia Roma or in downtown Mexico City, Barba Jacob was renting cheap hotel rooms, seducing—like Mexican dandy Salvador Novo did—bus conductors, soldiers, and street children, as well as consuming marijuana in the various secret places patronized by intellectuals, homeless people, and lost children of the city's middle classes. He knew that behind the National Palace, or in houses and pharmacies in Colonia Juárez or Roma, opium, marijuana, and heroin could be found. Barba Jacob took a photographer from El Heraldo to capture one of the very few images we have of this face of the city in 1919. Thus there is the picture of Juan El Moto ("Moto" was a popular name for a marijuana addict; it comes from "mota," marijuana), smoking marijuana in front of the camera on August 3, 1919. Jacobo Dalevuelta, one of the first Mexican investigative reporters who truly became a window into dark Mexico City, was probably the journalist from El Heraldo who followed Barba Jacob around. During the 1920s he reported on the consumption of marijuana in the Callejón de San Camilito, La Colonia de la Bolsa, Tepito, Balvuena, and Santa Julia, all dark spots on the city's map, but also on Bolivar Street and in downtown cabarets. And in Barba Jacob–like language he described Juanita (marijuana): "Gran señora y con porte de Reina, concede sus favores a todos por igual, al pobre que al rico; al triste que al alegre; al valiente que al cobarde. Buena parte de la juventud cultiva en México relaciones con la gran señora de penacho y caudal blancos y de sueños multicolores." (Great lady with the demeanor of a queen, yells her favors to all, as much to the poor as to the wealthy; to the sad as to the happy; to the courageous as to the coward. Much of the youth in Mexico engages in relationships with the great lady of white plume and caudal and of multicolor dreams.) He reported that clandestine theaters performed shows with marijuana as leitmotif, and he joined one of the proletarian sessions of *mariguanos* in which an old woman, Doña Tachita, rolled huge marijuana cigars, and eighteen people paid a fee to share them, combining the inhalation with bites of brown sugar (*piloncillo*). All were in a room "dirty with no paved or wooden floors; lighted with a small oil lamp with the bulb stained by smoke. With great effort, I saw an old and bony woman sitting on the floor, near a soap box holding a timber where they rolled their thick cigars." By the late 1920s Dalevuelta also reported the existence of a high-class marijuana club attended by wealthy young addicts who called cannabis "Juanita."

Barba Jacob described that city, the bohemian's vices with the moral lessons required by any major newspaper around 1919: "Aquí, hogares mendigos y hambrientos con el lujo de la miseria y del harapo; allá, lumpanares entre desmelenamiento de cabelleras de mujeres ébrias, que equivocaron su destino de ser madres para ser FLOR DE FANGO; y por todas partes esterialidad y ausencia de fuerza." (Here, vagrant and starved households with the luxury of misery and raggedness; there, brothels among drunken women losing their heads, who mistook their destiny of motherhood becoming flowers in the mud; and everywhere sterility and absence of strength).[39] Making use of the words of Porfirian novelist and doctor Fortunato Hernández, who talked about urban degeneration and vice, Barba Jacob described his own life as that of one of Hernández's characters: "There are moments in which we the atavist ones degenerate so much that I think at one point we must have been like pigs in the animal kingdom" (Hay momentos en que los atávicos nos dejeneramos tanto que creo que alguna vez hemos de haber sido cerdos en la escala zoológica).

But underneath the mandatory moral lesson was Barba Jacob's fascination with the bohemian life that granted him the possibility of reinventing both his art (poetry) and his persona. As he had written in 1911: "My pain made up for my madness/and no one has been happier than I!" (¡Compensé mi dolor con mi locura/y nadie ha sido más feliz que yo!). Bohemia was his art, his own self. His poetry was innovative thanks to a musicality based on free associations such as those caused by drug deliriums or listening to the city's streets. Thus sometime in 1918 or 1919 he wrote what was nothing but an ode to marijuana:

La dama de cabellos ardientes
La dama de cabellos encendidos
Trasmutó para mí todas las cosas,
Y amé la soledad, los prohibidos
Huertos y las azañas vergonzosas.[40]

The lady with burning hair
The lady with fiery hair
Changed everything for me,
And I loved the solitude, the forbidden
Gardens and the shameful deeds.

As irony would have it, in the same year, 1919, a Mexican writer in exile in Washington, D.C., Querido Moheno, had declared marijuana a plebeian Mexican drug that had neither a Baudelaire nor a Verlaine to sing it. He advised U.S. authorities, who were concerned with the arrival of the Mexican illness (marijuana), that young U.S. bohemians ought to be told that marijuana was not an addiction to be acquired in fancy salons of red silk and beautiful women: "its favorite ambiance is jails' galleries: its language the argot of thieves and murderers." It was an addiction born in *el petate* (Indigenous sleeping mat) in the midst of the lice and dirt of Mexican soldiers and proletarians. Little did Moheno know that as he was speaking marijuana was acquiring its Verlaine in Mexico City's underworld.

Barba Jacob used to visit poet González Martínez's house in Santa María la Ribera, and there he befriended López Velarde, his anathema. What López Velarde feared, and was fascinated by, was what Barba Jacob embodied: the city adrift. Barba Jacob claimed that he had initiated Spanish writer Ramón del Valle Inclán into the vice of marijuana in Mexico City. In 1919 José Vasconcelos helped Barba Jacob, as he did Bertram and Ella Wolfe or Pedro Henríquez Ureña, or Novo and Villaurrutia. Sometime in the early 1920s, however, Barba Jacob attacked Vasconcelos in newspaper articles and, according to Barba Jacob's biographer, Fernando Vallejo, Vasconcelos sought out Barba Jacob in his hotel room, where he found him naked in bed with a man; and it was there that Vasconcelos, the center of all intellectual groups before Diego Rivera reigned, was called by Barba Jacob "the dictator of Mexico's culture." Thus Barba Jacob became an outlaw within the Mexican intelligentsia.

A young man passing by in the streets of 1911 Mexico City inspired poems by Barba Jacob in which the main line read "Who makes flesh tremble with a restrained yearning . . ." (Que haga temblar las carnes con una ansía contenida . . .). In the same way, Novo, in 1919 a young and precocious teenager, observed the gazes of doormen, street boys, and bus drivers: urban sin *in potentia*. Around 1919 on a flat roof in Pino Street, Santa María la Ribera, he had his first sexual experience with the family chauffeur, a man with an odor of "proletarian gasoline"—an odor, he argued, that would mark his lifelong taste for proletarian men. In the early 1920s, together with a group of his peers, he rented a room on Donceles Street, the same street where Jack Johnson lived in 1919. There all sorts of members of the city's underworld joined Novo and his friends. Following what he then saw as a chic fashion for all things Mexican, Novo decorated the room with Mexican motifs: "an exhaustive nationalism pressed me to use a *jícara* [traditional small cup] as a deposit more in tune with the Vaseline necessary for the rituals." There, in that room, Novo met Barba Jacob, with his "repulsive ugliness" (*fealdad repulsiva*), who invited him and his friends to smoke marijuana. Novo collapsed. Of course, as a dandy and a homosexual, Novo knew of that other city inhabited by Barba Jacob, but Novo's political opportunism and aristocratic lifestyle always saved him. In 1974 Novo had a comfortable bourgeois death, crowned as the embodiment of the city itself (he was its official chronicler). His memoirs and narratives of the bohemian city remained unpublished until very recently. Barba Jacob died in 1941, sick and poor in a miserable hotel room (Sevilla, on Ayuntamiento Street). Novo was, said Barba Jacob, a "cheeky faggot with a lowered flag, I am a faggot with a wide-open flag" (nalgasobo puto con bandera arriada, yo soy puto con bandera desplegada). In 1919 Mexico City, Barba Jacob was to Novo what in Paris Mallarmé was to Victor Hugo.

In that other life of the city, bohemia, poetry, spiritism, orientalism, aesthetic ideas, politics, drugs, and sex blended. One large room on the third patio of an abandoned colonial convent became the emblem of that life. In 1931 Barba Jacob wrote Rafael Helidoro Valle and nostalgically referred to the "Nights of the Palacio de la Nunciatura." The reference implied that these scenes could not be easily spelled out. In fact, however, as he had done in 1919 with his urban articles, Barba Jacob published allegorical references to those nights in March 1922 in El *Demócrata*, where he told stories of Hindu wizards, fakirs, young men seduced by drugs and sensual pleasures. Two writers, Arqueles Vela and Rafael Arévalo Martínez, wrote stories that made into an urban epic that black hole of bohemia, that room in an old convent in the historical center of the city. Ironically, the convent was both the victim of postrevolutionary urban planning and soon the architectural paradigm to follow—the neocolonial style being massively produced at the same time as old convents were abandoned and destroyed.

Some of the attendees of those nights later wrote about them and told the story of a spirit that materialized and was named by Barba Jacob "Nalgalopio," then renamed Buda and later Timoteo. Arévalo Martínez recalled the "Man who looked like a Horse," as he described Barba Jacob, his incredible rhetorical explosions, his vice, his wisdom, and his total attachment to the city's pavement. In 1927 Arévalo wrote a text, half fiction, half journalism, mentioning names of attendees of those nights, such as Colombian poet Leopoldo de la Rosa (though it is never clear whether he was there personally or only through poetry), Salvadorean cartoonist Antonio Salazar (named as Toño Morazán), and Salvadorean poet Juan Cotto (named José Meruenda). In the narrative, Arévalo Martínez entered into a fictional dialogue with Aretal (Barba Jacob), marking the great creativity and the terrible desolation that was the bohemian city: "Pero Aretal, ¿se pronunció al fin sobre ti el anatema del Dios en quien creíste? Tu marijuana y tu alcohol y tu lujuria te sorbieron la médula de tal modo, que ya estás recluído en un manicomio y no te has dado cuenta." (But Aretal, did the curse of the God you believed in overcome you? Your marijuana, your alcohol, your lust brainwashed you in such a way that you are already imprisoned in an asylum and you have not realized it.) The stories of the Palacio de la Nunciatura seem to even have reached Jorge Luis Borges in Buenos Aires, through Alfonso Reyes. Borges often told some of the anecdotes of those grifos in an old abandoned convent in Mexico City, always concluding with the sentence: "The world of fantasy already worked by itself. Doesn't it seem like a Chesterton's tale?"

Barba Jacob embodied the bohemia of the city, but he also sought community and innocence—as did López Velarde and many of the U.S. radicals who doggedly sought lost innocence and origins in the city. In sum, wrote Arévalo Martínez, "Said Mr. Aretal: we know nothing yet feel something; this, what is felt can be called this: innocence, equality, unity." Indeed, Barba Jacob had lived in Porfirian, revolutionary, and postrevolutionary Mexico City. On many occasions he left the city, for Guatemala, for Monterrey, for Colombia, but he always came back. His was the city of sin and bohemia that so many claimed to live in, but hardly knew. Small wonder his "Balada de la Loca Alegría" started with the wine of Anáhuac (Mexico City):

Mi vaso lleno—el vino del Anáhuac—
mi esfuerzo vano—estéril mi pasión—
soy un perdido—soy un mariguano—
a beber—a danzar al son de mi canción . . .
ciñe el tirso oloroso, tañe el jocundo címbalo.
Una bacante loca y un sátiro afrentoso
conjuntan en mi sangre su frenesí amoroso.
Atenas brilla, piensa y esculpe Praxiteles.

My cup full—wine of Anáhuac—
my vain attempt—my passion, sterile—
I am a stray—I am a marijuano—
let me drink—let me dance to the sound of my song . . .
the fragrant wreath fits, the satisfying cymbal tolls.
A mad bacchanal woman and an insulting satyr
in my blood their loving frenzies fuse.
Athens shines, thinks and sculpts Praxiteles.

Barba Jacob was, as Arévalo Martínez characterized him, a *poète maudit*, a cynic like Voltaire, and yet a positivist like Kant, homosexual like Plato, and "like Teresa of Avila, ascetic like two drops of water from the same ocean." He found in the city the possibility of being and not being, the freedom of no identity, the fear and joy of experiencing the worst possibilities of human nature that the city's stones allowed—"and there are days that we are so squalid, so very squalid,/like the dark entrails of a dark flint" (Y hay días en que somos tan sórdidos, tan sórdidos,/como la entraña obscura de obscuro pedernal). But he also found the possibility of reborn innocence—"and there are days when we are so placid, so very placid . . . /decadence of childhood! Sapphire lagoons!" (Y hay días en que somos tan plácidos, tan plácidos . . . /—iniñez en el crepúsculo! ilagunas de zafir!—). For it was said that Barba Jacob claimed that, in order to reach human superiority, one has to reach total orphanhood: "to hate the fatherland and to abhor the mother" (odiar a la patria y aborrecer la madre). He found such orphanhood, and thus he became the city, the city that tempted so many, the city that became a fashion, but which very few fully surrendered to.[41]

Unknown to radicals and slackers in the city, even to the visitors to the Palacio de la Nuniciatura, in 1920 a young professional folklorist explored the city that Barba Jacob lived, and thus provided an inside/outside picture of those spaces (from the perspective of the ethnographer, the non-drug-addict). A Viennese amateur botanist, V. A. Reko, who had moved to Mexico City in 1921, also described the uses of marijuana in the city, and his description is that of Barba Jacob's physical and poetic impulse: "Then he [a marijuana addict] returns to his usual work, to his daily occupations, until his devil assaults him again sooner or later; once again his addiction to the pleasure drives him to repeat the dangerous experiment."[42] But the description by the young folklorist constitutes the clearest record of the dark room that embodied an urban bohemia: a room in a patio of an old convent rented by "a group of elegant youth":

To get to the room where they go only by night, you must cross some very long and somber corridors that were at one time the cloisters of the convent. They have the room covered in black and adorned with skulls and bones and when they bring a neophyte to it, they use as lamps some pans where they light alcohol with salts to produce a greenish light perfect for producing macabre wanderings in their future smokers. In these meetings they regularly dedicate themselves to reading selected poems, recited with excessive religiosity and they all claim to never take more joy in their favorite literature than when they are high [marijuanos].[43]

This was the city, and this is why López Velarde wanted to take refuge in parsimony, in "restraint," in escaping to "those things that did good to me." This is why it was better to escape to the confines of either an exotic and pristine Indigenous Mexico or the hope of the international revolution. Better than succumbing to the city's sin was to read in 1920 in Manuel Gamio's ethnographic journal, Etnos, a tune collected in Tepito—and "Is there someone who will ask these quiet people," went Isaac Berliner's Yiddish ode to Tepito, "Why such joy amid such bitter poverty?" The tune collected in Etnos went:

Suni, suni, cantaba la rana
ahí te van los polvos de la mariguana.
Mariguana estoy que no puedo
ni levantar la cabeza,
con los ojos retecolorados
y la boca reseca, reseca.[44]

Suni, suni sang the frog,
there goes the dust of marijuana.
I am so high that I cannot
even lift my head,
with my eyes bloodshot
and my mouth very dry, very dry.

End

Modernist Mexico City, in all its peripheral modesty, achieved at once a lasting victory and a great defeat. On the one hand, by the 1920s the meaning of Mexico had more global connotations than ever before: a hitherto unknown and powerful notion of the "native," of the authentic, an indisputable version of what such anthropologists as Edward Shils called in 1919 "genuine culture," or what countless world commentators identified as the lost community that fascinated such avant-garde personalities as Diego Rivera, Edward Weston, Aaron Copland, and Hart Crane. On the other hand, such meanings discredited the laboratory (the city) where such meanings were made possible. The city became invisible, lost in the midst of its romantic third-worldism. The city, of course, lost nothing with the silencing; it kept growing in size as well as in cultural, economic, and political significance. For experimentation, however, the silencing was a loss; it weakened the experimentalism that originated important political solutions and new and lasting cultural trends that marked the first three decades of the twentieth century. But it is true: the city was not, as the old Mexican saying goes, "monedita di'oro pa' caerle bien a todos" (a little gold coin to be liked by all).

PART III THE BROWN ATLANTIS

Idées fixes are like cramps, for instance in the foot—
the best cure is to stamp on it.
— S. Kierkegaard, *Diaries*, July 1838

What is that "Out-dam" thing [*The Outlook Magazine*]
requesting? . . . It is simply asking for a Mexican painter
to send them an album of national types, of the most
typical types . . . Don't they want Mexicans? They will
have their Mexicans.
— Salvador Arteaga, a painter, protagonist of Federico
    Gamboa's *La reconquista* (1908)

Eternity is the only thing on my mind permanently . . .
One good thing about Mexico, you just get high and dig
eternity every day.
— Jack Kerouac's letter to Carolyn Cassady, June 3, 1952,
    Mexico City

Thus—I hear some saying—you do not believe in the
existence of a picturesque Spain. By any chance are you one
of those supporters of the Europeanization of Spain? . . .
I do not believe that there is still something to collect beyond
the Pyrenees by the pursuers of the picturesque. They should
start by quitting the idea that they will find it there, where it
is proclaimed the most.
— Mario Praz, *Penisola pentagonale* (1928)

THE BROWN ATLANTIS

Like a pyramid belongs to Egypt, a pagoda to China, a geisha to Japan, or the conspicuous *abacaxi* in Carmen Miranda's sombrero to Brazil, the idea of "Mexico" belongs to a series of well-known tropes produced and consumed domestically and internationally. The very notion of Mexico has been a commodity in the international cultural market for nearly 150 years. The characteristics of this merchandise are as palpable as they are relatively fixed: ruins and cacti, "traditional" arts and crafts, pristine and "authentic" Indigenous people; Spanish or Moorish patterns in architecture or in the eyes of exotic *señoritas*; *mestizaje* and such heavy moral categories as family, community, fiesta, death, color, race, and violence, all packaged in their brown wrapping. Pots, drugs, pistolas, sombreros, siestas, Rivera, Kahlo, Azuela, Paz, and Fuentes are consumed, and little else. The world's demand for the commodity is steady, as is the supply. Of course, Mexico, the country, its people, have changed tremendously over the last century, but not its image. Like a triumphant actor of a wearily performed single sketch, the idea of Mexico is trapped in its own modern success—a powerful modernist image that, nevertheless, decades of presumed post-this and post-that considerations have only made more alluring.

I want to dissect how Mexico came to be somehow frozen as a modern metaphor of atemporal race, endless community, and redemptory violence—what I call the search for the "Brown Atlantis": "Mexico" first and foremost as an intellectual longing. Echoing the way many travelers, ethnographers, anthropologists, and commentators described Mexico (an Atlantis), the notion of Brown Atlantis specifically refers to the creation of the idea of Mexico, by foreigners and Mexicans alike between circa 1870 and 1940.[1] I study the formation of an enduring view of Mexico seen through the interaction between many accounts about Mexico and Mexico City, the central location of the thinking and social mingling of the author of these accounts.[2] It is the story of solid stereotypes about the meaning of Mexico, silencing the very presence of the city—a *ciudad* that betrayed their expectations of *comunidad*.

Brown Atlantis connoted a racial obsession—brown—and a place—Atlantis—whose essential reality was not topographic but moral, made precisely by the fact of being simultaneously a robust presupposition (that Atlantis existed) and a relentless search (it had to be found). By 1920 the Atlantis was a modernist imagined place that presumed its own existence, but at the same time had been sought time and time again for more than a century. Therefore it was a cultural undertaking necessarily linked to at least three modern issues that made the Atlantis both a noun and a verb; namely, evasion (to evade), authenticity (to authenticate), and discovery (to discover). To be sure there were, and are, various forms of evasion, authenticity, and discovering, depending on how, when, and by whom Mexico is or was defined. But what I consider relatively constant is the very need of evasion, authenticity, and discovery in defining such a thing as Mexico.

Yet, it needs to be said, the idea of the Brown Atlantis is only an irony. Mexico, the city, the country, its peoples, had never been truly an exotic paradise of either dystopias or utopias. And whether Mexicans were or are brown, black, white, or blue is, or should be, a non-issue. To make it so, a non-issue, I offer the irony of the historical obsession with brownness in the making of Mexico as an Atlantis.

I want to truly essay the concept of the Brown Atlantis in the way nineteenth-century essayists handled their multifaceted craft. Thus this is the map of what follows: 1. A postcard of the issues this essay seeks to dissect. 2. On how the idea of and search for the Brown Atlantis came to be. 3. On how Mexico City was seen and not seen by the searchers for the Brown Atlantis and on some first, inevitable, thoughts on the race obsession. 4. More on the obsession with race, because it is hard to avoid the topic, and on the emblematic case of Stuart Chase. 5. On a great mystery: how the Atlantis came to Mexico, particularly to Mexico City, and on how its arrival made the city invisible. 6. On the high maintenance that the Brown Atlantis has demanded, and on how race, again, and revolution made it so strong and lasting. 7. In conclusion, on who on earth the inhabitants of the Brown Atlantis were.

1. A Postcard of the Issues
This Essay Seeks to Dissect

At the beginning of the twentieth century a number of people fled the intellectual and social discontent of Europe and the U.S. by moving to either Paris or the tropics. Some even went to Taos, New Mexico, and a few more went further, crossing what was little more than a loose territorial border into

Mexico. Crossing the border meant a different time scale, another civilization, and, above all, immersion in a racial other. Yet the border was often too close physically as well as conceptually, for Mexico had long been privately used and abused by U.S. and European historians, amateur archaeologists, and anthropologists, as well as by all sorts of orientalists, as a necessary background for the self-definition of their own racial self-esteem and positioning within evolution. Mexico was an uncomplicated contrast. Easier to access than China or Japan, it was a familiar escape from industrialism and modern disenchantment, a truly accessible primitiveness that did not require special knowledge of Kanji alphabets or Confucian philosophy. Mexico represented economic opportunity and cultural comfort. It was, as an 1884 investment pamphlet put it, "a magnificent but underdeveloped mine—our India in commercial importance—our Cuba and Brazil in tropical products—our Italy in climate and attraction—our Troy in antiquities and classic history."[3]

A 1927 lithograph by the U.S. artist Everett Gee Jackson captured in a single image the civilizing jump that was narrated before and after by countless journalistic reports, novels, poems, letters, and paintings. E. G. Jackson was one of the many artists who traveled to Mexico between 1915 and 1940 searching for pristine authenticity and alternatives to industrialism. His childhood recollections of tamales in a small Texan town took him south in search of lost innocence. Mexico was different, it was argued as late as 1940s by yet another book on Mexico, because there "the latitude of the mind, the longitude of the blood" were somehow different.[4] That is what Jackson showed in his depiction of the crossing of the border with the U.S. as urban lights and high buildings, with Mexico a "different" civilization of Indigenous people, burros, cacti, nature, community, and an attachment to land found everywhere in the brown country (figure 5.1).

Everywhere except, of course, Mexico City, which is where most of the world's intelligentsia that went to Mexico between 1915 and 1940 ended up living and mingling with each other, as well as with Mexicans. Jackson visited the murals, as many did in those decades, and found that "the people represented in the paintings seemed to me to be quite true to the people I was seeing in the streets of Mexico City. In fact, the people I was seeing in the streets now looked to me as though they had come right out of the murals." Of course, like many before and after him he was looking at the city with non-city eyes: "I had learned that way of seeing in Chapala and Guanajuato, and now I was applying it in Mexico City."[5]

Mexico City was not Mexico. That lesson was learned in European modernist disenchantment, both in the late nineteenth-century German sociological thought of Oswald Spengler and Georg Simmel, and in pioneering U.S.

5.1. E. G. Jackson's illustration, *It's a Long Road to Comondú:*
Mexican Adventures since 1928 (College Station: Texas A & M University Press, 1987),
courtesy Texas A & M University Press.

anthropological studies of *Gemeinschaft* vs. *Gesellschaft*, community vs. mass
society. Or rather the lesson was a command, observed by two generations
of modernist intellectuals and learned in canonic texts such as T. S. Eliot's
The Waste Land, a blend of mythology, ethnography, and modernist rhetorical innovations that conveyed that cities were inauthenticity par excellence.[6]
Thus for a 1909 U.S. traveler, "the capital is not truly Mexico," and a 1940s
U.S. journalist could repeat as unquestionable truth: "Everybody agrees that
Mexico City is not Mexico, and indeed there is something strange about this
metropolis . . . It is, someone says, as if Kansas City had been set down in the
middle of China." And the conventional wisdom prevailed to the point that
even a prominent contemporary historian can blend historical specificity with
myth: "Yet the real Mexico, and in particular the Mexico of the Revolution, was
provincial Mexico."[7]

2. On How the Idea of and Search
for the Brown Atlantis Came to Be

By the 1920s, observers, German, British, and French, had in some respects
already been to Mexico. The work of Alexander von Humboldt, William Prescott,

George Ticknor, Washington Irving, Madame Calderón de la Barca, and H. H. Bancroft had been common knowledge for at least two generations. Explorer and archaeologist Guillermo Dupaix, painters Léon Gautier, Ernest Wadsworth Longfellow, Conrad Wise Chapman, and Frederic Church, chronicler Ernest Vigneaux, novelists Lucien Biart and Gabriel Ferry, and ethnologist Alexandre Lambert de Sainte-Croix paralleled in French the stories told by Bancroft, Prescott, or Irving about Mexico and Spain.

In addition to these long-lasting views, the image of Mexico in U.S. progressive journalism was as much a part of U.S. political culture as it was part of revolutionary Mexican leaders' thinking. (Francisco I. Madero, a Mexican progressive à l'américaine, is a good example). Progressive journalists visiting the slums of New York City or Chicago, or denouncing the destruction of rural communities in the Midwest by big business, also researched Mexico, but not Mexico City. Mexico for them meant, of course, not Mexico City, but the "real" Mexico. John Kenneth Turner's Barbarous Mexico (1911), John Reed's Insurgent Mexico (1914), Herbert Croly's articles in The New Republic in the 1920s, and Mary Austin's 1930 essays on Mexico constituted a progressive common sense about Mexico. An important California journalist, Carleton Beals, reached Mexico City by 1918 and founded an enduring progressive perspective of Mexico that, as a natural extension of epochal racial and historical truths, was extended to "Latin" America.[8] Diego Rivera's illustrations of Beals's reporting on Mexico conclusively synthesized this racio-civilizational-revolutionary view of Mexico.

Small wonder then that young writer Katherine Anne Porter decided to change her plans and, instead of heading to Paris, went to Mexico in 1920.[9] Swapping Paris for Mexico was common in those decades: U.S. poet Hart Crane, English writer D. H. Lawrence, and many others did so as well. Such French artists and writers as Jean Charlot, Antonin Artaud, and André Breton also succumbed to the attraction of Mexico City in different moments; it was known that André Gide often thought of traveling to Mexico. At any rate, Waldo Frank (today a forgotten author but a pretentious and famous U.S. intellectual in the 1920s) went and appointed himself the André Gide of the Americas. For Breton it was clear in 1939 that "a part of mental landscapes has Mexico as a frontier."[10] And significantly, another artist changed Paris for Mexico City: Rivera left Paris in 1921 for Mexico City. Paris was indeed in Mexico City, at least for a while.

For long this kind of appeal was supported by a vast literature. Travel books ranged from the many editions of Terry's Guide to Mexico to countless accounts from U.S., British, German, and French travelers. Between 1870 and 1913, nearly 150 books about Mexico were published by travelers, naturalists, amateur archaeologists, and anthropologists.[11] The titles of these books and periodicals represented the common sense of Mexico at the time: "Itla Itechpa in Mexicapan in Echitopan in Tonatiuh Icalaquiyan" (Things about Mexico, Egypt of the West, and of General Literature), "The Egypt of America," "Viva Mexico!," "Aztec Land," "Wonderland of the South," and, of course, "The Mayan Atlantis."[12] These books consolidated and concretized the fixed images marking the path from north to south—from the U.S.-Mexico border to Yucatán—or from Veracruz to Mexico City, and then to the south. For these books the further south things were, the more authentically Mexican. These titles were later paraphrased in a new generation that, although using different words, spoke to the same longing for an exotic land: "Idols Behind Altars," "Mexico: a Study of Two Americas," "Mexican Maze," "Visiones solaires," or "Anahuac ou, L'Indien sans plumes."[13] Time and time again Mayan ruins, Mitla, Tula, or Teotihuacán were reproduced. A quasi-Lombroso-like fascination with looks and skull shapes, especially of Indigenous people, were shown in countless books, reproducing pictures of Indigenous men and women—or what were militantly defended as "pure" Indigenous people—in the countryside or in small villages. These books created a canon of relatively fixed narrative tropes: the encounter with colonial buildings; bullfights; *cargadores*; naked children; woman peddlers; and all, of course, refusing to admit Mexico City. There was also the ethno-eroticism of the Tehuana, an obsession that foreigners shared with Mexicans. This tropical woman from Tehuantepec was described by Mexican writer Federico Gamboa as a sublime image of desire, female power, and freedom, similar to John Dos Passos's description of her as a woman with the strong nature of Marie Antoinette.[14] The books often used the same images, and thus there are thousands of copies of impressions by U.S. photographer C. B. Waite, and German photographers Hugo Brehme and Guillermo Kahlo.[15] Alicia Azuela, Iztel Rodríguez, and I gathered hundreds of images from all these books, but they are only variations of the same fifteen or twenty images: *cargadores*, burros, ruins, specific colonial buildings, pyramids, Indian faces, street peddlers, dirty semi-naked children . . .

Of the many books about Mexico that were published in Europe and the U.S. throughout the nineteenth century and up to 1940, only one dealt specifically with Mexico City. The author, Olive Percival, was a book collector and clerk from California. In 1900 she saw in the city a crowded urban landscape, full of "such astonishingly poor creatures and sorrowful eyed!" Her book was all about walking and busy people, a Simmel-like description of the city: "Where could they all be going?," she wondered. She saw homeless people and countless beggars. When she tried to take a picture of a rotten wooden colonial door she was stopped by one of the city's inhabitants: "one young man, of perhaps eleven, [who] thinks it ridiculous to photograph old worm-eaten doors and balconies." Thus "he gives a little whoop to attract my attention, takes off his hat with a 'See me, young lady,' and charitably allowed me to get his likeness." The lesson Percival drew in 1901 from this episode tells us how deep-rooted a disappointment the city was as a real expression of Mexico. She concluded that the "young man" was "of the generation that will favor gringos and their cameras and their railroads." This is a strange but revealing conclusion. We might wonder if the young man had posed for her as a native Aztec in the city—as many did—would the conclusions have been different?[16]

3. On How Mexico City Was Seen and Not Seen by the Searchers for the Brown Atlantis and on Some First, Inevitable, Thoughts on the Race Obsession

Books about Mexico written by travelers, scientists, artists, and publicists often devoted a few pages to describing the city. They created through repetition the emblematic images of monuments (Cuauhtémoc, Columbus, Juárez), colonial buildings (the Cathedral, the National Palace, the villa de Guadalupe), and Porfirian buildings and urban spaces (the Post Office buildings, Plateros and Cinco de Mayo streets, Alameda). As a whole, these images were not treated in and of themselves, but were rather used to show the contrast between cosmopolitism and modern comfort on the one hand, and the inexorable primitivism of burros, *cargadores*, and street peddlers, on the other.

There are also occasional panoramic views of streets, taken from flat roofs, but in these urban images people are conspicuously absent. Mexicans only appear in their role as the spectacle of a non-city within the city, as incongruous muleteers, *cargadores*, peddlers, and close-ups of faces. As such, they often serve to illustrate an irrepressible need for modern versions of casta paintings. Often the captions would read "pure Aztec," "Mestizo woman," or "Indian in his ancestral dressing." In 1880 the U.S. consul in Mexico City had the old well-known journalist and illustrator David Hunter Strother (better known as Porte Crayon) draw his servant, and then what he called an Aztec child, even though both were the same person. In 1920 well-known German painter Winold Reiss, who had previously painted African American and Native American faces, came to Mexico and painted "Mexican Types," including "pure Aztecs."[17] This typological mania could be found even into the 1940s.

I could reconstruct a series of (literally) renewed casta paintings for the reader to sense how enduring and, unfortunately, common this view was. I could start in 1860 or 1880, but let us start in 1909. A cluster of pictures in W. E. Carson's *Mexico, the Wonderland of the South* (1909), labeled "The Ancient Race," depicted people who could have been from anywhere but were, according to the author, members of the ancient race (figure 5.2). The same book

5.2. "The Ancient Race." From W. E. Carson,
Mexico, the Wonderland of the South
(New York: Macmillan Company, 1909).

5.3. "Lola, our *portera*." From J. W. F. Stoppelman, *People of Mexico* (New York: Hastings House Publishers, 1966).

Lola, our *portera*, holding her sister's baby.

Two young Aztecs who came to stay with Lola.

included pictures of "Typical women of the upper class," in sharp contrast with "Indians" in public schools. As late as 1966, another U.S. book on Mexico included the Mexican-types kind of pictures, one with the caption "two young Aztecs who came to stay with Lola," which were pictures of urban children and a woman, Indigenous or not (figure 5.3).[18] The artistic account of Mexico by U.S. modernist photographer Paul Strand was also a sort of ethnographic account of Mexican castas, as he, together with U.S.-Australian photographer Anton Bruehl, escaped the city and took trips to shoot "authentic" types. In 1941 a writer from the southern U.S., Hudson Strode, visited Mexico to repeat the same old story about Mexico City. There he met Diego Rivera, left the city for Patzcuaro, and found Prisciliano, a boatman at Patzcuaro Lake. "I know [he is] authentic Tarascan and not a studio creation," he argued. The picture: a handsome brown man in a 1940s proletarian outfit who, by decree of the observer, was a pure Indian. Of course the photo used cacti as background. He might have been "pure," but after all what was and what is a pure Indian?

Though one could present countless additional pieces for this puzzle of modern casta paintings, allow me to use a final image: Herbert Cerwin's 1947 picture *These Are the Mexicans*, a truly contemporary casta painting including the

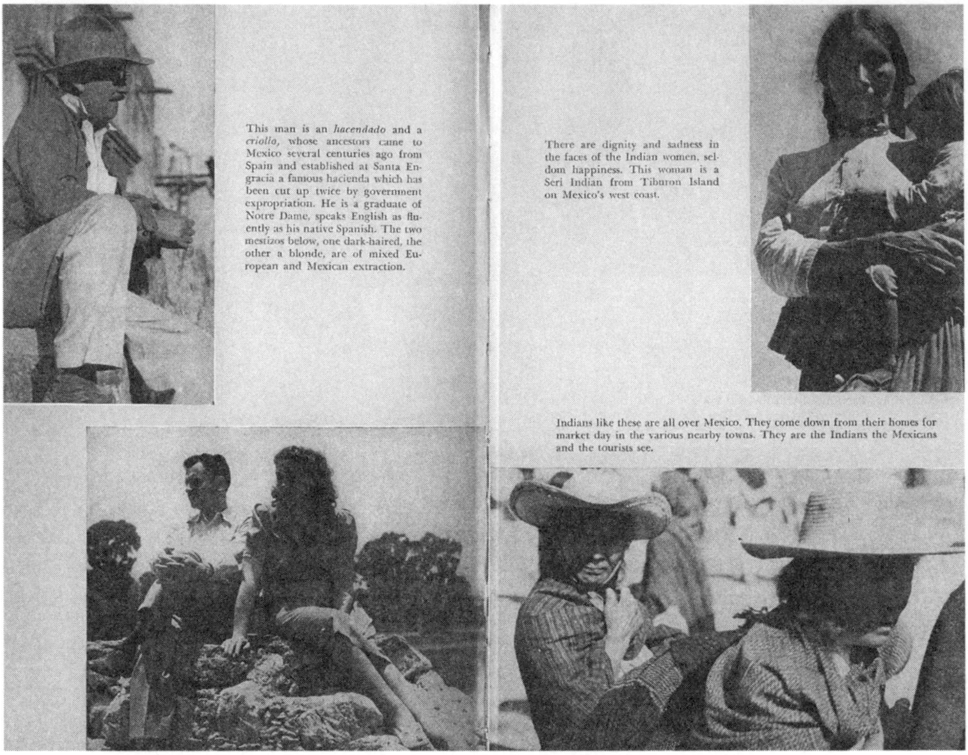
This man is an *hacendado* and a *criollo,* whose ancestors came to Mexico several centuries ago from Spain and established at Santa Engracia a famous hacienda which has been cut up twice by government expropriation. He is a graduate of Notre Dame, speaks English as fluently as his native Spanish. The two mestizos below, one dark-haired, the other a blonde, are of mixed European and Mexican extraction.
There are dignity and sadness in the faces of the Indian women, seldom happiness. This woman is a Seri Indian from Tiburon Island on Mexico's west coast.
Indians like these are all over Mexico. They come down from their homes for market day in the various nearby towns. They are the Indians the Mexicans and the tourists see.

5.4. Contemporary "casta paintings." From Herbert Cerwin, *These Are the Mexicans* (New York: Reynal & Hitchcock, 1947).

criollo, the mestizo, and the pure Indian both in and outside the city—a typical rendition of Mexico as a utopia of racial specificity. Mexicans, in sum, were either not Mexicans—bourgeois Europeans—or Mexicans belonging to a racial structure that the city both created and contradicted.[19] And this was as recent as 1947 (figure 5.4).

When faces are stamps in casta paintings they are not real people, an indifference to faces complemented by a total disdain of urban interiors. This was the case before 1920, but the discovery of the city as a capital of a radical world accentuated and affirmed this tendency. Post-1910 Mexico, after all, was seen as the return to authenticity in the form of race. Stuart Chase's *Mexico: A Study of Two Americas* (1931)—for three decades a worldwide best seller about Mexico—put it clearly: in 1910 Mexico "turned from prostrating herself before white men from all points of the compass, and regarded her own brown men, their imperishable traditions, their authentic artistic gifts, their gentleness and essential dignity." The book, of course, was illustrated by Diego Rivera, who

5.5. Illustration by Diego Rivera. In S. Chase, *Mexico: A Study of Two Americas* (1931),
© 2011 Banco de México, Diego Rivera Frida Kahlo Museums Trust,
Mexico, D.F. / Artists Rights Society (ARS), New York.

recycled some of the sketches he had done for various murals. His illustrations
in Chase's book included only one with an urban setting: bourgeois dubious
sorts of Mexicans having coffee in a gaudy Porfirian interior, the window looking out to the unfinished Porfirian Opera House (figure 5.5).[20] The bad city is
there in that depiction of the wrong, bad, and unauthentic Mexico: the urban

and the bourgeois.[21] Thus, according to the seekers of the Brown Atlantis, postrevolutionary Mexico became what they expected it to be from the beginning.

4. More on the Obsession with Race, Because It Is Hard to Avoid the Topic, and on the Emblematic Case of Stuart Chase

Mexico City's dwellers were seen as either real Indians or as unauthentic mestizos, or worse, white "Westernized" elites—as if they could be non-Western. The observer, whether male or female, could be a simple traveler or, say, Edward Weston, who found an Indian in any brown person, and hated Mexican elite interior spaces and white people. He ended up in the city but tried to live far from the center, finding towns and cities other than Mexico City "less spoiled . . . , the natives more genuine," and candidly writing, "Mexico City is not Mexico at all." Or the traveler could be other photographers, like Anton Bruehl and Sally Lee Woodall, who hated Mexico City because it changed and accepted change. For them the real Mexico was "in the secluded places, in the one-room adobe hut of the primitive places, in the brilliance of the Indian stubbornness."

Foreigners and Mexicans alike shared this racial obsession. Foreigners, however, were more concerned with racial specificity than Mexicans, as if in keeping clear percentages of racial purity, history, geography, and culture could remain unchanged. With these modern racial casta paintings Mexico's image stayed, to paraphrase Ramón López Velarde's poem, "always faithful" to the mirror (see chapter 4) where foreigners found their own images of alienness, hope, or hate. Mexicans, as racist as they could be, had a long history of dealing with racial vagueness.

The obsession with race combined with both a dislike of the city and with revolutionary dreams. We can see this in the reception of Stuart Chase's famous book. The author contrasted industrialized Middletown (following sociologist Robert Lynd's *Middletown: A Study of Contemporary American Culture*, 1929) and the enchanted beauty of a real community, Tepoztlán—based on Robert Redfield's *Tepoztlán: A Mexican Village*. The latter book, themed on fakeness opposed to authenticity, was called *A Study of Folk Life* (1930). In Europe Chase's book was read often as a sort of tourist guide, but also as an anticapitalist manifesto. "It's a great book," opined French writer Jean Prévost in 1939. "It establishes the comparison between an aboriginal and rustic civilization [Tepoztlán], without machines, and the American civilization . . . the book's prejudices—quite mild—would favor the Mexican Indian. These comparisons powerfully help us to see things as they are and to choose the best of oneself."

Despite slight aesthetic and political differences, all those searching for the Brown Atlantis in Mexico shared Prévost's basic opinion.

Aldous Huxley, however, found in Chase's book the obvious dilemma that Mexico City actually presented for everybody: that the myths seemed more important than the cruelty of the urban reality. Chase's kind of views formed an unsolvable dilemma. "The question which confronts us is this," Huxley wrote in a 1934 commentary on Chase's book, "can we evolve a new society which shall combine the virtues of primitives with those of civilized, but exhibit the vices of neither? . . . How much of what is good in North American civilization can Mexico import and still remain Mexico?" Huxley knew that if Mexico developed, the Brown Atlantis would die. "School in Mexico is Dante, and the Indian mind has remained up till now barrenly Beatrice . . . Backed up by the Fords, the village schools will at last begin to do what they were meant to do— transform the national character. And then good-bye—yet once more—to Mr. Chase's Indian."[22]

Similar views were shared by a dandy from Mexico City, Salvador Novo. Writing in the 1930s, he argued that U.S. tourists went to Mexico City to buy "native" dolls, ask for pajamas made of *sarapes*, and wear *huaraches*. Then they published a book about Mexico, as Chase did, portraying

> The rural paradise of a non-mechanized Mexico, still full of villages where looms lace and weave the simple wool of the wide petticoats of the Indians, where the chairs of tulle netting are decorated like the curios that, when seen in a shop where English is spoken, produce an ecstasy as if one were standing in front of the Mona Lisa.[23]

Criticisms similar to Novo's can be found in a unique analysis of Chase's book, written not in a book or in an article but in the margins of a 1950 edition of Chase's *Mexico: A Study of Two Americas*. The author was a young Mexican-Texan folklorist recently returned from China and Japan, Américo Paredes.[24] I have found only one published account of Mexico City before 1940 written by a Mexican-American, Carlos Castillo's *Mexico* (1939). Castillo was a Spanish teacher in the U.S., and his opinions were not very different from most of the foreign views, except for his belief that women ruled the city.[25] But Paredes's reading of Chase is indeed illuminating.

Chase made the point that Tepoztlán constituted a real single race, while the U.S. was an "omelet" of various races. Pages before, he made the point that after 1910 Mexico proudly returned to its real brown race. There, on page 84, Paredes wrote for the first of many times, "he [Chase] is too conscious of race." While Chase described the *criollos* critically, Paredes found them similar to U.S. southerners and was surprised that Chase did not find the likeness.

By page 112 Paredes seemed to be tired of Chase's "racial viewpoint." When Chase described Mexicans as machineless people, Paredes thought otherwise. All Mexicans faced change, he thought, and what Chase talked about sounded like a dead society. When Chase argued that Mexicans were the worst mechanists in the world, Paredes wrote, "Does he consider it racial handicap?" When Chase considered whether Tepoztlán ought to be incorporated into modern times (Chase decided it should not), Paredes claimed unequivocally, "It has been." Chase criticized some Mexicans for claiming to be white; Paredes wrote: "[Chase] is too American and . . . too affected by American prejudices. Peons with blue eyes, rich Indians in the conservative party." Paredes could not believe the distortion the racial bias produced in Chase, which was so strong that Chase distinguished Indians from non-Indians by the consumption of bread and tortillas. Chase was adamant:

> This is the real cleavage between the Indian and the white Mexican way of life. The count has never been made, but I should estimate it at one to ten. In the recent cabinet of General Calles, there are eight whites, three mestizos, and one pure Indian.

Paredes simply asks, "Who classified them?" I also ask who did so, especially since we find this typological mania simultaneously in both sympathetic intellectuals and in Mexico bashers; Mexico bashing is a recurrent sport for certain U.S. politicians. James Sheffield, U.S. ambassador in Mexico City (1924–27), commenting on President P. E. Calles's cabinet, once wrote to Nicholas Murray Butler, an educator and social scientist who, one would think, deserved a complex explanation:

> There is little white blood in the Cabinet—that is, it is very thin. Calles is Armenian and Indian; Leon almost wholly Indian and an amateur bull-fighter; Saenz, the Foreign Minister is a Jew and Indian; Morones more white blood but not the better of it; Amaro, Secretary of War, a pure blooded Indian and very cruel.[26]

The typology is no different from what Chase argued, although he drew positive connotations. This is precisely what Paredes objected to. In his notes he finally had enough of the nonsense when Chase argued that Spaniards had deforested the Valley of Mexico in order to make it look like the barren hills of Spain. "How stupid can a supposed economist be?" he asked.[27]

One can find a few examples of unique clairvoyants who realized the irony of living in a great city while also dreaming of ancient small communities and the Revolution. Paredes saw the profound irony in the construction of an Atlantis based on an undue obsession with race. A U.S. artist, Ione Robinson, also saw this. Her naiveté seemed unbearable for many of the radical writers and artists also in Mexico City when she arrived in the city to study under Diego Rivera in 1932. But at times naiveté translates into necessary ignorance, an indispensable path to knowledge. She wrote to her mother in 1932 that she could not follow all the radical conversations, and did not understand all the political rituals that people like Rivera or her fiancé, U.S. dandy radical Joseph Freeman, kept up. Above all, as an artist she found less inspiration in the idealized and commercialized versions of Indian arts and crafts than in the great colonial art that she found around the city. "Not being a Mexican, I have little in common with the pure Indian," she wrote,

> although their struggles to live in the modern world have opened my eyes . . . [but] I have had too many centuries of Europe mixed into my blood. A man cannot become primitive overnight . . . Rivera may feel at home sitting on a pyramid of Chichen-Itza, but I feel more at ease walking through an arched corridor of a colonial building![28]

In fact, if truth were to be told, this was exactly the case for the great majority of the city's inhabitants, including Diego Rivera. But of course they were not as naïve as Robinson.

With Mexico City established as their capital, the inhabitants of the Brown Atlantis necessarily engaged in an endless search for new versions of casta paintings within the city. Anything—and anyone—that could not fit in these idealized racial paintings was invisible, too un-Mexican, too urban, and too fake. This is why the Atlantis needed to be brown. If it were not explicitly brown, it could not be a new Atlantis of radical political and aesthetic hopes against encroaching modernity. Great destiny that of the idea of Mexico; at times the product of sublime inspiration, commonly equal to something alien, but often the same idea repeated time and time again.

5. On a Great Mystery: How the Atlantis Came to Mexico, Particularly to Mexico City, and on How Its Arrival Made the City Invisible

Plato had never been to Mexico, according to Antonin Artaud, the well-known bohemian precursor of surrealism. However, he believed the Tarahumara Indians were "the direct descendents of the Atlantes" and "when the question is about an authentic tradition, the issue of progress does not exist." The Atlantis of Plato's Critias was eternal. Artaud held that for the Tarahumara Indians, as for him, "to live in a city is to err." Artaud claimed to have found the Brown Atlantis that mestizos could never reach.[29] Racial, cultural, and historical obsessions were an intoxicating elixir.

Earlier, in the 1890s, U.S. amateur archaeologist and poet Augustus Le Plongeon believed that the Atlantes were the Mayans, before the Egyptians and before the Solomon temple. In 1905, Konstantin Balmont, a Russian poet and admirer of Madame Blavatsky's theosophy, visited Mexico. Full of theosophical hope, he wrote:

> I know very well that the day is not so distant in which these secret words will be pronounced; then the rainbow of conjectures, covering the Atlantis which has disappeared, will reunite in a single unique square the vestiges of the Maya, the pyramids of Egypt, the Hindu temples, and the legends of Oceania.

Mexico would be a part of a universal Atlantis that, according to Balmont, would not include the Europeanized Mexico City but would encompass the truly Indigenous Mayan Mexico.[30] Legions of foreigners sought in the Mayans the authenticity that could not be found in urban, afrancesado, mestizo Mexico.

And sometime in 1921 Mabel Dodge, a modernist New Yorker in Taos, finally convinced young John Collier to visit Taos. She had convinced others—among them D. H. Lawrence and U.S. poet W. Bynner—to stay in Taos en route to or from Mexico. Dodge was then about to become Dodge Luhan for Tony Luján, a Native American whom she eventually married. Soon Collier too fell in love with Native Americans. As many did in those years, he found that the Taos Indians still possessed the "fundamental secrets of human life." He had found a "Red Atlantis," one still living but soon to disappear. In the 1930s, Collier—like his anthropologist wife Laura Thompson, anthropologist Elsie C. Parsons, and writers D. H. Lawrence and W. Bynner, to mention but a few—pursued their search further south, expanding the Red Atlantis and finding the Brown Atlantis. Small wonder then that Collier joined efforts with Mexican indigenistas such as Manuel Gamio, to whom he dedicated his Indians of the Americas (1947).[31] For two decades they corresponded, but their interactions had a lot more to do with the interactions of big capital cities, with the bureaucracies and intellectuals of Mexico City, Washington, D.C., and New York, than with Taos or Teotihuacán or Mitla. Until the 1940s, however, the capital of the Brown Atlantis was Mexico City, both its raison d'être and its volte-face.

By the 1920s, for the many radicals who found in Mexico City a capital for their ideas and socializing, a full acknowledgment of the city's import to their own plotting and thinking would have been a betrayal of the principle that brought them to Mexico City in the first place. For Mexico City's commoners, on the other hand, the city had long been both a recognizable and desired (albeit ambivalently so) reality. This was not only because the city meant comfort and civilization, but also because there was a great advantage—and an anguished freedom—in accepting the city's greeting, in giving up the possibility of, say, becoming an ethnographic character in a study of Tepoztlán. On the contrary, for a great majority of the founders of the Brown Atlantis between 1915 and 1940 the city was, like capitalism, mechanization, or hyperindustrialization, a roadblock to Mexico's Brown Atlantis destiny. This is why, in the 1950s, anthropologist Oscar Lewis became an "innovator" in the discipline simply by claiming that there was "culture" in the midst of urban poverty in Mexico City. Thus, Mexicans were either "authentic" natives or children of Sánchez—the title of one of Lewis's popular 1950s ethnographies of Mexico City.[32]

For Mexican intellectuals and artists, as well as for many common people who migrated to the city, the city/not-city distinction was not even a conceivable conceptual option. But for foreigners Mexico City was an urban path of return to the small village. "The return to the small village from the city," said Ashis Nandy in commenting on a Gandhi-like bucolic trend in Indian thought, "is frequently the search for an alternative cosmopolitanism. That cosmopolitanism possesses a place for the humble vernacular, commonly incompatible with the iconography of the Nation-State, with the compulsions of the global market, with the demands of global knowledge industry."[33] Indeed, many would have preferred to reach the revolutionary world that Mexico City represented without the city itself. They did not seem to know that the city was not a neutral space that they simply visited, inhabited, something that they had or wore. The city was something that had them, something they indeed were or became. Their denial of the city was their strongest affirmation of what the city meant. When they escaped the city they expanded it, they took it within themselves to Coyoacán, to Tepoztlán, or to New York.

The dislike of the city was consubstantial to the rejection of the city's own intelligentsia by the advocates of the Brown Atlantis. Unless they suffered a Rivera-like transformation the city's intellectuals were seen as too French, or too Western. 1900s progressive journalists in Mexico such as J. K. Turner or John Reed, or radical U.S. slackers in 1920s Mexico City, or U.S. and European intellectuals in 1930s Mexico shared the same basic complaint: too much of Mexico's intelligentsia was urban, too concerned with Nietzsche, Paul Valéry, Henri Bergson, Francisco de Quevedo, or Émile Zola, and not concerned enough with the "real" Mexico, the small towns and the great ancestral traditions of the country. In July 1931 Hart Crane wrote to Waldo Frank from Mexico City that Mexico is indeed magic, but only because of the real Indigenous people and not due to "the average mestizo." Neither Spanish poet León Felipe nor Mexican poet Genaro Estrada—whom Frank recommended to Crane as contacts—was worth the effort. They were not interested "one iota in expressing anything Indigenous; rather they are busy aping (as though it could be done in Spanish), Paul Valéry, Eliot." The same thought occurred to Stuart Chase and Edward Weston. Of course Diego Rivera shared these sentiments, busy in the late 1920s making himself into the archetype of the real—racially, culturally, revolutionarily—Mexican artist. Thus he wrote to his biographer, Bertram Wolfe, his views of other Mexican artists like Orozco: "Criollo que dice que en un pueblo de indios se siente como en China" (a criollo who claims that in an Indigenous town he feels like he's in China), who better expressed the spirit of the city than that of the real Mexico. Rivera used the opposition to the city and its un-Mexican intellectuals to make himself—a man who lived in Paris and Mexico City almost all of his life—the real Mexican artist.[34]

By the 1930s, however, the citizens of Mexico City had long been aware of the world's search for a Brown Atlantis in their city. Both the city's intellectuals and common people knew that the Brown Atlantis did not exist, but were also aware that many still looked for it. In the city, at least since the 1900s, photojournalism, bohemian life, vaudevilles, essay writers, and cartoons mocked the seekers of the Brown Atlantis. Salvador Novo's sarcasm often mocked foreign luminaries in Mexico City as either overly perturbed or overly enchanted with urban beggars. Many cartoons and jokes took the exotic fetish of Mexico in the city for their subject matter. One, by an artist known as Fa-Cha in the popular periodical *Revista de Revistas* (1934), best embodies this lasting mockery. The cartoon is a collage of many emblematic Brown Atlantis moments: an elegant woman painting a "typical" Mexican woman carrying a baby on her back— "Wait a minute!," says the painter (in English), while the "authentic" woman answers in Mexico City's language: "¿Ya acabó 'aste? Ya se me tulleron los pieses." It is impossible to translate the rich class, ethnic, and cultural connotations of "aste," "tulleron," and "pieses," but it approximates "Have you finished? My feet already have fallen asleep." In another scene a local character speaking city slang says, "I sold my *cuete* to a gringo" (*cuete* meaning pistol in the city's slang), and "told him that it was Villa's."[35] The reader should bear this irony in mind when reading the dissection of the Brown Atlantis.

6. On the High Maintenance that the Brown Atlantis Has Demanded, and on How Race, Again, and Revolution Made It So Strong and Lasting

Mexico City—as the capital of an Atlantis for a world's generation of travelers, activists, and artists—often shows itself to the historian as an escape from home, industrialism, persecution of socialists or pacifists, from the decadence of the West, and from a lost community. By the 1920s Mexico City was a refuge and a reliable escape, not only from the draft in New York City or from the Great Depression, but also from Mexico City itself. The escape continued toward Tepoztlán or Tehuantepec, wherever the city was not, for as a utopia of harmony and beauty the Atlantis was inevitably conceived in the city without being urban.

The Atlantis demanded evasion to exist, demanded the search for authenticity vis-à-vis the fakeness surrounding modern daily life, especially modern life in places like Mexico condemned—by modern Western thought—to be immune to modernity. Every new discovery in the search for authenticity needed to be authenticated, and this authentication was in fact the living and building of the Brown Atlantis. Every new traveler, every new radical, and every new artist claimed his or her Atlantis to be the true one. Thus there were many contradictions and conflicts among intellectuals and artists in Mexico City during the 1920s and 1930s. Some claimed the real utopia to be a communist one, against the revisions of some soft petit bourgeoisie. Others claimed to be authentic discoverers of Mexico, as opposed to either fake idealizers or insurgent bashers of Mexico.

But something kept the many evasions, authenticities, and discoveries that the Brown Atlantis implied together, something as strong as two fundamental certainties that merged in Western thought between the 1880s and the 1900s—race and revolution. Mexico became a lasting Atlantis, but above all it was a Brown Atlantis. Race makes the Brown Atlantis intelligible to us inhabitants of the twenty-first century in a way that, for instance, Johan Huizinga's account of medieval pessimism does not.[36]

Race made the Brown Atlantis something that could be mapped in space, in time, and in human evolution: Mexico the nation-state, whose racial composition made it more visible to the world than anything modern cartography could offer. Entering Mexico was above all to enter not a physical territory, but a racial dimension in which purity and hybridism, difference and longings, evasions and discoveries, were possible. In Mexico City itself Mexican intellectuals had long thought of the nation in racial terms, either in the prize of the mestizo and the whitening hopes sustained by Porfirian intellectuals, or in the mestizofilia and indigenismo of postrevolutionary ideologues. It is thus in terms of racial differences, dreams, and obsessions—rather than in hectares—that we ought to measure the territory of the Brown Atlantis. This made it a ductile territory both spatially and temporally.

The most enduring version of a Brown Atlantis, one that synthesized a century of views and prejudices about Mexico while adding new modernist longings and revolutionary utopias, was articulated in Mexico City between 1920 and 1940 by Mexican and foreign activists and intellectuals alike. This version took advantage of the moment, the streets, comfort, bohemia, and rich cultural environment that the city offered. For that Brown Atlantis dictated race, true race, which was furnished only by authenticity, discovery, and an evasion from oneself and all modern things. Thus the Brown Atlantis was an urban entelechy that doggedly referred to *campo*, *milpa*, sombrero, sarape, fiesta, pueblito, and *communities* (that sacrosanct term of modernist English that still enchants us). Yet those were precisely the things that the city (or any city) was not. That is why the Brown Atlantis was especially visible in urban personalities. It was Stuart Chase living in Mexico City, but talking about Tepoztlán. Or it was Gamio in Mexico City, or Columbia University, writing about Teotihuacán. Or it was poet Hart Crane getting drunk in downtown Mexico City, searching for lovers among the city's brown male servants (and brown meant Indian for him), only to then search for poetic inspiration in Taxco or Tepoztlán when writing a poem on the Conquista.

Revolution was the ingredient that merged with race in the 1910s, and did so in an era in which revolutions acted as vanguards and utopias of the political, social, and aesthetic. The result was an extremely powerful synthesis, both politically and aesthetically. Modernist enchantments and disenchantments, as well as early twentieth-century aesthetic innovation, blended with socialist, communist, populist, and anarcho-syndicalist criticisms and their attendant utopias. The Brown Atlantis thus acquired lasting connotations that still survive in contemporary conceptions of Mexico. It brought us to a dimension of rural things, of communities and small towns, preferably Indigenous, anchored in one vision or another of racial atavism. Of course the Atlantis was extremely cosmopolitan, but it was militantly nativist. This was not an idea conceived by Indigenous people—the cities of God constructed in the many *parroquias* and *confradías* within Mexico City, and the entire country, for nearly three centuries were more "Indigenous"—but it was actively *indigenista*. The Brown Atlantis hated the city, yet needed it in the same way that it accepted *mestizaje* by necessity while dreaming of purity and permanence. Finally, the Brown Atlantis implied a certain enchantment with limited violence, the kind involved in any revolutionary change, the kind required to make justice, the kind inevitable to an Atlantis always made of racial subjects on the verge of miscegenation.

7. In Conclusion, on Who on Earth the Inhabitants of the Brown Atlantis Were

Yes, who were they? Were they a bunch of intellectuals? In fact, if we take "inhabiting" in a literal sense the answer is "no one." The Brown Atlantis had no material existence. However, when trying to discern the meaning of the very term "Mexico" it is fair to say that the inhabitants of that mythic Brown

Atlantis were not only a bunch of intellectuals, living decades ago, but also still includes us all today. In eloquent Spanish, one of those U.S. intellectuals from the 1930s who participated in the lasting articulation of the Brown Atlantis, Lesley Simpson, put things in a nutshell in the introduction to the 1970s translation of his landmark book, *Many Mexicos*: "As a theme of discussion Mexico presents such emotional charge that it does not leave the specialist a mental refuge removed from the extremes of love and hate."[37] This emotional charge is the legacy of the Brown Atlantis. If it is about feeling the confines of the Brown Atlantis, I kindly ask the reader to consider whatever Mexico currently means in the world. The reader could easily discover herself an inhabitant of a Brown Atlantis that efficiently linked race and revolution with fiesta, siesta, sombrero, pistolas, Diego Rivera, Frida Kahlo, and pyramids. Mexico, the name, has not as yet become independent from its Brown Atlantis connotations.

TRANSPARENCY

There was once an imaginary Brown Atlantis that nevertheless counted on a material capital—Mexico City. Thus the Atlantis's silhouette comes into sight as a hologram hidden in the many images and no-images made of the city between the 1880s and the 1940s. In order to decode, as it were, the hologram and show the imaginary contours of the Brown Atlantis—alas fleetingly, for its outline no sooner reveals than fuses into a mass of conventional truths about Mexico—, I examine variegated realms of images: Bodies, Unurban Panoramas, Pulquerías, Children, the City as Souvenir, Actual Urban Scenes, Women, Impersonations, Unmissable Sin, the City Imposing Its Presence, and The City at Last for Poets Know Better.

What follows deals with all sorts of photos, paintings, drawings, and narratives, but from the outset it needs to be stated: before 1950, the foreign photographers and artists who observed the city rarely directed their eyes to their own backs or their own feet; that is, to the city that hosted them all regardless of their trips to towns around the nation. Mexican photography itself of course had a different trajectory—the city and photos were born together. There were thus the works of a growing number of Mexican urban reporters and photojournalists in the 1910s representing the actual city in the city's media. Unlike media during the Porfirian regime, newspapers from the 1920s and 1930s made the entire city, including its morally unacceptable parts, the principal subject of their reporting. The work of Manuel and Lola Álvarez Bravo, Nacho López, Agustín Jiménez, and Juan Guzmán (Hans Gutman) perhaps best expresses these urban views during the late 1940s and through the 1950s.[1]

There were, however, important exceptions for foreign photographers and artists. Some of the works—but not the most important part of his Mexican portfolio—by Henri Cartier-Bresson in 1934, some pictures by Edward Weston in 1922 (who photographed patios and flat roofs), and Tina Modotti's images of meetings and workers' organizations in the city. Robert Capa, the great photographer of the Spanish Civil War, also spent six months in Mexico City during 1940 drinking in Hotel Montejo and, trapped in a contested election, capturing images of repression and violence against supporters of presidential candidate General Almazán. The images were published in *Life*.[2] There were also images taken by journalists and tourists coughing in the 1913 fire of the *decena trágica* in Mexico City—dead bodies, a mountain of corpses burning, street barricades, and damaged buildings. But, of course, when the city was reduced to violence, barricades, death, and armed sombrero-people, the city became the Brown Atlantis. And in 1941, Helen Levitt, as I will show, did become one of the most telling foreign photographers who truly found the city worth depicting.[3] But even today international images of Mexico tend to avoid Mexico City, with its pollution and lack of Indigenous flavor.[4] Simply by searching Internet sites in English, French, or German about Mexico will the reader see what I mean.

Bodies

All views of the city began with the specific argument that even though the city was not really Mexico, too cosmopolitan and Westernized, there were some things worth seeing. "Mexico City might be described," explained a 1909 guide book, "as a sort of Americanized Madrid," since all its new buildings, including those that followed art-nouveau trends, were contracted to U.S. companies. It was anticlimactic to find so much familiarity in a place that was supposedly an escape.[5] C. B. Waite's endlessly reproduced photographs included some shots of Mexico City, especially *cargadores*, monuments, empty streets, toreros, cockfights, archaeological museum halls, sombrero and pottery stores, and street peddlers (figure 6.1).[6]

This kind of invisibility, cloaked by the lure of the exotic within the city, was common. If we are to avoid pages and pages of *cargadores*, toreros, and sombrero stores, allow me to present later versions of the same images: for instance, Herbert Cerwin's 1947 image of a *cargador* in Mexico City (figure 6.2). The image was a common nostalgic focus of the old city, not an image representing the present.

Mexican artists, of course, depicted *cargadores*, but as a way to capture the city. Sometime in the 1900s Germán Gedovius painted "Cargador," but the canvas studied facial expressions: a sad gaze, the depiction of poverty and overwork, and nothing to do with the circus-like fixation on the *cargador* as a human mule. And in 1922 García Cabral reproduced a similarly structured collage of the city's old water fountain and a water carrier interpreted with nostalgia.

In García Cabral's case it was simply urban nostalgia for the colonial city, but what about the many actual *cargadores*, captured by foreign views? Was this

6.1. *Cargador* in Mexico City, circa 1904, by C. B. Waite.
Courtesy Archivo General de la Nación, Mexico.

6.2. *Cargador.* Herbert Cerwin, *These Are the Mexicans*
(New York: Reynal & Hitchcock: 1947).

simply to contrast modern urban scenes and ancient forms of transportation, to compare industrial production and sombreros? What explains this invisible city behind the *cargadores* and sombreros? The Atlantis was above all brown, a brownness matched with backwardness and atavism, as well as particular views of the brown body. Sombreros, brown bodies, and *calzones blancos* were part of the same rhetorical package. "Although there are mules and burros in great numbers," reads a popular travel account from 1907, "the *cargador* is still the great burden bearer and takes the place of the fast freight in the commerce of the sections away from the railway lines. A traveler can take his mule and send his baggage by a *cargador*, and the latter would reach the same stopping place each night and some times ahead of the man on the mule."[7]

In 1886 J. Hendrickson McCarty, a Protestant clergyman, found Mexico City to be "the Paris of the western world," but went on to add that the city was full of ignorant Aztecs who did not understand English, and stupidly responded to all questions with "*sí señor.*" "Do you know that you are a very stupid Aztec?," he told a servant. "Sí señor, was his courteous reply." Stupid Aztecs ignorant of English, for they should speak . . . what? Aztec? Spanish? Of course Mc-Carty saw *cargadores*, finding in them as many did after him an atavist Mexican nature: "It is an actual fact, amply vouched for, that after making long trips thus heavily loaded, on their return they will fill their baskets with stones, their striven and distorted muscles seeming to require the burden to which they had been accustomed."[8]

The city itself disappeared, swamped by the obsession with brown bodies. Any brown body was considered Indigenous by cultural decree, an erotic fascination that is present in the very image of the *cargador*. Charles Macomb Flandrau's *Viva Mexico!* (1908) put it clearly: Mexicans look like "home-made cigars" at first sight, but if one looks closer, "there is among all classes an extraordinary amount of beauty." He found the strength of their small, brown "effeminate" bodies remarkable: "However great may their muscular development be from trotting up and down perpendicular mountain trails with incredible loads of corn, or pottery, or tiles, or firewood, or human beings on their backs, the muscles themselves never stand out." The contrast was shaped vis-à-vis familiar bodies:

> The legs of an American "strong man" look sensually like an anatomical chart, but the legs of the most powerful Totonac Indian—and the power of many of them is beyond belief—would serve admirably as one of those idealized extremities in which women's hosiery is displayed . . . There is in the general aspect of their physique more of prettiness than of vigor, more grace than virility.[9]

To be sure these could be considered the opinions of some travelers. But when considering the contentions in the context of a major city in the 1900s or in the 1930s, and when one adds the hundreds of images of *cargadores* that were taken until the 1950s, then the reader may conclude that this obsession was indeed a deep-rooted sensual and racial fixation. Unfortunately, this was not very different from the more sophisticated views of the modernist inhabitants and creators of the Brown Atlantis, like poet Hart Crane. In a letter to an unknown recipient, Crane wrote from Mexico City:

The nature of the Mexican Indians, as Lawrence said, isn't "sunny," but he is more stirred by the moon, if you get what I mean, than any type I've ever known. The fluttering gait and the powder puff are unheard of here, but that doesn't matter in the least. Ambidexterity is all in the fullest masculine tradition. I assure from many trials and observations. The pure Indian type is decidedly the most beautiful animal imaginable, including the Polynesian—to which he often bears a close resemblance. And the various depths of rich coffee brown, always so clear and silken smooth, are anything but negroid.[10]

Cargadores and bodies are inseparable, constituting a race, a body, an obsession, and desire. Crane went to Mexico City to find his Brown Atlantis precisely because the Taos intellectual mafia told him that Indian men in Mexico were as sexually accessible as Turkish men. The same obsession showed, as late as the 1940s, in German-American photographer Fritz Henle's view of Mexico—subsidized by the Mexican government—that included few views of Mexico City. He too believed that the real Mexico existed outside Mexico City, sharing what had been a common view since, for instance, 1886: "the Mexican character is a compound of Indian stolidity and Castilian haughtiness, with him change is slow, time has no meaning to him."[11] However, Henle did include a picture of a native in a pool, repeating the sensual fascination with the authentically Mexican male body.[12]

Unurban Panoramas

The city itself remained obscure. In 1878 Albert Zabriskie Gray, a traveler whose orientalist credentials were verified as the author of *The Land and the Life, or Sketches and Studies in Palestine*, drew views of the city according to its well-known colonial profile, emphasizing downtown and the Spanish character of the city.[13] Jasper T. Moses, the director of the Presbyterian Institute in Monterrey, represented these modern views of the city when he included a chapter on street scenes in his 1909 book *Today in the Land of Tomorrow: Sketches of Life in Mexico*. The scenes were parades, picturesque images of burros, and what appeared to the author to be native people. The images also included new buildings in the fancy Porfirian city, completely devoid of people, and scenes of important busy streets, but with people lacking personality and not even looking toward the camera.[14]

Frequently, the repeated images of the city in the many books about Mexico were panoramas demonstrating a longing for the rural. In Mexico City itself an urban view of the city had been developing in the media and in the scientific literature for a long time. In the 1900s several important Mexican publications showed panoramas, like that produced by the Ciudad de México balloon in 1910. Although these common panoramas of the city were devoid of people, they were nevertheless truly urban in that they lacked the stereotypical views of volcanoes and the longing to escape urban greed and flat roofs. Although Mexicans participated in their own exoticization, they resisted a rural view of the urban.

U.S. writer Charles Morris's travels in early revolutionary Mexico ironically paralleled the Ciudad de México balloon image. In his *The Story of Mexico* (1914) he included a rare view of Juárez Avenue with many automobiles, a *charro*-like person, and many urban dwellers, as well as a balloon flying in the horizon. No attempt to ruralize Mexico City, but the caption left no doubt of his intention to contradict dominant views of Mexico: "This broad and beautiful Avenida Juárez in the city of Mexico, with its handsome buildings and a long line of automobiles, is something of a revelation to those who are accustomed to thinking of Mexico as a crude and barbarous country. Note the balloon in the upper part of the picture."[15] Another urban landscape appeared in *La Semana Ilustrada* (figure 6.3), a beautiful Mexican scene of urban melancholia.

Works by famous citizens of the Brown Atlantis—Frank Tannenbaum, Carleton Beals, Anita Brenner, Stuart Chase, Rosa E. King— had very few images of the city. Exceptions include Covarrubias's cartoon of a labor strike and factory in Tannenbaum's *Peace by Revolution*. Rivera's illustration in Chase's book included one single view of the city (see chapter 5).[16] Once again, as in many other metaphors, the Brown Atlantis was confined to race and revolution; urban motifs were either insufficiently brown, or insufficiently revolutionary, or both.

As the capital of a Brown Atlantis, Mexico City was acceptable to foreign eyes as long as it fed the images of an ancient civilization. The 1860s depiction of Mexico City in the travel account by J. W. von Müller—a distinguished German naturalist whose accounts of Africa and Mexico were widely read—was a sort of urban mirage of Baghdad in the midst of a bucolic landscape (figure 6.4).[17] As late as the 1930s a popular travel guide included an illustration in which the city appeared as the mirage of a Brown Atlantis, in the process of being discovered by Cortés and his allied Indian soldiers (figure 6.5). Entire maps of the country, spread throughout countless books, in which the city is smaller than Oaxacan pottery or pyramids, fit the commonplaces of the Brown Atlantis. This was the case even with books by radical writers like Frances Toor and Anita Brenner. The city became only fiesta and sombrero (figure 6.6).[18]

6.3. Urban landscape. From *La Semana Ilustrada* (September 9, 1910).

Pulquerías and Other Urban Attractions

Pulquerías (*cantinas* where *pulque*, the traditional alcoholic beverage of central Mexico, was sold) and *fiestas* (bullfights, the burning of Judas, or cockfights) were also common urban images. The names of *pulquerías*, as well as the paintings on their walls, became common points of reference. Late nineteenth-century travel books mentioned the strange names of *pulquerías*, and in 1913

6.4. J. W. von Müller's view of Mexico City. From *Reisen in den Vereinigten Staaten, Canada und Mexico*, vol. 1 (Leipzig: F. A. Brockhaus, 1864–65).

Nervin O. Winter listed names like "Delight of cactus," "The seventh heaven," "The food of gods," "La *cruda* [hangover] of Juan Bautista," and "The retreat of the Holy Ghost." Writer Stephen Crane wrote about them in his Mexican short stories, and even Edward Weston made endless lists of the names he read in the *pulquerías* on the streets. Weston was taken in by the irony and wit of the names, attracted and repelled by the establishments themselves, full of the race and authenticity that he (and many other travelers) were looking for. (Unfortunately the places themselves stank: "I have always had the desire," he wrote, "to frequent the *pulquerías*, to sit down with the Indians, drink with them, make common cause with them," but "most of them are dirty!") In turn, Hart Crane was convinced, in 1931, that he was the only American present at the ceremony of the emergence of *pulque* in Tepoztlán.

In the early 1930s, artists of the Mexican vanguard considered it fashionable to paint the walls of *pulquerías*, which thus became a Mecca, a rite of passage, for young artists. In the Brown Atlantis ideology, consumed throughout the world, *pulquerías* were a picturesque aspect of the city and rarely problematized. The most illuminating image of a *pulquería* is from British journalist R. J. Mac-Hugh. In 1913 MacHugh, after following the Serbian army in the Balkan War, was sent by *The Daily Telegraph* to cover Mexico. His picture of a *pulquería* shows

6.5. From Leonidas Willing Ramsey, *Time Out for Adventure: Let's Go to Mexico* (Garden City, N.Y.: Doubleday, Doran & Co., 1934).

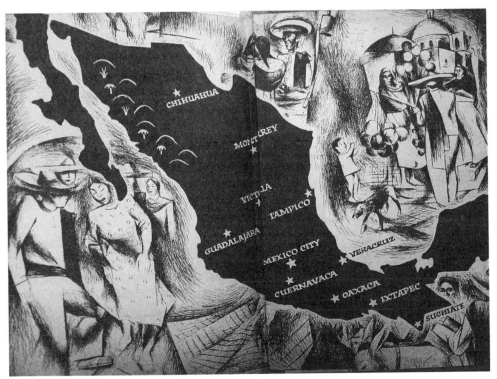

6.6. Max Miller, *Mexico Around Me* (New York: Reynall & Hitchcock, 1937).

the porch with men, women, children, ordered and clean, looking to the camera. *Pulquerías* stood for Indigenous people, backwardness, tradition, drunkenness, and delusion; nothing was more suitable for the Brown Atlantis.[19]

Here, however, is where the views of Manuel Álvarez Bravo, and especially of Helen Levitt, show the real contrast between looking at the city with the eyes of the Brown Atlantis and looking at it with the same urban eyes one would use to look at New York. Levitt came to Mexico City in 1941, living on Sonora Street in Colonia Roma. She went to Mexico with Alma Agee (and later Uhse and Neuman) and her son. Levitt went to Mexico to see city, as she would do with New York for decades; Agee was in the city escaping from the abandonment of her husband, the famous James Agee of *Let Us Now Praise Famous Men*.[20] In Levitt's images of *pulquerias* from 1941 there are none of the typical sombreros, no clean or picturesque views, just human misery, drunkenness, women, men, and children. There is life, urban ugly life, in the pictures. Small wonder then that these images were not published or included in the many books about Mexico as Brown Atlantis produced during this period. In fact they were not published until the 1990s, thanks to the efforts of historian James Oles (figures 6.7 and 6.8).[21]

What Levitt accomplished in black-and-white photographs had been done before in narrative colors, though difficult to understand for the majority of the city's inhabitants because they were written in Yiddish. To see the city as I. Berliner did one needs, of course, to be a poet, but also to walk it as he did working as a door-to-door salesman. What is needed above all is the conviction that the city is an escape with no escape. It had to be a Jewish poet who saw the brilliant dirt of the city, one who came to Mexico because, as many others did, he was unable to reach the U.S. due to immigration quotas. Berliner was a Jew with no other place to escape to. As M. Rosenberg wrote in the introduction to Berliner's *Shtot fun palatsn* (City of palaces), "It was the wind that had uprooted it from its home and had brought it hither. And here, in the desert of all places, the seed grew and bloomed." In his poems, Berliner did with a *pulquería* what Levitt did with her photos:

> Two half-doors balance at the opening of two thick licking lips
> impure mouth emitting pestilential odors into the intricate streets
> and inside, Juan and his friend drink from the same pitcher.

Berliner captured the city's misery, but also its creative and obscene irony. He did so with a humor that only a connoisseur of the city's language could capture in the walls and words of a *pulquería*:

6.7. *Pulquería*. Helen Levitt (1941). © Estate of Helen
Levitt. Courtesy Laurence Miller Gallery, New York.

A poster on the wall: a naked woman plays a lyre with her fingers
Juan holds up a clay pitcher in his impure hand, on the wall, her glassy
    look.
And he says: Believe me, brother, no kidding,
I'm ready to exchange my blabbermouth of a wife for that frisky
    whore right this minute.

Levitt's and Berliner's views were, of course, by and large ignored because they
documented something other than the Brown Atlantis.[22]

Cargadores, pulquerías, buildings, landscapes, and monuments constituted
the city for many travelers, regardless of the date of their visit or their ideological position. These motifs are found continuously in graphic and narrative records. Tramps, though mentioned regularly by all sorts of observers, were rarely
represented graphically. "One of the worst features of Mexico City," wrote Carson, "is the swarm of beggars, who constitute a serious nuisance. Filthy, dirty
and truly worthy of the title 'Verminous persons,' the lame, the halt, the blind,
and able bodied rogues and vagrants are encountered almost everywhere, de-

6.8. Children. Helen Levitt. © Estate of Helen Levitt.
Courtesy Laurence Miller Gallery, New York.

manding centavos."[23] Between 1870 and 1940 the presence of beggars regularly disturbed everyone from common travelers like Carson, to radicals such
as M. N. Roy, Charles Phillips, and Bertram Wolfe, to acute observers like
Clare Sheridan, Edward Weston, and Graham Greene. The radical cartoonist
Hendrik (Henry) Glintenkamp, working for *The Masses*, captured urban characters for the English section of *El Heraldo* (1919), but not the beggar. Beggars

were not picturesque characters. In a modern Catholic metropolis, beggars were an institution linked to the visual performance of pity and suffering, a performance unacceptable for many foreign visitors. Glintenkamp's characters were thus less arresting—"*La placera*," "Tortilla Vendor," "*El papelero*," and of course the "Burden bearer," "*El chamaco*," and "*Azteca*" (simply a woman from the streets of Mexico). Glintenkamp soon after dedicated his work to depicting small towns and rural people, leaving urban characters to rest in peace.

Children

The *chamaco*, however, was not just Glintenkamp's atypical depiction of a street boy in Mexico City. Something about the city made the presence of children unmistakable to its many visitors.[24] Children were often part of the composition of the modern clashing with the traditional, or the racial casta painting images produced by photographers and artists. Female street peddlers were often shown with their children, and racial classifications of faces, families, and groups included children to show how a particular race looked in childhood. Important illustrators, such as René D'Harnoncourt and Miguel Covarrubias, painted images of little brown girls and boys with beautiful big black eyes, *rebozos*, white *calzón de manta*, and petit sombreros. There is even a series of books from the 1930s on Mexican children with photos and illustrations, but rarely did these books include children that were openly and explicitly urban. Marion Lay (wife of the 1932 Guggenheim fellow in Mexico City, H. L. Davis), Stella Burke May (U.S. travel writer and journalist), Anne Merriman Peck (U.S. traveler and painter), and Catharine U. Stoker (U.S. children-stories writer) published books with images of Mexican children. The images in most of the foreign books avoided disturbing images of urban children, even though the children they depicted very likely lived in the city. The depictions were picturesque and frequently staged with costumes and postures. Peck's children functioned as part of a larger imaginary package. The children could be in a traditional Mexican kitchen, accompanying Indian-looking mothers, *ollas*, *sopladores*, and *comales*. They could be burden carriers, or children staged with old plows and *milpa*, or children with *metate*, cacti, and tortillas.

The urban child in the street was both disturbing and appealing to foreigners. Poverty and childhood were disturbing because they provoked sympathies in observers, many mothers and fathers themselves, and yet appealing because children tempted them to find even more authenticity, even more of the unspoiled other, in what were already authentic and pristine characters. Poet Mina Loy felt in 1918 the challenge of urban children: "One leans praying against a wall, a naked child sits straight up between his legs, has little arms crossed on his chest as children beg here, his sleeping eyes upturned to the morning sun . . .

The nirvana of infancy, the state before understanding."[25] When breaking with Roberto Haberman in 1924, Bertram Wolfe used the image of children to contradict Haberman's pro-Calles view of Mexico as a socialist paradise. (However, at the time Wolfe never published anything about this, doing so only in his 1981 memoirs.) He told Haberman that the Mexico City he found, a city full of homeless boys, was far from a socialist paradise, and thus he would not write propaganda essays for him. His depiction, however, makes clear that children were indeed present in the minds of so many seekers of the Brown Atlantis: "homeless boys . . . begging and picking pockets by day, and tearing down billboards after nine o'clock . . . sleeping on the sidewalk with nothing but the billboards to lie on, and perhaps a flea-corroded dog to wrap in."[26]

The ironic fascination with children, when the common urban child was invisible in the writings of many expatriates in Mexico City between 1920 and 1940, is especially striking if we consider the many visitors who left children behind, got pregnant in Mexico, or had abortions in Mexico City. Mina Loy, Alma Neuman (Agee), and Anita Brenner all left children behind, taking Mexico City's great offer of cheap servants. Bohemian Mexico City, in part about love and passions and betrayals among radicals and avant-garde artists, often meant babies, wanted or not depending on the situation. Frida's obsession with getting pregnant contrasted with Katherine Anne Porter's abortion in that city of young radicals and children everywhere. Neuman, like Edward Weston or Clare Sheridan for a short while, brought a child with her. Sheridan's photo of her son in a creek at Molino del Rey during a fancy picnic with Mexico City's elites makes an interesting aesthetic statement for a liberated female sculptor who traveled everywhere with her son.[27] The foreigners could not be indifferent to the urban children, so they compensated by making them inhabitants of the ideal Brown Atlantis.

Urban children had been an important social and artistic subject of Mexican scientists, journalists, and artists since the late nineteenth century. This preoccupation is linked to the emergence of social science in the city and of the welfare state. However, it is important to distinguish between idealized views of urban children and revealing views of the diversity and beauty of children in a booming city. For instance, the cover of the fancy magazine Arte y Letras in 1914 reproduced, in color, an image of "tipos nacionales" embodied in a little girl carrying a baby. This was an approach to urban poverty and children quite similar to foreign views. However, it is important to note, it was published in one of the city's worst years of hunger and poverty. The child in the photo might have been one of the many children who followed the revolutionary troops. The aesthetic and social composition was found in the use of colors, in capturing such an image in the city and publishing it in a highbrow literary magazine (figure 6.9).

6.9. Tipos Nacionales. Cover of *Arte y Letras* (May 16, 1914).

The 1910 *Centenario* produced simple urban scenes and records of moments of elite philanthropy, which were not meant to be explicitly about children. Nevertheless, the pictures included the faces and expressions of urban children that otherwise would not have been captured. In those pictures we find records of the faces and the expressions of poverty, yet also happiness, in the lives of Mexico City's Oliver Twists. A little boy carrying a basket on Cinco de Mayo street in overalls and a cap is particularly beautiful because he is so urban (figure 6.10). He is also very Mexican and could be an image of the coexistence of childhood and city anywhere in 1910.[28]

Curiously Tina Modotti, a young female Italian radical living in Mexico City during the 1920s and a seeker of the Brown Atlantis, saw similarly urban children. One of her photos was titled by its publishers, with an apparent lack of irony, "A Stall in the Alameda selling Indian wares": a picture of two urban children. They are a boy and a girl, poor, astute with a beautiful urban gaze possessing clear street savvy. Although the "stall" is most likely selling tourist souvenirs, rather than anything Indians would actually use, the children were indeed Mexico City. In another untitled picture circa 1926 Modotti captured the common scene of a child defecating in the streets. The picture is nothing more, just the dirty urban soil and a kid busily inspired in his labor. In another photo, Modotti produced an incredible rendition of two little urban children in front of the huge baskets used to transport vegetables and fruits in the city (figure 6.11). Although all of Modotti's pictures are from 1926, it is as if she had found the same urban little boy from 1910 in Cinco de Mayo street. Her rendition of the well-established urban boy with overalls, cap, and bare feet contrasted with the urban boy more recently arrived from the countryside, who also wore overalls but with a palm sombrero. This intriguing image references the 1910 boy of the *Centenario* and serves as a prologue to the images produced by the Spanish-exile film director Luis Buñuel in the 1940s. These renditions, however, were the lesser known of Modotti's pictures. They seem to be cast aside as urban outliers in the collective documentation of the revolutionary, radical, avant-garde Brown Atlantis.

By 1940 photojournalists in Mexico City had reported on the city's poor for two decades with children, of course, as principal subjects. A 1938 photojournalist essay in *Hoy* showed children in the streets as singers and thieves, and girls who were to become "maids or prostitutes." These are the same children who I. Berliner saw in the 1920s, writing: "Where are the mothers/of indolent children/who teem on the corners . . . ?" In the *Hoy* essay there are incredible images of children sleeping on the asphalt, standing out against very young children crossing train tracks, with a revealing caption: "No, this is not a Diego Rivera painting made for tourists. It is the reality of innocence

6.10. Little boy on Cinco de Mayo street, 1910.
Courtesy Genaro García Collection, Nettie Lee Benson Latin
American Benson Collection, The University of Texas, Austin.

6.11. Tina Modotti's Children, Mexico City—Tina Modotti, Untitled (Two Barefoot Boys with Baskets), n.d. Gelatin silver print; 3 5/8 in. × 2 3/8 in. (9.21 cm × 6.03 cm). San Francisco Museum of Modern Art. Purchased through a gift of the Art Supporting Foundation, John "Launny" Steffens, Sandra Lloyd, Shawn and Brook Byers, Mr. and Mrs. George F. Jewett, Jr., and anonymous donors.

6.12.
Photojournalist
essay, *Hoy*
(May 14, 1938).

crossing the 'trenches of life' without knowing its destination."[29] The essay
also shows street children playing the guitar while a middle-class girl on roller
skates passes through the same park—in the same city—in the background
(figure 6.12).

City as Souvenir

The city somehow forced its image beyond *cargadores*, *pulquerías*, beggars,
and children by the 1930s and early 1940s, as it became impossible to miss the
urban and social transformation it was experiencing. "Mexico" as an idea was
well-established as a world trend by the middle of the 1930s. Arts and crafts
that were considered Mexican could be found all over the world, while the city
itself retained a marginal image. The capital was still defined by great panoramas without real people, interiors, or context, lacking urban gazes toward
its urban reality. Images from the 1930s and 1940s consistently contrasted
tradition and modernity, generally with gaudy scenes where the good from
modernity gets destroyed by tradition that cannot in turn maintain its purity
from modernity. Tourism was the main leitmotif for many of these images.
Although they included information about newer hotels and the comforts of
the city, the places to visit in the city remained the same: colonial buildings
within the ideal city, the Guadalupe temple, etc. *You Must Go to Mexico: Down the
Pan American Highway* (1947) included collages of the city center taken from
flat roofs showing busy streets, cars, buses, and trucks, but—in common with
past urban vistas—lacking a sense of people.[30] That same year *This Is Mexico*,
a popular book, showed images of monuments, streets, and some factories.[31]
The new monument of the Revolution, massive and stern, contrasted with the
landscape of streets full of buses, high-rises, and non-picturesque people. The

book reproduced a view of a family including dogs and a pig, still insisting on tradition and backwardness in the midst of the big city.

Mexicans themselves produced images of a "real" Mexico meant for international tourism, blending images of the city together into the ancient, the pre-Hispanic, and the hypermodern. The combination can be seen on the cover of *Real Mexico*, a magazine produced in English in Mexico City by the Consolidated Railroad and Pullman Company (1934). The cover combines the new architecture of the city and the doggedly copied Cuauhtémoc monument, contrasted with airplanes and pyramids. As the Spanish saying goes, *al cliente lo que pida*. The same was portrayed in a magazine produced by the Mexican government, *Mexican Review*, in the 1920s. Mexico was equated with abundance, sombreros, tradition, and señoritas. Mexicans and foreigners alike produced the boundaries of the Brown Atlantis, even if they were mirages.

Unmissable Sin

One of the most interesting books in this long list of vistas of the Brown Atlantis was written by the journalist Max Miller (1899–1967), who in the early 1930s acquired a certain fame for his waterfront coverage for the *San Diego Sun*.[32] Miller's *Mexico Around Me* (1937), like all the other books by travelers and radicals, included the common images of burros and peasants. The author visited Cardenista Mexico City and found a sharp contrast between the new socialistic city and the countryside. "No special valiance is needed," he wrote, "for calling a strike in Mexico these days, since government and labor are one and the same. That is, labor in the cities. But the Indians out in the country continue carrying the loads as usual, as in the beginning." He described a May 1 parade in Mexico City as the most un-Mexican thing he saw. For Miller only the hungry Indian children were the real Mexico.

The book included illustrations by Miller's fellow San Diegan, artist Everett Gee Jackson, whose ingenious lithographs profoundly summarized the meaning of the Brown Atlantis. Jackson included in Miller's books, once again, the burros, sombreros, and "Indian" men and women, as well as neoclassical columns resembling those from the then unfinished Palacio de Bellas Artes. This collage, to be sure, is equal to the best images produced by Mexican officials and foreign travelers, with its gaudy denigration of the new and enduring embrace of the old. Somewhat uncommon in Miller's role as urban reporter was his visit to the city's slums. Like Henri Cartier-Bresson, Manuel Álvarez Bravo, José Clemente Orozco, and Manuel Rodrígues Lozano, Miller described prostitutes—city dwellers par excellence—in a saloon: "I referred to '80' [a saloon] as an intermediate between the level of a 'salon Mexico' and the Cuauhtemotzin [the city's lower-class prostitution street]." He added:

but here again I may be jumping to conclusions. Although the girls did advertise their business rather diligently while dancing, and though it is difficult for us to reconcile ourselves to such frankness while the bedrooms are so conveniently near, we did go to another place at the end of Cuauhtemotzin Street. The place is not supposed to be a "house" at all. This was a cabaret, in which the "hostesses" were not allowed to do anything under its roof except dance and collect their tips.

Miller observed a hotel sign advertising Simmons mattresses on Cuauhtemotzin Street.[33] The vistas of the Brown Atlantis rarely include depictions like the Jackson image included in Miller's book. The picture is of a prostitute on Cuauhtemotzin Street (the same street where Cartier-Bresson captured his famous 1934 photos of Mexico City), including a sign that read "Rosa" with the legend "Viva Cristo Rey," the motto of the Cristero rebellion, then in its final moments (figure 6.13). The images above all showed the sharp contrast between Catholic rectitude and the hypocrisy of urban sin. Perhaps it was also a reaction to the views of Mexico centered on the Cristero rebellion like those of Graham Greene and the Catholic U.S. priest Francis C. Kelley.[34]

These kinds of foreign views, however, were rare. They echoed the Mexican views of someone like Manuel Álvarez Bravo, photos of criminal records, Mexico City's own photojournalists, and Orozco's and Rodríguez Lozano's drawings. They touch upon an important aspect of the Brown Atlantis's borders: its women.

Women

If Indigenous male bodies were incorporated into the myth of the Brown Atlantis, the views of women were just as essential to maintaining the myth of a vivid and pristine brown space, despite the change and chaos found in the actual city. Foreign women created many of these views themselves, and the relatively high number of female foreigners writing about Mexico since Madame Calderón de la Barca is rather surprising. Emma-Lindsay Squier, Mariam Storm, Rosa King, Catherine Ulmer Stoker, Zelia Nutall, Elsie C. Parsons, Anita Brenner, Frances Toor, Laura Thompson, Ione Robinson, Alma Agee, and Clare Sheridan were among the most prominent, although all were from very different backgrounds.[35] Their work resulted in the tiringly repetitious and ethnographically sensual image of the Tehuana, as well as countless images of female peddlers, tortilleras, urbanites in rebozo surrounded by stereotypical children, and alluring female servants. Edward Weston, Ella Wolfe, Katherine Anne Porter, Alma Agee, Anita Brenner, and M. N. Roy all talked about their maids as if they had a piece of real Mexico at home thanks

6.13. Prostitute, by Everett Gee Jackson. From Max Miller,
Mexico Around Me (New York: Reynall & Hitchcock, 1937).

6.14. La criada. Sonora
News Company (private
collection, Mauricio Tenorio).

to them. Accordingly, it should come as no surprise that since the 1900s,
postcards of "criadas" were produced by the Sonora News Company (figure
6.14). Ever since the 1840s, various travelers dedicated many pages to female
servants, especially curious about their long, untied, and bright black hair. Bob
Brown, a U.S. slacker living in the city during 1919, insisted that some of the
slackers expressly aimed to sleep with the servants.[36]

There were also strong opinions about specific female roles in Mexico City,
especially as seen through submission to men and the rules of courtship. In
1897 a French traveler reported that "one should not say that the Mexican
woman is intelligent, lively, and spiritual. Far from it. But idleness is a seduc-
tive temptress."[37] Foreigners were ambivalently attracted to the stereotypical
Indigenous female body and look. It was ambivalent because, in the high valley
of Mexico, no consensus was stronger than that on the sensuality of tropical
women. There was, of course, a general dislike of high-class city women, who
only did bad impersonations of U.S. or European women.

"Most charming are the women of Mexico," read a 1902 travel book: "In physique small and delicate, with a wonderful wealth of raven black hair, in which the shadows of midnight sleep. And beautiful eyes, the light of the stars sparkling in their warm depths." The writer was so enamored that he believed "a Raphael would paint glorious pictures of womanhood in Mexico." The book, however, referred mostly to women living in small towns or tropical places. The only thing it had to say about the city itself had to do with beggars, and how they sang—in 1902!—to Dona Marina about the fall of the capital of the Aztecs. Although to my knowledge no one, not even folklorists, ever recorded the song in either the nineteenth or the twentieth century, poetic license was the right of the makers of the Brown Atlantis.

W. E. Carson's *Mexico, the Wonderland of the South* (1909) looked directly at urban women, comparing their beauty to women on New York's 5th Avenue or San Francisco Street in Mexico City, a street where no beauty could be found, "so far as the white element is concerned." Indian women were not considered very attractive, and "at present no strictly defined Mexican middle class exists, although both the upper class and what would be equivalent to the minor business classes in this country are more Moorish than European in their treatment of their sex." Carson wrote on women's issues—mainly divorce—and thus dedicated a chapter to women in Mexico in his book. However, he concluded with a rejection of elite women and a lesson on the ugliness of the lower classes. "As a rule," he wrote,

> the Mexican women are not beautiful. They are generally of medium height and slight build when young though, as they progress in years, they tend to obesity. Mexican beauties may be divided into two classes: the slight, delicate girl with big, soft black eyes, with features somewhat suggestive of the Madonna type; and a stout, voluptuous young woman.[38]

The stereotype of the serenade abounded, and the architecture of balconies for the service of sexual jealousy can be found everywhere in the city. Images of a serenade, like those of *cargadores*, were repeated from the 1880s through to the 1940s. C. B. Waite's image of a serenade is reproduced in many books since the 1900s (figure 6.15). Radical cartoonist Glintenkamp did the same with an image from 1919. In 1934 *Gringa: An American Woman in Mexico* produced a new performance of the same scene (figure 6.16).[39] Singing happened everywhere in the city, not only in conformist serenades. Street vendors, for example, sang the virtues of their products. People sang at work, and people in the streets or bars would sing.

Women and courtship serenades were a focus of the limited urban attention

6.15. C. B. Waite's serenade, Mexico City, circa 1900. Courtesy Nettie Lee Benson
Latin American Collection, The University of Texas, Austin.

6.16. Serenade, picture by John Bransby, in Emma-Lindsay Squier,
Gringa: An American Woman in Mexico (Boston: Houghton Mifflin Co., 1934).

from Mexico City's visitors. The subject combined so much together: ideas about machismo, female seclusion, and protection of virginity, as well as romantic Latin lovers. These images were, to be sure, stereotypes fed by desire, hate, and love. The emotions longed, both for brownness and for Spain, to be understood through Washington Irving's eyes.

Impersonations

The Brown Atlantis of Mexico City invited visitors to go native in a way that the more dangerous and uncomfortable small towns could not. Impersonations in Mexico City were a common habit, with foreign travelers and writers dressing like what they believed to be Mexicans, and elite Mexicans impersonating stereotypically native Mexican women or men. If the city could not offer the "real" Mexico, the "real" Mexico materialized in the fake city. A 1901 travel account proudly captures a parade in the city where modern Indians dressed like old Indians, offering the viewer a uniquely authentic experience. Both conventional travelers and avant-garde artists disliked it enormously when brown people dressed differently from how they understood brown people ought to dress. Of course, Frida Kahlo is today considered authentic, but not back in the 1920s and 1930s, when her persona was seen as a performance, as a constant impersonation of different "Indigenous" types. Dressing as Tehuanas or as *charros*, Mexicans and foreigners alike made impersonations part of their Mexican experience. English aristocrat and sculptor Clare Sheridan visited Mexico City with her young son in 1921. She dressed elegantly native, producing one of the more enigmatically modernist images from the many impersonations foreigners made in Mexico City as an evanescently modern beauty in *rebozo*.[40] Even communist activists and surrealist artists performed the ritual of going native, like U.S. activists Ella Wolfe in the 1920s and Joseph Freeman in the 1930s, Austrian painter Wolfgang Paalen in the late 1930s, John Dos Passos in the 1920s, and Robert Redfield in the early 1930s (figure 6.17).

The need to impersonate gradually became an expected part of the Mexican tourist experience. It also became a scarecrow with a life of its own, still alive today. It seems every new generation must have their Fridas and their U.S. tourist or anthropologist in native outfits.

The City Imposes Its Presence

Making Mexico City famous in the world as the capital of a mythic Atlantis while simultaneously ignoring its urban reality was profoundly ironic. But by the 1930s the city managed to impose its presence upon a few international and national writers, artists, and commentators. Year after year the city became

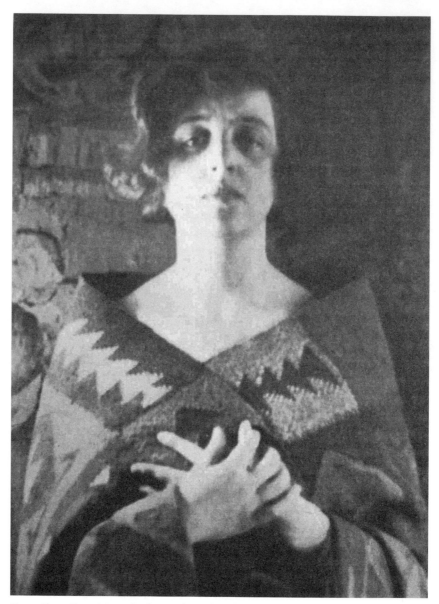

6.17. Clare Sheridan and *rebozo*. Clare Sheridan,
My American Diary (New York: Boni and Liveright, 1922).

harder and harder to ignore. Helen Levitt's 1941 photographs, as I have argued, were a real fracture. Their significance is not that the city finally became a metropolis in 1941; the city had been a city before 1941, and would remain an invisible, although indispensable, site for the myth of a Brown Atlantis. Edward Weston's son Brett compared Mexico City to others, saying in 1925, "I don't like Mexico City any better than Los Angeles, Glendale or any other city." Weston noted in his diaries, "If it is to be a city, let it be a real city, New York or San Francisco." Mexico City had been a city all along, but for visitors it had been just not Mexican enough, making it fallacious both as Mexico and as a city.[41]

Levitt came to Mexico City in 1941 and ventured outside the comfortable confines of Colonia Roma and kept her distance from the Coyoacan, Tepoztlán, and Taxco circle. Instead she went to the back to the National Palace and Lagunilla, and took pictures as she had done in New York City. The compositions are all very Mexican, all as daily life, with nothing particularly exotic about it. These incredibly urban and incredibly beautiful images of the city were never seen from any of Levitt's contemporaries, foreign artists and writers alike, except, of course, in H. Cartier-Bresson's portfolio (1934) of Mexico City (figure 6.18).

Another character who felt the call of the city was John Dos Passos. In 1926, and then in 1927 through 1928, he began his well-known interest in Mexico. His watercolors of Mexico were similar to the *tipos populares*, analogous to the racial fixation with the "real" Mexican. But Dos Passos was unique in his engagement with the city's literati. He talked about the city as a cosmopolitan center, full of people from around the world as well as Americanized—but also distinctly red—Mexican poets. He actually translated one of Maples Arce's particularly urban poems, "Urbe." Unlike Waldo Frank and Anita Brenner, who interacted with the city's intelligentsia only to document the Brown Atlantis, Dos Passos produced the only English translation of how the city's poetry existed to its inhabitants.[42]

Of course, such photographers as Edward Weston had photographed interior patios of *vecindades* in the 1920s (see chapter 3), but these *vecindades* were from Xochimilco, where quasi-anchorite Mexican artist Francisco Goitia lived and painted. However, Weston's *vecindades*, together with some of his shots of and from flat roofs, were unusual avant-garde violations of the overwhelming invisibility of the city. But more interesting were the depictions of a less well-known artist, Caroline Durieux, who came to Mexico in 1926—and left ten years later—as the wife of a General Motors representative in Mexico, Pierre Durieux. She did not look for the exotic, painting the aristocratic world she

6.18. Henri Cartier-Bresson, Mexico City (1934). © Magnum Photos.

6.19. C. Durieux, "Acolytes" (1935). Courtesy Ogden Museum of Southern Art, University of New Orleans.

lived in instead. Perhaps, as Anita Brenner argued in 1934, her aesthetic norm was just different—meaning not the then conventional *indigenista* revolutionary aesthetic. Durieux found irony in the gaudy and pretentious aspects of city life. Like García Cabral, she mocked urban life, and mockery and urban life are often one and the same. See her painting of Café Tupinanba, where Mexican and Americans businessmen went (1934); or her depiction of supreme *cursilería*, a satire of both Catholic formalities and Mexican tackiness—acolytes in a Mexico City church (1935) (figure 6.19). Her painting of a high-class interior, seen through a window, shows two bored women playing cards in a Porfirian-like interior. This was a Kurosawa-like take on Rivera's drawing in Chase's book. Instead of conceiving the scene from the point of view of a corrupt and bourgeois interior, the boring interior was seen instead by Durieux from the exiting city. Her beautiful parody of Mexican cabaret dancers is particularly revealing of Mexican popular standards of female beauty at the time.[43]

Humor was a good medium for breaking the consensus on a Brown Atlantis. It allowed Durieux to show the city as flashes of various roles in gaudy performances, showing that there was more than Indians, fiesta, sombrero, *cargadores*, and *pulquerías*. Durieux used irony and humor in the short play she sent to Anita Brenner, intended to circulate domestically among the gringos of Mexico. "Flight from Pampan, Story of a Mexican Village by Agapito Garrapata" parodied the characters of 1930s Mexico City, including Rivera (named Jesús Flaco [Jesus the Thin One]), Siqueiros, and Kitagawa (see chapter 7). It tells the story of a U.S. archaeologist discovering a lost town in the highlands of Guerrero, in which the Indians speak pidgin English and wear shorts with polo shirts. Durieux mocked the discovery and authenticity mania in the searchers for the Brown Atlantis by creating a mirror town where—finally—Americans could see what they were really doing in Mexico City.[44]

Similarly Bob Brown, writing a novel about U.S. slackers in Mexico City in 1918 and 1919 and a slacker himself, also used humor and irony as treatment of the self-importance of U.S. radicals. He, however, shared the desire for exotic and easily accessible bodies. "All [U.S. slackers in 1919 Mexico City]," he wrote,

> had sweethearts of different degrees back in America, and only a few could thoroughly satisfy themselves with the anxious-to-please quick Mexican girls who came to court and remained to eat. Born hungry for food and men in revolution times, they snatched at scraps of meat and snips of masculinity, cunning little lady animals gaily smearing their olive cheeks with egg yolks and kisses.[45]

The urban life of slackers in Mexico that Brown recalled was often marked by ideological disputes among socialists, communists, and anarchists. However, their Mexican urban experience by and large followed the path of late nineteenth-century travelers. Of course they hated the modernized and capitalist city, but they enjoyed tremendously the cheap life, servants, sin, revolution, and authenticity at hand. Many of them wrote articles and books, or drew images, about Mexico, including M. N. Roy, Charles Phillips, Bertram Wolfe, Mark Gold, and Hendrik (Henry) Glintenkamp. Almost all were radical, searching for the Brown Atlantis—except, that is, for the rare case of Evelyn Trent.

Trent was an intriguing inhabitant of the city. Originally from the U.S., she came to the city as the radical wife of M. N. Roy, the South Asian Indian who founded the Mexican Communist Party (see chapters 4 and 8). Very little information about her remains, as she slipped out of the historian's field of view after her return to the U.S. in 1925 (she died in 1970).[46] However, thanks to Evelyn's friendship with Charles Phillips, a U.S. slacker in Mexico, she was able to publish her book *Mexico and Her People* in installments. By 1919, she edited the English section of *El Heraldo*—the newspaper owned by the powerful revolutionary General Alvarado—together with Phillips, Mike Gold, Henry Glintenkamp, and others. Trent's book, almost totally unknown, sharply contrasts with the many books published by other U.S. travelers and slackers around that time. It constituted a search for an exotic utopia, but a modernist one with no idealistic endorsements, nor racial rejection or racial idealization of the Mexican Indigenous population. It was, in fact, one of the very few foreign pre-1930s books that advanced a unique, positive, and realistic view of urbanites, or what Trent called the mestizos who were, for her, the "real" Mexicans.

She called urban mestizos "the middle class," considering them real pragmatic republicans who were ready to experiment with, and appropriate, any available local or global trend. This was "the middle class which formed the unhappy link between oppressed barbarism and civilized oppressor, sharing the blood of each but belonging to neither, and whose soul awoke the first vague conception of national entity and who first called himself with a sense of pride, Mexican, in place of the opprobrious mestizo or Creole."[47] This consideration of the Mexican sharply contrasted with the common kind of "progressive" or "racist" hatred of the mestizo. Hart Crane, Stuart Chase, Robert Redfield, Antonin Artaud, Edward Weston, Carleton Beals, and all the rest disliked the mestizo as an unauthentic, urban, character. Mexican intellectuals and scientists had, for their part, been constructing an entire "mestizology" since the 1880s, realizing that Mexico was and will be either mestizo or nothing. Foreign scientists, however, followed—for different reasons—the "mestizophobia" of the radical foreign intellectuals in Mexico. In 1921 Yale professor Ellsworth Huntington, commenting on Mexico City's mortality rates, characterized the mestizo: "it is a biological law that the mixture of diverse types tends to produce extremes. This is obviously true of the mestizo. Some are completely dominated by the sluggishness of their duller Indian ancestors, while others show only the brilliant and adventuresome spirit of their best Spanish ancestors."[48] By the 1950s, the world intelligentsia had fully endorsed the great Mexican idea: *mestizaje*.

But long before, Trent observed what very few of her contemporaries witnessed in their radical Mexico City. Mexicans were not, for Trent, the stereotypical exotic characters that countless Americans, and her Bengali husband

M. N. Roy, believed them to be. She did not expect Mexico to become endlessly more Indigenous and, thus, more "real." For her the Mexican was, in fact, a pragmatic political character who tries, errs, succeeds, fails, and learns: "The Mexican of today is quick to glimpse new ideas and his mind is a receptacle for impressions from every source . . . he is not imitative." Thus, she observed, anything and everything could be found in Mexico, from the Pullman car, the electric light, and futuristic art to decadent literature and "the atheism and new thought cults that flourish in Mexico side by side with Indigenous institutions and beliefs."[49] Trent was aware of the common primitivist idealizations of Indigenous forms of life and the equally frequent racist consideration of Mexico as atavistic backwardness. Her book was meant to demystify those concepts based on a two-fold axis that, on the one hand, recognized the pragmatic empowering of urban dwellers, thus granting them the possibility of democratic national experimentation; and on the other, saw the need for a new internationalism that could stand up to the common enemies of materialism and consumerism.

A sad and yet auspicious piece of information for Trent was the fact that two neighboring countries like the U.S. and Mexico could remain so different— "a reflection upon the insular policy of each"—since "such mutually splendid isolation seems to make true internationalism remote indeed."[50] The U.S. internationalism of intellectuals like Charles Beard and Randolph Bourne could not be realized with either reactionary U.S. policies toward Mexico or with Mexico's strong nationalism, and especially not with exoticist views of Mexico. Cultural protectionism had value, but a common destiny ought to be found for Mexico and the U.S. in the long run. Trent's Mexico City was, in sum, very different from both the common *indigenismo* of Mexicans and the exoticism of other Americans.

The City at Last for Poets Know Better

The city had been a city for a long time, but by the 1940s the urban transformation was all too conspicuous. This is not to say that by the 1940s the city was impossible to miss. As we have seen, the city would be invisible for many whether in 1910 or in the 1950s. In the late 1930s through the 1940s Mexico City became a capital of various exiles. Many Spaniards reached the city after escaping the Nationalists' victory in the Civil War. Among them were great urban observers, like Juan Rejano, who escaped the Brown Atlantis: "I am not seeking the picturesque, nor the exotic. I couldn't care less about that [*Eso me trae sin cuidado*]. I seek the city itself, that which, in the simplest and most naked part of the city, can reveal to us the sole image of its intimacy."[51] He could write about the end of picturesque Mexico. To walk Juárez Avenue, he argued, was to encounter cars and shops, Hungarians, Chinese, U.S., Spanish, and Germans. "Where?" he asked, "Where is the serape, and the rugged sombrero, and the *charro* embroidery?"[52]

The city had always been there; it was a matter of will to see it or ignore it. A Catholic poet, Joan Sales, saw in the 1940s the city as Berliner and other foreign poets did: an ugly but indispensable human refuge. Like Berliner, he wrote in an uncommon language (Catalan). "Night at Mexico City" (title originally in English) portrays the urban metamorphosis between night and early morning, the closest available metaphor between chaos and cosmos. "The city, when touched by night, transfigures itself," reads the poem. Little by little the night city opens like an enormous fruit that "worms have worked from the inside." The fruit, a city, is rich in "larvae lives and secret labyrinths." The city provides beautiful infernos at night for the rich and the poor. But,

Del crepuscle diürn la mirada malsana
demà descobrirà, per tota la ciutat,
els veterans del pulque i de la mariguana
estesos pels carrers com després d'un combat.

Tomorrow, in the early twilight,
the unhealthy gaze will determine, all around the city,
veterans of *pulque* and marijuana
spread out in the streets as if after combat.

The city at night thus becomes the chaos that allows for the appreciation of the early morning cosmos. Sales experienced Mexico City's unique summer storms, describing prostitutes, urban life, hope, desire, and tragedy in the rain. But for this survivor of the Spanish Civil War the city was above all a truce between the tragedies of the past and the insecurities of the future. There is no exoticism in finding the "gaze that has made us" in the city:

Senyor, fins la virtut ens és un egoisme
    que masteguem molt en secret
i ens va seguint pertot l'Absurd—antic abisme
    a la mida de Qui ens ha fet.[53]

Lord, even virtue is for us a selfishness that we chew very much in secret
and follows us throughout the Absurd—ancient abysm
made to measure that who has made us.

Indeed, to dwell historically outside the boundaries of the capital demanded by the Brown Atlantis, one needs to return to insightful observers such as Micrós or Salvador Novo, Saturnino Herrán, Nacho López, A. Jiménez, Juan Guzmán (Hans Gutman), or the many photojournalists. Yet in thinking through the city seen by foreign eyes between 1920 and 1940 my mind goes back to poems, to those by Sales, I. Berliner, and two other Yiddish poets in Mexico City between 1920 and 1960, J. Glantz and M. Glikowski. Somehow they were equipped with a sense of their own fragility, allowing them to realize how knowing a city is to feel its cruelty beyond utopias: "O city of the muddy puddles" (Berliner):

> So many generations have tread upon your body
> and you have endured all the more, loathed and withered
> . . .
> and now, in each house one of your tears is a tenant.

To see past the Brown Atlantis more than just a mental escape was necessary. The first generation of Jewish survivors in Mexico was less concerned with the racial profile of others than with their own. "We were white," recalled a Lithuanian woman, "for them we were like something new" ("Éramos blancos, para ellos éramos como nuevos"). The father of Jack Kalb stayed in Mexico City because no one called him a "Yid." Another Jew from Aleppo recalled that many Jews back in Syria looked toward Mexico City because there were electric light and freedom.[54] David Zabludovsky, who came from Bialystok to Mexico City in 1925, learned stories of poor Jews in his hometown in La Merced while selling pieces of cloth. In Cuauhtemotzin he saw not only exotic brown prostitutes, but also his own people's misery when he ran into Jane, a woman from his hometown. In Mexico City he read Yiddish descriptions of the Bialystok ghetto, learning of a "renowned maskil [a title of honor] of riddles. Each day he had something to say, each day a new verse, a new word, until one obscure morning he fell in the street and fainted." So it was that in Mexico City he learned of his father's death.[55] These observers sarcastically sang to each the song of desperation, for having reached a city full of problems and poverty—but also of joy—they were safe and alive.

Rubinstein, another immigrant, welcomed the great, ugly city for the freedom of a place where no one asked about or stopped them for being Jews. Glikowski wrote novels with Mexico City as their main setting and main character. Some of the tales are of Jews who know only twenty words in Spanish trying to establish all sorts of businesses in the city. One of his characters receives a letter in Mexico City: "Apart from that everything in Bitristke is in order. Last month no Jews were beaten, and this year for Easter there were no accusations of ritual killings." The novel depicts the homeless and blind in the city. For those who have nowhere to escape, the city was real:

Mexico, I travel through your streets, where my ancestors have never stepped. I want to put their steps on your soil, but they don't take root. I stroll in a city whose breath is strange to me. I was not born in this land, I did not see it even in dreams, and nonetheless you have made me your own.

Although Mexico City was poor it was nevertheless an exciting invitation to ruminate on one's condition, to walk the streets "like a shadow." To do so is to walk in one's own "dark night," suffering, but also enjoying both the bright and dark colors of life like Glantz: "Here in this earth, in the bright shine,/a summer loneliness walks on the streets." Some found the reinvention and escape offered by the city sad yet indispensable. Glantz again: "[Mexico] I am from those who are used to drinking/the poisonous fortune like sparkling wine." Perhaps because there was no escape from escape these poets found in the city its many cities, everything except calm: "Does anyone know where calm spends the night?" One can imagine the poet in exile, at the city's twilight, upset at the city and the world, yet enlightened, tempted by the very possibility of finding happiness in watching the sun go down once again over a city that had, after all, saved him. Glikowski:

Don't cry, hushed dusk of mine
don't cry at the death
of your newly sacrificed brother:
the day.
. . .
clean is the man
who doesn't know happiness
Oh, don't come to take my sadness with you![56]

It is a small wonder that the Diego Rivera who illustrated Berliner's poems was an alien of the Brown Atlantis. One of his collages included the many contradictions of the city: modern buildings; modern bourgeois memorabilia like wedding portraits, or a portrait of a military man kissing a woman; a car; an airplane; a colonial arch with the emblem of the city; and the poor house of a proletarian family. Through Berliner's eyes, Rivera finally turned his gaze to the Mexico City he inhabited. He managed to see a drunk, semi-naked, and sick woman lying on the asphalt, a drunk man on the sidewalk within the

6.20. Diego
Rivera's illustration,
I. Berliner's *Shtot
fun palatsn* (1936).
© 2011 Banco de
México, Diego Rivera
Frida Kahlo Museums
Trust, Mexico, D.F. /
Artists Rights Society
(ARS), New York.

shadow of the Porfirian Opera House, and lots of garbage (figure 6.20). This
was no Brown Atlantis. The city reigns when Mexico is not a racial or social
utopia but, finally, a real place.

End

Even when it remained invisible to the Brown Atlantis, the real city persisted, making possible the many images and words that Mexico meant as a
cultural season. The need for a Brown Atlantis was such that it obscured the
city's cultural might. The seekers of the Brown Atlantis thought they were active agents of discovery, authentication, and escape. They thought they were
the city's center of attention. Tom O'Sullivan's illustration, "The Bohemians
Come," in Carleton Beals's *House in Mexico* (1958), could be used to close the
circle: the mythical inhabitants of the capital—all depicted as stereotypical
Indians—gaze at the bohemian Beals with a pipe and a typewriter, as though
he were an animal in a zoo cage (figure 6.21). The desired irony is that of the
observer being observed. The irony I want to leave the reader with is more

VII

THE BOHEMIANS COME

6.21. Tom O'Sullivan's "The Bohemians Come," in Carleton Beals,
House in Mexico (New York: Hastings House, 1958).
Courtesy of Hastings House Publishers.

disturbing, and more revealing of why the Brown Atlantis has endured. The image is not simply a fictional Odysseus singing back at the enchanting mythic Sirens. It is a collective Homer unconsciously, yet conclusively, convinced that the chants and adventures of his own mythic characters are real.

PART IV ODALISQUE-MANIA

Cuando la última odalisca,
ya descastado mi vergel,
se fugue en pos de una nueva miel
¿qué salmodia del pecho mío
será digna de suspirar
a través del harén vacío?
— Ramón López Velarde ("La última odalisca," 1919)

During his melancholy longing at midday
what did Adam recollect?
Primeval emotion is like a cloud,
like infinitely sweet love.
It floats on the other side of memory
far beyond my reach.
— Hagiwara Sakutarō ("Most primitive emotion," 1923)

JAPAN

I seek to understand a peculiar form of orientalism, especially related to Japan (chapter 7) and India (chapter 8) in Mexico City between the 1880s and the 1930s, which I call odalisque mania. But "odalisque," I have been warned, is a rather uncommon term in English. Orientalism, I was told, better conveys the search for odalisques I examine. And yet I keep the term "odalisque," for the word is not mine: my historical characters use it, as the term was commonly used in various Romance languages between the 1860s and 1950s. Starting about 1860 countless essays, novels, and poems used the term to describe a state of mind, an epoch, or a style in eroticism. Thus in the metaphor of the odalisque, "a female slave or concubine in an Eastern harem" (*Oxford American Dictionary*), I include the larger epochal impulse: *ecstasy* ("getting beside or outside of oneself"), which was indispensable in order to achieve, and to try to overcome, any form of modern knowledge in cities around the world.[1]

As in French, odalisques meant many things in Spanish in the last part of the nineteenth century: exotic women, scenes from what was known in Spanish as *Las mil y una noches* and in English as *The Arabian Nights*, certain types of interiors, neo-baroque architecture, Rubén Darío's revolution in the Spanish language, or the simple sensual fascination with exotic trends, bodies, and styles.[2] Countless essays, novels, and poems used "odalisque" to describe a state of mind, an epoch, or a style in eroticism. The term was so common in Mexico City that as late as 1957, the film *La odalisca número 13* ("Odalisque Number 13") directed by Fernando Cortés and starring the legendary comedian Germán Valdés, aka Tin-Tan, was not only a very popular Mexican movie but also a complex parody that involved Mexico City's turn-of-the-century modernist fascination with odalisques, Matisse-like paintings of odalisques, Lebanese migration to the city, and the "Americanization" of Mexican life. *Odaliscas* thus is the term I use to group an ample cultural trend.

I, however, do not attempt to enter into the vast criticism, and self-criticism, of orientalism all over the world. I simply study a peculiar form of orientalism: Mexico's odalisque-mania, with Mexicans as multifaceted participants in a world obsession embodied by the term "odalisque." They are multifaceted because almost all the historical characters of this odalisque-mania story were also advocates of, say, the international recognition of Mexican popular arts and crafts, *indigenismo*, avant-garde literary or artistic trends, spiritualism, or socialism. They sought odalisques for the same reason that they sought a pristine and authentic Mexican art in Indigenous children or the emergence of a truly Mexican literary synthesis or functionalist architecture for the new revolutionary city. The obsession encompassed here has four main foci of concerns: the allure of the alien; the wisdom of what is ancient; the sensuality of a variant sexuality; and the sublimity of longevity and authenticity.

But before essaying Mexican evocations of Japanese odalisque, some disclosures are in order regarding such basics as cultural originality, the equation of the East and the West, periodization, cultural intermediacy, and, finally, the meaning of *lo oriental* in Mexican Spanish. Hence, Mexican odalisque-mania could seem a simple history, a nice supplement; for instance, for those who saw in Mexico an exotic and non-Western land, orientalism in Mexico City was nothing but Mexican *afrancesados* imitating European fashions. And yet, who, in modern cities, was not a complex and unstable character as well as an impersonator, regardless of her geographical situation? I examine the odalisque mania in the city as a way to essay undeniable global features as they acquired local expressions, which in turn generated unique reverberations that at times are seen by historians as "authentically" Mexican, other times as "fake" urban imitations, and quite often are simply ignored as "epochal" nonsense.

But there is the matter of East and West. How could I deal in the same lines with Mexico City, India, Japan, the U.S., and France? A careful analysis of the confines of India's, Japan's, and Mexico's histories reveals the evasiveness of the concepts of East and West. Within and among these three regions, East and West have meant very different things. When the English writings of an 1880s Bengali nationalist and intellectual are as non-Western as the Spanish writings of a nineteenth-century nationalist and anti-Western intellectual in Mexico City, or a late nineteenth-century Japanese thinker, non-Westernness becomes absurd. Indeed, it is precisely in the omnipresence of the East-West distinction that we see India, Japan, and Mexico together. In other words, it is only because of the modern appearance of such a distinction (East-West) that we may claim to be in the same boat, though what exactly East and West *are* remains vague and changing. Therefore, the limits of what follows are not East and West, but rather, the making of East and West in the late nineteenth and early twentieth centuries.

Regarding periodization, I believe that the period ranging from the 1860s to the 1940s was a time in which many cities of the world danced, or seemed to dance, to the same tune; not only because it was then that "globalization" or "Westernization" gathered speed, but also, because all pasts and all futures were, at the same time, reformatted according to our (still) conceptual and geographical lingua franca—that of a world of nations and states. Nations and states are the other name of a concentrated nineteenth century that constitutes the indispensable axiom for our contemporary way of thinking. It is a foundational idea. It is a concept that rests on our current state of being post-this or post-that, and on our innocent conviction of situating ourselves in, and being, "Europe," "Asia," the United States, or even the America that is still strangely and "nineteenth-centurally" called "Latin." This era, which is that of the formation of states, nations, and identities, serves as the most well-constructed division between past and present. From it, even contemporary historians derived their position as citizens and as storytellers. Because the nation-state not only has a history (it came to be in this way), it also has a code of ethics (as it should be). Here lies the great communality among many regions.[3]

But, because India, Mexico, and Japan belong to this global, fixed concept of the nineteenth century, the cultural interactions between and within the three regions are inevitably marked by the intermediacy of what we call Europe or the U.S. And this is so either conceptually—if we deal with the issue of Pan-Asianism or Pan-Latinism, or with the different forms of self-ethnology and nativism—, or empirically—if we, in Mexico City, believe that it was such prominent French orientalists as the Goncourt brothers, or the great U.S. Japonista Ernest Fenollosa, or the modernist poet Ezra Pound who taught us Japanese poetry, or if we trust the German, French, and English translations of what Max Müller called the "Sacred Books of the East," or if we satisfy our odalisque-mania by reading Indian thought (without noticing it) in Nietzsche. My ignorance of the Japanese and Indian languages does not allow me to elaborate on the other side of the story, but somehow I believe that if any image of Mexico existed in Japan or India before the 1940s, it had already been filtered by U.S. or European scholars and travelers. This suspicion seems confirmed by some of the stories told in this history of odalisque-mania.

Finally, it is important to bear in mind that both highbrow and lowbrow urban Mexican cultures grouped together very different geographical and cultural references. China and Japan were often considered in the same cultural context as Egypt, Arabia, and India. Thus Mexico's odalisque-mania shared this lack of specificity, which is, after all, the raison d'être of this mania. Of course the city's intelligentsia often distinguished between a clean, sensual, progressive Japan and a dirty, corrupt, opium-smoking China. Perhaps Francisco Bulnes—Mexico's Voltaire at the turn of the century—best epitomized this distinction when traveling to Japan as an engineer in 1874–75. In Japan he saw clean cities, sensual prostitutes, and well-organized government and scientific institutions; while in Hong Kong he smoked opium and saw dirty cities: "Los chinos sucios como la conciencia de un demonio" (Chinese: dirty as the devil's conscience).[4] But Mexicans tended to group in such terms as *chinos* or *orientales* very different people.

Japan between 1880 and 1930 was a common point of reference in Mexico City's intellectual, political, scientific, and artistic circles. Mexican scientist Francisco Díaz Covarrubias, traveling in Japan on an astronomical mission, reported to his government that Japan was a country that achieved in eight or ten years what "the civilized world" had taken four centuries to accomplish. Besides, in Japan the powerful Emperor had voluntarily laid aside his absolutist power in favor of constitutional arrangements. Japan was thus a true and apropos model for Porfirian Mexico to pursue.[5] That is why early Mexican social scientists, such as Andrés Molina Enríquez, in the 1900s studied Japan's development as a best-case scenario for Mexico's future. He praised Japan as a natural model for the development of Mexico's Indigenous character. "I have understood and favored Japanese development and success," he argued, "hoping that Japan's strength as a world power would save the Asiatic peoples [including Mexico] from the barbarous Western imperialisms." For Molina, Mexico's two clashing cultures (Spaniard and Indigenous) leaned, on the one hand, extremely West and, on the other, extremely East. He wanted instead a new race of mestizos, which necessarily had to temper their anti-Americanism by maximizing Mexico's Oriental character, but unmistakably following a Western path.[6]

Efrén Rebolledo published a novel of his experience in Nikko, translating a Japanese saying to Spanish with modernist authority (figure 7.1):

Nikko wo minal uchi wa
Keko to iu na.
No puede decir magnífico
El que nunca ha visto Nikko[7]

Who has never seen Nikko
cannot say magnificent.

However these kinds of political and poetic evidences conceal innumerable historical instances of shared views and mutual interactions. One needs to go

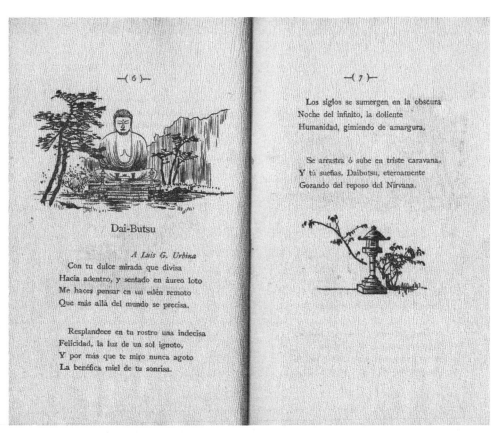

The illustration includes the following printed text:

-(6)-

Dai-Butsu

A Luis G. Urbina
Con tu dulce mirada que divisa
Hacia adentro, y sentado en áureo loto
Me haces pensar en un edén remoto
Que más allá del mundo se precisa.

Resplandece en tu rostro una indecisa
Felicidad, la luz de un sol ignoto,
Y por más que te miro nunca agoto
La benéfica miel de tu sonrisa.

-(7)-

Los siglos se sumergen en la obscura
Noche del infinito, la doliente
Humanidad, gimiendo de amargura,

Se arrastra ó sube en triste caravana,
Y tú sueñas, Daibutsu, eternamente
Gozando del reposo del Nirvana.

7.1. Efrén Rebolledo, *Rimas japonesas* (Tokyo: Shimbi Shoin, 1901), illustrated by Shunjo Kihara.

back to Martyrs and Other Basics (1) in order to then understand some Bizarre Interconnections (2). From there, new topics surface for the analysis: a unique Mexican *Japonista*, José Juan Tablada (3), Science (4), A Japanese Exhibition in Mexico City (5), Poetry (6), and of course Desire (7) and the Arts (8).

On Martyrs and Other Basics

Beginning in 1565 Japan and New Spain were connected, at least to some extent, by the *Nao de China*, the boat that also linked New Spain with the Philippines and China.[8] New Spain's religious orders were also linked to Japan. It was in Japan that Franciscan friar Felipe de Jesús (a New Spaniard), along with other friars and Christianized Japanese men, was sacrificed in February 1597. In 1862 the friar was canonized as San Felipe de Jesús, the first saint from Mexico. Mexico thus owed Japan a great honor.[9] New Spain's art found lasting proof of Mexico's Westernness (i.e., Christianity) vis-à-vis Japan's East-ernness in the imagery of San Felipe, the martyr surrounded by the evil faces of Japanese pagans and criminals.[10] In this imagery heaven is for souls dressed in white, while color belongs to the evil killers of Christianity. This symbolism was repeated many times, aiming to make the martyr the most significant sym-bol—after Guadalupe—of Mexico's criollo patriotism.[11] The symbol's strength declined over the years, only to be resurrected by Catholic-Mexican patriotism in the nineteenth century, when the martyr was finally canonized. The devotion to San Felipe reached all parts of the country, and a town in Nuevo León—whose patron saint was and remains San Felipe—was named China, Nuevo León. (Japan or China? The same thing for Mexican norteños.) San Felipe could have reached Guadalupe's heights—imagine this San Felipe, this epic struggle of East and West, as a founding myth of Mexico. Although Guadalupe won, hers is an image masterfully orientalist and decisively urban in itself: an exotic brown Catholic virgin in the valley of Anáhuac.

Around the time the friars were sacrificed a Mexican-born Spaniard named Rodrigo Vivero y Velasco, nephew of New Spain's viceroy and provisional gov-ernor of the Philippines, became a distinguished traveler in early seventeenth-century Japan. In 1609 he spent ten months in Japan and wrote an intriguing account of that country's life and culture in the era of Tokugawa Ieyasu.[12] He brought a Japanese delegation to Mexico City in 1610. Nahuatl urbanite Do-mingo de San Antón Chimalpahin Quahtlehuanitzin recorded the visit; in his opinion, Japanese envoys looked like girls (they were short, with long hair and delicate shoes) and were too stern and quiet, like eagles. Chimalpahin saw them similarly to the way they were seen by any European writer at the time: as exotic pagans from Japan, the same place, for Chimalpahin, as China. When another Japanese delegation reached Mexico in 1613 it was also a great event for the city.[13]

Another instance of contact between Japan and New Spain took place through the intermediation of the Jesuits. Namban art was an artistic school developed by Japanese artists who were inspired by Portuguese and Spanish techniques and styles. Namban art circulated heavily in Japan, Portugal, and Mexico. The seventeenth-century Mexican Namban biombos in Mexico City's palaces showed the presence of Japanese Namban artists in the city, as well as illustrating how art traveled from Portugal to India and Japan, and from there to New Spain.[14] It was the art, as a great Portuguese poet described it in the twentieth century, of the "Pasmo de povos de repente/frente a frente"; the biombos were "Alvoroço de quem vê/o tão longe tão o pé" (Astonishment of peoples suddenly/face to face . . . Delight of the one who sees/the so far away so at hand.)[15]

After 1870, with the advent of relatively stable and modernizing governments, both in Tokyo and Mexico City, mutual interactions became more visible and institutionalized. At that time scientists like Díaz Covarrubias and writers such as Francisco Bulnes, José Juan Tablada, and Efrén Rebolledo traveled to Japan. Diplomats from both countries, using as a leitmotif the fears and threats of the U.S. and the possibility of Japanese investment and immigration, engaged in several exchanges. Bulnes wrote about his impressions of Japan, which are full of references to geishas and to the great progress of a people who worked hard and should be an example to Mexicans.[16] Rebolledo produced odalisque-like poetry, illustrated by Shunjo Kihara, which were the envy of the city's bohemia.[17]

In 1891, with the knowledge and permission of the U.S., Japan and Mexico exchanged ambassadors. Their efforts did not lead to significant Japanese immigration or investment, but they did open lines of cultural and political communication. The Mexican foreign minister to Japan, Carlos Américo Lera, assiduously reported on Japan's social, cultural, and political life from 1899 to 1906. He received many odalisque-mania requests from Mexican intellectuals and politicians—Lera had to buy clothing, paintings, and books, and kept feeding Mexicans's curiosity with regard to Japanese traditions and industrial development.[18] For his service to Japan and Mexico he was decorated by Japan with the Great Cross of the Order of the Imperial Dragon.[19]

Japanese immigration remained tied to U.S. migratory policies, and Japanese investment except for one large transportation company was meager. A study shows that in the 1900s no more than 150 Japanese citizens per year, on average, were granted official access to Mexico, and that these immigrants had a hard time once they arrived. But 1906 and 1907 were exceptional, as more than 9,000 Japanese people migrated to Mexico, coming mostly from the U.S. as a result of the expansion of the Chinese Restriction Act to Japanese citizens.[20] Though it is hard to know for certain, some stayed in Mexico City, but the official attempt was to create a Japanese colony in Chiapas backed by both governments (1890s)—it was known as the Enomoto Colony. The results were rather insignificant, though some Japanese-born citizens remained in Chiapas and formed a small community.

After the 1880s Japan promoted itself all over the world commercially, militarily, and culturally, as a symbol of a unique blend of tradition and modernity. Mexico City was an active Japonista subject and an attractive target for Japanese propaganda. During Porfirian times Japan was a common point of reference among military officers, a military orientalism that lasted until World War II. Japan was seen as an example of a similar race that, nevertheless, had a strong military that was especially visible to Mexican officers during the

Russo-Japanese War. In 1907 Colonel Luis G. Palacios, commenting on the psychology of the Mexican soldier, used Japan as the model to follow. Japan's victory was due to its superior strategy, of course, but also to the high morale of the Japanese soldier who, being smaller and weaker than the Russian soldier, had "an unbreakable faith in the success of his cause, loving fanatically his Emperor and the honor of his country." Thus a country recently opened to the West "assimilated" "rapidly" all modern innovations, blending them with its own traditions. For Colonel Palacios the Mexican soldier, after all a creature with an "Oriental fatalism," could become a Japanese-like soldier through education and patriotism.[21]

Then, of course, there was the network of intrigues and conspiracies involving Mexico, the European powers, Japan, and the U.S. From 1910 to the beginning of World War II countless reports by Mexican, German, American, and Japanese spies were exchanged, most of them having to do with Japanese intentions to acquire territory, lend money, and establish colonies of millions of people on the U.S.-Mexico border. U.S. authorities responded to the threats in a Pavlovian fashion, to the utter satisfaction of the Mexican revolutionary leaders and presidents who were able to play the "Japanese card" to obtain minor economic, military, and political concessions from the U.S.[22]

These fears, if they had been more publicly known, would have ignited popular anxiety because intellectual odalisque-mania and, to some extent, popular odalisque-mania, existed simultaneously with a strong xenophobia directed especially at the Chinese immigrants arriving in Mexico since the 1880s. From the 1880s to the 1930s Chinese men and women were constantly harassed, both in the large Chinese communities in the northern part of the country and in Mexico City. Tokojuro Inukai, a Japanese immigrant who had reached Mexico City in 1916 after his expulsion from the U.S., recalled in the 1970s how all Orientals were hated because they were competition. Mexican people, he said in his unique blend of Japanese-Spanish, "es muy bajo culto, gente buena, maldita es el político" (are low in culture, good people, evil are the politicians).

The xenophobia was not precisely an elite, state-oriented xenophobia. It was also the popular reaction of small merchants and poor urban residents to the presence of Chinese workers and merchants and, consequently, to that of any Oriental-looking people in Mexico City including the Japanese and Koreans. Chinese people were considered ugly, weak, and smokers of opium. It is no surprise, then, that since the 1880s there were popular demands in various states to expel the Chinese, and to ban intermarriages involving Orientals. In 1886 and 1888 there were reports in Mexico City of Chinese men seriously beaten in the streets by a variety of poor urban residents. The police did not

Manif-stáción espontánca á un hijo del. . . . . . Celeste Imperio (Tomado del natural.)

A esto jijo de la...Chir a
Que come muchos ratones.
Bailándole el Chin-Chun-Chan,
Lo dejaron sin calzones,
"Pelo yo que hago á Usteles"
Dice el chino Alí jajá

Y los muchachos responden.
¡Alí yú! Chintarará
Pero luégo llega el choco
Sin andarse con mouserga;
Los llevan á la Jefatura
Y allí les meten la. . . . . . .mul a.

7.2. Popular xenophobia in Mexico City. *La Guacamaya* (August 18, 1904).
"A este jijo de la . . . China" suggests the expression "A ese hijo de la chingada."

react, as it seemed to be a form of popular entertainment. In 1904 a Mexico
City workers' periodical, *La Guacamaya*, reproduced an image of the physical
harassment of Chinese people in Mexico City. The cartoon depicted various
urban types: the recently arrived migrant from the countryside, the *lépero*, the
dandy, and the small shopkeeper, all beating a Chinese man in the streets (figure 7.2). A poem accompanied the cartoon. "They left that son of a . . . who
eats mice without underwear." By 1911 this popular xenophobia reached such
a level that a massacre took place in Torreón where between 249 and 303 Chinese men were killed. By the 1920s various northern state governments, under
pressure from the masses, decreed the official expulsion of Chinese populations. In 1911, in the midst of the massive killing of Chinese immigrants in the
north of the country, cartoonist Rafael Lillo imagined Mexico City taken over
by Chinese people, the Mexican Eagle fighting the terrible Chinese influence,
all as the dream of a Chinese man. By the 1930s even the Communist publication in Mexico City, *El Machete*, proposed a nationalist campaign, arguing that
the Chinese, the Jews, and the U.S. imperialists were ruining the country.[23]

How could odalisque-mania occur in the midst of this xenophobia? For dwellers of Mexico City, it seemed, there was no contradiction between their orientalist dreams and their xenophobia, just as U.S., French, and English intellectuals found no problem in craving Japanese and Chinese arts at the same time that the "yellow peril" was often discussed within their societies. In Mexico City this xenophobia, though it did somewhat affect the few Japanese immigrants, was particularly directed at the Chinese population since they were the largest Asian group in the city. Additionally, urban intellectuals with their odalisque-mania were removed from the concerns of the urban poor and the small shopkeepers. When the urban lower classes began to crave odalisque images in the city's vaudevilles, it became clear that desiring geisha-like divas was one thing, but tolerating Chinese men marrying Mexican women was quite another.

On Bizarre Interconnections

Xenophobia could not mask the fascination of Mexico City's bohemian and avant-garde intellectuals, whose obsession with Japan was directed through French, English, Italian, and German intermediaries. The existence of intermediaries to the East was also a reality for Ernest Fenollosa—the U.S. professor at Tokyo University and the most prominent U.S. Japanist of the late nineteenth century. He in fact was Ernest Francisco, the son of Malageño musician Fenollosa y Alvarado. Fenollosa claimed, during his studies at Harvard, that "my very great, great grandfather, I am bound to believe, was Xicotencatl, chief of the Trascalans [sic] in Mexico at the time of Cortes's invasion, whose chief gave his baptized daughter, Louisa, to the Spanish Capitan Alvarado."[24] In his history of Japanese art, Fenollosa used Aztec art to display the chronological evolution of Japanese artistic creations and trends. Moreover, in Japan Fenollosa started what Mexican artists would eventually produce in Mexico City: the revalorization of traditional artistic techniques in art education. Indeed, Fenollosa's influence in the arts and poetic traditions of Japan, the U.S., and Mexico is lasting.[25]

In turn, José Juan Tablada, friend of prominent U.S. scholar and publicist of Japan Lafcadio Hearn (1850–1904), connected Mexican and Japanese art forms both in his beautifully illustrated account of the Japanese painter Hiroshiqué and in his history of Mexican art.[26] He even planned to write De aztecas y japoneses, an account of the similarities between Japanese and Aztec art. Tablada was thus Mexico's greatest Japonista. It is no wonder, then, that Miguel Covarrubias (a prominent cartoonist in the city, with a long residence in New York) depicted Tablada as a great Mexican Buddha with nonsensical, Japanese-looking inscriptions (figure 7.3).

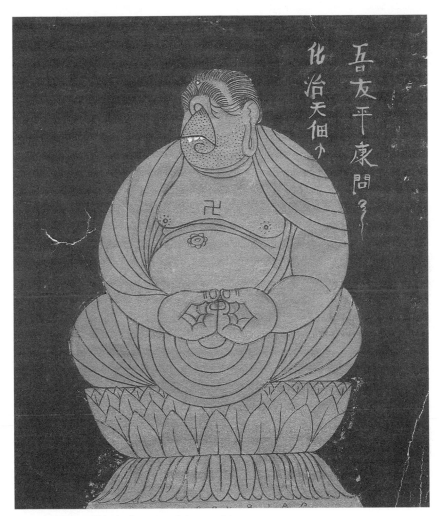

7.3. José Juan Tablada, by Miguel Covarrubias.
Courtesy Archivo Gráfico José Juan Tablada, Colección J. J. Tablada,
Universidad Nacional Autónoma de México, Instituto de Investigaciones
Filológicas.

The Japanese presence, artistic and otherwise, was prominent at both the French and American World's Fairs. At these events the Mexican/Aztec contrast was always part of a subconscious mental exercise performed by the viewers, either at the History of Housing Exposition in Paris (1889), the 1893 Chicago White City Exposition, or at the 1904 Saint Louis Fair—at which the individual in charge of Mexican antiques and arts, Frederick Starr, also oversaw the display of Japanese art and people. Starr gathered Mexican antiques and Indigenous people, also traveling to Japan in 1904 in order to bring Ainu people to the Fair.[27] Mexico and Japan played a sort of mirror game, in which Aztec, Mayan, and Mexican elements often crossed paths with the images brought from Japan. In fact, for many the goal was to see them in a sort of continuum.

Japonisme and Mexican exoticism have coexisted since the 1876 World's Fair in Philadelphia.[28] At that point the links between the Orient and Mexico were well established as one single cognitive sphere. Many Mexicans and foreigners found Japanese, Chinese, or Hindu connections in native Mexican pottery, architecture, and languages. World orientalism knew no real boundaries within the realm of the exotic.[29] In 1877 amateur ethnologist, archaeologist, and medical doctor Gumesindo Mendoza found, as many did at the time, Chinese influences in an Aztec figure. Following a discussion at the 1875 Congress of Americanists in Nancy regarding P. E. Foucaux's theory of Buddhist influences in Mesoamerica, Mendoza found in the Aztec figure a definitive proof of the ideas of Foucaux, a pioneering scholar of Tibet and India as well as a professor at l'École Nationale des Langues Orientales in Paris. Mendoza also found Japanese traces in another Mexican image, thus showing what he believed was indisputable evidence of the link between Japan, China, and Mesoamerica. The figures he displayed constituted a selection of stereotypical views of what Japanese and Chinese faces ought to look like. If Nahuatl artisans of the Mexican valley were able to carve these figures, it was because of their undeniable Oriental origins.[30]

Early anthropological and archaeological studies had already established that Mexico was somehow Japan or China, and Japan was, in a way, Mexico. This grouping made it possible for Mexico to become a second-class East, but it also made Mexico's own orientalism possible. Mexico and Japan were grouped together in the Western view partially because both were sites of ecstasy. What Fenollosa proposed in his poem *East and West* (1893) was, in fact, performed on an almost daily basis from the 1880s to the 1940s by U.S. intellectuals and artists using Mexico as their East, their own private Japan. Fenollosa wrote:

> I've flown from my West
> Like a desolate bird from a broken nest
> To learn thy secret of joy and rest.[31]

Four years after Fenollosa's *East and West* Tablada wrote, in Japan, his *Musa Japónica*, which like the poem was an escape from his own West, with ecstasy as a vice:

[Japón] Tú eres el opio que narcotiza,
y al ver que aduermes todas mis penas
mi sangre—roja sacerdotisa—
tus alabanzas canta en mis venas.[32]

[Japan] You are the opium that narcotizes,
and upon seeing that you soothe all my troubles,
my blood—red priestess—
sings your acclamations in my veins.

The fact that "backward" Mexico represented a form of ecstasy for foreign travelers trying to escape industrialization was, in a way, inevitable. But Japan's rapid modernization was neither a secret for observers from the United States nor for those from the Spanish-speaking world. For Spanish-speaking intellectuals it was difficult to match Japan's image as the eternal wisdom of tradition with that of capitalist and military development. Henry Adams sought, both in Tokyo and in Mexico City, an escape from his West, but instead found that to be impossible given that both nations, he believed, had been tempted by the very Western lore of money and power he wanted to escape.[33] But Adams or Tablada saw Japan not only in Japan, but also in such French writers as the Goncourt brothers, Théophile Gautier, and Pierre Loti.[34]

Tablada

José Juan Tablada was the greatest advocate of Japonisme in turn-of-the-century Mexico City. His translations and reports about Japan were published in the most important literary journals of his time. In 1900, for instance, the prominent Revista Moderna published one of Tablada's pieces on Japan, which included his own illustrations.[35] Tablada's Japonisme, as he recalled in his memoirs, started with his friendship in Mexico City with the Spanish diplomat Pedro de Carrere y Lembeye, who eventually moved to Coyoacán, where he died in 1913.[36] Tablada bought de Carrere's library on Japanese art. The later influence of the Goncourt brothers and U.S. orientalism made Tablada the greatest Mexican Japonista (although he never learned the language). He traveled to Japan during 1900 and 1901, writing several essays there that were later published as En el país del sol in 1919. His descriptions are an unmatchable synthesis of modernist poetics, romantic ecstasy, and sensualism.[37]

His chronicles often compared Japanese places with their European and Mexican "counterparts": Hiroshigué becomes the Japanese Rembrandt; fancy Ginza Avenue in Tokyo becomes Mexico City's Platero Avenue; Mount Kōya is

Tepoztlán. Tablada became a self-appointed translator for Mexicans regarding everything Japanese, though he himself used French and English translations. His odalisque-mania knew no limits. In the main streets of the fancy districts of Tokyo, he said, "every story of every house is a harem; behind the thin bars [on the windows], silent and inert odalisques appear seated upon the fluting of the finest bamboo."[38]

In 1905 Tablada saw the West's parallel stereotyping of Mexico and Japan. He claimed that for many years in Mexico there were three "documents" used to imagine Japan in Mexico City: "the *tabor*, the folding screen, and Pierre Loti's *Chrysanthème*" (El tabor, el biombo y la "Crisantema" de Pierre Loti). These "documents" echoed Western views of Mexico, which were nothing but "the feathered headdress, the naked and glossy body, and the obsidian *tentetl* [nail] gleaming in a pierced lip" (El tocado de plumas, el cuerpo desnudo y embijado, y el "tentetl" de obsidiana chispeando en el labio perforado). He was surprised to see how, upon his return from Japan in 1901, friends in the city asked whether Japan was as civilized "as we [Mexicans] are." He acknowledged that Japan had become a snobby trend, but he still hoped for Mexico to be as civilized as Japan.[39] Ignorance had created the stereotypes, and he consciously made of his work a two-fold demystification of the world's image of Mexico City, and of Japan's image in the city. In doing so, however, he contributed to both the stereotyping of modern Mexico—no longer a stereotype of headdresses, naked bodies, and obsidian, but of fiesta, siesta, sombrero, and Mexico as a Brown Atlantis—and the stereotyping of Japan, not as the country of Loti's Chrysanthème, but as that of haikus. He was, in short, a major modernist creator.

Tablada's *Hiroshigué: el pintor de la nieve y de la lluvia, de la noche y de la luna* (1914) was a detailed analysis of the works and life of the famous Japanese painter, full of orientalist stories, as well as references to the Goncourt brothers and Loti (the book was dedicated to Edmund de Goncourt). The book was one of the few things that survived 1914, when Tablada had to abandon his house in Coyoacán because he collaborated with the regime of antirevolutionary general Victoriana Huerta. His house had been a Japanese paradise in Mexico, including a Japanese pagoda and garden.[40]

Tablada's account of Hiroshigué and Japanese art was part of a larger representation of Japan in Mexico City that included many copies of Japanese images he had himself drawn, as well as his own house and persona. But it was in his study and transformation of Japanese poetic structures where Tablada was a real innovator. His haikus, snapshots of natural images and everyday occurrences, were filled with great irony and suggestive language. The structure was inspired both by Japanese haikus and by the relationship of the poems to graphic images. The content, however, of Tablada's poems combined Mexican and cosmopolitan textures by including words in English and French. His haikus were, indeed, innovative poetic "illustrations" rarely seen in Spanish, a loquacious tongue that, throughout the nineteenth century, regarded thriftiness in language as a sin. It is no wonder he became, as we shall see, so influential to other poets in the city. Consider, for instance, the following image of a mushroom that becomes, in Tablada's eyes, the Japanese-like umbrella of a *Japonista* toad:

El hongo.
Parece la sombrilla
Este hongo policromo
De un sapo japonista.

The mushroom.
looks like an umbrella;
this polychrome mushroom
of a *Japanista* frog.

Tablada captured these glimpses of reality, while also consciously contrasting the extremes of many dichotomies: Mexico vs. the Orient, supreme beauty vs. supreme ugliness, and sonorous popular urban words vs. ornate language. Observe, for instance, the contrasts in the description of a common donkey:

El Burrito.
Mientras lo cargan
Sueña el burrito amosquilado
En paraísos de esmeralda.

The little donkey.
While they load him up,
the donkey, *amosquilado* [surrounded by flies], dreams
of emerald paradises.

In other poems there is an urban lowbrow. What he called his *Dramas mínimos* (short dramas) were beautiful, common occurrences made into brief, linguistic illustrations. A dog barking at a train becomes heroism:

Heroísmo.
Triunfaste al fin perrillo fiel
Y ahuyentado por tu ladrido
Huye veloz el tren . . .

Heroism.
You have triumphed at last, loyal little dog;
and, scared off by your bark,
the train quickly flees.

Or it was the beautiful consideration of hope and romantic enchantment as unattainable things. The secret for Tablada is in the search, not in the attainment:

Como el agua, el ensueño
Si cuaja es sólo
Hielo.[41]

Like water, a dream,
if it materializes, is merely
ice.

These renditions imitated Japanese poetic structures, but above all they were unique creations, a sort of juggling within the confines of the Spanish language and performed by a poet consciously seeking Japanese poetry even though he did not know Japanese. If he had been more faithful to the original Japanese, would he have been as creative? It is hard to tell. Tablada's creativity was also shown, almost simultaneously, in his crafting of a Mexican poetic style. He promoted precisely what the searchers for an exotic Mexico viewed as authentic, though these things were already the result of the poet's orientalism. "Yo tengo furor de mexicanismo. Casi me siento xenófobo" (I feel enormous enthusiasm for Mexicanism. I almost feel xenophobic), he wrote in a 1923 letter.[42] The illustrations of Tablada's haikus by the prominent art educator and artist Alfredo Best Maugard conspicuously featured Mexican motifs and styles. Postrevolution exile—mostly in New York—turned Tablada into a nostalgic nationalist, albeit an ironic one who dreamt of the smells, textures, and colors of the food and places he saw as a child. However, unlike the seekers of an exotic, pristine, and brown Mexico, he was fully aware that discovering the Mexican essence in himself was impossible—as a modernist poet, a

Japonista, a nationalist, a deep *chilango*, and a New Yorker, he was already too many persons in one.[43]

Thus his *Japonisme* paralleled his Mexicanism. He could blend together, in his nostalgia, his orientalist and nationalist motifs, as when he imagined a feast with all his friends at which Xochitl—the goddess of *pulque*—and the Persian poet Omar Khayyam would have been together:

Aromas de epazote y de chile pasilla
Anuncian como heraldos la sopa de tortilla.
Las garrafas ubérrimas de licor nacional
De todos los colores fingen un Carnaval,
Pulques de apio, de almendra, de huevo, de tuna,
¡Oh magníficos pulques donde vivas están
La regia alma de Xóchitl y la de Omar Khayam!

Aromas of *epazote* and *chile pasilla*
announce, like heralds, tortilla soup.
The bountiful carafes of national liquor
of all colors feign a Carnival—
celery, almond, egg and prickly pear *pulques*.
Oh, magnificent *pulques*,
in which the regal soul of Xóchitl, and that of Omar Khayyam, live on!

In addition to his haikus and his Mexican poems, Tablada experimented with Chinese themes. In *Li-Po y otros poemas*, published in Caracas in 1920, he mixed symbolic poetry with graphic poems. In it Tablada used as his inspiration the eighth-century Chinese poet Li-Po, who was well known in the West for his poems on drinking and love (Ezra Pound wrote versions of Li-Po's poems). Tablada's Li-Po poems were collages of Japanese, Chinese, and Mexican graphic styles, with wine and drinking as their subjects. Tablada was what any creator ought to be: a magnet for styles and ideas. Thus, his findings and collections were useful to seekers of Mexico as a Brown Atlantis, but he was not (for he was a *chilango*) considered a first-class orientalist by foreigners.

Science

Mexican poets saw in Japan the same importance that Mexican scientists and politicians saw: that is, the possibility of modernization by a simultaneous Easternization and Westernization. Mexico could simultaneously become more alluring as a deeply Eastern, exotic, profound, and spiritual land, yet remain resolutely Western. This is what Mexican technocrats saw in the military development of Japan, combining expertise in judo with modern weaponry. This is what Mexican writers saw in Japanese debates about the appropriateness of a "Westernized" Japanese literature. This is what Tablada's haikus were about.

Díaz Covarrubias's research on Japan as a technocratic model was followed by three other important scientific considerations of Japan and the Orient by engineers Miguel Ángel de Quevedo and Roberto Gayol, and doctor Carlos Glass (figure 7.4). Quevedo and Gayol had a significant impact on the development of Mexico City. Glass was a physician in the Mexican navy, assigned to the military ship Zaragoza, which went around the world in 1897. Glass reported his impressions of different parts of the world in El Mundo Ilustrado. He talked about the military power of Japan and conventional impressions of the faraway East, sending various pictures from China and Japan including "Execution in China," which photography historian Olivier Debroise considers a pioneering image of Mexican photojournalism.[44]

Quevedo, who studied in France in the 1880s, was known until the 1930s as the "Tree Apostle" and, when establishing conservationist techniques for Mexico City and the Pátzcuaro Lake in Michoacán, brought over Japanese professors Matzui and Yamachita, the second of whom was the former director of the Tokyo fishing industry.[45] Gayol, in turn, was one of the first sanitation engineers in Mexico City, influential to the development of sewer and irrigation systems in the city and other parts of the country. He was sent to both India and Japan to study irrigation systems from July 1908 to February 1909.[46]

The admiration for Westernized Japanese science was unanimous, unlike the admiration for the Westernization of Japanese literature. In Japan there were calls to stop the imitation of the West, a call echoed by various Mexican intellectuals destined to gain control of the city's culture in the 1920s, insisting on the emergence of a totally Mexican literature and an end to imitations of European cosmopolitism. Yet their nationalism was their most successful version of cosmopolitism. For indeed by the 1900s, for Mexico as well as for Japan, cultural "Westernization" meant "Americanization," a vulgar form of cosmopolitism for both Mexican and Japanese nativists. And a fait accompli that people in Mexico City both feared and avidly sought.

A Japanese Exhibition in Mexico City

Mexico City participated in the creation of the East, both through its Indigenous people and past, and through its own version of Japonisme. In 1904 Mexico City had its own version of Madame Butterfly in the popular opera En el Japón and, almost simultaneously, Tokutomi Roka's Hototoguisu was published

7.4. Díaz Covarrubias's view of Japan. Francisco Díaz Covarrubias, *Viaje de la Comisión Astronómica Mexicana al Japón: para observar el tránsito del planeta Vénus por el disco del sol el 8 de diciembre de 1874* (Mexico City: C. Ramiro y Ponce de León, 1876).

in a Mexico City newspaper (*Namiko* was the Spanish title, very likely a translation from either French or English). *Revista de Revistas* was still talking about the novel in 1919 (October 19). Tokutomi Roka was seen as the "Japanese Tolstoy," a comparison that, as I will show (chapter 8), blended two different Mexican odalisque-manias: one that longed for Japan, and another desiring the great Russian intellectual synthesis of the last part of the nineteenth century.

In 1907, at the peak of Mexico's own archaeological boom, the government commemorated the union of *indigenismo* and *Japonisme* with a Japanese garden at the foot of the Pyramid of the Moon, in the newly reconstructed Teotihuacán archaeological zone.[47] Curiously, in 1908 a Mexican traveler in Japan—perhaps Rebolledo or Tablada—published (in *El Mundo Ilustrado*) a long and detailed account, full of pictures, of Japanese gardens and cherry blossom festival in Japan. The account was a poetic description of the beauty and melancholy of Japanese gardens, echoing Lafcadio Hearn's accounts. Those who have not seen cherry trees in the spring in Japan, said the report, cannot fully imagine beauty. Then in 1910 the Egypt of America, Teotihuacán, included a Japanese garden.[48]

Consumption was another realm where orientalism, art, and science coincided in Mexico City. In April 1914 various downtown merchants in Mexico City organized a store-window competition. The public, by a vague voting process, preferred the Nuevo Mundo store windows. The picture of the winning display shows a Hindu-Arabic collage of textiles, carpets, and odalisque-looking mannequins.[49] The irony was total. Shoppers from a city often considered the Cairo of America found themselves fascinated by the orientalism of a store called "Nuevo Mundo" (New World). For these same shoppers the presence of Japan was a daily reality in Mexico City thanks to the Nuevo Japón shop. The shop was established by a Japanese immigrant in 1906 as a small shop for Japanese imports, mainly porcelain pieces and furniture. However, by 1913 it was called by La Semana Ilustrada one of Mexico's most important and elegant commercial establishments. There the city dweller could see Japanese porcelain, and even cherry trees in bloom.[50] Curiously, in 1910 a student protest responding to the lynching of a Mexican citizen in Rocksprings, Texas, stopped at the Nuevo Japón store, where the owner presented them with two flags—the Japanese and the Mexican.

These interactions culminated with a London-like exhibition of Japanese arts and crafts later in 1910, including a garden inaugurated for the festivities of the Centenario (figure 7.5). The exhibition occupied the Crystal Palace, the iron and crystal structure originally created for a future World's Fair in Mexico that ended up serving as a museum of natural history (see chapter 1). Shintaro Morimoto, envoy of the Compañía Oriental de Navegación, was the main advocate and organizer of an exhibit that, at the majestic Centenario celebration, represented a view of cosmopolitanism visited by both the lower and the upper classes. All the products—pottery, woodworks, technology—had already been sold to wealthy Mexico City elites, eager to establish their ownership of a Japanese salon at home. The exhibition coincided with the Baron and Baroness Yasuya Uchida's visit to Mexico. They were housed at the luxurious home of the widow of Braniff in El Paseo de la Reforma, and José Juan Tablada himself was put in charge of the Japanese delegation to the Centenario celebration. The exhibit included products that had no obvious Japanese influence, surprising the public because "they appeared to have been made in some European factory, given the fidelity and exactness with which Western art was reproduced."[51] Japan was then what Mexico had never managed to become: a perfect impostor.

This exhibition was an echo of international Japonisme, but also of East-West encounters. Exactly the same year, from May to October, the Japan-British

7.5. The Japanese exhibition. Courtesy Genaro García Collection, Nettie Lee Benson Latin American Collection, The University of Texas, Austin.

Exhibition was organized at the White City in London, where Japanese art fascinated the Bloomsbury group. The British exhibition was presented as an artistic affair, as opposed to the purely commercial motivations of the Mexican event. Both cases made the obsession with Japan clear, and established the new relationships of both Mexico City and London with this emerging world power.[52]

On Poetry and More

Despite the trends in art, it is in the tremendous popularity of Japanese poetic forms that the odalisque-mania of Mexican intellectuals is most visible.
Given the complexities of Japanese poetry and the insurmountable problems
of translation, one wonders how Japanese and Chinese poetry became so
prominent in the Spanish, French, and English languages. I believe Mexican
and European poets translated not the richness of a particular poetry, but the
hope of having a poetry of their own as particular.

Japanese haikus became a genre of their own in Mexico. The haiku, as a
modern critic has argued, is a "form of existence," especially suitable as "the
most selective container of the lightening process of illumination."[53] Poets,
at least in Mexico City, learned from the haiku "the possibility of reducing
the universe to sixteen syllables and the infinite into an exclamation."[54] As
I have argued with regard to Tablada's poetry, the Mexican haiku was a true
creation that, as the Spanish critic J. M. González de Mendoza affirmed,
eliminated "that ephemeral surprise for which the Japanese poet prepares the
reader." Thus Mexican haikus, said González de Mendoza, "are not an imitation of the Japanese ones . . . but rather, in a certain sense, an adaptation.
This can also be seen in the freedom of their metrics, which rarely adapt to
the difficult and scarcely harmonious classic measure."[55] Of course, Mexican poets had no knowledge of Japanese, but at least Tablada and Rebolledo,
unlike Ezra Pound or the Goncourt brothers, had lived in Japan for several
months.[56]

Japanese poetry was published and commented on widely in Mexico City's
literary journals. In 1900 various translations of Japanese poetry appeared in
Revista Moderna and, because they do not seem to come directly from Japanese, the cadence of the poems was significantly Mexicanized.[57] In 1925 in *La
Antorcha* (José Vasconcelos's magazine), González de Mendoza wrote about
the haiku and the synthetic poems in Mexico; he believed that the haiku was
too close to the Spanish *copla*—a traditional popular rhyme, usually in four
lines—and that, in order to conserve the richness of the Japanese haiku, Mexican poets ought to maintain its delicate and suggestive eroticism (otherwise,
they would write mere *coplas*).[58]

Japonisme faded over time in Mexico City, though it was still present in
the 1920s, when revolutionary governments established socialist-like policies. Haikus were then formatted as popular proverbs, including *Japonisme*,
populism, Mexican radicalism, and even Mexican anti-Semitism. Socialist
aesthetics, as an avant-garde obsession with both the manifesto rhetoric and
the beautiful utility of the short command for popular consumption, found a
home in the haiku style. Gutiérrez Cruz wrote in 1924:

La democracia, la obediencia y dios
Son tres maneras del amo
Para robarte mejor

Democracy, obedience, and God
are three ways the master has
of better robbing you.

And

Ellos crucificaron a Jesucristo
Nosotros crucificaremos
A los judíos.[59]

They crucified Jesus Christ;
we will crucify
the Jews.

According to Tablada, Gutiérrez Cruz (despite these pamphleteer pieces) also managed to write a perfect haiku in Spanish: "El Alacrán" (The Scorpion):

Surge de algún rincón
Enmedio [sic] de un paréntesis
Y una interrogación.[60]

From some corner it emerges,
between a parenthesis
and a question mark.

In 1922 writer and politician José Rubén Romero, inspired by Tablada, wrote a book of haikus (Historia de Tacámbaro). Apparently President Álvaro Obregón memorized these haikus—he was famous for his good memory—and altered them in order to add profanities, reciting them at official gatherings. The haikus were humorous, and although ostensibly inspired by the Japanese's poetic brevity, they were in fact echoes of popular wit. Here are two examples, full of deep irony and graphic plasticity difficult to convey in English:

El pueblo:
panaroma de Nacimiento.
Un buey, un gallo y un jumento.

The people:
panorama of the Nativity scene.
An ox, a rooster and an ass.

And

El granero.
Buscando huevos de gallina
por los rincones del granero
hallé los senos de mi prima.[61]

The granary.
Looking for hens' eggs
in the corner of the granary,
I found my cousin's breasts.

In 1923 haiku writer Francisco Monterde García Icazbalceta (about whom Tablada said "es haijin sincero y cabal" (he is a sincere and perfect *haijin*), wrote a haiku, linking late nineteenth-century social Darwinism and new Mexican *Japonisme*:

Atavismo.
Con el asombro de ayer,
Animales y campesinos
Miran en éxtasis al tren.[62]

Atavism.
With yesterday's astonishment,
animals and peasants
look in ecstasy at the train.

J. M. González de Mendoza was a haiku scholar and writer himself, and he wrote an excellent haiku about ambition:

La gota de agua
cayendo, cayendo,
se sueña Niágara.[63]

The drop of water
falling, falling,
dreams of being Niagara.

I recall vividly my first encounter with this haiku tradition as a child, a discovery so urban and so revealing. While walking in Paseo de la Reforma, on a huge wall surrounding some construction site, I saw the image of a slice of watermelon, and I read what I still know by heart: "del verano/roja y fría/ carcajada de sandía" (from the summer/red and cold/a watermelon laughter). Some odd city authority had put Tablada's haikus on the walls of the city, for us, city dwellers, to enjoy their fleeting beauty and wisdoms while we walked the streets.

In the early twentieth century this *Japonisme* reached beyond poetry to the novel in Rubén M. Campos's 1906 *Claudio Oronoz*. Campos was an amateur folklorist, a well-known collector of tunes and popular lyrics in the city. His novel was—oddly enough for Mexican literary tradition in the early twentieth century—an urban one, depicting bohemian Mexico City and thus including sensual scenes with a lot of *Japonisme* in the description of modern styles and sensual women.[64] Japan was thus not only a bucolic motif but also at the root of Mexico's urban novel. In the same way, in the 1920s Alfonso Teja Zabre's *La esperanza de Hati-Ké* transformed *Japonisme* into a novel about rural environments.[65] In it the author (a historian, writer, and politician) used what was vox populi—the presence of Japanese doctors and soldiers in the Mexican Revolution—in order to achieve a spiritualist version of Mexico's odalisque-mania. The novel, set in 1914, tells the story of Doctor Togo Matsumoto, an immigrant in Minantitlán, Veracruz, and his friend, the military man Hati-Ké, who was in love with a Mexican woman named Piedad. Hati-Ké is profound and disciplined, passionate and stern: "Fierce, brave, yellow, you love Piedad and you love Mexico, you are one of us, O Bushi, O Ronin, O Samurai, O Daimyo." The end of the novel constitutes a quintessential emblem of *Japonisme à la méxicaine*. Hati-Ké says: "I am not going to die. I know I will be reborn, wherever I want. I know I will be reborn in some town in the province of Yyó, near my family's people. And when the time comes, I will return with all of the dead. We will all return! Tanha, Tanha! Don't forget, you are Kaisahaku; I must fall face first, like this, like this."[66]

Desire

In Mexico City, as in cities in the U.S. and Europe, the image of Japan was marked by the desire of odalisques, especially because Japan, through what were known as *makuna-e, abuna-e, shunga,* and *warai-e,* had furnished modernist bohemians with the means to break away from nineteenth-century Catholic morality, as well as repressed eroticism. In the city's bohemia, Tablada and the Mexican modernists exchanged erotic sexual drawings from Japan. These constituted an Oriental orgasm for middle-class Mexican bohemians, immersed in a Catholic milieu that, until the 1930s, did not allow the publication of "bad words" or provocative images.

In 1875 Francisco Bulnes sought in Japan the kind of women whom French orientalist Pierre Loti would also find in the 1880s, thus describing beautiful and cold prostitutes full of *candor* (innocence and coyness) and mothers who sold their daughters to foreigners. Whereas in 1887 Loti asked for mothers who were "simultaneously dry cleaner, interpreter, and discreet agent for the crossing of races," before, in 1875, Bulnes praised this sexual commerce: "foreigners buy them at the price of a bull in Mexico, and to support them is not more expensive than a horse of good breed." Japanese women were a dream come true of total flesh, with no intellect to speak of. Said Bulnes:

> In them [Japanese women] there is sex, but the woman is nullified in their halo of intellectual incompetence . . . they have neither tears nor disdains, they smile for the buyer in an official manner, they never ask for a thing, they never whisper, they do not complain, they never get happy. Many of them speak English, but since they do not think, any possibility of conversation is absurd.[67]

Pure desire, with no intellectual obstacles, was a modern dream Mexicans like Bulnes found in Japanese women. Curiously, Mexican-American folklorist Américo Paredes echoed this blend of desire and racism vis-à-vis Oriental women in his 1940s reports from the East to the Mexico City newspaper El Universal. Like Bulnes, Paredes traveled to both China and Japan (also to Korea), and like Bulnes, his erotic hunger was better satisfied by Japan than by China.[68]

In turn Efrén Rebolledo, in his Tokyo-composed *Rimas japonesas*, wrote that Tokyo at night brought to him:

> En rachas tempestuosas de loca furia
> A mi oído excitado llega el bullicio
> Y las teñidas bocas finas de vicio
> Rebosan del veneno de la lujuria.[69]

> In tempestuous bursts of wild fury;
> the uproar reaches my excited ear
> and the fine, painted mouths of vice
> are brimming with the venom of lust.

Drawings and paintings of Japanese desire were also produced. In 1901 Julio Ruelas, one of Mexico City's most prominent illustrators, painted his

7.6. Roberto Montenegro's Odalisca. Courtesy Blaisten Collection, Mexico City.

own Oriental odalisque: a Chinese Venus. In 1911 the young painter and social critic José Clemente Orozco, in addition to drawing images of Mexico
City's prostitutes, praised opera singer Regina Vicarino in the role of Madame
Butterfly because, like a Japanese woman, "está para comerse" (she looks good
enough to eat).[70] David Alfaro Siqueiros also painted a stylish odalisque: an
Oriental ballerina, graciously jumping into the air. The colors and contours
of the images created an archetype of ecstasy through the image of exotic
women.[71] In 1920 artist Roberto Montenegro produced stylish blends of
Japanese motifs with modernist notions of beauty and fashion for the cover
of *Revista de Revistas*. This odalisque depiction would often reappear in Montenegro's art (figure 7.6).[72]

As we will see, even though some artists in the city—like Rivera—were strongly opposed to Mexico's odalisque-mania, Orozco and Siqueiros experimented with it. Granted, most of this experimentation was in the ephemeral format of magazine illustrations, precisely because it was in the ephemeralness and immediacy of periodicals where all sorts of cultural experimentation took place.

In turn, to dress like a geisha, or to organize Japanese kermises and parties, became commonplace in the city. The social pages of newspapers and magazines often reproduced those events. For instance the Catholic newspaper El Tiempo Ilustrado reported on one of these kermises in 1904: geishas selling tamales and atole.[73] Likewise, during the 1910 Japanese exhibition, both Japanese and Mexican women dressed in kimonos and were pictured in the Japanese setting par excellence: a Japanese garden.[74]

However, this geisha-fascination was not uncontested in Mexico City's cultural and social circles. In 1910, after a stylish social gathering to celebrate the birthday of a Japanese ambassador, a social magazine reported on the great costumes because all the women had dressed in beautiful geisha style. At the party there were recitations in French as well as the representation of "a day in Japan"—an idealized, sensual, and exotic version of the life of Japanese women. The magazine reported that "we saw the private life of the Japanese woman; two of them appeared lying on velvet cushions, and then the maids came in, dressed them, and served them breakfast in rich, fine porcelain cups."[75] But Tristan de Lyra, the pseudonym of a feminist thinker who wrote for the influential intellectual magazine Arte y Letras, explained what a geisha meant in terms of sexual exploitation, adding:

> You see, kind [woman] reader, the disgraceful creature you represent when, in fantasy dances, you turn into the Japanese woman; you free and respected woman . . . there exist, for the transformations of your ballroom, [different] types of free women, of women who boast the seal of the ideals that have elevated the female sex up to par with men.[76]

If male Mexican intellectuals found in the geisha a way to attest their Westernness, Mexican feminists (both male and female) found, in the negation of such a trend, the affirmation of their true Westernness. But geisha-mania knew no limits. One of the greatest moments of this collective geisha infatuation took place in 1912, when the popular Mexican diva Esperanza Iris appeared as Geisha Rolly Polly in the Abreu theater (figure 7.7).[77] Likewise, the magazine Arte y Letras published, in 1908, a translation of "O'Hana," a tale by A. de Gériolles (aka Mme. L. Génu de Régiol, an author of various orientalist narratives), with illustrations by C. Godoy. O'Hana was irresistibly beauti-

7.7. Esperanza Iris as a geisha. *La Semana Ilustrada* (June 5, 1912).

7.8. C. Godoy's illustration, A. de Gériolles's "O'Hana," *Arte y Letras* (June 1908).

ful and, at the same time, an evil Japanese priestess of the goddess of light, Amaterasu. She seduced a samurai and killed him to win the throne for his brother. Godoy's illustrations displayed a Japanese geisha and a valiant samurai doomed by lust, including many stereotypical, odalisque-mania-like views of Japan (figure 7.8).[78] However, it is important to bear in mind that the same influential modernist publications like *La Revista Azul* could also publish poems by modernists, full of Nahuatl references, representing another form of aesthetic experimentation.[79] Indeed, *Japonerie* was not antagonistic to *aztequisme*: it belonged to the same modern command.

Art: Ranchero *Yōga*

In painting, Mexican *Japonisme* found a bizarre accomplice: Mexican artists painting *nihonga* (traditional Japanese-style paintings) were complemented by Japanese artists producing *yōga* (Japanese Western-style paintings) à la ranchero. As I have shown, Tablada was known in Mexico City as the local *nihonga* painter. Moreover, in 1918 three Mexican artists—Marius de Zayas, Juan Olaguíbel, and Pal-Omar—exhibited their work in New York. There is not much information available about this exhibit, but it seems that the three painters used Oriental motifs.[80]

Even more interesting is the concept of Mexico as an inspiration to Japanese artists, especially for Kitagawa Tamiji and Foujita. Kitagawa arrived in Mexico in the early 1920s and was involved in the aesthetic experiment of the Escuelas de Pintura al Aire Libre (EPAL). The EPAL aimed in the 1920s and 1930s to recover the authenticity and naiveté of "real" Mexicans (preferably Indigenous children), in order to create both a Mexican and a universal form of art. Artist Alfredo Ramos Martínez conceived of these schools as pedagogical and social tools for aesthetically improving the nation (he studied and lived in Paris for fourteen years, later moving to California). The EPAL were part of a unique form of Mexican cultural nativism that found, in Indians and in children, the seeds of a new art form. This was a unique form of primitivism, one not overlooked by Japanese painter Kitagawa.

Kitagawa left Japan in the second decade of the twentieth century—he was not the firstborn son of his relatively wealthy father—but not before being introduced to *yōga* by Miyazaki Shoogo. After arriving in New York he studied with John Sloan, one of the Group of the Eight, a socialist who was then fighting against canonic art in the U.S. He was involved with Mexico City's various artistic mafias as art editor of *The Masses* in 1912–16, including U.S. artists like Maurice Becker, Henry Glintenkamp, and George O. "Pop" Hart. They were three radicals close to Sloan who, as pacifists, escaped to Mexico and found a natural complement to their aesthetic and political experimentation in "local colors" and the Revolution. Kitagawa was thus included in the circle of seekers of the Brown Atlantis.[81]

After a period of poverty in which Kitagawa, like many recent immigrant Jews, sold religious images door-to-door in Mexico City, he began studying at the EPAL in Churubusco, on the outskirts of Mexico City. He later worked as a teacher in the Tlalpan school from 1925 to 1932, ending up as director of the Taxco school in the state of Guerrero from 1932 to 1936, where he was visited by Japanese artists Foujita and Yasuo Kuniyoshi, and Japanese-American Isamu Noguchi.[82]

Mexico was the "rustic" component needed to overcome industrialism. Kitagawa, however, eventually moved from the city to the village and the countryside, thus joining a pilgrimage made by many others. He became a great admirer of the pedagogical technique of Ramos Martínez and a committed follower of the naiveté and flexibility of the Indigenous Mexican artistic mind. He tried to achieve this naiveté in his own self-portrait, blurring the difference between East and West and forming an East-East identification—a Japanese artist who looked like a Mexican *campesino* or "obrero leyendo."[83] He pursued a sort of reverse odalisque-mania, painting celebrations and scenes in Taxco and other places, or depicting, in the invitations to his own wedding in Mexico to Tetsuko Ninomiya (1929), the representation of La Catrina—the image of death popularized in the 1900s by José Guadalupe Posadas's lithographs, which were massively distributed in Mexico City in colorful papers. By the late 1920s, La Catrina had been, as it were, gentrified by avant-garde painters as a form of Mexican authenticity, and in Kitagawa's wedding invitation it served as an uncanny blending of love, irony, and death—a Mexican-inspired skeleton drawn by a Japanese painter in the act of uniting husband and wife (figure 7.9).

Kitagawa thus became a common icon for the discovery of a Brown Atlantis by artists and travelers. Travel guides, like 1935's *Mexican Odyssey*, included a description of Kitagawa and his Taxco. He was also a character in stories by U.S. radical journalist Josephine Herbst, who lived in Mexico in 1932. In her story "The Governor Does Not Come," villagers wait for the coming of the governor (who never comes!). Kunigoya, a local Japanese art teacher, wants to impress the governor with his paintings, and those of his students, wanting to become the next Riveras. Kinigoya, of course, represented the Kitagawa whom Herbst likely met in her travel to Taxco in 1932.[84] The move from the U.S. to Mexico was but one small geographical and cultural step, a step toward escaping what Kitagawa identified as "goodness that does not presuppose bad intentions, a beauty that does not imply production, stimulants that are not toxic and a country that does not have the possibility of miracles."[85]

Kitagawa eventually returned to Japan, implementing the EPAL method with Japanese children. His later paintings, like those of many of his U.S. masters, showed a renewed interest in chaotic urban scenes and in the unavoidable visions of the disappointing yet real land of postwar Japan. However, the influence and impact of Mexico City and Taxco on Kitagawa's work remain clear. Those cities were, to him, what Japan was to many Mexican artists: a staging point for a period of moral and aesthetic experimentation searching for purity, authenticity, and unseen beauty. Small wonder, then, that in 1928 Díaz de León considered Kitagawa's paintings a good example for foreigner artists in Mexico to follow. He, according to Díaz de León, was a great painter who—unlike other foreigners in Mexico—did not "teach us [Mexicans] what our soil is, what our customs and our art are." Kitagawa had not learned the "Berlitz of painting," and thus painted Mexico as he "speaks Spanish: because of *convivencia* (living together)." His art would never be tourist art, although Díaz de León admitted that Kitagawa constantly reproduced stereotypical na-

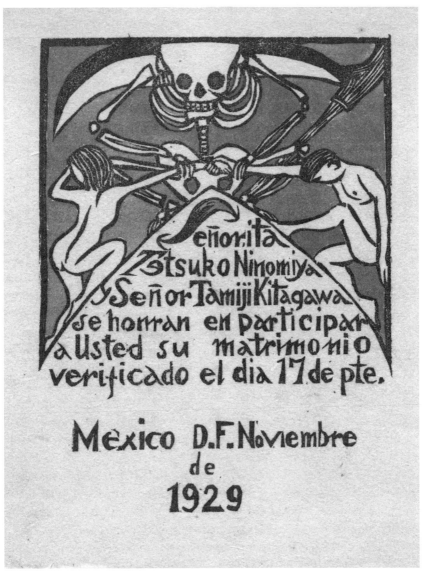

Señorita Tsuko Ninomiya y Señor Tamiji Kitagawa se honran en participar a Usted su matrimonio verificado el dia 17 de pte. Mexico D.F. Noviembre de 1929

7.9. Kitagawa's wedding invitation, Mexico, 1929.
Courtesy Blaisten Collection, Mexico City.

tional types only because "in those types he finds a familiar air (a hypothesis explained by the Bering Strait)."[86] Thus old and new Mexican orientalism were joined. Kitagawa was also praised by vanguard writer Xavier Villaurrutia, a poet and painter who did not follow the revolutionary nationalism of the 1930s. Kitagawa elaborated a portrait of Villaurrutia in which the melancholic eyes, almost effeminate, are naturally those of the poet who had, by coincidence, written that he felt "una languidez" (a feebleness), "cansancio, casi de relato/pueril . . ." (a tiredness, almost of a puerile tale . . .), as if

en el claroscuro envejecido
de un melancólico retrato.

in the aged chiaroscuro
of a melancholic portrait.

Kitagawa's melancholic portrait included a Japanese inscription: "1930 by the Western calendar. By request of Villaurrutia. By Kitagawa"[87] (figure 7.10).

This artistic Japanese-Mexican interaction was eventually reproduced on a larger scale in other artistic circles in Japan. Historian Bert Winther-Tamaki refers to the "Mexican boom" in Japanese art, whose main expression was the sizeable exhibition of Mexican art at the Tokyo National Museum in 1955. Mexican authorities and intellectuals organized the exhibit, as they had already done at other national museums. Japanese critics, for their part, found the ideas of total continuity from ancient pre-Hispanic times to modern art, and from mythical, non-Western, pristine milieus to a modern, alternative, and authentic art, credible. Japanese intellectuals and artists of the 1950s, like Kitagawa in the 1920s, satisfied their odalisque-mania by viewing a racially and revolutionarily powerful Mexico—especially in terms of the body. "The admiration for powerful Mexican embodiment," explains Winther-Tamaki, "was further articulated by the frequent recurrence in the discussion of terms that reference the human body, such as 'muscular optimism,' 'peak attainment of figurative art,' 'powerful smell of humanity,' and 'vital racial power.'" Hence the 1950s Mexican boom in Japanese art accentuated the ever-present stereotype of Mexico. For Mexican artists this was partly self-inflicted and partly imposed from the outside by the "cage" of the Brown Atlantis.

While in Mexico, Kitagawa received Japanese painter Foujita, who lived in Paris, and during 1932 and 1933 traveled with his lover, dancer Madeleine Lequeux, to Argentina, Brazil, Cuba, and Mexico. Foujita knew Rivera from the bohemian circles of Paris. Rivera had, in fact, painted a cubist canvas of Foujita and his friend Kawashima Riichiro in classic Greek outfits, which they liked to wear in the Parisian scene of Rivera, Modigliani, and Picasso. Foujita visited Rivera and Kitagawa in early 1933 and stayed in Mexico City for seven months. He consumed Rivera's self-perpetuated legend as a man who needed to shoot his guns for inspiration, and was absorbed by the murals. Although little evidence remains, he held an exhibition at precisely the Ministry of Edu-

7.10. Xavier Villaurrutia by Kitagawa. Courtesy Luis Mario Schneider papers, Biblioteca Pública Municipal, Malinalco, Mexico. Published in *Xavier Villaurrutia: entre líneas, dibujo y pintura*, edited by Luis Mario Schneider (Mexico City: Ediciones Trabuco y Clavel, 1991).

cation where Rivera painted walls. The exhibition, Kitagawa recalled, was a total failure. Foujita painted "typical" Mexican characters—sombreros, native faces—but mostly painted his own French companion, Madeleine, in Mexican scenes. "The entire exhibit," reported a critic, "was the pictorial presence of Señora Foujita, who even in her nakedness . . . is chaste."[88] Upon returning to Japan with Madeleine, Foujita painted an odalisque version of her surrounded by, *comme il faut*, cacti and Mexican commonplaces.

As I said, Foujita visited Kitagawa in Taxco, where the two characters exchanged artistic views about Mexican and Japanese art. Whereas Kitagawa's cosmopolitanism was a Mexicanized version of naïve social art, Foujita became a strong proponent of muralism in Japan. In 1934, already back in Japan, Foujita painted a large mural for a Brazilian coffee showroom in the Ginza. He also exhibited some of the art he produced during his travels to Mexico, Cuba, Argentina, and Brazil. To French critics Foujita epitomized the exotic Japan they longed for. He even illustrated (among other works) Pierre Loti's *Madame Chrysanthème* in 1926, blending French nineteenth-century *Japonisme* with 1920s avant-garde art. For Mexicans like Rivera, Foujita was the exotic Japanese traveling through Mexico with a liberated French woman, a man who could speak perfect French and whose Oriental origins necessarily matched Mexico's own efforts at returning to authenticity. Cosmopolitan Mexico in the 1930s left a mark on Foujita as well, a fact not missed by Japanese critics upon Foujita's return to Japan. His works, wrote the critic Araki Sueo, were but *ukiyo-e* paintings with an alien Mexican view. "He has been enraptured by the sight of Mexico, and with the same gaze he directs to foreign lands he traces his dreams about the old ways of his native land." That is, whereas Mexican *Japonisme* à la Tablada reinforced the search for local authenticity, Mexico reinforced and renewed Foujita's faith in the local.[89]

End

I have shuffled images that have gone from a sixteenth-century Mexican martyr killed by Japanese soldiers to Kitagawa's Mexican canvases; from Mexican scientific and economic studies of Japan to the haiku renovation of Mexico's poetry; and from geisha dreams to Fujita's European odalisque painted on stereotypical Mexican backgrounds. These images show the intricate textures of the cultural life of Mexico City; a culture that flowed in a turbulent river where many currents clashed and interacted. There was then already an indisputable fact that is better explained by an anecdote. In the 1950s popular Japanese singer Yoshiro Hiroishi came to Mexico City after his successful adaptation of "Sabor a mí" ("you taste like me" or "you carry my flavor"), a very popular piece by bohemian songwriter and singer Álvaro Carrillo. Dressed in traditional Japanese ceremonial clothing, Yoshiro appeared at Carrillo's night-club and intoned "Sabor a mí" before the singer; since that night, the anec-dote has been retold countless times. Neither Yoshiro nor Carrillo could have known that the whole scene—the two of them, their popular success in Japan and Mexico, and *the song*—would become the irrefutable lesson in unusual cultural interactions. The lyrics contained all that needs to be said about these dances between the presumed East and presumed semi-West:

> . . . que yo guardo tu sabor
> pero tú llevas también, sabor mí.

> That I keep your flavor,
> but you also keep mine in you.

8

INDIA

"I want to say that I can understand, to a certain extent, what it means to be Indian [from India] because I am Mexican."[1] So wrote Octavio Paz, Mexican ambassador to India from 1962 to 1968. India indeed was and is an essential spirit for the modern world. For him, India shared Mexico's cultural extremity to the extent that India was Mexico itself. It was as if in Mexico's long-lasting odalisque-mania, a true common ontology could be found in East and West—or at least between the East (India) and the semi-East/semi-West (Mexico). In fact, what Paz said about India has, today, the feeling of a relatively well-documented and common Western orientalism, for the true story of Mexico City's cultural attraction to Indian cultures has a longer and more complicated history.

The allure of India was felt in the city in variegated cultural domains. Language and religion were one, through both the nineteenth-century philological importance of Sanskrit and the modernist vogue of all sorts of Indian philosophies all over the world. Poets in Mexico City also had an Indian affair—what can be called the Rabindranath Tagore moment. Moreover, like Japanese odalisques, Indian odalisques also impacted the perceptions of bodies and desire in the city. Finally, I also submit that in the early 1920s there was in Mexico City an Indian odalisque mania in politics: the activities and presence in the city of a Bengali Quixote, Manabendra Nath Roy, the founder of the Mexican Communist Party (see chapter 4). It could be objected, of course, that all these domains are unrelated, that Mexican philology had little to do with India and even less to do with Hindu-like Tehuanas; that the history of communism—historical materialism—ought not to be blended with otherworldly spiritualist trends. And yet, all these bizarre interactions took place in Mexico City between the 1880s and the 1920s; therefore, please allow me to at least reveal to you how India nurtured, if secretly, a modernist city with words, ghosts, poetry, desire, and utopias.

Sanskrit and Spirit

India, unlike Japan, did not furnish Mexico with a saint. But it did give Mexico the celebrated image of Catarina de San Juan, "La China Poblana," an Indian woman born in Delhi who was sold as a slave, brought to the Philippines, and then sent to Mexico in 1619. She established herself as a model of purity and proletarian elegance for the urban poor in Puebla. According to legend "La China," born Mirraha, was the daughter of a magician or a yogi. Her fame and supposed power led to the creation of a popular cult, seen in popular Mexican celebrations as well as in countless travel books. She became the symbol of dark Mexican beauty, dressed in a Hindu-like—yet Mexican—sari.[2]

This mystical import of India has been a lot more important than Indian migration to Mexico City. In the nineteenth and early twentieth centuries Indians did not migrate to Mexico in very significant numbers, though there is some evidence of Sikh migration to northern Mexico in the 1920s (the Sikhs were linked to the U.S. migration quotas and nationalist movements in India).[3] India's presence in Mexico came from different sources. India was, at the time, not yet a nation-state, and Indian nationalism—until the diffusion of Rabindranath Tagore's thought—was questioned in the Mexican media. Mexico City's liberal media viewed India's revolutionary violence with skepticism; India's secession from the enlightened British Empire would be a disaster.[4] But in the second part of the nineteenth century, India became an important source of aesthetic, religious, and political ideas. This was mainly thanks to philology—a well-developed discipline in the Spanish-speaking world—and Hinduism—which had significant impact all over the world as an alternative to modern industrialism.

In Spanish-speaking countries, nineteenth-century comparative philology brought about the study of many Native American languages, as well as Sanskrit. Before the "philological revolution" of Friedrich Schlegel and Franz Boop (both advocates of the study of Sanskrit in Europe), Lorenzo Hervás y Panduro pioneered comparative philology in Spain. Thus, by the second half of the nineteenth century the philological canon established the unity of all Indo-European languages. A search for traces of an original, primitive Sanskrit had begun all over the world.[5] Amateur anthropologist Gumesindo Mendoza proved the existence of Oriental origins in Mexico through the bonds between the mother tongue, Sanskrit, and Nahuatl. Mendoza spoke Otomi and Nahuatl, so he claimed to have the authority to comment on the connections between these languages and Sanskrit.[6] He presented a lengthy list of correlations between the two languages, his evidence that Sanskrit lay at the origin of the Aztec language. Science and religion, he argued, agree upon a sole common origin of humankind, and philologists could easily prove this fact by demonstrating how all Indo-European languages came from the languages of "Brahmans."

Mendoza, furthermore, believed in the existence of both Atlantis and contacts between ancient American and Indo-European civilizations. He focused on linguistic links: *Ap*, meaning "water" in Sanskrit, became *apantli* in Nahuatl, meaning "water creek" or "water passing by." *Apam*, "ocean" in Sanskrit, was for him the root of *Apam*, a town in the modern State of Hidalgo where, as it so happens, there is a lagoon and thus the relation to "ocean." *Sitara*, according to Mendoza, was a Hindu word derived from Sanskrit meaning "star," and was associated with *Sitalla*, the Nahautl word for star. *Astika*, the Sanskrit term for believer, related to *Azteka*: "raza creyente y muy religiosa" (a race of strong faith, and very religious).[7]

One of the most prolific Mexicanist anthropologists of the late nineteenth century, Daniel Brinton, was the first collector of Nahuatl poems, which he titled (following his own India-like odalisque-mania) *Rig Veda Americanus*.[8] Brinton called Mendoza's exercise "a misdirected erudition," as it was all too obvious to Brinton that the language of the Aztecs came from Mongolia![9] Francisco Pimentel, one of the most distinguished Mexican philologists in the nineteenth century, was also very critical, both of Mendoza's idealization of the sublime character of Otomi as the mother language of Nahuatl, and of the relationship between Otomi-Nahuatl and Sanskrit. For Pimentel, language was instead something that had been given to humankind. It was a natural thing, a spontaneous occurrence, and thus related to God. Pimentel believed that there was no basis on which to prove the sublimity of Otomi, or the Sanskrit origins of Nahuatl, and that many relationships could be found in all language because of the spontaneous character of language as a divine gift. He was adamant in his own orientalism:

> A sublime language—that is, elevated, lofty, rich—not only has a term for every capital idea, but also for their diverse modifications. In Spanish, for example, to express the different degrees of the same love, we say *to esteem, to care for, to love, and to adore*. What an appropriate gradation of our feelings! We esteem our friends, we care for a relative, we love our children, and we adore God. Perhaps the language richest in synonyms is Arabic, as may be observed in Hammer's memoirs, entitled *Das Kamel*, in which he states that that language has 5,744 words just for *camel*.[10]

The study of Sanskrit—and philology in general—was thus also a battlefield for different forms of Mexican odalisque-mania. Throughout the nineteenth century, in fact, the study of Sanskrit was a priority for philologists of the Spanish languages. Consider, for example, Manuel J. Rodríguez's *La fuente del idioma español; o, Formación de más de 7.000 vocablos castellanos, derivados de 90 raíces tomadas del sánscrito, del griego y del latín, con expresión etimológica y filosófica del desarrollo natural de las lenguas indo-europeas* (1900).[11] Along with Sanskrit, the Hebrew language, since the fifteenth century, had been a subject of study and revelation for Spanish intellectuals. Hence, for instance, Hebrew fascinated a physician and educator in Aguascalientes, Jesús Díaz de León, who translated the Song of Songs from Hebrew (as well as other texts). He advocated the study of Hebrew in various books and in *El Instructor*, a scientific periodical he edited from 1884 to 1907. But in addition to a scholar of Hebrew and Greek, Díaz de León was an early promoter of Mexican *indigenismo* in Mexico City.[12] In the same way Luis Cabrera—one of the most prominent intellectuals in the Carranza faction of the Revolution and a nationalist promoter of Mexican arts and crafts—also translated the Song of Songs from Greek (1919).[13]

Studying ancient Eastern languages became such a mark of erudition and sophistication that, at the beginning of the twentieth century, a telling anecdote circulated in Mexico City about Minister of Education Justo Sierra asking distinguished (and pretentious) Sanskrit philologist Maestro Rivas what was he studying. He responded: "Estoy muy ocupado con la gramática del arameo" (I'm very busy with Aramaic grammar), to which Sierra responded: "Pretencioso, Usted ya no ara no más mea" (aren't you pretentious, you, sir, no longer plow [*ara*], only pee [*mea*]).[14] Sarcasm aside, philologists in Mexico City were simply trying out available theories in order to understand Mexico's complex linguistic landscape, becoming active participants in world philology—fertile soil for orientalisms.

Language, however, was only one facet of Mexico's turn-of-the-century India odalisque-mania. Another source of fascination with India and the Orient came from the widespread blend of spiritualist, New Thought, and theosophical trends. Freemasonry, to be sure, remained a widespread source of secret rites and symbols in Mexico, the U.S., and France. As far as its secrecy allows the historian to know, Freemasonry's cult of science at times immunized it from the fever of Hindu, spiritualist, and theosophical trends of the last part of the nineteenth century; at times, however, it overlapped with Hindu-like philosophies. A great example of this in Mexico was the German doctor Arnold Krumm-Heller, who was in Mexico City in the 1900s, returned to Germany in the 1920s, and wrote vastly on the racial superiority of the Aryan and Aztec races. He blended theosophy, Freemasonry, racial theories, and his own orientalism vis-à-vis pre-Hispanic Mexico. By 1914, for him, Carranza's Mexico would resist the lure of the American (U.S.) mermaids, and would follow Germany's spiritualist call, rediscovering their Aztec (quasi-Aryan) past.[15]

In 1868 a spiritualist movement began in Guanajuato and Guadalajara. By 1900 there were several spiritualist associations in Mexico City, many with their own publications. Gradually, this purely spiritualist trend began to combine with different forms of New Thought, occultism, and theosophy. This was especially true of the ideas propagated by Madame Helena Blavatsky in England, France, and the U.S. Many Indian religious texts were thus introduced to Mexico.[16] Various Mexicans signed an attachment to the famous 1900 Spiritualist World's Congress declaration in Paris, among them General José de Bazethany, Doctor Pascual G. Molina, and journalist Luis G. Rubri. Foreigners like Russian symbolist poet Konstantin Balmont were, in turn, inclined to visit Mexico through theosophical inspiration. Balmont went to Mexico in 1905 searching for the theosophical connection between India, the Mayans, and Egypt. As late as the 1930s Antonin Artaud still viewed all "Brahman and Jewish exotericisms" through the same conceptual framework as Mexico's *Chilam Balam* or *Popol-Vuh*: "Who does not understand," he wrote, "that these exotericisms are one single exotericism that seeks to say, in spirit, the same thing?"[17]

In order to grasp this odalisque-mania in Mexico City we ought to understand these trends as forms of progressive, avant-garde, and "spiritual" enhancements in an increasingly materialistic and scientific era. Common ideological references in Mexico included liberalism, republicanism, positivism, as well as social and political Catholicism, but as the nineteenth century advanced, the prevalence of scientific, materialistic, and Jacobin trends somehow led intellectuals and urban middle classes to search for spiritualist complements.[18] Spiritualism in Mexico City was, therefore, a form of modernity in the same way that positivism was. It is no wonder, then, that spiritualism was often propagated as an imitation of the Masonic organization.[19] Such an imitation occurred in all parts of the world, as many socialists were also followers of New Thought in some form or another. In Mexico City spiritualism and theosophy were especially useful for balancing a deeply rooted religious belief in a supreme spiritual power with modern ideas of progress and science. Krausism played a similar role in Spain, combining a form of idealism (the belief in a supreme being) with scientific progress. The various forms of spiritualism, New Thought, theosophy, and transcendentalism were linked throughout the Americas and Europe with shared associations and publications. Emerson, Thoreau, Schopenhauer—all widely read in Mexico City—and many other authors are examples of these links. The World's Parliament of Religion, connected with the 1893 World's Fair in Chicago, popularized the modern discussion of Indian philosophy and the teachings of Vivekananda.[20]

Nothing represents the mutual interaction of Indian and Western thought in the last part of the nineteenth century better than theosophy. It derived mostly from Indian thought, including elements of the Vedas, the Upanishads and the Bhagavad-Gita ("Song of the Lord"), as well as Islamic Sufism, Buddhism, and Taoism. The Theosophical Society of New York, founded in 1875 by Helena Blavatsky and Henry Steel Olcott, was instrumental in popularizing these ideas. Both Blavatsky and Olcott moved to India in 1878 and established a center at Adyar. Blavatsky published various works, like her *Isis Unveiled* (1877) and *The Secret Doctrine* (1888), that were widely discussed throughout the world. Theosophy claimed to work toward a universal brotherhood of humanity without distinction of race, creed, sex, or color, while also proposing an ecumenical doctrine based on the study of comparative religions examining the unexplained laws of nature and the latent powers of human beings.

Though many forms of New Thought did not explicitly claim any "orientalist" connections in their origins or spiritual doctrines, it eventually became essential to prove links to the source of true "spiritualism"—India. Theosophy was thus "Indianized" little by little. The first major influence came from the handsome Indian Brahman, Mohini Mohandas Chaterjee. "Indians were to prove sexually fascinating for many theosophically inclined European women," argues historian Peter Washington. The myth of supreme Indian spirituality blended with the myth of Oriental sensuality in many instances, such as the appeal of many gurus or—in a variation of New Thought—the radical nationalism and socialism promoted in Mexico City by M. N. Roy, another handsome Brahman who moved from Hinduism to Marxism and nationalism.

In Mexico City theosophical society publications disseminated the spiritual supremacy of Indian thought. In 1914, for instance, the theosophical magazine *Flores de Loto* published (along with an homage to Helena Petrovna Blavatsky) the poem "La India" by Esther Valle, a member of the Mexican Theosophical Society:

¡Oh Indostán! El que te mira
por la vez primera, siente
una atracción reverente
hacia tu credo que admira.
Quiere, cuando en él se inspira,
romper las férreas cadenas
que unen las vidas terrenas,
como el yogui que lo eterno
halla en el santuario interno,
libre de goces y penas.[21]

O Hindustan!
He who looks at you
for the first time feels
a reverent admiration
for your admirable creed.
When by this creed he is inspired, he wants
to break the iron chains
that bind together the worldly lives,
like the yogi that finds what is eternal
in the inner sanctuary,
free of pleasures and of pains.

India was a "reverent attraction" already linked, in Mexico, to modern ideas. The idea of *Indostán* was as modern as the inventions of Thomas Alva Edison (himself a known theosophist), or as truly Mexican as the belief in a supreme order and the morality of self-sacrifice and respect to authority.[22]

José Juan Tablada, the prominent seeker of Japanese odalisques and manufacturer of goods for consumers of the Brown Atlantis, also tried theosophy and Indian thought. To essay was to exist, as in his 1923 poem "Meditación teosófica" where he gave evidence of his excursions into theosophy:

Yo fui loro en la Luna . . .
Me lo ha dicho la Teosofía
Y aquella que fue una
Alma inocente y gárrula, es hoy el alma mía.[23]

I was a parrot on the Moon . . .
Theosophy has told me,
and that soul that was
innocent and garrulous is, today, mine.

Tablada, according to J. M. González de Mendoza, started exploring theosophy in the early 1920s, in particular through the writings of P. D. Ouspensky (also Uspenskii).[24] The mélange of four-dimensional mathematics and Buddhism fascinated Tablada. He advocated Ouspensky's ideas in Spanish, writing the prologue for the Spanish edition of Ouspensky's *Tertium Organum*.[25] Tablada's letters in the 1920s often talked about the supreme spiritualism reached through Buddha and New Thought, and his 1924 novel *La resurrección de los ídolos* tells the story of a theosophy teacher facing the temptation of carnal love (this is the same topic, as we will see, of Amado Nervo's poem).[26] The novel blends *indigenista* themes with theosophy, turning Mexico City into an evil cosmopolitan agent corrupting the real (Quetzalcoatl) humanist spirit of Mexico vis-à-vis the purity of a small town. In the novel the well-known statues of the "Indios Verdes" in Mexico City are resurrected because "it is an axiom of occultism that statues are true prisons for the fleshless souls who remain captured in them."[27] As critic Serrato Córdova has shown in his study of the novel, *La resurrección de los ídolos* is a political novel critical of the violence and corruption in revolutionary Mexico City, searching for a primitive essence through theosophical arguments so complex that the reader needs a theosophical dictionary to finish the novel. However, Tablada's affair with theosophy was not as significant as those of other Mexican artists, intellectuals, and politicians.

Art historians Fausto Ramírez and Renato González Mello have recently maintained—somewhat controversially—that in some of Diego Rivera's and José Clemente Orozco's murals a secret esoteric dialogue takes place—a dialogue full of Hindu, Masonic, and theosophical symbolism. It seems that indeed at some point Rivera belonged to the Quetzalcoatl lodge of the Antigua y Mística Orden Rosa Cruz. It is also clear, as González Mello shows, that Alma Reed introduced Orozco to the Delphic Circle, a 1930s New York literary salon where Indian nationalism and esotericism were influential, especially through the presence of Sarojini Naidu—the prominent Bengali nationalist, sister of Virendranath Chattopadhyaya, and thus close to the M. N. Roy nationalist circles in New York and Mexico City (see chapter 4). Orozco found in Naidu an admirer of Mexican "untouchables"—*campesinos*—, as he recalled in his autobiography. I, however, am incapable of truly following the Hindu or Bengali input in Rivera's and Orozco's murals—especially considering Rivera's criticism of Tagore and Vasconcelos (see below). But the interested reader should not miss Ramírez's and Gonzlález Mello's provocative arguments.[28]

In fact, Amado Nervo (1870–1919), Francisco I. Madero (1873–1913), and, of course, José Vasconcelos (1881–1959) were the Mexican thinkers who best epitomized the uses and abuses of Indian philosophy in its different versions. Their understanding was filtered by Spanish Catholic mysticism, spiritualism, theosophy, transcendentalism, and the writings of French, German, and British orientalists. The significance of these three men in the history of the city and the country as a whole speaks to the important mark left by this odd odalisque-mania. Nervo was without doubt the most prestigious Mexican poet at the turn of the century. Madero was no less than the father of the Mexican Revolution, and Vasconcelos (along with Alfonso Reyes) was the most prominent intellectual of the first half of the twentieth century.

Amado Nervo's reputation as a modernist poet—and as a popular poet— has often obscured his Hindu inspiration, which can be attributed, first, to his strong sense of religion, full of mysticism, stoicism, and skepticism; second, to his readings of Maurice Maeterlinck, French symbolism, and Ralph Waldo Emerson; and finally, to his relationships with Spanish, Argentine, and Mexican *Krausistas*, theosophists, and spiritualists (especially after the death of a Platonic love).[29] After reading Belgian writer Maurice Maeterlinck—a Catholic whose texts were full of symbolism and mysticism influenced by Novalis and Emerson—and Catholic Spanish poet Miguel de Unamuno, Nervo began his own search for transcendental thought. There he found profound inspiration in Hindu ideas. In his poem "Predestinación" he left traces of his endless philosophical search:

> ¡Estaba escrito así! No más te afanes
> por borrar de mi faz el torvo enigma;
> Impélenme furiosos huracanes,
> Y voy, entre los brazos de Ahrimanes
> A las fauces hambrientas del Enigma.[30]

> It was so written! Don't strive anymore
> to erase the baleful enigma from my face.
> Violent hurricanes impel me,
> and I go, in the arms of Ahrimans,
> toward the hungry jaws of Enigma.

He referred to the symbolism of the Ahrimans, a group of female vampires, rebels of the Shabbat and relatives of the Tremeres, who according to vampire mythology, lived in the catacombs of Mexico City. For a second generation of theosophists like Rudolf Steiner, Ahrimans were evil spirits forcing mankind to rely only on the mind and senses; that is, the spirits of science that destroyed true spirituality.[31] Nervo felt trapped in a scientific era, falling into the abyss of enigmas. However, in Hindu renunciation and transcendentalism he found an effective relief for his doubts. Nervo's ideas were thus both eternal and, above all, extremely modern. Yet at the same time he criticized the moral laxity of modern decadentism:

> ¡O, Siddharta Gautama!, tú tenías razón:
> Las angustias nos vienen del deseo; el edén
> Consiste en no anhelar, en la renunciación
> Completa, irrevocable, de toda posesión
> Quien no desea nada, dondequiera está bien . . .
> El deseo es el par del esplín, de la hartura.

O Siddharta Gautama! You were right:
anguish comes from desire; Eden
consists of not yearning
[and] of the complete and irrevocable renunciation of all possessions.
He who desires nothing is fine wherever he is . . .
Desire is the match for "*esplín*" [melancholy] and glut.

Buddhism, the achievement of spiritual happiness through complete renunciation, was a welcome idea for this Catholic poet of Franciscan tendencies: "Este es el sueño de Buda:/no anhelar nunca nada, mas superarlo todo"
(This is the dream of Buddha:/do not ever yearn for anything; overcome everything).[32]

His book of poems El *estanque de los lotos* (1915), begins with quotes from Vivekananda ("Be in the world, but do not be from the world, like the *flor de loto*,
whose roots are grounded in the mud but remain always pure and clean") and
Buddha ("The water that surrounds the *flor de loto* does not wet the petals").
Here Nervo, in poems, tells the story of Miguel, a poet in love with a young
woman who does not love him back. Miguel turns to Krishna, his inner voice,
and finds no need for a Western-style Faustian pact to achieve wisdom and
love. He opts instead for the suppression of desire. When the young woman
finally offers her love, Miguel rejects her. He has finally overcome Maya,
achieving Nirvana. "¡Ya rompí mis cadenas," cries Miguel, "ya estás muerto,
anhelar!/Ya destruí del Maya la malla resistente . . ./ya tomé por asalto la ciudad del Nirvana" (I have broken my chains:/you are dead, longing!/I have destroyed Maya's resistant netting . . ./I have taken the city of Nirvana by storm).
Maya, the illusory "real" world, is defeated by the only real world—that of
the spirit.

Like other orientalists in Mexico City, Nervo referenced Tolstoy's blend of
Christian and Oriental values, which combined in Nervo's view Confucian,
Buddhist, and Jewish elements. Vasconcelos also found—first in Tolstoy and
later in Dostoyevsky—his true prophets of modernity in Russia—an agricultural and not fully Western country, just like Mexico.[33] Mexico City intellec-
tuals, when confronted with the conflicting extremes of Eastern esotericism
and their own Catholicism, were lured by Russia's great synthesis of either
Tolstoyan Christianity or the Bolshevik Revolution.[34] As a result, Soviet poet
Vladimir Mayakovsky, while in Mexico in the 1920s, received the warmest welcome in both socialist and antisocialist circles. José Vasconcelos's magazine
La Antorcha published articles and pictures of the poet in Mexico; apparently
Vasconcelos's strong anticommunism was put aside by Russian literature's
everlasting allure as a supreme spiritual synthesis.[35]

Russia's appeal as a great synthesis drew in Nervo, but Hinduism's attraction was stronger. "Everyone knows about my sympathies for Vedantism," Nervo argued. Yet while he claimed to be skeptical of a totally Pantheist view, he still felt the need to point out both the appeal and danger India represented for young writers:

> I understand that, in these undoubtedly admirable [Indian] ideas, there is, on the one hand, such subtle metaphysics that it seems, because of its sharpness and coldness, like a chlorine bleach for style; and on the other hand, such a thick skein of occultisms and inferior forms of magic (dear to the mediocre souls), that I would not induce my friends to board that bamboo boat [which travels] along the sacred Ganges . . . at the same time; I believe that there is great danger for the young souls in not digesting these theories (sometimes too beautiful and profound), and in suffering, at the height of their development, the disillusionment of all actions. Perhaps Vedantism (without Kabbalas or Sanskrit resurrections) is a sweet delicacy for modern men, because in it they begin to perceive, from its boat, the shore of death.

Precisely this appealing danger affected young politician Francisco I. Madero.[36] At an early age Madero became a profound spiritualist, an attraction developed first in Paris and later in the U.S. He was a successful businessman from a prominent family, a liberal convinced of the need to democratize Mexico's political system after three decades of economic progress, and also an active spiritualist medium in contact with his dead brother. Were these facets of Madero connected in any way? As with Nervo, Vasconcelos, and Tablada, Madero is known for those aspects of his personality connected with the traditional notion of his "true" Mexican authenticity. In Madero's case this meant his liberalism and struggle for an electoral democracy in Mexico.

In 1919 José Vasconcelos, commenting on the Bhagavad-Gita, included Madero's view of the book while suppressing anything in Madero's observations with spiritualist or occultist connotations. The aim was to produce an image of Madero as a democrat who, despite his idealism, fought against the treason of barbarism. In Vasconcelos's account, Madero was not a man participating in various spiritualist and theosophical societies, or a man donating money to many of these endeavors while believing to be an effective medium for the Lethe word. Vasconcelos's Madero was instead simply a true democrat and good Christian, whose efforts ironically paralleled Arjuna's story in the Bhagavad-Gita:

> It ends up being incredible to imagine what Madero [must have been] thinking when he found himself in the Mexican fields, in the situation of

Arjuna, willing to fight an army of enemies whom he did not hate—the Mexican Arjuna, in the noble battle of strength—and then he forgave them with loving Christian spirit; but only to be a victim of Judas, in the darkest and cruelest of all betrayals.[37]

Vasconcelos's Arjuna-Madero is defeated not by Krishna's divine argument about the need to fight violently in order to fulfill a destiny—like in the Mahabharata—but by an archetypical Judas. Along these lines, one could indeed argue that Madero was defeated not by Huerta (the Judas), but by the violent Krishna spirit of revolutionary change. Vasconcelos misrepresented Madero's spiritualism and Hinduism, turning a complex Mahabharata struggle of duty, courage, divine destiny, human hesitation, doubt, uncertainty, and foreseeable bad consequences, into a Manichean Catholic story of Judas and Christ.

Enrique Krauze, Madero's biographer, finds relationships between Madero's spiritualism and his specific political actions. Krauze's Madero, however, is still a Christian liberal democrat who happens to have spiritualist impulses, rather than an esoteric favoring the gradual democratic opening of what he believed to be a largely successful caudillo regime.[38] Indeed, Madero was closer to a mystic than to a lay apostle of democracy. His passion for Allan Kardec's writings engaged him in all sorts of spiritualist sessions, as well as in the organization of spiritualist associations, publications, and congresses like the First and Second Spiritualist Congresses that took place in Mexico City in 1906 and 1908.[39]

Thus Madero's spiritualism was linked to the orientalist trend of seeking muses and wisdom in faraway places like Arabia and India. He eventually blended his spiritualism with various forms of theosophy and Hinduism. In January 1904 he wrote to Mexico City's Centro Esotérico Oriental asking for more information about esoteric Buddhism because, he said, he had only read Smith's [sic] book on the subject. He invited the publishers of La Luz to combine spiritualism and theosophy.[40] In January 1906 he asked Manuel Salamanca—an important member of Mexico City's Theosophical Society—and other theosophists to join the First National Spiritualist Congress in Mexico City. Madero believed, like Nervo, in reincarnation, thus advocating a kind of Hindu spiritualism.

Madero believed spiritualism could accommodate all real and rational beliefs because, as he argued in a letter to a socialist journalist, it was not an "immutable dogma" but an open invitation to "the speculations of the intelligence."[41] Madero sought a theosophy that could go with his spiritualism. Thus his search for theosophy occurred within the parameters of spiritualism, the neutral point where he believed religion and science met.[42]

In either 1908 or 1909 Madero published his *Manual espírita* (under the name of Bhima) in the spiritualist publication *Helios*. In the work he combined common spiritualist techniques with Indian philosophy. Krishna was the son of the virgin Debaki, and only Christ could match Krishna's morals. Madero found in the ideas he took from theosophical readings—karma, reincarnation, and the suppression of desire—a natural complement to both his Catholic beliefs and his ideas of human fraternity. While president of the Republic, in either 1912 or 1913, in the midst of the country's terrible turmoil, he published in *Helios* an annotated version of the Bhagavad-Gita using a Spanish translation. He called his dense annotations "comentarios de un adepto" (comments by a follower), referring often to the many points of comparison between spiritualism and profound ancient Indian thought.[43] He saw, for instance, a parallel between spiritualist communications and notions of Nirvana. Madero also found problems in R. Borrell's translation, in view of Sanskrit's multiple meanings, though, of course, Madero did not command the language.

The Madero who commented extensively on the Bhagavad-Gita exhibited a form of odalisque-mania, searching for supreme wisdom in ancient Eastern texts through the intermediation of English and French theosophy. He was no more of a visionary (or, as it may be, a lunatic) than many of the English, French, and U.S. intellectuals following these trends. Nonetheless Madero's odalisque-mania has been treated as accidental, a simple peccadillo. Vasconcelos's own odalisque-mania tried to free Madero of theosophist connotations, as he believed theosophy constituted a vulgar fascination with India. But one can only marvel imagining the scene: Madero in the National Palace, at the center of a city and a country, in the verge of collapse, annotating the Bhagavad-Gita.

Vasconcelos, in turn, was a distinguished *maderista* during the Mexican Revolution who came of age in an intellectual milieu where positivism, racial theories, Bergsonian philosophy, spiritualism, and all forms of odalisque-mania were prevalent. His childhood near the border gave him a cultural background in the classics, as well as new philosophical and scientific ideas, all from U.S. public libraries. He could have been a Yankee philosopher, or so he said in recalling his childhood years in Eagle Pass; he would have studied at the University of Texas. "A Santayana from Mexico and Texas?" he wondered.[44] But instead he moved to Mexico City, becoming both a philosopher of the city—exploring odalisques in women, ideas, and trends—and a quasi-prophet of the oxymoronic *spiritual* superiority of a *racial* mixture.[45]

As a young man Vasconcelos, like Madero and others, read Allan Kardec with the hope of finding the "principio sobrenatural perdido" (the lost supernatural principle). He went through a crisis of faith, but later renewed himself as a Catholic, an anti-Semite, and an enemy of everything associated with the U.S. or Protestantism (a not uncommon combination in Mexican patriotic ideologies). Vasconcelos visited spiritualist lodges and experimented with spiritualist rites.[46] His skepticism did not allow a full embrace of the spiritualists, but he was interested enough to research the philosophical basis of spiritualism, theosophy, and New Thought.

Over his years of exile after the *maderista* revolution, Vasconcelos researched Indian philosophy, composing in 1919 *Estudios Indostanos*, which began with an odalisque-mania-like poem by Amado Nervo: "Leer los libros esenciales" (To read the essential books), said the poem, with "tu Pitágoras, tu Biblia, tus indios inmortales" (your Pythagoras, your Bible, your immortal Indians), who ". . . nos brindan los eternos manantiales!" (that the eternal springs offer us!). He studied Indian philosophy, art, history, and literature, but—as he confessed in *Estudios Indostanos*—he based his work on French, English, and U.S. analyses of India. "The truth is," wrote Vasconcelos in the prologue to the third edition of *Estudios Indostanos* (1938), "that my goal was not to produce a work of orientalist proselytism, but simply to inform, which I believe to be an indispensable part of the synthesizing that we, in America, are forced to undertake."

Vasconcelos was a prophet searching for an authentic Hispanic spirit: India thus was an important inspiration for a somehow racial ethos with a spiritual superiority. Vasconcelos discussed his Indian preoccupations with Pedro Henríquez Ureña and Alfonso Reyes in the streets of Mexico City in the 1900s. They were all searching for a philosophical synthesis of spirit and matter in the Spanish-speaking world, and the three of them were some of the few intellectuals who could be fully considered "Latin American" (if such a term ever had a material point of reference). In Vasconcelos's words, they talked about "all matters directly affecting the spirit. No teaching has left us satisfied, and none of the great fundamental questions has ceased to deeply interest us. [We were] unhappy with our own environment and disappointed with Europe, which was going through that period of materialistic corruption which preceded the war."[47] So they studied Vishnu, Shiva, Krishna, Brahmanism, Saktas, Kabir, Upanishads, Bhagavad-Gita, Nyaya, Tagore, and Vivekananda.[48] According to Vasconcelos, India had, before Greece, conceived of ideas and spirit rather than matter and science. Thus India was a source of "boundless benevolent idealism and [of] a devotion that has never been marked by the cruelty of fanaticism." Yet unlike his mentors and protégés, who found sexual liberation in Indian and Japanese eroticism, Vasconcelos opposed the "lujuria indostánica" (Hindustani lust) while finding in Christianity similarly distasteful moments at which "el espíritu se contagia del cuerpo" (the spirit was infected by the body).[49] He remained, however, convinced that the spiritual value of India would find in "América Latina" the best soil in which to grow. "In no place," he said, "will [the renaissance of Indian ideas] be as fecund as in Latin America and among the Spanish race, a race which is always on the alert for mystic undertakings."

In Tagore and Vivekananda Vasconcelos found an Indian synthesis suitable for his spiritualism, which became an artistic Mexicanism in service of a larger pan-Latinism. In his words, "Tagore's and Vivekananda's works . . . prove that Hindustani [sic] no longer wants to be divided into Buddhists, Hindus, or Jains, etc. Its greatest spirits are succeeding in melting all of the old truths into a new and sublime universal doctrine."[50] It is thus not surprising that when distinguished English sculptor Clare Sheridan (Winston Churchill's cousin) met Vasconcelos in 1921, she was astonished by Vasconcelos's knowledge of India. "He said he cared nothing for the civilization of the Occident," Sheridan wrote. "He understood better the Orient, and followed in the train of Tagore, whom he talked of with great admiration."[51]

Vasconcelos's view was not that of a nationalist *indigenista*; instead it was consciously expressed as a Western thinker, albeit one from the periphery. In his role as a self-appointed Westerner he called for "Latin" Christianity to participate in India's synthesis, asking: "Are we Christians going to remain confined in our precepts, even at the risk of shrinking our mental space, at the risk of turning into a sect; or will we know, as before, how to put all the resin of the old logs on the bonfire of our consciences, so that the sky may be filled with splendors?"[52] To further drive home this point, he finished his book on Indian philosophy with a telling mystic poem of the Spanish Golden Age by Fray Luis de León. One could, in fact, find similarities in the type of introspection common to classic Spanish mysticism and Indian philosophies. The interesting point, however, is to see how Vasconcelos's (or for that matter Nervo's) take on Hinduism is indistinguishable from their devotion to Catholic mysticism. It is difficult to say which came first.[53] Vasconcelos blended Indian philosophy with Catholic mystics, Bergson, J. G. Frazer, Heidegger, Nietzsche, Santayana, José Ingenieros, Tolstoy, José Enrique Rodó, and others, assuming what we may call a Mexican Western perspective. But in so doing—and in his search for a universal spirit—he blurred the distinction between East and West.

The Tagore Moment

Vasconcelos's odalisque-mania, especially in relation to India, manifested itself both in his studies on Indian philosophy and in his praise of the great Bengali poet, Nobel laureate Rabindranath Tagore. Tagore epitomized what India meant for Vasconcelos, who was the ideologue of a continental "Cosmic Race" (the title of his cultural manifesto written as a travel account to Brazil,

Uruguay, and Argentina in 1922). Of course, before Tagore there had been other "Eastern" poetic philias in Mexico City, such as the above mentioned interest in the *Song of Songs*, or that in Omar Khayyam and Khalil Gibran. Khayyam's *Rubáiyát* was very influential with modernist artists and poets.[54] But Tagore was the hero for intellectuals like Vasconcelos in Mexico, Victoria Ocampo in Argentina, and Gabriela Mistral in Chile. In 1924, when Vasconcelos was Minister of Education, the National University published an affordable anthology of Tagore's works including *La luna nueva, Nacionalismo, Personalidad, Sadhana*. The translation was written anonymously by someone from the university, but according to Guillermo Sheridan it was done by writers Heliodoro Valle and Ortiz de Montallano. Three earlier translations of Tagore, completed from English versions, were published in Mexico City by Heramba Lal Gupta, Pedro Requena Legarreta, and Luis Cabrera. And in 1921, also during Vasconcelos's ministry, Tagore was invited to Mexico City for the centennial celebration of the completion of Mexico's independence (1821). He never reached the city, as he was captivated by another city and by a woman: Buenos Aires and Victoria Ocampo.

Gupta in particular is an intriguing character. He appears to have been one of the radical Indian nationalists in Berlin and New York during the early twentieth century, friend of nationalist doctor, resident in New York, Chandra H. Chakrabarty.[55] He seems to have been known by U.S. and German intelligences as H. L. Gupta, a member of the Ghadar Party, which had cells in Moscow and New York. That is how he met M. N. Roy, and thus went to Mexico City. By the mid 1920s there was one "Herambalal" Gupta apparently living in Mexico City. This Gupta translated Indian literature into Spanish, published regularly in José Vasconcelos's periodical *La Antorcha*, and cooked Bengali food for Anita Brenner, Carleton Beals, Edward Weston, Rafael Sala, and Monna Sala. He wrote in Mexico City on the poet Kālidāsa, the legend of Nala and Damayanti (part of the Mahabharata), and Urvashi (Rig Veda). Unfortunately, I have been unable to find further details on him.[56]

But in Mexico City he did publish a translation of Tagore's *Chitra*—a play based on an episode of the Mahabharata in which, after a drama edging on homoerotics, Arjuna seduces Chitra, a noble woman raised as a man. Gupta's version was based on Tagore's English version of his own Bengali text, but Gupta claimed that he, being a Bengali himself, could better interpret in Spanish Tagore's ideas. This is how Arjuna sounds in Spanish when Chitra asks him whether he is to fulfill his twelve-year vow of chastity: "vos habeis deshecho mi voto de castidad como la luna deshace el voto de oscuridad de la noche" (thou hast broken my vow like the moon breaketh the night's vow of darkness).[57]

In turn, Requena Legarreta was a well-known Mexican poet living in New

York, whose translations of—and devotion to—a mystic version of Tagore led to his study of religion and the Bengali language. After Requena's premature death in 1918 his friend René Borgia wrote that Tagore was not Christian but rather a more authentic mystic than Dante, Santa Teresa, or San Juan de la Cruz. The prologue to the handsome edition of *Gitanjalí* (a 1918 translation of one of Tagore's books) stated that Requena learned Indian philosophy and Bengali rhyme and interviewed Tagore in New York in order to faithfully translate the book. The verses, however, display as gaudy a spirit as the orientalist cover of the fancily produced book (figure 8.1). This is how Tagore sounds as Darío (impossible to translate):

> El silencioso mar de la mañana
> rompió en ondulaciones vaporosas
> de cantos de aves y rumor de cosas,
> que se fundieron en melifluo trino

Whereas in 1918 Requena was indeed famous among the city's literati, soon, as critic Gabriel Zaid argues, he "went from being read, to being dismissed, without being read."[58]

In turn, in about 1919 Luis Cabrera translated some of Tagore's poetry (all from English), constructing the poet's verses as high-class Spanish aphorism: "Hallar lo que buscaba, no he podido/No puedo comprender/lo que querría saber" (To find what I sought, I have not been able/I cannot understand/what I'd want to know). But like many others, Cabrera's translations paralleled his own poems with a reliance on Nahuatl motifs.[59] However, the translation and adaptation of Tagore's work by Spanish poet Juan Ramón Jiménez and his wife Zenobia Camprubí de Jiménez were what made Tagore a literary hero in Spanish America.[60] (Again, all translations were based on English versions.) The couple, said Paz, "made the Bengali poet into a Spanish poet," even though Tagore seems to not have been influenced by poetry in Spanish.[61] Tagore's image was often used to represent ancient wisdom. In 1925 Mexican artist Gabriel Fernández Ledesma published in Mexico City a drawing of Tagore to accompany a translation of a Tagore tale about an ignorant parrot that died from his master's attempts to educate him (figure 8.2).[62] The drawing was but one of many Tagore portraits, texts, and interviews published in Mexico between 1915 and 1940 (by, for instance, Montenegro and Garcia Cabral). Tagore's image in Mexico City was that of an Indian Prince, of the guru of the long-sought blend of deepness and simplicity, a view that matched Tagore's ideas about the materialistic decadence of the West.[63]

In Mexico City, however, Tagore's poetry was not received with the same fer-

8.1. Cover, R. Tagore's *Gitanjali* (Mexico City, s. n., 1918).

vor as in Buenos Aires, Madrid, or Rio de Janeiro. Victoria Ocampo confessed that her affair with Tagore—both with the man and with his poetry—awoke her from a very sad moment in her love life. For Juan Ramón and Zanobia Jiménez, Tagore represented a necessary dose of spiritual optimism in the midst of profound pessimism. This can be seen as a dose, as Dipesh Chakrabarty called it, of overcoming what was "real" in India (or one might add Argen-

8.2. Gabriel Fernández Ledesma, drawing of Tagore. *La Antorcha* (January 1925).

tina or Spain) in order to see the sublimity of India (and for that matter the "Latin" "Cosmic Race").[64] Even Placido Barbosa, the first Brazilian translator of Tagore, saw the poet as a way to overcome the terrible tragedy of the loss of a son. "In tears I decided to translate him, in tears I translated him," he wrote in his translation of *The Crescent Moon* (1916). Indeed, Tagore was a sort of self-help for many, a therapeutic poetic medication. Could it be that in a postrevolutionary Mexico City, during a rapid and mostly optimistic cultural, economical, and political reconstruction, "Tagore therapy" was less necessary than in Argentina and Spain? It is hard to say.[65]

But Tagore and India had an interesting effect on the music of Mexico City; it was as if odalisque-mania could make music both universal and profoundly Mexican. In 1927 prominent Mexican musician Manuel M. Ponce, a pioneering figure in the collection and adaptation of Mexican folk tunes, set two Tagore poems to music. (He did the same with pieces by Mexican and Russian poets.) Tagore's poems "I plucked your flower, O World" and "One morning in the flower garden" were put to music with curious French and Indian intonations.[66] From Mexico City, Ponce played an essential role in the gentrification of Mexican folk music, producing marvelous pieces from the oral tradition. He studied in Mexico City and Europe, where he learned to use folklore in classical music through the compilation of Mexican and other American forms of music. Ponce and folklorist Rubén M. Campos were the greatest collectors of popular tunes in the city. Ponce formed an alliance of mutual convenience with Andrés Segovia, the most prominent Spanish guitar player of the twentieth century. Thus Ponce would write pieces for guitar, and Segovia would make those pieces known throughout the world. This Mexican-Spanish alliance best fit an Irving-like view of Spain's stereotypical image; the Arabic instrument—the guitar—playing Mexican *serenatas*.

Ponce's rendition of Tagore furthered his multifarious experimentation with Mexican folklore and German, French, and Spanish music. Tagore's poetry seemed like a great addition to this mixture due to its profound spirituality, although judging from Ponce's music, Tagore could not offer the romantic richness of popular Mexican ballads. (The pieces were Debussy-like, and not the best part of Ponce's musical legacy.)

"India-mania" and Tagore love were mocked by left-wing intellectuals, as these concerns were considered too urban, petit bourgeois, unrevolutionary, and un-Mexican. In a letter to communist comrade artist Xavier Icaza (November 2, 1926) Diego Rivera—then a strong supporter of Mexico's Communist Party—expressed his discontent with Vansconcelos, who had originally hired him to paint the walls of the Ministry of Education. In Rivera's opinion, Vasconcelos's *Estudios Indostanos* were nothing but "mediocre translations from English of pages of Oriental, esoteric vulgarization." Vansconcelos, said Rivera, was fighting "a sentimental campaign against Western civilization" ("[Una] campaña sentimental en contra de la civilización occidental"): "agitación socio-cristo-anarco-burgo-nacio-hispa-boli-rodo-confu-budi-pita-gore-pepe-vasconceliana." This is difficult irony to translate: something like "a socio-Catholic-anarchist-bourgeois-national-Hispanic-Rodó-like-Confucian-

Buddhist-Pythagoras-like-José-Vasconcelian agitation." In the letter he included the original sketch for the mural "Corrido de la Revolución Proletaria," then in production on the Ministry of Education's patios. In the sketch he depicted "sabios" (wise men), urban intellectuals who were not part of the real Mexico, and painted, at the center, a caricaturized version of Tagore with Vasconcelos, with its backside to the observer, sitting on a white elephant, writing in the letter to Icaza: "para que no digan, un elefante sagrado" (so they can't say anything, a sacred elephant). José Juan Tablada appears watching Bertha Singer, a then-famous *declamadora* (poetry reader). Tablada, for Rivera, was yet another Mexican intellectual fascinated with the Orient and totally unaware of the real conditions of the country. Another *sabio* with glasses plays a lyre, while Ezequiel Chávez (an official of the Ministry of Education and an educator himself) appears at rest on top of a pile of books. These Mexican *sabios* are observed in the sketch by a peasant with wheat stalks, a worker with a hammer, and a soldier. Together they hug each other and laugh, clearly mocking the scene of the *sabios* (figure 8.3). In the final version of the mural (finished in 1928), Tablada appears playing the lyre, with the worker, peasant, and soldier substituted with a different group of popular characters. Tagore appears to be transmitting wisdom to the Mexican *sabios*, a bunch of sissy, urban, cowardly, ignorant, and unrealistic imitators of Western orientalism who aim to criticize the West without seeing the real conditions of their country. The "lyrics" accompanying the mural (it was, after all, a *corrido*) read, "Quisiera ser hombre sabio de muchas sabidurías/mas mejor quiero tener que comer todos los días" (I would like to be a wise man with a lot of great wisdom;/but I would rather have something to eat every day).

If Vasconcelos's "Hinduism" was indeed, as Rivera put it in the letter to Icaza, "indigestión Tolstoina" (Tolstoyan indigestion), then Rivera's muralism and criticism were clearly part of that other form of "indigestion": Bolshevik Socialist Realism.[67]

Manuel Gamio was yet another critic of odalisque-mania. Gamio, the most prominent Mexican anthropologist in the first part of the twentieth century, was also a distinguished advocate of *mestizaje*. In his legendary 1916 collection of essays, *Forjando Patria*, he clearly distinguished different types of Mexican intellectuals, including the useless and false intellectual species of odalisque-maniacs. Gamio called them *cismáticos*, or imitators of the West and adversaries of all things Mexican: "La 'cultura cismática' es patrimonio de pedantes y de imbéciles" (The 'schismatic culture' is the patrimony of pedants and morons). For Gamio—as for Rivera—odalisque-mania was a false shroud covering the possibility of an authentic Mexico. But unlike Rivera, Gamio believed that the "real" Mexico was neither in the proletarian revolution nor in

8.3. Sketch of "Los Sabios," Rivera's letter to Icaza, November 2, 1926.
Courtesy Bertram and Ella Wolfe Papers, Hoover Institution, Stanford University.

Mexico's Indigenous population. In Gamio's opinion the "real" Mexico was yet to come, and the "morons" were only delaying its emergence. However, since many intellectuals (Ponce, Tablada, and Vasconcelos to name a few) were, in fact, creating the nationalist synthesis Gamio dreamt of, one wonders the extent to which Mexican orientalism was also, somehow *forjando patria* (forging fatherland).[68]

Bodies

India produced a great erotic fascination in Mexico City. Poet Jesús Urueta saw erotic performances by Persian and Indian belly dancers while in Paris in 1898. Afterward he imagined stories of sexual attraction and final triumph of true love in some of the most odalisque-like language ever composed, with words such as *harén* and *lujuria* (lust) blending with images of black female slaves and perfumed ivory-like breasts, all tempting the memory of a true chaste love: "no quiero que los senos de marfil y de ébano sean la copa de mi sed y el reclinatorio de fatiga!" (no translation could convey the flavor of this odalisque mania).[69]

An important manifestation of the Indian erotic fascination took place in 1934 during a true odalisque moment. Indian dancer Nyota Inyoca visited Mexico City and was widely revered; numerous poems were written about her naked belly and her dancing. Pictures of her exotic body and style of dress circulated with the argument that she would be appreciated in the city as she had triumphed in Paris because of her blend of erotic and spiritual powers: "The evocations of Brahmanic India are all inspired by sacred motifs. Vishnu, the god who conserves the Trimurt in his seventh reincarnation, [Rama] fights against Ravana, the king of the demons. Krishna [is] the eighth reincarnation of Vishnu, who personifies the lover in Hindu legends." Inyoca was, for the city, the reincarnation of that exoticism. Of course Mexico's Catholic morality had to tame this odalisque: "No levanta Inyoca el pie hasta la Cabeza como Siva [sic] . . . el estilo de la danzarina es casto" (Inyoca does not raise her foot up to her head like Shiva . . . the dancer's style is chaste). Such an awkward moderation was the result of a particular kind of Mexican lascivious chastity.

India-related odalisque-mania images often appeared in the city's literary and social periodicals. In *Arte y Letras* (1914), Carlos D. Neve, an artist who would later become famous for his comics, submitted an illustration called "La Bayadera" (figure 8.4). The theme is the *Bayadère*, an 1877 ballet by French choreographer Marius Petipa set in India. The ballet involves Brahmans, women, love, and—in Neve's depiction—Indian, Arab, Chinese, and Japanese motifs blended with the erotic contours of the dancer.[70] In 1918 "La Bayadera" still produced sensual reactions in the city; for instance, the young poet Carlos Pellicer composed an extremely erotic rendition of the image, combining unusual adjectives and words in rhetoric emulating the undulating character of the performance:

Genuflexa en la alfombra, se pandea
en rotatoria lentitud que ahonda
la onda lujuriante en que bucea
la perla azul de seducción, redonda.

She genuflects on the rug, arches
with rotatory slowness that deepens
the lust wave in which
the round, blue pearl of seduction is submerged.

8.4. Carlos D. Neve, "La Bayadera," *Arte y Letras* (August 22, 1914).

In Pellicer's "La Bayadera," her legs are "mínimas pagodas/erectas a la gloria de los Buddas [sic]" (slight pagodas,/erected to the glory of the Buddhas).[71] She is but one example from a long list of Indian-, Arabian-, Japanese-, and Egyptian-like divas who inspired incredible fascination in Mexico City. Included on that list were Italian dancer and actress Gabriela Besanzoni, as well as the incredible Sevillian dancer, amateur ethnomusicologist, and feminist Tórtola Valencia, the original choreographer for a 1910s version of *La Bayadera*. In 1919 Besanzoni was widely praised for her performances as Dalila in Mexico City. The popular magazine El *Universal Ilustrado* shows this mixture of odalisque-mania and eroticism with a marvelous cover illustration by García Cabral and text by Ramón López Velarde. In turn, Valencia's performances of Hindu-inspired dances became a true obsession in the city. López Velarde and poet Rafael López published poems about her in El *Universal Ilustrado*, in the form of two columns bracketing the image of the dancer. López Velarde's fascination with Oriental references led to his well-known enigmatic metaphors. Two verses of a poem dedicated to Tórtola read "tu rotación de ménade aniquila/la zurda ciencia, que cabe en tu axila" (Your maenad-like rotation obliterates/the left-handed science, which fits in your armpit).[72] Carlos Pellicer (author of the above-quoted poem "La Bayadera") also wrote a poem inspired by Valencia titled "La Gitana." "Esta es la gitana, la soberana," and "Es Tór-

8.5. Alfredo's Best Maugard's Tehuana (ca. 1920). Courtesy of Instituto Nacional de Bellas Artes, Mexico. Reproducción autorizada por el Instituto Nacional de Bellas Artes y Literatura, 2011.

tola Valencia la tal gitana," who "parece que a requiebros la mujer quema/los ritmos de la danza tan insolente" (This is the gypsy, the sovereign . . . Tórtola Valencia is that gypsy [. . . it] seems that, with gallantry, the woman burns/the rhythm of the insolent dance).[73] Tórtola Valencia in Mexico City impersonated an India that had been for long part of the erotic imagination of the city's intellectuals.

Alfredo Best Maugard, one of the most prominent artists in early revolutionary Mexico, created similar images of exotic divas. He was known for painting Tehuanas, native women from the southern tropical region of Tehuantepec, representing an exotic and sensual fantasy for Mexicans and foreigners alike throughout the nineteenth and early twentieth centuries (figure 8.5).

But Best Maugard depicted the Tehuana as a typical figure in classical Indian painting.[74] He had returned to Mexico City in 1913 after a long stay in Paris and New York, where he started to combine orientalist and *indigenista* motifs. In Mexico he developed a painting technique based on primitivist appropriations of simple, childlike drawings. Of course he was also somehow a nationalist. He choreographed Mexican nationalist ballet pieces with Anna Pavlova.[75] His unusual Tehuana combined two different cravings for the exotic; for Tehuanas, and for exotic women from India. The composition embodied both first-class Easternness (the Tehuana was as sensual as a female figure in classical India) and first-class Westernness (the Hindu Tehuana was created by the same Mexican painter who drew illustrations for *Freddy the Pig*, a classic of U.S. children's literature by Walter R. Brooks).[76] Best Maugard's Tehuana belonged in a series of drawings by the artist that included Oriental, pre-Hispanic, Hindu, and European motifs, such as a black dancer with Hindu traits. Curiously, a critic who saw these pieces in Best Maugard's studio in New York considered them proof of the artist's nationalism. Best Maugard had gone beyond the imitation of European art, for "beneath the Spanish and Oriental, Chinese, Korean and Japanese colonial influence, one can perceive the spirit of the ancestors, who expressed, in stone and in clay, more beautiful things than any other people in the world, except the Greeks."[77] This series of drawings was, in fact, part of the odalisque-mania of the time and was as "Europeanized" and as Mexican as Mexican art had always been.

Roberto Montenegro, as we have seen, was yet another prominent artist making use of Oriental motifs. His Parisian and Spanish training in the early twentieth century led him to all sorts of vanguard styles, among them orientalism in various forms. His illustrations for a Spanish version of Aladdin's story are the best expression of his Oriental experimentation (figure 8.6). The illustrations are colorful collages of Japanese, Chinese, Indian, and Arabic features, tragic Oriental faces blended with generic Oriental-looking textiles. These illustrations often became raw material for his later murals in Mexico City combining Oriental with native motifs, as well as for the children's literature officially and massively distributed in 1924 by the revolutionary government. These children's books combined Montenegro's illustrations with stories and extracts from the Vedas, Katha Upanishad, Ramayana, Panchatantra, Tagore, *Arabian Nights*, and Greek mythology.[78]

This fascination with Oriental divas was not simply an elite fashion; it reached popular dimensions. To be sure, Tórtola Valencia, Esperanza Iris, and the famous María Conesa in the roles of Hindu or Japanese odalisques were not meant for the urban poor. However, those same odalisque dreams reached large sectors of the population in Zarzuelas, *tandas*, *carpas*, and the first movie

8.6. Montenegro's illustration for *La lámpara de Aladino*
(Barcelona: Librería de las Galerías Layetanas, 1917).

theaters. By the 1930s the early movie industry had absorbed these images, and thus odalisque-like divas became popular sources of delirium, from the *chinitas* Kalantán and Su Muy Key to the 1980s icon Lyn May. Popular forms of urban obscenity have long been linked to these odalisques.[79]

A Bengali Quixote

In Mexico City during the 1910s and 1920s social radicalism constituted a collective call to the exotic in which the U.S. was an essential and ever-present catalyst, as if East and West were inconceivable without U.S. participation (see chapter 4). At that time revolutionary Marxist politics in Mexico City represented, I believe, a philosophical and aesthetic version of Mexican odalisque-mania. There were thus exotic objects—Mexicans themselves—converted to exoticist subjects fascinated with Russian stories of czars, samovars, and revolutions, or there were workers organizations constituted by networks of Mexican, Catalan, Indian, U.S., and Japanese ideologues. For revolutionary ideas were, for Mexicans, a clear attempt to overcome the exotic through a well-defined form of universalism: the working-class struggle.

Hence in 1919, Bengali nationalist M. N. Roy founded in Mexico City the Mexican Communist Party, as later he would found the Indian and Chinese Communist parties. For Mexico City was then exoticism in motion, a city where European, Asian, and U.S. radicals lived out their exoticist Mexican dreams. In Mexico City they found the necessary quota of both oddness and authenticity, but they also contributed to a universal canon of class struggle and revolution.[80] In 1921, the Mexican Communist Party appointed Roy as the Mexican envoy to the second meeting of the Comintern. Once in Moscow, however, Roy became the representative for anti-imperialist India, thus creating a conflict among the Mexican Communists. José Allen, secretary-general of the new Mexican Communist Party, had provided Roy and his wife, Evelyn Trent, with Mexican passports (see chapters 4 and 5). Roy became Roberto Allen y Villagarcía, a rather aristocratic combination of English and Mexican names for an Indian revolutionary who justified his poor Spanish on the basis of his affluent upbringing. At the same time, Linn A. Gale (a U.S. slacker) had introduced a mixture of socialism and New Thought into Mexico, struggling with Roy for leadership of the new party and the availability of international communist funds.[81]

Roy's first ardent efforts in life were directed toward Indian independence (as well as the superiority of Indian spirituality over Western materialism and English imperialism). In Mexico City, Roy reshaped his nationalism, becoming first a socialist and then a communist thanks to the influence of his wife Evelyn Trent and her U.S. radical circle in the city, as well as Roy's encounter with Michael Borodin—Moscow's envoy to the American republics—in Mexico City. As I have shown (chapter 4), Evelyn Trent traveled to Mexico City with Roy. The two met in Stanford, California, through the mutual acquaintance of Indian students and professors, especially Dhan Gopal Mukherjee.[82] Roy connected with the branch of U.S. orientalism that provided a window of opportunity to display himself, namely the New York branch of the Ramkrishna-Vivekananda Mission.[83] He searched in the U.S. for an old mystic message, uniting the former odalisque-mania of theosophy and Hindu thought with the new one of socialism and nationalism: "Having heard, while in India, so much about the spread of Vedanta in the U.S.A.," he wrote, "I made it a point to attend the branches of the Ramkrishna-Vivekananda Mission also in San Francisco and Los Angeles. The same spectacle everywhere; it proved that the materialist

West would not yet atone for its sins and respond to India's spiritual message. It was a disappointment for a believer in India's mission."

Once in Mexico City—and after he had converted to Marxism—Roy was less eager to find Indian mysticism, especially not with the help of U.S. radicals. Linn A. Gale's New Thought Church in Mexico City offered services performed by Gale and his wife. He preached a combination of socialist ideas, the importance of birth control, and Indian philosophy, while also publishing *Gale's Magazine*. At the church, recalled U.S. slacker Charles Phillips, "[Gale] preached Sunday sermons . . . wearing a black cutaway morning coat. The blond Magdalena [Gale's wife] stood at the foot of the pulpit, barefoot, in a white flowing robe."[84] *Gale's Magazine* was distributed in Mexico City as a publication for "reasonable radicals," full of New Thought optimism—a combination of Christian Science, Hinduism, and socialism.[85]

In Mexico City Roy no longer had any patience or tolerance for U.S. Indian orientalism. He vividly described meeting Gale and his wife, who were both eager "to hear some words of wisdom from a son of that holy land," right in the midst of Mexico City:

> I came at the appointed hour and was received at the door by the charming . . . Magdalena who had bundled herself clumsily in a loose garment, presumably to be taken for a *sari*. She had painted her feet red and went without shoes and wore a garland of white flowers on the head. It looked all very dramatic. The room was full of thick incense fumes, through which one could dimly see pictures of gods and saints and prophets hanging on the walls. The host led me towards one which looked like a picture of an Indian—a handsome face with sharp features and longish black hair . . . Standing worshipfully, the host enquired if I had the good fortune of ever meeting Lord Krishnamurti. Who was he? My naïve question dumbfounded the host, and Magdalena nearly fainted.[86]

In Mexico City—unlike in the U.S.—this sort of odalisque-mania seemed simply corny to Roy, who was engaged in the serious business of the revolution—not apparently a mystic business. In fact, Gale linked himself to labor leader L. N. Morones's faction when he could not procure funds from Roy (who always seemed to have plenty of resources), until Gale was expelled from the country along with other U.S. radicals in 1921. (It seems that Gale was also a spy for U.S. military intelligence monitoring the activities of U.S. subversives in Mexico City.) Roy had recently converted to Marxism, although he was still a vegetarian Brahman. It appears, then, that neither was Gale as much of a mystic as he appeared to be, nor was Roy as much of a materialist as he claimed to be. The odalisque-mania connections were everywhere. "It appeared to me," Roy later wrote, "that the revolutionary faith of Bolshevism had a religious devour, which did not harmonize with its materialistic philosophy."[87]

By 1918 Roy published a book in Spanish in which he presented his view of Indian history to a Mexican audience. "Thanks to the imperialist writers' poor interpretation of history," he wrote, "the entire world thinks that, before the British conquest, India never had a national life."[88] This argument echoed Mexico's liberal and revolutionary reconstruction of its own history, which constantly recalled how the "real" Mexico existed before the arrival of the Spaniards. In turn Roy found that, in Mexico City, political autonomy was not enough to defeat imperialism because Mexico was dominated by U.S. imperialism, despite its political sovereignty. Roy's views also resonated with arguments of racial and spiritual superiority. Around the same time as Roy's writings, Vasconcelos spoke of Mexico as la raza cósmica, meaning the blend of the best from Iberia and Indigenous America. India, Roy asserted, was the great summation of the mental energy of the Dravidians and the physical might of the Aryans.[89]

Roy's experience in Mexico City can be seen as the intersection of odalisque desires for a variety of reasons. First, he embodied for U.S. and Mexican radicals alike a path toward ecstasy that passed through several deep-rooted cultural needs related to the search for authenticity, antimodernism, exotic ideas and bodies, and radical innovative aesthetics. A young U.S. woman (Trent) and a handsome Indian (Roy), both radicals, appeared as a sort of avant-garde canvas of what new notions of beauty and social solidarity ought to be. It was mestizaje at its best. The spiritualism intrinsic to Roy's Indian heritage, like that of Tagore—along with his command of the cosmopolitan English language—made him the center of what was, after all, a bubble of cultural and political revolutions in Mexico City. Indeed theosophy, New Thought, and Hinduism were never far away from Mexican Marxism, which—as filtered through Roy, and their Mexican affiliates—represented a long-developing and powerful cultural amalgam of Tolstoy plus Tagore; spirituality, sensuality, and the ecstasy of faraway wisdom; and promises of eternal peace through divine violence. For local Mexican radicals a Bengali Quixote in Mexico City proved the validity of both socialist and indigenista myths. Insightful Spanish-speaking radicals in the 1920s, like Peruvians José Carlos Mariátegui and Luis E. Valcárcel, believed that "civilization" had not awoken the souls of Indigenous peoples in the Americas, but rather, el mito. As Valcárcel stated, the idea of the socialist revolution is "the same myths, the same ideas, [as are] the decisive agents in the awakening of other ancient peoples, of other ancient collapsing races: India, China."[90] Indeed Roy, Evelyn, and 1920s Mexico City formed a truly odalisque tableau of awakening myths through exoticism, radicalism, innovation, and all sorts of personal and ideological betrayals.

Second, Roy and Evelyn Trent's experience in Mexico City can be seen as the overlapping of odalisque desires because U.S. and Mexican radicals seemed to be enchanted, as Tablada or Fenollosa were in the late nineteenth century, by images of odalisques. The difference is that this time around the enchanter was a new revolutionary odalisque in the form of a Bengali Quixote. Oddly enough, in the midst of many narratives about ideological struggles, betrayals, and conspiracies, one could always find references to Roy's beauty. He was an icon. Roy, wrote Carleton Beals, was "tall, with long, slim expressive hands and black-white eyes that flashed frequent wrath out of a dark face." The wife of the German ambassador to Mexico apparently painted a portrait of Roy. J. T. Murphy, a British delegate to the Second International Congress, described him as "a tall fine figure of a man, with black hair and glittering eyes, a handsome Brahman . . . most arrogant." Agnes Smedley, arrested in New York for her part in the Hindu-German conspiracy, described him in a later novel as a "very dark, thin, tall and handsome" Indian revolutionary.[91] Roy himself appeared to have been aware of his own looks, as when he let himself be seduced in the city by radical Mexican women (such as Elena Torres) or men (such as Borodin, who was totally enchanted by Roy). Roy was a product of the odalisque-mania in Mexicans and foreigners alike. An exotic male odalisque was the ideal medium for the diffusion of what were, after all, equally exotic ideas for either Mexicans or foreign radicals in Mexico City.

Finally, Roy and Evelyn embodied odalisque-mania because of their deep-rooted familiarity with the ideas of both East and West. Sibnarayan Ray, a biographer of Roy, saw in Roy a new Tagore, an intellectual who was able to be at home with Western radicals and intellectuals. But Mexico City was Roy's West. Roy found in Mexico City a simplified West, one that could show him the extent to which his own Easternness blocked his participation in a truly global revolution. For Mexicans the fact that Roy, aka Roberto Allen y Villagarcía, could travel with two U.S. citizens to Berlin and Moscow as the Mexican envoy to the Second International Congress blurred the distinction between East and West. When a universal revolution was at stake, a Bengali Quixote could be Mexican. But the mirage did not last.[92]

End

In sum, the simultaneous repulsion and fascination that Mesoamerican Indigenous groups produced in the European imagination seem to overlap with that produced by India and Japan in Mexico. To match the Japanese national myth of isolation or the "oddness" of India, Mexicans compensated with their own private odalisque-mania. The odalisque-mania in Mexico City met the expectations of the West, when acting as a sort of self-exoticism or *indigenismo* that aimed at creating a particular world cultural product (Mexicanness). But Mexico's odalisque-mania also sought a modern profile that could synthesize other cultures (thus Mexico's fascination with Japan and India). What seems clear is that this fascination exhibits the main problem of the East-West dichotomy as applied to Mexico: a twofold form of self-contradicting gibberish. On one side there is the candid argument that Mexico constitutes a "minor" or an "incomplete" West. On the other, there is something even more nonsensical: Mexico as a second-class East, as it is neither India nor Japan. Mexico City, the world capital, the site and inspiration of all the above-told cultural adventures, for the world remained caught between its shoddy Westernness and its even cheaper Easternness.

PART V SCIENCE AND CITY

Presumes que eres la ciencia
y yo no lo comprendo así
¿por qué siendo tú la ciencia
no me has comprendío a mí?

You boast that you're science
I can't believe it
Why, if you're science,
haven't you unraveled me?
— "Tan afortuná que soy," La Serneta, traditional Cante
Jondo, Andalusia, Spain

9

SCIENCE AND THE CITY,
STORIES FROM THE SIDEWALK

The history of so peripheral a city as Mexico City shows that science and the modern city are mirrors for each other. The modern city embodied the prestige and the usefulness of science, and in fact became a science (*urbanisme*). The rampant problems of the modern city resulted in new sciences (social science), but also in the insurmountable realization of the limits of science—the modern city found itself being labeled "scientific" and yet being both a mystery and a challenge for science. Here I deal with science and the city, on the one hand, by zooming out, essaying a general way to understand their relationship; on the other hand, by zooming in, examining three specific topics within the interaction of science and the city; topics that I derive from a simple imaginary urban walk over the sidewalk: the conspicuous presence of the street dog; the omnipresence of the beggar; and, finally, the astonishment and scientific problems produced by history in stones.

City: Circles of Knowledge

From the 1870s to the 1930s, science and the city, whether in Mexico, the U.S., or Europe, ought to be considered within a broad range of knowledges, out of which we tend to emphasize—precisely because we belong to that range—the separation between artistic, aesthetic, social, human, religious, and scientific knowledges. I prefer to see modern science and cities as modernist phenomena, belonging to surroundings of ideas and beliefs that, if difficult to fully characterize, are as hard to disaggregate as they are to disregard. By the second part of the nineteenth century, there were a set of references, rhetorical styles, and scientific formulas along which urban problems were thought. Native cognitive traditions blended, reacted, and adapted to this dynamic set of references that were believed to be absolute—either truth or beauty. In turn, truth and beauty were aspirations that could not be easily called only scientific or only artistic. They were both at all times and in all places.[1]

To be sure, it is but natural to examine these phenomena in the decades between 1890 and 1930, since these years constituted, according to our early twentieth-first-century Decalogue, the "first globalization" in which the city and science truly had something to do with each other. Long before, however, the city and science had constituted each other and in a "global" fashion. But surely, starting in the second part of the nineteenth century, the city and science acquired a scandalous coexistence, all too evident not only in the massive sanitary transformations, city enlargements, and replanning of large capital cities, but also in the scientific management of the cities' governments and monies. Even the ideas of town planning or urbanism, according to some historians, flourished around 1910, right at the time when Otto Wagner projected a scientific plan to make Vienna an *unbegrenzte Großstadt*, capable of growing to the borders of the empire. These were scientific cities, and also a new science of the city. During these years, Barcelona scientifically expanded, following the large garden-city-like project by Ildelfonso Cerdà, exceeding the Roman and medieval walls of the city. Then Buenos Aires, with its 1.5 million inhabitants, became by 1914 not only the Paris of the Americas but also the Chicago of the Pampas.

As the locale of science production, the city is not new. It has always been like this, especially in the Iberian tradition. It is only in the twentieth century that small cities were devoted to science solely, in a way impossible for Charles Fourier, Claude-Henri de Saint-Simon, or Edward Bellamy to even dream of— think of such cities as Arzamaz in the Urals or Akademgorodok in Siberia or Los Alamos or the many university towns in the United States. For indeed the utopia advanced by those whom Marx called "utopian socialists" was made not of poetry but of science. Fourier estimated the exact geography, the optimum number of people and buildings, to form his dreamt communities. His cities were governed by reason and science, whether in Boston, New Jersey, or Texas. And they failed. These ideal cities, like nineteenth-century Universal Expositions, were conceived as miniature versions of ecumenism governed by science.[2]

Along similar lines, think of Mexico City as a summary of worldviews, of interactions between knowledge and the city: a pre-Hispanic city designed according to specific military, religious, astronomical, and agricultural knowledges. The colonial city that appropriated native knowledge and applied European technologies did the same to face the ecological and social problems resulting from the conquest of space and souls. These were sciences of the city because they were theologies of the city. Too much science was produced then to deal with the water problem, the problem of governance of two republics (that of Indians and that of Spaniards), the knowledge of new environments, the architectural problems of a city upon a lake, and the ethnology of natives . . . and all that over the heavy weight of history, in itself a wisdom believed, as in Bernardino de Sahagún or Francisco Xavier Clavijero, akin to science. More emphatically than Dutch New York or British Philadelphia, Mexico City was from the outset a scientific report that was periodically updated, and a history in stone rewritten on daily bases.

To be sure, as a locale of science, colonial Mexico City has a long history. A major university was founded in the capital of New Spain in 1553. It was also the site of an important scholarly community, including various scientific associations.[3] But it was beyond doubt during Porfirian times that science acquired a new institutional impulse. Then, old and new scientific institutions gained state sponsorship. Natural history, geography, statistics, social studies, archaeology, and anthropology acquired a vibrant existence in the university, the museums, cafes, and scientific tertulias. The Instituto Nacional de Geografía y Estadística, created in 1833 (and which later became the Sociedad), by the 1880s and 1890s produced the first general maps of Mexico and Mexico City and the first national statistics in all sorts of realms. During the 1870s, the National Museum was created, the National Observatory was rehabilitated, and the Mexican Society of Natural History attained a new life. These institutions became important parts of the scientific life of the city, and indeed of world scientific communities.

The National Museum became a major collection of pre-Hispanic objects and of anthropometric samples of American racial groups. The museum benefited from the major sanitary reforms of the 1890s and 1900s that brought about several important archaeological discoveries in the city. While the city was sanitized, museum halls were filled with the city's underground treasures. In addition, in 1888, the National Medical Institute was created to study the flora and diseases of Mexico. And in 1884, the most important scientific society of nineteenth-century Mexico, the Sociedad Científica Antonio Alzate, was created. Almost all men of letters and science belonged to it. As a result of this renewed scientific impulse, turn-of-the-century Mexico City boasted important scientific publications in which all sorts of sociological, anthropological, and philosophical themes were discussed back-to-back with poetry and art. Mexico City thus became an important site of science, so much so that it was for the first time internationally sanctioned as such through the organization of the first Congress of Americanists that took place in the "tropics" (the eleventh, which took place in Mexico City in 1895), as well as the Second Panamerican Medical Congress and the 10th International Geological Congress (1896).

Notwithstanding, in 1910 a massive popular revolution erupted. As a capital of science, Mexico City took some time to recuperate after the violent part of the Revolution. But by the late 1920s, Mexico City was already a world capital of a cultural revolution concerned with social reforms and welfare. Many scientific ideas were involved in these new concerns with housing, work conditions, zoning, sports, and social security. And Mexico City was not only the location where these new studies were being implemented, but also the object of study for Mexicans and foreigners alike interested in these subjects. The city and its surrounding towns became the rendezvous of international radicals and scholars who not only praised technology and urban life with avant-garde poetry but also believed in a scientific, historical materialist path of human civilization. The city became an inevitable reference point for the power and nostalgia of the new science—from the new workers' housing projects designed by avant-garde architect Juan O'Gorman to those designed by Hennes Meyer; from the idea of the folk-urban continuum of Robert Redfield to the notion of "culture of poverty" of Oscar Lewis; from Mexico as the 1920s socialist capital of the Americas to André Breton's view of Mexico as the world center of surrealism.

In a sort of endless circle, science and the city interact, and whatever knowledge is produced somehow returns to its original laboratory, the city, even if it is not a knowledge specifically produced about the city. In this circle of constant interaction, we may obtain the optical illusion that at some point the city is the object of study, as in the science of urbanism or in the emergence of social science. We can also have the momentary illusion that in fact the city is only the location where science occurred. Finally, in this circle of interaction we may also be tempted to sustain the existence of distinctive and autonomous forms of knowledge. Hygiene could be seen as a unique science different from, say, urban planning; or urban sociology autonomous from town planning. Indeed, all these are but momentary illusions of our knowledge. The circle never stops, and science and the city have been and are in constant interaction and mutual transformation.

I do not want to fully dissect the functioning of this circle and the kind of knowledges it has historically produced. But consider the following opinionated contentions about the interaction between science and the city. First, through the city we acquire knowledge, and we apply knowledge, which is of a marked local makeup, and yet by the very fact of being on or about the city, it is also potentially a universal knowledge. And any local urban solution becomes potentially a universal principle. On the other hand, any science applied to a specific city becomes a "local knowledge." The official periodicals of the city governments of any city of the Americas, from the 1870s to the 1930s, are full of this thinking out loud with an eye to the universal echoes of urban problems and solutions, and another eye on the local mess. If the concern was about prostitution and venereal diseases, for instance, sanitary codes and the experiences of cities all over the world were published and studied. Also, the opinions of experts and the resolutions of international congresses were collected. But at the same time, local studies were undertaken to explain, classify, or control the specific sexual characteristics of, say, Mexico City's men and women.

A second contention is that the interaction between science and city makes it all the more evident that all knowledge is political in both senses, namely, it is about power and it is about the solution of social problems. The institutions of science, the application of knowledge, the city as site and as organism—all this is political. The circle of interaction between the city and science is a political one as much as it is a scientific one.

Finally, I believe that between science and the city there are constant arrhythmias in terms of the production and appropriation of knowledge. City and science are experienced differently in different places depending on local circumstances. Thus the final result of the interaction between science and the city is not only comfort, control, security, or ecological destruction and devastation, but nostalgia. City and science have interacted in such a rapid cycle over the last 200 years that human nostalgia and yearning first accelerated to Proustian excesses, and then seemed to start on a path toward extinction, only to become the current industry of wash-and-wear nostalgia. The same urban experience generates simultaneous, shared lores, which are learned and lived as unique and unrepeatable. Although it is rather difficult for the historian to depict, the inhabitants of a city lived their city in a matchless and unrepeatable manner. We can see this through the perception of poets and writers who lived in very similar urban circumstances: modernization, mechanization, demographic growth, poverty, loss of past references, nostalgia, sexual freedom. Yet each one assumed this experience not only as a specific but above all as a personal occurrence. The poetic expression of such an exaggerated individuality constitutes precisely the universality of the urban.

To bring these ideas down to earth, I offer some vistas from the sidewalk, for it has been essential to the notion of *urbanidad*. From the eighteenth to the twentieth century, all etiquette manuals included sections on that essential component of *urbanidad*: walking sidewalks and streets. The most popular etiquette manual in Mexican Spanish, the *Manual de urbanidad* by M. A. Carreño, published devotedly from the 1890s to the 1940s, included a thorough section on how to behave when on the sidewalk—such matters as the walking speed, gazes, and voices. "Ceder la acera" (yield the sidewalk) was the most imperative concept discussed in these manuals—an instantaneous and solemn give and take based on a social map of the sidewalk. The sidewalk, that apparently free domain, embodied rigid social interactions, even in large cities: "for the use of the sidewalk there are fixed rules, which cannot be overruled without clearly breaking with *urbanidad*."⁴ And yet, walking the sidewalk inevitably meant both an invitation to *ensimismamiento* and a confrontation with the sanitary, moral, and cultural challenges that the modern city inflicted in the urban dweller. Here three of these *ensimismamientos*/challenges: dogs, beggars, and stones.

Dogs

hablo de la ciudad . . .
de los perros errabundos, que son nuestros franciscanos y
nuestros bhikkus, los perros que desentierran los huesos del sol . . .
— Octavio Paz, "Hablo de la Ciudad"

The interaction between science and the city can be seen through an obscure character of the sidewalk, an unmissable one in the streets of Mexico City in 1880, in 1930, or today; namely, the dog. Dogs have been the companions of beggars and street children and the indispensable presence in markets and *vecindades*; they have been loved, feared, and killed; matter of science and matter of literature. In pre-Hispanic times, dogs were urban companions, sources of much-needed animal protein, and also the escorts in the one-way trip to the underworld. Bernal Díaz del Castillo found the dogs of Tenochtitlán astounding with their quasi-hairless nature and their peculiar attribute: no barking. In the *barrio* of Acolman, an entire market was devoted to the commerce of these voiceless dogs. The various kinds of *itzcuintli* (pre-Hispanic dogs) gradually procreated with the dogs brought by the Spaniards, and by the eighteenth century the city was a pack of dogs. A part of the city was then known as *la isla de los perros*, because, as historian Artemio del Valle-Arizpe records, during the many floods suffered by the city, dogs found refuge in high areas of the city, waiting for the water to come down so that they could go in search of needed food.

In fact, even in the pre-Pasteurian era the countless dogs were a steady problem for the city—they were believed to carry illness, odors, and dangers, especially when they trudged the streets in packs. In 1792, according to the curious chronicler Francisco Sedano, Viceroy Revillagigedo ordered the first of the many massacres of dogs that would continue for three centuries. Sedano explained that there were so many dogs in the city that *guardafaroles* (men in charge of lighting lampposts) were paid four pesos for every hundred dead dogs, and thus, said Sedano, by 1792 dogs were gone from the city, but only to become a problem once again the next year. By 1798, for instance, dog killers reported 2,718 sacrificed dogs in February alone, and 9,213 in January 1799.[5]

By 1820, the city government still paid for dead dogs, and an official report on the overpopulation of dogs stated that people protected stray dogs unaware of dogs' dangers, especially for women. The odd report feared of course not rabies but women who "have for dogs a vehement passion, though when dogs are in heat they rapidly hug anyone who offers them any warmth and thus they are very dangerous and should never be allowed inside girls' toilets."[6]

Starting in 1880, with the steady growth in size and prosperity of the city, dogs once again became a very serious problem, especially if seen through the new Pasteurian sanitary concerns of scientists and bureaucrats. In 1888, sanitary codes from all over the world were studied, and Eduardo Liceaga, the most important hygienist of Porfirian Mexico, traveled to the Pasteur Institute in Paris to bring the rabies vaccine. Thus he traveled back to Mexico with rabbits carrying the vaccine.[7] The new science of the city thus started to make of dogs dangerous inhabitants of the sidewalk. A new sanitary code was passed, and Liceaga, together with engineers Roberto Gayol and Miguel Ángel de Quevedo, was placed in charge of cleaning the city and redesigning its sanitary profile.[8] But over the Porfirian years a new technology against rabies was developed: decades of dog massacres.

In late nineteenth-century Mexico City, dogs seemed to be totally out of control. In the surroundings of the city, people feared the attacks by packs of wild dogs that traveled from the city to nearby towns. In the marketplaces, where food was abundant, the dogs were epidemic. Starting in the 1890s, the city government signed yearly contracts with private contractors to exterminate dogs. The science was there to justify such an action; although many advocated similar measures regarding rats, especially in periods of Bubonic plague and typhus epidemics, no other animal seems to have been targeted as strongly as dogs in Mexico City. Horses and mules were often part of the sidewalk experience in Mexico City, and people often complained of the mistreatment of animals in the streets. But only dogs, as El País put it in 1904, "ramble over streets and plazas in complete freedom and as if protected by the exclusive privileges of their species."[9] Indeed, dogs ruled the streets.

The contract signed in 1902 with Rafael M. Carmona for the killing of dogs is emblematic of the various contracts that were signed between 1890 and 1909. The city's government, through the Junta de Saneamiento, visited the establishment (in Santa Cruz Acatlán) where the dogs were kept after capture. The government specified that dogs with no identification be collected and kept in captivity for twelve days, and if they were unclaimed, killed in special cremation ovens, which were designed according to a new technology of massive killing: gas chambers and cremation ovens that collected and used dog fat. This kind of contract was complemented by other contracts signed in the 1900s with entrepreneurs specialized in placing chunks of poisoned meat in different parts of the city to kill street dogs. The person in charge of this killing reported monthly and by section of the city the number of dogs killed.[10] For ten years, many contractors were hired to kill, poison, liquidate in massive gas chambers, and cremate in gigantic ovens thousands of dogs. In one single month in 1905, for instance, one of the eight districts of the city reported up to 800 dogs killed. And that was only one month and one district.

The final solution, however, did not work. During the difficult years of hunger and violence, 1914 and 1915, dogs were a real threat in the nearby countryside and within the city. In 1915, the revolutionary city government, like the Porfirian one, hired a private contractor to massacre dogs in the streets of the city. As in Porfirian times, people complained, for poisoned meat was placed through the city, and many non-stray dogs died. By 1928, the city established laws for the possession of dogs.[11] Over the revolutionary years, dogs abounded in the city, while in the surrounding area, they increased their numbers with the coming and going of revolutionary troops. Every revolutionary platoon, either Zapatista or Villista, included many dogs. Famous photos of the Revolution have seemed a depiction of peasants, sombreros, and *soldaderas*, but if one looks carefully, there it is: the dog.

By 1920, the city government estimated a population of thirty thousand stray dogs, and sought more humane approaches; many people seemed to object to Porfirian-like final solutions. Dogs were defended by people, stated a 1920 report, for both sentimental and practical reasons: they were companions of beggars, street children, and vendors, as well as part of the life of *vecindades*. But also their feces were useful in treating leather, and dogs cleaned streets and plazas of dead birds and rodents; they protected against thefts; and above all they provided warmth and companionship: people and dogs, said the 1920 report, made public displays of physical affection "¡horrible inhumanidad!"[12]

In fact, the dogs won against both the city and the Revolution, and survived so that nowadays they populate the entire city's streets, the *taquerías*, cantinas, and markets. And in some part of the city, dogs survived to exercise, as in European cities, the only new form of citizenship imagined by the Western world since the French Revolution: dogship and catship—the new first-class citizenship of European cities.

Science, dogs, and streets were not only a matter of extermination. Dogs were also important participants in the growth of scientific institutions in Mexico City. In view of their availability, dogs were used in laboratories to investigate typhus, rabies, and even the effects of marijuana and *pulque* consumption. In 1910, doctors reported the story of a dog fed only with *pulque* for a fortnight. The animal became slow, sleepy, and grew fat until his liver and belly exploded.[13] In epic research on typhus fever, many dogs were used as flea and lice carriers and as rat catchers. And in markets dogs served as tasters of all sort of foods.

School recitations, popular verses, and the urban language as a whole had also incorporated the dog. In the 1890s, one of the most popular poets, one who was recited aloud in schools and public events, M. J. Othón, using the voice of a dog, expressed, alas in a very tacky fashion, dogs' loyalty:

> no temas mi señor: estoy alerta
> y si llegara con paso taciturno
> la muerte, con mi aullido lastimero
> también te avisaré . . . ¡descansa y duerme!

> Fear not, my lord, I am alert
> and if death with silent step were to come
> with my pitiful howl
> I'll also warn you . . . you rest and sleep!

And the most modernist literary magazine, La Revista Moderna, included an illustration by Roberto Montenegro—the expressive and tender face of a dog called Mr. Bonifax—and a poem by Diego Fernández Espiro, whose dog, Monsieur Bonifax, was not a dog but a Nietszchean superman:

> Por mi parte he llegado a pensar y no yerro,
> que Monsieur Bonifax, superhombre,
> se ha ocultado en la forma de perro.

> For my part, I have come to think and I don't err,
> that Monsieur Bonifax, superman,
> has hidden in the form of a dog.

After the Revolution, when the city regained its centrality, once again the dog gained the attention of urban dwellers. Describing a walk, 1920s poet Miguel Aguillón Guzmán wrote a vanguard description of the sidewalk in which the dog became the central place of memory: "Se desploman de sueño los semáforos . . . /El ladrido de un perro se me ha enredado al cuello" (The stoplights collapse of sleep . . . /The barking of a dog has wrapped around my neck). The dogs' voice became thus part of the melancholy produced by the sidewalks. For poets and ramblers not only feared stray dogs, but also loved them, pitied them. In 1912, in a modernist magazine a young Gregorio López y Fuentes—who would eventually become a prominent novelist of the Revolution—published his fascination with the dog in the streets: "So life looks at the rheumatic dog, and as it is a life of meditation, after meditating the dog finds the ennui and then, raising its pointed snout, howls; howl that only it and the other dogs can tell whether is a moan or a song inspired by nocturnal peace . . ."

The dogs frequently constituted a metaphor of loyalty, sacrifice, and victimhood that was even more relevant in view of their natural background: the unbound city. In 1925, poet Juan B. Delgado wrote an urban story in verse in which the dog is the city's soul and spirit, betrayed by humans' cruelty and by progress and technology: "Like a formless mush" an emaciated dog lay beside the road, killed by a car, and a passerby cum philosopher claims:

> —hombre cruel, si así pagas el cariño
> del que te amaba con sinceros mimos,
> que ha de esperarme a mí, que latigazos
> recibo como premio a mi trabajo.
> Malhaya sea el hombre y su progreso
> si la muerte ha de dar con sus inventos.[14]

> Cruel man, if thus you pay the love
> of that which loved you with sincere affection
> what is in wait for me, that get lashes
> as a reward for my work.
> Cursed be man and his progress
> if death is to come from his inventions.

The emergence of urban short stories and novels meant the transcription of the feeling that the dog produces in the streets. In 1907, Ricardo Colt wrote the novel *Es el amor que pasa . . . La novela de los perros*: modernist love equated to a bitch in heat, followed by many strays dogs in the streets of the city, expressing in their desire all the atavism that science, romanticism, and liberalism assigned to Mexicans.[15] Carlos Noriega Hope, an urban bohemian, artist, and vanguard writer, wrote a short story in 1923 in which Ernesto, a typical urban *inadaptado* (misfit), reached his house and faced a stray dog's gaze: "On the threshold, curled up, slept a stray dog, pressing his ribs against the wall as if

9.1. Poor neighborhood, by Helen Levitt (1940s).
© Estate of Helen Levitt, Courtesy Laurence Miller Gallery, New York.

eagerly seeking a centimeter of protection. Ernesto did not pay attention to the dog until its two timid little eyes fixedly gazed at his greatcoat (hopalanda). It was a gray gaze full of a mute despair, which could do nothing, which only sought, as sole offering, a little bit of oblivion." The dog, like Ernesto, was an *inadaptado* in the city.[16]

The same kind of brotherhood in desperation is found in some photographic images of the city by the 1940s. Helen Levitt's images of poor neighborhoods are especially telling (see chapters 4 and 7). These pictures awaken one to the bizarre textures of coexistences on Mexico City's sidewalks, textures that surprise us both with familiarity—the capturing of a known daily occurrence—but also with grievance—any walker develops ingratitude and blindness in order to live and survive the sidewalks of Mexico City (figure 9.1).

Thus dogs were at once a scientific problem and an essential part of Mexico City's urban experience. Unsurprisingly, even in the twentieth-first century dogs and Mexico City remained inevitably linked, as in the harsh depictions in the successful Mexican film *Amores Perros* (2001).

Beggars

. . . los presentes no son mendigos de ocasión, sino de raza: mendigos por heren-
cia, vagabundos atávicos que llevan en la sangre aquella levadura que caracteriza
al gitano andante, porque los presentes son muestra del hongo social . . . forman
una casta que parte y de generaciones en generaciones y a través de maravillosas
adaptaciones, participan de circunstancias propias de las bestias.

. . . these are not ocassional beggars, but beggars by race: beggars by inheritance,
atavistic vagrants who in their blood they carry the yeast that characterizes the
errant gypsy, because these are samples of the social fungus . . . they are a breed
that from generation to generation, through wonderful adaptations, shares the
circumstances of beasts.
— Ángel del Campo (Micrós).[17]

Since colonial time, Mexico "swarmed more with beggars (*pordioseros*) than
with flies," said Artemio del Valle-Arizpe.[18] The capital of New Spain grew
and flourished and its beggars grew and flourished with it. There was the
widespread belief that there were too many professional beggars who abused
their neighbors' Christian pity by feigning poverty, blindness, handicap. The
sidewalks were full of their baroque tragic laments: "¡Mira mis tristes años y
amancíllate de este pecador!" (Look at my sad years, humble yourself before
this sinner!), "¡Por la Virgen Santísima de Guadalupe, nuestra madre, den un
corto socorro a este infeliz, comido por la miseria!" (For our very Holy Lady
of Guadalupe, our mother, give a morsel of relief to this miserable one, consumed by poverty!), "¡Santa Lucía bendita les guarde los ojos!" (Blessed Santa
Lucia keep your eyes healthy!).[19] These cries, which became part of the memory
of the city, appealed to a bizarre sense of we in the sidewalk: we all, the piteous
Christians.[20]

Today's foreign visitors in Mexico City—often en route either to the beach
or to their own take on the "real Mexico" (small towns, the countryside, Indigenous "communities")—are frequently dazed by the beggars on the sidewalks,
not only because of their poverty but also because of their disturbing theatri-
cality, an unwanted medieval urban spectacle, a show of misery. For indeed
the beggar has challenged the senses of social justice (how come so much
misery?), time passing (should not they be extinct?), and beauty (why should
one be forced to witness such grotesque scenes?). A popular U.S. travel guide
of the early twentieth century warned the potential visitor to Mexico City: "One
of the worst features of Mexico City is the swarm of beggars, who constitute
a serious nuisance. Filthy, dirty, and truly worthy of the title 'Verminous persons,' the lame, the halt, the blind, and able bodied rogues and vagrants are

encountered almost everywhere, demanding centavos." Over three centuries, countless travelers have echoed this warning.[21]

In turn, Mexican urban observers had not missed the beggars in their rambling of the streets. Ángel del Campo, the most prominent urban observer of late nineteenth-century Mexico City, used scientific—criminological, biological, anthropological, and sociological—metaphors in his descriptions of the city life. When Mexican urban reportage began in the 1900s, Mexican reporters also found themselves taken by images of beggars on the sidewalks; they were chucked not only by misery, not solely by the grotesque, but also by the beggars' physical attachment to sidewalks, to pavements. In the 1910s, *Visiones de la calle* (views from the street) and *A través de México* (Through Mexico City), by Porfirio Hernández and "Pentronio" respectively—the latter very likely Hernández's other *nom de plume*—, in the magazine *Arte y Letras*, were some of the first print media sections devoted fully and solely to examining and documenting Mexico City's streets. The sections reported on beggars, street vendors, unemployed people, and *transeúntes*—perhaps the closest Spanish word for a proletarian *flâneur*, a beautiful word for it possesses something of *ensimismamiento*. In 1914, Hernández described—in a quasi-tactile prose—a beggar as part of pavements: he "sadly drags his mutilated limbs through the streets, in the midst of the hubbub of *transeúntes*, showing the nakedness of his flesh—which the wind dries—with an inconceivable impudence and cynicism. Some rest on the asphalt as true larvae, lurking in the face of the first who passes for minimal traces of sympathy."[22]

These images captured by the first urban reporters constituted a blend of Christian compassion, plain disgust, and scientific curiosity. For graphically the beggar had become a modernist challenge for artists (such as Saturnino Herrán) who were able to achieve pious yet realistic images of street beggars. This was a challenge because of the difficulty of rendering a modern, as it were photographic, accuracy—which included the depiction of physical handicaps and sickness—, along with Christian compassion without sacrificing stylistic innovation. The goal was to reach human compassion beyond common religious imagery. Herrán's beggars (circa 1910), for instance, captured their gazes and facial expressions over the city as background (figure 9.2). His beggars were profoundly mystical—linked to lasting images of pity and compassion—and yet were decisively both Mexican and urban. The secret was in the technical treatment of the gaze and the flesh in the facial expressions: a modernist treatment of blindness and misery.

In 1919, Artenack, an illustrator of the popular *Revista de Revistas*, who worked at the vanguard of commercial propaganda and modernist art, depicted "El ciego del barrio": the common local beggar of any *barrio* of Mexico

9.2. Saturnino Herrán's beggars ("Los ciegos"). Courtesy Museo Regional de Aguascalientes, Instituto Nacional de Bellas Artes. Reproducción autorizada por el Instituto Nacional de Bellas Artes y Literatura, 2011.

9.3. Artenack's beggar. *Revista de Revistas* (March 29, 1919).

City, for beggars had their own *barrios* (figure 9.3). Thus, they represented misery, compassion, and sickness but also familiarity, for every site had its own private beggar in Iberian cities. Artenack's beggar is a blind street singer accompanied by a little girl, for beggars often adopted or kidnapped street children, as it was stated in medieval stories or in the accounts (1904) of one of the first Mexican criminologists, Carlos Roumagnac, or in Luis Buñuel's film *Los Olvidados* (1950). Artenack's depiction also sought the quasi-photographic accuracy, playing both with gazes (the girl who asks for money) and with a picaresque depiction of the beggar's mouth, fingers, and clothing.[23]

But it was *Arte y Letras*—after all the pioneer publication in urban reporting—that included the first telling photographic accounts of beggars. In 1910,

9.4. Beggar. Cover, *Arte y Letras* (February 3, 1910).

it published the expressive face of a beggar, with no visible background, just face and gaze in a studio photo that echoed Herrán's artistic efforts (figure 9.4). The gaze did not respond yet to the fully scientific approach to beggars, but these kinds of gazes eventually would sustain the sociology of beggars. In 1912, *Arte y Letras* published the photo of a beggar, a violin player, with a girl, an image captured by the camera in the streets, *au naturel*; bear in mind this was the cover of a prominent artistic and literary magazine. The image was not meant to be a social or scientific statement, but an artistic depiction of street melancholy. In 1914, the magazine published yet another photo, identified as an "artistic photography," by a photographer identified as Machado. It was not meant to be an objective representation, but art. It represented a beggar wearing glasses, eating a piece of bread. The beggar thus began to be a part of the telling of the sidewalk—simultaneously as reminiscences of medieval

9.5. Petronio, "A través de México."
Photograph by Tostado. *Arte y Letras* (September 26, 1914).

Christian feelings, experiments in urban reportage, and artistic innovation. But beggars gradually gained status as subjects of social science.[24]

Before moving to the scientific account of beggars, *transeúntes* deserve a special treatment. Beggars were not *transeúntes*, for the former lived in the streets, while *transeúntes* rambled the city. They were vendors or jobless people with no fixed schedule, as Petronio identified them in one of his 1914 urban reports. Petronio sought in the city's benches parallel lives: bench and person as a unity in the city. The photos (by Tostado) in Petronio's reportage had captions such as "Pasan las horas y no saben ni cuándo" (hours go by and they [*transeúntes*] don't even know when) and "Una postura artística" (an artistic posture): rare images of simple urban characters in the streets, captured by the camera in their rest; as Petronio said, no past and no future, only an endless present (figure 9.5). In sum: the city, any city.[25]

Unlike beggars, *transeúntes* found no practical goal in rambling the sidewalks and plazas. For them the sidewalk was not about survival, commerce, networking, social visibility, or sex; for them the sidewalk was the invitation and possibility of *ensimismamiento*.

For a long time, social welfare in Mexico City was by and large the responsibility of the Church and private institutions.[26] Therefore the Constitutionalist government in 1915 was torn: how to appropriate the resources and property of those institutions—often linked to the great Porfirian fortunes—when the city needed their services more than ever? A study of the private welfare institutions was undertaken in order to establish whether they were funded by, endowed by, or linked to the Church or whether the ancient-regime wealthy people still directly funded them. The study found that out of sixteen officially registered welfare associations, only three were created before Porfirian times—Asociación Francesa Suiza Belga de Beneficiencia y Prevensión de México founded in 1845, the Mexican Red Cross, and the oldest private welfare institution in the continent: Hospital de la Purísima Concepción y de Jesús Nazareno, created by Hernán Cortés in 1547. The rest of the officially registered institutions were Porfirian centers—shelters for male beggars, *mujeres incurables*, and orphans, as well as schools for poor boys, Catholic schools for girls, hospitals including the Spanish and American welfare associations. Between 1909 and 1913, ten welfare associations were approved but not yet fully registered. And there were fifteen centers that by 1915 had been neither approved nor registered, mostly endowments (for instance, by Isabel de Teresa viuda de Sobrino, Paula Torres viuda de Arciniegas, Rafael Benavides, and Rafael Donde), but also the workers' children daycare center, Casa amiga de la Obrera, founded by Carmen Romero Rubio de Díaz, and the Mexican Red Cross, established in 1864. The 1915 report still claimed that the Red Cross was a rather chaotic institution with "no sense of discipline and total lack of hygiene." Starting in the 1920s, all these institutions had to be, as it were, modernized, made into matters of science and state actions.[27]

Charity was of course linked to the streets' beggars, but begging itself was a larger and older institution than private charity in Mexco City. Porfirian and postrevolutionary amateur sociologists considered *mendicidad* as solid an institution as the Church or the state. An institution historically attached to the Church's labors and teachings, but also to baroque forms of popular religiosity that since Bourbon times had been anathema to stern and centralized forms of pity.

As such, as an institution, the beggar became a matter of scientific scrutiny from the 1910s until the full establishment of a modern welfare state in the 1930s. There were many reports on *mendicidad* from the 1920s to the 1940s in official and scientific publications, but perhaps there is no better window to observe the emergence of the new scientific view of the beggar than a book and a periodical: first, a study officially sponsored by the Mexican government, undertaken by a Mexican lawyer cum sociologist and economist, Ramón Beteta, and by the young U.S. economist E. N. Simpson, who had traveled to Mexico

City in the 1920s in order to study the Mexican agricultural institution, the ejido. The study was published in 1931 as La mendicidad en México. And second, the 1930s journal Asistencia, a monthly publication of the city's official welfare agency (Beneficencia Pública).[28]

In La mendicidad en México the old Christian/journalistic/modernist gaze was made into a fully scientific account of mendicidad, beyond urban reportage and yet still containing the compassion aspect and the modernist trend—which after all are inherent traits of the social science project everywhere. The study was in part a statistical report on numbers of beggars, diseases, origins, and mortality rates. It established that there were in Mexico City about 5,000 beggars in 1930 (a city of about a million inhabitants), and only in downtown's main streets there were about 338 male and 156 female beggars. Most had an urban rather than a rural origin, which reinforced the sociologists' belief in the city's destructive nature vis-à-vis genuine "communities." The statistical causes of mendicidad, according to the authors, were poverty, sickness, physical handicaps, unemployment, alcoholism, and what was called in nineteenth-century sociology urban anomie—and that Beteta and Simpson called "desorganizantes de la vida citadina" (disorganizing factors of urban life). However, the study also identified the cultural factor: mendicidad as a deep-rooted institution, merging popular religiosity with Catholic charity. Beyond statistics, begging was an institution sanctioned not only by the Church but also by the city's entire culture, with a clear sense of supply and demand as well as rituals of performance. Beggars were as intrinsic to the city as the heavy colonial temples.

The study also undertook a mapping of the beggars in the city's space, trying to find patterns, and establishing the relations between origins of beggars and the city's lack of services. Moreover, the study utilized what 1920s social science had done with urban reportage to make it into a scientific tool, that is, life stories based on observations and interviews. This is the anthropological technique that in the 1940s Oscar Lewis would make into mainstream science in Mexico City, but it had been used long before in the city by criminologists (Roumegnac), journalists (Petronio), and economists (Beteta). Of course, in La mendicidad en México the report of the life of certain beggars was full of the modernist rhetoric so common in the old gaze to the sidewalk. But the very fact of using such a resource in combination with statistics and other social science tools made the narratives something more than mere literary pieces. When considering solutions, like relocation in special institutions, the study combined the old rhetorical skills with the new scientific findings: "Piling them in a building? What would thus be gained from the point view of the city or of the beggars themselves? What would be gained from institutionalizing people as radically different as Juan Jiménez Aguilar the lame seller of heroin, Guadalupe

9.6. Juan Jiménez Aguilar. From *La mendicidad en México* by Ramón Beteta and Eyler N. Simpson (Mexico City: Beneficencia Pública and A. Mijares y Hermanos, 1931).

Casas González the girl abused by her parents, María Feliz García the paralytic woman, or Manuel Pinto the old drunkard?"²⁹

Finally, *La mendicidad en México* relied as much on artistic and modernist impressions as did *Arte y Letras*'s images. The photo of a beggar, Juan Jiménez Aguilar, a cripple, a heroin vender, and an addict, was advanced as the study's documentary evidence (figure 9.6). Seeing it in the continuum of beg-

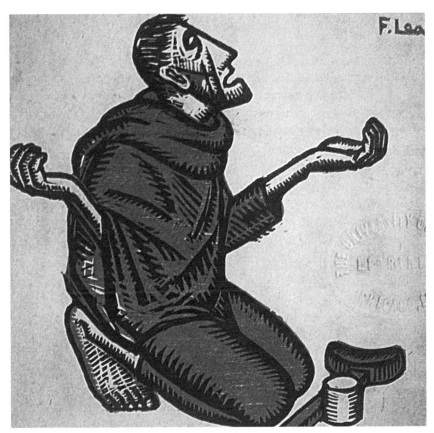

9.7. F. Leal's cover. *La mendicidad en México* by Ramón Beteta and
Eyler N. Simpson (Mexico City: Beneficencia Pública and A. Mijares
y Hermanos, 1931).

gars' depictions, the image is just another instance of the same trend, at once
Christian, scientific, and artistic. In addition, the book's cover used an artistic illustration of beggars rather than a photo: a color illustration by painter
Fernando Leal, a member of the radical artistic circle that included Rivera
and Siqueiros. The cover displayed in few strokes, in a minimalist fashion,
the beggar's expression that had for long fascinated artists and reporters
(figure 9.7).

In turn, the 1930s *Asistencia* made the radical switch from beggars as a matter of Christian and private compassion to beggars as a subject of state and scientific intervention. It stated that it was the state, neither private charity nor the
Church, that was in charge of beggars and other inhabitants of the sidewalk.
The revolutionary state had become a modern welfare state, and the scientific

turn meant the end of old forms of social welfare, and the emergence of a new tacky rhetoric to speak of the social:

> Medieval mysticism proclaimed private charity as the only remedy for the needs of the poor. The lay individualism that moved and organized the world in the nineteenth century was opposed by the feeling of brotherhood; and the spiritual reactions that straightened during the second half of the nineteenth century, as a reaction to positivism, furnished legal theorists with the flag of philanthropy in order to justify charity. [Thence followed the notion of solidarity] which, as an inescapable social fact independent of man's will, finally untied utilitarian and egotistic mankind, thus justifying social welfare as a sole duty of the state in order to avoid destruction of the social body.[30]

The journal published many articles devoted to sidewalks' inhabitants: beggars, street children, and, curiously, homosexuals (often considered the unmentionable inhabitants of the sidewalk). If Marx himself had included beggars and homosexuals within the lumpenproletariat, Mexican scientists also saw the homosexual as part of the chaos of streets and sidewalks. But Mexican scientists found in biology the way to preserve the honor of the city's social environment. That is, the city was indeed made of miasmas and mess, with a peculiar history that had allowed the existence of beggary as an institution, but the city was not so bad as to produce the aberration of homosexuality. Dr. Alfonso Millán, director of the National Mental Health Hospital (manicomio), disserted in Asistencia about homosexuals in the streets (1934): the homosexual was an antisocial character, a biological mistake, "no hay alma todo es cuerpo" (there is no soul only body), for in Mexico City, he argued, men were men and women women, and the city's culture was not refined enough as to produce the common feminization of other latitudes: "Indeed, among us the homosexual is seen with repugnance and disgust, and he cannot in any way be the product of the environment." If there was a Greek sense of friendship in the city, it was not among the popular classes, but among intellectuals. That is, a very macho city could not explain the emergence of homosexuals in the streets of Mexico City. It was a biological problem.[31]

All in all, Asitencia's prose clearly depicted the traces of the old modernist gaze; its graphic depiction of beggars had not overcome the blend of artistic, Christian, and scientific concerns of an Herrán. Thus the watercolor that depicted beggars drinking the coffee distributed by the Beneficiencia Pública—drawn by Luis León Díaz—advancing conspicuous echoes of gazes, facial expressions, and the picaresque so characteristic of the long fascination with this inhabitant of the sidewalk, the beggar. Moreover, it had curious undertones of the famous nineteenth-century Spanish romantic painter Leonardo Alenza, whose *La sopa boba* has an uncanny similarity to León Díaz's water-color—which was taken, as it was stated, *au naturel*.[32]

Stones

> . . . e serei, mergulhado no passado,
> cada vez mais moderno e mais antigo.
> — Ledo Ivo, "Acontecimento do Soneto"

Finally, I want to ruminate on the reddish stone, known as tezontle, that the walker finds in the walls of the historical center of the city. These volcanic stones, in the past very common in the valley of Mexico, belonged to the temples and houses of the Aztec city. Absorbed by these stones, one cannot help pondering the weight of history in Mexico City, which has been reconstructed several times. There are various cities breathing through that porous stone. This pondering is necessarily about history, the science of history, but also about the science of constructing new histories, new cities, over old ones.

From the onset, said Luis de Velasco, first viceroy of New Spain, Mexico City was a total gaffe: "fue yerro" (it was a mistake), he said, "not to inhabit another town of Spaniards, . . . , for there are good sites . . . where Spaniards little by little could have moved, now what cannot be done is a necessity, for there are neither enough people nor enough money to move them."[33] But blunders became historical incentives for both political and scientific innovations. Throughout three centuries of Spanish rule, Mexico City was a carefully studied site, a learning that included destruction but also dialogue and mutual appropriation between native and European knowledges.

The political decision to found the capital of New Spain in Mexico-Tenochtitlán constituted an incredible technological, political, and cultural challenge—the test of an immense valley, with a complex system of saline lakes and lands, almost 3,000 meters above sea level, with a monumental city in the middle, constructed with sophisticated canals and roads and inhabited at the time of the conquest by nearly 180,000 people (larger than any city in Spain at the time). A city that functioned as the axis of a religious and military power whose borders went as far south as Central America and as far north as the deserts of today's Sonora.[34] A city plan that from the outset aimed at the creation of a central city for the Republic of Spaniards, and a peripheral city for the Republic of Indians.

Countless technological problems emerged during the construction in this setting of a sixteenth-century Spanish capital, when Madrid itself was yet to be fully completed and the Moorish city of Granada had recently been "reconquered" by the unified kingdoms of Castile and Aragón. The Aztec city was, for Spanish eyes, more bizarre and alien than Constantinople. And yet their first decision was to reconstruct the Aztec roads and canals and then to build an entire new Spanish center, utilizing the materials of the Aztec structures. Aztec artisans and masons were put to work in the destruction and reconstruction of the same reddish stone they had carved before. But the stones were only a part of the technological dilemma. The management of water, to be sure, was from the beginning until the present one of the greatest predicaments.

But all technological challenges acquired meaning when considering politics. The reddish stones were part of the architecture of power. It is on the level of the politics of conquest that the historian finds the justification for, and actual success of, the relation between science and the city in colonial Mexico City. If the goal was gold and the conquest of souls, the decision to build the Spanish capital over the Aztec city proved to be right. In less than a century, the Spaniards achieved relatively stable political control over a vast territory. They hoped that, through Indian labor and tribute, the city would be built, but countless social and demographic problems had to be faced. They greatly depended on native knowledge, alliances, and labor force to deal with the city, and the Indian population started to diminish drastically, especially due to contagious epidemics. Soon the Spanish crown experimented with complex administrative and legal forms, including the separation and protection of la república de indios. New forms of land tenure, distribution of land, and religious indoctrination emerged during the sixteenth and seventeenth centuries. And gradually, despite various riots and protests, Mexico City became indeed the main capital of the Spanish kingdoms of the Americas, a city of gold, aristocracy, art, and science, making all the technological errors and gains in dealing with nature and history worthwhile.

During the Hapsburg period the city gradually became the "noble" and "imperial" capital of the kingdom of New Spain; a city formed, socially, by different religious orders, guilds, Indian communities, barrios, and cofradías. Religious-political rites ordered a complex baroque city that obeyed different jurisdictions, but with a clear predominance of convents and parishes—the main urban property holders. The late eighteenth-century Bourbon reforms aimed at homogenizing space, time, and society within the city. Plazas and streets would have to be ordered and tianguis and public spaces and finances centralized. But the old imperial city survived until the mid-nineteenth century, when liberal reforms radically transformed the structure of space and the rites of the city by appropriating land, social functions, and symbolic forces previously monopolized by the Church and religion.[35]

The Mexico City of the seventeenth and eighteenth centuries already included forms of urban control that would eventually be considered scientific. The first *enquêtes* were made house by house by priests eager to census the class, status, number, and gender of the population, as well as their observance of their religious rituals. A new zoning of the city was also derived from the religion-centered administration of the city.

Indeed, the city, the pre-Hispanic center, had seduced the Spaniards, and they made it into the symbol of both their power and their knowledge from the sixteenth to the nineteenth centuries. "Que quanto llega a ser intelligible," said Bernardo de Balvuena, the poet of the city, in 1604, "Quanto un entendimiento humano encierra," "los gallardos ingenios desta tierra/lo alcanzan, sutilizan y perciben/en dulce paz o en amigable Guerra" (All that can become evident . . . for what human knowledge entitles/the gracious wisdom of this land/can reach it, can perceive it and make it subtle/in either sweet peace or friendly war).[36] But in fact it was the historical power of the space that had created the scientific challenges and above all had made it possible for science to be applied to a city. In this sense, the historical weight of a space is not the externality of science, something that science must overcome, but its raison d'être.

After 1821, the capital of the newly created nation-state, as a scientific dilemma and as the site of knowledge, faced various environmental, military, and sanitary problems. The depopulation of the city was one problem after years of regional wars and political instability. Other problems were the result of the logistical needs of a city as a war zone. But by the 1870s, Mexico City and science experienced a renewed relationship, much closer to our contemporary notion of modern urban transformation, and a relationship that seemed to have overcome history.

After 1870, the city was radically transformed during two distinguishable periods: first from the 1870s to 1910, the year of the Mexican Revolution; and then from circa 1920 to the late 1940s. The first period can be seen as the making of "la ciudad científica." We can call the second season "la ciudad revolucionada," because this new city derived from a violent popular revolution, new political arrangements, and a radically new global perspective on cities and science. The transformation of the "ciudad revolucionada" sought to embody the Revolution, understood not as a romantic cultural or social phenomenon, but as an inevitable, objective, scientific, and natural development. And the *ciudad revolucionada* was truly revolutionary: it rapidly transformed the Mexico City of the reddish stones from a peripheral small "city of peasants" into one of the largest world metropolises: revolutionized and revolutionary, indeed.

In fact, by the 1920s the world had changed, but not the faith in science: Paris, London, and Vienna were seen as scientific results and works of art—

capitals finally scientized and great metropolises of science. By the 1930s, Leningrad, New York, and Buenos Aires were seen as places of social mobilization and urban innovation, thanks to knowledge, thanks to what industrial technology and science were able to produce, and thanks to the new science, social science. Whereas science was at the core of Haussmann's transformation of Paris, science was also the justification of the social architecture of 1920s Germany and Austria and of the zoning of 1920s Chicago.[37]

It could be argued that between 1880 and 1930, the arts were gradually subjected to science, architecture to engineering, worthless contrivance to utility, and sterile and pompous creativity to methodical, efficient, modern productivity. Moreover, history seemed to be surpassed by the scientific management of the historical nature of space. The final triumph of science. The city itself, that historical chaos, seemed to make sense finally. The best epitomes of this apparent triumph of science over the city as overflow historical tradition, as the chaos of time, are three very important cities that, like Mexico City, were turned into science between 1850 and 1910: Constantinople, the ancient capital of Byzantium, and the two cities par excellence: Athens and Rome.

Modern Istanbul, one of the centers of the world since 330, when Constantine moved the capital of the Roman Empire from Rome to Byzantium, and since the fifteenth century the capital of Islam, underwent an accelerated urban Westernization from the 1880s to the 1910s. The ancient Byzantine map of the city, which had been altered by the Muslim city, was reformed geographically and administratively according to what was believed to be superior scientific ideas that came from Europe. In fact, until 1924, when Ankara was declared the capital of modern Turkey, Istanbul was a unique example of the significance of the most dense and chaotic history and space; it became a modern city in the nineteenth-century manner, loaded with the symbols and architectonic styles that characterized all late nineteenth-century cities. The past seemed overcome, and it only periodically returned—and returns—to stain the modern scientific, civilized, comfortable, and safe city. Or so it seems, because indeed as a Roman city (after all, a military and holy center), Istanbul was precisely knowledge in stone. An entire science made into a city. As a Muslim capital, with its apparent mess of curvy streets and demographic and spatial agglomeration, it was also a holy city, a Polis from a world the West saw as upside down. The last metamorphosis of Istanbul, the one that resulted from the defeat of the Ottoman Empire by Greece, did not mean the final encounter of science and the city. It was a simple, quite brief stage in a long history of science and the city.[38]

The same was true for Athens, which was by decree made into the capital of the modern Western myth of the nation-state; the capital of post-1834

Greece, the romantic and modern emblem of Europe. And it was made so both by Europeans and by Greeks, and against other Greeks who sought to make other Greek city-states (Argos, Tripoli) the capital city of modern Greece. And it was history, so torrential for Greece and unforgettable to nineteenth-century Europe, that made Athens succeed. Prussian monarchs redesigned it to make it even more ancient and yet more modern.

The new Athens became a collage of improvisations that included American-style urban experiments, Parisian transformations, solutions like those undertaken in Calabria after an earthquake in the 1780s. Athens, like Washington, D.C., was an example of the founding of the total power of a state in a neutral place. In Athens, new cathedrals, universities, and academies were created to give centrality to a nonexistent nation and to furnish the West with a space of memory, if ephemeral, as solid as the Agora or the Acropolis. This despite the fact that Athens's inhabitants remained attached to a variety of local senses of belonging. Through nineteenth-century urban knowledge, Athens could become a modern, central, true capital city of Greece. But it was and had already been science. It was and had already been a city—thanks to its historical weight.[39]

Rome followed a similar path. It was classical antiquity's cosmopolis, the renaissance capital of Christianity, and by decree the modern capital of the Italian state finally unified by the Piedmont kingdom in 1861. In 1870, Rome was occupied and incorporated into the new nation. Through various commemorative projects, which manipulated the symbolic importance of the Roman past, the new Rome, modern, scientific, and sanitary, emerged. The peak moment of this transformation was the reorganization of the city according to Alessandro Viviani's plan (1882). The impression was, once again, that for the first time science and the city joined. But this was another city among other cities; a new city that, like those with an analogous mythological profile (Istanbul, Athens, Mexico City), had to deal with history in a unique fashion and, unlike many other cities, could not easily disperse the density of the past.

Between 1880 and 1930, Mexico City was, I argue, of this hue of cities, perhaps the only one of this kind on the American continent. And not because Mexico City was made into a world metropolis in those decades—the best example of that could be New York, São Paulo, or Buenos Aires—, but because it was, as Francisco Xavier Clavijero as well as later many historians and architects of the Porfirian period, put it: the Athens of America. It was not the only pre-Hispanic capital, but it was the only one that was carried on to the modern era as a capital.

Indeed, nineteenth-century Mexico City reinvented science and thus reinvented itself. It reenacted the original equation of chaos and cosmos; from the chaos of spatial disorder, uncontrolled history and tradition, the world upside down, to the cosmos of civilization, of scientific space. The city became an integrated cosmos of knowledge and education that joined religion, art, and wisdom in a space that in turn does not recognize itself as mere art or as pure science or as simple power. Mexico City grew to be a modern city, an epitome of the true and natural order, a laboratory city, an experiment, an ephemeral metaphor of change and progress. In the last analysis, it is impossible to know what was first—the city as an allegory of God? The city as an organism? God as the city? The human body as an urbane society? History, embodied in *tezontle*, was not overcome by science; the modern, scientized, city was made possible by the very weight of history.

ON LICE, RATS, AND MEXICANS

This is the story of the post-Pasteurian moment in science and cities, specifically of the search for the etiology of and cure for what was called in Nahuatl *matlazahuatl* and was known in Spain and New Spain as *tabardillo*: the typhus fever that endemically persisted in Mexico City and that, since colonial times, periodically reached epidemic proportions.

Between the 1900s and the 1930s, Mexico City and typhus underwent multifarious and overlapping incarnations: the city as a dangerous human abomination that germinated disease, the city as a scientific object of study, the city as a major world laboratory, and the city as the host of the passions and adventures of the world's bacteriologists. The story of so many incarnations involves a plot inevitably made of filthy scenes, great miscalculations, and important scientific eurekas; heroes and antiheroes, one hundred dead scientists and thousands and thousands of victims; Nobel Prize winners and forgotten scientists; novelists and the many anonymous urban rats, fleas, and lice that are at the center of the story.

The story can be told as a tragicomic drama in two acts, requiring a minimum introduction as to the setting, the main cast of characters, and the basic leitmotifs in the unraveling of the plot in order to subsequently proceed to the two main acts: 1910 and 1931. The action in both takes place in Mexico City; moreover, this is a plot about the city as a focal point upon which various historical currents (from Mexico, the United States, Africa, and Europe) converged between the 1900s and the 1940s.

Before the Curtain Goes Up

Cities kill people. This is an unquestionable statement in either 1800 or in 1900, and is especially true for such cities as Mexico City, one of those cities that blended modern growth and human agglomeration with what was seen by nineteenth-century scientists as atavistic backwardness and uncleanliness. But typhus and Mexico City have had a peculiar parallel trajectory, a shared modernist history, for it was between around 1880 and the 1940s that the world's typhus research acquired an accelerated pace, and this acceleration occurred in Mexico City. To be sure, this was but an episode in the long history of cities and diseases; an episode marked by three factors: first, typhus fever's unique bacteriological nature, which was only slowly and painfully unraveled; second, the scientific habits created by the world's Pasteurian revolution; and, finally, by Mexico City's own long entanglement with the disease.

The Strange Life of the Main but Mute Character of the Story

The final denouement of the plot is the least interesting part of the story. It needs, however, to be told in order to understand why the city and its scientists seemed to operate in a labyrinth. It is now known that typhus fever is not one but various diseases caused by Rickettsiae: a parasite that cannot be grown artificially and that was named Rickettsiae precisely because of the plot and actors in this story. Rickettsiae include various bacteria, producing different kinds of typhus, a fact that made the research all the more complicated. All forms of typhus are known to have arthropods as their agents, but each has a unique way of entering the human body. The two forms that are important for the story are the so-called epidemic typhus, produced by *Rickettsia prowazekii*— first fully described in 1916 by the Brazilian doctor Henrique da Rocha Lima at Hamburg's institute for tropical medicine. The specific arthropod carrier for this strain of typhus is the *piojo blanco*, or body louse, on humans. Research on this strain was made more difficult by the fact that it is not actually the louse's bite that produces the disease but something far more disgusting: when a louse feeds on a human, it simultaneously defecates; when humans scratch their bites, the feces (which carry the contagious agent) are introduced into the wound. Body lice were common in overcrowded cities, especially in cities with large pauperized populations and with temperate weather punctuated by seasonal or daily episodes of cold, leading inhabitants to keep their warm clothing in perpetual use and unwashed.

The second strain is the murine typhus, also known as Mexican typhus, first proposed by some Mexican doctors (Miguel Otero, Ángel Gaviño), by a Swiss doctor resident in Mexico City, Hermann Mooser (1928), and finally described by U.S.-German doctor Hans Zinsser and Mexican doctors Maximiliano Ruiz Castañeda and Gerardo Varela between 1931 and 1940. The arthropod that transmits the disease is the flea, via the city's rats. The murine and the epidemic types combine, the former as an endemic disease and the latter in epidemic outbreaks, such that once humans are infected with the murine type they can develop the other type and spread it through lice to other humans.

The murine type is more benign, but both present similar symptoms: weakness, extremely high fever, headaches, muscle aches, and rashes composed of both spots and bumps (first on the back, chest, and abdomen, then on the arms and legs). It often lasts seven to twelve days, and in the worst cases produces swelling in the heart muscle or in the brain and, finally, death. Most of the infected survive and develop immunity. The murine causes about twelve days of reduced forms of these symptoms, but rarely advances. Between 1870 and 1915, the typhus mortality rate was between 17 and 25 percent. Typhus is thus the protagonist that until the 1930s was present, but unknown and feared by the city's inhabitants.[1]

The Pasteurian Fever

Whereas Thomas A. Edison epitomized the inventive nature of an era, Pasteur became the model for the observant, logical, and philanthropic scientist able to improve the lives of cities, countries, and empires. Pasteur's discoveries, style of research, and institutionalization of a science linked to state intervention constituted a revolution not merely in the biological sense. Pasteurism also became a social, cultural, and personal way of interacting with sickness, cities, wars, and "science as a vocation." Typhus and many other diseases became calls to action for the many would-be Pasteurs. In the 1930s the most prominent typhus expert of the twentieth century, Charles Nicolle, recalled that he and his colleagues were called *les pasteuriens* because they were like members of a religious order. The fact that every scientist seemingly had to reach Pasteur's genius, state patronage, and fame surely fostered previously unparalleled scientific research. But it also made all the more conspicuous a facet of modern science sometimes considered to be a remnant of a more archaic period, namely, the encounter of egos, the crude exchange of kicks under the table of science.

Indeed, post-Pasteurian interactions between disease and cities constituted an unsettling fight of suspicious, egotistical, and entrepreneurial characters. Many died in the effort, others emerged as heroes, and yet others became science's betrayed heroes. All thought of themselves as underrated geniuses whether they lived and worked in Paris, New York, or Mexico City.[2]

The Setting and Its Cast of Characters

European and colonial wars had been the natural stage for the struggle against typhus. Millions of people acquired the disease in the many nineteenth-century European wars—in trenches, hospitals, and prisoners' camps. Some have estimated that in European Russia alone between 1917 and 1923 nearly three million people died of typhus.[3] Mexico was no exception to this rule: the hero of the defense of Puebla against the French imperial troops, General

Ignacio Zaragoza, died in 1862 in the epidemic that killed thousands of imperial and Mexican troops. Until the 1900s, few measures were successful in fighting the disease. The fight against typhus occurred in metropolitan laboratories (in London, Paris, Berlin, Santiago de Chile, Rio de Janeiro, Boston, Mexico City, and New York) as a result, especially, of the global Pasteurian revolution.

Wars were only one of typhus's natural environments. Cities were the other, and by the end of the nineteenth century there were two main capitals of both typhus and its research: Tunis and Mexico City. Both suffered from periodic epidemics and both had the political and scientific institutions necessary to host research. As a French protectorate, by 1910 Tunis had for two decades been the French laboratory for the study of all sorts of diseases, but especially of typhus and syphilis. Pasteur Institutes were established in many cities, including Tunis. By the early twentieth century, one personality, French biologist Charles Nicolle, dominated typhus research in Tunis.

Mexico City, for its part, had suffered several typhus epidemics throughout colonial and independent times, which devastated streets, barrios, hospitals, and prisons. Mexico City's mortality rates were slowly but surely diminishing starting in 1900, from 49.8 per thousand inhabitants in 1891–1900 to 29 in 1921–24, while the population grew from approximately 400,000 inhabitants in 1910 to a bit more than a million in 1930.[4] But according to Dr. Fernando Ocaranza, between 1800 and 1921 Mexico City had suffered twelve typhus epidemics: 1812–14, 1824, 1835–39, 1848–49, 1861, 1867, 1875–77, 1892–93, 1901–2, 1906–8, 1911, and 1915–17.[5] But the disease was endemic, though not the main mortality factor in the city—a distinction that, until the 1930s, was held jointly by pneumonia, tuberculosis, diseases of the digestive systems, and liver disease (mostly cirrhosis and amoeba infection of the liver). Mexico City's nineteenth- and early twentieth-century statistics were concerned with finding geographical, climatic, and social patterns in typhus. It was established that typhus and the winter were clearly correlated, peaking from December to March. The founding Mexican document of modern typhology was written in 1844 by Dr. Manuel Jiménez: *Apuntes para la historia de la fiebre petequial o tabardillo que se obseva en México*. Thereafter followed countless studies by Mexican scientists, especially in and about Mexico City.

Mexico City, however, remained an efficient killer at the end of the nineteenth century. It underwent periodic outbreaks of typhus and cholera, as well as yearly periods of dust storms, and fecal stench. In 1876 a first Congress of Medicine was convened to deal with the city's diseases. Typhus was prominent at the congress, though its origins remained unknown. It was believed that miasmas and their fecal stench were related to the disease. Some doctors, like the prominent Dr. José Lobato, advanced unfounded but then trendy explanations, making use of the theses of scientist Max von Pettenkofer, who maintained that diseases were the result of imbalances between ground and underground water reservoirs. Hence for Lobato typhus was produced neither by a bacterium nor by a virus, as some were already suggesting in Mexico, but by "an infectious miasma that spreads periodically."[6] All in all, more than following essentially backward European theories about miasmas, Mexican doctors experimented with whatever ideas became available. Jiménez, rather than pursuing well-established theories, based his argument on observations, distinguishing typhus from typhoid and suggesting that Mexican typhus was different from European typhus. City inhabitants, however, kept dying of typhus and the city continued to impose the search for new solutions and new lines of thought.

In 1893 a colorful flyer, featuring a woodcut illustration by José Guadalupe Posada, was distributed in the streets of Mexico City: "awful and terrifying devastation" read the leaflet, "caused by bad harvests and the horrible typhus epidemic that has caused such commotion in Mexico City." Posada's illustration depicted people crying, the transportation of corpses through city streets, and the conspicuous urban dog—at once a symbol of human pain and a potential cause of human diseases. That same year, Dr. Luis E. Ruiz, director of the Hospital Juárez, observed an increase of typhus patients from 1,471 in 1889 to 2,597 in the first semester of 1893 alone. As Ruiz put it, if typhus was not the most *mortifera* disease, it was certainly the most "devastating . . . not only because in the winter months it becomes positively epidemic, but also because of the panic aroused by its contagiousness." By 1922 typhus was listed as number twenty-one in an enumeration of causes of mortality in the city; in 1937 it was the twenty-eighth (though in terms of people 1922 saw 670 typhus patients as opposed to 991 in 1937). As late as 1922, however, 4.7 percent of the city's mortality was still due to typhus, while in such cities as Washington, D.C.—not exactly the most hygienic city in the world—typhus was responsible for 0.0000009 percent of the mortality rate. London had presented 190,000 cases of typhus in 1862, and yet by 1910 typhus was virtually unknown. As occurred in London or Washington, Mexico's gradual defeat of typhus was the product not of a single vaccine or miracle cure, but a mixture of sanitary measures, medicine, insecticides, and education.[7]

Starting in the 1880s, the city's relative peace and stability produced the institutions necessary to deal with the epidemics. In addition to researchers in the Hospital General, the Hospital Juárez, and the American Hospital, two institutions became essential: the Instituto Patológico (created in 1896 as direct offshoot of the Museo Patológico), and the Instituto Bactereológico Nacional (created in 1905). These institutions—and their direct postrevolutionary successors—commanded typhus research from the 1900s to the 1930s, and the cast of personalities they contained, though generally unknown, exhibits a robust and distinguished cross-section of figures in modern world bacteriology: Ángel Gaviño, José Terrés, Manuel Otero, Gerardo Varela, and Maximiliano Ruiz Castañeda as well as two foreign bacteriologists in Mexico City, the French Joseph Girard, and the Swiss Hermann Mooser. With and/or against all of them other prominent foreign scientists worked between 1909 and 1932.[8]

This sets the stage and introduces the characters of the story.

Act I. 1910: The Louse Moment

The 1910 moment of typhus, lice, city, and scientists commenced far away from Mexico City. In 1909, in the midst of a severe typhus epidemic in Tunis, Charles Nicolle, the prominent *pasteurien*, entered a hospital full of typhus patients and then eureka: "It was at that very moment that I saw the light." Then and there he realized it: the louse, that filthy arthropod, was the agent that spread typhus. He had solved the great mystery at his beloved Tunis Pasteur Institute. As late as 1931, while in Mexico City, he maintained that it was then, in 1909, through this vision, that the key to the prevention of and cure for typhus was discovered. Truth be told, in 1909 the mystery was far from solved, but Nicolle had kicked off a comedy of errors that would last until the middle of the 1930s.[9]

Nicolle's discovery appeared to be the first transmission of typhus from infected men to monkeys through lice. But his discovery had not been the mythic scientific illumination that he—also a novelist, after all—described a posteriori. It was, rather, a lucky experiment tried many times before; one that was not replicated until Mexican and U.S. doctors succeeded in Mexico City in early 1910. Many had tried before, including Dr. Miguel Otero in San Luis Potosí, who in 1906 experimented with flies, fleas, lice, and thus with dogs, horses, and rats, but could not come out with a final conclusion, wrongly identifying the typhus germ as what he called "amoeba mexicana petequialis." He thought it was unique to Mexico. He was of course wrong, and did not truly understand the role played by lice, and the cellular function of the typhus agent. But he was right in thinking, as would later be proved, that there was something uniquely Mexican about the whole affair. But in 1909 even Nicolle could not isolate the bacteria or virus that caused typhus.[10]

Also in 1909 there was an epidemic outbreak of typhus in Mexico City that would prove a seminal event for global typhus research. After almost three decades of stability, the city had been physically and intellectually transformed, and the 1910 *Centenario* was drawing near. In this context, the conventional interaction between city and science that had existed for at least two decades became a whirlpool of interconnected stories: first, the saga of state intervention in scientific research through monetary prizes, which in 1909 reached unprecedented levels. In the 1880s, Mexico's National Academy of Medicine had created a permanent commission to grant a prize of 500 pesos for "observations that advance knowledge of the disease in terms of its nature, etiology, prophylaxis, or treatment." There were calls for proposals in 1879, 1881, and 1882 but there was no winner. In 1891, in the context of the dissemination of the miasma measures proposed by Max von Pettenkofer, the study by Fernando Zárraga and Luis E. Ruiz was awarded the prize. The study, of course wrongly, concluded that in 1891 there had been a correlation between changes in the levels of underground water and the frequency of typhus—the lower the levels of underground water the more typhus. But in 1909 Porfirio Díaz himself offered a first prize of 50,000 pesos and a second prize of 20,000 pesos for the discovery of the typhus agent and its cure.[11]

Second, there was the story of the international post-Pasteurian scientific race for fame and prestige and the frantic hunt for germs of all sorts, among them, typhus. Thus, with Mexico City's 1909 epidemic under way and with the prize announced internationally, four teams rose to the fore in Mexico City: one from the U.S. Public Health Service commanded by Joseph Goldberger and John Anderson; another from the University of Chicago, formed by Howard T. Ricketts and his student Russell Wilder; still another from Ohio State University, made up of E. McCampbell and James Conneffe; and finally a team that, unlike the others, was not present in Mexico in 1909 but was nonetheless the engine of the 1909–10 whirlpool, namely, Nicolle and the authority commanded by his discoveries.

Third, there was the story of the Mexican community of bacteriologists that in 1909 was divided by fierce competition between its central institutions: the Instituto Patológico, the Instituto Bacteriológico Nacional, Hospital General, the Hospital Juárez, and the American Hospital in Mexico City. The main actors, among many, in this local battle were, in 1909, Ángel Gaviño, Miguel Otero, Joseph Girard, and Hermann Mooser.

Finally, there was another current in this maelstrom—the story of the city, its miasmas, jails, rats, and lice. The result of this whirlpool of stories was a tragicomedy of errors, although not one without intermittent successes.

In 1909 and 1910 Mexico City provided the stage for a multifarious hunt for lice, rats, flies, and tifosos in hospitals, prisons, and vecindades. Ángel Gaviño, a prominent, if controversial, Mexican scientist and the founder of the Instituto Bacteriológico Nacional, had been engaged in the hunt for quite some time when the news from Tunis and the rush of scientists reached the city. At Gonzalo Sandoval street, in Popotla—beyond the Calzada Verónica, the northernmost limit of the city in 1910—, Gaviño had formed a team of scientists, among them his closest collaborator Joseph Girard, whom he had hired at the Pasteur Institute in Paris.[12] In the 1900s, in the midst of an accelerated transformation of Mexico's academic institutions, the Porfirian government hired foreign scientists, Girard among them, who worked in Mexico from 1906 to 1913. Of course, in order to attract foreign scientists to the city, Mexico had to offer plenty of lice and diseases or lots of money or, better yet, both.[13]

Hoping to win the typhus race, Gaviño and his team had been fighting internally with the Instituto Patológico in order to concentrate the prestige, equipment, and resources necessary for typhus research. Dr. Ygnacio Prieto, from the Instituto Patológico, claimed in 1906 to have found the typhus germ, but Gaviño and Girard were adamant: it was simply a kind of streptococcus having nothing to do with typhus. The struggle between Gaviño and Prieto was fierce—a matter of science and honor. Prieto said of Gaviño: "He is plenty in quotations and opinions, but fast in scientific standards." Gaviño, in turn, demanded apologies and involved Dr. Antonio J. Carbajal and some of the highest scientific authorities of the time in his quest for moral reparations. The ultimate stake in this fight was control of the resources to fight typhus. Gaviño and Girard did ultimately advance typhus research but, unfortunately, both wrote in Spanish and in local publications with little chance for international exposure.[14]

But "No hay científico que aguante un cañonazo de 50,000 pesos" (There is not a scientist who can withstand having 50,000 pesos fired at him).[15] The news of Nicolle's experiment in Tunis reached Mexico in the midst of a serious typhus epidemic that had involved the Mexican government like never before: the 50,000 peso prize (then about $25,000—at a time when the yearly salary of an American university professor was about $2,000) attracted many scientists. Gaviño and Girard, along with other Mexican scientists at the Hospital Juárez (Luis Ruiz) and Hospital General (F. Orvañanos and E. Escalona), seemed to have advantages over the foreign teams that started arriving in late 1909. The Mexican teams had plenty of patients, experience, and enough lice to replicate Nicolle's experiment. Most especially they had biological immunity and access to the terrifying Belém jail, a palace of lice, fleas, diseases, passions, and corruption; the place where such stories as that of Miguel Cao Romero—told by Heriberto Frías in 1891—occurred daily. A jealous man, Cao had killed his lover, and lived for years in Belém, sick with love for the dead woman; just before completing his time in prison, recounted Frías, "typhus dug in its claw . . . Acute illness arrived on the scene to finish off the man who loved the dead girl." Belém was indeed a unique reservoir of passions and diseases, and though Mexican doctors also granted access to it to Goldberger and Ricketts, they knew that this was a risky move for foreigners. Whereas Wilder described Belém as a "hotbed of typhus," in 1909 writer and prisoner Carlos Toro wrote stories about typhus inside Belém: "What is astonishing is not that typhus so violently propagates inside Belém's walls, but that typhus has not yet completely obliterated the jail's population." A mystery that Gaviño understood: he had immunity to the disease thanks to years of coexistence with typhus patients.[16]

Gaviño and Girard had plenty of patients and lice, but lacked the right monkeys on which to experiment. The ones brought from Tehuantepec (spider monkeys, *Ateles geoffroyi vellerosus*) were suitable for inoculation with blood from typhus patients, but not for experiments involving inoculation with lice from monkey to monkey. Gaviño and Girard, however, worked with these monkeys, and experimented with dogs, horses, pigs, and finally guinea pigs, which they proved were suitable carriers of the disease. In due time, in the 1920s, the inoculation of guinea pigs would prove highly significant. In May 1909 they transmitted the disease to monkeys using injections. In August 1910, they reported that guinea pigs and Tehuantepec monkeys were carriers of typhus, but that they had failed in isolating the exact typhus's microorganism. In early 1911, Nicolle reported the finding of a microorganism in infected guinea pigs, and therefore Gaviño claimed—for years to come—that it was his team, before Nicolle (May 1910 vs. June 1911), that was the first to prove transmission to monkeys and to guinea pigs. In fact, since 1909 Gaviño's team had tried to prove the central tenet of Nicolle's hypothesis. They neither proved nor disproved Nicolle's louse hypothesis, but Gaviño continued to maintain that his experiment had been undertaken before Nicolle's.[17]

This was not the only feeling of betrayal Gaviño and his team expressed in 1909 and 1910, for the other teams that reached Mexico in late 1909 produced a domino effect of resentment, jealousy, and as yet unseen international cooperation. All of these scientists interacted among themselves; many of the foreigners publicly claimed ignorance of the prize, and each was suspicious of the other. The lice and the city they lived in, however, could not care less about the scientists' disputes, their monkeys, and their greed: by mid-1910, all of these doctors had been infected by lice, and two, Ricketts and Conneffe, were dead.

E. F. McCampbell contacted Ricketts in November 1909, asking him to join on a trip to Mexico City in search of the typhus germ, in view of both the great economic reward and Nicolle's recent discoveries, which required further demonstration. Ricketts was then well known for his research on Rocky Mountain spotted fever—for which he discovered the germ and the method of transmission (ticks). At the time he was contacted by McCampbell, he was awaiting response from the government of Montana in order to return to the study of diseases similar to the spotted fever. Later on, Ricketts and his student Wilder, as well as Ricketts's biographers, would claim that he had planned to go to Mexico City before learning about the monetary prize. In fact, it was McCampbell's letter, along with his own studies on spotted fever and the news of Nicolle's discoveries, that turned Ricketts's attention to Mexico City. As he wrote to his wife, Myra, on December 14, 1909, "There is only one way to go into this kind of a job, and that is in a careful and . . . business like way." On December 15, he wrote, "If I find the microbe there will be 10,000 in it" (for he would have had to share it with Wilder). But the fact remains that before departing for Mexico, he agreed to collaborate with McCampbell, concurring that McCampbell would depart for Mexico first.[18]

Goldberger and Anderson, however, had outsmarted both Ricketts and McCampbell. They left for Mexico before Ricketts and McCampbell; by the time Ricketts and McCampbell were discussing their collaboration, they had already been in Mexico for four weeks. Ricketts followed suit, departing early for Mexico and sending McCampbell nothing more than a cursory note from the road, sparking the latter's outrage. By December 17, Goldberger and Anderson were well located in Mexico's Hospital General, Ricketts and Wilder were just arriving in Mexico City, and McCampbell and Conneffe were still on their way. At this point, of course, Gaviño and Girard were well advanced in the competition, not to mention Nicolle, who by then was well along in his candidacy for the Mexican typhus prize.

Goldberger had not been in Mexico City, but he had been in Tampico in 1902 during the yellow fever campaign. He was a new soldier in the modern army of hygienists, bureaucrats, and bacteriologists that post-Pasteurian progressive governments had assembled. He was a Jew, born in the Austro-Hungarian Empire (arrived in the U.S. in 1883), and as such the career of sanitary inspector was easier to achieve than that of an upscale doctor in New York City. Like Ricketts later on, he publicly recognized the help of Mexican doctors while privately dismissing them. "Mexicans are too polite to be thorough," he had said about Mexico's yellow fever doctors in 1902.[19] For him, the city was a true hygienic disaster, and yet he was there, working in Mexican institutions, with Mexican doctors, perhaps treating Mexican patients as mere guinea pigs, as if he were working in the Amazon. To the city, however, he was simply another typhus fighter whom it enchanted with its insurmountable problems, its institutions, and its vibrant urban life.

In view both of the 1909 Mexico City typhus epidemic and of the Mexican prize, Goldberger joined efforts with John F. Anderson (director of the Harvard

Hygiene Laboratory), and renewed contact in Mexico City with his former university peer, Dr. A. Goldman, then the resident doctor at the Ferrocarril Nacional, who helped him find a laboratory and to receive official permission. Thus Goldberger and Anderson claimed to have been the first in Mexico (November 1909) to inoculate monkeys with blood from typhus patients—though Gaviño and Girard insisted that they had done it almost simultaneously. "For once in the history of the Service," Goldberger wrote back home, "we have gotten on the scene of action first."[20]

Goldberger and Anderson managed to inoculate suitable laboratory monkeys (*Macacus rhesus*) that they brought from Washington—and that was their advantage over the Mexican team, although they generously acknowledged the support of Mexican scientists (Liceaga, Otero, and Orvañanos, among many others). Thus José, Adela, and Andrea—all monkeys—were injected with blood from typhus patients. Subsequently the scientists attempted transmission from monkey to monkey. They experimented with fleas and head and body lice, and found the body louse to be the carrier of the disease, but could not specify how and could not isolate the actual typhus agent or virus. Adela, José, and Andrea, like the sick men from the Belém prison from whom the blood samples were taken, died.[21]

As I said, upon learning of Goldberger and Anderson's presence in Mexico, Ricketts left the United States immediately; he needed, as he wrote to his boss in Chicago (Dr. Ludvig Hektoen), "to get in the game" as soon as possible. By mid-January, Ricketts wrote to his wife that Goldberger was heading back to the States, sick with typhus, though Ricketts lied to his wife about the actual nature of Goldberger's illness. Previously, McCampbell had sent news of Conneffe's illness, advising extreme precaution to Ricketts and the others, despite their mutual dislike. By February 1910, McCampbell reported to the Mexican Academy of Medicine that in his work at the Hospital General and the Hospital Juárez he had been able to transmit typhus to monkeys, but did acknowledge that he had done it "as Goldberger, Anderson, and Ricketts have done." He claimed, though, that Mexican typhus was identical to European typhus. Lice were truly to be blamed. Ricketts, in turn, was churning out articles as fast as possible, obsessed with getting to the heart of the matter and paying little attention to McCampbell's discoveries and warnings.[22]

As late as April 1910, Ricketts wrote to Goldberger: "I am a lucky fellow . . . we are both lucky, mighty lucky . . . when you think of the fate of the man from Ohio, we two differ having been down here for 3 or 4 months without being infected." Indeed, "the man from Ohio," Conneffe, died of typhus in Columbus in January 1910, surrounded by such fear that his hometown, Philadelphia, refused to accept the return of his corpse. Goldberger was indeed lucky, not because he did not get infected, but because he survived; Ricketts had no such luck.[23]

McCampbell acknowledged the collaboration of Orvañanos and Figueroa, López, and Gerardo Escalona in his work at the Hospital General. Goldberger acknowledged Gaviño and Escalona. Ricketts and Wilder acknowledged Gaviño, Fernando López, and Escalona. All of them were in de facto collaboration, in public friendship, but privately engaged in fierce competition and, most often, dislike. Ricketts would not leave the laboratory of the Instituto de Bacteriológico for fear that his monkeys and research would be either stolen or sabotaged. From January to April 1910, he wrote to Myra about his fears and his eagerness to publish his findings as soon as possible, in view of the competition and of constant "spying" by Mexican scientists. "An impertinent bunch," was how he described Gaviño and his collaborators at the Instituto. According to Ricketts, Gaviño and the Mexican doctors were guilty of such outrageous transgressions as asking questions and wanting to learn more about his research. The fact that he was in Gaviño's laboratory did not seem to be for Ricketts any excuse for the Mexican doctors' undue curiosity. Ricketts and Wilder did not leave their notes on the laboratory desks, not even when they left for lunch. Mexicans were, he thought, stealing their lice and observing their monkeys. "We have few friends among Mexican physicians," he wrote in April 1910, and added: "I know that the institute hates us, a Mexican French newspaper attacks us, still credit to the Frenchman Nicolle."

Ricketts was right, Mexican scientists in 1910 were not terribly different from the Stockholm academy in their preference for French over American scientists. And yet Ricketts and Wilder received all the official and unofficial credentials and honors that the city could have bestowed upon them. They were housed by the city's institutions, assisted by Mexican servants and colleagues, and, although there is no direct record of their social lives, it seems that they enjoyed the city's weather, restaurants, museums, avenues, and high social gatherings. Granted, the city killed one of them, but after reading Ricketts's private opinions of the city and its people, I cannot help but feel a certain sense of poetic justice in the city's revenge.[24]

Ricketts's fight was for the discovery of the germ, and the duplication of Nicolle's transmission experiment; Gaviño's fight was for recognition of the first actual lice transmission; Goldberger and Anderson struggled less against Ricketts, Gaviño, McCampbell, or Nicolle—though they questioned Nicolle's interpretation of the infection of monkeys—than they did against Nathan Brill, a New York scientist who in 1910 had identified a kind of fever in New York City, claiming it to be different from the Mexican typhus: a kind in itself. Goldberger and Anderson claimed to have shown that "Brill's disease, which is apparently endemic in New York City, is identical with the typhus fever of Mexico." The fight continued into the 1920s. It would eventually be proven that the fever Brill had discovered in New York was indeed typhus, but it was likewise shown that there existed a unique Mexican strain.

In these U.S. disputes, Mexico City was used as a mere laboratory; whatever Mexican scientists produced was only secondarily considered and more as a sort of ethnographic raw material than as true scientific knowledge. In a way the relationship of American scientists to Mexican research in 1909 and 1910 was not far removed from the still common epistemological claim to authority, best epitomized by the phrase "this hitherto has not been [said, argued, discovered, concluded] in English." For to this day, if I were writing this essay in Spanish it would be but material to document *barbarie*, in silence waiting to be made into real knowledge by the graceful touch of an English-speaking researcher. Indeed, in 1910 the city and its inhabitants were raw data, a randomly selected setting for the scientists' disquisitions, and never the raison d'être of their work or their careers.[25]

In April 1910, Gaviño, Ricketts, and Wilder visited the Belém prison in search of lice. They were confident in their scientific capabilities, though the risk of infection was high. Although Gaviño continued to work on typhus and would develop the first versions of a vaccine during the terrible 1915 epidemic in Mexico City, in 1910 he did not publish his findings and ideas in any reputable journals, whereas the forceful Ricketts managed to publish four essays in four months (January to April 1910), mostly in the *Journal of the American Medical Association*. These were the results of Ricketts's efforts in Mexico and the basis of his solid reputation. These essays were Ricketts's way of marking his domain, typhus, as a lion pees.

Ricketts's final act, the transmission of typhus through lice, and his epic death on May 3, 1910, made him the hero of the messy 1910 moment in typhus research. When Henrique da Rocha Lima finally identified the typhus germ in April 1916, he called the agent *Rickettsia prowazekii* in honor both of H. Ricketts and of the Bohemian doctor—and friend of da Rocha—Stanislaus von Prowazek (who died fighting the disease in World War I). Two dead heroes in the history of typhus. But what Ricketts and Wilder did was, first, to refine Nicolle's early experiments and interpretations. Second, they showed that whatever caused typhus was not a normal, easily isolated germ. Third, they tried to test Mexican doctors' suspicions regarding the uniqueness of Mexican typhus vis-à-vis European typhus. In their first article, they suggested that the transmission factor could be lice. In their second installment, they proved transmission by lice, and argued: "As to whether these experiments on transmission are to be considered as substantiating that of Nicolle, or whether they should be regarded as new observations, will depend on the identity or non-identity of tabardillo with the old world typhus." In their third article, they acknowledged that Gaviño, Girard, Goldberger, and Anderson had described organisms, but they claimed to have found an agent that could not be grown under normal laboratory conditions. They affirmed that tabardillo was different from Rocky Mountain spotted fever, but they could not ascertain whether Mexican typhus was identical to the European kind. And then Ricketts died.

On April 29, 1910, Myra Ricketts received the first news of her husband's illness from Russell Wilder. She left for Mexico City that very day. By April 30, Ricketts's condition had seriously worsened, and he died on May 3 in a special tent whose construction he had requested in the gardens of the American Hospital in Mexico City in order to avoid contagion. The Mexican government organized an elaborate celebration to honor the heroic doctor. The minister of education and the U.S. ambassador, as well as Gaviño and Wilder, were in charge of the honors. A commemorative plaque was inaugurated at the laboratory where Ricketts, Wilder, Gaviño, and Girard worked in the 1910 battle against typhus. In his speech, Wilder proudly argued that Ricketts traveled to Mexico unaware of President Díaz's handsome prize, and claimed that in the end "the merit of authorship is of no importance," as each of them, all scientists working in Mexico City, had collaborated. Gaviño was as generous as Wilder, though he clearly revealed his feelings about what Ricketts had meant for the 1910 typhus struggle: "Wishing to arrive before other researchers at the frontiers of truth in the study of typhus, he could not see that he was headed for certain death . . . disdaining the dangers that surrounded him and refusing to heed the prudent advice of those of us who saw him full of such overconfidence." Gaviño asserted that he had collaborated with Ricketts in good faith, and that he was ready to be the first to applaud his success and lament his death. Like any good war, the one fought against typhus in 1910 had achieved its own compelling epic, complete with its own heroes. Thus in 1945, at the fourth Inter-American Typhus Meeting, in Mexico City, a medal was distributed among the participants: engraved upon it were the faces of Ricketts, Nicolle, and Hans Zinsser.[26]

The Ricketts legend continued, though da Rocha himself never stopped claiming authorship of the great typhus-related discoveries. For da Rocha, Ricketts was one of the many *navengantes* that preceded Columbus; he, da Rocha, believed himself to be the Columbus of typhus, or so he said in 1951.[27] Thus as late as the 1950s, the scientist who had given Rickettsia its name claimed that neither Nicolle nor Ricketts had in the end unraveled the mystery of typhus. Also as late as the 1950s, the Mexican doctor Rubén Saucedo Fuentes wrote a novel inspired by Ricketts's life. He too claimed that Ricketts was not moved by the monetary prize. For him, Ricketts remained disinterested due to his "greatness of spirit." Saucedo Fuentes described a fictional Ricketts rambling the city, encountering a priest and engaging him in dialogue, with the wise and stern Ricketts learning that diseases are not God's punishment but God's challenge to human intelligence. Ricketts faced the challenge—in Saucedo's novel—with Franciscan stoicism. The legend thus continued.[28]

Still, by the end of 1910, and with the outbreak of the Mexican Revolution, epidemics were to come, and the only real winners still seemed to be the louse and the city unbound. The refined Porfirian city then seemed an ephemeral mirage of cosmopolitanism, which under this facade was a savage village that killed people and was once again on its way to revolutionary violence. And yet, despite all odds, that the Porfirian city had been the capital of a major period in global typhus research was not a mirage but a fact in 1909 and in 1931.

In February 1911, the National Academy of Medicine considered the applications for the typhus prize. Nicolle had mailed his 1909 papers and a letter explaining why he had been the first to decipher the typhus mystery. The Mexican panel was made up of prominent doctors—Manuel Toussaint, José P. Gayón, Octaviano González Fabela, Ernesto Ulrich, and José S. Saloma—, and they decided not to award the prize. No one won the competition. The academy's decision was disputed by Nicolle and Mexican doctors for years to come. Nicolle often referred to Mexican doctors' ignorance—he was convinced that he deserved the prize. The academy claimed that, although in the long run it was proven that the transmission agent was the louse, Nicolle's 1909 experiment had neither identified the active germ nor conclusively proven the function of lice—both finally proven by da Rocha in 1916.[29]

As late as 1931, when Nicolle was in Mexico City, he maintained once again that in 1909 he had shown the role of lice in typhus transmission, and had found the definitive solution for the problem, and thus "divested of all value the epidemiological arguments of Terrés." Nicolle refers here to José Terrés, who in 1922 still defended the academy's 1911 decision, denying the role of lice in the disease. In the 1930s another Mexican doctor, in flowery prose, also defended the decision against Nicolle's demonstrations, pointing out that in 1909, "details were lacking in the laboratory and in the illustrious reasoning of scholars; it was as if that vile insect had them hidden in its gut, refusing to allow microscopes, cultures, and inoculations, along with prevailing knowledge, to extract them from the hiding place which had for centuries concealed them with such reserve." The academy, then, had been as wise as the louse was treacherous. Still, the fact that, in 1922, Terrés and others still denied the role of lice, and that Nicolle still claimed that he had solved the mystery in 1909, is living proof of the wisdom of lice in the old Spanish *refranero*: "El piojo puesto en altura, todo se le vuelve locura" (When the louse becomes paramount, everything else becomes insanity for it).

In the end, Nicolle's 1928 Nobel Prize in Medicine—for his work on typhus—seemed to demonstrate beyond any reasonable doubt the stupidity of 1909 Mexican doctors. Again, let us rely on the wisdom of the louse in the *refranero*: "Piojo que a persona asciende, no se acuerda de que fue liendre" (something like "a louse sitting atop a human being, forgets it was ever a nit"). Nicolle, in 1909, was far from having solved the typhus mystery. In old age, freed from the confines of *politesse*, the prominent Mexican scientist Maximiliano Ruiz Castañeda put it bluntly: Nicolle "wanted to make our lives impossible! Fortunately, we cut him down to size (*redujimos*)." And indeed Ruiz Castañeda and Hans Zinsser "redujeron" (reduced, made small) Nicolle's early findings, but that was in 1931 and in Mexico City, when the city experienced what the saying predicted: "El piojo resucitado es el que más pica, porque coge sangre nueva y se desquita" (The louse which has been brought back to life is the one that bites the most because it gets new blood and takes its revenge).[30]

Act 2. The Rat Moment

For Mexico City the post-1910 *desquite* (revenge) of lice and typhus was indeed intense both in human and scientific terms. Multiple epidemics attacked the city before the disease finally disappeared as a public health matter. The city experienced a major epidemic in the revolutionary years of 1915 and 1916, which was, according to Fernando Ocaranza, one of the most serious typhus epidemics in the city's history, infecting more than ten thousand inhabitants in 1916 alone. According to Dr. Silvino Riquelme, between November 1915 and May 1917 there were 21,344 persons infected, and just between January 1916 and May 1917, 2,119 died of typhus. It was difficult for the revolutionary city to deal with the disease in 1915, though the old Porfirian doctors and institutions worked hard to keep the outbreak under control in the midst of chaos and political antagonism. Gaviño, for instance, was accused of collaboration with Victoriano Huerta's counterrevolutionary regime, though later he reestablished his reputation, while Girard returned to Paris after confrontations with Gaviño.[31] At any rate, the insecure and violent city was not appealing for international bacteriologists during this period. They were already using all of their resources to fight typhus in World War I. In those years the international Epidemic Commission (originally called the Typhus Commission) was created precisely to fight lice in armies and camps.

After the Revolution, between 1925 and 1928, city authorities engaged in a disinfection crusade—against lice—and in an educational campaign, including the free distribution of pamphlets, posters, and film exhibitions, with such titles as "Luchemos contra las ratas" (Let us fight rats), "El tifo," and "La tuberculosis." But despite all efforts the disease continued to present a problem, and in 1931 another epidemic outbreak occurred that seemed to have started at the Belém prison before spreading throughout the city. Compared to the 1915–16 epidemic, the 1931 outbreak was minor, but it constituted a major event: it provided the opportunity and the environment in which a new generation of microbe hunters, Mexicans and foreigners alike, finally solved the last mysteries of the disease.[32]

Whereas 1909–10, "the louse moment," had centered on finding the essential epidemiology of typhus, 1931 was about the rat. The process of transmission during epidemic outbreaks was known; however, the question remained as to what happened with the triggering factor between outbreaks. This basic question gradually turned into a matter of identity: whether or not European and Mexican typhus fevers were the same disease; if the same, why the endemic character of the disease in Mexico City and not in other places? If different, was the dissimilarity a temporary matter between endemic and epidemic moments or a more biologically fixed difference? Dealing with these questions meant granting the rats of the Belém prison a leading role in the unraveling story of disease, science, and the city.[33]

Many of the scientists who fought the disease during World War I—among them Nicolle, Zinsser, Simeon B. Walbach, and Polish bacteriologist Hélène Sparrow—in due time played some kind of role in this "rat moment," in the same way that those students of typhus who were in the city in 1931 ended up in some ways influencing the struggle against typhus in World War II, especially through the development of vaccines. Throughout World War II in Europe, for instance, both the Zinsser–Ruiz Castañeda and Mooser-Varela vaccines (both rat-based) were used in various European cities and war camps.[34]

The 1931 rat moment serves as a lens through which one can observe how the interaction between city and science transformed understandings of typhus. This gradual transformation gives shape to the four scenes of the 1931 act: first, a lasting Mexican trial and error; second, the social personality of the Mexico City rat; third, the cultural and scientific conflicts over the final solution to typhus; and finally, Mexico City as a magnet and stage for truly peculiar personalities. For it was almost as if the louse, the flea, and the rat, each all too aware of its trashiness, recruited as their chroniclers not stern spirits but flamboyant scientists cum writers and poets.

Enter a Lasting Trial and Error
In 1931, scientific and social views on the city and its diseases went back to the first postrevolutionary summary of findings about typhus in the city: the

Segundo Congreso Nacional del Tabardillo, which took place in Mexico City in December 1921.[35] By 1921, typhus in Mexico City had put Mexican bacteriologists back in business, and their congress rekindled the internal political and scientific struggles, now involving both old and new actors. In view of the sanitary effects of war on the city, the revolutionary governments had established new institutions to deal with sanitary issues, among them the Departamento de Salubridad Pública (1917), a federal agency created to deal with sanitary regulations and to handle epidemics, and the Escuela de Salubridad (1922). Both old and new Mexican research joined at the 1921 Congress, highlighting what had been a long process of trial and error, but also bringing to the fore lasting jealousies and antagonisms.

Once the typhus debates reached an accelerated pace, between 1928 and 1931, old Mexican solutions to the disease's mysteries were once again intoned. Maximiliano Ruiz Castañeda recalled in the 1950s that after experiments with atypical, lice-transmitted, forms of typhus (starting in 1917)—by Kenneth Maxcy in the southwestern United States, M. H. Neill in Texas, and Mooser in Mexico City—, it was clear that "already in 1904 in Mexico it was thought that bedbugs might be a typhus vector, and José Terrés doubted that the louse could be the only one. In 1923 Federico Molás also pointed out the notable correlation between cases of typhus and the abundance of rats in the very center of Mexico City." In the same way, in 1928, at the outset of the new trend that eventually established two main types of typhus and two main vectors (lice and rat fleas), Mooser wrote, not in an academic paper, but in a letter (in English) to Hans Zinsser about the history of the research in Mexico City. In the letter, Mooser gave voice to his own cultural conflicts with Mexico, but also explained the long Mexican process of trial and error (of which he was very much a part), as well as new international discoveries: "Mexican authorities on typhus, if such a thing really would exist, claimed for a good many years that tabardillo and typhus are different diseases and many of them do not believe in the louse theory of transmission. Doctor Maxcy of the United States Public Health Service is also convinced that endemic typhus of the southern United States is not transmitted by lice." Options and theories, of which Mexicans had a long track record, were once again reconsidered.[36]

But old wounds were also reopened. At the 1921 Congress, for instance, as already mentioned, the influential doctor Terrés still vehemently denied that lice were the main vector of the disease. Of course, Terrés's denial was not only a matter of science, but also a personal matter, tightly wrapped up with his support of the academy's decision against Nicolle. Throughout the rest of the 1920s Terrés would act as the great dean of Mexican *tifólologos*, butting heads most frequently with Nicolle and the young doctors who worked around Mooser and Zinsser.

Unlike 1921, however, 1931 did represent a significant paradigmatic and generational shift in the trial and error surrounding typhus in Mexico. Old bacteriologists, including Terrés, had been born in the 1880s, trained in Mexico, with at best short stints in Europe (France and Germany by and large). The generation that headed the 1931 rat moment was born in the 1900s and was trained in Mexico City, but engaged in lengthy studies and many collaborations in U.S. institutions, in part through the support of both U.S. researchers and the Rockefeller Foundation. When, in 1915, the American media reported up to 30,000 typhus cases in Mexico City, it also announced the joint efforts of the International Red Cross and the Rockefeller Foundation. By 1931, Mexico City's government had received Rockefeller funds to establish a local central health administration (assigning around $16,000 between 1928 and 1933). In 1933, Zinsser sought to help both Mexican medicine and his friends in Mexico City—especially Mooser and Ruiz Castañeda—by lobbying the Rockefellers (in the middle of the Depression, one might add) to increase funds for typhus research in Mexico. In fact, the large post-1940 Rockefeller funding of research in Mexico on various diseases and agricultural developments has obscured this early funding of typhus research; a kind of funding that can be seen beyond the common consideration of philanthropy vs. imperialism. It seems instead to have been the result of small networks of scientists in Mexico City, New York, and Boston concerned with immediate sanitary crises in Mexico City and various U.S. cities.[37]

Indeed, out of trial and error, out of the ashes of the Revolution, and out of new international sponsorship of research in Mexico, a new generation of Mexican scientists emerged. They were young doctors trained by the experience of the prominent generation that came of age in 1910. They faced a very different city, country, and world: a revolutionary Mexico experiencing a rapid industrialization, a booming city about to become one of the first, and the largest, twentieth-century megalopolises, and a world contemplating massive annihilation. Unlike the previous generation, among the new Mexican scientists there were several who, realizing that their knowledge of both city and sickness constituted an entry into the global scientific community, sprung onto the international scene. As a result, they learned the new lingua franca, English. Maximiliano Ruiz Castañeda and Gerardo Varela are the most prominent representatives of this trend. Both demonstrate the advantages and limitations of being what they were: scientists in Mexico City.

The careers and visibility of Mexican bacteriologists were of course limited by their location (Mexico City) and language (Spanish), but ironically in the case of typhus research it was through the city that they were able to become truly international figures. They were the children of the city's excellent Porfirian institutions, and the city furnished them with the epidemics, rats, and, very importantly, the biological immunity that made them indispensable for international bacteriologists. In September 1928, experimenting at Harvard with rats and the Mexican strain of the disease, Zinsser became sick but survived, and decided not to involve further any other members of his laboratory. That was the root, Zinsser recalled in his memoir, of Hermann Mooser's greatest gift to him—his faithful collaborator Maximiliano Ruiz Castañeda.[38]

But it was also in the city that Varela and Ruiz Castañeda began collaboration, at the American Hospital, with Mooser, and it was there that they worked with rats at the Belém prison and had access to epidemics, plenty of patients to experiment on with impunity—sometimes even recklessly. In late 1929, for instance, the Mexican doctor José Zozaya, director of the Instituto de Higiene, on the one hand, and Mooser, on the other, inoculated humans with early versions of vaccines. Zozaya's results are unknown, but all four of Mooser's patients almost died. "I have no intention to repeat human experiments, I got a big scare," wrote Mooser to Zinsser. Doctors continued, nonetheless, to use the city as their laboratory. Dr. Varela and several others, for instance, experimented—this time successfully—with twenty-three patients of the Hospital General and three at the National Mental Health Hospital (manicomio).[39]

Unlike Gaviño and his team, the new bacteriologists reached the mainstream of their discipline, believing for a while that they were a part of the global scientific community, only to find that when all was said and done they were returned to their provincialism both by what Mexico City represented in political terms, and by their foreign peers. Co-opted or distracted by the new revolutionary politics in the city, and ninguneados (underestimated) by their foreign peers, by the 1960s those Mexican bacteriologists who had been mainstream in the 1930s sounded like disenchanted heretics from the temples of nationalism and cosmopolitan science.

In 1931 and its aftermath, Mexican scientific experimentation was marked not by the lack of scientists or scientific concerns, but rather by the peculiar politicking that the revolutionary government established as its modus operandi—popularly known today in Mexico as grilla. That is, every major change at the head of the national or city government brought about a total change of personnel in universities, health councils, and laboratories. Power in academic institutions became part of the larger politicking in the country. The year 1931 was particularly auspicious for typhus research not only because of the epidemic but also because it was then that Dr. Rafael Silva became director of the Departamento de Salubridad. He was a recognized ophthalmologist, trained in Europe, but also a cosmopolitan scientist and a musician who fostered international collaboration and who personally invited Nicolle and Zinsser to come to Mexico, charming them not only with the availability of rats in the Belém prison, but with long chats and dinners where literature and music were discussed. He was—Zinsser described him in his memoirs, witnessing the socialist (Cardenista) turn in Mexican institutions—a member of Mexico's "upper class which will probably disappear as an expensive sacrifice to socialism. Wealthy, highly cultivated and polished, almost a professional musician, a pupil of D'Albert, in his own name a composer of considerable accomplishment."[40]

Mexican scientists had to face constant changes in institutions, as well as the temptation to themselves become part of the national revolutionary family. That is why, later in his life, Ruiz Castañeda recalled his early years in the city as a golden age, when he worked at the Instituto de Higiene under the direction of the enlightened Dr. José Zozoya (1928 and 1929). When a new director was appointed, he was left with no source of income besides his afternoon work, poorly paid, at the American Hospital with Mooser. The new director, he recalled in the 1970s, accused him "of wasting the nation's funds on enemas (lavativas) for lice." Incidentally, this was not an entirely unfair accusation: when Ruiz Castañeda reached the Harvard laboratories to work under Zinsser he was recognized as the expert in rectal inoculation of lice. In late 1929, Ruiz Castañeda wrote to Zinsser that the new director "apparently has not scientific inclinations and I was told to occupy myself with something more useful than typhus and lice. . . . I have the intention to leave the country."[41] La grilla, then, as much as ninguneo by foreign scientists, was the main obstacle to Mexican scientific trial and error.

Enter the Rat

No account of scientific egos and works is complete without first establishing the more-than-scientific profile of these famous, if undesired, characters: Mexico City's rats. Rats have been to cities what fire is to hell. Their conspicuous and hated urban presence has an established literary, scientific, and popular tradition. In Mexico City in 1915, reports of a wild and unbounded rat infestation were so common that the rat became the stuff of legend. At the time officials were confronted with the numerous sanitary issues that plagued the revolutionary city—garbage collection, typhus, disposal of corpses, and dogs and rabies.[42] Whatever the reality of the matter was, the legend has it that Álvaro Obregón sought to kill two birds with one stone: his program aimed to eliminate both rats and Catholic opposition to his anticlerical, prolabor mea-

10.1. Fleas and death: Rat International Congress, Paris 1928,
*Première Conférence Internationale du Rat (Paris–Le Havre,
16–22 mai 1928)* (Paris: Vigot frères, 1931).

sures—he had expropriated the San Jerónimo Church and given it to radical labor organizations. He offered monetary rewards for rats captured alive. The legend recounts the instance when the ladies of the Perpetua Congregación at the San Jerónimo Church approached the National Palace in protest, Obregón ordered the release of the rats, producing chaos amongst the pious ladies.

Despite the 1915 measures, the city's rats remained in their liberated Jerusalem—revolutionary Mexico City—, becoming as the city grew an endemic problem paralleling that of any major city. In the early nineteenth century there were places in the city known as "Callejón de las ratas." *Rata* in the *calo* (slang) of the city referred specifically either to a thief (closer to the 1910s and 1920s neologism *carrancear*, from "Carranza") or, more generally, to a repulsive person. Moreover, in the urban culture a very popular tune involved all the odd characters of these stories—rats, lice, and fleas. "El piojo y la pulga se van a casar," begins the tune, which enjoyed a long popularity—louse (masculine in Spanish) and flea (feminine) are about to get married (figure 10.1). Then all of these stories' mute protagonists enter into action: a mouse becomes the godfather and another flea becomes the godmother, and as a result of the wedding all *changos* (meaning both monkey and "guys") cannot stop scratching themselves.

As the city grew, rats were involved in shocking stories such as one reported in the late 1940s by Dr. Federico Gómez of the city's Hospital Infantil (children's hospital): a pair of baby twins had arrived at the hospital with their faces devoured by the enormous rats that inhabited the proletarian quarters of the city. Even in the 1950s urban rats retained their literary status, for instance, in the graphic recollections of Guadalupe Dueñas, whose short story talks of a proletarian undertaker describing the intermingling of rats and corpses in a city cemetery:

> I tell you, it's quite exciting, especially when a body arrives. What intelligent creatures! They can guess the exact time of arrival. You'll see: as soon as a grave is covered a noise like hail runs through the cemetery; one can hear them smashing into each other in the subterranean labyrinths; like colts they careen along their terrifying path to attend a banquet heralded by the fetid air. They come from all over, like people from the *rancherías* when they hear that a pig has been slaughtered. One can hear the starving rats fight for their piece of stale meat. There is the muffled crackle of insides, torn apart by their fangs . . . With their snouts they drag along the remains of hair, strips of skin, pieces of sticky intestine which they have vomited up . . . The fat and slow beasts amble in the sun. Their bellies, swollen like canvas bags full of weight, waiting to digest the rot.[43]

Whereas in the 1920s lice had become a matter of legend, in the 1930s rats became the obscure object of scientific desire and the source for the anecdotal drive of scientists, poets, and other people of all sorts. Dueñas's undertaker was a revival of stories told in the 1930s by Ruiz Castañeda and Hans Zinsser: Ruiz Castañeda tells of Macario Aguirre, the warden at Belém, who was well acquainted with both its rats and its prisoners. Instead of putting traps in specific locations to capture rats—as Ruiz Castañeda had done, only to see them stolen—, Macario decided, much as Obregón had, to pay a peso per rat. Macario's success in capturing rats apparently led Mooser to hire him as an assistant in his scientific endeavors. There was nothing like a real connoisseur of the city to capture rats, to procure lice, to inoculate people in the poor *barrios* of the city, even if, on one occasion, Mooser had to wait for Macario to leave prison, as he had "apaleado a su dulce suegra" (beaten his sweet mother-in-law with a stick)—or so Mooser wrote to Ruiz Castañeda with a touch of good Mexican irony. In turn, Zinsser's Gustavo story was his version of the 1931 capture of the all-important rats of the Belém prison. Zinsser was a lavish storyteller and an accomplished writer, thus one cannot be sure where his poetic license ends, but his version of the capture goes as follows: Gustavo was the main rat catcher working for Zinsser and Ruiz Castañeda. With his trademark blend of *buena pluma* and racism, Zinsser recounts that Gustavo looked like a rat, and that he had turned, atavistically, to rat catching, which had been the family profession for generations. Gustavo "understood their [rats'] psychology, the routes they were likely to take, and the places where food would not look suspicious." He was, for Zinsser, a typical *indio*, "very greasy," and when Zinsser asked locals whether he could really catch rats, the response was "¿El hijo de un pez puede nadar?" (Can the son of a fish swim?). Or at least that is how Zinsser recounted the story. Whatever the truth of the story, eighteen infected black rats were caught. The color of the rodents is important, as will later become clear.[44]

In 1931 another legend told of Ruiz Castañeda and Zinsser's steamship trip from Boston to Mexico City, carrying healthy rats as well as rats infected with the strain of typhus they had cultivated at Harvard. They were on their way to undertake the experiment they had envisioned for the 1931 Mexico City typhus outbreak. The only way to transport the strain, however, was in live rats. Young poet Hart Crane, who had met Zinsser at a dinner party the night before the steamship was to depart, was on the same ship. He was on his way to reach the enchanted country that would inspire him to write the poem about the Spanish Conquest of Mexico for which he had procured funds from the Guggenheim Foundation. Crane would soon find himself in Mexico City getting drunk with an Irish revolutionary, pursuing male servants, and rediscovering himself— feeling at times, as he wrote, "unraveled, umbilical anew."

There they were, three friends, Ruiz Castañeda, Zinsser, and Crane—very different characters, each in search of a very different Mexico. Crane visited the rats in the doctors' cabin, amazed by the stories of lice, fleas, and typhus told by the doctors. The flamboyant Zinsser could talk with him about English, American, and German poets, while Ruiz Castañeda briefed Crane on the cultural life of Mexico City. Zinsser knew by heart many of Heine's poems, and must have been hard pressed to miss the connection of Crane's poetic interest in the Conquest, with Heine's own "Vitzliputzli" (Huichilopoztli): a long poem about the Conquest in which Heine, like Crane in his writings, imagined the Indians' revenge. Crane never finished his poem, immersed as he was in his mystic ecstasy and in his tequila. But he found in Ruiz Castañeda and Zinsser the medical assistance his alcoholism demanded over the months he spent searching for his own Vitzliputzli.

By contrast, Ruiz Castañeda was simply going home, in search of rats at the Belém prison, and also to encounter not an exotic ecstasy but his fiancée, a Mexican dental technician. Zinsser, while searching for rats, was also seeking the exotic images that nurtured his stream-of-consciousness prose. Ultimately, the friendship almost had a tragic finale there on the steamship, all thanks to the rats. During a stop in Havana, the three dined together and continued their chat with a bottle of Bacardi they brought on board. When the scientists realized that the infected rats were about to die, they infected healthy ones in order to keep the strain alive, and summarily tossed the dying animals overboard. In the midst of his drunkenness, Crane saw the swimming rats, for as Zinsser vividly described the scene, "contact with the cold water revived the animals and we could see their glistening bodies swimming against the current, trying to get to one of the outboard ropes." Witnessing the swimming rats, Crane began to melodiously repeat aloud:

the doctor has thrown rats into the harbor of Havana
the doctor has thrown typhus rats into the water
there will be typhus in Havana
the doctor has thrown rats into the harbor

Fortunately for Zinsser and Ruiz Castañeda, by the time they reached Havana, Crane's alcoholic reputation was well established among the crew, who remained unaware of the existence of the experimental rats. They therefore paid no attention to Crane's cries. As luck would have it, nearly a year later Crane would return to Boston on the same steamship, throwing himself overboard somewhere near Havana and drowning, just like the scientists' rats. Crane, the poet who sang the glories of the Brooklyn Bridge, drowned himself, as he wrote from Mexico to various friends, because he felt "caught like a rat in a trap." A year or so after Crane's suicide, Ruiz Castañeda and his wife, traveling from Boston to Mexico aboard the Orizaba, threw flowers out to sea near Havana, honoring the drunk and brilliant poet who had befriended Ruiz Castañeda, the rats, and Zinsser. While in Mexico City, Crane had written "Havana Rose," a prose poem in which Zinsser, the rats, and Havana fused in images in which rats and colors were used in allusions to typhus and death: "Poets may not be doctors, but doctors are rose poets when roses leap like rats—and too when rats make rose nozzles a pink death around the teeth." Of course, Crane's poetic license reigned in his allusions to the disease, to the scientists, and to his own sense of tragedy. No less poetic, however, was Zinsser's license in describing both the anecdote and the entire history of the disease in his *Rats, Lice, and History* (1935): a quasi-epic story of typhus and human beings, full of historical, literary, and poetic circumlocutions.[45]

The many anecdotes involving rats written around 1931 blended with the scientific profile of the rodent in its relation to the city and its diseases. True, rats had been a part of Mexico City long before 1931. Moreover, rats, diseases, and cities have a long shared history. Legends of plague and city slums come readily to mind. Bucolic dreams of open spaces, fresh air, rat-free places, and disease-free people are by now part of the romantic and modernist disdain for urban places. Starting in the early twentieth century, but most especially between World War I and World War II, typhus brought about a scientific redefinition of this well-established link between rats, cities, social undesirables, and diseases. Hence, soon enough, the city's poor, rats, Jews, and Gypsies were one with typhus, and not only in a lyric but in a truly scientific fashion. Rats, with their fleas and lice, with their potentially rabies-laden bites and their overwhelming predominance in crowed dirty swamps, were caught up in the notion that there existed "natural" carriers of diseases; that is, the unclean, the uncivilized, the poor, the animal-like people. In Nazi Germany this association constituted an industry in science, literature, and propaganda. Jews, lice, and rats became the same thing. In World War II, typhus became an instrument in opposition both to Bolshevik Russia and to Nazi Germany. It was indeed, as M.-A. Balinska has argued, an ideologized disease. In turn, for a long time Mexico City's uncleanliness, *pelados*, *léperos*, rats, and typhus had been a single concept. In the Mexico City of 1931 rats were important because the intersection between rats and cities gave rise to the scientific reincarnation of a well-established belief.[46]

But rats also became important in 1931 thanks to a random combination of ecological, epidemiological, and social factors that, although it is still not fully explained, led scientists to refocus on typhus research. This had to do with both short- and long-term trends. The longue-durée was constituted by an internal civil war between rats, namely between the so-called black Alexandrine rats and the brown rats. A civil war well known in many parts of the world, in which the brown (*Rattus norvegicus*) ultimately won over the black (*Rattus rattus*), assisting in the reduction of diseases like the plague. This was a result of the brown rat's nesting habits. Of course international bacteriologists like Nicolle and Zinsser initially paid scant attention to these peculiarities in Mexico City, as they had no knowledge of the different local species and of their specific habits in the city, especially during and after 1915. But for local scientists like Maximiliano Ruiz Castañeda, one of the clues to understanding the new science of typhus in 1931 was in the peculiarities of rats and in their interaction with the city.

It was known that both brown and black rats were potential carriers of human disease via fleas and lice, as a result of their constant proximity to humans. But Ruiz Castañeda saw a more specific relationship between the peculiar ecology of Mexico City, its revolutionary conditions, and the rats' civil war. Brown rats tend to nest underground. In Mexico City this meant that they nested in humid places—too hot in the summer, too cold in winter, too filthy all the time. Thus they tended not to carry as many fleas, and were as a result less prone to becoming vectors for the transmission of typhus. The old-world black rat nested, on the contrary, at surface level, in fresh, less filthy environments, making it, in the specific ecology of Mexico City, the ideal carrier for fleas. The black rat's contact with humans thus explained the endemic character of typhus in the city. In 1931, outside the Belém prison no black rats were found, particularly no rats with infected brains—where the typhus agent was often found—except for one found by Dr. Gerardo Varela in the *pabellón de infecciones* of the Hospital General. This fact suggested to Ruiz Castañeda that the Belém prison might be the black rat's last refuge in the long fight between the black and the brown rats.

The prison had been founded in the mid-nineteenth century in an old convent and school, and remained a major national prison, even after the 1900 inauguration of a modern panoptic prison in Mexico City. It remained a prison until 1933, when it was finally destroyed. In 1931, as I argue below, the specific relationship between rats and the city led Ruiz Castañeda and others to a controversial environmental/social conclusion about Belém. They saw the evidence and concluded that the 1931 typhus epidemic was linked to the survival of the black rat and its peculiar nesting habits.[47]

Finally, the nature of Mexico City's rats also became a question of age. Mexican scientists were concerned with establishing whether the Mexican mouse (*Microtus mexicanus*), whose pre-Columbian existence had been archaeologically established, was a carrier of typhus. If the mouse was a typhus carrier, that could prove the long-held Mexican belief that a Mexican kind of typhus preceded the arrival of the European kind. In 1934, Gerardo Varela put it clearly: "*Microtus mexicanus* . . . seems to induce an invisible disease, remaining, as we have shown, in the brain. These rodents are better adapted to murine typhus, as they have been infected for longer." Mexican rats thus proved for Varela and others what, from fifteenth-century chronicler Bernal Díaz del Castillo to nineteenth-century scientist Nicolás León, had been suspected—that there was typhus in Mexico before the arrival of Europeans. Mexican rats had infected old-world black rats, and thus spread the Mexican, endemic, typhus throughout the world. All in all, my point is that these infusions of local knowledge about rats produced important bacteriological conclusions.[48]

Enter the City, the Lab, and Civilization

The actual unfolding of the science of the 1931 rat moment can be explained as the result of the contentious encounters of clashing and collaborative views of science, the city, and its inhabitants. Beyond the scientific minutia of the many papers and experiments, three different approaches seem to emerge—first, the aforementioned approach that, in addition to global scientific trends, took into consideration the social and biological ecology of Mexico City (Gerardo Varela, Maximiliano Ruiz Castañeda, and Hans Zinsser); second, a more laboratory-focused approach (mostly represented in this story by Hermann Mooser and Hélène Sparrow); and finally, a more civilization-centered and moral approach to the disease (Charles Nicolle). These approaches blended, clashed, and collaborated on different occasions and in variegated ways. They were not mere scientific differences but also cultural- and ego-related stands.

The 1931 typhus epidemic in the city offered a unique opportunity to test many ideas that had been launched by two bacteriologists from the U.S. Public Health Service (M. H. Neill and Kenneth Maxcy), as well as by a series of new discoveries produced by Hermann Mooser in Mexico City in 1928 and 1929. In different studies of typhus-like fevers in the southwest, Neill and Maxcy had proposed new ideas about, first, the identity of the fevers in the southwestern United States—the fevers identified by Brill—with the Mexican-like typhus; and second, the possibility that typhus might survive in nature in rodents capable of transmitting the disease to humans through fleas. In 1924, Zinsser isolated from cases of the so-called Brill's fever a strain of typhus that proved to be of the louse-borne variety. Zinsser believed that Brill's cases in New York City were recrudescences of infections originally acquired years before by European immigrants. Thus this silent mode of the disease, what Nicolle called the unobservant type of the disease, served to maintain its continuity by bridging gaps in the chain of human-louse-human propagation.

The key to these discoveries were experiments on guinea pigs: the Mexican strain produced a scrotal swelling in guinea pigs, which was not produced—at least before 1932—by other strains of the disease.[49] In Mexico City, Mooser produced a plethora of experiments and papers (in Spanish, English, and German), all of them centering on scrotal swelling in guinea pigs in an attempt to determine whether the Mexican typhus was a unique form of endemic typhus, found in nature in rats. This was the possibility that Zinsser mentioned to Nicolle while congratulating him for the Nobel Prize in 1928. During 1928 and 1929, Mooser published four papers by himself and three in collaboration (with Varela, Ruiz Castañeda, and Sparrow), and he and his Mexican and Polish collaborators were indeed the center of the revolution in typhus research that peaked in 1931.

Based on detailed laboratory observations, Mooser had gradually moved from mere suggestions of the identity of Mexican typhus and Brill's disease in the U.S. to the more radical proposition that Mexican typhus was a unique

disease, entirely different from the European typhus. In doing so, he antago-
nized Nicolle and many others. A prominent bacteriologist, S. B. Wolbach,
basing himself on Nicolle's findings, maintained that European and Mexican
typhus were identical. Mooser, for his part, began to have doubts: he pains-
takingly proved the existence of scrotal swelling in guinea pigs infected with
the Mexican type. But in early 1928 he still maintained, in the *Gaceta Médica
de México*: "But let it be understood, this inference by no means indicates that
we are dealing with two different diseases." By the summer of 1928 he had
done extensive experiments and claimed that there was indeed an American
variety of typhus (*Transactions of the Royal Society of Tropical Medicine and Hygiene*).
By September he had identified the peculiar intracellular diplobacillus in the
"tunica vaginalis of guinea-pigs reacting to the virus of Mexican typhus (tabardillo). Considerable evidence is forward [sic] that this diplobacillus is the
causative agent of typhus" (*The Journal of Infectious Diseases*). And by 1929 he repeated experiments and emphatically claimed the existence of a unique Mexican (murine or endemic) form of typhus, which passed from rats to humans
via fleas, potentially gaining at that point the characteristics of the European
(historic) form of typhus, transmitted from human to human by lice, but never
returning to its murine form (*Sonderabdruck aus der Schweizerischen Medizinischen
Wochenschrift*). Varela and Ruiz Castañeda collaborated with Mooser in these
laboratory experiments, and eventually they all would come up with a common
laboratory-based hypothesis postulating two different typhus fevers, and with
an ecologically and Mexico City–centered perspective on the origins of typhus
in the city's rats.[50]

Varela and Mooser also put forward their views in English: "We have then
this situation in Mexico: from rats, from endemic cases of typhus, and from
cases during short epidemics, murine strains only could be isolated; whereas
from a long standing serious epidemic, strains were obtained which correspond to strains of historic old world typhus. But not all of our epidemic
strains agree completely with Nicolle's strain of old world typhus. . . . It was
in Mexico, indeed, that the work of Nicolle and his collaborators on the infection of the guinea pig with typhus was first confirmed, and it is not conceivable that the conspicuous scrotal reaction characteristic of all murine strains
should have escaped the observation of so many investigators." This last part,
about the impossibility of Ricketts, Girard, and Gaviño not having noticed the
swelling in the 1910s, would be an important conclusion for the Mexican researchers, as we will see below.

The discovery of a murine type faced the initial opposition of such important scientists as Nicolle. Mooser himself, in view of his continued laboratory work, later changed his mind, coming to insist on the identity between

Mexican and European strains of typhus. As late as 1932, after Nicolle, Zinsser, Mooser, Ruiz Castañeda, Varela, and Sparrow had done work together in Mexico, Nicolle wrote to Zinsser, "For the moment it seems impossible to me that your claims do justice to the true importance of Mooser's Rickettsia," and, "The rats are not sick enough for the fleas abandoned them to go and byte men. What is certain, is that the Mexican strain of typhus (murine typhus) exists in Europe."[51]

As I noted above, Ruiz Castañeda had gone to Boston, and was working with the so-called Mooser bodies, and in the second half of 1930, just before traveling to Mexico, Zinsser and Ruiz Castañeda produced a series of papers laying the groundwork for what would be the major experiment of 1931 in Mexico City. These papers, together with Mooser's and Varela's, were the most important element of the new global typhus research. Zinsser and Ruiz Castañeda essentially followed Mooser's lead, carefully and slowly coming over to the hypothesis of a unique Mexican typhus, and to the role of rats and fleas in its transmission. But unlike Mooser, who by 1929 had no problem attacking Nicolle's hypothesis, Zinsser was cautious in stating his doubts, attempting to not antagonize Nicolle. For Nicolle, the center of the research must remain the louse (his discovery and the source of his Nobel Prize), which also provided fodder for his "civilizational" conclusions about the disease: "Western hygiene had vanished lice," he argued in the 1920s, and typhus had as a result disappeared in Europe; that is, the threat of the "uncivilized tendencies of civilized nations" no longer existed in Europe, or so he believed. For, he argued, "typhus presents itself to us as both a plague and a moral lesson. It tells us that man has only recently emerged from barbarity." Nicolle was then more than a laboratory "rat"; he was a man of letters, a global celebrity who did not welcome contestation of his findings from within the minutiae of laboratory research—for him merely local obstacles to his grandiose civilizing mission.

Nicolle's views of Mexico and typhus thus reflected his personal trajectory from scientist cum philosopher of civilization to the disenchanted believer in reason who ultimately found refuge in the Catholic faith. In Mexico City in 1931, Nicolle still believed that human civilization was nothing more than nature. Thanks to progress, propelled by reason, civilization had broken its organic equilibrium with nature. He perhaps viewed his travels, discoveries, and fame as those of a genius, destined to restore civilization's link to nature. But geniuses were also natural products for Nicolle, not found amongst women and certain races, especially not mixed races—which produced, he believed, "cerebral sterility." In Mexico City in 1931, Mexico and its typhus research must have seemed to Nicolle to be deviations awaiting the civilizing role of both France and of his own genius. By the mid-1930s, however, after professional and personal disappointments, he became disenchanted with the power of reason and sought faith. Though for different reasons, he died as his Mexican colleague Ruiz Castañeda had, disenchanted with science and with the politics of his guild. He died in 1936 as a devout Catholic at his beloved Tunis Pasteur Institute.[52]

Within this antagonistic context Zinsser and Ruiz Castañeda planned their experiments during Mexico City's 1931 epidemic. Early in 1931, Zinsser wrote to Mooser that they had come up with an idea for an experiment in Mexico City:

> We [Zinsser and Ruiz Castañeda] would like to enlist your collaboration, not only because we would value your assistance and advice, but because if this came out right we would like to have you associated with us in it as a small acknowledgement of your consistently generous attitude toward other workers in this disease . . . The sudden suspicion which has lingered there for some time and probably has occurred to you that in nature typhus may be kept alive perhaps either in a rodent like the rat or rabbit or even perhaps in ticks; that it is transmitted from such an unapparent reservoir to bedbugs or ticks to man, and then kept going in man by lice.

Thus the need to go to Mexico, where typhus was both endemic and epidemic in order to catch rats at the Belém prison and inject their liquified brains into guinea pigs. In his posthumous biography of the disease, Zinsser explained what they did: "Our work in Mexico consisted of mapping the typhus foci in the city, selecting houses in which cases were occurring, and then setting to work catching as many rats as possible, also collecting resident bedbugs; when the rats were trapped, they were carefully gone over for fleas and rat lice. The rat brains (where typhus virus would be found if the animal were infected) were injected into guinea pigs; likewise the well-ground bodies of bedbugs, fleas and so forth."[53]

By the second semester of 1931, the typhus epidemic that had started at the Belém prison had spread throughout the city. Varela's map of the epidemic shows the high frequency of the disease at the center of the city, near the Belém prison, and dots here and there through the rest of the city, very likely following class lines, the circulation of rats in sewer systems as well as a degree of randomness. As Ruiz Castañeda suggested, the Revolution had changed the social and biological ecology of the city; over the revolutionary years the city became a major importer and exporter of diseases. But not only that: by 1931 the city experienced a construction fever, expanding horizontally and vertically, in all likelihood producing a whirlpool in the city's sewer systems, underground pipes, and within the overall rodent population. Ruiz Castañeda, Varela, and Mooser came to the realization that the city they made the subject of their research was a very different city from the one in which Ricketts, Girard, and Gaviño had worked.

In 1934 Zinsser wrote to Nicolle in surprise: "You have perhaps seen a long article by Mooser and Varela on the relationship between Mexican typhus and classic typhus in which they again return to the notion that the two varieties of the disease are caused by a single virus." He added with professional tact: "For the moment, I am not of the same opinion as Mooser. I think, as you do, that the two viruses derive from the same origin and easily change course from one to the other [changes l'un dans la direction de l'autre.]" In fact what was happening after the 1931 discoveries in Mexico City was that, while some (such as Wolbach) believed in a temporary difference between strains of typhus, Zinsser, Ruiz Castañeda, and Varela (at least until 1934) maintained a structural distinction between the murine and the European varieties. Zinsser sought the support of Nicolle after 1931, eventually recruiting the famous French scientist to the camp of the two strains.

In 1933 Mooser and Sparrow proved definitively the occurrence of rat-to-rat contagion in nature, and this significant laboratory experiment helped to convince Nicolle, not least because his collaborator, and lover, Sparrow was involved in it. But Mooser's laboratory approach continued, and by late 1934 he had shown that over time both types produced scrotal reaction in inoculated guinea pigs. At that point Nicolle rejected Mooser's new conclusion precisely because Mooser had arrived at this conclusion in a laboratory: it was an artificially forced conclusion for guinea pigs that were not normal carriers in nature. Zinsser agreed: the two forms could be induced to mimic each other only under experimental conditions, and only temporarily.[54]

By 1935 Mexican scientists, however, had all come to believe in two distinctive typhuses, and naturally so since Varela and Ruiz Castañeda were so involved in the discoveries that had led to this conclusion. This was, nevertheless, a hard consensus to reach among Mexican scientists tired of being found lacking, unique, or different in civilizational and/or biological attributes. Before Mooser's 1928 experiments, at the 1921 typhus Congress, the prominent Dr. Fernando Ocaranza rejected the suggestions made by young Mexican doctors regarding the unique Mexican ecology of the disease. It has been suggested, he said, "that Mexican tabardillo is not the typhus that exists in other countries," and he added laconically and ironically, "I am unsure of whether the significance attributed to this argument is specific or racial."[55] Ocaranza meant to warn doctors against the conventional stereotyping of Mexicans. The success of the 1931 generation of Mexican bacteriologists rested precisely on finding the uniqueness of Mexican typhus not in Mexicans' racial or civilizational profile but instead in the ecological and environmental conditions of the city and its rats.

In 1935, Hans Zinsser published in *The Atlantic Monthly* the first installment of his biography of typhus, *Rats, Lice, and History*. Though by then many new discoveries both on prophylaxis and on vaccines were yet to come, Zinsser saw the 1931 Mexico City rat moment as the final piece in the puzzle of the epidemiological cycle of typhus that had for so long fascinated scientists and devastated cities and war camps. It could finally be agreed that there were murine and epidemic typhus fevers, and that they were interrelated in the epidemiological cycle. The ecological concerns sustained by Zinsser, Ruiz Castañeda, and Varela had proven fruitful. The cycle was clear, as Zinsser explained in 1935: "Domestic rats carry the infection. In them, it is perpetuated by transmission from rat to rat by rat fleas and by rat lice. Rat fleas will feed on man when driven to seek a new host . . . From the bite of the infected fleas the human being contracts typhus. This is the sporadic or endemic case. If the victim is lousy, group infection may result. If he lives in a louse infected community, the consequence is an epidemic."[56]

For Mexican scientists, however, the cycle resulted in other conclusions. As Ruiz Castañeda put it on the fiftieth anniversary of Ricketts's death: of course Mooser's observations of scrotal infection in guinea pigs had proved that Mexican typhus was one of a kind and thus "we"—as Ruiz Castañeda put it in a confusing third-person plural (which could mean Ruiz himself or the typhus laboratory of the new Hospital General, founded in 1936)—"we simultaneously isolated both strains of the infection and bore witness to the gradual disappearance of murine typhus to the point of being eradicated in Mexico City." For Ruiz Castañeda, nevertheless, it should have been impossible back in 1910 for Gaviño or Girard to miss the murine type, as the scrotal infection in guinea pigs was unmissable. Thus he reasoned that "it would not be a stretch, therefore, to suppose that at that time murine typhus was rare, and that it only acquired importance years later, coinciding with the great upheavals of the Revolution."[57] That is, though there was a consensus on the existence of two main kinds of typhus, there were doubts about the historical origins of these strains in Mexico City.

As I have previously explained, Mexican doctors also proved that the murine type existed in the old Mexican mouse, thus proving that typhus had existed in Mexico prior to the arrival of Spaniards. Mexican scientists' emphasis on the history and locality of the disease allowed bacteriologists to conclude what Zinsser summarized in his biography of the disease: "Man, in the biological sense, is a recent host, and in him Rickettsia invasion arouses a physiological resentment. A struggle between invader and host ensues which manifests itself as disease." In such a way the evolutionary argument was completed.[58]

Until his death in 1940, Zinsser was engaged in vaccine production with Ruiz Castañeda and others. But *Rats, Lice, and History* already marked, with uncanny clairvoyance, the different paths the struggle against typhus would take over World War II. He pointed to anti-lice campaigns as the key to preventing and eliminating the disease, utilizing the louse as a twofold justification: of the chemical war against it, and of the struggle against Nazi Germany. "Unlike the flea," he argued, "[the louse] can neither hop nor live for any length of time separated from its human host, it possesses qualities of dogged persistence and patient diligence which arouse that admiration, thinly masked by a pretense of loathing, which men similarly feel for competing races whom they fear and, therefore, persecute." And he added, as a clarification of this last sentence: "we refer to the blond Aryan complex."[59]

In 1940, while returning from China, Hans Zinsser realized that he had developed leukemia. The doctor cum poet wrote:

> Now is death merciful. He calls me hence
> Gently, with friendly soothing of my fears
> Of ugly age and feeble impotence
> And cruel disintegration of slow years.
> . . .
>
> How good that ere the winter comes, I die!
> Then, ageless, in your heart I'll come to rest
> Serene and proud, as when you loved me best.

As he prepared for his own death and legacy—with notes of gratitude to his Mexican collaborator Maximiliano Ruiz Castañeda—, he urged the Mexican scientists, who had developed a typhus laboratory, to accelerate the production of their—Zinsser and Ruiz Castañeda's—vaccine using rats. He also defended the authorship of those vaccines, even against Ruiz Castañeda, who in 1939 was wrongly credited with the invention of the vaccine. Ruiz wrote back, "It gives me now the greatest of pain to feel in your letter as if you consider me guilty of not giving you due credit in typhus work. How could you—think such a thing after years of knowing me and knowing that in Mexico and particularly in my laboratory and in my home you are worshipped?" But the fact is that by 1939 the stationery used by Ruiz Castañeda and Zinsser read "Departamento de Salubridad Pública" and the seal "Zinsser-Castañeda vaccine typhus laboratory Mexico, servicio de exportación."

Later on, Ruiz Castañeda informed Zinsser of the export of 500 doses to South Africa and in 1942 a free delivery of vaccines to Poland—whose production was paid for by Mexico City's Jewish community in collaboration with American Jews.[60] But the trajectory of the vaccine was interrupted by the new approach to the disease developed over World War II and in its aftermath—the massive use of insecticides against lice.

As Zinsser and Ruiz Castañeda rapidly sought to produce a cheaper and more effective vaccine in Mexico City in view of the imminent start of a new massive war, the Rockefeller Foundation's virus laboratory was engaged in research on insecticides to fight mosquitoes, lice, and fleas. This eventually resulted in the final defeat of typhus during World War II, when, as Ruiz Castañeda later recalled, "hyper-civilized men," in order to attain massive destruction, had first to defeat the louse. But that was over by the end of the war. The story of the use of DDT and other insecticides during World War II and first experimented with in Mexico in the 1940s goes beyond the confines of this tragicomic account. Suffice it to say that the center of the research moved from Harvard and Mexico City—after Zinsser's death—to the virus laboratory of the Rockefeller Foundation in New York. John C. Snyder and William Davis directed the effort and in 1943, again in collaboration with Ruiz Castañeda, the louse lab's field test was carried out in Mexico, successfully developing the anti-lice powder that was massively used in World War II and afterward.[61]

Enter Ninguneo and the Poetic Will

In the impressive accomplishments of typhus research, wrote Zinsser in 1935, "French, Swiss, American, British, German, Mexican, and Polish investigators have engaged in the sort of exciting, friendly, and eager competitive collaboration or collaborative competition which gives our profession a zest and charm and a freedom from nationalistic chicane found in few others." By the 1970s, Ruiz Castañeda, who had survived his old mentor and collaborator by more than thirty years, was less romantic regarding his line of scientific work, especially in Mexico: "El que diga que trabaja para la humanidad es un farsante" (Whoever claims to work for humanity is a fraud), for in Mexico scientists discovered things out of their own curiosity and by chance, as all institutional efforts were sooner or later interrupted by political changes and by the clashes of national and international egos. In order to show that the "collaborative competition" was far from the harmonious one described by Zinsser, one does not need to fully subscribe to the cynicism of Ruiz Castañeda's old age. To be sure there were all sorts of prejudices (national, cultural, racial) wrapped up in typhus research. Of course there were competing egos involved, and to be sure one has to count the poetic attraction and repulsion of the city by many of the *tifólogos*. Besides, up to the 1930s there was still the problem of that seeming oxymoron: science in Mexico City? Mexican scientists?[62]

The collaboration of Ruiz Castañeda, Varela, Mooser, and Zinsser between Mexico City and Boston seemed to be the best proof that, unlike Gaviño's team in 1910, Mexican scientists had finally become part of the mainstream of global scientific developments, with local and international effects. Their various collaborative papers are a testament to this common cause. In private, Zinsser often wrote to Ruiz Castañeda praising their friendship. Upon returning from Mexico City, Zinsser wrote: "May I again express my unceasing appreciation of the intelligence and loyalty with which you have always worked with me?" In 1937, he still wrote: "The years that we worked together will always remain in my mind as among the most pleasant and productive of my career and we worked in such perfect partnership that I will always look upon all this typhus work as belonging to both of us together." And still in 1938: "I always miss you and I shall never forget the five happy years we spent together, working together like two brothers."[63] But this brotherhood did not withstand the "civilizational" gap that, in the eyes of the foreign doctors in Mexico City in 1931, separated the Mexican from the scientist.

In Mooser and Zinsser's correspondence the collaboration with Mexicans acquired a different tone. Mooser lived in Mexico City until 1937, when he returned to Zurich. In fact, in 1928 he had accepted a position in Cincinnati but returned to his work at the American Hospital in Mexico City despite the lower salary—he disliked the weather and the United States. He spoke and wrote excellent Spanish; moreover, from the recollections of Mexican scientists it is quite clear that Mooser had an uncommon wit in Spanish, often mocking Ruiz Castañeda in Spanish, Zinsser in English or German, and then Nicolle in French. Once he congratulated Ruiz Castañeda for his wedding (Ruiz Castañeda had married by power of attorney in Mexico City while he was in Boston) with a quintessentially Mexican double-entendre irony: "es mejor casarse por poder que divociarse por no poder" (it is better to marry by power [of attorney] than to divorce for lack of power [*por no poder*, meaning for lack of sexual powers]). And when Nicolle was in Mexico City, Mooser had no difficulty mocking Nicolle's opposition to his, Varela, and Ruiz Castañeda's findings, blending his jokes with well-established European prejudices about Mexico. Traveling in Puebla, Ruiz Castañeda recalled, Nicolle had asked Mooser— who was having his shoes shined by a *bolero* in Puebla's main plaza—about the status of lepers in Mexico; with a mixture of scientific superiority and cultural sarcasm, Mooser explained in French to Nicolle that the *bolero* who was shining his shoes, "was a typical leper with the characteristic *leonine facies*." Indeed, the anecdotal evidence accessible to the historian shows Mooser as a genuine cultural, ironic, and truly local inhabitant of the city and its language.

But his irony could not break apart the civilizational gap that Mooser perceived. While he had recommended Ruiz Castañeda to Zinsser, in late 1929 he wrote to his colleague revealing his ambivalence toward Mexicans: "[what Ruiz Castañeda] needs is a better training and better methods. Make him do also the most insignificant things at the start, because all Latins lack a sound foundation, especially the Mexicans. After they have been in the U.S. or abroad for a year they think they know the last secret of nature and science. Fortunately Dr. Ruiz is not of that kind." Yet he could not help but refer to a Mexican raciocultural profile. The same was true for Zinsser, whose public respect for Ruiz Castañeda coexisted with a deep-rooted racial view of Mexico. When Mooser considered moving permanently to Zurich, Zinsser wrote expressing views of Mexicans not far from Mooser's own: "I have in some respect a high regard for the Mexicans and I have a great affection for Ruiz, but I fear that their national pride proceeding from a curious inferiority complex will never permit them to give support and enthusiastic acknowledgment to a foreigner."[64]

What Zinsser said about Mexican xenophobia might have been true, especially in the 1930s, when there were anti-Chinese, anti-Spanish, anti-American, and anti-Jewish movements in the city, but what is important is the shared commonsensical views about Mexican atavisms. Science in Mexico City in 1931 was caught in the crossfire between Mexican anti-Americanism, U.S. and European racial views of Mexico, and the mutual distrust between American and French science. A comedy of errors that did not hinder scientific advancement, but that did reproduce cultural barriers between science in—and for—Mexico and science in—and for—the United States and Europe.

What Zinsser or Mooser thought about Mexicans had nothing to do with Ruiz Castañeda, Valera, or the Mexico City that hosted them in 1931. It was a well-established belief; they did not find these atavisms in Mexico City in 1931, they just confirmed them then and there. In his memoirs, Zinsser blended his findings in Mexico City with long-standing beliefs: "As a matter of fact, the Indian population is Mexico, and that is the main reason why we do not understand the Mexicans. Their developing civilization starts from a base line quite different from our Anglo-Saxon, fundamentally commercial one." For Zinsser Mexican food, habits, Latinness, and rhetoric . . . all led them to vagueness and chaos. It should come as no surprise that, despite all collaboration, Zinsser always saw Mexican scientists more as Mexicans than as scientists.[65]

Mooser's racial views of Mexicans were paired with his anti-French feelings. On the one hand, as had been the case for Goldberger in 1910, for Mooser in 1931 Mexicans were too Latin to be rigorous; on the other hand, Mooser saw

Americans as being too religious. It was for this reason, he claimed, that the U.S. media exaggerated the curative powers of Ruiz Castañeda and Zinsser's vaccine in 1930: "Finding a cure [for Americans] is serving man and God." But ironically Mooser himself identified with doctors in the Americas. Therefore, for him it was clear that any doctor either in the U.S. or the American continent had no chance of being recognized by the Stockholm academy, or so he wrote to Zinsser in 1928 upon learning of Nicolle's Nobel Prize: "[Nicolle's] demonstration that typhus is transmitted by the body louse prolonged the war. I also think that Theobald Smith should finally be honored with the prize, because he showed first that diseases can be transmitted by arthropods. If he were a Frenchman, he would have received it."

Mooser's irony and his anti-French feelings were wrapped up in the struggle of scientific egos: Mooser vs. Nicolle, Mooser vs. Ruiz Castañeda. In mid-1931, Mooser wrote to Ruiz Castañeda requesting revision of a simple essay published in the Mexican review *Medicina* because it appeared to be exclusively authored by Ruiz Castañeda instead of being a report on research undertaken by Ruiz Castañeda, Zinsser, and Mooser: none of them, Mooser remonstrated, had the right to publish anything without recognizing the rest.

The defense of their respective authorships was mixed with the articulation of their cultural views about Mexico, and also with a curious poetic will that seemed unstoppable in such characters as Mooser, Zinsser, and Nicolle. "Mala situación económica," Mooser wrote to Ruiz Castañeda commenting on Mexico City during the Depression, but added an expressive illustration of his own poetic will (in Spanish): "I wish I were a bachelor and could eat bread and onions like Sancho Panza, the simpleton. Yesterday I was reading *Don Quijote de la Mancha* looking for the page where Sancho comments that they must be getting close to the Equator because the little animals who wandered around on his belly had disappeared. I didn't find it, but I've continued reading so that I can illustrate my tales of typhus with classic literature. Regards to *el jefe* Juan Zinsser." Indeed, one could say of Mooser what one of his colleagues wrote to him on his eightieth birthday (1971): "Literatur zu hohem Ansehen gebracht hättest" (literature would have brought him a high reputation).[66]

The same collage of rivalries and literary impulses can be found in Zinsser and Nicolle—who introduced Zinsser to a number of French novelists (Balzac, Flaubert, Madame de la Fayette, and l'Abbe Prévost). Zinsser traveled to Paris and Tunis in 1932, on his own behalf and on that of Ruiz Castañeda and Mooser, to convince the Parisian "genius"—as Mooser put it ironically—of the findings of the new research on fleas and Mexico City. Nicolle in turn consulted Zinsser before his trip to Mexico. Rafael Silva invited Nicolle, but the former requested that his collaborator and lover Hélène Sparrow be invited as well. She worked in Mexico City along with other places with Nicolle, and indeed she constitutes an intriguing and influential female character in the typhus story; she worked at the Tunis Pasteur Institute until her retirement in 1960, but Nicolle's intellectual debt to her was never recognized.[67]

Before his trip to Mexico City, Nicolle had been in Uruguay and Argentina, received as the king of French science thanks to his Nobel Prize. In Mexico, he was granted all the official scientific and political honors and, together with Sparrow, engaged in laboratory work at the Hygiene Institute of Mexico. Zinsser was not in Mexico at the time, but they were hosted by Mooser, Varela, and Ruiz Castañeda. And in the city, Nicolle could let of go of his cultural, "exoticist," and anti-American views. From Mexico City, he wrote to fellow doctor and writer Georges Duhamel, complementing his anti-American opinions with racial views of Mexico motivated by notions of cultural atavism: "Mexico . . . grande ville peuplée d'indiens et de métis, plutôt sale" (Mexico . . . large city populated by Indians and mestizos, rather dirty). There were no racially unmarked people, and no clean people in the city in 1931, despite more than a million inhabitants, 2,185 medical doctors, and nearly 2,300 engineers. The city also provided an occasion for the arousal of Nicolle's anti-Americanism to the extreme of French imperial nostalgia: In Mexico "Americans are very dangerous. The [French] Mexico expedition was a brilliant idea, but was badly carried out." For him, Mexicans looked to France in literary matters, but not in scientific questions, and that was due to an inopportune U.S. competition. He actually proposed to Mexican authorities the creation of a Pasteur Institute in Mexico with Mexican doctors trained in Tunis and other French possessions in Africa, in view obviously of the Mexican laboratories that were emerging, full of individuals trained in the United States and with the support of the Rockefeller Foundation. For Nicolle, U.S. competition in Mexico was "even more dangerous because it represents, for many young Mexicans, a civilization better adapted to modern life than our own. . . . the Americans, in Mexico, are admired, feared, and hated." His views of Mexico were marked by his sense of coming from a superior civilization, much like his views of typhus: "France tenaciously opposes to the hypocrisy of the United States and its materialistic civilization, the humanitarian goals and the ideal of our own civilization." He was as anti-American, as much an advocate for the superiority of French civilization, as was his writing mentor, Georges Duhamel, who had described Americans as "civilisation hargneuse dont la hideur défie toute description" (an aggressive civilization, whose hideousness defies all description).[68]

Both Nicolle and Zinsser had literary pretentions, for which Mexico became one of many motifs. The subtitle of *Rats, Lice, and History* already marked the stream-of-consciousness type of rhetoric that made Zinsser both anachronis-

10.2. E. García Cabral, "Inútil todo afán, el mal soy yo" (1921).
Courtesy Taller Ernesto García Cabral A.C., Mexico City.

tic—as this rhetorical device was a return to the nineteenth-century English essay tradition—and modernist—William James and Proust were obvious inspirations. Thus his book became a best-selling work popularizing science. The subtitle was: *Being a Study in Biography, which, after Twelve Preliminary Chapters Indispensable for the Preparation of the Lay Reader, deals with the Life History of Typhus Fever also known.* . . . His vivid descriptions of fleas and lice recalled the epic story of all those who lived through the 1931 rat moment in Mexico City:

> My insect hunting has been concerned mainly with bedbugs, lice, ticks, and fleas, though lately also with mosquitoes. But the lice and fleas have furnished the most satisfaction. Bedbugs are a vulgar game. They are dull beasts and offer little play for skills or intelligence; are easily sneaked up on, and docile when caught. Fleas are the noblest game of all. They have speed and elusiveness, and, despite the evidence of flea circuses, are not easily domesticated . . . With fleas it is a matter of toujours de l'audace.

With such prose, it comes as no surprise that in 1934 Nicolle, the scientist and the novelist, wrote to Zinsser—perhaps discussing a translation of Zinsser's book—, "If I were near you I would place myself at your service to help you move forward in French. It would not be too difficult, for you already possess the spirit of our language. And the spirit is what is essential . . . in the end you would become a scientific and literary author in the French language."[69]

Nicolle was the man whose exoticist stories, full of orientalist motifs, were prized by Duhamel. As a scientist, he seemed to want his literature to complement the dryness and vulgarity of his subject—lice, fleas, rats; as a writer, he wanted his science to make him into both a modern researcher and an authoritative renaissance man. In one of his stories, a fictionalized female shadow says to the scientist who stands in for Nicolle in his writings: "I love your meticulous and precise spirit, somewhat stiff even on occasion as a result of your maniacal scrupulousness—I believe that you will be faithful to me. I trust your fear of decrepitude, a fear to which every word of your writing testifies. I am eternal youth, which nothing can wither and which never withers on its own." This was science as a literary vocation, and literature as a scientific *Beruf*.[70]

Mexican scientists had little to do with this crossfire between the nationalist and cultural feelings of foreign scientists. Trapped, on the one hand, by the city's political and social life and, on the other, by the *ninguneo* of international sciences, they kept facing every new sanitary crisis as such: as emergencies that needed to be dealt with rapidly. In 1938 the prominent doctor Ignacio Millán accused old doctors of "individualistic medicine," which was "una medicina remendona" (patchwork medicine), and called for the emergence of social medicine. But even after the creation of a vast system of social medicine, health in the city remained by definition remedial, a matter of improvisation and patching. In the early 1920s, cartoonist Ernesto García Cabral mocked the city's doctors in a telling cartoon: "Inútil todo afán, el mal soy yo" (all efforts are useless, I'm the problem): Death rules over the efforts of psychologists, surgeons, and bacteriologists (figure 10.2). Thus some of the Mexican *tifólogos* are represented in the cartoon: José Terrés appears behind Death, sternly looking at the representation of death, and a guinea pig appears on the shoulders of Fernando Ocaranza, who also holds an experimental dog on a leash. The efforts of the city's doctors were thus multiple and variegated but, in the irony of the cartoon, useless. Once the interrelation between science and city embarked on the massive modernizing move toward becoming a megalopolis, such interaction followed that wise, if vulgar, Mexican saying (once again based on the louse): "Encarrerado el peine" (once the comb is on its path), "chinguen su madre los piojos" (the lice can fuck off). And indeed through the bizarre interaction of science and city in Mexico City, lice disappeared as a public health problem, leaving the city and its science to face the many other old, new, and renewed problems.[71]

PART VI LANGUAGE

. . . a palavra falada . . . Dita, morta.

. . . the spoken world . . . once said, it's dead.

— Fernando Pessoa, *A língua portuguesa*

vete de mí.
Seré en tu vida lo mejor
de la neblina del ayer
cuando me llegues a olvidar,
como es mejor el verso aquel
que no podemos recordar.

get away from me.
In your life I will become
the best thing of the mist of yesterday
when you get to forget me
in the same way that it always seems much better that verse
we are unable to remember.

— "Vete de mí," popular tune, 1936,
    by Argentine composers Homero and Virgilio Espósito

WHISPERS

It is language that historians of culture seek and produce. Words and cities, however, are evasive. The written word, said Fernando Pessoa—a magnificent listener of cities—, is a cultural phenomenon, while the spoken word is a natural occurrence.[1] In listening to the languages of the past, one never knows whether what one hears are the whispers of past voices or the echoes of our own. We can attempt, of course, a command of the philosophical argots of the past in order to decipher, say, politics.[2] But will we ever truly be enabled to hear the mundane and promiscuous language of a late nineteenth-century city? How did Mexico City's many voices become distinctly *chilango?*[3]

From the 1880s to the 1930s, Mexico City underwent its most dramatic linguistic transformation, comparable only to its conversion from a Nahuatl-speaking center to a Spanish capital.[4] To be sure, New York and Buenos Aires were then the most modern linguistic laboratories of the Americas. In comparison, Mexico City was merely a local phenomenon, reflecting above all a long history of the Mexicanization of the Spanish language. Mexico City, however, was an important stage for the formation of a language that, at the beginning of the twenty-first century, we are just starting to examine with some distance. Our current words—whether scientific, popular, colloquial, artistic, or sentimental—were synthesized throughout the nineteenth century, but especially in the decades between the 1880s and the 1930s, when Mexico lost, as poet Ramón López Velarde then put it, "la inteligencia del lenguaje usual" (the intelligence of day-to-day language).[5]

In what follows I wish I could take comfort in an academic listening to the "subaltern." I cannot. Listening to past cities is never truly possible and, above all, has no rational or political why. Not unless, as if in a spiritualist session, one hopes to converse with past words for roughly the same reasons that one talks to oneself—"The city's voice itself is soft like Solitude's."[6] I am far from claiming to give voice to the common people of Mexico City's past; I merely want to listen, hoping surreptitiously to chitchat with those past sounds that still murmur in my own language.

The language of Mexico City studied here is thus a collection of simultaneous echoes: written tongues and oral traditions. These echoes form the iceberg of which we only know the literary, political, and scientific peaks. The iceberg itself is only partially translatable to our ears, because it is loaded with ephemeral and vivid blasphemy, tenderness, humor, and irony. With time, these feelings lose their meaning and gain conceptual autonomy from the present; they live only in being what they were and only in the moment that they were and solely for those to whom these feelings meant something. But let us try to hear such city whispers as *pregones* (crying vendors), dichos (sayings), *coplas* (short traditional verses), *refranes* (proverbs), popular tunes, and, finally, the whispers of the sayable but unpublishable: *palabrotas* (swearing).

Sayings

When I was a child, I marveled at the shouts of merchants in the city's *barrio* markets and *tianguis* (flea markets). Maximizing profit for the ice-cream peddler meant to shout, consciously mis-accentuating the verbs: "¡Cargalés calor, cargalés!" (you, heat, hit them with heat, hit them). "Mugrosas pero sabrosas" (dirty but tasty), shouted the watermelon seller to any potential client, while his competition melodiously counterattacked: "vendo sabor no color" (I sell taste not color). For the city was and is an unstable chorus of rumors that at times deafen, at times enchant the walker who is surrounded by *pregones* (crying vendors), shouts, music, proverbs, machines, cars . . .

From what one can gather, since colonial times *pregones* were the base of the city's collective voice. Memoir writers, novelists, and travelers often mention *pregones* and their motley intonations across the city. Madame Calderón de la Bara was enchanted by the *pregones* of the city, and a city dweller in the early twentieth century still recalled: "On all of the streets Indians mulled around, in much greater numbers than nowadays, and with a more primitive, more derelict appearance: they were usually vendors who couldn't speak Spanish correctly . . . they displayed and shouted out their wares, be they *petates* [bedrolls] or carved stones for distilling water or exquisite white fish from nearby lakes, which have since then dried out . . . They hawked each item with a special song, languid and penetrating."[7] By the 1930s, folklorists began collecting this component of the city's voice, which, they believed, was becoming extinct due to rapid modernization. They gathered melodious sounds that were part of the collective memory of *barrios*: "¡Carbooón . . . ciu, Carbooón . . . ciu! (carbón de encino, oak charcoal); a peddler of a kind of sweet (*trompadas*, which also means "punches" in Mexican Spanish) played upon the word's double meaning to sell his product: "Aquí traigo las trompadas, a centavo las voy a dar; quien no compre mis trompadas, trompadas le voy a dar" (Trompadas for sale, I'm selling them for a cent, he who doesn't buy trompadas [candies], will get trompadas [punches] from me).[8]

These sounds stuck in the memory of residents of the city, taking on the feel of a lost language, a disappearing paradise of eloquence and domesticity. But they were also spontaneous constructions of popular languages that, despite their continual evolution, got frozen in time by the writer of a memoir or a folklorist. Rhythm, irony, humor, blasphemy, and appeals to a sort of collective unconscious were vital for these pregones. One pastry seller on Cadena street used to shout:

pastelitos y jalea
pa' la chula y pa' la fea.

cakes and syrup,
for cute and ugly girls alike.[9]

(Throughout the essays in this part of the book, I underline the tones, words, spellings, and phrases that correspond to the city's language in order to highlight their unique flavor.)

There are many more such cries of the city's street vendors, transcribed in memoirs and in the notebooks of folklorists, but pregones were devoted above all to selling—pastries, fruits, fish, sweets, charcoal . . . Irony and spontaneity had their limits. Cursing was off limits. But dichos or refranes (popular proverbs) were other rumors of the city that had no such constraints upon them. Mexico City's proverbs of course cannot be separated from the long and vast refranero tradition in the Spanish language, or even from the sayings of other related languages like Catalan, Portuguese, and Gallego. The tradition is so old and enduring that, in terms of proverbs, Sancho Panza is still our master.

The promiscuity of popular wisdom—thank God—has no real geographical or temporal borders. "La Llorona," a tune made popular in the early twentieth century by radio singers—but whose verses were a collection of lasting popular refranes—, included the verses:

No sé lo que tienen las flores, Llorona,
las flores del campo santo,
que cuando las muebe el viento
parecen que están llorando.

I don't know what it is about the flowers, *Llorona*
the flowers in that cemetery,
but when the wind moves through them
it looks as though they are crying.

But the same verses can be found in a nineteenth-century Gallego proverb:

Miña nai, non sei que teñen
as froles do camposanto
que cuando o vento as abala
parece que están chorando.

Mother, I don't know what it is about
the flowers in that cemetery,
when the wind moves them
it looks as though they are crying.

For indeed popular proverbs offer a unique analytical lesson to be applied to culture as a whole: it is useless and nonsensical to wonder about origins and authenticity. Proverbs were language games to express rapid, robust, and summary logic, often advising actions; they have been extensively studied in the Spanish languages.[10] What is interesting is to examine how these *refranes* were either made or rephrased at the start of the twentieth century in Mexico City—a moment of rapid change that fortunately inspired many to collect them. The language of Mexico City built upon this *refranero* tradition, ultimately manifesting as the collective enjoyment of multifarious meanings and double-entendres, fast, witty, rhythmical, and blasphemous aphorisms that such folklorists and philologists as Darío Rubio described in the 1920s:

> It is true that we Mexicans are, and this no one can deny or avoid, very daring in matters of language, just as we also have a very sensitive ear for any bad-sounding expression. This last fact makes us all the quicker to employ that voice that is equivalent to the one we wish to avoid, or a phonetically similar voice, with the aim of softening the force of the expression by the sound of it, without missing the bad intention of the bad word.[11]

Yet, at the time of their collection—between 1870 and 1930—many of these sayings were too blasphemous to be published. As a result of the nineteenth-century world's obsession with language, however, German, Portuguese, Chilean, Argentinean, and Mexican philologists collected many proverbs all over the world. Following suit, Mexico's most prominent nineteenth-century intellectual, Francisco Manuel Altamirano, compiled a collection of the proverbs he came across in Mexico City. He never published his list, although he might have sent it to the German colleague who requested it. As a result of this request we count on a good uncensored sample of some of the city's most popular proverbs in the 1880s.

The proverbs that Altamirano found were very "Mexico City," including one that still is used in many different contexts, a proverb that mocks the egocentrism of the capital: "Fuera de México todo es Cuautitlán" (outside Mexico City everything is Cuautitlán), although today the irony is that Cuautitlán (a former small town near the city) is very much a part of the city's metropolitan area. Some other proverbs in Altamirano's collection were echoes of well-established sayings in the Spanish language, full of gender connotations, such as "mujer que sabe latín ni se casa ni tiene buen fin" (a woman who speaks Latin will never get married, nor will she have a good destiny), a Spanish proverb that, in its Mexico City version, was laced with anti-Spanish sentiment: "Ni mujer que hable latín ni hombre que hable como gachupín . . ." (Neither a woman who speaks Latin, nor a man who speaks like a Spaniard . . .). Some proverbs of the city included Nahuatl words; Altamirano, being a native Nahuatl speaker, had no trouble collecting and translating them: "Diligencia mochihuiliz, amo san Dios dara" (in Spanish, "diligencias harás no sólo Dios dará," meaning "help yourself and God will help you").

Many of the proverbs compiled by Altamirano made use of the Indian as the buffoon, as the illiterate, the poor, the urban outcast, in much the same way as their Iberian counterparts made use of the urban poor. Mexico City's proverbs were often cruel and racist, but also witty and revealing of the mores and language of the city: "Los inditos y los burritos de chiquitos son bonitos" (little Indians, like little donkeys, are beautiful as babies). Indeed, from language, when truly popular, one can expect wit, wisdom, and eloquence, but cannot ask for any sort of correctness.

A saying that expressed a greater degree of class-consciousness was "Indio con puro ladrón seguro" (an Indian with a cigar is surely a thief). It is hard to find more eloquence, and more racism, in a briefer form. And then there were those proverbs that addressed sex, and the unique "way of life" that permeated Mexico City at the time. These proverbs forced Altamirano to write down words that he knew could not be published: "Con pendejos ni a bañarse, porque hasta el jabón se pierde" (with pendejos one can't even bathe, for even the soap disappears). Or better yet: "Persona muy lunareja o muy sabia o muy pendeja" (A freckled person is either a wise man or a fool). Of course *pendejo* was as *chilango* and as vulgar a term as there could be—meaning asshole or fool and derived from the Spanish term for hanging (often in reference to pubic hair) but which in Mexico City had and has a very different meaning. Another vulgar proverb was "No me echen ungüento que voy de alivio," a popular proverb collected in Mexico City in the late 1930s, pronounced "No me *chin'güento* que voy de alivo," meaning "don't mess with me" in exceedingly vulgar (and beautiful) terms.

Sexual proverbs gave anatomically inspired advice on courtship and copulation: "Mediano culo aguado, *chinguitito* y pan tostado," which is hard to translate, something like "enjoy soft asses." Another proverb described a woman who was "espesa, babosa y fría como la chía" (heavy, slimy, and cold like the beverage made of chía seed). A more specifically anatomical warning about the dangers of women was "Puede haberlas más chichonas pero no que de más leche" (There might be some with bigger tits, but they don't give more milk). Again, here we have great eloquence in the briefest form together with supreme vulgarity (both things often come together). In the 1920s, folklorist Vicente T. Mendoza collected similar sayings, wordplays, and popular prejudices in Mexico City, such as "Las mujeres al querer son como el indio al comprar: aunque las despachen bien no cesan de regatear" (Women loving are like an Indian buying; even if you give them a good deal they won't stop haggling).

The nature of all these sayings, whether with sexual or social content, was the riddle. For it was riddles that the streets demanded in order to survive in their changing order of wit, *ninguneo*, and honor; riddles like "Un perdido muy perdido que de perdido se pierde, si se pierde, qué se pierde, si se pierde lo perdido" (A very lost lost person, who by virtue of being lost gets lost, if he gets lost, what gets lost, if the lost gets lost?).[12]

Coplas

The city was also a center for the production of *coplas*: an old Spanish tradition of short popular rhymes, which became part of the oral mores of many cities, at times used in gatherings at plazas or at the entrances of *vecindades*; at times repeated by storytellers on the street, other times included as verses in popular songs. *Coplas* of course were above all about love, betrayal, and sex (what else is there to talk about?). In the twentieth century, Mexican philologists arduously worked to collect *coplas* across the country and, not surprisingly, Mexico City turned out to be a great repository of *coplas*. Many of these *coplas* were, as a result, profoundly urban, deeply "Mexico City," as if they were sponges that absorbed the city's need for new terms to name new technology, streets, and social phenomena. Thus one of the *coplas*, using the city's post, cables, and telegraphs as source of metaphors, went:

Por el hilo de un alambre
voy a ir a tu balcón;
como mi pasión es grande
no tiene comparación;
haz favor de constestarme
cuál es tu resolución.

On a [telephone, electric] wire
I will travel to your balcony;
as my passion is boundless
and has no equal;
please do me the favor of answering me
and letting me know your decision.

Many *coplas* used city parks and plazas as loci to fix memories and rhythmical feelings of revenge and desperation, laconically telling a passionate short story that needed no further elaboration:

Árboles de la Alameda
¿por qué no han reverdecido?
¿qué dicen, calandrias: cantan
o les apachurro el nido?[13]

Trees on the Alameda
why have you not turned green again?
What is that I hear, larks; will you sing
or shall I smash your nest?

The city furnished the distance and anonymity that allowed for rambling, walking, looking onto balconies, and into windows, blended with feelings of love and betrayal, all of which were sources of *coplas*:

Tanto pasar y pasar
tanto pasar por aquí
yo gozando mis huaraches
y otro gozando de ti.

So many times I have walked and walked
so many times I have walked around here
me enjoying my sandals
and another enjoying you.

At times the city's loci became excuses for rich blasphemy, as in a *copla* incorporated into a popular song ("Mariquita," collected in Mexico City in 1908):

> y si alguno no le gustan
> mis versos ni mi tonada,
> que se vaya a la . . . Alameda
> ahora que está bien regada.

> And whosoever doesn't like
> my verses or my tone
> can go . . . to the Alameda
> now that it is well watered.

Any Spanish speaker in the city understood that it was not to the Alameda park where the unappreciative ought to go but to *la chingada*. All in all, women were the leitmotif of many *coplas*, as they were the source of all happiness, sadness, and guilt. Thus the *copla* (incorporated into a song) that must have been very popular at the Belém prison:

> ¡Ay! que sonido de llaves
> ¡ay! que altura de paredes
> ¡ay! si en esta carcel me hallo
> la culpa es de las mujeres.

> Oh! the sound of keys
> oh! the high walls
> oh! if I find myself in this prison
> women are to blame.

But the city's popular language was too precise and logical to simply blame women alone for men's misfortunes. God was to be blamed too:

> La primera la hizo Dios
> y Eva engañó al padre Adán,
> cuando esa la hizo Dios
> las demás ¡¿cómo serán?!

> The first woman was made by God
> and Eve betrayed Father Adam

if that one was made by God
how must the rest be?!

In addition to such indisputable logic, these *refranes* and *coplas* exhibit popular biblical common sense akin to that found in many nineteenth-century African-American tunes from the U.S. south. Popular language was indeed wise and rich, but also ran the gamut of social, gender, and racial prejudices, as in this comparison between women and mules, complete with sexual innuendo:

La mujer en el amor
es cual mula de alquiler
empieza a todo correr
y se para en lo mejor.[14]

A woman in love
is like a rented mule
she starts out at a run
and stops during the best part.

Other resonant themes in the city's language were common expressions that had become widely used. In 1918, a Mexican philologist, Salvador Cordero, explained them to high-school teachers so that they could avoid them, as the expressions were either vulgar or incorrect. These were expressions that became deeply ingrained in the city's language, such as "Cobrarse a lo chino" (take revenge the hard way), "Dorar la píldora" (literally to gild the pills, meaning to fool someone by making bad news look good), and the beautiful and cheering Spanish expression "Hacer de tripas corazón" (turning guts into heart).[15] Some of these expressions are still used in Mexican Spanish today.

Tunes

Popular tunes, of course, were the other constant theme in the city; they were, folklorists like Vicente T. Mendoza believed, the *almacén de la tradición* (warehouse of tradition), the archive, library, and engine of popular traditions.[16] In fact, between 1870 and the emergence of radio in the early 1920s, Mexico City was the magnet that attracted, blended, and transformed many lyrical traditions. But it was the massive dissemination of the radio that made the city into a linguistic capital, not only nationally but internationally. This was accomplished through the massive diffusion of the sounds of the city, and by blending these sounds with everything from everywhere. The tunes are thus very indicative of popular feelings, although not because of their "authentic" rooting in a static popular language but rather because of their great capacity for linguistic innovation and adaptation.

The old rumors of songs are hard to fix in one single location, one single class, but folklorists and popular publishers collected Mexico City's musical legacy even before the emergence of radio as they believed those traditions to be rapidly disappearing. By the 1880s, the songs of the city already included a mixture of lowbrow and highbrow: nineteenth-century Spanish romanticism, rural tunes, and city speak. By the end of the nineteenth century, one of the most popular songs that could be heard everywhere was "Marchita el alma," which used words and rhymes coming from canonic Spanish romanticism:

Marchita el alma, triste el pensamiento,
mustia la faz, herido el corazón
atravesando la existencia misera
sin la esperanza de alzcanzar tu amor.

My soul is withered, my thoughts are sad
my face is fallen, my heart is injured
I move through this miserable life
with no hope of earning your love.

Of course it is likely that many of the street singers who sang the phrase "mustia la faz" did not understand its meaning; all the same, they found the grace of the lyrics appropriate to a subject requiring elegant articulation: love. The song was so popular that in 1916, in a fit of populist nationalism, Mexican classical composer Manuel M. Ponce used "Marchita el alma" as the inspiration for a piece of classical music.

In turn, regional lyrical traditions reached Mexico City, and there they were transformed and appropriated, like the following tune, believed by folklorists to be from Sinaloa, which was transcribed from a street singer in Mexico City in the 1930s (El lirio):

Y ya con esto comprenderás, bien mío,
que yo te adoro con férvida pasión.
Yo te suplico que cese tu desvío
calmando el fuego de aqueste corazón.

With this you will understand, my love,
that I love you with a fervent passion,

I beg that you cease your rambling
and come calm the fire that burns in this heart.

The lyrics are already a popular appropriation of the flowery prose of high Spanish, with such characteristic words as "férvida," a linguistic anachronism deriving either from rural imitation of upper-class language, or from urban efforts to speak in a more "classical" style (using such terms as "aqueste," an old form of "este"). A better example of this popularization of aristocratic language is in "El Murciélago," a song from the 1880s that was essentially the city's "top hit" well into the 1940s—an urban gothic piece:

En noche lóbrega galán incógnito
las calles céntricas atravesó
y bajo *clárica* ventana gótica
templó su citara y así canto:
Virgen purísima de faz angélica
que entre las sábanas durmiendo estás,
despierta y ábreme que entre mis cánticos
suspiros prófugos escucharás.

On a dark night an unknown gentleman
traversed the downtown streets
and beneath an illuminated gothic window
tuned his zither and sang as follows:
Purest virgin of angelic features
up there sleeping between the sheets
wake up and open your window, for between the verses of my song
you will hear my fleeting sighs.

In fact, this tune sought to parody the use of verb tenses, the metaphors, and the syntax of the late seventeenth-century gothic revival—with such words as *murciélago, citara, lóbrega,* and *ventana gótica*—even if it required the use of made-up terms like *clárica* for *clara* (clear). These kinds of parodies would eventually become a genre for the Mexican comedians of the 1930s and 1940s—Cantinflas, Piporro, Tin-Tán, and Joaquín Pardavé, all of whom sang tunes full of invented terms, generally with ridiculously long words accented so as to produce a comic effect: instead of *te hablaba* they would use *hablabate,* rhyming with *fallote,* a sonorous word for *te falló* (you failed, you missed it).

Rural jargon was, of course, the delight of the city. The streets borrowed, sang, and imitated the many rural variants of Mexican Spanish, especially those coming from Jalisco, which eventually would become, much as Andalusia did for Spain, the source of the national image reproduced on the radio, in movies, and, later, on TV. In the 1890s, this Jalisco tune was often sung in the city:

No te eches de lao, Petronila,
y no creas que por juliona yo te olvidé,
si tú te hubieras visto como yo me vide:
Con to' el hocico arrepegado a la pared.
Ojalá y te jueras para otras tierras,

. . .

reteorgullosa y felónica mujer

Don't move away, Petronila,
don't think because you are so forceful I forgot you
If you had been as I was:
With your mouth smashed against the wall
I wish you would go far away . . .
you proud and unfaithful woman.

In this tune we have rural expressions and names that were naturalized in Mexico City's slang: Petronila was a rural name that often maids would use in the city; lao for lado, as in to' for todo was a very regional (Bajío) habit of abbreviating the suffix -do (also common in Andalusian Spanish) that became popular in the city. The change of J for F and H—as in "jueras" for "fueras" (from ir, "to go") or jullir for huir (to flee)—became a mark of class in Mexico City. Nineteenth-century philologists believed that these kinds of linguistic changes were the result of the influence of Nahuatl on the Spanish spoken in Mexico City. Jesús Sánchez listed the following common "mistakes" derived from Nahuatl: óido for oído (heard or ear), vesitar for visitar (to visit), prencipal for principal, medecina for medicina, afigurarse for figurarse (to figure out), afusilar for fusilar (shoot), rete for muy, aiga for haya (has), aigre for aire (air), ansina for así (like this), ñeto for nieto (grandchild), and faitura for factura (bill). All these terms were an essential part of the city's language, but it is unclear whether and how they were appropriated from Nahuatl.[17]

In the song cited above, rural anachronisms (terms used in old Spanish, but absent from more proper, urbane language) are more prevalent than Nahuatl influences. The use, for example, of trujiste instead of traer (to bring) dates from Don Quixote, but became a prominent marker of class and was found by

American and Mexican philologists in Texas in the 1890s (today, it can still be found in some rural Texas communities). A prefix used for augmentation or exaggeration that was typical of Mexico City was *re-*, used in terms such as *reteorgullosa* (very proud) or in a number of well-known Mexican words including *refritos* or *reteque . . . bonitos*, meaning very fried or fried more than once, and very, very beautiful. But the song also demonstrates popular usage of more formal terms: the word *felónica*, coming from *felonía* (betrayal), was not considered correct when used as an adjective.

The appropriation of rural language became so popular that a sort of Mexican Chaplin, Joaquin Paradavé, used it in his 1928 "La Panchita": a veritable anthology of the terms and mannerisms that philologists would later identify as remnants of rural language in Mexico City.

> Y cuando me ve enojado se rie y se <u>carcajia</u>,
> y cuando me ve temblando me llena de <u>labia</u>;
> no sé que hacerle, mamá querida, <u>pa'</u> que me <u>quera</u>
> que esa Panchita me tiene loco con su <u>vacilón</u>.

> And when she sees me angry she laughs and guffaws
> and when she sees me tremble she lets me have it
> I don't know what to do, dear mother, to make her love me
> that Panchita makes me crazy with her taunts.

The underlined terms—constituting the rhyme scheme of the piece—are all rural expressions that were fully appropriated by the city (especially beautiful is the expression "me llena de labia," literally "fills me with lips," meaning "fills me with words"). Likewise, the use of *quera* instead of *quiera* is particularly evocative, for the moment one deletes the i from *quiera* one effects a change of worlds: from the canonic universe of establishment Spanish to the streets of Mexico City.

Other songs talk about the technology of the city, adapting rural languages to the subject, as this one from the 1890s (originally from Zacatecas but adapted to the urban life of Mexico City):

> luz eléctrica, tú que en el Zócalo estás
> con tus faroles iluminas la catedral
> <u>vide</u> pasar a mi amor,
> pero !ay! no le pude hablar,
> luz eléctrica, de noche me has de alumbrar.

Electric lamp, there in the Zócalo
lighting up the cathedral
I saw my love walk by,
but oh! I couldn't say a word to her
electric lamp, at night you'll light my way.

And science also was proletarized, parodying the vast new scientific jargon
that was everywhere as a form of popular common sense, like in a Bajío song
collected in Mexico City in 1898: the song talks about being capable of fully
loving Mariana because:

Yo se la química, retórica, botánica,
botánica, retórica y sistema decimal.
Volaré del uno al otro polo,
imitando a los globos areostáticos
hasta encontrar la piedra filosófica
cuadrada o triangular.
Porque yo soy físico, retórico, poético,
astrónomo, filósofo y político;
sin duda soy el hombre más científico
que en el mundo puede haber.

I know chemistry, rhetoric, and botany
botany, rhetoric, and the decimal system.
I'll fly from one pole to the other
like a hot air balloon
'til I find the philosopher's stone
be it square or triangular.
Because I am a physicist, a rhetorician, a poet,
an astronomer, philosopher, and politician;
without a doubt I am the most scientific man
to be found in the entire world.

Needless to say, very few of those singing or listening to this tune could
understand the meaning of every single discipline mentioned, but one can
only imagine their delight in hearing the tune's rhythmical repetition, a sort
of logic of love. Wittgenstein would have seen the lyrics as exemplary of the
limits of language; chilangos found in it the unspoken possibilities of language.[18]

Palabrotas

Palabrotas (bad words) act in a way as the iodine label in an X-ray of Mexico City's language from the 1880s to the 1940s. Let us listen to words, the "bad" ones, utilizing an utterance as a guide, say, *pendejo*, which in its semantic origins, as I have explained, had sexual connotations, but which came to adopt a variety of meanings across the Spanish-speaking world. While in Chile *pendejo* simply meant little boy, and in Perú designated an astute but ill-intentioned person, in Mexico the term was and is commonly used to characterize a stupid, slow-thinking, ill-intentioned, and pusillanimous person. It was also the root of the term *pendejada*, referring to actions of *pendejos*. The meanings of this word, its powerful resonance in the city, and its conspicuous absence from printed material tell us a lot about the languages of the city. For Mexico City's highbrow language was ultimately a secret version of the vulgar eloquence of the city. Mockery, irony, and vulgarity formed the indispensable scaffolding supporting the structure of the highbrow eloquence of the city.

Words were, and are, dangerous weapons. Such expressions as *pendejo* were, the dictionaries stated, "cosas de hombres" (men's matters), and to misuse these words could have a consequence as dire as death. Duels, thus, were often what followed the misuse of words, as it was the case in a famous duel between Santiago Sierra (Justo's brother) and Ireneo Paz (Octavio Paz's grandfather) that ended in Santiago's death, and the many occasions in which poet and politician Salvador Díaz Mirón dueled.[19] Nothing particularly Mexican about it, of course. In almost any language in the nineteenth century, words and duels were linked. Above all, no one dared to write and publish words such as *pendejo*, not even in the many dictionaries of *mexicanismos* published between 1870 and 1910. A few criminological texts did mention these terms and their meanings in popular argot. In the late 1930s, Darío Rubio's *Estudios Paremiológicos* included various popular proverbs with the word *pendejo* collected by and large in Mexico City during the 1920s and 1930s: "navegar con bandera de pendejo" (pretending to be a fool in order to obtain higher goals, a proverb still used in Mexican Spanish today) or "No hay carta de pendejo sin posdata" (what comes from an ill-intentioned fool always has something added).[20] Other proverbs stated that "Un pendejo callado es oro molido" (a quiet fool is pure gold) and "Tacones que no hacen ruido, de pendejo o de bandido" (he whose heels do not make noise is either an idiotic coward or an outlaw). This last proverb, Rubio noted, was going extinct in the city due to the appearance of rubber heels, but "if this proverb were to disappear, no jewel would be lost." These proverbs, one must assume, had been around for a long time before Rubio collected them. The beauty and rich obscenity of these terms were thus common, but never published.

Some Spanish dictionaries of the nineteenth century included the term "pendejo"—Pages de Puig's dictionary registered the somehow pejorative connotations of the word but not in the way the term was used in Mexico City. Since Joaquín García Icazbalceta never reached the letter *p* in his dictionary of *mexicanismos*, we will never know whether he planned to include it. His decorum, however, led him to deprive his compilation of Mexican Spanish of the monumental verb *chingar*, about which so much has been said. An influential late nineteenth-century geographer, Antonio García Cubas, recalled the chats in the back rooms of stores and coffee shops where they debated about the origins of what he called the H word, "que usan nuestros léperos" (which is used by our lower classes). He never identified the H word, whose real identity was obviously *chingar*. In the 1920s, Victoriano Salado Alvarez—a passionate searcher of words like few others—perhaps for the first time transcribed and deciphered *chingar* in all of its many connotations. By the 1950s, well-known writers such as Octavio Paz and Carlos Fuentes built an entire phenomenology of the word. With a bit of psychoanalysis and a pinch of long-standing stereotypes about the Mexican thrown in, and *viola!*: never before had all Mexicans belonged in such a way to the many variations of a single word, *la chingada, chingadera, chingar, chingón.* And yet so much psychoanalysis of *chingar* can be seen not solely as a product of the 1940s global identitology, but above all as part of a long-lasting fascination with popular language, and as a sign of the inevitable gentrification of vulgar eloquence by highbrow intellectuals. In any case, whereas in the 1940s *la chingada* was the symptom of an intellectual epidemic of psychoanalysis, by the 1980s, *la chingada* became the epidemic itself in very popular local tunes: old fears of epidemics in the city were expressed by a very popular local rock band as a rats epidemic, meaning corrupt politicians, and thus, the tune wonderfully went, "se ha soltado una epidemia de jijos de la chingada" (an epidemic of sons of a bitch has let loose).[21] Words have their own, and better, life beyond the confines of the city's intellectuals.

F. J. Santamaría's dictionary of *mejicanismos*—an unauthorized continuation of García Icazbalceta's efforts—did include *pendejo*, but that was in the 1920s. It registered the printing of such a term in the 1920s memoirs of a revolutionary general (Francisco Urquizo). The fact is that such prominent figures of the revolutionary novel as Urquizo and Mariano Azuela, in his renowned attempt to "speak popular," never wrote the entire word letter by letter, but a simple "pen . . ." Eloquence was then shyness but that does not mean that the entire written word did not take part in the urban orgy of words. Liberalism was conceived of as a mythical, homogeneous, and applicable system of thought. The existence of a highbrow eloquence was similarly mythologized. But no paradise of good or bad words existed.

This is a nineteenth-century phenomenon, for printed language had more freedom in the sixteenth, seventeenth, and eighteenth centuries, at least in terms of words that did not allude directly to God. Miguel de Cervantes and Francisco de Quevedo had eloquently used blasphemy. Shakespeare too, thus the popularity of Family Shakespeare in nineteenth-century England. Ironically, it is thus harder to hear the echo of words loaded with the sexual and social meanings in the Mexico City of the nineteenth and early twentieth centuries (chronologically just around the corner from us) than it is to experience the linguistic orgy of eighteenth-century Spain. Then, for instance, Nicolás Fernández de Moratín in print described, without periphrasis, the encounter of a priest and a prostitute. The priest sought sex, which is what many did in the nineteenth century but no one wrote about it: "Alzo el sus habitazos cazcarriosos/presentando un mangual como una torre" (He lifted up his muddy robes/revealing a shaft like a tower), but the poor man found "un clítoris llagado,/sin un labio y pelado a repelones" (a clitoris covered in sores/missing a lip and shaved in strips). Fernández de Moratín tells in detail how the priest, astutely, uses his headdress as a condom and then puts it back over his head: "la capilla que chorrea,/jabonando el cerquillo y la corona/blanco engrudo, simiente de persona" (the headdress drips/lathering the bald head and the crown/white glue, seeds of humans). These echoes of blasphemy, rudeness, vulgarity, irony, and creativity are not to be found in print in the late nineteenth century. That century purified our tongues.

The vocabulary of liberal treaties and histories was a Victorian expurgation of the broader language of the city. To write history, poetry, or simple prose was not, as it has been doggedly argued, to mimic European rhetorical forms (could Mexico City's intellectuals do otherwise?). It meant to tame the multiple echoes received from the daily life of the city. In our post-Victorian era, in which we believe everything to be sayable, the closest thing to that taming process would be the experience of a Mexican, Argentine, or Spanish writer who would consciously aim to tell a local story in a Spanish that is native and yet not parochial, not solely comprehensible by the inhabitants of Mexico City, Buenos Aires, or Madrid.

But before the moral liberalization of the written word, behind the published political or scientific prose there were mockery, blasphemy, obscenity, and disbelief, and this was the background of the intellectuals' selective readings of theories and ideas. The oratory that accompanied the inaugurations of monuments, the words used in textbooks and in scientific prose, constituted this Victorian expurgation. This language was also formed by a constant struggle to overcome this expurgation. Thus the metaphor commonly used for language was war, for there were battles in search of and against styles.

There was, on one hand, the need to control the circulation and weight of words; on the other, an obsession with newness and a linguistic laissez-faire. Within these limits, political and social concerns struggled to be articulated in a changing reality; these were battles in which those best suited to irony and allegorical allusions (never directness) within the liberal and Victorian rhetoric won.

To our contemporary ears, the printed echoes of the city sound too refined and essentially tacky. However, if those early twentieth-century intellectuals were to read the post-1960s urban novels and chronicles, they would understand not only the words but also the fact that the streets had won the battle of the tongues. Early twentieth-century intellectuals sought liberation in the most extreme possibilities of the language, at times through the abundance of adjectives and synonyms, at others rediscovering austerity: "Decir lo que decir hemos sin hojarasca de palabras inútiles" (Say what we need to say without the detritus of useless words).[22] But the liberation of language went beyond the strict boundaries of what was considered lengua culta. When intellectuals wrote about race or nation, they could not ex nihilo invent a new language, they had to speak within a clearly demarcated cosmopolitan chorus. The same could be said about the entire language: the possibilities for creativity and innovation were enormous, yet there remained clearly demarcated rhetorical limits. In English, explained Virginia Woolf in 1914, Victorian coyness ruled; the origins of modern literature, for Woolf, could be dated to the printing of the first obscene word—around the 1920s. For Spain, in 1944 Ramón Gómez de la Serna wrote that it was Ramón del Valle Inclán who first went beyond the conventional Victorian style, by creating a language that existed neither in brothels nor in elegant saloons: "el chulesco literario," the language that only Valle, said de la Serna, "could use and save from going sour." Therefore, de la Serna wrote, Valle was able to overcome what Darío called, in private and in his cups, of course, "la pendejada de la época" (the epoch's stupidity) (de la Serna transcribed the expression in his 1944 biography of Valle Inclán).[23]

But in the Mexico City of 1910, someone like Federico Gamboa, who was acquainted with the city's brothels, never once wrote the word puta or pendejo, though he wrote an entire novel (Santa) about the life of a city's prostitute. But of course 1910 Mexico City's intelligentsia welcomed like a king the great master of turn-of-the-century linguistic revolution in Spanish: Rubén Darío, the Bismarck of new adjectives and metaphors. Soon after 1910, Darío's language would look like a simple transitional stage in the orgy of words that rapidly made his French-like syntactic turns anachronistic—though he would not have minded being surpassed, as he said it eloquently in 1910 to a priest in

Mexico: "yo no tengo escuela, no sea usted <u>pendejo</u>" (I have no school, don't be such an idiot sir).[24]

But swearing and obscene language were an insurmountable aesthetic temptation. Writers, folklorists, and philologists searching for popular languages did not have to travel very far to experience verbal laissez-faire: it was among them, city intellectuals, when they were in cantinas and brothels and on the streets. Philologists such as Max Leopold Wagner and C. Carroll Marner did transcribe and print many "bad words," but in doing so they made museum pieces of the words. Philologists and criminologists collected words as botanical specimens, inoffensive objects in a laboratory; "tanto valdría," said Nervo of the philologists who collected isolated words, "buscar la arquitectura en los ladrillos" (it would be just as useful to attempt to grasp the architecture of a building in its bricks). The long list of words found, for instance, by Wagner in the Colonia de la Bolsa seemed to have no real life, when in fact the city's intelligentsia knew how to use many of those words. Enrique González Martínez, the guru of the city's letrados between 1914 and 1925, told stories of Saturdays at the beginning of the twentieth century, in which he and his intellectual friends heard comedies on López and Independencia streets. He lamented that the tuguriosos (lowly) verses of those evenings in cafes and streets could not be reproduced: "people knew them by heart [but] the printed letters are too shameful [las letras de molde son por demás pudorosas]. . . . They don't like to reveal the secrets that are heard in the intimacy of literary circles." Alfonso Reyes himself, perhaps the most erudite of the city's intellectuals, longed to write a piece titled "El Hombre Desnudo" (The naked man), which, without falling into "anthropological nonsense . . . would do justice to the fruits of my life at 7 Cedro Street, recording my observations on the intonations of the plebs on every street corner. What on one is / / / / / on another is /////
[sic]."[25] This was thus the city's highbrow eloquence obsessed with the popular speech and yet unable to print it.

José Sánchez Somoano, a Spaniard who lived in Mexico and the U.S. at the end of the nineteenth century, did not hesitate to publish words in their own contextual meaning in a way he would have never done for obscene words from his native Spain.[26] He found in Mexico City countless voices with strange connotations for a Spaniard, and collected several "bad" words not because he was living among the rotos of the city, but precisely because he listened to the streets and to the language spoken in the social gatherings of intellectuals, professionals, and politicians. To be sure, Sánchez Somoano did not aim at achieving a scientific record of the Mexican parole, but rather sought to express the irony of certain voices. What in Mexico meant a total transgression of a linguistic code was in Spain a simple joke. For example, the strong Spanish insult *gilipollas* had, and has, no real life in Mexico; the term simply sounds hilarious, despite its insulting sexual connotations. Sánchez Somoano heard, wrote, and published:

Aquí [en Epaña] se paran los pies
al que se propasa en algo,
y allá se les para a todos
militares y paisanos.

Here [in Spain] he who makes an inappropriate advance
is stopped in his tracks [*se le paran los pies*]
there [in Mexico] everyone gets a hard-on [*se les para*]
military and countrymen alike.

He found a verb meaning "to stand up" being imbued in Mexico City with male sexual connotations. Simply put, men from both the high and the low classes used the reflexive verb *se me, se les, se nos para*: an ecumenical universe created out of men's sexual arousal. Sánchez Somoano also tells us about such profoundly *chilango* expressions as *enchílame otra* (meaning fix me another enchilada, but actually connoting something close to the contemporary U.S. "whatever"), *xidos* (nice, cool), *rotos* (low, poor, vulgar), *como agua para chocolate* (ready to exploit), *los blanquillos* (hen's eggs), *los barbajanes* (insolent, trashy), *los calzonudos* (in Mexico, Indians; in Spain, he who is ruled by his wife), and *la chiripa* (good luck). All these expressions circulated the city, across *barrios* and classes. They were expressions that combined ironic coyness with sexual connotations. For instance, *blanquillo* was a way not to say egg (*huevo*), a term with serious genital meaning in Spanish.[27]

Sánchez Somoano knew well the cultural valence of verbs: "¿Y coger? ¡Quién lo diría!/es un verbo empecatado;/no hay que dejarse coger/ni siquiera por la mano" (And *coger*? Who would have known!/a loaded verb;/one must not allow oneself to be grabbed/even by the hand). How and when did the verb "*coger*" (to catch, to take, to grab, to grasp) come to mean "to fuck" in Mexico City? Impossible to know, but the fact is that by the end of the nineteenth century, we should assume, that verb had a ubiquitous presence in the city, across all social classes. It was nevertheless not printed with that meaning in any legal or literary text until almost the 1950s.

And thus Sánchez Somoano wrote:

Al que en los tratos sociales
no demuestra ser experto

en vez de llamarle tonto
le dicen que es un pendejo.

He who in social situations
shows a lack of expertise
is not called *tonto* (stupid)
but instead is called a *pendejo*.

Here we have the term in print, in 1892. Sánchez Somoano's irony elucidated the fact that the language of the city was, as was the city itself, corrupt, promiscuous, uncontrollable, unpredictable, rich, creative, and, at times, virtuous. Another Spaniard, Valle Inclán, was in Mexico City around the same time as Sánchez Somoano, and returned in 1921 to write his famous *Tirano Banderas, novela de tierra caliente* (1926) (see chapter 4). According to the author, the novel was an appropriation of the language of an unidentified tropical country. In fact, the language of the novel was a potpourri of what the great Spanish novelist believed to be Mexico City's language—which impressed his Spanish readers. The traces of the language of Mexico City are visible in the use of such words as *pendejo, chamaco, jefesito,* and *chingado*. One of the dialogues included: "¿Qué se teme Usted, una pendejada?" (Are you afraid that I am going to mess with you?). At moments Valle Inclán's use of those words reveals how much his linguistic appropriation was a form of orientalism, one with no real knowledge of the meanings and uses of words: "Deja paso, y mira, no me manches el charol de las botas, gran chingado" (Let me get by and don't sully my boots, *gran chingado*). *Gran chingado* is an uncomfortable use of the term, one clearly written by a Spaniard trying to speak Mexican.[28] And another Spaniard did likewise, one who reached Mexico City after the defeat of the Republic in the Spanish Civil War. A. Artís-Gener's *Paraules d'Opoton el vell* (1968) in Catalan told the story of the conquest of Spain by Indians, using a language that Artís-Gener (Tisner) claimed to have learned by talking to Indigenous people in Mexico City. The irony was in the translation from Catalan into Spanish that the author himself composed in the 1970s: the language he used was pure 1950s Mexico City *calo*. The city ruled.[29] This would be like claiming East LA slang as the old language of the natives of California.

There were two other domains in which the term *pendejo* and other vivid components of the city's language were captured. One domain followed an unanimated and published fashion; the other an animated yet not totally public style. The first is, as I have mentioned before, the genre that contained the many dictionaries of *calo* and *germanía* (the language of criminals) published from 1880 to 1940.[30] The second domain is one that is difficult to label, but constituted the first conscious attempt to really speak *chilango*. This endeavor I have found by mere coincidence, particularly in the language of bohemian women consciously crafting themselves as modern, Mexican, and liberated ladies of the city between the 1910s and the 1930s.

Max Leopold Wagner (b. 1880), a distinguished German philologist who studied many romance languages, is emblematic of the search for words that characterized the logophilia (see chapter 12) of early twentieth-century Mexico City. In his trip to Mexico in 1919 he studied the language of La Colonia de la Bolsa, which was then called a "colonia de rateros: colonia de la bolsa, gente de toda broza" (thieves' *barrio* inhabited by the worst of the worst). He based his analysis on the many studies done around the world of *calo, germanía,* Gypsy language, and the terminology of criminals, especially in Cuba, Spain, Italy, and Germany. In the verbal sparring of the city, Wagner did not register the term *pendejo*; after all, the word should have been nothing particularly apropos criminals in the city. But the words he found, his analysis of them, seem like still images of what should be a moving picture. For instance, he registered two important words that speak broadly to gentrification of lowbrow language: *acuache (acuachi)* and *xido.* Following Rovelo and Ramos i Duarte, Wagner defined the first as "friend, comrade, ally," coming from the Nahuatl *acoatzin,* meaning water snake, though Wagner added, based on Fray Alonso de Molina's Spanish-Mexican dictionary (1571), *coatl* indeed meant snake, but also twin. Wagner quoted Lucio de Mendieta's *Historia Eclesiástica de las Indias,* where it was explained that the Aztecs believed that when twins were conceived either the mother or the father would inevitably die. Wagner found the expression in popular newspapers that employed the city's vernacular; that is, *La Guacamaya* (which Wagner defined as "Centavo-Blatt mit Gesprächen in volkstümlicher Rede"), in which he discovered the illustrative phrase "me tocó ganar, ya era justo *cuatito*" (it was my turn to win, it was only fair *cuatito* [little brother, pal, chap]). In any case, this word is at the origins of *cuate* (friend), without which the *chilango* language could not exist. *La Guacamaya* provided a forum for the imitation of the city's voices, and it is clear that by the early twentieth century, *cuate*—a *chilango* term par excellence—was already indispensable. By the 1920s it was a common term, truly a part of the language of the city, no longer a *Rotwelsch.* So much so, as I show below, that women aiming at crafting their own proletarian style often used *cuate, cuatita, cuatazo.*

The second word, *xido,* is equally important. Wagner found that its meaning in La Colonia de la Bolsa was "good," "acceptable," "nice," coming, he surmised, from Portuguese and Gallego *calo,* with the same meaning. Very likely Wagner was right, but in fact this is the register of the word *chido*: the mark of Mexico City's popular language throughout the 1940s and 1950s, which by the 1980s was appropriated by elites and is now a *chilango* trademark. In the 1980s, Mexico City's most popular rock band, El Tri, sang that Mexicans constituted "la raza más chida/del reino animal" (the coolest people/in the animal kingdom).[31] *Chido* less than the mark of being Mexican was and is the mark of speaking Mexico City.

Wagner found other telling words still in regular use in the city's language: *mayate* (literally a kind of flying insect; the word was used in La Colonia de la Bolsa in 1919, according to Wagner, to mean *aktiver Päderast* and is still in use in the *calo* of Mexico City with the same meaning), *meco* (from *chichimeco*, meaning Indian: urban poor), *mota* (marihuana; use of the word found also in Cuba), *chile* (penis), *cuico* (policeman), and the contemporary term *buey* or *güey*, then meaning, according to Wagner, *aktiver Päderast*, which today is the ultimate all-purpose word used to address a friend or an ally, to call someone stupid, or simply to connect sentences. Wagner also found other terms which are less common today: *gumarros* (testicles), *jaño* and *jaña* (man and woman), *tener grima* (being afraid), *yemis* (I, mine), and *berbear* (to say).

Wagner's logophilia led him to collect *altisonante* words in Mexico City's La Colonia de la Bolsa, in Barcelona, in the language of *Pachucos*, and in the language of Lisbon.[32] Mexican criminologists, among them the well-known Julio Guerrero and Carlos Roumagnac, also collected *calo* in Mexican prisons. Roumagnac in 1904 gathered criminals' words, such sonorous words—also found by Wagner—as *molleja* (watch), *xido*, *mayate*, and *gacho* (a mean person)—the latter a very important word by the 1930s, indispensable in the language of the city, which nonetheless in 1904 meant, according to Roumagnac, "fake witness." Roumagnac also included life stories, which were edited to avoid swearing and bad language; he included, nevertheless, some snapshots of vulgar eloquence, such as "Arapame la sutia para sutiar a teseo" (hand me the knife to hit this one) or the telling "Berbeale a teso" (say something to this one).[33] By the end of the 1940s, a Mexican-American linguist, Renato Rosaldo, researching Mexico City's colloquial expressions, found *gacho* to mean "lacking in gracefulness," *pinche* to mean "disgraceful," and of course *pendejo*, which he translated as "unpleasant person, dope, sty poor."[34] Without *gacho*, *pinche*, and *pendejo*, *chilangos* would be mute.

As late as 1942, the collection of words in Mexico City continued. Then Alfredo M. Saavedra, in "El caló de la delicuencia y la expresión sexual," joined logophilia with the psycho-identitology and Freudian trend that prevailed in Mexico and the world during the 1930s and 1940s and gave rise to such books as *El pérfil del hombre y la cultura en México* (Samuel Ramos, 1934) and even *El laberinto de la soledad* (Octavio Paz, 1950)—both books, to be sure, draw heavily on the lasting fascination with popular language. "An obsession with the vulgar and the scatological," argued Saavedra, "is typically found in this vocabulary as an expression of psychological states linked to inadequacy, ignorance, malice, and satire that violate the nobility of sex."[35] This was probably explained by a long-standing Mexican inferiority complex. Saavedra recorded important *chilango* terms such as *abuzado* (be ready, be careful), *bato* (chap, friend, colleague), *caifaz* (yes), *cuarenta y uno* (a homosexual man), *chota* (police), *empedarse* (get drunk), *grifa* (marijuana), *mordida* (bribe), *valedor* (a friend, a trustworthy person), and *coger* (to copulate). He also found sonorous terms that today are not often used in *chilango* and show the same creative obscenity: *castigadita* (a woman who can stand the sadism of a pin), *leo* (a homosexual man), *argolla, ojete, remolino* (anus), *bacalao* (for female genitalia), *bajonazo* (oral sex), *cabezón* (penis), and *mecos* (semen). As evocative as all of these terms are, they provide, nonetheless, only a snapshot of the city's language, not a full account of its life and dynamism.

But *palobrotas* in action can be found in past evidence elsewhere. We know that in private, Mexican bohemians inhabited the language of the city and used blasphemy and obscenity, but they never attempted to truly speak *chilango*. Likewise, poor urban women were masters of *chilango* with their eloquent swearing. But these anonymous women were not writers, painters, or intellectuals so as to leave record of their language. By 1920, however, there were women who, in trying to craft their identities as independent, revolutionary, avant-garde, and sexually liberated women consciously tried to speak genuine *chilango*. Of course, they were not the only people doing it, and perhaps they were exceptions, but the fact remains that this conscious attempt to fully speak *chilango* appears (at least in my research) only in the private letters of women. In speaking as if *entre hombres* (among men), they inhabited and helped to mold the language of the city. I am referring to such women as Frida Kahlo, Lupe Velez, Guadalupe Marín, Esperanza Domínguez, Concha Michell, Anita Brenner, and Frances Toor.[36]

As late as the 1940s, such female writers as Magdalena Mondragón wrote novels about the city, using vivid metaphors but never actually attempting to speak *chilango*.[37] Another strong woman, Guadalupe Marín, who was part of the world of female bohemians living in the 1920s and 1930s—and was married to Diego Rivera and then Jorge Cuesta—, in her autobiographical novel, *La única* (1938), did speak in the voice of the city, sadly without any swearing. In commenting on the misdiagnoses by various doctors of her illnesses, she wrote in a melodic and graphic *chilango* still hindered by the decorum required of the printed word:

Entre las tripas de vaca . . . y las lenguas de toro. Junto a los gusanos de maguey . . . y los acociles. Junto a los vendedores de nopales . . . y del ahuatle. Con el olor del papaloquelite y del cilantro, del orégano . . . y la cebolla. Llamaré a las de los ahuilores, y los capulines, a la de los camichines, y allí en medio de esa gente quiero decir mi discurso, en medio de esa gente gritaré: a ellos son a los que quiero libertar de la explotación y de la farsa, y me oirán hablar así: Médicos de todo el mundo: médicos de las ciudades; . . .[38]

This is impossible to translate fully:

Amidst cow guts . . . and bull tongues. Between maguey worms and crawfish (*acociles*). Next to *nopal* and *ahuatle* [a type of insect egg] vendors. With the smell of *papaloquelite* [summer cilantro] and cilantro and oregano . . . and onion. I'll call the women who sell *ahuilores*, the one who sells *capulines* (a type of cherries) and the one who sells *camichine* and there, in between those people I will pronounce my speech, in the middle of those people I will yell: it is you I want to liberate from exploitation and farce, and they will hear me speak as follows: Doctors worldwide: city doctors . . .

In private, of course, Marín had no problem telling her friends that her late husband, Jorge Cuesta, was "un puto inmundo" (a repulsive fag). Inhabiting this language became the path to becoming a truly modern Mexican revolutionary woman.

Let us listen to the development of this language by women. In September 1924, Frida Kahlo wrote to Anita Brenner, in a consciously crafted *chilango* that was published nowhere at the time: "Tú eres de las meras buenas, Anita linda, cuate del alma, tu carta me dio hartos impetus de aguantar a lo machín la pedrada. Pensé que hay todavía gente 'riata' en este pinche mundo y tú eres de las meras 'güenas' que no se rebientan ni a mentadas de madres" (You are one of the best, beautiful Anita, dear friend, your letter gave me lots of reason to keep on going. It made me think that there are still good people in this fucking world and you are one of the very good ones who don't fall apart even when having insults hurled at them). Of course, the translation does not convey the strong attempt to speak like the streets. In discussing her relationship to Diego Rivera she wrote to Brenner that "por Belcebú o por gestas, que chingaderas son estas." (Impossible to convey the sonorous nature of this. Something like "For the Devil's sake, for whatever, what the fuck is all this.") Diego had asked her to return to him, "pero estoy todavía 'clachando' hasta que punto tiene uno la cabeza 'agüeyada.'" (Meaning, but not really, "I'm still figuring out whether I'm in my right mind.")[39] Here we have a sample of pure and sonorous *chilango*, of course consciously articulated to the point that Kahlo herself used quotation marks when making use of the language of the city. She used, as Brenner did, the terms *pendejo*, *pendejada*, and *pendeja* freely and sonorously. And she called Anita's daughter *chilpayatita*, a term often registered by philologists as the way the urban poor in Mexico City referred to children. Frida used this language as she used her Tehuana outfits: at certain times, with great care for the context, and with the aim of carefully crafting her own personality as a modern woman, artist, and political actor. Most of her letters were written in a more standard Spanish prose. For instance, in October 1934, after her separation from Rivera, she wrote to Ella and Bertram Wolfe in clear and eloquent Spanish: "Hace tanto tiempo que no les escribo que ya no sé ni por dónde empezar esta carta. Pero ya no les quiero dar largos y aburridos pretextos y decirles luengas historias de por qué no les escribí en tantos meses. Ustedes saben todo lo que ha pasado, y creo que entenderán mi situación, aunque no les diga los detalles. Nunca había sufrido tanto y nunca creí resistir tantas penas." (It has been so long since I've written you that now I don't even know where to begin this letter. But I don't want to bore you with long and tedious pretexts and to tell you protracted tales about why I have not written you in so many months. You both know everything that has happened, and I believe that you will understand my situation, even if I don't give you the details. I had never before suffered so much and I never believed I could put up with so much grief.)[40] On another occasion, however, in 1936, Frida wrote to the Wolfes inviting them to visit her in Mexico City using a mixture of English and *chilango*: "What do you wait kid? Please don't te rajes y don't te cuartees, pues ya me estoy haciendo hartas ilusiones pa' cuando ustedes lleguen a este populoso y nunca bien ponderado Mexicalpán de las tunas."[41]

In the same way, Frances Toor appropriated *chilango* in her effort to assimilate—as an American woman—into revolutionary Mexico. She wrote in 1932 to Diego Rivera describing how she and Concha Michell sang ballads collected in the city, full of *palabrotas*. She signed off with evident pride at her *chilango*:

> Te mando muchos besos
> Grandes abrazos y harto amor,
> Que no te los quite la Chicha [Frida Kahlo],
> Huevona, cabrona y sin pudor.
>
> I'm sending you many kisses,
> Big hugs and so much love,
> Make sure la Chicha [Frida Kahlo] doesn't take them away from you
> Shameless bum that she is.

Rivera—who unlike Kahlo never truly commanded English—responded as "Diego el Conquistador":

Les restregué en la jeta [to some communists]
sus pendejadas en México
y no hubo un solo cabrón
que abriera su gran cajeta
pa' responder al jalón
que les vacié en la maceta.

I rubbed in their [some communists'] faces
all their *pendejadas* in Mexico
and there was not a single jerk
who opened his big mouth [also vagina]
to respond to the reproach
I threw in their face.

Anita Brenner, in turn, in her own diary used *chilango* often, commenting, for instance, on a love affair (January 12, 1925): "Me lo trago. Jovencito que yo creía logrado aparentemente no resultó . . . soy una desgraciada. . . . vida de pendeja . . . . . . !qué diablos me importa!" (I'll suck it up. The young guy I thought I had in my pocket didn't come through . . . I'm a wretch. What a mess all over again . . . miserable life. . . . . . what the hell do I care!) In her diaries Brenner constantly mixed the language of Mexico City with English, and talked of parties, meetings, and groups as if speaking *chilango* were very chic among certain intellectuals. And it was, especially after 1920. At last the high-class language of the city completed its gentrification of the language of the streets, becoming the latest fashion.

Very likely aware of this gentrification, common among women, another female intellectual and sponsor of many cultural bohemians, Antonieta Rivas Mercado, consciously tried to be a modern, liberated woman (she was the lover of José Vasconcelos) without adopting *chilango*. "No soy una mujer moderna," she wrote to a friend in 1929, "si por moderna se entiende que domina, como virtuoso, el problema sexual . . . No soy moderna porque doy al amor en general y al acto sexual en particular, una importancia otra que lavarme la boca o tomar un baño." (I am not a modern woman if what is understood by modern is a woman who dominates the sexual question as if it were a virtue . . . I am not modern because I take love in general, and sex in particular as something more than washing out my mouth or taking a bath.) It was her genteel Spanish more than her ideas about sex that demonstrated that she did not want to be a "modern woman." To speak *chilango* was becoming an integral part of the profile of the modern bohemian woman, but Rivas Mercado wrote in 1931: "I want to immerse myself in what is purely Mexican, without 'jicarismos' [blind imitation of local forms], without anyone thinking to bring up 'local color.'"[42]

Soon, the movie industry began using this local language in films set in the city—of course in a sanitized version. And in 1932, a novel by Rubén Salazar Mallén, *Cariátide*, was published in installments in the magazine *Examen*, which was censored as a result. Its publication created a vociferous scandal—and the year was 1932! The novel was never published in its entirety, but what was published was in pure *chilango* and was uncensored. Just a sample, with no translation:

> "La güera atraviesa el jardín. En una banca fuma un vagabundo joven que silba entre dientes
> —uuuuuh, piruja . . .
> La güera se acerca a un Ford verde que está frente al Salón México, sube al lado del chofer.
> —¿qu'ihbo?—pregunta éste.
> —ni la cruz me he hecho—contesta ella.
> —ya te lo he dicho, ya te lo he dicho—rezonga el chofer—Por aquí ni que te pongas a que das cachuchazo. . . . Lo mero bueno está en Argentina, por ai [*sic*] sí hay un bute de majes.
> . . .
> —si me empedo no l'importa a ningún jijo de la chingada—replica el chofer
> Pinche carcacha.[43]

This novel, and the aforementioned women, constituted the first records of the full use of *chilango*. Neither folklorists nor avant-garde writers and artists could yet say or represent the unrepresentable that was, nevertheless, all too prevalent in the city: a scene dominated by obscenity and vulgarity. Therefore, the appropriation of the vulgar was always a *colección*, a selection, an adaptation of popular forms, language, and music, never their spontaneous expression. But the process was far from a Machiavellian or one-sided phenomenon: the popular classes themselves were providing the necessary "popular" features for the collection to be titled "popular culture," and thus were stimulated to produce one and not other forms or styles, and in turn were blending different popular styles and appropriating more refined styles.

End

These are a few glimpses of the noises and intonations of the city that ended up constituting the *chilango* language. To this eloquence I can add no more.

THE STREET MUSE

In city streets everywhere resides *la musa callejera*, the street Muse, as writer, politician, and liberal leader Guillermo Prieto named her, for "a rua é a transformadora das línguas" (the street is the transformer of language), as wrote João do Rio, a carioca flâneur, in 1902. The Muse appears in the streets as an anonymous and unexpected form of inspiration. A young Alfonso Reyes found, in 1912, that it was in the *vulgo* of his city that the natural meaning of words and things could be discovered. The meaning of things, he said, *se ha refugiado* in the *vulgo*, which speaks in riddles: the night becomes "the black lady," and the morning "the blond."[1] Thus the street Muse inspired the development of Mexico City's unique language. She was made of the magnetism of rapidly changing utterances, the overwhelming descriptive temptation produced by buildings, people, windows, faces, façades, and gazes. The Muse was just as much at the root of the incessant draw of the obscene, the vulgar, and the anonymous as she was the inspirer of an obsession with scientific and literary neologisms or the unstoppable search for new and unique styles. The growing modern city inhabited the blend of three centuries of encounters of European and Indigenous languages, and its growth gave rise to the renaming of all things, and to a nostalgia for old names.

The street Muse inspired Prieto to capture the language of the city in his accounts of its daily events in various newspapers and magazines (chronicles that were published in 1883 as *Musa callejera*). But there is something to words that ensures that any play on them is neither totally new and random nor absolutely isolated and calculated. In literature, in the 1860s Francisco Manuel Altamirano had pioneered the movement to create a national literature by articulating the "genuine" language of the people, especially rural people. In fact, this translation and transcription in a way marked the end of oral traditions, because "the language of the city tends to become petrified in formulas and 'slogans' and thus suffers the same fate as popular art, becoming an industrial artifact."[2] And yet, Prieto tried to capture the street Muse in the form of the old

Spanish *letrillas*, *romances*, and *cancionsillas*. He blended what he constructed to be the popular speech of the urban poor with romantic, liberal, and scientific similes. Luisa and Tules, for instance, young women living in one of the city's *vecindades*, tell each other of their respective amorous yearnings. Tules is in love with the son of a launderer; she is a woman who is "rediabla/industriala muy aquello" (astute with wicked intentions, made so by the rough experiences of life) and whose mouth is like a "boca de infierno" (one of the inferno's entrances), making free use of obscenities. Her prospective mother in law is thus a woman feared in the day-to-day battle of tongues on the street. When Tules's mother and the mother of Fidencio (the man in question) do verbal battle on the street, Fidencio exercises his street eloquence, an eloquence that, at least in Prieto's ironic rendering, dignifies popular speech—generally considered "bad" Spanish—by applying it to universal concepts of freedom and equality:

—¡Juera curiosas!—Siñoras
muncha atención y silencio:
será Tules mi siñora
mas que rabien los infiernos.
Vayasté, siñora madre:
Suegra amada, el peje quieto,
Que yo soy un suidadano
Y conozco mis derechos.[3]

Get out of here you gossipy women! Ladies, listen closely: Tules will be my wife, however much hell may rage. Leave, mother; my dearest mother-in-law, keep your mouth shut, for I am a citizen, and I know my rights.

These verses allude, in evoking the sounds of Mexico City's *barrios*, to an urban language. But they do no more than allude to this language, for the transcriptions inspired by the street Muse were simultaneously an ethnology of and a dialogue with the developing language of the city's growing working class, servants, immigrants, middle class, and outlaws. It was thus never a question of simply transcribing such utterances, it was above all the revolt of words.

In order to at once chitchat with the street Muse and somehow explain her appeal, I submit various vista points, all of which converge, from different angles, in the street Muse. Logophilia is the first point from which to observe a global nineteenth- and early twentieth-century trend—the fascination with words all over the world—in its local expression. A second vista point is the coyness of words; that is, a view to the moral, poetic, and social introversions of the city's words in print, what they said, what they might mean to say. In turn, the street Muse as the dual process of gentrification of popular language (*anacamiento*) and proletarization of highbrow language (*acatrinamiento*) is another angle from which to look at the dynamic and promiscuous mélange of words in the city. But to truly grasp the language of the city between 1880s and 1930s, the 1910 Revolution needs to be considered like the French or the Soviet Revolution: as attempts to name the unnamable, to coin a new idiom for a new era. Thus the Revolution becomes a last point from which to observe the revolt of the vulgar, the emergence of a new social rhetoric, and the impact of radio and the Revolution on the city's language.

Logophilia

Beginning in the late eighteenth century and throughout the nineteenth century, there arose an obsession with the origins of language; scholars and the popular press were fascinated with Champollion and the Rosetta stone. In Madrid, for instance, by 1900, there had already been an attempt to modernize the Spanish language in literature. Carlos Arniches sought to speak like "the people" for, much like the German romantics, he considered the real spirit (*genio*) of a country to reside in the language of its people. Benito Pérez Galdós—the most prominent Spanish writer of the late nineteenth century— was said to have sought inspiration from no classical Muse, no Clio, but rather from *Mariclío*, the Muse of History who wore only *paños menores* (underwear), inspired by the traditions of the street and popular oral traditions. By the 1920s, José López Silva had forged a rich and vibrant language for Madrid. Indeed, since the mid-nineteenth century, Spain's literature had included what were called *hablas dialectales*, exemplified, for instance, in *Escenas andaluzas* by Serafín Estébanez Calderón or in *Cuentos andaluces* by Fernán Caballero.[4] Along similar lines, turn-of-the-century Buenos Aires, at the time a dynamic linguistic mélange, embarked upon the canonization of the Gaucho speech of Martín Fierro. Writers such as Leopoldo Lugones and Evaristo Carriego brought to life the language of the city, proving that Spanish could lose some of its verbosity while remaining conceptually baroque—a transformation of the Spanish language that would reach its sublime climax in another *porteño*: Jorge Luis Borges who was, as we know, mesmerized by the street Muse in Buenos Aires.

In the world of Mexican letters, José Joaquín Fernández de Lizardi's *El periquillo sarniento* (1816), a novel inspired by the Spanish *novela picaresca*, already sought to put the language of the streets into print. Lizardi told stories that brought to light the self-consciousness of the urban poor, aware of the ways their language differed from that of the upper class, employing what would later become common expressions in the city, terms such as *achicharrado* (scorched), *barbaján* (someone who is rough/uncouth), and *chiripa* (luck, a fluke, chance).[5]

Perhaps one of the most visible allures of the street Muse was that very obsession with language that boomed in Mexico City as a part of the pan-Hispanic linguistic consciousness that flourished between the 1880s and the 1930s. Late nineteenth-century cities, in both the Americas and Europe, developed in the shadow of their respective national languages, and hundreds of "erudite" experts on language emerged to protect, transform, regulate, and study the nuances of languages. The scientific zeitgeist and the romantic search for uniqueness and genuineness found in language a perfect marriage.[6] Evolutionary and sentimental schemata were developed to explain the origins of language and of the genius (*genio*) of different peoples. By 1921, after years of language research, Edward Sapir found it necessary to call for a return to the concept of "drift" to overcome the mystical quality of language and thus see it as constant and directionless change.[7]

What was then known as the German school of philology was paramount to the study of language in all countries, regardless of the language at hand. Wilhelm von Humboldt and August Schleicher became players in many national histories. In Mexico, Francisco Pimentel, considered in the nineteenth century to be one of Mexico's greatest philologists, summarized the achievements of the German and French schools in his *Cuadro descriptivo y comparativo de las lenguas indígenas de México: o tratado de filología mexicana* (1874–75). Manuel Orozco y Berra and Joaquín García Icazbalceta were two other important modern philologists in the latter half of the nineteenth century; the former mapped Mexican languages, the latter undertook the first dictionary of Mexican Spanish (of *mejicanismos* or *mexicanismos*), although he never finished it—he died in 1894 with the dictionary only having reached G. Francisco Javier Santamaría, an important philologist from the 1920s, undertook the continuation of García Icazbalceta's labors. He completed it in 1959 at the age of seventy; it remains the most authoritative dictionary of Spanish in Mexico.[8]

The *genio* of Spanish speakers in Europe and America, however, was seen to reside in Spain. Thus the Hispanism of the late nineteenth and early twentieth centuries coincided with the dictates of a long-standing romantic philology that attempted to locate the spirit of the people in the language of the commons. In this sense Mexico City was at the center both of a reevaluation of the language of Cervantes and of numerous nationalist quests to discover the spirit of the Mexican people in its language.

From Marcelino Menéndez y Pelayo, Julio Cejador y Frauca, Adolfo Bonilla, and Ramón Menéndez Pidal, to Francisco Giner de los Ríos, Miguel de

Unamuno, Ángel Ganivet, and José Ortega y Gasset, the Spanish language acquired a hitherto unknown archival, ethnological, political, philosophical, and philological consciousness of itself. An important part of this enterprise was the search for the spirit of popular language. In the eyes of its students, the Spanish language appeared as a beautiful example of Spanish heroism and greatness vis-à-vis the ugliness and power of other languages and other nations. This spirit was sought by philologists in Mexico, such as Féliz Ramos i Duarte, for whom "the interior life of a people is revealed in its language, which is people's way of life, their heart . . . their all." But "real" languages needed to be purged of "those vicious locutions and turns of phrase that we have heard amongst commoners and read in newspapers, books, [. . .] speeches, etc., which we have substituted for the proper [castizo] ones."[9] It was in the twentieth-century philosophy of José Vasconcelos that this romantic view of casticismo (pure Castilian) most fully expressed itself in Mexico; it was a casticismo that gradually accepted the mestizaje in language not solely as a Mexican patrimony, but also as renewal in the New World of the great spirit of Spain.

But language itself, in the obsessive consciousness of its architecture and function, was a contested realm. Mexican philologist Miguel G. Revilla opposed Spanish writer Cejador y Fracua's views, and argued for the tight control of the evolution of language as well as for the superiority of erudite over vulgar Spanish. Another Mexican philologist, Darío Rubio, complained both of the mejicanismos collected by Ramos i Duarte and of the negligence of the Spanish Royal Academy, which did not accept the entire list he and his collaborators had sent to the academy. Of the 1,285 words from Mexican Spanish, only 652 were published in the twelfth edition of the Diccionario de la Real Academia de la Lengua. Rubio insisted that those mexicanismos accepted by the academy presented an absurdly distorted vision of the language.[10]

In 1921, Santamaria, while completing García Icazbalceta's dictionary, wrote the most ironic critique of the general lack of comprehension of mexicanismos. He condemned both Ramos i Duarte's dictionary ("the worst offense to Mexican philology") and the recently published Suplemento de todos los diccionarios enciclopédicos españoles, by Ranato de Alba. Of the latter's definition of the Mexican term jipato (someone who is pale) as "someone who is hysteric," Santamaría wrote, in a sentence dripping with irony and faux respect, "esto tiene las trazas de un disparate que merece el honor de llamarse solemne" (this has all of the signs of an act of idiocy that deserves the honor of being called superb).[11]

Words were thus circulating throughout the Spanish-speaking world, and every one was contested. Lépero, one of Mexico City's terms par excellence, describing the urban poor, was defined by the academy as: "Dícese de la ínfima plebe en la Ciudad de Méjico" (applied to the poorest plebs in Mexico City) but was never actually described as "applied to persons." Rubio complained: "because the definition is written in such a way, those that form that class of Mexicans that the academy refers to have not even reached the category of persons, remaining instead in an inexplicable and unknown zoological category." For Rubio, *léperos* were people and they certainly did not belong to the *ínfima* strata, for in Mexico City, he explained, plebe is "the dregs of Mexican society, within which there are no possible gradations or classifications; it is a uniform group."[12] In Rubio's mind, vulgarity was the supreme equalizer. For his part, Santamaria rejected de Alba's definition of *cajeta* (relegated by de Alba to describing a small box). For Santamaria, *cajeta* meant much more: any kind of candy, a sweet, and a specific Mexican version of caramel. The word, however, also had vulgar connotations in Mexico City: "*Cajeta* connotes the intimate parts of a woman in the language of *léperos* and loose women . . . this usage of the word has no other origin than that of comparing a sort of sweet or a candy to that part of the woman that incites the carnal desires of man."[13] Of course, these nuances were lost in de Alba's understanding of *cajeta*. But Santamaria's own formality did not allow him to see the furtive eloquence of the vulgar use of *cajeta*, which combined its multiple meanings, "small box" and "candy," a combination that increased its vulgarity, but also its marvelous expressiveness.

Local linguistic forms, both popular and erudite, had irreversibly marked the language of the city. Revilla, a great supporter of the unity of the language, heard in Mexico City's speech a unique slow cadence, different from that of peninsular Spanish. The language of Mexico City tended to lengthen the last or second-to-last syllable when the accent falls there. This furnished the city's language with a *lánguida dulzura* (languid sweetness) that was, to many, a welcome addition to the abrupt and coarse language of Madrid. But Mexico City's people spoke with too many useless connectors (*este*, ¿*no*?, and *pues*), which were a real *peste* in the language, or so Revilla thought. Nevertheless, "it is rare to hear in that land [Mexico City] disagreeable or high-pitched voices." The language of Mexico City did not experience, then, the radical experimentation of Buenos Aires, but neither did it retain the sharpness of Madrid; language in Mexico City, for all of its provincialisms, was often considered to contribute to the politeness of the Spanish language.[14]

Nothing illustrates better the logophilia of the late nineteenth and early twentieth centuries than the search for the *romances*—ancient Spanish popular stanzas. This was ultimately a search for the authenticity and wisdom of the Spanish language. Mexico City was one of the leaders in this quest. Menéndez y Pelayo first, and then, famously, Menéndez Pidal and his group that congregated at the Centro de Estudios Históricos de Madrid undertook massive ethnographic and philological work across Spain and throughout the rest of the world. They sought popular *romances*, which retold events and recounted stories of love and betrayal in a language that blended refined terms with popular forms. These *romances* were found everywhere in the written and oral memories of towns and cities, in their frequent use by authors, and in orally transmitted local versions of songs and poems. Until the late nineteenth century, Menéndez Pidal explained, it was believed that no *romances* existed in the Americas. But starting in the 1890s, thousands of different versions of *romances* were found in the Americas by folklorists and philologists—including by Menéndez Pidal himself, who traveled to Peru, Colombia, Ecuador, Argentina, and Uruguay.[15] A great exchange of information and collaboration took place among the Peruvian, Argentinean, Mexican, Spanish, Catalan, U.S., Galician, Portuguese, and Sephardic scholars in search for the traditional voices. Notebooks and the first (wax) phonographic devices were used to record these linguistic discoveries. Ardent logophiles had to mingle with their "informants," those who spoke the language of the city.

Menéndez Pidal found that since the Conquest, "in the memory of each captain, each soldier and each businessman, there was a trace of the then wildly popular Spanish *romancero.*" With the help of philologists of the Americas, many *romanceros* were published between the 1890s and the 1930s. Many local philologists not only undertook the search for Spanish *romances*, but also unearthed local songs, tonalities, and terms. Juan León Mera in Ecuador published *Cantares del pueblo ecuatoriano* (1892); in Santiago de Chile, Julio Vicuña Cifuentes distributed among his students his *Instrucciones para recoger de la tradición oral romances populares* (1905) and recorded the language of criminals in Santiago. Also in Chile, Rodolfo Lenz found many *romances*, children's stories, and what in Chile were called *corridos*—precisely the same forms that were found across Mexico: popular verses that told stories of events, battles, loves.[16] Simultaneously, in Portugal for the first time the songs of the medieval troubadour tradition were collected in libraries and oral traditions, serving as an important asset for the renewal of twentieth-century Portuguese and Galician literature and popular culture. The search for and obsession with popular language reached not only Mexico, but also New Mexico and Texas. The New Mexican philologist and folklorist Aurelio Espinosa collected Spanish children's stories and studied the popular Spanish of New Mexico. One can see the twentieth-century search for *corridos* by Texan folklorist Américo Paredes precisely along these lines, not only because *corridos* were evidently part of this long linguistic matrix, but because Paredes's very search was a part of the lasting effort to recuperate the popular roots of different versions of the Spanish language.[17] In this sense the *corrido* originated in rural society but was above all an urban discovery; it was not Texan, but neither was it Mexican; it was Spanish, Chilean, and Peruvian. In short, it was, and is, of the Spanish language.

Mexico City was an important site for those sharing in this obsession with language and words. As a result of this search for popular linguistic forms, in 1923 Pedro Henríquez Ureña taught a course at the Escuela de Altos Estudios of the National University on the popular elements of Spanish-American literature. One of his students, Bertram Wolfe, an inhabitant of what was then a very radical Mexico City, collected hundreds of *corridos*. Wolfe was not the only American doing this: from 1920 through the 1940s people like Frances Toor, Joseph Freeman, and also the Columbia-affiliated German anthropologist Franz Boas did the same. In 1931 *Mexican Folkways* produced a collection of Mexican popular songs, not all of them *romances*, but traditional stanzas nonetheless; the *Cancionero mexicano* even included a flattering blurb stating that "Mexican tunes used in Aaron Copland's El Salon Mexico were taken in part from this Cancionero."[18]

It was hard to find examples of *romances* in Mexico City and the surrounding area because, explained Henríquez Ureña, the *romance* had been buried "by the enormous blossoming . . . of popular poetry in Mexico, of songs and *corridos* or tragedies." Two of the most famous of these songs—in fact two old Spanish *romances*—were "La Delgadina," the story of an incestuous relationship, and "La adultera," the old story of a man gone to war and returning in disguise to seduce his own wife in order to test her faithfulness. Bertram Wolfe found these songs in Mexico City around 1920. Of course, these *romances* had been Mexicanized, and thus instead of talking about wars in Europe, "La adultera" talked about Puebla and the French army: "por las señas que me ha dado/su marido muerto es/el que en un sitio de la Puebla/lo mató el traidor francés" (From all the indications you have given me/your husband dead is/[he is] the one who somewhere in Puebla/was killed by the French traitor). In turn, the Mexican "Delgadina" talked not about a Castilian town, but about Morelia, but still mentioned as the incestuous character a king, Delgadina's father, as in *romances* collected in the Spanish peninsula or in Iraq's Sephardic communities.[19]

In 1912 and 1913, Franz Boas collected stories and songs in the areas surrounding Mexico City (Milpa Alta). What he found were striking parallels between the tales and stories found in Mexico City and those found in New Mexico by Aurelio Espinosa and by anthropologists studying African-American communities in the southern United States. Boas surmised that most of these stories must have the same Spanish origins. Many of the beautiful songs he found in the Mexican valley contained a delightful mixture of old Spanish poetry with a genuinely *chilango* flair.

In turn, in 1920, Mexican philologist Pablo González Casanova investigated Hispano-Aztec *corridos* in the Nahuatl-speaking environs of the city. He found what he called *corridos macarrónicos*, which were as burlesque and innovative in their use of Spanish as Italian seems in comparison to Latin. Since Nahuatl had been the lingua franca of central Mexico, many of the old Spanish *romances* and new oral ballads were full of Nahuatl terms.

In sum, Mexico City participated in full in the global bout of logophilia that struck at the end of the nineteenth and the beginning of the twentieth century. Various participants in this phenomenon lived and worked in the city, and the city was studied constantly because of the bizarre linguistic mixtures that it fostered. The intriguing history of Mexican philology is yet to be written, but any such history would naturally have to revolve around Mexico City, both as the point from which people looked outside, to towns and to the countryside, in a romantic search for an authentic Mexican language, and as a linguistic laboratory in its own right. The most important names in Mexican philology are to be found between 1880 and 1940: Miguel Salinas, Darío Rubio, Francisco Javier Santamaría, Francisco Castillo Nájera, Alberto María Carreño, José López Doñez, Nicolás León, Féliz Ramos i Duarte, Manuel G. Revilla, Alfonso Reyes, Pedro Henríquez Ureña, Amado Nervo, Mariano Silva y Acebes, Rubén N. Campos, and Pablo González Casanova. All of them—except for León and García Icazbalceta—lived and worked in and around Mexico City, although they also studied and wrote about the languages of other regions.

Foreigners were also important, and as a rule of thumb there seem to always be one or two German scholars for any given language in the world. Max L. Wagner (1880–1962), as I have explained (chapter 11), was a prolific philologist who pioneered the study of poor *barrios* in the city, such as La Colonia de la Bolsa. He was likewise a student of many other romance languages, especially Sardinian, but also Portuguese, Italian, Catalan, Sephardic Spanish, and even Mexican Pachuco in the United States. Other foreign scholars contributed to the study of the languages of Mexico, including F. Semeleder, Sommer, C. Carroll Marden, and Franz Boas. Nascent concern with language was solidly institutionalized in the creation of the Mexican chapter of Spain's Royal Academy of Language, the Real Academia de la Lengua: an important moment for the official study of language in the late nineteenth century. The branch was established in 1874 with a mandate to intervene in what was seen to be the dire situation of Spanish in Mexico. The first Mexican members of the Academy to study the language were all from Mexico City. Many intellectuals participated in the academy between 1880 and the 1940s, but despite its output and authority, the academy remained relatively marginal in the "logophilic fever" of the late nineteenth century.[20] For, as Mexican poet and dandy Manuel Gutiérrez Nájera put it in 1894, "before the academy accepted . . . the word *pulque*, there was already *pulque* [in the city] . . . We cannot say: let us drink the anonymous liquid."[21] The academy was a language police no one but writers obeyed.

The Coyness of Words

Precisely when cities were growing and languages were being dramatically transformed by the urban environment—when folklorists, novelists, poets, and philologists were enchanted by popular speech—Victorian-romantic mores made it impossible to print one of the largest portions of popular speech—that involving obscenity and swearing. Manuel Payno's *Los bandidos de Río Frío* (1889) emulated the language of outlaws in the highlands of Puebla and the Federal District, but no bad words were used. Luis Inclán's *Astucia, el jefe de los hermanos de la hoja, o Los charros contrabandistas de la rama* (1865–66) was perhaps one of the most interesting literary appropriations of the popular speech of the highlands of Michoacán and the State of Mexico, and yet it contains not a single swear word.[22] Better yet, in 1908 a philologist and writer—and member of the Mexican branch of the Real Academia de la Lengua—, Cayetano Rodríguez Beltrán, published *Pajarito*, a novel that with Victorian shame captured the melodious popular language of the Veracruz coast—an untranslatable rhythm of allusive but clean words: "ái ejtá la infelí de mi nieta que se le jué muriendo el marío en un sujpirar, pa dejarle el defunto un chorro de muchachoj ateníos al 'échame nana.'"[23] For the manifestation of this Victorian morality in Mexico was more complicated than a simple class distinction. It separated two speaking worlds—the world of the printed word and the oral *palabrería* of both masses and elites. Ultimately, the restrictions imposed by Victorian mores did little more than make popular cursing all the more appealing and the idea of a truly refined style seem all the more unreachable and outmoded.

Because of Victorian morality, these two worlds of words were more defined by male-female distinctions than by *catrín-roto* (rich-poor) differences. Wealthy men of the city, in the brothels and cantinas, surely used bad words and knew and exercised the utterances of the popular languages. Women from the lower class, as in Prieto's example, could have mouths like a *boca de infierno*, but any woman considered minimally decent was totally barred from the world of popular urban words. Language at its most laissez-faire was by and large *cosa de hombres* (men's business), although lower-class women joined in the "revolt of words," and women, as those who most directly imparted language to children, were clearly important actors in shaping the language of the city.

There were, of course, popular figures who became legends within intellectual circles thanks to the force of their tongues, but they were, so to speak, sanitized. The most popular was the eighteenth-century personality of the Negrito Poeta, whose verses were later included in the popular *Calendario del Negrito Poeta*, several editions of which were published throughout the nineteenth century. Ironically enough, Negrito's name was a pseudonym for none other than an eloquent José Vasconcelos (not to be confused with the twentieth-century intellectual with the same name). Negrito was a popular character in Mexico City, and Guillermo Prieto and many others repeated his anecdotes. It is impossible to know the real authors of the many Negrito anecdotes that circulated during Porfirian times. Nevertheless, his aphoristic irony and enjoyment of the textures of the city's languages were then legendary, and still resound today. In one piece, Negrito wrote of a friend, a Maldonado who sought to live within a Franciscan convent:

Nunca serás bien Donado
aunque digan que eres santo;
bajo el franciscano manto
siempre serás Mal-Donado.

You will never be blessed/gifted [bien donado]
even if they call you a saint
beneath the Franciscan cloak
you will always be cursed/poorly gifted [mal donado].

This form of ironic play with the nuances of language was so beloved, even without the use of swear words and "bad language," that it became a popular diversion both in literary salons and common cantinas. In another excellent example, a legend describes one friend of Negrito's becoming jealous of his girlfriend's admiration for Negrito. Negrito (Vasconcelos) responded:

El objeto idolatrado
Que es causa de tus desvelos
Cuando verlos has intentado
Siempre has ido y Vas-con-celos.

The idolized object
Which is the cause of your insomnias
Once you have tried to see them [the insomnias]
You have always and always will proceed with jealousy [Vas-con-celos].

In Spanish the stanza is simply a confession: your enemy is Vasconcelos (Negrito). Negrito was just one of the mythical heroes of the vernacular. Fernández de Lizardi mentioned him as part of the linguistic tradition of the city.[24] Negrito's rhetorical style became more than a person, a genre. Between 1880 and 1930 Luis G. Urbina, Gutiérrez Nájera, Rubén N. Campos, Jesús Valenzuela, José Juan Tablada, Salvador Novo, and Elías Nandino, among many others, were the great exponents of this genre. This was sanitized street Muse, when published, but by the 1920s the old anecdotes could be told without censorship. As a result, the historian is able to truly feel the texture of the *chilango* language percolating on the streets of the city. Rubén M. Campos recalled how a famous humorist, Federico Hernández, asked by someone on the street why he looked sad, improvised the following verse full of wit and vulgarity:

Eneas, mi perro querido,
murió, y aunque no lo creas
tanto, tanto lo he sentido
que aun estando bien dormido
sueño que me lame Eneas.[25]

Eneas, my beloved dog,
died and, though you may not believe it,
I missed him so, so much
that even in a deep sleep
I dream that Eneas is licking me [*me lame Eneas*].

Me la meneas also means "you play with my penis."

And Gutiérrez Nájera, Campos recalled in the 1920s, frequently wrote Negrito-esque verses. When he was introduced at the Palacio de Cristal Bar in Mexico City to lawyer Nicolás Bejarano, Gutiérrez Nájera improvised:

No me gusta, Bejarano,
tu apellido singular,
porque empieza por vejar
lo más delicado, ¡hermano!

I do not like, Bejarano,
your unique last name,
for it begins by humiliating [*b/vejar*]
the most delicate part [anus], brother!

The genre was the delight of city bohemians who, in private, used the language of the street in full. At times highbrow language blended with common "vulgar" expressions in this tradition of socializing and killing in verse. Musician Miguel Lerdo de Tejada, who began his career as a band conductor in the 1910 *Centenario* and whose fame soared in the 1920s with his Orquesta Típica Mexicana, was satirized by the modernist and refined poet Luis G. Urbina for wearing a military uniform:

Con tu vestido de cuero
y tu banda de reclutas
¿y de qué batallón de putas
serás capitán primero?[26]

There you go with your leather suit
and your band of recruits
tell me, in what battalion of whores
are you the first captain?

I hope the reader is able to feel the unique ironic texture of these verses, for this is what the city's language was made of, requiring, as the reader can imagine, wit and alertness, as well as a constant readiness to jump into the war of words. This is what early Mexican comedians played with, though of course they were limited by censorship. The genre, with the same erotic connotations, was used in the 1920s, though ultimately only released publicly in the 1980s, by the vanguardist bohemians of the city. Elías Nandino recalls that after Salvador Novo in 1920s outed him, poet Xavier Villaurrutia, Jorge Cuesta, and Alfonso Lazo as homosexuals (which they were) on a public bus, Nandino, Cuesta, and Villaurrutia wrote a poem for Novo:

Romula
Remula
de la antigua Roma
a quien todos llamamos Novalisa
y no es nova ni lisa ni por broma
Mujer corrida y sin punto ni coma
Debora Dora de la Longaniza
más vulgar que la torre de Pisa . . .[27]

Little could be added to these words, and a translation would only destroy the intense humor and vulgarity of the piece. And all of them, Novo, Villaurrutia, Nandino, Cuesta, and Lazo, were not only well-respected intellectuals, but erudite minds who spoke various foreign languages in addition to *chilango* and other forms of Mexican Spanish.

All in all, more than books, it was the ephemeral periodicals of Mexico City between the 1880s and the 1910s that violated linguistic and moral canons with humor and irony. There were *El fandango: bisemanal destinado exclusivamente a la defensa de la clase obrera, decidor de verdades, no farolero, y sostenedor de cuanto dice en cualquier terreno (no son papas ni mucho menos alverjones)* (1892) and *El Valedor: periódico joco-serio, ladino, chismoso, médico, loco y de todo un poco, lo que se llama entrón de al tiro!* (1884–85). Others were *El Nahual* (1885), *El Hijo del Valedor* (1886), *El Nieto del Valedor* (1888), *Don Pepito* (1892), *Juan Cuerdas* (1892), and *La Guacamaya* (1900s). Other periodicals, like the well-known *El Hijo del Ahuizote*, though ironic and humorous, did not seek to appropriate the popular language except sporadically.

These periodicals did what studious intellectuals attempted: they disseminated and gentrified popular speech. This was done by and large by workers who knew how to read and write and had access to presses. They followed trends similar to those occurring in popular songs, proletarizing highbrow language. *El Chahuistle* in 1910 engaged in a delicious mockery of the modernist language of the tune "El Murciélago" (see chapter 11), loaded with class resentment:

Alma gláuca
soy un pictórico versificante
de melenáceas, longas guedejas
de pectorales sensiliformes
y aglutinantes opalescencias,
fluviales chispas encefaloides inspiratrices,
esferoideas tonificantes—
espirituosas que en craneana caja abulean . . .[28]

". . . en craneana caja abulean," meaning "in a head": these elaborate and flowery Spanish wordplays were also satirized by important twentieth-century literary trends. Don Juan de Mairena, the fictitious rhetorics professor created by Spanish poet Antonio Machado in the 1930s, was perhaps the most lucid critic of the Spanish prose, and he was ironically imitated in "Murciélago." In one of his lessons, Mairena asks a student, first, to write the phrase "los eventos consuetudinarios que suceden en la rúa" (the habitual events that occur on the avenue); next, he asks the student to translate the phrase into a real poetic language. The student writes "lo que pasa en la calle" (what's going on on the street), and Mairena responds "No está mal" (not bad).[29] What Machado did, with economy of language, for pompous nineteenth-century Spanish prose, popular urban language did in Mexico City by taking that pomposity to absurd extremes.

In Porfirian times El *Valedor*—meaning, as German and Mexican philologists recorded it in the poor *barrios* of the city, trustful friend—was a longstanding workers' periodical that disseminated popular *parole*. The sarcastic and critical tone of the periodical was enabled by the changing name of its editor—to avoid censorship and to keep the joke running. On occasion the chief editor was (in characteristic *chilango* terms) Sacramento Chafa (fake sacrament), at other times Lucas el Brincón (rebellious madman). In 1885 a satire affirmed: "Tenemos orita, orita al de jumento [Fomento] vendiendo las tierras, tenemos toditos de votar, porque pareso semos suidadanos, y si no tomamos parte en las eleisiones, no tenemos derecho pa' quejarnos" (Right now we have the Public Works Ministry selling lands, we all have to vote, it is for that reason that we are citizens and if we don't participate in the elections we have no right to complain).[30] This was social criticism by militant and literate workers who consciously produced a sanitized version of the language of the streets, maybe in order to obtain popular support, maybe simply to show their radicalism by putting such language into printed letters.

In turn, La *Guacamaya*, a workers periodical that remained in print from the 1880s to the 1900s, was "un periódico hablador y de buen humor rebasilador y decididor de verdades, no papero no farolero, azote de los burgueses y defensor de la clase obrera"—a talkative and *rebasilador* (very funny) paper and a speaker of truths, not a *farolero* nor a *papero*, an antagonizer of the bourgeoisie and a defender of the working class (*farolero* was a common term in the city for pretentious, *papero* a way to say "brown-noser"). Its editorial line consisted of political criticism based on a "gentrification" of the language of the city, although it avoided any swearing. Its dialogues were inventive re-creations of the fluid and rapid exchange of words on the street:

> —pos nada, mano, que encontré a Matilde González, la muñequita, Felisa la moreliana y otras jañanas, nos juimos a revalsarla a Santanita y que nos vamos encontrando al jorobado
> —¿A cuál manario?
> —¡Como a cuál! aquél que se llama Rafael y que es las pilas de versador.[31]

This language—impossible to translate—is an exercise in the fast wit, the rhythmical nature, and the eloquence of popular words. Such a lively and fast-paced re-creation of the immediacy of street *parole*, however, sharply contrasted with what workers themselves wanted to write about. La *Guacamaya* offered a page for its readers to publish their own literary pieces, and in them, unlike on the editorial page, what we find is the usual, proletarian desire to discuss love, almost always in "high-class" Spanish, which then meant a gaudy blend of flowery romantic and modernist prose. In 1902, *La Guacamaya* thus featured a poem by Canuto Godínez Godínez, to Lupe:

> Pero, ven tierna paloma,
> de mi pecho flor galana,
> ven mi Lupe, ven ufana,
> que esto huele a sepultura;
> y ivamos!! se me figura
> que me he de morir mañana.[32]

> But, come here, tender dove
> handsome flower of my breast
> come here Lupe, come here cheerful one
> for it smells like a tomb to me;
> in sum, it seems to me
> that I must die tomorrow.

Not a single "vulgar" use of language appears in this poem; on the contrary, the excerpt demonstrates clear attempts to be *culto* (well-read): *ufana*, for example, or the use of *ivamos!!*, an elegant way of saying "in sum." In 1903, an anonymous reader published a sonnet in *La Guacamaya* in which this kitschy language was once again employed, this time in the service of proletarian resentment (with no attempt to gentrify the city's language, but proletarize the highbrow language):

> Deshoja el cierzo el árbol corpulento
> y eleva hasta las nubes la basura
> en fealdad se convierte la hermosura
> y en mendigo se trueca el opulento
> . . .
> y el mundo la sumerge en el olvido
> porque es ahora la sin par mesera
> una asquerosa e inmunda tortillera.[33]

> The northern wind tears the leaves off the robust tree
> and lifts garbage up to the clouds

all that is beautiful becomes hideous
and the affluent man becomes a beggar

. . .

And the world submerges her in oblivion
for the insurpassable waitress
is now a disgusting and filthy *tortillera.*

So the waitress, who had been the poet's lover, is paid back with this high language meant to ridicule her for being less than a waitress—a vulgar tortilla maker. (In current slang, *tortillera* also means a lesbian. I have found no reference to this meaning of the term in the collections of Mexico City slang from the 1870s to the 1930s. In Spain, however, *tortillera* had had that connotation since at least the 1920s.) Under the Porfiriato, it seems, the publishing and appreciation of popular language was the domain more of folklorists and politically minded intellectuals and editors than of a linguistically empowered working class.

In turn, during the revolutionary years urban journalists appropriated the language of the city for political and comic ends, often mocking politicians. In 1914, *Multicolor* published "La voz de la plazuela," criticizing the new revolutionary elite using a sanitized version of the city's common slang:

Son purititos bueyes
los que creen que todo
Se arregla con leyes.[34]

They are nothing but stupid
those who believe that everything
can be fixed with laws.

The poem ended with a laconic "Vamonos manario" (*mano* and *manario,* instead of *hermano,* brother, were commonly used in the city), a *cuico* (a police officer) is coming. Some of the reports of "La voz de la plazuela" even used English words, already commonplace on the streets, as a way of mocking elite language (1914):

Qué de noticias
las qui ora train,
son todititas
muy rete fáin.[35]

They bring
so much news
They are all
very *rete* fine

El *Microbio*—"diario muy tres piedras y un ojo parado"—also used street
language to mock and criticize such revolutionary luminaries as Francisco
I. Madero, often through sexual innuendos. In one instance, Madero was
criticized for having done nothing to break up the *pulque* monopoly: "Te
hemos ayudado a subir al guayabo y ahora que 'tas en él nos 'tás tocando el
instrumento" (We helped you to climb up the guava tree and now that you
are up there you are mocking us).[36] Guava tree has sexual innuendos, as well
"tocando el instrumento" (touching our sexual tools). The revolutionary government publications also jumped on board, following the latest fashion of
adopting and disseminating popular language. In official government publications poems appeared that most likely required translation for their elite
readers:

Ya sabes que te guardo en los nopales
pa' dar un vacilón, pos tengo ganas
de mercarte un culebro, unas campanas
y unos calcos lo menos de a diez riales.

You know that I'm waiting for you in the *nopales*
to give you a nice surprise, because I want
to give you a *culebro* (*rebozo*); some *campanas* (petticoats)
and some *calcos* (shoes) worth at least ten *riales*.

The writer footnoted the poem: *culebro* = *rebozo*; *calcos* = *zapatos*; and *campanas*
= *enaguas*.[37] In sum, the language of the city had become an insurmountable
aesthetic and political need. A need that was, nevertheless, limited both by the
impossibility of publishing "bad words" and by the very ephemeral character
of any popular language.

But undoubtedly one of the most sonorous appropriations of the common
language of the city over the revolutionary years was to be found in a simple
phrase in *El mero petatero* (1912), one that displays all of the vulgar eloquence
of the street: a woman speaking says, "Por diosito que soy como la ruda, que
jiedo más si me untan."[38] Touché!, I can neither translate nor paraphrase such
supreme eloquence.

Anacamiento, acatrinamiento

I suggest an admittedly all too general view on the function and operation of the street Muse in Mexico City from the 1880s to the 1930s. On the level of long-lasting historical phenomena, Mexico City was the stage for the daily linguistic revolt of the *rotos* (urban poor). This revolt was due, in part, to the growth of the city, the migration of thousands of people from different parts of the country to the capital, a dynamic that ultimately resulted in a radical metamorphosis of the language of the city. People from all parts of the country, but especially from the central states, moved to the capital, bringing with them their various versions of the Spanish language, their Indian languages, and their numerous and varying forms of "vulgar eloquence." Between 1895 and 1910, Mexico City received more than a fourth of the total internal immigration of the country. According to census information, the Federal District received about 188,000 immigrants in 1895 and 329,000 in 1910.[39] Based on the 1921 census, Pedro Henríquez Ureña estimated that by the early 1920s there were nearly a million Nahuatl speakers, the vast majority of them in the center of Mexico, especially in and around the capital.[40] Mexico City was also full of people from such states as Guanajuato, Jalisco, Michoacán, Queretaro, and Veracruz—all Spanish speakers, but with dissimilar words, intonations, and with their own unique, and often beautiful, vulgar vernaculars.

In addition, as Andrés Lira has shown, in the last part of the nineteenth century the Indian communities in and near Mexico City were fully incorporated into its urban development.[41] This marked the end of the "picturesque" dissonance between a rural Indian lifestyle and the urban life of the city: the Indian accent and intonation in Spanish now became an important component of the city's language. Indians were very much a part of the city; their language and mores were both rejected and absorbed; they were the *léperos*, the *nacos*, the *mecos*, the *calzonudos*, as the various dictionaries of *mexicanismos* registered them. The first major dictionaries, not of native languages, but of *aztequismos* in the Spanish language, appeared between 1860 and the 1920s, delineating for the first time a definitive profile of Mexican Spanish.[42] Over the course of the revolutionary years, Pablo González Casanova, Jorge Engerrand, and Franz Boas studied the storytelling of Milpa Alta and Xochimilco—Nahuatl-speaking towns very close to Mexico City. In these studies, transcribed in Nahuatl, the many Spanish words already included in the original versions stand out.[43]

For both locals and outsiders, the Indian influence was paramount in the creation of the language of the city. Philologist and writer Victoriano Salado Álvarez in the early twentieth century was adamant in his fight to keep a classical and "pure" Spanish on the streets of Mexico City: "Indians horribly destroy the language due to their lack of education, although this is also because of their capricious nature and their stubbornness; they say some words partially, refuse to make subject and verb agree, confuse masculine and feminine forms, don't follow the rules of conjugations, resulting in a gobbledygook that is sometimes funny and beneath which the naïve think they see the innocence and candor of the Indian, but that in truth only conceals wickedness and falsehood."[44] Before, in the 1880s, Salvador Quevedo y Zubieta, like many other writers up to the present, were both attracted by the sonority and repelled by the incorrectness of the Indian words and intonations employed by the Spanish of the city. One needs to hear the Mexican Indian, he wrote, "with the indolent and languid emission of his words in *xitli*, in *etl*, in *illi*, in *iltsi*, etc . . . to understand what the Greeks meant by song of honey (mellodia)."[45] In fact, during Porfirian times, when Mexican philologists sought to uncover the mysteries of Mexican Spanish—fighting against purist philologists in Spain—, they were just as fascinated by the influence of Nahuatl on the language of the city—thus the many dictionaries of *mexicanismos* and the extensive folkloric research—as they were eager to expand the teaching of "correct" Spanish to the lower classes.

But from the point of view of long-lasting trends, the effect of internal migration on the linguistic mélange that was Mexico City is only part of the story in this "revolt of the vulgar." Cosmopolitanism is another important facet. Foreigners arriving in late nineteenth-century Mexico City had an important social presence. According to the 1910 census, there were nearly 120,000 foreigners residing in Mexico, and only 9 percent of them in agricultural regions. Mexico City, at the turn of the century, had around 60,000 foreign inhabitants, mostly Spaniards and Americans, but also well-established French, English, Lebanese, Spanish, and German communities. Since the 1880s, the city counted American, French, and German schools.

French residents and the French language had an overwhelming presence among the city's elite. French was undisputedly the private code of the elites; it was taught in all the city's private and public schools, and any well-educated person was supposed to be able to recite a passage from Victor Hugo in French. "Maître Corbeau, sur un arbre perché, tenait en son bec un fromag . . . ," recited a little boy in the *barrio* school described by Ángel del Campo in the late 1890s—though the poem was indeed by Jean de la Fontaine.[46] French was everywhere in Mexico City but, unlike English today, its impact was reduced to its digestion by the elites and to their transmission of it to the masses.

By contrast, since the 1880s English has impacted not only the high classes, but has also been directly consumed by the country as a whole, thanks to the media and, above all, continuous migration back and forth between Mexico and the United States. By the 1940s, the *pachuco* language was made possible both by the existence of large Mexican communities in the southwestern United States and by the belief in the existence of a metropolitan, cosmopolitan Mexican Spanish, whose capital was Mexico City. Already in the 1940s, the so-called *pachuco* language started to be recorded in Mexico City's criminal and popular slang.[47]

In the early 1920s, American English and French were popularly mocked. A good example is a parody of the popular Adelita song, composed around 1910 and distributed in short-lived sheets of cheap paper. In it, the "Americanization" of women is criticized—women with short-hair, *pelonas*—and the French terms and American influences are blended with the Mexican terms (*enaguas* for the Spanish *naguas*):

Si Adelita estuviera pelona
una peluca la había de comprar
sus enaguas a la tut-ans-amon [*sic*]
para llevarla a Chicago a bailar.[48]

If Adelita were a *pelona*
we would have to buy her a wig
and her slips at the *tut-ans-amon* [*sic*]
to take her to Chicago to dance.

Starting in the 1880s, English became the bête noir of Mexican philologists and writers. Americans began to impact the language of the city through their presence in schools, sports, and industrial clubs, and through the introduction of American technology, as well as through massive investment by Americans in the city's infrastructure. English names, words, and phrases gradually became commonplace in the urban panorama. As the city grew, technology became more and more accessible, and people became familiar with the new meanings and words disseminated in instruction manuals and fashion magazines. It was not only intellectuals in the city, from Amado Nervo to Maples Arce, who found themselves fascinated by technology. Common people too were constantly exposed in the streets to the new technology and to the new names and terms that appeared on signs and all sort of machinery. "Portland" became a popularly used word, while the modernization of the city's infrastructure and social life was often seen as Americanization.

English was already so much a part of the city's voices that local advocates for the purity of the Spanish language began to complain. "Our language is undergoing today," wrote the Mexican philologist Alberto María Carreño in 1925, "one of the most blunt challenges: inventions, sports, and our constant and commercial contact with the North." Carreño decried the use of such words as "garage," "beisbol," "pichar," "batear," "cachear," "mitin," "líder," and chauffer." Along similar lines, Féliz Ramos i Duarte complained of the use of the word "dandy" in one of Justo Sierra's *Cuentos románticos* (1896). In seeking to eliminate these "barbarisms" from the Spanish language, he quoted a grammar manual produced in Madrid by the Real Academia de la Lengua (1895) that aimed explicitly at the "protection" of the language. The academy disapproved of the use of such terms as "dandy," "fashionable," and "meeting"—"one should say *caballeret, lechugino* [dandy], *elegante, estar de moda* [fashionable], *reunión, junta,* or *asamblea* [meeting]."[49] In turn, a city dandy, Gutiérrez Nájera, as early as 1890, complained about the Americanization of the city's language. The streets were full of English words and American investors who did not speak Spanish. They were, Gutiérrez Nájera argued, like Catalans, willing to risk everything but their language.[50] Still, in 1919, English was the reason to mock the modern woman, as in a poem "Enigmática" by Otilio González:

Burlesca no comprendes a Pierrot;
volar en automóvil te extasía;
ejecutas right turns con sangre fría,
y mueres por el tennis y el fox trot.[51]

Shameful woman, you don't understand Pierrot
[but] to run fast in an automobile enraptures you
making right turns in cold blood
and you love tennis and the fox trot

It was a consensus: English was the great enemy, and as late as the 1940s important intellectuals such as José Vasconcelos—who had himself grown up on the border and was fluent in English—and Alfonso Reyes—a man who had learned English to read Emerson and Wilde, at Henríquez Ureña's suggestion—mocked and rejected the use of English in Mexico. English would prevail, wrote Reyes, but not because of its lucidity and intelligence, but rather thanks to power and money.[52]

In turn, starting in the 1920s, Lebanese and Chinese influences became important elements of the urban linguistic panorama, especially in the area of La Merced and Independencia Street. Moreover, in the 1920s and 1930s, Yiddish, Ladino, and Hebrew were spoken by newly arrived Jewish communities.[53] Of course, the influence of Chinese on the city streets and in its vaudevilles became a running joke, demonstrated particularly by the popularity of such comic dramas as *Chin Chun Chan*.

In addition, for centuries, Spaniards from different linguistic backgrounds (Gallegos, Asturians, Catalans, Extremeños, Basque) had shaped the language of Mexico in ways often difficult to map. From the 1870s to the 1940s, moreover, Spaniards were actively involved in the promotion, rescue, protection, and standardization of the languages from the peninsula, including Catalan, Gallego, and Euskera, but most importantly of an "officially recognized" Spanish, the one promulgated by the Real Academia de la Lengua.[54] These peninsular languages and intonations continued to act upon the city throughout the dynamic era of logophilia spanning the period from the 1870s to the 1940s. Catalan publisher Santiago Ballescá was an important cultural figure in late nineteenth-century Mexico City, and after 1936 the city became an important center for the publication of books in Catalan.[55]

At the level of long-lasting historical processes, migration and cosmopolitanism are merely the visible parts of the fundamental lesson that the city teaches: that in language the seemingly sharp partition between the elite and the popular is deceptive. Cities are built upon anonymity and promiscuity, and these features of a city inhabit its language. As a result, from the 1880s to the present, Mexico City has experienced, at an ever-increasing rate, two consequences of the vernacular's urge toward innovation and hybridization. These are, to use terms from the vernacular, *acatrinamiento* (the constant vulgarization of highbrow language, both national and international) and *anacamiento* (the constant gentrification of popular language). *Acatrinamiento* describes the unstoppable drive for the refinement of popular speech; that is, the popular desire to possess and to speak a *catrín* language. On the other hand, the process of *anacamiento*, based on the nineteenth-century city term *naco* (referring to the urban poor, the inelegant, the Indian), describes a process acting upon the middle and upper classes, and even the intelligentsia of the city. In this process, middle- and upper-class language was itself transformed by inevitable contacts with the vulgar eloquence of the street, and by the obsessive late nineteenth-century drive to collect, rescue, and embrace popular speech.

Indeed, from a horizontal historical perspective, at any given point in time there was and is a highbrow and a lowbrow in the city: a refined upper-class language and, simultaneously, an upper-class slang, coexisting with a lower-class elegance and a lower-class argot. But from a vertical historical perspective, such divisions appear too ephemeral and, above all, lose their capacity to distinguish one from the other. Through the decades, with language forced to interpret anger and suffering, love and blasphemy, virtue and sin, the boundary between popular and elite language became blurred. There were and are sharp distinctions between oral and written language. But *acatrinamiento* and *anacamiento* reduce the notion of a stable, distinguishable, popular speech to an illusory ideal, just as the very possibility that the city's elite might preserve an unpolluted and orthodox *castizo* language was nothing more than an antiquated utopia.

Elite zarzuelas and operas, which introduced a special vocabulary to speak about love, betrayal, and comedy, gradually filtered down to the masses, who in turn used these terms in popular lyrics and songs. These songs soon entered the repertoire of "decent" men. Commenting on the language of the urban poor (in the convoluted modernist prose of the 1900s, albeit one that still honored the vulgar language), Rubén M. Campos wrote: "O shell of humanity, iris-tinged slime bubble, emerald-green fly that arises from the detritus and alights on the flowering almond tree! In what river would the lobster eater have to wash you so as to retrieve your naked and white soul, like a mermaid who singing, singing, was caught in the coral as she fled the changing tides? . . . He [lépero] drank bile and vinegar while nursing, and his blood brothers were the pups of the wolf, misery." It is hard to imagine a discussion of the vulgar language written in a more *catrín* prose. Campos then imagines how the *lépero* would respond to the *catrín*:

> I am waiting for the promised redemption, a task you have left to the state and its schools because you have not had time enough to dedicate to politics. . . . And if a century has passed and you have still only incorporated me into your pleasures and vices, don't suppose that crushing and exiling me is the only solution. Leave me to my cynical transparency, so that you see yourself in me as in a mirror. Leave me to my defects and my vices, which are of your own making. Let me enjoy myself as you enjoy yourself, now that the cinematographer has let me in on your private shame and your moral failures. Who knows which one of us is the more foul![56]

Campos thus gave voice to the inevitable coexistence of *acatrinamiento* and *anacamiento*. Although this coexistence was almost unstoppable, some scholars, especially within the Mexican office of the Royal Spanish Academy of Language, opposed the *anacamiento* of the language, and were horrified by such love of popular speech. By 1920, one already notes nostalgia for the more honest and direct forms of rural speech, for the cries and songs of Indian vendors in the streets, and also for the clear distinctions between aristocratic and vulgar intonations in the language. By the 1930s, the fruitful promiscuities of classes and regions and the willful development of new literary styles had generated even more nostalgia. Old nineteenth-century words and intonations had been decreed passé, and new avant-gardes experimented with all sorts of styles. The old elegance in things and words was thus appropriated by the growing urban masses, resulting in the tacky popular intention to appear elegant, comparable only to the equally tacky and equally frequent bourgeois intention to speak the popular language.

The Revolution in Urban Language

In terms of language, the Revolution in the city ought to be seen as belonging to the era of logophilia. During and after the Revolution, the passionate study of language continued, with equal homogenizing and educational goals as in Porfirian times, but with a new *indigenista* tone. Masters of revolutionary *indigenismo*, such as Moisés Sáenz and Manuel Gamio, were experts on Nahuatl-speaking communities within and around the city, although still great promoters of correct Spanish as the country's only unifying civilizational element. There were revolutionary plans, in part implemented in rural bilingual schools, to use Nahuatl as an intermediary language while public education in Spanish reached the masses. But Nahuatl was found to be too *aglutinante*, like German, allowing too many concepts in a single word, hindering the command of Spanish, for example in the word for railroad: *ohtli* meant road in Nahuatl, and *tepoztli* iron, thus railroad was the long and difficult word *tepozohtli*. Moreover, Nahuatl was too rich—some estimated 20,000 words—, thus becoming an additional obstacle to the immersion of people in Spanish. Sáenz, searching in the 1930s for "unpolluted" Indian communities to experiment with the incorporation of Indians into the national revolutionary language and development, found in Purepecha-speaking Carapan a rich linguistic reservoir, as well as involuntary poetry: when an eighty-three-year old Carapan man was asked what a minute was, he answered: "pus minuto ma hor' zapichu, un minuto así, una hora chiquitito" (a minute: a very, very small hour).[57]

Rafael Ramírez undertook a survey of Mexican philologists in order to establish a linguistic policy for the revolutionary government. And his concluding advice to rural teachers is quite revealing of the similarity between pre- and postrevolutionary linguistic approaches: "Listen here, my dear rural teacher, up until now we have considered you a valiant agent for the incorporation of the Indigenous race into the heart of our own, precisely because we believed that you began your work by teaching the Indians to speak *castellano* . . . But if you . . . speak to them in their own language, we will lose all faith in you, because you yourself are in danger of being incorporated [into Nahuatl]."[58]

More revolutionary were the attempts to simplify Spanish instead, to make it easier for an illiterate population to command, and to show, with the nationalist sentiment characteristic of the time, Mexico's linguistic independence from Spain. In 1930 in Mexico, much as in Germany and Portugal around the same time, many philologists sought to simplify the anachronistic orthography and syntax of the national language. A teacher in Mexico City proposed an entirely new spelling for the national language, which he used to prove his point: "no estoi estorbando el paso de la umanidad presente, sino aselerando su formal estado de adelantar más i más" [sic] (I am not blocking the progress of current humanity, but accelerating its state of constant advancement). He very logically proposed the elimination of the silent and useless h and the non-sensical q, which sounds as a simple c. He also suggested the use of s for all ce, ci, za, zo, and zu sounds, and the removal of the y in favor of a simple i.[59] The goal was to write as people speak, so as not to delay any longer "nuestra positiba liberasión, i poder estampar en el papel lo ce nos ordena nuestro berbo al gritar: biba mejico! Biba la independensia!" [sic] (our genuine liberation, to be able to print on paper that which our tongue intones when we shout: Long live Mexico! Long live Independence!). No one, of course, followed his advice, and the vast literature that resulted from the Revolution was as adamant about its canonical linguistic correctness as it was about continuing to depict bucolic rural scenes. Again, even after the Revolution, literature contained no trace of *malsonantes* (swearing).

Indeed, what the Porfirian city had begun was radically accelerated by the Revolution, by the exile of city folk, by the invasion of troops from across the country and, finally, by the victory of northern provincial elites, who used the city as the base from which they projected their power. The revolt of the common people, seen in the continuum from the 1880s to the 1930s, in fact consisted in the formation of a specific and important version of the Spanish language, namely, the *chilango*, the language of a Mexico City that has in turn become the standardized version of Mexican Spanish—and even, nowadays, of international Spanish, given the profound influence of Mexican Spanish on life, media, commerce, and industry in the United States.

The Revolution, however, left a lasting mark in the language of the city that I believe recuperated the romantic tradition but projected it toward a re-consideration of Mexicanness as a universal and revolutionary mark. It was a renewed rhetoric linked to anthropological studies, folklore, revolutionary sponsorship, radical thought, and radical movements. It combined the metaphors, then in vogue, of evolution, revolution, and proletarianism with the language of the noble savage. Voices in this chorus ranged from Dr. Atl's studies of popular art, to the creation of official *calendarios* and announcements, widely disseminated throughout the city, to the formation of the DAPP (Autonomous Department of Publicity and Propaganda) in the 1930s; it spanned the establishment of a well-sponsored notion of real revolutionary art, prose, and architecture, and the gradual achievement of a nationalist, city-centered, welfare rhetoric. This chorus digested modernist motifs while at the same time spitting out innovative terms for referring to social issues. The very prevalence by the late 1920s of such expressions as "nuestra raza mestiza" (our mestizo race) "obreros" (workers), "clase obrera" (working class), "nacionalismo revolucionario" (revolutionary nationalism), and "lo popular" can be seen as a sign of the emergence of this chorus.

The revolutionary general and writer Francisco Urquizo was believed, at least by Francisco Santamaría's *Diccionario de mejicanismos* (1959), to be one of the few to use "bad terms" in his prose in the context of the novel of the Revolution. In Urquizo's *Tropa vieja* (192?) characters spoke as they never had before in Mexican literature, yet their manner remained urbane, clean: "Cabo Reynaldo Aguirre que es tan mal hablado, viendo que ya nadie se pica con su palabrería insolente, ha tenido que inventar algo más nuevo y enredado: él no dice nomás:—tizna a tu madre', sino que dice,—'anda y retizna a tu rehijo de una tiznada madre, tal por cual'. Hasta bonito se oye la retahíla de insolencias; algunos a quienes se las mienta, hasta se ríen en sus meritas barbas." (Corporal Reynaldo Aguirre, who has such a dirty mouth, seeing that people were no longer shocked by his insolent language had to come up with something newer and more involved: he no longer just says—"tarnish your mother," but instead says—"go on and tarnish your big son of a tarnished mother," just like that. The string of insults sounds somewhat pretty; some of those he tries to insult even laugh in his very face.)[60] This was supposed to be the Revolution's greatest linguistic contribution—at last people speaking like the people. In fact, it was business as usual, writers fascinated with and sanitizing popular speech.

Although logophilia in Mexico was older and more comprehensive in its effects than the Revolution, troops and war had a significant impact on the language of the city. The songs of the soldiers were heard in the streets, images of *soldaderas* and of cantinas full of soldiers became commonplace, and accents and provincialisms of all sorts were heard in the city. Refined words and spaces were taken over by the motley languages of new arrivals in the city. Such words as *acocote* (originally the name of a kind of long squash used to extract the *aguamiel* of the *maguey*) and *mitigüeson* became echoes of violence: the first was used to refer to a kind of Mauser rifle, and the second was the Mexicanized name of popular Smith and Wesson pistols. New verbs, adjectives, and names, which came from the provinces or had been circulating the city for a long time, were popularized by the experience of the Revolution: *achicopalarse* (to have fear), *carrancear* (to steal, popular after Carranza's invasion of Mexico City), *indiada* (all Indians, and by extension all popular classes mobilized during the Revolution), *pelones* (soldiers), *niguas* (originally an insect, but used as a synonym of "no"), *güilas* (prostitutes), *afusilar* (to shoot a person by firing squad), *apochado* (meaning a person who had become *pocho*: affected by the north, Americanized), *culero* (a fearful man), and many popular expressions that became all too visible (*daca, diónde, cuantimás, güélvamos, alueguito, titipuchal, újole*).[61]

Sonorous nicknames and anecdotes circulated about the revolutionary heroes; each epithet was more than a name, it was a story, which often included songs, anecdotes, and countless references. A *carrancista* capitain, Pablo M. Garza, was known in the city as *Mamuza*, a term born of his own, self-deprecatory play on words—the legend was that he repeated constantly: "mamuza, pretérito pluscuamperfecto del verbo mamarse" ("*mamuza*," pluperfect of *mamarse* [to get piss-drunk]). Babies were baptized with new and strange names, particularly, in the 1920s, names taken from the titles of various socialist experiments (for instance, in Tabasco with Garrido Canaval, who established socialist baptisms), and as a result of the emergence of the radio and the indigenist turn of the city's language. *Masiosare* became a boy's name (derived from a stanza of the national anthem: "Mas si osare un extraño enemigo . . ."), but also *Alcazelser* (after the popularity of Alka-Seltzer), *Xochitl, Tenoch, Cuauhtémoc, Tonatihu* (the biblically named Lázaro Cárdenas named his son *Cuauhtémoc*).[62]

The new rulers of the city gradually developed a rhetoric for the city, a mixture of the new terminology used to refer to social and political issues in a world of mass politics with traces of Porfirian aristocratism and paternalism, and a willingness to "speak like the people." This language evolved slowly; even during the 1921 *Centenario* the language of politicians, newspapers, and intellectuals was closer to that of the nineteenth century than to the social language of the 1930s (see chapter 1). A 1937 periodical produced by the Mexican government, *La palomilla*, which sought to create revolutionary children, can be used as an example of the rhetoric that was being formed to refer to social and political issues. One issue explained to children that they were living in an *época de pugnas tremendas* (an era of tremendous conflicts) and in an *agitación que invade a las actuales razas* (agitation that invades the existing races), but that good children would never take refuge in individualism: "no debes constituirte en un ser individual, tienes que adecuarte a la constitución social" (you should not build yourself up as an individualistic self, you must adapt to the social constitution). These words blended nineteenth-century science and epic bellicosity with socialist tones (one can almost hear Marx and his "social being," together with state-centered developmentalism): "Niño el país necesita que se produzca, que el comercio aumente" (Child, the country needs production, it needs commerce to grow). Obviously, children must have been scared by this kind of language as, we ought to assume, the tone used to speak to children in the city remained the familiar one more closely affiliated with notions of intimacy, authority, and religion.[63]

In the 1920s, however, the emergence of the radio radically expanded the linguistic and musical might of the revolutionary city. In 1923 the first radio station opened in Mexico City, CYL (El Universal Ilustrado, La Casa de la Radio). It was linked to the newspaper El Universal. The same year also saw the inception of CYB, owned by the cigarette maker El Buen Tono. By the end of the decade there seem to have been twenty-five radio stations operating in Mexico.[64] In 1930 XEW was founded, and by the early 1940s it had become the most important radio station in Mexico, although it didn't have the strongest signal. Radio Nacional also appeared in 1931 and rapidly grew to serve many official purposes. In 1937 XEDP and XEX were created to serve the DAPP.[65] In the 1920s, an official military publication mapped the radio stations of the country, showing that for the first time words were circulating all over the country.[66] This was a key element in the transformation of the language of the city. With the radio, words circulated and transgressed parameters in a previously unknown fashion. The city became receptive to the influence of a number of different slangs and terminologies, both national and international, and in turn the city dispersed its own language, which had been in the making for many years, across the country.

Rubén M. Campos and Vicente T. Mendoza especially hated the influence of U.S. culture on Mexican language and music. A report on Mexican broadcasting, published in English by the Mexican government in order to attract U.S. tourism, stated: "American jazz . . . is scarcely conductive to Mexican art or ideals and . . . it should be subject to severe scrutiny by the regulatory authorities." But other commentators, like Salvador Novo, realized that radio would transform Mexican words although, like Pessoa ("dita, morta") or Dante ("quanto è corto il dire"), Novo knew how ephemeral language and words had become: for him the advent of radio would ensure that "the word gives way more and more to pure sound . . . remember that it is going to be heard, and not seen, nor read. By its very essence of being a resident of the air, the word spoken on the radio cannot aspire to eternity."[67]

The combination of Revolution and radio had four main effects on the language of the city. First, the above-mentioned gradual formation of an officially sanctioned tone of voice to refer to politics, society, and culture—a mixture of socialist rhetoric, romantic paternalism, and nationalism. Second, a process of rapid proletarization of the old Porfirian eloquence, especially in its sentimental and amorous connotations. Third, the triumph of the "Bajío" (from

Jalisco, and parts of Michocán and Guanajuato) as the national style.[68] Finally, modernizing revolutionary elites and the emergence of the radio left the city open to foreign, most notably American, influences.

In 1930, the linguistic panorama of the city was dramatically affected by the appearance of XEW. The motto of XEW was "La voz de la América Latina desde México" (The voice of Latin America from Mexico), and indeed it was. On September 18, the station was inaugurated with singers Alfonso Ortiz Tirado and Juan Arvizu (both former opera singers transformed by the new popular romantic and *ranchero* tunes), the famous Orquesta Típica conducted by Miguel Lerdo de Tejada (the prominent musician who had been one of the first to appropriate popular tunes in the late Porfiriato) and Agustín Lara—who became Mexico's most popular and prolific composer of love songs. Since the mid-1920s, revolutionary *corridos* were part of the noise of the city (*La Adelita, La Rielera, La Valentina*). The radio had turned the bucolism, tragedy, and violence of the Revolution into common fare. And countless *ranchero* songs from the Bajío that gradually appropriated the accents, the words, the style of the *charro* as the stereotypical image of the real macho Mexico became the culture of the city, the country, and the world.

But the city also standardized a notion of popular sentimental eloquence. The radio continued the appropriation of old-school eloquence through romantic music and songs. In 1922 Mario Talavera put to music a poem by the modernist poet Amado Nervo ("Flor de Mayo") and made it an instant radio success. In 1925, a poem by the Porfirian poet Gutiérrez Nájera was made into a song, "Tímido Amor." In 1922, Alfonso Esparza Oteo produced one of the most popular tunes of twentieth-century Mexico (lyrics by Adolfo Fernández Bustamente), "Mi viejo amor" (see chapter 4): a masterpiece of malleable romanticism, a proletarization of the highbrow, and a gentrification of the lowbrow, all because of a pair of *ojazos* (big eyes) black as *penas y amores* (sorrows and loves). Through the image of crying eyes the tense of the song was frozen in an eternal present: it is no longer in the past, because "un viejo amor ni se olvida ni se deja" (an old love can be neither forgotten nor abandoned); it is in the present of endlessly crying eyes.

The best example of the development of an urban romantic language, however, is Agustín Lara. In the 1920s, Lara's songs, according to Baltasar Dromundo, described "the lights, the characters, the customs, the language, women's spats, half-tones, the way of dressing, the bone-chilling miseries, in sum, life, with all the appropriate scenery."[69] Lara was a man who at early age played the piano in brothels in the late Porfirian city. A man who in 1927, in a bar in the *barrio* of Santa María la Rivera, had had his face slashed with a broken bottle by a woman, "Estrella," giving the popular composer his well-known scar-face. He was, as he himself put it, *cursi*, and had "la fortuna de nacer feo; eso me salvo del exceso" (the good fortune to have been born ugly; this saved me from excess).[70] His lyrics summarize an evolution in the city's language. He was, wrote poet Xavier Villaurrutia in a letter to Salvador Novo (1936), "a better musician than Ponce, and a less bad poet than Nervo."[71] The streets of Mexico City sang Lara's tunes, in a beautiful mixture of romantic, modernist, and tawdry Spanish. In 1930, hence, with the inauguration of XEW radio station, in the city the most popular song was "Hastío" (ennui, a nineteenth-century both word and vice), a masterfully tacky piece:

Has perdido la fe
y te has vuelto medrosa y cobarde.
El hastío es pavoreal
que se aburre de luz en la tarde.

You have lost faith
and you have become pusillanimous and coward.
Hastío is a peacock
bored with light at dawn.

The *chilango* masses of the 1930s were still caught up in the tackiness of the nineteenth century. But there was, and there is, no way to capture a fixed version of the language of the city. The city, its people, inhabit the language that cannot be lived in the same way over different streets and over time. The city is never the same, always welcomes words. That is why nostalgia; that is why, as the old tune goes, that old verse we seem unable to remember always seems to be superior.

FINAL WORD

In 1935 Jorge Luis Borges realized that translations of *The Arabian Nights* into various European languages were subject to vigorous disputes over taste, loyalty to the original text, and authenticity. Antoine Galland's version, he wrote, was the weakest and most unfaithful to the original. Yet, he added, "It was the best read. Those who got close to it grasped happiness and astonishment."[1] Despite Galland's success, Enno Littmann's 1920s German rendition was the most authoritative and faithful version of Scheherazade's stories. "I hear that the Arabists agree," on this contention, Borges claimed, adding: "it doesn't matter that a mere man of literature—and one from a merely Argentine Republic—prefers to dissent" ("Oigo que los arabistas están de acuerdo . . . nada importa que un mero literato—y ése, de la república meramente Argentina—prefiera disentir").[2]

Of course a writer from a republic "merely Argentine"—that is, "of or resembling silver"—could never know any better than Europeans. Borges's irony knows no boundaries, and it encapsulates the essential paradoxes of Mexico City as a world capital. When Borges expressed his opinions about the verisimilitude of *The Arabian Nights* translations, he stretched the irony even further by assuming the authority of a writer from a republic that was "merely Argentine." If there is an "Argentine Republic," where is the golden one? Borges recognized his peripheral status, yet he managed to make his voice heard through sharp wit within an already existent current of thoughts and interests. This current ran deeply through the European languages in which Borges read and wrote, and in which he hoped to be read and be written about. Thus he dissented from the accepted opinion in 1935. He held that Littmann, despite its accuracy, was not the best translation of *The Arabian Nights*:

My reason is this: Burton's, Madrus' and even Galland's versions only allow themselves to be conceived after the existence of a literature. Whatever their flaws or merits, those characteristic works presuppose an elaborate previous process [presuponen un rico proceso anterior].[3]

Hence the reading of the Oriental document enters an existing linguistic current already including what the late Edward Said would have called a "culture of empire."[4] Borges considered himself a part of that current, albeit from the periphery. Like the characters in these essays, Borges shared the concepts and verbs included in the Spanish, French, English, and German languages. Is Borges then, like many of the characters in the stories I have told, simply a Europeanized intellectual from a "merely Argentine Republic"? Are the global flows explored here merely an elitist inauthentic participation in the larger culture of empire, which led the people of Mexico City or Buenos Aires to experiment either with neoclassical monuments, *Japonisme*, science, or Scheherazade?

The overlapping mirror images I have explained in these essays ought to create doubts about the assumptions included in such questions. When we speak of cultural regions like Mexico City in the last part of the nineteenth century, we face a twofold dilemma. First we see individuals expressing their own modern urban selves within their shared daily language. That language— always a variation on an import from Europe—is a condition of their own self-meaning; that is, their "authenticity" as modern creators was unattainable without inhabiting the "unauthentic," chaotic, modern, and a-modern games of words that surrounded them. In order for each one to modernly be him- or herself, they had to be someone else. Or so it seems.

Second, there is the dilemma of the well-established meaning of "Mexico" as a globally assumed collective self, a portrait from which no one attempting to modernly conceive Mexico could escape. That portrait has been for quite some time the "authentic" self that various European languages pronounce and can say no more and no less about; in Wittgenstein's words, "A *picture* held us captive. And we cannot get outside it, for it lay in our language and language seemed to repeat it to us inexorably."[5]

The first is a dilemma only if one believes in a creative cultural existence outside the confines of one's own language. But if one does not believe in such a possibility the dilemma is nothing more than the unsolvable problems faced everywhere by anyone attempting to speak, write, paint, or otherwise express culture. The second dilemma assumes that any individuality ought to pale in comparison to the assumed collective self. No voice can be vocal unless it is articulated within the parameters of such an assumed collective self. That is why it seems that the first task of any cultural creator in Mexico City was to pronounce what was believed to be Mexico's authentic version. Mexico as the relatively fixed portrait of a collective self remains today a dilemma because the portrait has been pronounced not only in English and French but also in Spanish, for the portrait itself has come to constitute the unavoidable language available when speaking about anything Mexican.

When such terms as "Westernized," "Europeanized," "afrancesados," "un-Mexican," "imitation," and "copies" are used to describe individual creations in Mexico City, the implication is that those creations could have been something else. This assumption is, in simple linguistic terms, an absurdity. By the last part of the nineteenth century—in Mexico City as in half of the continent—common people were, as were elites, modern Spanish speakers. Like Borges, they all considered themselves in a way peripheral. But they were also conscious of their participation in the local and global eddies of a cultural flow encompassed by the widely spoken Spanish language. Mexican intellectuals, scientists, and politicians were consciously writing and rewriting translations, twisting meanings within the confines of their broad yet limited horizon, understanding their existence as late nineteenth- and early twentieth-century Spanish-speaking inhabitants of modern times.

Through, say, orientalist or Old English themes Borges explored "big" concepts (death, life, destiny, reality, dreams), offering a key to unlock the meaning of the cultural existence available to a writer from a "merely Argentine" republic. This is an existence found in neither a mythical local East nor an equally mythical West; neither in authenticity nor in fixed identities. Instead, that existence resides in narration itself, in the inevitable experimentation, appropriation, transformation, and infringement of an existent cultural current. To essay, to be essayed: to experiment with everything available, and then to exist.[6]

Mexico City participated in a chaotic process of storytelling, self-narration, invention, and discovery: a grand experiment from various angles. All this made the perception of an assumed time and place known as "Mexico" possible. Every time Mexico's late nineteenth- and early twentieth-century artists, intellectuals, and urbanites consumed or created a cultural product, they did so within the confines of the Spanish language's already-established cultural current. Whatever they did, even when they transformed or reversed the current with original ideas or phrases from Nahuatl, Japanese, Chinese, French, English, or German, they did so within the global parameters of the well-established Spanish domain. That Spanish was by then already part of the culture of empire is undeniable, yet the cultural interactions Spanish implied were not only imperial impositions. Spanish was their language and (most of the time) the only one they owned, transformed, and manipulated, and the only one that owned them, transformed them, and manipulated them. This included Mexicans, both poor and elite, Spaniards, Argentines, and many others. Rubén Darío, even with the

French undertones of his poems, owned, and was owned by, Spanish as much as a Mexican *lépero* sabotaging highbrow meanings of words in unique and unthinkable ways. There was no choice but to dive in and submerge oneself in that current, for either the fancy intellectual or the common inhabitant in Mexico City. That was the only available cultural existence.

Mexico, however, does possess a relatively fixed definition. It is like a "cage," the Brown Atlantis, constructed not only by centuries of travelers, studies, and commentaries, but also by many forms of self-imposed confinement in definitions that have echoed and nurtured global views of Mexico. When Lysander Kemp (a true cultural intermediary who made authors like Octavio Paz, Juan Rulfo, and Carlos Fuentes accessible to the English-speaking public) first translated *The Labyrinth of Solitude* in 1961, the arguments of *la chingada*, *mestizaje*, and identity anguish became clichés of *mexicanidad*. These were, indeed, aspects of Paz's argument. But another aspect—arguably the most important part of the book—was solitude, how for the first time solitude had made Mexicans "contemporaries to humankind." Yet to this day, despite years of both exalting and bashing Paz's ideas, the aspect of solitude has mostly escaped from the idea of Mexico. Paz, creator of stereotypes, was also Paz the world poet, the Mexican orientalist in love with India, the philologist, and the thinker of human solitude. But the constraining frame of Mexican authenticity is so powerful that Paz is known outside his country mostly as the creator of *pachucos*, *malinches*, and *chingadas*.[7] Mexico the idea, the image, is a cage and, says a popular proverb, *aunque la jaula sea di'oro . . . no deja de ser prisión* (even if the cage is of gold . . . it remains a prison).

I have sought to show how the narration of the city, or of the nation, of the exotic, narrating one's self as exotic, the tale of science, history, and language was vivid and widespread in the modern city of Mexico. The city was nothing more and nothing less than this. To recall Borges once again, the right question for the peripheral intellectual is whether or not to seduce the world with the stories it demands from a cultural product such as Mexico. Such a seduction reproduces an everlasting form of authenticity; yet the peripheral intellectual can also seduce and be seduced with less comfortable, although less exotic, arguments. Borges wrote a poem in English for his own European "odalisque," as it were, Beatriz Bibiloni Webster de Bullrich, in which he explained the offer: he offered her "explanations of/yourself, theories about yourself/authentic and surprising news of yourself" and, in exchange:

> I can give you my loneliness, my darkness, the
> hunger of my heart; I am trying to bribe you
> with uncertainty, with danger, with defeat.[8]

NOTES

INTRODUCTION

1. Hernando Alvarado Tezozómoc, *Crónica mexicáyotl*, trans. from the Nahuatl by Adrián León (Mexico City: Imprenta Universitaria, 1949). Throughout these essays I spare the reader that common scholarly gibberish of self-references.

2. J. M. Eça de Queiros, *Prosas bárbaras* (Lisbon: Livros do Brasil, 1969), 185.

3. For a long time, the study of Mexico City in the nineteenth and early twentieth centuries was scarce. The last three decades have seen an important growth in the literature, growth from which these essays have been both contributors and beneficiaries. The pioneer efforts by Alejandra Moreno Toscano—*La Ciudad de México. Ensayo de construcción de una historia*, 2 vols. (Mexico City: INAH, 1978)—were the beginning of demographic, urban-planning, cultural, artistic, social, and political approaches to the history of Mexico City. Throughout these essays I will extensively use this literature. Here I mention just the basics: Vicente Quirarte, *Elogio de la calle: biografía literaria de la ciudad de México, 1850–1992* (Mexico City: Cal y Arena, 2001); Ariel Rodríguez Kuri, *La experiencia olvidada: el ayuntamiento de México: política y gobierno, 1876–1912* (Mexico City: El Colegio de México, 1996); Ariel Rodríguez Kuri, *Historia del desasosiego: la Revolución en la Ciudad de México, 1911–1922* (Mexico City: El Colegio de México, 2010); Andrés Lira, *Las comunidades indígenas frente a la Ciudad de México* (Mexico City: El Colegio de México, 1983); Federico Fernández Christlieb, *Mexico, ville néoclassique: les espaces et les idées de l'aménagement urbain, 1783–1911* (Paris: L'Harmattan, 2002); Ismael Katzman, *Arquitectura del siglo XIX en México* (Mexico City: UNAM, 1973); Ricardo Sánchez Puentes and Eric Van Young, eds., *La ciudad y el campo en la historia de México* (Mexico City: UNAM, 1992); John Lear, *Workers, Neighbors, and Citizens: The Revolution in Mexico City* (Lincoln: University of Nebraska Press, 2001); Jorge H. Jiménes Muñoz, *La traza del poder* (Mexico City: Dedalo, Codex, 1993); Priscilla Connolly, *El contratista de don Porfirio: obras públicas, deuda y desarrollo desigual* (Zamora-Mexico City: El Colegio de Michoacán-UAM, Fondo de Cultura Económica, 1997); Manuel Cohen Perló, *El paradigm porfiriano: Historia del desagüe del valle de México* (Mexico City: UNAM-Porrúa, 1999); Pablo Piccato, *City of Suspects: Crime in Mexico City, 1900–1931* (Durham: Duke University Press, 2001); Katherine Elaine Bliss, *Compromised Positions: Prostitution, Public Health, and Gender Politics in Revolutionary Mexico City* (University Park: Pennsylvania State University Press, 2001); Patrice Elizabeth Olsen, *Artifacts of Revolution: Architecture, Society, and Politics in Mexico City, 1920–1940* (Lanham: Rowman & Littlefield, 2008); Rubén Gallo, *Mexican Modernity: The Avant-Garde and the Technological Revolution* (Cambridge: MIT Press, 2005).

4. Georg Simmel, "Metropolis and Mental Life" (1903) trans. Karl Wolff, *The Sociology of Georg Simmel* (Chicago: University of Chicago Press, 1950), 410–11; Octavio Paz poem "Hablo de la ciudad," trans. Eliot Weinberger.

5. My academic approach began with the influence of many scholars, from Richard Morse to José Luis Romero in the history of modern Iberian cities, and from Carl E. Schorske to Marshall Berman in more general approaches. Richard M. Morse, *From Community to Metropolis: A Biography of São Paulo, Brazil* (Gainesville: University of Florida Press, 1958); and his essays in *New World Soundings: Culture and Ideology in the Americas* (Baltimore: Johns Hopkins University Press, 1989); Carl E. Schorske, *Fin-de-siècle Vienna: Politics and Culture* (New York: Knopf, 1979); José Luis Romero,

Latinoamérica: las ciudades y las ideas (Mexico City: Siglo Veintiuno Editores, 1976); Marshall Berman, All That Is Solid Melts Into Air: The Experience of Modernity (New York: Simon and Schuster, 1982).

6. Gabriel Zaid, "La carretilla alfonsina," Letras Libres, no. 1 (January 1999), n.p.

7. Julio Sesto, La ciudad de los palacios: Novela mexicana, illustrated by Duhart, Gutiérrez, and Zaldivar (Mexico City: El Libro Español, 1917), 133.

8. Cover, Adolfo Prantl and José L. Grosó, La Ciudad de México: Novísima guía universal de la capital de la República Mexicana . . . (Mexico City: Juan Buxó y Cia. Editores, 1901).

9. "Mi ciudad," popular song by Guadalupe Trigo circa 1970.

10. Karl Kraus, Sprüche und Widersprüche (1909), www.textlog.de/39307.html.

11. Jorge Cuesta, Poemas y ensayos: Ensayos I, prologue by Luis Mario Schneider, ed. Miguel Capistrán and L. M. Schneider (Mexico City: UNAM, 1964); Edmundo O'Gorman, México, el trauma de su historia (Mexico City: UNAM, 1977); Roger Bartra, La jaula de la melancolía (Mexico City: Joaquín Mortiz, 1988); Roger Bartra, Anatomía del mexicano (Mexico City: Plaza & Janés, 2002); Roger Bartra, La sangre y la tinta: ensayos sobre la condición postmexicana (Mexico City: Editorial Océano, 1999); Claudio Lomnitz, Las salidas del laberinto: Cultura e ideología en el espacio nacional mexicano (Mexico City: Joaquín Mortiz, 1995); Claudio Lomnitz, Deep Mexico, Silent Mexico: An Anthropology of Nationalism (Minneapolis: University of Minnesota Press, 2001); Claudio Lomnitz, Death and the Idea of Mexico (Brooklyn: Zone Books, 2005); Christopher Domínguez, Diccionario crítico de la literatura mexicana (1955–2005) (Mexico City: Fondo de Cultura Económica, 2007); Christopher Domínguez, La sabiduría sin promesa: vidas y letras del siglo XX (Mexico City: Joaquín Mortiz, 2001); Charles A. Hale, The Transformation of Liberalism in Late Nineteenth-Century Mexico (Princeton: Princeton University Press, 1989); Charles A. Hale, Emilio Rabasa and the Survival of Porfirian Liberalism (Stanford: Stanford University Press, 2008); Ricardo Pérez Montfort, Expresiones populares y estereotipos culturales en México, siglos XIX y XX: diez ensayos (Mexico City: CIESAS, 2007); Rocardo Pérez Montfort, Cotidianidades, imaginarios y contextos: ensayos de historia y cultura en México, 1850–1950 (Mexico City: CIESAS, 2008).

12. Benedetto Croce, La historia como hazaña de la libertad, trans. Joaquín Díaz Canedo (Mexico City: Fondo de Cultura Económica, 1942); Constantin Fasolt, The Limits of History (Chicago: University of Chicago Press, 2004); F. R. Ankersmit, Sublime Historical Experience (Stanford: Stanford University Press, 2005); Richard McKean, "Has History a Direction? Philosophical Principles and Objective Interpretations," and "Freedom and History," both included in Richard McKeon, Freedom and History and Other Essays, ed. Zahava K. McKeon (Chicago: University of Chicago Press, 1990), 126–241.

13. Marc Bloch, Apologie pour l'histoire ou Métier d'historien (Paris: Masson & Armand Colin Éditeurs, 1993).

CHAPTER 1

1. Virginia Woolf, "Mr. Bennett and Mrs. Brown" (1924), reprinted in Collected Essays, vol. 1 (London: Hogarth P., 1966).

2. "Programa definitivo de las ceremonias y fiestas oficiales para la celebración del Primer Centenario de la Independencia en la Ciudad de México (acordado el 28 de julio de 1910)" (SRE, Le. 101).); Genaro Garcia's Crónica oficial de las fiestas del Centenario de la Independencia de México (Mexico City: Secretaría de Gobernación, 1911); E. Barros, Álbum gráfico de la república mexicana (Mexico City: Müller Hermanos, 1910). The estimated total budget of the centennial celebration was 317,000 pesos. Michael Johns, The City of Mexico in the Age of Díaz (Austin: University of Texas Press, 1997),

makes use of parts of the Genaro García collection (N. L. Benson Latin American Collection, University of Texas, Austin). My sources and approach are very different from the latter work. Annick Lempérière, "Los dos centenarios de la independencia mexicana (1910–21): de la historia patria a la antropología cultural," *Historia Mexicana*, 45, 2 (1995): 317–52; Lillian Briseño Senosiain, "La fiesta de la luz en la Ciudad de México: El alumbrado eléctrico en el Centenario," *Secuencia*, 60 (2004): 90–108. Michael González elaborates further my first installment on the subject (1996) and adds interesting data on the finances of the *Centenario*; see Michael González, "Imagining Mexico in 1910: Visions of the *Patria* in the Centennial Celebration in Mexico City," *Journal of Latin American Studies*, 36 (2007): 495–533.

3. Eric Hobsbawm, *The Age of Empires* (New York: Pantheon Books, 1987).

4. "Iniciativas" can be found in AGN GOB Centenario. Proposal submitted by a little girl named María de la Luz Islas, June 1910, AGN GOB 910-3-1.

5. La Reforma was the liberal reform movement, accompanied by a civil war, which culminated in the constitution of 1857. Benito Juárez led this movement and was Mexico's president from 1858 to 1872.

6. Federico Gamboa, *Mi diario: Mucho de mi vida y algo de la de otros, segunda serie*, vol. 2 (Mexico City: Eusebio Gómez de la Puente Editor, 1938), 181–93; F. Starr, *Mexico and the United States: A Story of Revolution, Intervention, and War* (Chicago: Bible House, 1914), 33–72.

7. Emilio Rabasa, *Evolución histórica de México* (Mexico City: La Vda. de C. Bouret, 1920), 163.

8. Quoted in Andrés Molina Enríquez, *Los grandes problemas nacionales* (Mexico City: Impr. de A. Carranza e hijos, 1909), 65.

9. Molina Enríquez, *Los grandes problemas nacionales*.

10. El Foro (March 19, 1889). Reprinted by the author in *Iniciativa para celebrar el Primer Centenario de la Independencia de México con una Exposición Universal* (Mexico City: Secretaría de Fomento, 1893), 15–19, 25–51; Antonio A. de Medina y Ormaechea, *La Exposición Universal del Primer Centenario Mexicano* (Mexico City: Secretaría de Fomento, 1894).

11. *Gran Exposición Internacional de México que se abrirá el día 15 de septiembre de 1895 y que se clausurará el día 3 de abril de 1896* (Mexico City: Imp. de F. Camacho, 1894), 310.

12. Jorge H. Jiménez Muñoz, *La traza del poder: Historia de la política y los negocios urbanos en el Distrito Federal: de sus orígenes a la desaparición del Ayuntamiento (1824–1928)* (Mexico City: Dedalo, Cotex, 1993); a reproduction of Malo's *ensache* for Mexico City can be found in Fernando Benitez, *La Ciudad de México*, vol. 6 (Mexico City: Salvat, 1984) (there is no reference to the original location of the map, and I have not been able to find its original source). Barcelona's *eixample*, designed by Ildelfonso Cerdà, was one of the most notable examples of city development in the nineteenth century.

13. *Mexican Financier* (June 14, 1890): 323. Historian Paolo Riguzzi has found seven insolvency cases against Malo. I thank him for all this information; see P. Riguzzi, *¿La reciprocidad imposible? La política del comercio entre México y Estados Unidos 1877–1938* (Mexico City: El Colegio Mexiquense, El Colegio de México, 2003).

14. Agreement made between Mr. John R. Dos Passos, as legal representative of the Mexican National Exposition and Land Company, and Vicomte R. de Cornely, in San Francisco, México, April 22, 1896. AGN EXP, Box 99, Exp. 22.

15. Secretaría de Fomento, *Memoria de la Secretaría de Fomento, 1897–1900* (Mexico City: Secretaría de Fomento, 1908).

16. Cornely-Limantour, July 15 1897, Limantour-Cornely, July 17 1897, Archivo José Yves Limantour, Centro de Estudios Historia de México Carso.

17. Malo-Limantour, April 20 1899, Archivo José Yves Limantour, CEMC.

18. AGN GOB. 909-3-1.

19. I express my ideas about celebrations in the twentieth and twentieth-first centuries elsewhere. My views on 1968 are marked by my conversations with Ariel Rodríguez Kuri (whose as yet unpublished study of the 1968 Olympic Games I await). Two first installments of the project are: "El otro 68: Política y estilo en la organización de los juegos Olímpicos de la Ciudad de México," *Relaciones*, no. 76 (Fall 1998): 209–29; and "Los primeros días: una explicación de los orígenes inmediatos del movimiento estudiantil de 1968," *Historia Mexicana*, 53, no. 1 (2003): 179–228. See also Luis Castañeda, "Beyond Tlatelolco: Design, Media, and Politics at Mexico '68," *Grey Room*, 40 (Summer 2010): 100–126.

20. Luis G. Ortiz, *Prontuario . . . de acuerdos, bandos, circulares, decretos, leyes, reglamentos y demás disposiciones vigentes de la Secretaría de Gobernación y sus despachos* (Mexico City: Secretaría de Gobernación, 1908–10).

21. Santiago Quesada, *La ciudad en la cultura hispana de la edad moderna* (Barcelona: Universitat de Barcelona, 1992); Jorge Hardoy, "Theory and Practice of Urban Planning in Europe, 1850–1930: Its Transfer to Latin America," in Hardoy and Morse, eds., *Rethinking the Latin American City* (Baltimore: Johns Hopkins University Press, 1992), 20–49; Jérôme Monnet, *La ville et son double* (Paris: Nathan, 1993), 19–36; and Federico Fernández Christlieb, *Mexico, ville néoclassique: les espaces et les idées de l'aménagement urbain, 1783–1911* (Paris: L'Harmattan, 2002).

22. Salvador Novo, *Los paseos de la Ciudad de México* (Mexico City: Fondo de Cultura Económica, 1974); Barbara Tannenbaum, "Streetwise History—The Paseo de la Reforma and the Porfirian State, 1876–1910," in William Beezley, Cheryl English Martin, and William E. French, eds., *Rituals of Rule, Rituals of Resistance: Public Celebrations and Popular Culture in Mexico* (Wilmington: SRbooks, 1994), 127–50; and Carlos Martínez Assad, *La patria en el Paseo de la Reforma* (Mexico City: UNAM, Fondo de Cultura Económica, 2005); Archivo Histórico del Ayuntamiento, 3583, Exp. 17, 1889–1893.

23. John Lear, *Workers, Neighbors, and Citizens: The Revolution in Mexico City* (Lincoln: University of Nebraska Press, 2001); Michael Wagenaar, "Conquest of the Center or Flight to the Suburbs? Divergent Metropolitan Strategies in Europe, 1850–1914," *Journal of Urban History*, 19, 1 (November 1992): 60–83; and Pablo Piccato, *City of Suspects*.

24. José Luis Romero and Luis Alberto Romero, eds., *Buenos Aires, historia de cuatro siglos*, vol. 1 (Buenos Aires: Editorial Abril, 1983); Jorge Hardoy and Margarita Gutman, *Buenos Aires* (Madrid: Fundación MAPFRE, 1992), 113–62.

25. Francisco J. Bullrich, "La arquitectura: el eclectisismo," in Romero and Romero, *Buenos Aires*, vol. 1, 173–200.

26. Jiménez Muñoz presents the most complete panorama of colonias. Jiménez Muñoz, *La traza del poder*.

27. Andrés Lira, *Las comunidades indígenas frente a la ciudad de México* (Mexico City: El Colegio de México, 1983).

28. Wagenaar, "Conquest of the Center," 63–71.

29. For clear mapping of this area, see the various maps of colonias and nomenclatura included in

Archivo Histórico del Ayuntamiento, 4765. Especially, see the map titled "Comisión permanente de nomenclatura de la ciudad de México, cuarteles V, VI, VII, VIII," 1908.

30. AGN GOB 909-10-4-3; Archivo Histórico del Ayuntamiento, 4753, "Postes para Avenida Juárez," "Postes que van de la estatua de Carlos IV al Portal de Mercaderes y San Fernando"; see also Senosiain, "La fiesta de la luz en la Ciudad de México."

31. Lear, Workers, 130.

32. Manuel Torres Torrija, in Francisco Trentini, Patria: El florecimiento de México (The Prosperity of Mexico) (Mexico City: Tip. de Bouligny & Schmidt sucs., 1906), 64.

33. Most of the elite resided within the limits of the new ideal city. However, Porfirio Díaz had owned a house since the 1870s in Cadena Street (in the old part of the city, today Venustiano Carranza). For a detailed description of the origins and characteristics of this house, see Carlos Tello, El exilio: Un retrato de familia (Mexico City: Cal y Arena, 1993).

34. Ramona Isabel Pérez Bertury, "Parques y jardines públicos de la Ciudad de México, 1881–1911," Ph.D. diss., El Colegio de México, 2003.

35. Regarding this park, see Archivo Histórico del Ayuntamiento, Legajo 603, Exp. 6.

36. Presented to Porfirio Díaz and Eduardo Liceaga, SSA Box 6, Exp. 33. Quevedo argued that the total cost of the Balbuena park was 100,000 pesos.

37. Alan Knight, "Revolutionary Project, Recalcitrant People: Mexico, 1910–1940," in Jaime Rodríguez, ed., The Revolutionary Process in Mexico: Essays on Political and Social Change, 1880–1940 (Los Angeles: University of California Press, 1990), 233–35.

38. Federico Gamboa's novel Santa (1903): the story of a country girl who migrates to the city and is corrupted by the city's evil, becoming a prostitute.

39. See letter by the secretary of the Centennial Commission, J. Casarín, to Juan Bibriesca, secretary of the Ayuntamiento of Mexico City, in which he accepted the proposal by the influential physician Luis E. Ruiz (February 1910). AGN GOB 910-3-1; see also Archivo Histórico del Ayuntamiento, Legajo 2276, Exp. 36-38 and 61; Joe Nash, El Paseo de la Reforma (Mexico City: R. Esquivel, 1959); Francisco Sosa, Las estatuas de la Reforma (Mexico City: DDF, Secretaría de Obras y Servicios, 1974).

40. Regarding this monument, see Archivo Histórico del Ayuntamiento, Legajo 60, Exp. 1; Legajo 2276, Exp. 58; and regarding the origins of a national fund for the construction of the monument, see Legajo 2276, Exp. 35.

41. AGN GOB 909-10-4-3. About the monument, see Archivo Histórico del Ayuntamiento, Legajos 1166 and 1167. See also José de Jesús Nuñez Domínguez and Nicolás Rangel, El monumento a la Independencia: Bosquejo Histórico (Mexico City: Dirección General de Acción Educativa, Recreativa, de Reforma y Social, 1930); and Samuel Ruiz García, Monografía de la columna de la Independencia, 1910–1958 (Mexico City: Departamento del DF, 1958).

42. There were twenty-eight "civilized" countries that attended: six as special diplomatic missions (Italy, Japan, the U.S., Germany, Spain, and France); eighteen with special envoys (Honduras, Bolivia, Austria, Cuba, Costa Rica, Russia, Portugal, Holland, Guatemala, El Salvador, Peru, Panama, Brazil, Belgium, Chile, Argentina, Norway, and Uruguay); and three countries that commissioned residents of Mexico to represent them (Switzerland, Colombia, and Venezuela). Great Britain could not attend due to the death of King Edward VII, and Nicaragua due to a coup d'état, though the Nicaraguan poet Rubén Darío, who was appointed envoy of Nicaragua before the po-

litical turmoil, was treated as a national guest of honor by Mexico's intelligentsia and government. See Genaro García, *Crónica*, and SRE LE 101.

43. SRE LE 101, 117.

44. Archivo Histórico del Ayuntamiento, Legajo 594, Exp. 4.

45. Manuel Perló Cohen, *El paradigma porfiriano: Historia del desagüe del valle de México* (Mexico City: UNAM-Porrúa, 1999); Priscilla Connolly, *El contratista de don Porfirio: obras públicas, deuda y desarrollo desigual* (Zamora-Mexico City: El Colegio de Michoacán-UAM, 1997).

46. This proposal was made by E. Lozano, R. Nervo, Carlos Lazo de la Vega, and R. Riveroll del Prado. AGN GOB 910-6-1.

47. AGN GOB 907-3-1.

48. See also "Resumen de la historia de los trabajos de la penitenciaria de San Lázaro leido por Angel Zimbrón secretario del gobierno del Distrito Federal." 1900 SSA Impresos Box 2 Exp. 2/61.

49. On the Hygienic Exhibition see Consejo Superior de Salubridad, *La salubridad e higiene pública en los Estados Unidos Mexicanos: Brevísima reseña de los progresos alcanzados desde 1810 hasta 1910* (Mexico City: Casa Metodista de Publicaciones, 1910); and SSA, Salubridad Pública, Congresos y Convenciones, Box 10, Exp. 1-19.

50. These included, among other things, the famous study by Dr. Orvañanos, *Geografía médica y climatología* (1889), studies on the eradication of yellow fever in Mexico by Dr. Liceaga, *Quelques reseignements sur la tuberculose à Mexique* (1899); "Obras que remite la secretaría del Consejo a la sección de exposición de higiene y conferencias relativas," in SSA, Box 10, Exp. 11. See also Claudia Agostoni, *Monuments of Progress: Modernization and Public Health in Mexico City, 1876–1910* (Calgary: University of Calgary Press; Denver: University of Colorado Press; Mexico City: UNAM, 2003).

51. Mauricio Gómez Mayorga, "La influencia francesa en la arquitectura y el urbanismo en México," in Arturo Arnaiz y Freg, ed., *La intervención francesa y el imperio de Maximiliano cien años después, 1862–1962* (Mexico City: Asociación Mexicana de Historiadores, Instituto Francés de América Latina, 1962).

52. On the Columbus monument, see Luis García Pimentel, *El monumento elevado en la ciudad de México a Cristóbal Colón* (Mexico City: Impr. de F. Díaz de León, 1879).

53. Nash, *El Paseo de la Reforma*; José de Jesús Nuñez Domínguez and Nicolás Rangel, *El monumento a la Independencia*; Samuel Ruiz García, *Monografía de la columna de la Independencia*; Sosa, *Las estatuas de la Reforma*; Tannenbaum, "Streetwise History."

54. For examples of these types of arches, see sketches found in Archivo Histórico del Ayuntamiento, 4753, arches for the Paseo de la Reforma, Juárez Avenue, and Independencia Street.

55. *Adamo e Sesto Boari, architetti ferraresi del primo Novecento: A cura di Alessandra Farinelli Toselli e Lucio Scardino* (Ferrera: Liberty House, 1995).

56. For data on Rivas Mercado see the biography of his daughter, Antonieta: Fabienne Bradu, *Antonieta* (Mexico City: Fondo de Cultura Económica, 1991). That Rivas Mercado's daughter became José Vasconcelos's mistress, that she was a patron of bohemian artists, and that she killed herself in Notre Dame in Paris all gave don Antonio some historical visibility.

57. Archivo Histórico del Ayuntamiento, Legajo 116, Exp. 9, 13, and Legajo 1167, Exp. 24.

58. "Informe leido por el señor ingeniero don Antonio Rivas Mercado, Director de la Escuela Nacional de Bellas Artes, en el acto de inauguración de la Columna de la Independencia, el 16 de septiembre de 1910," reproduced in García, *Crónica*, 74.

59. Fray Servando y Teresa de Mier, *Historia de la revolución de la Nueva España*, republished by

the Sorbonne (Paris: Publications de la Sorbonne, 1990), 569; Javier Toribio Medina, *Historia del Tribunal del Santo Oficio de la Inquisición en México*, facsimile ed. (Mexico City: Porrúa, 1987; originally published in Santiago de Chile 1903), 295–301; Gerard Ronan, *The Irish Zorro: The Extraordinary Adventures of William Lamport (1615–1659)* (Dingle: Brandon, 2004); and Fabio Troncarelli, *La spada e la croce: Guillén Lombardo e l'Inquisizione in Messico* (Rome: Salerno editrice, 1999).

60. Vicente Riva Palacio (ed.), *México a través de los siglos*, vol. 2 (Barcelona: Santiago Ballescá, 1887–89), 383–87.

61. Luis González Obregón, *D. Guillén de Lampart: La Inquisición y la Independencia en el siglo XVII* (Mexico City and Paris: Vda de C. Bouret, 1908), 232. He refers to Alberto Lombardo's pamphlet: Alberto Lombardo, *Injusticias históricas: Olvido del primero que concibió e intentó la Independencia de México* (Mexico City: Tipografía Económica, 1901). In fact, Alberto Lombardo also had written a historiographical reconsideration of Lampart: Alberto Lombardo, *D. Guillén de Lombardo* (Mexico City: Tipografía Económica, 1901).

62. Lombardo, *D. Guillén de Lombardo*, 3.

63. González Obregón, *D. Guillén de Lampart*, 235.

64. Vicente Riva Palacio, *Memorias de un impostor: Don Guillén de Lampart, Rey de México*, 2 vols. (Mexico City: Porrúa, 1946; originally published in 1872).

65. See Claude Nicolet, *L'idée républicaine en France, 1789–1924 : essai d'histoire critique* (Paris: Gallimard, 1982).

66. Archivo Histórico del Ayuntamiento, Legajo 3603.

67. Formed by distinguished and wealthy members of the Porfirian elite: José Landero y Cos, Gabriel Mancera, Carlos Rivas, Carlos Herrera, Genaro García (the only historian of the team), and Ignacio de la Barra. "Informe al presidente de la república respecto al monumento a Juárez," by de la Barra, June 1910, AGN GOB. 906-4-2.

68. "Informe al presidente."

69. "Discurso pronunciado por el señor Licenciado don Carlos Robles en el acto de inauguración del monumento a Benito Juárez, el 18 de septiembre de 1910," reproduced in García, *Crónica*, 80.

70. See results of the 1906 contest for a Juárez monument, especially the project in Zapoteco style (including illustration). Antonio Rivas Mercado, Nicolás Mariscal, Velázquez de Léon, in *El Arte y la Ciencia*, 7, 11 (May 1906): 281–89.

71. See original AGN GOB 909-3-1.

72. García, *Crónica*, 148–42. See original plan in AGN GOB 909-3-1.

73. Clara García Ayluardo, "A World of Images: Cult, Ritual, and Society in Colonial Mexico City," in William Beezley, Cheryl English Martin, and William E. French, eds., *Rituals of Rule, Rituals of Resistance: Public Celebrations and Popular Culture in Mexico* (Wilmington: SR Books, 1994), 77–94.

74. The state of Morelos was asked for 250 Indians. The governor decided to send them, but then he wrote to Casarín explaining that Indians decided not to travel to Mexico City, because "there are rumors that from Mexico City they will be sent to San Luis Potosí, where there is war, thus they don't want to go to Mexico City." AGN GOB 909-3-1.

75. The conference was simultaneously hosted in Buenos Aires, which was celebrating Argentina's centennial. For an analysis of scientific politics, see Charles A. Hale, *The Transformation of Liberalism*.

76. *Actas del XVII Congreso Internacional de Americanistas. Sección Mexico* (Mexico City: Secretaría de

Fomento, 1910). The president of the Mexican section of the congress was Justo Sierra. It was attended by mainstream scholars on anthropology and archaeology (among them Edward Seler and Franz Boas). For the history of these congresses, see Juan Comas, *Cien años de congresos internacionales de americanistas* (Mexico City: UNAM, 1974); and for the history of the International School of Anthropology, see Ricardo Godoy, "Franz Boas and His Plans for an International School of American Archaeology and Ethnology in Mexico," *Journal of the History of Behavioral Sciences*, 13 (1977): 228–42; and Carmen Ruiz, "Insiders and Outsiders in Mexican Archaeology (1890–1930)," Ph.D. diss., University of Texas, Austin, 2003.

77. *Actas del XVII Congreso Internacional de Americanistas*, 8.

78. In this regard see Jesús Díaz de León, "Concepto del indianismo en México," in *Concurso científico y artístico del Centenario* (Mexico City: Tip. de la Vda. de F. Díaz de León, 1911), 23.

79. Camilo García de Polavieja y del Castillo, "La crónica del Centenario de la Independencia de Méjico," *Boletín de la Real Academia de la Historia*, 60 (1912): 454–56; also by Polavieja, *Hernán Cortés (estudio de un carácter)* (Toledo: La viuda é hijos de J. Peláez, 1909); Francisco Fernández de Béthencourt, *Discursos leídos ante la Real Academia de la Historia: en la recepción pública de Camilo G. de Polavieja y del Castillo, Marqués de Polavieja, el 28 de enero de 1912* (Madrid: J. R. Martín, 1912). During the *Centenario* a pamphlet was published about Polavieja, *Vida y hechos del Excmo. Sr. Dn. Camilo G. Polavieja Marqués de Polavieja* (Mexico City: Linotip. de Braulio Acosta, 1910). See also Alfredo López Serrano, *El General Polavieja y su actividad política y militar* (Madrid: Centro de Publicaciones, Ministerio de Defensa, Secretaría General Técnica, 2002); and *1910: El arte en un año decisivo: La Exposición de Artistas Mexicanos*, staged at the Museo Nacional de Arte, Mexico City, May–July 1991, catalogue published by the Museo Nacional de Arte, 1992.

80. "Discurso pronunciado por el señor don Fernando Pimentel y Fagoaga, presidente del Ayuntamiento Constitucional de la ciudad de México, en el acto de dedicación de la Av. Isabel la Católica, el 31 de agosto de 1910," reproduced in García, *Crónica*, 45.

81. AGN GOB 909-3-1, AGN GOB 910-3-1. Out of the many films that were made during the *Centenario*, very few survived. For a detailed explanation of these films, see Juan Felipe Leal, Eduardo Barraza, and Alejandro Jablonza, *Vistas que no se ven: Filmografía mexicana, 1896–1910* (Mexico City: UNAM, 1993).

82. The proposal was sent from Veracruz by Huerta Vargas. AGN GOB 907-3-1.

83. Mario Praz, *El pacto con la serpiente*, trans. Ida Vitale (Mexico City: Fondo de Cutura Económica, 1988), 405; Ramón Gómez de la Serna, *Lo cursi y otros ensayos* (Buenos Aires: Editorial Sudamericana, 1943); Raoul Fournier, *El cristal con que se mira: la cursilería y padecimientos afines* (Mexico City: Editorial Diana, 1980). See also the similarities with Spain in Noël Valis, *The Culture of Cursilería: Bad Taste, Kitsch, and Class in Modern Spain* (Durham: Duke University Press, 2002).

84. About the general architecture during the *Centenario*, see Ramón Vargas Salguero, "Las fiestas del Centenario: Recapitulaciones y vaticinios," in Fernando González Gortázar, ed., *La arquitectura mexicana del siglo XX* (Mexico City: CONACULTA, 1994), 19–33.

85. Fausto Ramírez, "Hacia la gran Exposición del Centenario de 1910: el arte mexicano en el cambio de siglo," in the catalogue of the exhibit *1910: El arte en un año decisivo*, 19–63.

86. In 1898 no first prize was awarded, the second was granted to Boari, and the third, not unanimously, to "Majestas." AGN SCOP-Palacio legislativo, 530/28.

87. In fact, Boari came to Mexico in 1897 to participate at the contest for the Palacio Legistativo. He won the contest, but after much discussion and debate, the contract was granted to the

French architect, É. Bénard (see I. Katzman, *Arquictectura del siglo XIX*); *Álbum Histórico del Palacio de Bellas Artes, 1904–1934* (Mexico City: Moderna, 1934); Antonio Bonet Correa and Francisco de la Maza, *La arquitectura de la época porfiriana* (Mexico City: Secretaría de Educación Pública, Instituto Nacional de Bellas Artes, 1980); Jesús Galindo y Villa, "Los proyectos para el palacio del Poder Legislativo Federal," *Memorias y Revista de la Sociedad Científica Antonio Alzate*, II (1897); and AGN-SCOP Palacio Legislativo, especially 530/30 and 530/28.

88. Katzman, *Arquitectura del siglo XIX*, 325–26.

89. "Informe sobre el estado problable de las obras el 16 de septiembre de 1910," AGN SCOP Palacio Legislativo, 530/733. This report informs about the artistic works that were made in Paris. See also "Informe trimestral sobre los estudios, trabajos, y gastos hechos para la construcción del Palacio Legislativo Federal, del 1 de julio al 30 de septiembre de 1910." AGN SCOP Palacio Legislativo leg 530/733. There is also the same type of data for October 31-December; April 1911. After the Revolution, there were constant complaints regarding delays in payments. AGN SCOP Palacio Legislativo 530/675 and 530/318; *Adamo e Sesto Boari*.

90. AGN SCOP Palacio Legislativo 530/734-6. "Let in the marble-like castle/the feeling of ardent civic pride grow huge/and that in the midst of patriotic struggles/the Parliament sings hymns of concord."

91. Among the most prominent professors of architecture there were Antonio Rivas Mercado, Carlos M. Lazo, Emilio Dondé, the brothers Federico and Nicolás Mariscal, and Manuel Torres Torrija. All of them opposed the modern steel-and-concrete construction, which they identified as a flashy American style. Katzman, *La arquitectura del siglo XIX*, 68.

92. Nicolás Mariscal, *El desarrollo de la arquitectura en México* (Mexico City: Oficina tip. de la Secretaría de Fomento, 1901); and Federico Mariscal, *La patria y la arquitectura nacional: Resúmenes de las conferencias dadas en la casa de la Universidad Popular Mexicana del 21 de octubre de 1913 al 29 de julio de 1924* (Mexico City: Imprenta Stephan y Torres, 1915).

93. Both Boari and Bénard had spent time in the U.S., Boari as student and assistant at the Burnham Chicago office, and Bénard as builder for the University of San Francisco. Both were admirers of the technological innovations of American architecture. *Adamo e Sesto Boari*. For images of Bénard's projects and paintings, see Javier Pérez Siller and Martha Bénard Calva, *El sueño inconcluso de Émile Bénard y su Palacio Legislativo, hoy monumento a la Revolución* (Mexico City: Artes de México, 2009).

94. Juan Agea, Romón Agea, Santiago Mendez, Ignacio de la Hidalga, Antonio de Anza, Guillermo Heredia, Ramón de Ibarrola.

95. Commentary by Edward Gorezynski in *The Mexican Herald* (April 19, 1898).

96. See proceedings of the jury meetings AGN SCOP-Palacio Legislativo, 530/28. The secretary of the jury was Ramón de Ibarrola.

97. This story is told by Álvarez in his "Las universidades alemanas y las escuelas de ingeniería y de arquitectura," *Boletín Municipal, Órgano del Ayuntamiento de México* (January 5, 1912): 50–62. P. J. Weber also worked in Chicago.

98. AGN SCOP-Palacio Legislativo 530/448. Bénard's palace included a frontispiece with representations of *Juventud, Ley, Verdad, Trabajo, Paz, Raza, Fuerza, Edad Viril* (in that order from left to right). European sculptors such as Ruffier Noël and Laurent Marqueste were hired to design these representations. Crowning the buildings was a dome with a huge bronze eagle and bronze representations of Industry, Commerce, Agriculture, and Mining. AGN SCOP-Palacio Legislativo

580/675. I thank the Bénard family in Mexico City for the access to É. Bénard's papers, drawings, and paintings. Bénard's son and daughter took residence in Mexico after 1914. The most complete study of Bénard is Stéphanie Chouard, "Émile Bénard, un inspirateur méconnu (1844–1929)," 2 vols., Mémoire de maitrise, Sorbonne, Paris IV, Institut D'Art et D'Archéologie, 1995. See also Pérez Siller and Bénard Calva, El sueño inconcluso; A. Rodríguez del Campo, "La portentosa obra del Palacio Legislativo proyectada por Bénard," Obras Públicas, 2, 12 (December 1930); Antonio Rivas Mercado, "El Palacio Legislativo Federal," published in El arte y la ciencia, nos. 1, 2, 3, 5 and 6, 1900, and republished in 1902, same title (Mexico City: Imprenta de Francisco Díaz de León).

99. The opinion is from Paul Philippe Cret's conversation with Donald Drew Egbert, transcribed in Chouard's "Émile Bénard," 188.

100. Jules Claretie, "Art et littérature," in Roland Bonaparte, ed., Le Mexique au début du XX siècle, vol. 2 (Paris: C. Delagrave, 1904), 231.

101. Contract, Bénard's private papers, Bénard Family (Mixcoac, Mexico City).

102. SRE, 27-11-54. Crónica ficcional de los festejos conmemorativos del centenario de la consumación de la independencia de México 1922. For an example of an "epistemic" break between 1910 and 1921, see Annick Lempérière, "Los dos centenarios de la Independencia"; about 1921, see El Universal, "Edición conmemorativa del primer centenario de la independencia mexicana," tomo I, núm. 4, September 1,1921, suplemento de arte e información. The best general account of the 1921 celebration in Mexico City is Elaine C. Lacy, "The 1921 Centennial Celebration of Mexico's Independence: State Building and Popular Negotiation," in ¡Viva México, Viva la Independencia! Celebrations of September 16, ed. William Beezley and David Lorey (Wilmington: SR Books, 2001), 199–232.

103. El Universal, "Edición Conmemorativa del Primer Centenario de la Independencia."

104. Cervantes, Rodó, and Darío were mandatory references from 1900 onward as proofs of Hispanism. Montalvo, a cosmopolitan Ecuadorian writer who lived in exile most of his life (1832–89), was admired by liberal Porfirians, especially for his anticlericalism, but also for his imitations of Cervantes. Obregón was known, after the revolutionary battle against Villa's troops, where he lost an arm, as the Manco de Celaya.

105. Mechthild Rutsch, Entre el campo y el gabinete: nacionales y extranjeros en la profesionalización de la antropología mexicana (1877–1920) (Mexico City: INAH, 2007); Ruiz, "Insiders and Outsiders."

106. The "India bonita" contest has been examined, in different ways, in Carmen Ruiz, "La India Bonita: National Beauty in Revolutionary Mexico," Cultural Dynamics, vol.14, no. 3 (November 2002): 283–302; and Rick A. Lopez, "The India Bonita Contest of 1921 and the Ethnicization of Mexican National Culture," Hispanic American Historical Review,82, 2 (May 2002): 291–329.

107. Carlos Obregón Santacilia, El Monumento a la Revolución (Mexico City: Secretaría de Educación Pública, Dep. de Divulgación, 1960).

108. Italo Calvino, Invisible Cities, trans. William Weaver (New York: Harcourt Brace Jovanovich, 1972), 163.

CHAPTER 2

1. Senator James McMillan sponsored the creation of an advisory park commission. Constance McLaughlin Green, Washington Capital City (Princeton: Princeton University Press, 1963), 132–46; Peter Hall, Cities of Tomorrow: An Intellectual History of Urban Planning and Design in the Twentieth Century (Oxford: Blackwell Publishing, 1988),175–81; Thomas S. Hines, "The Imperial Mall: The City

Beautiful Movement and the Washington Plan of 1901–1902," in *The Mall in Washington 1791–1991*, ed. Richard Longstreth (Washington, D.C.: National Gallery of Art, 2002), 79–100; Frederick Gutheim, *Worthy of the Nation: The History of Planning for the National Capital* (Washington, D.C.: Smithsonian Institution Press, 1977); William Tobin, "In the Shadow of the Capitol: The Transformation of Washington, D.C., and the Elaboration of the Modern U.S. Nation-State," Ph D. diss., Stanford University, 1993. See also, for contrast, Andreas W. Daum and Christof Mauch, eds., *Berlin, Washington, 1800–2000: Capital Cities, Cultural Representation, and National Identities* (Washington, D.C.: German Historical Institute; Cambridge: Cambridge University Press, 2005); Thomas Hall, *Planning Europe's Capital Cities: Aspects of Nineteenth-Century Urban Development* (London: E & FN Spon, 1997); Arturo Almandoz, ed., *Planning Latin America's Capital Cities, 1850–1950* (London: Routledge, 2002); Wolfgang Sonne, *Representing the State: Capital City Planning in the Early Twentieth Century* (Munich: Prestel, 2003); and Jeffrey F. Meyer, "The Eagle and the Dragon: Comparing the Design of Washington and Beijing," *Washington History* 8, no. 2 (1996–1997): 4–21.

2. Warren Susman, *Culture as History: The Transformation of American Society in the Twentieth Century* (New York: Pantheon Books, 1984); Alan Trachtenberg, *The Incorporation of America: Culture and Society in the Gilded Age* (New York: Hill and Wang, 1982); Elise Marienstras, *Nous, le people: Les origins du nationalisme américain* (Paris: Gallimard, 1988); Merle Curti, *Roots of American Loyalty* (New York: Atheneum, 1968); David Waldstreicher, *In the Midst of Perpetual Fetes* (Chapel Hill: University of North Carolina Press, 1997); Christopher A. Thomas, *The Lincoln Memorial and American Life* (Princeton: Princeton University Press, 2002); Morton Keller, *Affairs of State: Public Life in Late Nineteenth Century America* (Cambridge: Harvard University Press, 1977). For a comparison with Australia and Germany, see Lyn Spillman, *Nation and Commemoration: Creating National Identities in the United States and Australia* (Cambridge: Cambridge University Press, 1997); Andreas Etges, *Wirtschaftsnationalismus: USA und Deutschland im Vergleich (1815–1914)* (Frankfurt: Campus, 1999); Wilbur Zelinsky, *Nation into State: The Shifting Symbolic Foundations of American Nationalism* (Chapel Hill: University of North Carolina Press, 1988); Cecilia Elizabeth O'Leary, *To Die For: The Paradox of American Patriotism* (Princeton: Princeton University Press, 1999); Jean-Louis Cohen, *La temptació d'Amèrica: Ciutat i arquitectura a Europa, 1893–1960* (Barcelona: Centre de Cultura Contemporània de Barcelona, Diputació de Barcelona, 1996); Lawrence W. Levine, *Highbrow/Lowbrow: The Emergence of Cultural Hierarchy in America* (Cambridge: Harvard University Press, 1988); William Novak, "The Myth of the 'Weak' American State," *American Historical Review* 113 (2008): 752–72.

3. Robert Harbison, *The Built, the Unbuilt, and Unbuildable: In Pursuit of Architectural Meaning* (Cambridge: MIT Press, 1994), 84–86.

4. Thomas, *The Lincoln Memorial and American Life*.

5. Richard Morse and Jorge Hardoy, eds., *Rethinking the Latin American City* (Baltimore: Johns Hopkins University Press, 1992), 32.

6. Andrés Lira, *Las comunidades indígenas frente a la ciudad de México* (Mexico City: El Colegio de México, 1983), 123. On the U.S. invasion of Mexico City and the consequences for the city, see Carlos Illades and Ariel Rodríguez Kuri, *Ciudad de México: Instituciones, actores sociales y conflicto político, 1774–1931* (Zamora: El Colegio de Michoacán, 1996); Luis Fernando Granados, *Sueñan las piedras: alzamiento ocurrido en la ciudad de México, 14, 15 y 16 de septiembre de 1847* (Mexico City: Ediciones Era, CONACULTA-INAH, 2003).

7. Keller, *Affairs of State*, 98–101.

8. There are many examples of this; see Michael J. Bednar, *L'Enfant's Legacy* (Baltimore: Johns Hopkins University Press, 2006).

9. J. L. Sibley Jennings, "Artistry as Design in L'Enfant's Extraordinary City," *U.S. Library of Congress Quarterly Journal*, 36, 3 (1979): 225–27; Santos Juliá, David Ringrose, and Cristina Segura, *Madrid: historia de una capital* (Madrid: Alianza Editorial, Fundación Caja de Madrid, 1994).

10. Green, *Washington Capital City*; William M. Gardner, "Native Americans: Early Encounters," in Francine Curro Cary, ed., *Urban Odyssey: A Multicultural History of Washington, D.C.* (Washington, D.C.: Smithsonian Institution Press, 1995), 3–19; Kenneth R. Bowling, *The Creation of Washington, D.C.: The Ideal Location of the American Capital* (Fairfax, VA: George Mason University Press, 1991).

11. C. M. Harris, "Washington's Gamble, L'Enfant's Dream: Politics, Design, and the Founding of the National Capital," *William and Mary Quarterly* 56, 3 (July 1999): 533.

12. Pamela Scott, *Temple of Liberty: Building the Capitol for a New Nation* (New York: Oxford University Press, 1995); Pamela Scott, "'This Vast Empire': The Iconography of the Mall 1791–1948," in *The Mall in Washington 1791–1991*, ed. Richard Longstreth (Washington, D.C.: National Gallery of Art, 1995); and Green, *Washington Capital City*.

13. Ciro Flamarion Cardoso and Paulo Henrique da Silva Araujo, *Río de Janeiro* (Madrid: Fundación MAPFRE, 1992); and Richard Morse, *From Community to Metropolis* (Gainesville: University of Florida Press, 1958).

14. Regina Hernández Franyuti, ed., *La Ciudad de México en la primera mitad del siglo XIX* (Mexico City: Instituto de Investigaciones Dr. José María Luis Mora, 1994); Andrés Lira, *Las comunidades indígenas frente a la ciudad de México* (Mexico City: El Colegio de México, 1983); and María Dolores Morales, María Amparo Ros Torres, and Esteban Sánchez de Tagle, *Ciudad de México, época colonial: Bibliografía* (Mexico City: Departamento del Distrito Federal, Dirección de Estudios Históricos, INAH, 1987).

15. Therefore, as Ariel Rodríguez Kuri has shown, in the 1820s Mexico City authorities did not want the city to be federalized, fearing the loss of the autonomy gained from 1808 to 1821. Ariel Rodríguez Kuri, *La experiencia olvidada: el ayuntamiento de México: política y gobierno, 1876–1912* (Mexico City: El Colegio de México, 1996), 21–23.

16. For the meeting of the American Institute of Architects in Washington in 1900, see Gutheim, *Worthy of the Nation*, 115–17.

17. Jorge Hardoy, "Theory and Practice of Urban Planning in Europe 1850–1930," in *Rethinking the Latin American City*, eds. Jorge Hardoy and Richard Morse (Baltimore: Johns Hopkins University Press, 1992); Margarita Gutman and Thomas Reese, eds., *Buenos Aires 1910: el imaginario para una gran capital* (Buenos Aires: Eudeba, 1999); Margarita Gutman and Jorge Hardoy, *Buenos Aires: historia urbana del área metropolitana* (Madrid: Editorial MAPFRE, 1992).

18. Quoted in Cohen, *La temptació d'Amèrica*, 25.

19. Francesco Passanti, "Le Corbusier et le gratte-ciel: aux origines du plan Voisin," in *Américanisme et modernité: L'idéal américain dans l'architecture*, eds. J.-L. Cohen and H. Damisch (Paris: Flammarion, 1993), 171–89; and Nicolau Sevcenko, *Orfeu Extático na metrópole: São Paulo, sociedade e cultura nos frementes anos 20* (São Paulo: Companhia das Letras, 1992).

20. Harbison, *The Built, the Unbuilt*, 41.

21. Green, *Washington Capital City*; and Edward Relph, *The Modern Urban Landscape* (Baltimore: Johns Hopkins University Press, 1987).

22. Cohen, *La temptació d'Amèrica*, 126; Hall, *Cities of Tomorrow*. For the final triumph of New York

as world capital of art in the 1950s, see Serge Guilbaut, *How New York Stole the Idea of Modern Art: Abstract Expressionism, Freedom, and the Cold War*, trans. Arthur Goldhammer (Chicago: University of Chicago Press, 1983).

23. Lois E. Horton, "The Days of Jubilee: Black Migration During the Civil War and Reconstruction," in *Urban Odyssey: A Multicultural History of Washington, D.C.*, ed. Francine Curro Cary (Washington, D.C.: Smithsonian Institution Press, 1996); and Green, *Washington Capital City*.

24. Domingo F. Sarmiento, *Viajes III, Estados Unidos* (Buenos Aires: La Cultura Argentina, 1922), 156–69, quotation on p. 158.

25. Justo Sierra, *Viajes en tierra yankee, Obras completas* (Mexico City: UNAM, 1948), 111–12.

26. It pains me to transcribe Ibargüengoitia's comments, as I have learned a lot from his irony. J. Ibargüengoitia, "Carta de Washington," in *Viajes a la América ígnota* (Mexico City: Joaquín Mortiz, 1972), 121–25.

27. M. A. de Quevedo, *Espacios libres y reservas forestales de las ciudades: su adaptación a jardines, parques y lugares de juego: Aplicación á la ciudad de México* (Mexico City: Gomar y Busson, 1911); Carlos González Peña, *La vida tumultuosa: Seis semanas en los Estados Unidos* (Mexico City: Editorial Botas e Hijos, n.d.), 62, 64.

28. Jorge H. Jiménez Muñoz, *La traza del poder (1824–1928)* (Mexico City: Dedalo, Cotex, 1993); María del Carmen Collado, *La burguesía mexicana: el emporio Braniff y su participación política: 1865–1920* (Mexico City: Siglo Veintiuno Editores, 1987); and Nora Pérez-Rayón, *Entre la tradición señorial y la modernidad: la familia Escandón Barrón y Escandón Arango: formación y desarrollo de la burguesía en México durante el porfirismo (1890–1910)* (Mexico City: Universidad Autónoma Metropolitana, 1995).

29. Green, *Washington Capital City*, 142; and Howard Gillette, *Between Justice and Beauty: Race, Planning, and the Failure of Urban Policy in Washington, D.C.* (Baltimore: Johns Hopkins University Press, 1995), 108.

30. For the debates in Washington between 1900 and 1920, see Alan Lessoff, *The Nation and Its City: Politics, Corruption, and Progress in Washington, D.C. 1861–1902* (Baltimore: Johns Hopkins University Press, 1994); Gutheim, *Worthy of the Nation*; and Tobin, "In the Shadow of the Capitol."

31. Yannis Tsiomis, "Athènes et Washington ou comment confondre l'origine et le progrès," in *Américanisme et modernité: L'idéal américain dans l'architecture*, eds. J.-L. Cohen and H. Damisch (Paris: Flammarion, 1993), 121–35.

32. Stanley Elkins and Eric McKitrick, *The Age of Federalism* (Oxford: Oxford University Press, 1993), 169–82.

33. The Federal District encompassed a radius of two *leguas* around Mexico City's central plaza. Lira, *Las comunidades indígenas*, 56; and Rodríguez Kuri, *La experiencia olvidada*, 21–22.

34. Irene J. Winter, "Homer's Phoenicians: History, Ethnography, or Literary Trope? A Perspective on Early Orientalism," in *The Ages of Homer: A Tribute to Emily Twonsend Vermeule*, eds. Jane B. Carter and Sarah P. Morris (Austin: University of Texas Press, 1995), 248.

35. Tsiomis, "Athènes et Washington, ou comment confondre l'origine et le progrès," 126.

36. Federico Bravo Morata, *Historia de Madrid* (Madrid: Fenicia, 1966); F. C. Sainz de Robles, *Por qué es Madrid capital de España* (Madrid: Aguilar, 1961); and Antonio Bonet Correa, "Los 'ensanches' y el urbanismo burgués del siglo XIX en España," *Storia della città* 23 (1982): 27–34.

37. For the exceptionality of Washington, see the introduction to Green, *Washington Capital City*; Gillette, *Between Justice and Beauty*, xi; and Lessoff, *The Nation and Its City*, 1–3.

38. Lisa June Hart, "Shepherd's Castle: Documentation of a Gothic Revival House in a Mexican Silver Mining Town," MA thesis, University of Texas, 1988.

39. Quoted in Gillette, *Between Justice and Beauty*, 68.

40. Annick Lampérière, "La sécularisation de la capitale. De l'espace sacré à l'espace civique: Mexico au XIXe siècle," in Jérome Monnet, ed., *Espace, temps et pouvoir dans le Nouveau Monde* (Paris: Anthropos, 1996), 71–100; Pérez-Rayón, *Entre la tradición señorial y la modernidad.*

41. Elkins and McKitrick, *The Age of Federalism*, 192–93.

42. Paul Boyer, *Urban Masses and Moral Order in America, 1820–1920* (Cambridge: Harvard University Press, 1978), 252–76.

43. Lira, *Las comunidades indígenas*, 42.

44. Therefore the city council performed the first rudimentary electoral manipulation—rudimentary if compared, for instance, to Chicago's or New York's sophisticated electoral techniques of the late nineteenth century.

45. M. C. Rolland, *El desastre municipal en la República mexicana*, 3rd ed. (Mexico City: Molina, 1952), 39.

46. Rodríguez Kuri, *La experiencia olvidada*; Lira, *Las comunidades indígenas*; Charles A. Hale, *The Transformation of Liberalism in Late Nineteenth Century Mexico* (Princeton: Princeton University Press, 1989); as well as Antonio Annino, "Prácticas criollas y liberalismo en la crisis del espacio urbano colonial," in Enrique Montalvo Ortega, ed., *El águila bifronte: Poder y liberalismo en México* (Mexico City: INAH, 1995), 17–63.

47. Yoshinobu Hakutani and Robert Butler, eds., *The City in African-American Literature* (Madison: Fairleigh Dickinson University Press, 1995).

48. Lira, *Las comunidades indígenas*; John Lear, *Workers.*

49. Lira, *Las comunidades indígenas*; Lear, *Workers*; and Pablo Piccato, *City of Suspects: Crime in Mexico City, 1900–1931* (Durham: Duke University Press, 2001).

50. Lira, *Las comunidades indígenas*, 113.

51. Fernando Escalante, *Ciudadanos imaginarios* (Mexico City: El Colegio de México, 1992).

52. Willard B. Gatewood, *Aristocrats of Color: The Black Elite, 1880–1920* (Bloomington: Indiana University Press, 1990), 39–68.

53. James Kirkpatrick Flack, *Desideratum in Washington: The Intellectual Community in the Capital City, 1870–1900* (Cambridge: Schenkman Publishing, 1975).

54. Gillette, *Between Justice and Beauty*, 27.

55. Green, *Washington Capital City*, 150; and Gatewood, *Aristocrats of Color.*

56. Green, *Washington Capital City*, 153.

57. Elbert Peets, "Current Town Planning in Washington," *Town Planning Review* 14, 4 (1931): 231–32, quoted in Lessoff, *The Nation and Its City*, 267.

58. Érico Veríssimo, *Gato prêto em campo de neve* (Rio de Janeiro: Editôra Globo, 1961), 70–71 (originally written in 1939).

CHAPTER 3

1. Higinio Vázquez Santa Ana, *Canciones, cantares y corrido mexicanos* (Mexico City: n.p., 1925), 75.

2. "La ciudad," and "Himno del dolor convergente," S. Novo, *Ensayos* (Mexico City: n.p., 1925), 99, 105–6; Rolf Lindner, *The Reportage of Urban Culture*, trans. Adrian Morris (Cambridge:

Cambridge University Press, 1996); Henriette Levillain, editor, *Poétique de la maison : la chambre romanesque, le festin théâtral, le jardin littéraire* (Paris: Presses de l'Université Paris-Sorbonne, 2005).

3. Alejandro Rebolledo, "Vecindades in the Traza of Mexico City," MA thesis, School of Architecture, McGill University, 1998; Wallace Thomson as quoted in Lear, *Workers*; Gonzalo de Murga, "Atisbos sociológicos, el fraccionamiento de tierras, las habitaciones baratas, curso pronunciado de recepción leído en la Sociedad Mexicana de Geografía y Estadística por el socio Sr. Don Gonzalo de Murga," *Boletín de la Sociedad de Geografía y Estadística*, 6 (1913): 474–86; *Informe y Memoria del Departamento del Distrito Federal que rinde el C. Jefe del mismo Lic. Aarón Sáenz por el periodo administrativo comprendido entre el 1 de julio de 1933 y el 30 de junio de 1934* (Mexico City: Departamento del Distrito Federal, 1934); María Soledad Cruz Rodríguez, *Crecimiento urbano y procesos sociales en el Distrito Federal (1920–1928)* (Mexico City: Universidad Autónoma Metropolitana, 1994).

4. Jorge H. Jiménez Muñoz, *La traza del poder* (Mexico City: Dedalo, Cotex, 1993); also Érica Berra, "La expansion de la Ciudad de México y los conflictos urbanos," Ph.D. diss., El Colegio de México, 1982; Ernesto Aréchiga Córdoba, "La formación de un barrio marginal, Tepito entre 1868–1929," María del Carmen Collado, ed., *Miradas recurrentes, la ciudad de México en el siglo XIX y XX*, vol. 1 (Mexico City: Instituto de Investigaciones Dr. José María Luis Mora, 2004), 271–93.

5. William Henry Bishop, *Mexico, California and Arizona* (New York: Harper and Brothers, 1889), 51; W. E. Carson, *Mexico, the Wonderland of the South* (New York: Macmillan Company, 1909), 134.

6. Martín Gómez Palacios, *A la una a las dos y a las . . .* (Mexico City: Editorial Cultura, 1923), 6.

7. Julio Sesto, *La tórtola del Ajusco* (Mexico City: Maucci hermanos y cia., 1915), 31. "There was very little to see in that miserable dwelling, very little indeed. At the entrance, to clean the feet, a frayed piece of cloth; on the left, in the corner, a poorly assembled stand holding a broken bust, under which was a covering of yarn, woven by the house's señora; the square corner cupboard was missing one of the curved legs, and instead of the leg maimed by time, there was the little piece of a brick; along the wall, on the left side, an archaic sofa with a carved back, supported by the wall, because the screws and the spikes that held the piece of furniture together no longer had the strength to hold the back, which complained of old age when anyone leaned against it; around the couch, turning the corner to the middle of the front wall, the armchair mates of that sofa, all battered, all nailed again and again every five years, just to get by, like the flaccid muscles of the deteriorated señora."

8. Carlos González Peña, *La musa bohemia: novela* (Valencia: F. Sempere y compañía, 1908), 21, 23.

9. "A saint with her lamp burning . . . pictures of bright colors depicting scenes of Attila and William Tell, soldiers cut with scissors, glued to the wall with house-made glue . . ." Quoted in Ana María Prieto Hernández, *Acerca de la pendenciera e indisciplinada vida de los léperos capitalinos* (Mexico City: CONACULTA, 2001), 23.

10. "Una excursión a la Colonia de la Bolsa," *Arte y Letras* (September 12, 1914); *Todo* (July 4, 1944); *Informe y memoria del Departamento del Distrito Federal que rinde el C. Jefe del mismo Lic. Aarón Sáenz por el periodo administrativo comprendido entre el 1 de julio de 1933 y el 30 de junio de 1934* (Mexico City: Departamento del Distrito Federal, 1934).

11. *Memoria de los trabajos ejecutados por el Consejo Superior de Salubridad en el año de 1901* (Mexico City: Tip. y Lit. La Europea de J. Aguilar Vera y Com., 1902).

12. *Memoria de los trabajos*, 83.

13. Julio Guerrero, *La génesis del crímen en México, estudio de psiquiatría social* (Mexico City, Paris: Li-

brería de la viuda de C. Bouret, 1901), 45, 165, 166; Ariel Rodríguez Kuri, "Julio Guerrero, ciencia y pesimismo en el 900 mexicano," *Historias*, no. 49 (September–December, 1999): 43–55; Piccato, *City of Suspects*. For Jourdanet's theory, see Denis Jourdanet, *De Mexique au point de vue de son influence sur la vie de l'homme* (Paris: J.-B. Baillière et fils, Baillière brothers, 1861).

14. *Memoria de las labores realizadas por el Departamento de Salubridad Pública durante el año fiscal julio 1931–julio 1932* (Mexico City: Talleres Gráficos de la Nación, 1932); *Memoria de los trabajos ejecutados por el Departamento de Salubridad del 1 de diciembre de 1920 al 31 de agosto de 1921* (Mexico City: Talleres Gráficos de la Nación, 1923); *Memoria de los trabajos ejecutados por el Departamento de Salubridad del 1 de mayo al 15 de noviembre de 1920* (Mexico City: Talleres Gráficos de la Nación, 1923); *Informe y memoria del Departamento del Distrito Federal que rinde el C. Jefe del mismo Lic. Aarón Sáenz por el periodo administrativo comprendido entre el 1 de julio de 1933 y el 30 de junio de 1934* (Mexico City: Departamento del Distrito Federal, 1934).

15. Oscar Lewis: *Life in a Mexican Village: Tepoztlán Restudied* (Urbana: University of Illinois Press, 1951); *Five Families: Mexican Case Studies in the Culture of Poverty* (New York: Basic Books, 1959); *The Children of Sánchez: Autobiography of a Mexican Family* (New York: Random House, 1961). These studies were commercial successes and had two followups: *Pedro Martínez: A Mexican Peasant and His Family* (New York: Random House, 1964); and *A Death in the Sánchez Family* (New York: Random House, 1969). See also Matilde Callari Galli, *Le storie di vita nelle analisi culturali di Robert Redfield, Oscar Lewis, Cora Dubois* (Rome: Edizioni Ricerche, 1966); Richard Critchfield, *Look to Suffering, Look to Joy: Robert Redfield and Oscar Lewis Restudied*, 3 vols. (Hanover, NH: American Universities Field Staff, 1978); and Susan M. Rigdon, *The Culture Facade: Art, Science, and Politics in the Work of Oscar Lewis* (Urbana: University of Illinois Press, 1988).

16. Oscar Lewis, *Cinco familias*, trans. Emma Sánchez Ramírez (Mexico City: Fondo de Cultura Económica, 1961). In English some of Lewis's book were illustrated by Alberto Beltrán—by the 1950s a well-established self-made newspaper and magazine illustrator, and a native of Tepito.

17. The Spanish publisher of the book was the prestigious Fondo de Cultura Económica—a state publisher. As a result of the scandal, President Gustavo Díaz Ordaz deposed the Fondo director. For a narrative of events see José Agustín, *Tragicomedia mexicana*, vol. 1 (Mexico City: Planeta, 1998), 236.

18. Lewis attempted several times to sell the rights for the film version of his books. His wife disapproved Hall Bartlett's script. Rigdon, *The Culture Facade*.

19. Guillermo Bonfil Batalla, *México profundo: una civilización negada* (Mexico City: Secretaría de Educación Pública, CIESAS, 1987).

20. Mario Praz, *Il patto col serpente, paralipomeni di "La carne, la morte e il diavolo nella letteratura romantica"* (Milano: Mondadori, 1973), 402.

21. "Si tuvo defensa el siglo XIX es porque aceptó lo cursi como ingrediente vital, como conservador de la paz, como anclaje seguro de su tiempo." Ramón Gómez de la Serna, *Ensayo sobre lo cursi* (Madrid: Eduardo A. Ghioldi, 1990), 33 (originally published in 1934). About Porfirian interiors, see Antonio Saborit, "El modernismo y los espacios interiores," *Nexos* (June 1991).

22. Salvador Novo, *Toda la prosa* (Mexico City: Empresas Editoriales, 1964), 98.

23. Charles Rice, *The Emergence of the Interior: Architecture, Modernity, Domesticity* (New York: Routledge, 2007); Rémy G. Saisselin, *Bricabracomania: The Bourgeois and the Bibelot* (London: Thames and Hudson, 1985); Penny Sparke, *The Modern Interior* (London: Reaktion, 2008); Beatriz Blasco Esquivias, *La casa: evolución del espacio doméstico en España* (Madrid: Ediciones El Viso, 2006).

24. Clare Sheridan, *My American Diary* (New York: Boni and Liveright, 1922).

25. Micrós, *Ocios y apuntes* (Mexico City: Imprenta de Ignacio Escalante, 1890).

26. While this book was in production, Laura González and Miguel Ángel Berumen published a newly discovered collection of photos, which also included some interiors of Mexico City's houses. See Laura González Flores and Miguel Ángel Berumen, *Otra Revolución: Fotografías de la ciudad de México, 1910–1918* (Mexico City: UNAM, 2010).

27. See, for instance, Elizabeth Heyert, *Metropolitan Places: Interiors from New York, Barcelona, Milan, Mexico City, Paris, West Berlin, London, Los Angeles* (New York: Viking Studio Books, 1989).

28. Walter Benjamin, *The Arcades Project*, trans. Rolf Tiedemann (Cambridge: Belknap Press, 1999), insertion 12, 6; Mario Praz, *An Illustrated History of Furnishing, from the Renaissance to the 20th Century*, trans. William Weaver (New York: G. Braziller, 1964), 20.

29. Adolf Loos, *Ins Leere gesprochen 1897–1900* (Paris: Éditions Georges Crés et Cie., 1921); Michelle Perrot, *Histoire de chambres* (Paris: Éditions de Seuil, 2009). .

30. "Don Thomás Braniff y su distinguida familia," by "Cronista de la S. S.," *Revista de Revistas* (October 23, 1921): 6.

31. For this orientalism, see chapters 7 and 8.

32. Víctor Manuel Macías-González, "The Mexican Aristocracy and Porfirio Díaz, 1876–1911," Ph.D. diss., Texas Christian University, 1999; *Savia Moderna*, 1 (April 1906): 107–13; Salvador Moreno, *El pintor Antonio Fabrés* (Mexico City: Instituto de Investigaciones Estéticas, UNAM, 1981).

33. Marte R. Gómez to Plutarco Elías Calles, June 12, 1930. Fondo Plutarco Elías Calles, Archivo Calles-Torreblanca, Exp 88, inv. 2400.

34. Gaston Bachelard, *La poétique de l'espace* (Paris: PUF, 2004), 120.

35. Gómez de la Serna, *Ensayo sobre lo cursi*, 35.

CHAPTER 4

1. William K. Klingaman, *1919: The Year Our World Began* (New York: Harper and Row, 1987); Anthony Read, *The World on Fire: 1919 and the Battle with Bolshevism* (New York: W. W. Norton and Company, 2008); Ulrich Kluge, *Die deutsche Revolution 1918–19: Staat, Politik und Gesellschaft zwischen Weltkrieg und Kapp-Putsch* (Frankfurt: Suhrkamp, 1985); Fausto Ramírez, *Crónica de las artes plásticas en los años de López Velarde* (Mexico City: UNAM, 1990). In this narrative my sources are too many. In order not to saturate the text with footnotes, I consolidate many references in each footnote.

2. Julio Torri, "A Circe," poem included in J. Torri, *Tres libros: Ensayos y poemas, De fusilamientos, Prosas dispersas* (Mexico City: Fondo de Cultura Económica, 1964).

3. Frank Seaman [Charles Phillips], "How to Travel on a Slim Pocketbook: Seeing Mexico through Your Parlor Window," *El Heraldo* (September 22, 1919); Seaman's poem, "In the Backwash," *El Heraldo* (October 27, 1919). The night of the earthquake is described by Juan Bustillo Oro, *Vientos de los veintes: cronicón testimonial* (Mexico City: Secretaría de Educación Pública, 1973); Julio Sesto, *La ciudad de los palacios* (Mexico City: El Libro Español, 1917), 217; Alberto J. Pani, *La higiene en México* (Mexico City: Imprenta de J. Ballescá, 1916); Ellsworth Huntington, "The Relation of Health to Racial Capacity: The Example of Mexico," *Geographical Review*, 11, 2 (April 1921): 243–64; *La mendicidad en México* (Mexico City: Beneficencia Pública del D.F., 1930); Ricardo Granillo, "La mortalidad en la ciudad de México," *Boletín del Departamento de Salubridad Pública*, no. 1 (1925): 11; Miguel Ángel de Quevedo, *Relato de mi vida* (Mexico City: n.p., 1943); Quevedo's comments in *México Forestal, órgano oficial de la Sociedad Forestal Mexicana*, 1, 2 (February 1923): 20; Felipe Teixi-

dor, PHO 4-104; J. González de Mendoza, "G. Apollinaire," and "Apollinaire en México," both in *Ensayos selectos* (Mexico City: Fondo de Cultura Económica, 1970); Octavio Paz, "Ramón López Velarde, el desconocido de sí mismo," in *Cuadrivio* (Mexico City: Joaquín Mortiz, 1965); Guillaume Apollinaire, *Correspondance avec son frère et sa mère, présentée par Gilbert Boudar et Michel Décaudin* (Paris: Librairie J. Corti, 1987); and "Français à Mexico" (1914), in Apollinaire, *Oeuvres en prose complètes*, vol. 3 (Paris: Gallimard, 1993), 184; Domingo Díez, "Nuestra cultura y el respeto a los monumentos colonias," *Memorias y Revista de la Sociedad Científica Antonio Alzate*, 37 (1919): 381–95.

4. Lopez Velarde's story: "Caro data vermibus," *Vida Moderna* (November 9, 1916); José Emilio Pacheco, "Ramón López Velarde (1970)," in López Velarde, *Obra poética*, edited by José Luis Martínez (Mexico City, Barcelona, Buenos Aires: Galaxia Gutenberg, ALLCA XX, UNESCO, 1998), quoted p. 588; Alfonso Reyes, "Epitafio," *Obras completas X* (Mexico City: Fondo de Cultura Económica, 1996), 84; Manuel Gamio, "La zahurda," in Gamio, *Vidas dolientes* (Mexico City: Botas, 1937).

5. Emilio Rabasa, *El cuarto poder* (1888) (Mexico City: Porrúa, 1970), 9–10; Julio Sesto, *La tórtola del Ajusco* (Mexico City: Maucci hermanos y cia., 1915); and *La ciudad de los palacios*; on symbolism between Mexico and Europe see Fausto Ramírez, "El simbolismo en México," *El espejo simbolista, Europa y México, 1870–1920* (Mexico City: Museo Nacional de Arte, 2005), 29–59. See Guillermo Sheridan, *Los Contemporáneos ayer* (Mexico City: Fondo de Cultura Económica, 1985), 83; Gabriel Zaid, *Leer poesía* (Mexico City: Fondo de Cultura Económica, 1987), 76; López Velarde, *Poesías*; Porfirio Barba Jacob, *Poesía completa*, edited and annotated by Fernando Vallejo (Mexico City: Fondo de Cultura Económica, 2008); López Velarde, 'Melodía criolla,' *Armas y Letras* (1917), in López Velarde, *Obra poética*, quote in p. 351.

6. José Clemente Orozco, *Autobiografía* (Mexico City: Ediciones Occidente, 1945); Julio Sesto, *La bohemia de la muerte; biografías y anecdotario pintoresco de cien mexicanos célebres en el arte, muertos en la pobreza y el abandono, y estudio crítico de sus obras* (Mexico City: Editorial Tricolor, 1929), 71.

7. Fausto Ramírez, *Saturnino Herrán* (Mexico City: UNAM, 1976); "Oracion funebre: Pronunciada en el 1er aniversario de la muerte de Saturnino Herrán en el Anfiteatro de la Escuela Nacional Preparatoria, por Ramón López Velarde," *El Universal Ilustrado* (October 16, 1919), reproduced in Ramírez, *Crónica de las artes plásticas*, 93–94.

8. Alfonso Toro, "El pintor de raza," *Revista de Revistas* (Nov. 17, 1918): 14, reproduced in Ramírez, *Saturnino Herrán*, 83. See Montserrat Gali i Boadella, *Artistes catalans a Mexic: segles XIX i XX* (Barcelona: Generalitat de Catalunya, Comissió Amèrica i Catalunya 1992, 1993).

9. Castro Leal as quoted in Ramírez, *Crónicas de las artes plásticas*, 120; Manuel Gamio, *Forjando Patria (pro nacionalismo)* (Mexico City: Porrúa Hermanos, 1916). Carlos Mérida illustrated Anita Brenner's book *Your Mexican Holiday: A Modern Guide*, maps and illustrations by Mérida (New York: Putnam, 1932).

10. *Revista Musical de México*, no. 1 (May 15, 1919): 11.

11. *Revista Musical de México*, no. 3 (July 15, 1919); Manuel M. Ponce, "Folk-lore musical mexicano," *Revista Musical de México*, no. 5 (September 15, 1919); and "Caruso en México, el arte exquisito de Caruso," *Revista Musical de México*, no. 7 (November 15, 1919): 6.

12. AGN Propiedad artística literaria, 1920; Julia Tuñón, "La Santa de 1918, primera versión fílmica de una obsesión," *Historias*, 51 (2002): 81–89; Baltasar Dromundo, *Mi barrio de San Miguel* (Mexico City: Antingua Librería Robledo, 1951), 98; Paco Ignacio Taibo I, *Agustín Lara* (Mexico City: Jucar, 1985).

13. Juan S. Garrido, *Historia de la música popular en México* (Mexico City: Extemporáneos, 1974); Jorge Mejía Prieto, *Historia de la radio y la televisión en México* (Mexico City: Octavio Colmenares Editor, 1972); Mario Talavera, *Miguel Lerdo de Tejada, su vida pintoresca y anecdótica* (Mexico City: Editorial Compás, n.d.), 64–65; *Atlas general del Distrito Federal, geográfico, histórico, commercial, estadístico, agrario: Su descripción más completa, profusamente ilustada con mapas, fotografías y gráficos: Se formó esta obra por orden del Sr. Dr. José M. Puig Casauranc, jefe del Departamento del Distrito Federal* (Mexico City: Talleres Gráficos de la Nación, 1930).

14. Pedro Henríquez Ureña and Bertram Wolfe, "Romances tradicionales en Méjico," in *Homenaje ofrecido a Menéndez Pidal*, vol. 2 (Madrid: Librería y Casa Editorial Hernando, 1925), 375–90. In 1932 Wolfe finished his MA thesis, "The Mexican Corrido," for the Romance Language Department, Columbia University. His literary excursions were helped by his friendship not only with Henríquez Ureña, but also with poet León Felipe and Columbia professor F. de Onís. Bynner's letter to Idella Purnell, March 12, 1924, Idella Purnell Stone Papers, HRC; Timothy G. Turner, *Bullets, Bottles and Gardenias* (Dallas: South West Press, 1935); Anita Brenner Papers, HRC, diary entry 1926; Albert's letter to Apollinaire, July 12, 1914, in *Correspondance avec son frère*; Alma R. Reed, *Peregrina* (Reed's lost memoirs, published by the University of Texas Press, 2007), 213.

15. M. N. Roy, *Memoirs* (Bombay, London: Allied Publishers Private Limited, 1964); Sibnarayan Ray, *In Freedom's Quest: A Study of the Life and Works of M. N. Roy*, vol. 1 (Calcutta: Minerva Associates, 1998); Tilak Raj Sareen, *Indian Revolutionary Movement Abroad, 1905–1921* (New Delhi: Sterling Publishers Pvt Ltd, 1979); Jack Johnson, *Jack Johnson Is a Dandy: An Autobiography*, with introductory essays by Dick Schaap and the Lampman (New York: Chelsea House, 1969); Charles Phillips, *It Had to Be Revolution* (Ithaca: Cornell University Press, 1993) (Phillips says that Johnson's opponent in Mexico City was an Argentine); Carolyn Burke, *Becoming Modern: The Life of Mina Loy* (Berkeley: University of California Press, 1996); Maria Lluïsa Borràs, *Arthur Cravan: Una biografía* (Barcelona: Quaderns Crema, 1993); Richard V. McGehee, "The Dandy and the Mauler in Mexico: Johnson, Dempsey, et al. and the Mexico City Press, 1919–1927," *Journal of Sport History*, 23, 1 (Spring 1996): 20–33.

16. U.S. War Department Files, military attaché, report, April 2, 1926, Edgard David, ACT 83 905 31 inv. 1543; Hoover Institution's Oral History Tapes, Ella Wolfe interview; Burke, *Becoming Modern*; Joseph Retinger, *Memoirs of an Eminence Grise*, ed. John Pomian (Sussex: Sussex University Press, 1972).

17. Roy, *Memoirs*, 223. For Allen, see Barry Carr, *Marxism and Communism in Twentieth-Century Mexico* (Lincoln: University of Nebraska Press, 1992). For this complicated period in the history of the international left in Mexico, see Carleton Beals, *Glass Houses: Ten Years of Free-Lancing* (Philadelphia, New York: J. B. Lippincott Company, 1938); Héctor Cárdenas and Evgeni Dik, *Historia de las relaciones entre México y Rusia* (Mexico City: Secretaría de Relaciones Exteriores, Fondo de Cultura Económica, 1993); Arnoldo Martínez Verdugo, ed., *Historia del comunismo en México* (Mexico City: Grijalbo, 1985); Ricardo Melgar Bao, "Redes y representaciones COMINTERNistas: El Buró Latinoamericano (1919–1921)," *Revista Universum*, 16 (2001): 375–405; and Paco Ignacio Taibo II, *Bolshevikis, historia narrativa de los orígenes del comunismo en México (1919–1925)* (Mexico City: Joaquín Mortiz, 1986). For Roy and Smedley, see Tilak Raj Sareen, *Indian Revolutionary Movement Abroad (1905–1921)* (New Delhi: Sterling Publishers Pvt Ltd, 1979); Ruth Price, *The Lives of Agnes Smedley* (New York: Oxford University Press, 2005); and Smedley's fictional autobiography, in which Roy

becomes Juan Díaz—a blend of M. N. Roy and H. Gupta—A. Smedley, *Daughter of Earth* (New York: Coward-McCann, 1929).

18. Felipe Alfau, *Locos: A Comedy of Gestures*, afterword by Mary McCarthy (Elmwood Park, IL: Dalkey Archive Press, 1988); PHO 4-104 (Felipe), PHO 4-114 (Monna).

19. Enric Critòfol Ricart, *Memòries* (Barcelona: Parsifal Edicions, 1995); Frances Xavier Puig Rovira, *El pintor vilanoví Rafael Sala* (Vilanova i la Geltrú: n.p., 1975), quote p. 46. See the book Sala produced sponsored by the Mexican government: *Marcas de fuego de las antiguas bibliotecas mexicanas* (Mexico City: Impr. de la Secretaría de Relaciones Exteriores, 1925).

20. Vicente Blasco Ibáñez, *El militarismo mejicano: estudios publicados en los principales diarios de los Estados Unidos* (Valencia: Prometeo, 1920). Ramón del Valle Inclán, *Tirano Banderas: novela de tierra caliente* (Madrid: Espasa Calpe, 1994); for Mexican subsidies and help to Valle Inclán, see his letters to Alfonso Reyes and Genaro Estrada, in Juan Antonio Hormigón, *Valle Inclán: Biografía, cronología y epistolario: Volumen III: Epistolario* (Madrid: Publicaciones de la Asociación de Directores de Escena de España, 2006).

21. Valle Inclán not only lived in the city in the 1890s but became part of the urban bohemia; the same in 1921, though as a guest of the Mexican government. Traven went to live near Acapulco. Lowy lived in Cuernavaca and Oaxaca, as he hated Mexico City. León Felipe, *Español del éxodo y del llanto: doctrina, elegías y canciones* (Mexico City: La Casa de España en México, 1939), 14; *Presente amistoso a Felipe Teixidor* (Mexico City: n.p., 1969), especially Josep Carner's essay on Teixidor's house; PHO, Felipe y Monna Teixidor; interview with Ella Wolfe, Hoover Institution; for Sala in Florence see the memoirs of his friend and fellow traveler Enric Cristòfol Ricart, *Memòries*; and Françesc Xavier Puig Rovira, *El pintor vilanovi Rafael Sala*; *Todo Valle Inclán en México*, ed. Luis Mario Schneider (Mexico City: Coordinación de Difusión Cultural, Dirección de Literatura, UNAM, 1992). Valle Inclán's poem in *México Moderno* (September 2, 1922).

22. Burke, *Becoming Modern*; Maria Lluïsa Borràs, *Arthur Cravan*; Committee on Cultural Relations with Latin America, *Seminar in Mexico*, reports, Mexico City, 1926–1937; *What Mr. John Dewey thinks of the educational policies of Mexico* (Mexico City: Talleres Gráficos de la Nación, 1926) (small pamphlet); John Dewey, *Impressions of Soviet Russia and the Revolutionary World, Mexico—China—Turkey* (New York: New Republic, Inc., 1929); B. Traven, *Ich kenne das Leben in Mexiko: Briefe an John Schikowski 1925 bis 1932* (Frankfurt: Limes, 1992); Leon Trotsky, *Mi vida*, trans. Fermín Soto (Mexico City: Compañía General de Ediciones, 1960), 280; and Karl Siegfried Guthke, *B. Traven: Biographie eines Rätsels* (Zurich: Diogenes, 1990), 30, 272.

23. Bob Brown, *You Gotta Live* (London: D. Harmsworth, 1932), 247.

24. U.S. War Department Files 10640-690 M.1.5 report on Roy's activities in Mexico by U.S. military attaché in Mexico in 1918. About the persecution of U.S. pacifists in the context of World War I and the German connection in Mexico, see F. Katz, *The Secret War in Mexico: Europe, the United States, and the Mexican Revolution* (Chicago: University of Chicago Press, 1983); Gregory Andrews, *Shoulder to Shoulder?: The American Federation of Labor, the U.S., and the Mexican Revolution* (Berkeley: University of California Press, 1991); Diana K. Christopolus, "American Radicals and the Mexican Revolution, 1900–1924," Ph.D, diss., State University of New York, Binghamton, 1980; W. D. Ratt, "U.S. Intelligence Operations and Covert Action in Mexico, 1900–1947," *Journal of Contemporary History*, 22, 4 (October 1987): 615–38; Daniel La Botz, "'Slackers': American War Resisters and Communism in Mexico, 1917–1927," Ph.D. diss., University of Cincinnati, 1998; Gilbert C. Fite and H. C. Peterson, *Opponents of War, 1917–1918* (Seattle: University of Washington Press, 1957);

Charles Chatfield, *For Peace and Justice: Pacifism in America, 1914–1941* (Knoxville: University of Tennessee Press, 1971); and Daniela Spenser, *The Impossible Triangle: Mexico, Soviet Russia, and the United States in the 1920s* (Durham: Duke University Press, 1999).

25. Fraina quoted in David Madden, ed., *Proletarian Writers of the Thirties* (Carbondale: Southern Illinois University Press, 1968); Freeman's letter to Bertram and Ella Wolfe, 1958, Bertram and Ella Wolfe Papers, Hoover Institution of War, Revolution, and Peace, Stanford University.

26. Both Sibnarayan Ray and Samaren Roy refer to Trent's 1950s "friendly" but cold encounter and communications with Ellen Roy—Ellen Gottschalk, M. N. Roy's last wife, who was assassinated in New Delhi in 1961 (apparently by a common city thief, but there were rumors of Chinese communist intrigues). Roy had died in 1958. Ray, *In Freedom's Quest*; and Samaren Roy, *The Twice-Born Heretic* (Calcutta: Firma KLM Private Limited, 1986), 191–204.

27. U.S. War Department Files 10640-690 M.1.5 report on Roy's activities in Mexico by U.S. military attaché in Mexico in 1918.

28. See the papers of H. Sneevliet, the Dutch communist organizer who was killed during the German occupation (International Institute of Social History, Amsterdam); a small amount of Evelyn Trent's papers (a single folder) (Hoover Institution of War, Revolution, and Peace, Stanford); and the following sources: M. N. Roy, *Selections from the Marxian Way and the Humanist Way* (New Delhi: Ajanta Publishers, 1999); *Political and Social Views*, edited by R. M. Pal, with an introduction by Sibnarayan Ray (Calcutta: Minerva Associates, 1998); Ray, *In Freedom's Quest*; Roy, *Our Differences* (Calcutta: Saraswaty Library, 1938); Samaren Roy, *M. N. Roy* (London: Sangam, 1997); N. Innaiah, *M. N. Roy, Evelyn, Ellen Bibliography* (Hyderabad: V. Komala, 1996); Sibnarayam Ray, *M. N. Roy, Philosopher-Revolutionary* (Delhi: Ajanta Publications, 1995); Roy, *Fragments of a Prisoner's Diary* (Calcutta: Renaissance Publishers, 1957); A. S. K. Hindi, *M. N. Roy, the Man Who Looked Ahead* (Ahmedabad: Modern Publishing House, 1938); Clyde Rathburn Brown, "M. N. Roy and the Communist International, 1920–28," MA thesis, International Relations Program, Stanford University, 2001; Samaren Roy, *India's First Communist* (Calcutta: Minerva, 1988); Ray, *The Twice-Born Heretic*; Robert Carver North and Xenia J. Eudin, *M. N. Roy's Mission to China: The Communist-Kuomintang Split of 1927* (New York: Octagon Books, 1977); N. Innaiah, *Evelyn Trent alias Shanthi Devi, Founder Member of the Exile Indian Communist Party* (Hyderabad: V. Komala, 1995); and John P. Haithcox, *Communism and Nationalism in India : M. N. Roy and Comintern Policy, 1920–1939* (Princeton: Princeton University Press, 1971).

29. Anita Brenner Papers, HRC, diaries, March–April 1928.

30. Joseph Freeman Papers, Hoover Institution, Stanford University; Ione Robinson, *A Wall to Paint On* (New York: E. P. Dutton and Co., 1946).

31. Archivo Calles-Torreblanca, Archivo de Cholita, Esperanza Dominguez's letters June 3 and August 8, 1926; September 6, October 19, and November 4, 1927, Roberto Haberman Ex 542, Cholita. See also M. H. Mohoney, *Espionage in Mexico: The 20th Century* (San Francisco: Austin & Winfield, 1997); La Botz, "Slackers"; Dan La Botz, "Roberto Haberman and the Origins of Modern Mexico's Jewish Community," *American Jewish Archives*, 43 (Spring/Summer 1991): 721; Gregory A. Andrews, "Roberto Haberman, Socialist Ideology, and the Politics of National Reconstruction in Mexico," *Mexican Studies/Estudios Mexicanos*, 6 (Summer 1990): 189–211; Andrews, *Shoulder to Shoulder?*; FBI records, R665, headquarters case files, call numbers 23, 25-218 through 25-230, box 19; especially report by agent Manuel Sorola, San Antonio, Texas, September 25, 1924; letter to FBI director William J. Burns, confidential reports October 21, 1922, March 1924, August 1921, and

May 1926 regarding Esperanza Domínguez entering the U.S. (Laredo), 25-230. For Haberman, M. N. Roy, and Thorberg, see Price, *The Lives of Agnes Smedley.*

32. "The list of illustrations" found in Bertram Wolfe Papers, Hoover Institution, Stanford University, letter by D. Rivera, March 19, 1939; letter to Frida, March 9, 1939; Freeman poem in box 6, file 42; Bertram Wolfe, *A Life in Two Centuries: An Autobiography* (New York: Stein and Day, 1981); Wolfe, *Diego Rivera, His Life and Times* (New York: Alfred A. Knopf, 1939); Wolfe, *Three Who Made a Revolution: A Biographical History* (Boston: Beacon Press, 1948); Joseph Freeman, *An American Testament: A Narrative of Rebels and Romantics* (New York: Farrar & Rinehart, 1936).

33. Edward Weston, *The Daybooks of Edward Weston: I: Mexico, II: California*, ed. Nancy Newhall (New York: Aperture, 1975), 52; *The Letters of Hart Crane, 1916–1932*, ed. B. Weber (Berkeley: University of California Press, 1965); Paul Mariani, *The Broken Tower: The Life of Hart Crane* (New York: Norton, 1999); Commission of Inquiry into the Charges Made Against Leon Trotsky in the Moscow Trials, New York, 1937, *Not Guilty: Report of the Commission of Inquiry into the Charges Made Against Leon Trotsky in the Moscow Trials* (New York: Harper & Brothers, 1938).

34. Anita Burdam Feferman, *Politics, Logic, and Love, the Life of Jean Van Heijenoort* (London, Boston: Jones and Bartlett Publishers, 1993); Jean Van Heijenoort, *With Trotsky in Exile: From Prinkipo to Coyoacán* (Cambridge: Harvard University Press, 1978).

35. Juan Rejano, *La esfinge mestiza* (Madrid: Cupsa, 1978), 56.

36. This section is based on Kahlo's correspondence with Ella and Bertram Wolfe, in B. Wolfe Papers, Hoover Institution, Stanford University, box 12; and my correspondence with Ella Wolfe in 1989.

37. López Velarde's poem in *El Heraldo* (February 6, 1920), from *Zozobras* (1919); Phillips's poem in *El Heraldo* (August 4, 1919).

38. For the English rendition of Berliner's poems, I rely on both the Spanish and English translations of his verses: *Tres caminos: El germen de la literatura judía en México*, trans. and ed. Becky Rubinstein (Mexico City: Ediciones El Tucán de Virginia, 1997); and Isaac Berliner, *City of Palaces*, drawings by Diego Rivera, trans. Mindi Rikewich (New York: Jacoby Press, 1996).

39. *El Heraldo* (May 8, 1919). Earlier, in 1909, *El Imparcial* (June 8, 1909); and *México Nuevo*, no. 231 (1909), had engaged in a short debate about drugs in the city. An anonymous author in *México Nuevo* talked about experimentations with drugs (maybe it was written by Barba Jacob), and José Juan Tablada responded in *El Imparcial*, opposing the promotion of the bohemian life of drugs—*El Imparcial* (August 24, 1909). Tablada mixed his criticism of the drug with his criticism of *México Nuevo*, a periodical close to Bernardo Reyes's political faction. Jacobo Dalevuelta was indeed Fernando Ramírez de Aguilar (he used the same pseudonym—Jacobo—as Barba Jacob). See his *Estampas de México* (Mexico City: n.p., 1930), 153–57.

40. Porfirio Barba Jacob, *Antorchas contra el viento: poesía completa y prosa selecta*, ed. Eduardo Santa (Medellín: Gobernación de Antioquia, Secretaría de Educación y Cultura, 1983), 47. Barba Jacob refers to F. Hernández, "La degeneración," but very likely he was referring to F. Hernández, *Desequilibrio*, 2nd ed. (Mexico City: Talleres Tipográficos de Pablo Rodríquez, 1907).

41. Querido Moheno, "Arte y marijuana," in *Cartas y crónicas* (Mexico City: A. Botas e hijos 192?); Fernando Vallejo, *Barba Jacob, el mensajero* (Bogotá: Planeta, 1997; 1st ed. 1984); Juan Bautista Jaramillo Meza, *Vida de Porfirio Barba Jacob: anecdotario-cartas-poemas* (Bogotá: Editorial Kelly, 1956); *Cartas de Barba Jacob*, selections and notes by Fernando Vallejo (Bogotá: Revista Literaria Gradiva, 1992); see articles in *El Demócrata* (March 17, 22, and 26, 1922); Rafael Arévalo Martínez,

El hombre que parecía un caballo, y Las rosas de Engaddi (Guatemala: Tipográfica Sánchez y de Guise, 1927); Rafael Arévalo Martínez, Las noches en el Palacio de la Nunciatura (Guatemala: Tipográfica Sánchez y de Guise, 1927); Barba Jacob, Antorchas contra el viento; Arqueles Vela, El café de nadie; Un crimen provisional; La señorita etc. (Mexico City: Lecturas Mexicanas, CONACULTA, 1990); Fabienne Bradu, Antonieta, 1900–1931 (Mexico City: Fondo de Cultura Económica, 1991); José Vasconcelos, Ulises criollo, la vida del autor escrita por él mismo (Mexico City: Ediciones Botas, 1935); Salvador Novo, La estatua de sal, prologue by Carlos Monsiváis (Mexico City: CONACULTA, 1998), 84, 105–6; Elías Nandino, Juntando mis pasos (Mexico City: Editorial Aldus, 2000); Ramón Gómez de la Serna, Don Ramón María del Valle Inclán, 2nd ed. (Buenos Aires: Espasa Calpe, 1948); Discreta efusión, Alfonso Reyes, Jorge Luis Borges, 1923–1959, correspondencia, crónica de una amistad, ed. Carlos García (Berlin: Iberoamericana, 2010), 120; Todo Valle Inclán en México, ed. Luis Mario Schneider.

42. V. A. Reko, "Marijuana," in Magische Gifte: Rausch- und Betäubungsmittel der neuen Welt (Stuttgart: Enke, 1935); Eugenio Gómez Maillefert, "La marijuana en México," Journal of American Folk-Lore, 33, 127 (1920): 28–33, quote p. 29.

43. Gómez Maillefert, "La marijuana en México," 29.

44. Version published in Etnos (1920), reproduced in Vicente T. Mendoza, La canción mexicana: Ensayo de clasificación y antología, estudios de folklore (Mexico City: UNAM, 1961). A very different version of the song was found and published by Gómez Maillefert ("La marijuana en México").

CHAPTER 5

1. Marco Ciardi, Atlantide: una controversia scientifica da Colombo a Darwin (Rome: Carocci, 2002); Chantal Foucrier and Lauric Guillaud, eds., Atlantides imaginaires: réécritures d'un mythe (Paris: M. Houdiard, 2004); and Pierre Vidal-Naquet, L'Atlantide: petite histoire d'un mythe platonicien (Paris: Belles Lettres, 2005). The myth has had uses not only to understand the New World, but also to understand the "East" from, say, Spain and Mexico. José Ortega y Gasset, Las Atlántidas, con unas figuras del Sudán y de la China (Buenos Aires: Editorial Sudamericana, 1943); Manuel Amábilis Domínguez, Los Atlantes en Yucatán (Mexico City: Editorial Orión, 1963). On the history of the term in the Americas, see Eustaquio Buelna, Peregrinación de los aztecas y nombres geográficos indígenas de Sinaloa: La Atlántida y la última Tule (originally published in the late nineteenth century) (Mexico City: Siglo Veintiuno Editores, 1991); David Brading, The First America: The Spanish Monarchy, Creole Patriots, and the Liberal State, 1492–1867 (Cambridge: Cambridge University Press, 1991); and the account of the uses and mixtures of the platonic myth in many New World cronistas (from Las Casas on) in Sabine McCormack, In the Wings of Time: Rome, the Incas, Spain, and Peru (Princeton: Princeton University Press, 2006).

2. Lizzetta LeFalle-Collins et al., In the Spirit of Resistance: African-American Modernists and the Mexican Muralist School {En el espíritu de la resistencia: los modernistas africanoamericanos y la escuela muralista Mexicana} (New York: American Federation of Arts, 1996); James Oles, ed., South of the Border: Mexico in the American Imagination, 1914–1947; México en la imaginación norteamericana, 1914–1947 (Washington: Smithsonian Institution Press, 1993); Andrea Boardman, Destination, México: "A Foreign Land a Step Away": U.S. Tourism to Mexico, 1880s–1950s (Dallas: DeGolyer Library, Southern Methodist University, 2001); Seth Fein, "Hollywood and United States–Mexico Relations in the Golden Age of Mexican Cinema," Ph.D. diss., University of Texas, 1996; Helen Delpar, The Enormous Vogue of Things Mexican: Cultural Relations Between the United States and Mexico, 1920–1935 (Tuscaloosa: University of Alabama Press, 1992); Alejandro Ugalde, "The Presence of Mexican Art in New York be-

tween the World Wars: Cultural Exchange and Art Diplomacy," Ph.D. diss., Columbia University, 2003; John A. Britton, *Revolution and Ideology: Images of the Mexican Revolution in the United States* (Lexington: University Press of Kentucky, 1995); Alicia Azuela, *Arte y Poder: renacimiento artístico y revolución social, México 1910–1945* (Zamora, Michoacán: El Colegio de Michoacán, 2005); Drewey Wayne Gunn, *American and British Writers in Mexico, 1556–1973* (Austin: University of Texas Press, 1974); R. Tripp Evans, *Romancing the Maya: Mexican Antiquity in the American Imagination, 1820–1915* (Austin: University of Texas Press, 2004); Rebecca M. Schreiber, *Cold War Exiles in Mexico: U.S. Dissidents and the Culture of Critical Resistance* (Minneapolis: University of Minnesota Press, 2008); Ronald G. Walker, *Infernal Paradise: Mexico and the Modern English Novel* (Berkeley: University of California Press, 1978); Cecil Robinson, *Mexico and the Hispanic Southwest in American Literature: Revised from With the Ears of Strangers* (Tucson: University of Arizona Press, 1977); Luis Leal, "The American in Mexican Literature," MELUS 5, 3 (1978): 16–25.

3. Alexander D. Anderson, *Mexico from the Material Stand-Point: A Review of Its Mineral, Agricultural, Forest, and Marine Wealth, Its Manufactures, Commerce, Railways, Isthmian Routes, and Finances: With a Description of Its Highlands and Attractions* (Washington, D.C.: A. Brentano & Co.; New York: Brentano Bros., 1884), 9.

4. Clifford Gessler, *Pattern of Mexico*, illustrated by E. H. Suydam (New York: D. Appleton Century Company, 1941), 1–2.

5. In his later days Everett Gee Jackson published his many drawings and impressions of 1920s Mexico. For his 1926 visit to Mexico City see his *Burros and Paintbrushes: a Mexican Adventure* (College Station: Texas A & M University Press, 1985), quote on p. 117. The lithography is reproduced in *It's a Long Road to Comondú: Mexican Adventures since 1928* (College Station: Texas A & M University Press, 1987). He was a lithographer, trained at the Art Institute of Chicago, and worked for many decades at San Diego State College. In 1936 he illustrated Max Miller's *Mexico Around Me* (New York, Reynall & Hitchcock, 1937).

6. Oswald Spengler, *The Decline of the West*, trans. C. F. Atkinson (New York: Alfred Knopf, 1926); T. S. Eliot, *The Waste Land and Other Poems* (New York: Harcourt, Brace and World, 1934); Wolf Lepenies, *Between Literature and Science: The Rise of Sociology*, trans. R. J. Hollingdale (Cambridge: Cambridge University Press; Paris: Éditions de la Maison des Sciences de l'Homme, 1988).

7. W. E. Carson, *Mexico, the Wonderland of the South* (New York: Macmillan Company, 1909), 123; Samuel Grafton in *St. Petersburg Times* (December 9, 1946): 4; Alan Knight, *The Mexican Revolution*, vol. 1 (Lincoln: University of Nebraska Press, 1990), 1.

8. Carleton Beals, *Mexico: An Interpretation* (New York: Huebsch, 1923); Beals, *Mexican Maze*, illustrated by Diego Rivera (New York: Book League of America, 1931); Beals, *The Stones Awake: A Novel of Mexico* (Philadelphia: J. B. Lippincott, 1936). His memoirs in Mexico are found in *House in Mexico*, with drawings by Tom O'Sullivan (New York: Hastings House, 1958). On Beals and Mexico, see John Britton, *Carleton Beals: A Radical Journalist in Latin America* (Albuquerque: University of New Mexico Press, 1987). On Turner, see Rosalía Velázquez Estrada, *México en la mirada de John Kenneth Turner* (Mexico City: Universidad Autónoma Metropolitana, INAH, 2004). On Reed, see Granville Hicks, *John Reed: The Making of a Revolutionary*, with the assistance of John Stuart (New York: Macmillan, 1936); Jim Tuck, *Pancho Villa and John Reed: Two Faces of Romantic Revolution* (Tucson: University of Arizona Press, 1984); and Mary Austin, *Earth Horizon* (Boston: Houghton Mifflin, 1932).

9. Gunn, *American and British Writers in Mexico*, 103–5.

10. Frank conversation with Jean Van Heijenoort, in Jean Van Heijenoort, *With Trotsky in Exile*

from Prinkipo to Coyoacán (Cambridge: Harvard University Press, 1978); André Breton, "La clé des champs," in *Recuerdos de México* (Mexico City: CONACULTA 1996); Fabienne Bradu, *André Breton en México* (Mexico City: Editorial Vuelta, 1996).

11. Helen Delpar identified a total of 95 between 1920 and 1935. See table in Delpar, *The Enormous Vogue of Things Mexican*, 56.

12. The first title comes from the *Hunt-Cortes Digest*, a periodical published in Mexico City (1904–1906) by Rev. A. M. Hunt-Cortes, an American who maintained a technical school in Mexico City in which English, Spanish, and "Aztec" were spoken. Charles Fletcher, *The Awakening of a Nation: Mexico of To-Day* (New York: Harper, 1898); Charles Macomb Flandrau, *Viva Mexico!* (New York: Appleton, 1908); translation of Désiré de Charnay's book, *The Ancient Cities of the New World: Being Voyages and Explorations in Mexico and Central America from 1857–1882* (New York: Harper & Bros., 1887); Carl Lumholtz, *Unknown Mexico: A Record of Five Years' Exploration among the Tribes of the Western Sierra Madre; in the Tierra Caliente of Tepic and Jalisco; and among the Tarascos of Michoacan* (New York: C. Scribner's Sons, 1902); by the same distinguished Norwegian explorer, *New Trails in Mexico: An Account of One Year's Exploration in North-Western Sonora, Mexico, and South-Western Arizona* (New York: Scribner, 1912); the long poem *Queen Moo's Talisman: The Fall of the Maya Empire*, by Alice D. Le Plongeon (New York: P. Eckler, 1902); Augustus Le Plongeon, *Maya/Atlantis, Queen Móo, and the Egyptian Sphinx: Sacred Mysteries among the Mayas and the Quiches, 11,500 Years Ago; Their Relation to the Sacred Mysteries of Egypt, Greece, Chaldea and India: Free Masonry in Times Anterior to the Temple of Solomon* (New York: R. Macoy, 1886); William Henry Bishop, *Old Mexico and Her Lost Provinces: A Journey in Mexico, Southern California, and Arizona, by Way of Cuba* (New York: Harper & Brothers, 1883). See also Maturin Murray Ballou, *Aztec Land* (Boston: Houghton, Mifflin, 1890); Frederick Ober, *Travels in Mexico and Life Among the Mexicans* (Boston: Estes & Lauriat, 1884); Gilbert Haven, *Our Next-door Neighbor: A Winter in Mexico* (New York: Harper & Bros., 1875); Carson, *Mexico, the Wonderland of the South*; Albert Evans, *Our Sister Republic: A Gala Trip through Tropical Mexico in 1869–70: Adventure and Sight-Seeing in the Land of the Aztecs, with Picturesque Descriptions of the Country and the People, and Reminiscences of the Empire and Its Downfall* (Hartford: W. E. Bliss, 1870); Wallace Owen Gillpatrick, *The Man Who Likes Mexico: The Spirited Chronicle of Adventurous Wanderings in Mexican Highways and Byways* (New York: Century, 1911); Channing Arnold, *The American Egypt, A Record of Travel in Yucatan* (New York: Doubleday, 1909); Thomas Rogers, *Mexico? Si, Señor* (Boston: Collins Press, 1893); Caecilie Seler-Sachs, *Auf alten Wegen in Mexiko und Guatemala: Reiseerinnerungen und Eindrücke aus den Jahren, 1895–1897* (Berlin: D. Reimer, 1900); Karl von Schlözer, *Mexikanische Briefe* (Stuttgart: Deutsche Verlags-Anstalt, 1913); B. Traven, *Land des Frühlings* (Berlin: Büchergilde Gutenberg, 1928); Joseph Lauterer, *Mexiko: das Land der blühenden Agave: einst und jetzt* (Leipzig: O. Spamer, 1908); Josef Maria Frank, *Mexiko ist anders; eine Reise ins Land der Azteken* (Berlin: Universitas, 1938); D. H. Lawrence, *Mornings in Mexico* (New York: A. A. Knopf, 1927); John Dewey, *Impressions of Soviet Russia and the Revolutionary World, Mexico-China-Turkey* (New York: New Republic, 1929); Graham Greene, *Another Mexico* (New York: Viking Press, 1939); Dana S. Lamb, *Enchanted Vagabonds* (New York: Harper & Bros., 1938); Evelyn Waugh, *Mexico, an Object Lesson* (Boston: Little, Brown, 1939); René D'Harnoncourt, *Mexicana, a Book of Pictures* (New York: A. A. Knopf, 1931); Howard Vincent O'Brien, *Notes for a Book about Mexico* (Chicago: Willett, Clark & Co., 1937); Anton Bruehl, *Photographs of Mexico* (New York: Delphic Studios, 1933); Charlotte Cameron, *Mexico in Revolution, an Account of an English Woman's Experiences & Adventures in the Land of Revolution, with a Description of the People, the Beauties of the Country & the Highly Interesting Remains of Aztec Civilisation* (London: Seeley,

Service, 1925); Stella Burke May, *Children of Mexico* (Chicago: Rand McNally & Company, 1936); Clarissa W. Collins, *Mexican Vignettes* (New York: Snellgrove, 1938).

13. Robert Redfield, *The Folk Culture of Yucatan* (Chicago: University of Chicago Press, 1941); Stuart Chase, *Mexico: A Study of Two Americas*, in collaboration with Marian Tyler, illustrated by Diego Rivera (New York: Macmillan, 1931); Anita Brenner, *Idols Behind Altars* (New York: Payson & Clarke Ltd., 1929), a famous book in English not translated into Spanish until the 1980s; Beals, *Mexican Maze*; Marc Chadourne, *Anahuac ou, L'Indien sans plumes* (Paris: Plon, 1934), is one of a few of these books to have even been translated to Spanish, as *Anáhuac, o, El indio sin plumas*, trans. Alfonso Teja Zabre (Mexico City: Ediciones Botas, 1935); Konstantin Dmitrievich Balmont, *Visions solaires: Méxique, Égypte, Inde, Japon, Océanie*, trans. Ludmila Savitzky, 4th ed. (Paris: Ed. Bossard, 1923). Chadourne published a book on China which was nicely illustrated by Covarrubias, the illustrator of many of the books by the inhabitants of the Brown Atlantis. M. Chadourne, *Chine*, illustrations by Miguel Covarrubias (Paris: Plon, 1931).

14. Federico Gamboa, *Mi diario* (Guadalajara: Imprenta de La Gaceta de Guadalajara, 1907–20), vol. 2; letter from John Dos Passos to Felipe Teixidor, Box 6 (circa 1937), AGN, Felipe Teixidor Papers.

15. Hugo Brehme, *México pintoresco* (Mexico City: Fotografía artística H. Brehme, 1923); on him see two catalogues, *México, una nación persistente: fotografías, Hugo Brehme* (Mexico City: Instituto Nacional de Bellas Artes, Museo Franz Mayer, 1995); and *Hugo Brehme Fotograf: Mexiko zwischen Revolution und Romantik*, ed. Michael Nungesser (Berlin: Ibero-Amerikanisches Institut Preussischer Kulturbesitz, Arenhövel, 2004). I thank Diana von Roemer for having guided my attention to some of Brehme's pictures. About Waite see Francisco Montellano, *C. B. Waite, fotógrafo: una mirada diversa sobre el México de principios del siglo XX* (Mexico City: CONACULTA, 1994). On Kahlo, see *Guillermo Kahlo, fotógrafo, 1872–1941: vida y obra* (Mexico City: Museo Estudio Diego Rivera, Museo Franz Mayer, CONACULTA, 1993). See also *Mexicana: fotografía moderna en México, 1923–1940*, ed. Salvador Albiñana and Horacio Fernández (Valencia: Generalitat Valenciana, Conselleria de Cultura, Educació y Ciencia, IVAM Centre Julio González, 1998); Rosa Casanova, Olivier Debroise, and Pablo Ortiz Monasterio, *Sobre la superficie bruñida de un espejo: fotógrafos del siglo XIX* (Mexico City: Fondo de Cultura Económica, 1989); and Oliver Debroise, *Mexican Suite: A History of Photography in Mexico*, trans. Stella de Sá Rego (Austin: University of Texas Press, 2001).

16. Olive Percival, *Mexico City: An Idler's Note-Book* (Chicago: H. S. Stone, 1901), 9, 39. On Percival as book collector see Ingrid Johnson, "Book Collector Extraordinaire: The Life and Times of Olive Percival," MA thesis, UCLA, 2004. By the 1930s some books were either translated from Spanish or published in English in Mexico City, dealing with some aspects of the city itself. Luis González Obregón, *The Streets of Mexico* (San Francisco: G. Fields, 1937); and Dorothy Stewart, *Hornacinas: Stories of Niches and Corners of Mexico City* (Mexico: Editorial Cultura, 1933). A book that dealt with Mexico City but with a religious point of view is Albert Judson Steelman, *Charities for Children in the City of Mexico* (Joliet, IL: E. M. Steelman, 1907); and a directory and account of Germans in Mexico City, Erich Günther, *Illustriertes Handbuch von Mexico, mit besonderer Berücksichtigung der deutschen Interessen* (Mexico City: E. Günther, 1912). This is in addition to German studies of Mexico City's language in the early nineteenth century: M. L. Wagner, "Mexikanisches Rotwelsch," in *Zeitschrift für Romanische Philologie*, 39 (1919): 513–50; and Sommer, "Über die mexikanische Gaunersprache," *Arch. f. Kriminal Anthropologie*, 28 (1907): 209–14.

17. *Porte Crayon's Mexico: David Hunter Strother's Diaries in the Early Porfirian Era, 1879–1885*, ed.

John E. Stealey III (Kent: Kent State University Press, 2006); and Cecil D. Eby, "*Porte Crayon*": *The Life of David Hunter Strother* (Chapel Hill: University of North Carolina Press, 1960): 195–207; Winold Reiss, "Mexican Types," *Survey* (May 1924): 153–56.

18. Joseph W. F. Stoppelman, *People of Mexico* (New York: Hastings House Publishers, 1966).

19. Carson, *Mexico, the Wonderland of the South*; Frank G. Carpenter, *Mexico* (Garden City, N.Y.: Doubleday, Page, & Co., 1925); Hudson Strode, *Now in Mexico* (New York: Harcourt, Brace, 1947); Herbert Cerwin, *These Are the Mexicans* (New York: Reynal & Hitchcock, 1947); Paul Strand, *Photographs of Mexico* (New York: V. Stevens, 1940), portfolio (twenty mounted plates), introductory essay by Leo Hurwitz.

20. For the history of Rivera and Chase collaboration, see Lyle W. Williams "Crossing Borders: The Weyhe Gallery and the Vogue for Mexican Art in the United States, 1926–40," in *Mexico and Modern Printmaking: a Revolution in the Graphic Arts, 1920 to 1950*, ed. John Ittmann (Philadelphia: Philadelphia Museum of Art; San Antonio: McNay Art Museum; New Haven: Yale University Press, 2006).

21. Chase, *Mexico: A Study of Two Americas*, 83. The book was translated into French but, to my knowledge, never into Spanish. About Rivera as illustrator, see Raquel Tibol, *Diego Rivera ilustrador*, commentaries by Alberto Beltrán (Mexico City: SEP, Dirección General de Publicaciones y Medios, 1986).

22. Aldous Huxley, *Beyond the Mexican Bay* (New York: Harper & Brothers, 1934).

23. Salvador Novo, *La vida en México en el periodo presidencial de Lázaro Cárdenas* (Mexico City: Empresas Editoriales, 1964), 53; Salvador Novo, *El joven* (Mexico City: n.p., 1922), 19; Frances Toor Papers, letter to E. Parsons, August 9, 1929, Elsie C. Parsons Papers, American Philosophical Society.

24. I found Paredes's annotated copy of Chase's book at the N. L. Benson Latin American Collection of the University of Texas. He used the 1950 edition published by Macmillan. He had the habit of signing his book with the year when he either acquired it or read it, and this was 1954. There are fresh references to Japan and Korea in his annotations. About Paredes's views of Japan see part IV.

25. Carlos Castillo, *Mexico*, ed. Burton Holmes, text by Carlos Castillo, illustrations by Burton Holmes (Chicago: Wheeler Publishing Company, 1939).

26. Letter, November 24, 1925, quoted in James John Horn, "Diplomacy by Ultimatum: Ambassador Sheffield and Mexican-American Relations, 1924–1927," MA thesis, State University of New York College at Buffalo, 1969. Frank Tannenbaum intervened in order to make the State Department realize that Ambassador Sheffield's conflictive relations with Mexican officials should be improved.

27. Similar fascinations with racial purity can be found in many other books about Mexico. For instance, H. S. Dunn's book on Zapata argues that Zapata's widow, María Flores, claimed, or so is transcribed in English, "I am Otomi. My father is the cacique of our race in Morelos. We are pure blood. We are better than the mestizos, and are proud of it." This is what Dunn wanted to hear. It is hard to imagine these phrases in Spanish, as Dunn could not have this conversation in Otomi. Dunn, *The Crimson Jester, Zapata of Mexico, Illustrated with Photographs by the Author* (New York: R. M. McBride & Company, 1933), 307.

28. The letter is included in Ione Robinson, *A Wall to Paint On* (New York: E. P. Dutton and Co., 1946), 202.

29. Antonin Artaud, *Les Tarahumaras* (Paris: Gallimard, 1971). Artaud published some of his essays in El Nacional in Mexico City. I use the annotated and expanded version in Spanish translation, *Los Tarahumaras* (Barcelona: Tusquets, 1995).

30. Balmont, *Visions solaires*, 56; Le Plongeon, *Maya/Atlantis, Queen Móo, and the Egyptian Sphinx*.

31. Collier was the chief of the Bureau of Indian Affairs (1933–45). John Collier, *From Every Zenith: A Memoir* (Denver: Sage Books, 1963); Collier, "The Red Atlantis," *Survey* 49 (1922); Collier, *The Indians of the Americas* (New York: W. W. Norton, 1947); William Willard, "The Plumed Serpent and the Red Atlantis," *Wicazo Sa Review* 4, no. 2 (1988): 17–30; E. A. Schwarts, "Red Atlantis Revisited: Community and Culture in the Writings of John Collier," *American Indian Quarterly* 18, no. 4 (1994): 507–31. See also the Taos connection in Lois Palken Rudnick, *Mabel Dodge Luhan: New Woman, New Worlds* (Albuquerque: University of New Mexico Press, 1984); the fourth volume of Dodge's memoirs, Mabel Dodge Luhan, *Edge of Taos Desert: An Escape to Reality* (New York: Harcourt, Brace, 1937); and Desley Deacon, *Elsie Clews Parsons: Inventing Modern Life* (Chicago: University of Chicago Press, 1997).

32. See chapter 3.

33. From Ashis Nandy, *An Ambiguous Journey to the City: The Village and Other Odd Ruins of the Self in the Indian Imagination* (Delhi: Oxford University Press, 2001), 27.

34. Letter to Waldo Frank, June 13, 1931, in *The Letters of Hart Crane, 1916–1932*, ed. B. Weber (Berkeley: University of California Press, 1965). Texts on various Mexican painters written by D. Rivera for Bertram Wolfe (B. Wolfe Papers, Hoover Institution, [ca. 1927]).

35. "A la sombra de los turistas" by Fa-Cha, *Revista de Revistas* (August 12, 1934).

36. Johan Huizinga, *The Autumn of the Middle Ages*, trans. Rodney J. Payton and Ulrich Mammitzsch (Chicago: University of Chicago Press, 1996), originally published in the 1920s.

37. Lesley Simpson, *Muchos Méxicos*, trans. L. Simpson and Luis Monguio (Mexico City: Fondo de Cultura Económica, 1976), 5.

CHAPTER 6

1. It is beyond the scope of this book's analysis, but López and Guzmán truly capture the city's uniqueness and its cosmopolitism. For more on them see John Mraz, *Nacho López, Mexican Photographer* (Minneapolis: University of Minnesota Press, 2003); Maricela González Cruz Manjarrez, *Juan Guzmán: una visión de la modernidad* (Mexico City: CONACULTA, 2004); Carlos A. Córdova, *Agustín Jiménez y la vanguardia fotográfica mexicana* (Mexico City: Editorial RM, 2005).

2. *Life*: June 10 (Nazis and Communists in Mexico); July 1 (Mexican presidential campaign); July 22 (violence in Mexico City); December 2 (about president Manuel Ávila Camacho). Richard Whelan, *Robert Capa: A Biography* (New York: Knopf, 1985); *Robert Capa: The Definitive Collection*, ed. Richard Whelan (London: Phaidon, 2001).

3. See, for instance, the private photo album by Chase Littlejohn, a mining engineer who was in Mexico City during the *decena trágica*. N. L. Benson Latin American Collection, the University of Texas.

4. On this topic my work relies on the lucid contributions of John Mraz and James Oles. John Mraz, "From Positivism to Populism: Towards a History of Photojournalism in Mexico," *Afterimage* 18 (1991): 8–11; Mraz, *Nacho López, Mexican Photographer*; Helen Levitt, *Helen Levitt: Mexico City*, with an essay by James Oles (New York: Center for Documentary Studies, W. W. Norton and Company, 1997). In the 1920s there was *Revista Cemento* and in the 1930s the *Revista Mexicana de*

Ingeniería y Arquitectura: Órgano de la Asociación de Ingenieros y Arquitectos de México. About this culture, see Guillermo Sheridan, *Los Contemporáneos ayer* (Mexico City: Fondo de Cultura Económica, 1985); Guillermo Sheridan, *México en 1932: la polémica nacionalista* (Mexico City: Fondo de Cultura Económica, 1999); Fausto Ramírez, *Saturnino Herrán* (Mexico City: UNAM, Dirección General de Publicaciones, 1976); Fausto Ramírez, Antonio Rubial García, and Gustavo Curiel, *Pintura y vida cotidiana en México, 1650–1950* (Mexico City: Fomento Cultural Banamex, CONACULTA, 1999); Fausto Ramírez, *Crónica de las artes plásticas en los años de López Velarde, 1914–1921* (Mexico City: UNAM, 1990); Rubén Gallo, *Mexican Modernity: The Avant-Garde and the Technological Revolution* (Cambridge: MIT Press, 2005).

5. W. E. Carson, *Mexico, the Wonderland of the South* (New York: Macmillan Company, 1909), 57.

6. According to historian Francisco Montellano, C. B. Waite did photograph urban scenes, such as poor naked children in the city's central Post Office, but—Montellano argues—these pictures are hard to find. Francisco Montellano, *C. B. Waite, fotógrafo: una mirada diversa sobre el México de principios del siglo XX* (Mexico City: CONACULTA, Grijalbo, 1994).

7. Nevin O. Winter, *Mexico and Her People of To-day: An Account of the Customs, Characteristics, Amusements, History and Advancement of the Mexicans, and the Development and Resources of Their Country*, illustrated from photographs by the author and C. R. Birt (London: Cassell, 1913), 98.

8. J. Hendrickson McCarty, *Two Thousand Miles through the Heart of Mexico* (New York: Hunt & Eaton, 1886), 171–73.

9. Charles Macomb Flandrau, *Viva Mexico!* (New York: D. Appleton and Co., 1908), 37.

10. Letter circa 1931, in B. Weber, ed., *The Letters of Hart Crane, 1916–1932* (Berkeley: University of California Press, 1952).

11. McCarty, *Two Thousand*, 190.

12. Fritz Henle, *Mexico: 64 Photographs* (Chicago: Ziff Davis Publishing Company, 1945).

13. Albert Zabriskie Gray, *Mexico as It Is, Being Notes of a Recent Tour to That Country* (New York: E. P. Dutton and Co., 1878).

14. Jasper T. Moses, *Today in the Land of Tomorrow: Sketches of Life in Mexico* (Indianapolis: Christian Woman's Board of Missions, 1909).

15. Charles Morris, *The Story of Mexico, a Land of Conquest and Revolution, Giving a Comprehensive History of This Romantic and Beautiful Land from the Days of Montezuma and the Empire of the Aztecs to the Present Time; Including a Graphic Description of the Mexican Country—Its Contrasts of Great Wealth and Abject Poverty—Its Magnificent Resources in Fields, Forests and Mines—Its Palaces and Cathedrals—Its Development in Civilization, Religion, Education, Industry and Military Affairs—Its Present Unrest and the Causes—the Long Rule of Diaz and His Fall—the Madero Revolution and the Tragic Death of Its Leader—the Huerta Régime and President Wilson's Policy—the Latest Diplomatic Developments and the Mexico of the Future, by Charles Morris . . . Illustrated with Nearly One Hundred Photographic Plates of Actual Mexican Scenes and Events and a Map of the Country* (Philadelphia: Universal Book and Bible House, 1914).

16. Rosa E. King, *Tempest over Mexico: A Personal Chronicle*, illustrated by Carroll Bill (Boston: Little, Brown, and Company, 1935); Frank Tannenbaum, *Peace by Revolution: An Interpretation of Mexico*, drawings by Miguel Covarrubias (New York: Columbia University Press, 1933).

17. J. W. von Müller, *Reisen in den Vereinigten Staaten, Canada und Mexico* (Leipzig: F.A. Brockhaus, 1864–65).

18. Leonidas Willing Ramsey, *Time Out for Adventure: Let's Go to Mexico* (Garden City, New York: Doubleday, Doran, 1934); Max Miller, *Mexico Around Me*, with illustrations by Everett Gee Jack-

son (New York: Reynall & Hitchcock, 1937); Emma-Lindsay Squier, *Gringa: An American Woman in Mexico*, illustrated with photographs by John Bransby (Boston, New York: Houghton Mifflin company, 1934); Frances Toor, *Frances Toor's Guide to Mexico* (Mexico City: A. Mijares y hno., 1934); Anita Brenner, *Your Mexican Holiday, a Modern Guide*, maps and illustrations by Carlos Mérida (New York and London: G. P. Putnam's Sons, 1932).

19. R. J. MacHugh, *Modern Mexico* (London: Methuen, 1914); Edward Weston, *The Daybooks of Edward Weston: I, Mexico; II, California*, ed. Nancy Newhall (New York: Aperture, 1975), 48; Nevin O. Winter, *Mexico and Her People of To-day* (Boston: L. C. Page, 1907).

20. Levitt, *Helen Levitt: Mexico City*. See also John Mraz's argument about the emergence of photojournalism, and the prevalence of the exotic in photographing Mexico in Mraz, *Nacho López, Mexican Photographer*; and Alma Neuman, *Always Straight Ahead: A Memoir* (Baton Rouge: Louisiana State University Press, 1993).

21. Levitt, *Helen Levitt: Mexico City*.

22. I. Berliner, "Pulquería," in *Shtot fun palatsn*, as translated in *Tres caminos: El germen de la literatura judía en México*.

23. Carson, *Mexico, the Wonderland of the South*, 66.

24. *Hendrik Glintenkamp, 1887–1987, un dibujante norteamericano en México, 1917–1920* (Museo Estudio Diego Rivera, Mexico City, September 1987; Museo de la Alhondiga, Guanajuato, October 1987).

25. Quoted in Burke, *Becoming Modern*, 259.

26. Bertram Wolfe, *A Life in Two Centuries: An Autobiography* (New York: Stein and Day, 1981), 305.

27. Neuman, *Always Straight Ahead: A Memoir*; Thomas F. Walsh, *Katherine Anne Porter and Mexico: The Illusion of Eden* (Austin: University of Texas Press, 1992); Clare Sheridan, *My American Diary* (New York: Boni and Liveright, 1922). Joel, Alma and James Agee's son, who was ten when in Mexico City, eventually wrote memoirs of his childhood in East Germany, where mother and son moved after Alma's marriage in Mexico City to German radical Bodo Uhse. Joel Agee, *Twelve Years: An American Boyhood in East Germany* (New York: Farrar Straus Giroux, 1981).

28. Marion Lay, *Wooden Saddles; The Adventures of a Mexican Boy in his own Land*, illustrated by Addison Burbank (New York: W. Morrow and Company, 1939); Stella Burke May, *Children of Mexico* (Chicago: Rand McNally & Company, 1936); Anne Merriman Peck, *Young Mexico*, illustrated by the author (New York: Robert M. McBride & Co., 1934); Catherine Ulmer Stoker, *Little Daughter of Mexico*, illustrated by Theobold Holsopple (Dallas: Dealey and Lowe, 1937); Margaret Loring Thomas, *Carlos, our Mexican Neighbor*, drawings by Willis Rudolph Lohse (Indianapolis: Bobbs-Merrill Company, 1938).

29. *Hoy* (May 14, 1938); Berliner, "¿Dónde están las madres," in *Tres caminos*.

30. Cecil Carnes and Fred Carnes, *You Must Go to Mexico: Down the Pan American Highway* (Chicago: Ziff-Davis Publishing Company, 1947).

31. E. Evalyn Grumbine McNally and Andrew McNally, *This Is Mexico*, maps by Valdemar Paulsen (New York: Dodd, Mead, 1947).

32. Max Miller, *I Cover the Waterfront* (New York: E.P. Dutton and Company, 1932); Miller, *Mexico Around Me*, with illustrations by Everett Gee Jackson (New York: Reynall & Hitchcock, 1937).

33. Miller, *Mexico Around Me*, 154, 174.

34. Francis C. Kelley, *Blood-Drenched Altars: Mexican Study and Comment* (Milwaukee: Bruce Publishing Company, 1935).

35. Mariam Storm, *Prologue to Mexico: The Story of a Search for a Place* (New York: A. A. Knopf, 1931): Catharine Ulmer Stoker, *Under Mexican Skies*, illustrated by Theobold Holsopple (Dallas: B. Upshaw, 1947).

36. See, for instance, the well-known account of Madame Calderón de la Barca, *Life in Mexico, During a Residence of Two Years in that Country* (London: Chapman and Hall, 1843); or the comments by the Empress Carlota's company, Paula Kollonitz, *Eine Reise nach Mexiko im Jahre 1864* (Vienna: C. Gerold, 1867); or the books that include a section on "domestics," such as Percy F. Martin, *Mexico of the Twentieth Century*, 2 vols. (London: E. Arnold, 1907), vol. 1, 181–89, and Bob Brown, *You Gotta Live* (London: D. Harmsworth, 1932), 103.

37. Alexandre Lambert de Sainte-Croix, *Onze mois au Mexique et au Centre-Amérique* (Paris: Librairie Plon, 1897), 52.

38. James Edwin Morris, *A Tour in Mexico*, photos by James Edwin Morris (London: Abbey Press, 1902), 195; W. E. Carson, *The Marriage Revolt: A Study of Marriage and Divorce* (New York: Hearst's International Library Co., 1915); Carson, *Mexico, the Wonderland of the South*, 157–60.

39. Emma-Lindsay Squier, *Gringa: An American Woman in Mexico*, illustrated with photographs by John Bransby (Boston, New York: Houghton Mifflin Company, 1934).

40. Clare Sheridan, *My American Diary* (New York: Boni and Liveright, 1922).

41. Weston, *The Daybooks*, vol. 1, 139.

42. John Dos Passos, "Relief Map of Mexico," *The New Masses* (April 1927): 24–25; Manuel Maples Arce, *Metropolis*, trans. John Dos Passos (New York: T.S. Book Company, 1925).

43. Anita Brenner, "La pintura de Caroline Durieux," *Revista de Revistas* (June 17, 1934); *Caroline Durieux Lithographs*, text by Richard Cox (Baton Rouge: Louisiana State University Press, 1977).

44. In Anita Brenner Papers, HRC, Box 59.

45. Brown, *You Gotta Live*, 204.

46. See the sources cited in chapter 4, note 28.

47. Evelyn Trent, "Mexico and Her People," chapter 3, *El Heraldo* (September 29, 1919). Trent also published the essay "La mujer mexicana y el movimiento feminista mundial," *El Socialista, semanario dedicado a la defensa del proletariado*, no. 38 (August 1, 1919).

48. Ellsworth Huntington, "The Relation of Health to Racial Capacity: The Example of Mexico," *Geographical Review*, 11, 2 (1921): 260.

49. Trent, "Mexico and Her People," chapter 2 (September 22, 1919).

50. Trent, "Mexico and Her People," chapter 2 (September 22, 1919).

51. Juan Rejano, *La esfinge mestiza: crónica menor de México* (Madrid: Cupsa Editorial, 1978), 71.

52. Rejano, *La esfinge mestiza*, 127.

53. Joan Sales, *Cartes a Màrius Torres: seguides de viatge d'un moribund* (Barcelona: Club Editor, 2007), 666–68.

54. Testimonies by Clara Peretzman de Guruich (144-22), Jack Kalb (144-36), and Isaac Dabbah (144-53), Oral History Project, Hebrew University of Jerusalem.

55. David Zabludovsky, *Años pasados*, private edition of Spanish translation, published by his son Jacobo Zabludovsky, 201, 333. I thank Julio Boton for allowing me to use his contacts and library on these matters.

56. M. Glikowski, *Blandzendike gasyster: poeme in proze* (Mexico City: Druk alma, 1929); I. Berliner, J. Glantz, and M. Glikowski as translated in *Tres caminos*.

CHAPTER 7

1. Mario Praz, *La carne, la muerte y el diablo en la literatura romántica*, trans. Rubén Mettino (Barcelona: El Acantilado, 1999); J. J. Clarke, *Oriental Enlightenment: The Encounter Between Asian and Western Thought* (London: Routledge, 1997). Of course somehow my treatment of Mexico's odalisque mania ought to be indebted to the focus on orientalism brought about by the late Edward Said. My approach, however, is rooted in the specificity of the Mexican phenomena, and only secondarily seeks to enter into the decades of debates about Said's major contribution. Edward Said, *Orientalism* (New York: Pantheon Books, 1978). For the idea that not all orientalisms start and end in Said, see Suzanne Marchand, *German Orientalism in the Age of Empire* (New York: Cambridge University Press, 2009).

2. Mohja Kahf, *Western Representations of the Muslim Woman: From Termagant to Odalisque* (Austin: University of Texas Press, 1999); and Donald Rosenthal, *Orientalism: The Near East in French Painting, 1800–1880* (Rochester: Memorial Art Gallery of the University of Rochester, 1982). On *Japonisme*, see Linda Gertner Zatlin, *Beardsley: Japonisme, and the Perversion of the Victorian Ideal* (Cambridge: Cambridge University Press, 1998); Siegfried Wichmann, *Japonisme: The Japanese Influence on Western Art in the 19th and 20th Centuries* (Greenport, N.Y.: Crown, 1981); Klaus Berger, *Japonisme in Western Painting from Whistler to Matisse*, trans. David Britt (Cambridge: Cambridge University Press, 1992); Shigemi Inaga, "Une esthetique de recontre, ou l'affinité de l'impressionisme avec le japonisme comme un malentendu et sa conséquence paradoxale au cours de l'implantation de l'impressionisme au Japon," *Word & Image*, 4, 1 (1988): 139–47; the catalogue of the exhibition, "Japonisme," *Le Japonisme* (Paris: Galeries Nationales du Grand Palais, 1988); Julia Meech and Gabriel P. Weisberg, *Japonisme Comes to America: The Japanese Impact on the Graphic Arts, 1876–1935* (New York: Harry N. Abrams Inc. Publishers, 1990).

3. This is what historian Harry Harootunian has called the "time lag" that characterizes our moral and empirical views of history. On the complexities involved in the drawing of a line between past and present, see Constantine Fasolt, *The Limits of History* (Chicago: University of Chicago Press, 2004), 3–29; and Harry Harootunian, *Overcoming by Modernity: History, Culture, and Community in Interwar Japan* (Princeton: Princeton University Press, 2000).

4. Francisco Bulnes, "Once mil leguas sobre el hemisferio norte," included in the reedition of Bulnes's works, *El porvenir de las naciones hispanoamericanas, Once mil leguas sobre el hemisferio norte* (Mexico City: Grijalbo, 1998), 187–95.

5. *Viaje de la comisión astronómica mexicana al Japón para observar el tránsito del planeta Vénus por el disco del sol el 8 de diciembre de 1874* (Mexico City: Imprenta Poliglota de Ramiro y Ponce de León, 1876), 242–43.

6. Andrés Molina Enríquez, *Los grandes problemas nacionales* (Mexico City: Imprenta de A. Carranza e hijos, 1909); "La guerra del Pacífico. Polémica con Rafael Nieto," included in *Anales del Museo Nacional* (1937), 31–69 (essays published in July 1925, *El Universal*).

7. Efrén Rebolledo, *Nikko* (Mexico City: Tip. de la Viuda de F. Díaz de León, 1910), 9.

8. Eva Alexandra Uchmany, "Los contactos entre la Nueva España y el subcontinente indio durante la época colonial," in *México-India: Similitudes y encuentros a través de la historia*, ed. Eva Alexandra Uchmany (Mexico City: Ispat Mexicana S.A. de C.V., Fondo de Cultura Económica, 1998), 69–103.

9. The significance of Felipe de Jesús's canonization may be better understood when considering how rare an occasion it was: some 140 years passed before another Mexican (Juan Diego) was

canonized in 2002. As the story goes, Juan Diego was visited personally by the Virgin of Guadalupe.

10. Zelia Nutall, *The Earliest Historical Relations Between Japan and Mexico* (Berkeley: University of California Press, 1906); Carlos Américo Lera, *Primeras relaciones oficiales entre Japón y España tocantes a México* (Tokyo: n.p., 1905); Eduardo Enrique Ríos, *Felipe de Jesús, el santo criollo* (Mexico City: Editorial Jus, 1962); *Compendio de la vida del protomartir del Japón, San Felipe de Jesús, patrón de México su patria, y devoción consagrada a celebrar su memoria el día cinco de cada mes . . .* (Mexico City: Imp. de I. Lovis Morales, 1852); Elena Isabel Estrada de Guerrero, "Los protomártires del Japón en la hagiografía novohispana," in Fausto Ramírez, ed., *Los pinceles de la historia; De la patria criolla a la nación mexicana, 1750–1860* (Mexico City: Museo Nacional de Arte, 2000), 72- 89. According to Estrada de Guerrero the first account of the events was written by witness Marcelo de Rivadeneyra; see *Historia de las islas del archipiélago Filipino y los reinos de la Gran China, Tartaria, Conchinchina, Malaca, Siam, Cambodge y Japón* (Barcelona, 1601). See also Alfonso Martínez Rosales, "Japón y México en un sermón," *Estudios de Asia y África*, 31, 2 (1996): 427–72; this text deals with an 1897 sermon in honor of the third centennial of San Felipe's martyrdom. (My narrative of events is taken from Estrada de Guerrero's rigorous account.)

11. On criollo patriotism see David Brading, *The First America: The Spanish Monarchy, Creole Patriots, and the Liberal State, 1492–1867* (Cambridge: Cambridge University Press, 1991).

12. Rodrigo Vivero y Velasco, *Relación que hace D. Rodrigo de Vivero y Velasco* (Barcelona: Imprenta Barcelonesa, 1904). See also Michael Cooper, "Shipwrecked in Japan, 1609," *History Today*, 25, 12 (1975): 834–42; Josef Franz Schütte, "Don Rodrigo de Vivero de Velasco and Sebastián Vizcaíno in Japan," *International Congress of Human Sciences in Asia and North Africa, 30th, Mexico, 1976, Asia and Colonial Latin America*, ed. Ernesto de la Torre Villar (Mexico City: El Colegio de México, 1981), 77–100; and *Documentos inéditos para la historia de España*, tomo 5, ed. M. Ballesteros Gaibrois (Madrid: Maestre, 1947).

13. Journal entry, December 16, 1610. I thank Kevin Terraciano and Sanjay Subrahmanyam for referring my attention to this source. I used the Spanish translation, published as Domingo Franciso de San Antón, *Diario*, paleography and trans. by Rafael Tena (Mexico City: CONACULTA, 2001). See also Ernesto de la Torre Villar, *La expansion hispanoamericana en Asia, siglos XVI y XVII* (Mexico City: Fondo de Cultura Económica, 1980); Lothar Kanuth, *Confrontaciones transpacíficas* (Mexico City: UNAM, 1972); Miguel León Portilla, "La embajada de los japoneses en México, 1614. El testimonio del cronista Chimalpahin," *Estudios de Asia y África*, 16, 2 (1981): 23–36.

14. Fernando García Gutiérrez, "Influencia del arte cristiano en el arte japonés," *Ars Sacra*, 24 (2002): 72–86; Gustavo Curiel, *Viento detenido: Mitologías e historias del arte del biombo* (Mexico City: Museo Soumaya, 1999); and Rodrigo Rivero Lake, *Namban Art in Viceregal Mexico* (Mexico City: Turner, 2005). For the Japanese and Chinese influences in New Spain's hand-painted fans, see V. Prieto, "El abanico a través de los tiempos," *Anales del Museo Nacional*, serie 4, 1–2 (1922–24): 84–95.

15. "Os biombos Nambam," in Sophia de Mello Breyner Andresen, *Nocturno mediodía*, bilingual ed. (Madrid: Círculo de Lectores, 2004).

16. Bulnes, "Once mil leguas sobre el hemisferio norte."

17. I have not been able to find more information on this artist. Rebolledo's fascination with Japan paralleled his fascination with Norway, where he married and had children. In addition to his poems he published two prose accounts of his trip to Japan. See Efrén Rebolledo, *Nikko*; and

Hojas de bamboo (Mexico City: Compañía de Editores Nacionales, 1910). For this curious interaction, see Hugo Gutiérrez Vega, "Rebolledo, los viajes, el decadentismo y el amor sexual," *La Jornada Semanal*, 360 (January 27, 2002).

18. SRE, Expediente Carlos Américo Lera. I thank Víctor Macías-González for having referred me to this source; see his "The Mexican Aristocracy and Porfirio Díaz, 1876–1911," Ph.D. diss., Texas Christian University, 1999.

19. SRE, Expediente Carlos Américo Lera. He was the successor to Mariano Walheim. He was accused by Consul Rodrigo Parra of some wrongdoing, the details of which are unclear in the record but which had something to do with his removal.

20. Moisés González Navarro, *La colonización en México, 1877–1910* (Mexico City: n.p., 1960), 91.

21. Luis G. Palacios, "Psicología del soldado mexicano," *Revista del Ejército y Marina*, 3, 13 (January 1907): 119–34, quotes on pp. 122, 124, and 131.

22. Friedrich Katz, *The Secret War in Mexico: Europe, the United States, and the Mexican Revolution* (Chicago: University of Chicago Press, 1981); Jerry García, "Japanese Immigration and Community Development in Mexico, 1897–1940," Ph.D. diss., Washington State University, 1999; and Archivo Calles-Torreblanca, Presidente Calles Exp. 35, Informe confidencial; *The Mexican Review* 3 (May 1909): 23.

23. Inukai's testimony in PHO 6-2. For the events in Mexico City in the 1880s, and for a general view of this xenophobia, see Moisés González Navarro, *Historia moderna de México: El Porfiriato: Vida social*, vol. 4 (Mexico City: Editorial Hermés, 1974), 170–73, and the cover of *La Guacamaya* (August 18, 1904). For the 1911 massacre see Juan Puig, *Entre el río Perla y el Nazas: La china decimonónica y sus braceros emigrantes, la colonia china de Torreón y la matanza de 1911* (Mexico City: CONACULTA, 1992); and *El Machete* (Primera Quincena, March, 1931). The most outspoken anti-Chinese politician in Mexico City was José Angel Espinoza; see his *El problema chino en México* (Mexico City: Porrúa, 1931). See also Humberto Monteón González and José Luis Trueba, *Chinos y antichinos en México: Documentos para su estudio* (Guadalajara: Gobierno del Estado de Jalisco, 1988); José Jorge Gómez Izquierdo, *El movimiento antichino en México (1871–1934): Problemas de racismo y nacionalismo durante la Revolución* (Mexico City: INAH, 1991). For Lillo's cartoon, see Armando Bartra and Juan Manuel Aurrecoechea, *Puros Cuentos: La historia de la historieta en México, 1874–1934*, vol. 1 (Mexico City: Grijalbo, 1988), cartoon reproduced on p. 144.

24. Biographical sketch quoted in Lawrence W. Chisolm, *Fenollosa: The Far East and American Culture* (New Haven: Yale University Press, 1963), 23.

25. In J. J. Tablada, *Hiroshigué: el pintor de la nieve y de la lluvia, de la noche y de la luna* (Mexico City: Monografías Japonesas, 1914); and his *Historia del arte en México* (Mexico City: Compañía Nacional Editora "Aguilas," 1927). He mentioned, in *Hiroshigué*, his forthcoming *De aztecas y japoneses*, although it was never published. See also José María González de Mendoza, "La obra inédita de J. J. Tablada," reprinted in J. M. González de Mendoza, *Ensayos selectos* (Mexico City: Fondo de Cultura Económica, 1970). On Fenollosa's input into Western poetic traditions, see Heraldo de Campos, "Ideograma, anagrama y diagrama: una lectura de Fenollosa," included in Heraldo de Campos, *De la razón antropofágica y otros ensayos*, ed. and trans. Roberto Mata (Mexico City: Siglo XXI, 2000).

26. Hearn was, argued an anonymous writer in the popular *El Mundo Ilustrado*, "an enthusiastic English citizen who has become Japanese and has dedicated to his new country (*patria*) the two most insightful and exact books [about Japan]: *El Japón desconocido* (Glimpses of unfamiliar Japan) and *Kokoro*." "La primavera en el Japón: La fiesta de los cerezos," *El Mundo Ilustrado* (May 24,

1908); Lafcadio Hearn, *Glimpses of Unfamiliar Japan* (Boston: Houghton, Mifflin and Co., 1894); and Hearn, *Kokoro: Hints and Echoes of Japanese Inner Life* (Boston: Houghton, Mifflin, 1896). There was a Spanish translation of *Kokoro*—*Kokoro: impresiones de la vida íntima del Japón*, trans. Julián Besteiro (Madrid: D. Jorro, 1907). Besteiro was a prominent intellectual who became an important socialist politician before and during the Spanish Civil War.

27. The history of philology, like the history of art, shows the interactions between nationalism, art, orientalism, and science. Maurice Olender, *Les langues du paradis: aryens et sémites, un couple providentiel* (Paris: Le Seuil, 1989). By Frederick Starr see: *The Ainu Group at the Saint Louis Exposition* (Chicago: Open Court Publishing Company, 1904); *Shinto, the Native Religion of Japan: An Address Given at Abraham Lincoln Centre, on Sunday, March 28, 1915* (Chicago: University of Chicago Press, 1915); *The Aztecs of Ancient Mexico: Syllabus of a Course of Six Lecture-Studies in Anthropology* (Chicago: University of Chicago Press, 1897); and the travel account *In Indian Mexico: A Narrative of Travel and Labor* (Chicago: Forbes & Company, 1908). Information on his trips to Japan in 1904 in search of Ainu people can be found in his personal papers, now held at the University of Chicago. His Japanese antiques and books were donated to the Library of Congress and his personal library, containing many books on Mexico and Central America, was bought by Tulane University in the 1930s. On the subject of Japan at World's Fairs, see Angus Lockyer, "Japan at the Exhibition, 1867–1970," Ph.D. diss., Stanford University, 2000; Carol Ann Christ, "'The Sole Guardians of the Art Inheritance of Asia': Japan and China at the 1904 St. Louis World's Fair," *Positions: East Asia Cultures Critique*, 8, 3 (Winter 2000): 675–709; Ellen P. Conant, "Refractions of the Rising Sun: Japan's Participation in International Exhibitions, 1862–1910," in Tomoko Sato and Toshio Watanabe, eds., *Japan and Britain: An Aesthetic Dialogue 1850–1930* (London: Lund Humphries Publishers Ltd., 1991). In the 1950s Nina Cabrera de Tablada, Tablada's wife, recalled that Tablada was in constant contact with Starr, with whom he discussed Japanese topics. Nina Cabrera de Tablada, *José Juan Tablada en la intimidad (con cartas y poemas inéditos)* (Mexico City: Imprenta Universitaria, 1954), 66.

28. Meech and Weisberg, *Japonisme Comes to America*; and Robert Rydell, *All the World's Fair: Visions of Empire, International Exhibitions 1876–1916* (Chicago: University of Chicago Press, 1984).

29. See, for example, Rafael Heliodoro Valle and Alberto Aria, "Bibliografía del Japón en México," *Boletín de la Biblioteca Nacional*, 7, 1 (January–March, 1956): 26–376; 8, 1 (January–March 1957): 24–35. See also Miguel Alonso Romero, "Refulgencias del espíritu nipón," *Memoria de la Academia Nacional de Historia y Geografía*, 14, 5 (1958): 5–18; Gumesindo Mendoza, "Ídolo azteca de tipo chino," *Anales del Museo Nacional de México*, 1 (1877): 39–42; and Mendoza, "Ídolo azteca de tipo japonés," *Anales del Museo Nacional de México*, 1 (1877): 91. See also Daniel G. Brinton, "Ethnology: On various Supposed Relations between the American and Asian Races," *Memoirs of the International Congress of Anthropology* (Chicago: University of Chicago Press, 1894); Thomas Stewart Denison, *The Primitive Aryans of America, Origin of the Aztecs and Kindred Tribes, Showing their Relationship to the Indo-Iranians and the Place of the Nahuas of Mexico in the Arian Group* (Chicago: University of Chicago Press, 1908); Alter Hough, "Oriental Influences in Mexico," *American Anthropologist*, 1 (1899): 199, 2 (1900): 66–74; Dhirendra Nath Mujerji, "A Correlation of the Maya and Hindu Calendars," *Indian Culture*, 2, 4 (1936): 685–92. A more modern scholar still maintained these connections; see Ángel María Garibay, "Semejanzas de algunos conceptos filosóficos de las culturas hindu y náhuatl," *Cuadernos del Seminario de Problemas Científicos y Filosóficos*, 15, segunda serie (1959). In 1962 Paul Kirchhoff still maintained that the diffusion of a religious system from India to Mexico

occurred through the dispersal of the Indian-Japanese calendaric classification of twenty-eight Hindu deities into pre-Hispanic Mexico. Paul Kirchhoff, "The Diffusion of a Great Religious System from India to Mexico," in *Congreso Internacional de Americanistas, XXXV, México, 1962: Actas y memorias*, vol. 1 (Mexico City: 1964), 73–100. Even in 1984 Kornelia Giesing, without sustained diffusion, established a parallel between the Indian deity Rudra-Shiva and Tezcatlipoca, arguing that they both fulfilled similar roles within their respective religious systems. Kornelia Giesing, *Rudra-Siva und Tezcatlipoca: ein Beitrag zur Indo-Mexikanistik* (Tübingen: Science and Fiction, 1984).

30. Mendoza, "Ídolo azteca de tipo chino" Mendoza, "Ídolo azteca de tipo japonés."

31. Ernest Fenollosa, *East and West: The Discovery of America and Other Poems* (New York: T. Y. Crowell and Company, 1893).

32. José Juan Tablada, *Poesías: Obras Completas* (Mexico City: UNAM, 1971); and see John Page, "José Juan Tablada, introductor del haiku en Hispanoamérica," Ph.D. diss., UNAM, 1963; Atsuko Tanabe, *El japonismo de José Juan Tablada* (Mexico City: UNAM, 1981).

33. Henry Adams, *The Education of Henry Adams: An Autobiography* (Boston: Houghton Mifflin, 1918).

34. Among the books available in Spanish there are Théophile Gautier, *Una noche de Cleopatra* (Barcelona: Ramón Sopena, 1900), and Judith Gautier, *El Japón* (Paris: Casa Editorial Hispano-Americana, 1912). *Revista Moderna* often published translations of works by Pierre Loti; see, for example, vol. 3, Primera Quincena (November 1903): 177.

35. *Revista Moderna*, Primera Quincena (May 1900). In the same periodical Tablada published an essay on Hokusai and Utamaro (pp. 140–41).

36. J. J. Tablada, *La feria de la vida (memorias)* (Mexico City: Botas, 1937), 209–10.

37. See, for instance, J. J. Tablada, "El castillo sin nombre," *Revista Moderna*, Segunda Quincena (December 1901): 378–80.

38. Tablada, "El castillo sin nombre," 380.

39. J. J. Tablada, "La mujer en Japón," El Mundo Ilustrado (April 16, 1905): 14–15. Tablada referred to Pierre Loti's novel *Madame Chrysanthème* (1887), the story of a Western sailor who seduced and abandoned a Japanese woman; it is full of stereotypical images of Japanese women and places.

40. J. J. Tablada, *Hiroshigué: el pintor de la nieve y de la lluvia, de la noche y de la luna* (Mexico City: Monografías Japonesas, 1914), 5. This was a very small and selective edition, full of beautiful illustrations.

41. All these haikus are taken from J. J. Tablada, *El jarro de flores* (New York: Escritores Sindicados, 1922), illustrations by Alfredo Best Maugard. Another book of Tablada's haikus was *Un día: Poemas sintéticos* (Caracas: n.p., 1919), which includes the following beautiful haiku: "Pavo real, largo fulgor,/por el gallinero demócrata/pasas como una procesión" ("Peacock, long luster/ like a procession you pass / by the democratic henhouse").

42. Quoted in J. M. González de Mendoza, "El espiritualismo de José Juan Tablada," included in J. M. González de Mendoza, *Ensayos selectos* (Mexico City: Fondo de Cultura Económica, 1970).

43. J. J. Tablada, *La feria: Poemas mexicanos*, illustrated by M. Covarrubias, M. Santoyo, and George (Pop) Hart (New York: n.p., 1928).

44. Francisco Díaz Covarrubias, *Viaje de la Comisión Astronómica Mexicana al Japón: para observar el tránsito del planeta Vénus por el disco del sol el 8 de diciembre de 1874* (Mexico City: C. Ramiro y Ponce de León, 1876); Carlos Glass, "Apuntes sobre el viaje alrededor del mundo en la corbeta Zaragoza, recogidos por Carlos Glass . . . 37,000 millas sobre los mares," El Mundo Ilustrado, published in

installments from September 15 to October 31, 1897. I thank Antonio Saborit for this reference. Olivier Debroise, *Mexican Suite: A History of Photography in Mexico*, trans. Stella de Sá Rego (Austin: University of Texas Press, 2001), 185.

45. Lane Simonian, *Defending the Land of the Jaguar: A History of Conservation in Mexico* (Austin: University of Texas Press, 1995); and Quevedo's autobiographical notes, *Relato de mi vida* (Mexico City: n.p, 1943).

46. *Arte y Letras* reported on Gayol's trip (January 16, 1910). He published stereotypical photos of buildings in India. See Gayol's first studies on irrigation, written before his travels. They include large sections on India and can be found in Roberto Gayol, *Dos problemas de vital importancia para México: la colonización y el desarrollo de la irrigación: estudios preliminares* (Mexico City: El Popular de Francisco Montes de Oca, 1906). See also his *Proyecto de desagüe y saneamiento de la ciudad de México que por orden del Ayuntamiento formó el ingeniero Roberto Gayol* (Mexico City: J. F. Jens, 1891).

47. See Enrique Cortés, *Relaciones entre México y Japón durante el Porfiriato* (Mexico City: Secretaría de Relaciones Exteriores, 1980); María Elena Ota Mishima, *México y Japón en el siglo XIX* (Mexico City: Secretaría de Relaciones Exteriores, 1976).

48. "La primavera en Japón: La fiesta de los cerezos," El Mundo Ilustrado (May 24, 1908). I thank Antonio Saborit for this reference.

49. *La Semana Ilustrada* (April 7, 1914).

50. *La Semana Ilustrada* (September 2, 1913); photograph of storefront, in El Tiempo Ilustrado (September 11, 1910).

51. This information is based on the Genaro García Collection, Benson Latin American Collection, the University of Texas. Genaro García was the official chronicler of the celebration. *Memoria de la Secretaría de Fometo*, 62.

52. On the fair, see Peter Stansky, *On or About December 1910: Early Bloomsbury and Its Intimate World* (Cambridge: Harvard University Press, 1996), 120–21; Ayako Hotta-Lister, *The Japan-British Exhibition of 1910: Gateway to the Island Empire of the East* (Richmond Surrey: Japan Library, 1999); and Angus Lockyer, "Japan at the Exhibition, 1867–1970," Ph.D. diss., Stanford University, 2000. Indeed, Lockyer does not deal with the Japanese presence at the many exhibitions between 1867–1910, but he does devote an entire chapter to the Japan-British Exhibition.

53. Alois M. Hass, "Poesía en la mística cristiana y el budismo zen," in Hass, *Visión en azul: Estudios de mística europea*, trans. from the German by Victoria Cirlot and Amador Vega (Madrid: Editorial Siruela, 1999), 67–88, quote on 86. See also W. R. LaFleur, *The Karma of Words: Buddhism and the Literary Arts in Medieval Japan* (Berkeley: University of California Press, 1986). The other side of the coin (the translation, from Western languages into Japanese, of political, historiographical, and aesthetics concepts) is examined in Douglas R. Howland, *Translating the West: Language and Political Reason in Nineteenth-Century Japan* (Honolulu: University of Hawaii Press, 2002).

54. Octavio Paz, "El sentimiento de las cosas: Mono no Aware," 365, and "La tradición del haikú," 361, both in Octavio Paz, *Obras Completas*, vol. 2 (Mexico City: Fondo de Cultura Económica, 1993).

55. José María González de Mendoza, "Los Hai-jines mexicanos," included in J. M. González de Mendoza, *Ensayos selectos* (Mexico City: Fondo de Cultura Económica, 1970).

56. "Tres momentos de la literatura japonesa" (1954), included in *Las peras del olmo* (Mexico City: UNAM, 1965); and "La tradición del haikú" (1970), in Paz, *Obras Completas*. According to Aurelio Asiain—perhaps the only Mexican poet who ever spoke fluent Japanese—while Tablada

based his translations on B. H. Chamberlain, Paul-Louis Couchoud, and others, Paz used Ei-
kichi Hayashiya, Donald Keene, R. H. Blyth, and Jacques Roubaud (communication with Aurelio
Asiain). I thank him for his generosity.

57. *Revista Moderna*, Primera Quincena (October 1900): 298. In the next issue of *Revista Moderna*
there were translations of poems by Emperor Uda (*Kokinshō*), Chisato, Fun'ya Asayasu, and Ono
no Komachi.

58. *La Antorcha* (February 7, 1925). This is a different version of the essay "Los Hai-jines
Mexicanos," published earlier (in 1924) in *La Revue de L'Amérique Latine*, and then included in
J. M. González de Mendoza, *Ensayos selectos* (Mexico City: Fondo de Cultura Económica, 1970).
The version in *La Antorcha*, which included the argument about the *coplas*, was not included in the
latter book.

59. Carlos Gutiérrez Cruz, *Dichos y proverbios populares* (Mexico City: Ediciones del PEN Club,
1924).

60. J. J. Tablada, *El jarro de flores* (New York: Escritores Sindicados, 1922).

61. José Rubén Romero, *Obras Completas* (Mexico City: Porrúa, 1970). It was in the 1960s, while
reviewing his 1920s haikus, that Romero confessed that he was not inspired by Jules Renard,
as Genaro Estrada had written, but by Tablada. "Granero" was a popular haiku. Not only did
Obregón make his own version of its sonorous obscenity, but Salvador Novo wrote a homoerotic
version: "Buscando de uvas un racimo/hallé los huevos de mi primo" (Looking for a bunch of
graves/I found my cousin's balls). Salvador Novo, *La vida en México en el periodo presidencial de Manuel
Ávila Camacho* (Mexico City: Empresas Editoriales, 1965), 259.

62. Francisco Monterde García Icazbalceta, *Itinerario completo*, prologue by José Juan Tablada
(Mexico City: Cultura, 1923).

63. González de Mendoza, *Ensayos selectos*.

64. Rubén M. Campos, *Claudio Oronoz* (Mexico City: J. Ballescá, 1909); José Juan Tablada,
"Claudio Oronoz: Novela por Rubén M. Campos," *Revista Moderna* (February 1906): 376–77; Pedro
Henríquez Ureña, "Notas sobre *Claudio Oronoz*," *Revista Moderna* (June 1902): 239–40.

65. The novel was published in installments in *El Universal* (1914), and republished by Alfonso Teja Zabre as *La esperanza y Hati-Ké: novela mexicana* (Mexico City: Compañía Editora Latino-
Americana, [1920s]).

66. Teja Zabre, *La esperanza*, 99.

67. Loti, *Madame Chrysanthème* (1887); Bulnes, "Once mil leguas sobre el hemisferio norte,"
178–79.

68. See his articles "Desde China" and "Desde Tokio" in *El Universal* (May 28, July 11, August 11, November 17, 1946). Paredes married a Uruguayan-Japanese woman he met on his trip.
Ramón Saldívar, *The Borderlands of Culture: Américo Paredes and the Transnational Imaginary* (Berkeley:
University of California Press, 2006). For a critical account of both Paredes's and Saldívar's views
of China and Japan see José E. Limón, "Border Literary Histories, Globalization, and Critical Regionalism," *American Literary History*, 20, 1–2 (Spring–Summer 2008): 160–82.

69. Efrén Rebolledo, *Rimas japonesas* (Tokyo: Shimbi Shuin, 1901).

70. *El Hijo del Ahuizote* (December 30, 1911).

71. Cover, *El Universal Ilustrado* (February 19, 1919).

72. *Revista de Revistas* (November 7, 1920).

73. *El Tiempo Ilustrado* (July 31, 1904): 500.

74. *El Tiempo Ilustrado* (September, 11, 1910), cover.

75. *Arte y Letras* (February 17, 1910), n.p.

76. *Arte y Letras* (March 6, 1910): 6–7.

77. *La Semana Ilustrada* (June 5, 1912).

78. *Arte y Letras* (June 1908), n.p.

79. *La Revista Azul*, translation of Loti (September 9, 1894): 302–04; Nahuatl poems (August 5, 1894): 212–13. In the same publication, even the prominent writer and Japanist Rubén Darío published poems with Nahuatl topics; (July 26, 1896): 211, for his poem about the Cacique Tutecotzimi.

80. *El Mundo Ilustrado*, 19 (Nov. 9, 1918); Tablada's report of the exhibit in *El Universal Ilustrado* (January 17, 1919): 3, 7. Tablada wrote an article praising Pal-Omar's work and lamenting his early death in 1920, a victim of poverty and starvation. *Excélsior* (December 12, 1920), sec. 1, p. 3. In 1921 once again told about their common life (he and Pal-Omar) in New York; see *El Universal Ilustrado* (March 10, 1921).

81. Richard Fitzgerald, *Art and Politics: Cartoonists of the Masses and Liberator* (Westport: Greenwood Press, 1973), 193–224; Gabriel Gilbert, *George Overbury "Pop" Hart: His Life and Art* (New Brunswick: Rutgers University Press, 1986); and Tablada, *La feria*.

82. For Kitagawa's arrival in Mexico see F. Díaz de León, "El pintor japonés en México," *Forma*, 7 (1928): 2–5. Painter and photographer Yasuo Kuniyoshi, born in Japan in 1893 but resident in the U.S. since 1906, also used Mexico as inspiration. In 1935, he went to Mexico (and Taos) to study Orozco's murals. Richard A. Davis, *Yosuo Kuniyoshi: The Complete Graphic Work* (San Francisco: Alan Wofsy Fine Arts, 1991).

83. The final title of the canvas was "Self-portrait," but F. Díaz de León reproduced the image in *Forma* with the label "Worker reading." F. Díaz de León, "El pintor japonés en México," *Forma*, 7 (1928): 2.

84. Dan Kitagishy Tsukamoto, "Kitagawa Tamidyi en las Escuelas de Pintura al Aire Libre: Un intento de la educación a través de las prácticas artísticas en el México post-revolucionario," tesis de maestría, Estudios Latinoamericanos, UNAM 1993; and Francisco Díaz de León, "Un pintor japonés en México," *Forma*, 7 (1928): 4. Kitawaga had, himself, written of his experiences, but I have used Kitagishy's translations. By Kitagawa see *Mekishiko no seishun* (Tokyo: Kobunsha, 1955). I thank Professor Toshiharu Omuka for his help in finding Kitagawa's material in Japan. Heath Bowman and Stirling Dickinson, *Mexican Odyssey* (Chicago: Willett, Clark & Company, 1935); Josephine Herbst, "The Governor Does Not Come," *The Magazine* (April 1934): 157–60, in Barbara Wiedemann, *Josephine Herbst's Short Fiction: A Window to Her Life and Times* (Selinsgrove: Susquehanna University Press; London: Associated University Presses, 1998).

85. This quote comes from Kitagawa's autobiography (p. 67), as translated into Spanish by Kitagishy Tsukamoto, "Kitagawa Tamidyi," quote on p. 26.

86. Díaz de Léon, "El pintor japonés," 4–5.

87. *Xavier Villaurrutia entre líneas: Dibujos y pintura*, ed. Luis Mario Schneider (Mexico City: Ediciones Trabuco y Clavel, 1991). I thank Susan Burns for the translation of the inscription. The poem's title is "Más que lento," included in Xavier Villaurrutia, *Obras: poesía, teatro, prosas varias, críticas*, ed. Miguel Capistrán, Alí Chumacero, and Luis Mario Schneider (Mexico City: Fondo de Cultura Económica, 1966). By 1964, the abstract painter Kishio Murata became another Japanese artist in Mexico. He died in Mexico City in 1992.

88. B. Winther-Tamaki, "The Mexican Boom in the Japanese Art World of the 1950s," unpublished paper (2007); "El pintor japonés, señor Foujita, que ha abierto una expocisión de sus obras en la sala de arte de la Secretaría de Educación," El Universal (December 6, 1932).

89. Most of Foujita writings, including his autobiography, are in Japanese. I have relied on Sylvie Buisson and Dominique Buisson, La vie et l'œuvre de Léonard-Tsuguharu Foujita, 2 vols. (Paris: ACR, 1987–2001); and Phyllis Birnbaum, Glory in a Line: A Life of Foujita, the Artist Caught between East and West (New York: Faber and Faber, 2006). Kitagawa's opinions are found in his autobiography. I relied on Kitagishy Tsukamoto, "Kitagawa Tamidyi." Araki Sueo's opinion is quoted in Birnbaum's Glory, 187. See also Pierre Loti, Madame Chrysanthème (Paris: Excelsior, 1926).

CHAPTER 8

1. Vislumbres de la India, in Obras Completas, vol. 6 (Mexico City: Fondo de Cultura Económica, 1996), 411; Julia A. Kushigian, "Ríos en la noche: Fluyen los jardínes: Orientalism in the work of Octavio Paz," Hispania, 70, 4 (December 1989): 776–86; Enrique Ruiz-Fornells, "La India de Octavio Paz: Testimonio y pensamiento," Cuadernos Hispanoamericanos, 595 (2000): 79–90; and Susnigdha Dey, "La influencia de la India en la obra poética de Pablo Neruda y Octavio Paz," XVII Congreso del Instituto Internacional de Literatura Iberoamericana: El barroco en América; Literatura hispanoamericana; Critica histórico-literaria hispanoamericana (Madrid: Centro Iberoamericano de Cooperación, Univ. Complutense de Madrid, 1978), 845–56; on Paz's reading of India, see Rubén Gallo, Freud's Mexico: Into the Wilds of Psychoanalysis (Cambridge: MIT Press, 2010).

2. Nicolás León, Catarina de San Juan y la China Poblana: Estudio etnográfico-crítico (Mexico City: Biblioteca Aportación Histórica, Editor Vargas Roa, 1946); José Juan Tablada, "A Mexican Type, La China Poblana," Mexican Art & Life, 5 (January 1939); Louise Stinetorf, La China Poblana (Indianapolis: Bobbs-Merrill, 1960); the literary account by Eula Long, Pirate's Doll: The Story of the China Poblana (New York: Knopf, 1956); Agustín Grajales Porras, "La China Poblana: Princesa india, esclava, casada y virgen, beata y condenada," in México-India, 105–35; and La China Poblana: Revista Artes de México (2003).

3. Isabel Duque, Kiran Saxena, and José Silvestre Revueltas, "Encuentro entre sikhs y mexicanos: Paralelo 48," in México-India, 139–55.

4. See, for instance, article by J. P. Wilson, in Revista de Revistas (September 4, 1921).

5. H. Pedersen, The Discovery of Language: Linguistic Science in the Nineteenth Century (Bloomington: Indiana University Press, 1962); Manuel Murelle-Lema, La teoría lingüística en la España del siglo XIX (Madrid: El Soto, 1968); Francisco Javier Pérez, Orientalismo en Venezuela: Historia de la lingüística sánscrita (Caracas: Universidad Católica Andrés Bello, 2004); Alberto Bernabé, "El descubrimiento del sánscrito: Tradición y novedad en la lingüística europea," Revista Española de Lingüística, 13, 1 (January–June, 1983): 41–62; and Francisco Pimentel, Cuadro descriptivo y comparativo de las lenguas indígenas de México, 2 vols. (Mexico City: Impr. de Andrade y Escalante, 1862–1865). On Sanskrit and Europe, see Marchand, German Orientalism in the Age of Empire.

6. In reply to Pimentel, Mendoza claimed to be a native speaker of Otomi, while Pimentel did not speak any native language. Pimentel, "Réplica al Sr. Gumesindo Mendoza, acerca de su disertación sobre el idioma otomí," in Obras completas: Publícanlas para honrar la memoria del autor, sus hijos Jacinto y Fernando, vol. 5 (Mexico City: Tipografía Económica, 1903–4), 604.

7. G. Mendoza, Estudio comparativo entre el sánscrito y el nagüatl (Mexico City: Ignacio Escalante,

1878), also published in *Anales del Museo Nacional de México*, I (1877): 75–84. To support his theory, Mendoza quoted the Argentine Fidel López and his study of the relationship between Quechua and Sanskrit.

8. Daniel Brinton, *Rig Veda Americanus; Sacred Songs of the Ancient Mexicans, with a Gloss in Nahuatl: Edited, with a Paraphrase, Notes and Vocabulary*, originally published in 1890 (New York: AMS Press, 1969). About these poems and their real pre-Hispanic origins, see Pablo González Casanova, "¿Tuvieron poetas los aztecas?," *Anales del Museo Nacional*, serie 5, 1 (1934): 325–28.

9. Brinton's assessment of Mendoza's theories is in D. Brinton, *Essays of an Americanist* (Philadelphia: Porter & Coates, 1890), 57.

10. Francisco Pimentel, "El idioma otomí: Observaciones a la disertación en la Sociedad Mexicana de Geografía y Estadística, por el Sr. Gumesindo Mendoza" (1872), in Pimentel, *Obras Completas*, vol. 5, 581–99, quote on p. 596.

11. Written in collaboration with M. Albert Wolf (Paris: Garnier, 1900). For the history of Sanskrit studies in the eighteenth and nineteenth centuries in Spanish-America, see the excellent work by Pérez, *Orientalismo en Venezuela*.

12. Jesús Díaz de León, *Concepto del indianismo en México* (Mexico City: Tip. de la Viuda de F. Díaz de León, 1911); *El cantar de los Cantares de Salomón: traducido del hebreo*, trans. Jesús Díaz de León (Aguascalientes: Perdoza, 1891); also *Lamentaciones de Jeremías*, trans. Jesús Díaz de León (Aguascalientes: Imp. R. Rodríguez Romo, 1913). For his Hebrew studies, see Rafael Heliodoro Valle, "Judíos en México," *Revista Chilena de Historia y Geografía*, 81 (1936): 215–36.

13. Luis Cabrera, *Musa peregrina*, published in Mexico City by the author himself (1920), reedited in 1947 (Mexico City: Imprenta Nuevo Mundo), including a translation of the Song of Songs from the Greek.

14. Anecdote as related in Rubén M. Campos, *El folklore literario de México: Investigación acerca de la producción literaria popular (1525–1925)* (Mexico City: Publicaciones de la Secretaria de Educación Pública, 1929), 584.

15. Gian Mario Cazzaniga, *La religione dei moderni* (Pisa: ETS, 1999); R. William Weisberger, Wallace McLeod, and S. Brent Morris, eds., *Freemasonry on Both Sides of the Atlantic: Essays Concerning the Craft in the British Isles, Europe, the United States, and Mexico* (Boulder: East European Monographs; New York: Columbia University Press, 2002); Arnold Krumm-Heller, *Mexiko, mein Heimatland!* (Saale: Dr. Krumm-Hellersche Verlagsanstalt, 1919); see also his novel of manners (including sexual manners) *Alfredo, deutscher-mexikanischer Roman* (Halle: Maennel, 1918). On Krumm-Heller and Mexico, see Ricardo Pérez Montfort, "El doctor Arnold Krumm Heller en México, 1910–1935," in his *Cotidianidades, imaginarios y contextos: ensayos de historia y cultura en México, 1850–1950* (Mexico City: CIESAS, 2008), 249–74.

16. Jean-Pierre Bastian, "Jacobinismo y ruptura revolucionaria durante el Porfiriato," *Mexican Studies/Estudios Mexicanos*, 7, 1 (Winter 1991): 29–46; and José Mariano Leyva, *El ocaso de los espíritus: El espiritualismo en México en el siglo XIX* (Mexico City: Cal y Arena, 2005). Among the publications, there were: *La ilustración espíritu; El Siglo Spírita; Revista Luz; Helios; Flores de loto; La ley de amor: Revista quincenal del Círculo Espirita "Peralta"* (Merida, Yucatán); *El Alma: Revista mensual de estudios psíquicos y morales*; and *Boletín del Círculo Espiritista "Paz y Progreso"* (Orizaba, Veracruz). Kardec was first translated into Spanish in the 1860s; see Allan Kardec, *El espiritismo en su más simple espresión; exposición sumaria de la enseñanza de los espíritus y de sus manifestaciones* (Barcelona, 1869). For a different kind of spiritualism, based on popular Catholic beliefs and messianism (that of Father Elías) in 1970s

Mexico, see Kaja Finkler, "Dissident Sectarian Movements, the Catholic Church, and Social Class in Mexico," *Comparative Studies in Society and History*, 25, 2 (April 1983): 277–305. The author, however, calls this movement a kind of spiritualism that is "largely ignorant of Kardec." Indeed, the Father Elías movement had more to do with long-lasting millenarian movements in Mexico than with spiritualism itself.

17. *Congrès spirite et spiritualiste international de 1900 tenu a Paris du 16–27 sept.* (Paris: Imprimerie Daniel Chambon, 1902); Konstantin Balmont, *Visions solaires: Mexique-Égypte-Inde-Japon-Océanie*, trans. Ludmila Savitzky (Paris: Éditions Bossard, 1923); A. Artaud, "El hombre contra el destino," in A. Artaud, *México y Viaje al país de los tarahumaras* (Mexico City: Fondo de Cultura Económica, 1984), 122.

18. Charles A. Hale, *The Transformation of Liberalism in Late Nineteenth Century Mexico* (Princeton: Princeton University Press, 1989); Jesús García Gutiérrez, *La masonería en la historia y en las leyes de Méjico* (Mexico City: n.p., 1957).

19. Krausism was an especially Spanish trend, based on the influence of the German philosopher Karl Christian Friedrich Krause (1781–1832), who contrary to his contemporary, Hegel, defended the metaphysical existence of a supreme being (*Urwesen*), along with a strong belief in human fraternity, and the power of science. Juan López-Morillas, *El krausismo español: perfil de una aventura intelectual* (Madrid: Ediciones Fondo de Cultura Económica, 1980); and María Asunción Ortiz de Andrés, *Masonería y democracia en el siglo XIX: el Gran Oriente Español y su proyección político-social (1888–1896)* (Madrid: UPCO, 1993). For the influence of Krausism in Mexico, see Charles A. Hale, *The Transformation of Liberalism*.

20. Wendell Thomas, *Hinduism Invades America* (New York: Beacon Press, 1930); Arthur Christy, *The Orient in American Transcendentalism: A Study of Emerson, Thoreau, and Alcott* (New York: Columbia University Press, 1932); Dale Riepe, "Emerson and Indian Philosophy," *Journal of the History of Ideas*, 28 (1967): 115–22; Frederic Ives Carpenter, *Emerson and Asia* (Cambridge: Harvard University Press, 1930).

21. *Flores de Loto: Revista mensual gratuita: Estudios de teosofía, ocultismo, naturismo, orientalismo, etc.*, etc., 1, 3 (May 1914): 6–7.

22. "Del pensamiento primero, el pensamiento vibró, tomó forma y la luz fue hecha." *La Luz: Revista científica, órgano oficial del Centro Esotérico Oriental de México*, 1, 1 (November 1903).

23. Tablada, *La feria*, n.p.

24. J. M. González de Mendoza, "José Juan Tablada y el espiritualismo," in González de Mendoza, *Ensayos Selectos*. Ouspensky was a Russian thinker and a longtime resident in England and the U.S. who, upon being influenced by Eastern religions, theosophy, Hindu thought and dancing, and George Gurdjieff's ideas, developed a mystic idea of a new order for the universe. His book *Tertium Organum*, which was widely recommended by Tablada to various friends, was a best seller in the U.S. in the mid-1920s, and was a great success among European intellectuals belonging to what we may call the "intimist" moment; for example, Proust and Bergson. See P. D. Ouspensky, *Tertium Organum: una clave para los misterios del mundo*, trans. Antonio Manero, prologue by J. J. Tablada (Mexico City: Editorial Botas, 1937).

25. Published as P. D. Ouspensky, *Tertium Organum: una clave para los misterios del mundo*, trans. Antonio Manero, prologue by J. J. Tablada (Mexico City: Editorial Botas, 1937).

26. The novel was published in 1924 by *El Universal Ilustrado*, with illustrations by Duhart. José Juan Tablada, *Obras Completas VII: La resurrección de los ídolos: Novela americana inédita, publicación ex-*

clusiva de El Universal Ilustrado (1924), prologue and annotations by José Eduardo Serrato Córdova (Mexico City: UNAM, 2003). For Tablada's theosophical influences, see prologue, 11–37.

27. Tablada, La resurrección, 125.

28. Renato González Mello, La máquina de pintar (Mexico City: UNAM, 2008); Fausto Ramírez, "Artistas e iniciados en la obra mural de Orozco," in Luis Cardoza y Aragón, et al., Orozco: una relectura (Mexico City: UNAM, 1983), 61–102; Fausto Ramírez's entries in Los murales de la Secretaría de Educación Pública, CD compiled by F. Ramírez (Mexico City: UNAM, 1997); and J. C. Orozco, Autobiografía (Mexico City: Ediciones Occidente, 1945).

29. Esther Turner Wellman, Amado Nervo: Mexico's Religious Poet (New York: Instituto de las Españas, 1937); Roderick A. Molina, "Amado Nervo: His Mysticism and Franciscan Influence," The Americas, 6, 2 (October 1949): 173–96; and G. W. Umphrey, "Amado Nervo and Hinduism," Hispanic Review, 17, 2 (April 1949): 133–45.

30. Amado Nervo, Obras completas: Edición estudios, y notas de Francisco González Guerrero (prosas) y Alfonso Méndez Plancarte (poesías), vol. 2 (Madrid: Aguilar, 1955–1956). (All of the poems by Nervo quoted in the following pages were taken from this edition of his Obras).

31. Regarding the Ahrimans, see Peter Washington, Madame Blavatsky's Baboon (New York: Schocken Books, 1993), 145–62.

32. "Las voces," 1904.

33. José Vasconcelos, El viento de Bagdad: Cuentos y ensayos (Mexico City: Letras de México, 1945), 55–61, 194, for Vasconcelos's explanation of why Dostoyevsky is the best prophet of modern times.

34. I thank Professor Sheila Fitzpatrick for recommending that I pay more attention to what was, after all, a conspicuous Russian reference in the sources I consulted.

35. La Antorcha (August 1925).

36. About Madero, see Gabriel Ferrer Mendiolea, Vida de Francisco I. Madero (Mexico City: Secretaría de Educación Pública, 1945); Pedro Lamicq, Madero, por uno de sus íntimos (Mexico City: Oficina Editorial Azteca, 1915); and Enrique Krauze, Biografía del poder: Caudillos de la Revolución Mexicana (1910–1940) (Barcelona: Tusquests, 1997), 23–76.

37. José Vasconcelos, Estudios Indostanos, in Obras Completas, vol. 3 (Mexico City: Editores Mexicanos Unidos, 1959), 157–62, quotation on p. 162.

38. Krauze, Biografía del poder, 59. Regarding Madero's Porfirism, see Francisco I. Madero, La elección de 1910 (Mexico City: n.p., 1909).

39. Mexico, Secretaría de Hacienda y Crédito Público, Archivo de don Francisco I. Madero, Epistolario (1900–1909), vol. 1. (Mexico City: Secretaría de Hacienda y Crédito Público, 1963), 41.

40. Madero, Epistolario (1900–1909), vol. 1, 98. It is not clear, but very likely, that Madero was referring to Alfred Percy Sinnett's Esoteric Buddhism (Boston: Houghton, Mifflin and Company, 1884), a translation of which was published some time in the early twentieth century in Madrid as El Buddhismo esotérico, trans. of the 6th English ed. by Francisco de Montoliu, with annotations by José Melian y Chiappi (Madrid: B. Rodríguez Serra, n.d.). Sinnett was a well-known theosophist whose radical interpretations of Buddhism, full of esoteric and spiritualist fantasies, produced as many followers as enemies (among those who were impressed with him were W. B. Yeats and Madero). Washington, Madame Blavatsky's Baboon; and also Ronald Davidson, Indian Esoteric Buddhism: A Social History of the Tantric Movement (New York: Columbia University Press, 2002).

41. Letter to Luis G. Rubín, December 1, 1907, Madero, Epistolario, vol. 1.

42. Francisco Madero, *Obras completas, Escritos sobre espiritismo*, vol. 7 (Mexico City: Clío, 2000), 53

43. Madero used *Diálogos entre Krishna y Arjuna, príncipe de la India: Bhagavad-Gita (el canto del Señor)*, trans. Roviralta Borrell (Barcelona: Tipografía La Académica, 1896). This edition claimed to be a translation of the English and French versions of the Mahabharata. A 1910 edition— *Bhagavad-Gita: (Canto al Señor): coloquios entre Krichna y Arjuna, príncipe de la India*, 2a ed., trans. and annotated by R. Borrell (Barcelona: Tip. de Carbinell y Esteva, 1910)— claimed to have been based directly on the Sanskrit. Indeed, Borrell was a well-known Catalan translator of English and German—his translations of Shakespeare and Goethe are still in use. But it is doubtful that he actually read Sanskrit; he probably made that claim upon converting to theosophy. In fact, he translated a theosophy glossary written by Madame Blavatsky.

44. José Vasconcelos, *El Ulises criollo, Obras Completas*, vol. 1 (Mexico City: Libreros Mexicanos Unidos, 1957), 43.

45. Vasconcelos is a very complex character who merits a more profound analysis than the one I offer here. He embodied almost all of the dilemmas of the twentieth-century Mexican intellectual, all of their temptations—power, erudition, religion, fame, desire, ideology, race, spirit. He was, above all, one of the greatest memoir writers of twentieth-century Mexico. No definitive biography of Vasconcelos exists, but there are partial biographies: see José Joaquín Blanco, *Se llamaba Vasconcelos: una evocación crítica* (Mexico City: Fondo de Cultura Económica, 1977); Claude Fell, *José Vasconcelos, los años del águila, 1920–1925: educación, cultura e iberoamericanismo en el México postrevolucionario* (Mexico City: UNAM, 1989); and John Skirius, *José Vasconcelos y la cruzada de 1929*, trans. Felix Blanco (Mexico City: Siglo Veintiuno Editores, 1978).

46. Vasconcelos, *El Ulises criollo*, 436–37.

47. Vasconcelos, new introduction to the 1938 edition of *Estudios Indostanos*, included in *Obras Completas*, vol. 3 (Mexico City: Editores Mexicanos Unidos, 1959), 87–90.

48. By 1920, there were at least two versions of Vivekananda's ideas in Spanish, though it is hard to tell how well known these versions were: Seva Swami Vivekananda, *Karma Yoga: la manera de que el hombre realice su propia divinidad mediante las obras y el cumplimiento del deber* (Buenos Aires: Sociedad Vedanta, 1914); and Seva Swami Vivekananda, *Pláticas inspiradas, cartas selectas y otros escritos* (Buenos Aires: Ramakrishnan Ashrama, 1937).

49. Vasconcelos, *Estudios Indostanos*, 93, 135.

50. Vasconcelos, *Estudios Indostanos*, 95–96, 301. However, in 1919, Vasconcelos was in favor of India's independence, unlike many others who expressed their views via the Mexican media. Nationalism, for him, was a result of the British conquest. And nationalism, he thought, would bring about the unity of India's many languages and groups; and the India that would emerge would be a "nación extraña" ("strange nation"), i.e., not homogeneous, because India "cannot renounce its history and its soul." Vasconcelos, *Estudios Indostanos*, 113.

51. Clare Sheridan, *My American Diary* (New York: Boni and Liveright, 1922), 214.

52. Vasconcelos, *Estudios Indostanos*, 302.

53. On this subject, see Rudolf Otto, *Mysticism East and West: A Comparative Analysis of the Nature of Mysticism*, trans. Bertha L.Bracey and Richenda C. Payne (New York: Macmillan, 1932). Regarding the Spanish mystics and Indian and Chinese thoughts, see José Ángel Valente, *Variaciones sobre el pájaro y la red, precedido de La piedra y el centro* (Barcelona: Tusquets, 1991).

54. R. Arévalo Martínez, *Las noches en el Palacio de la Nunciatura* (Guatemala: Tipografía Sánchez

de Gurse, 1927); *Cartas de Barba Jacob*, ed. Fernando Vallejo (Borgota: Revista Literaria Gradiva, 1992); Khalil Gibran, *Obras selectas*, trans. Safick Kaim (Mexico City: Editorial Comaval, 1959); and Gibran, *El loco: sus parábolas y poemas* (Mexico City: Orión, 1952).

55. U.S. War Department Files, 100640-640. M.I. 5, Report on M. N. Roy's Activities in Mexico by the United States Military Attaché in Mexico in 1918.

56. Letter to Jerry Aron, September 24, 1923, Anita Brenner Papers, HRC; *La Antorcha* (November 1924 and December 1924); for the many parties and interactions of this circle with Gupta, see Edward Weston, *The Daybooks of Edward Weston*, ed. Nancy Newhall, vol. 1 (Millerton, N.Y.: Aperture, 1973).

57. *Chitra, un drama en un acto por Rabindra Nath Tagore, traducción del original bengali al inglés por el autor, traducción al castellano por Heramba Lal Gupta* (Mexico City: Linotipografía La Helvética, 1919), 32.

58. R. Tagore, *Gitanjalí, poemas místicos por Rabrindanath Tagore*, trans. Pedro Requena Legarreta (Mexico City: n.p., 1918); "Tagore y Pedro Requena," included in Requena's *Poesías líricas* (Mexico City: Miguel E. Castilleja e Hijos, 1930), xxi; Gabriel Zaid, *The Secret of Fame* (New York: Paul Dry Books, 2008), 75.

59. Cabrera, *Musa peregrina*. Poems included were "Gardener," "Ask Me," and "The Unread Letter."

60. The earliest translations by the Jiménezes include *Mashi y otros cuentos*, trans. Zenobia Camprubí de Jiménez (Madrid: Fortanet, 1920); *Ofrenda lírica, gitanjali, poemas*, trans. Zenobia Camprubí de Jiménez (Madrid: n.p., 1918); and *Pájaros perdidos: sentimientos*, trans. Zenobia Camprubí de Jiménez (Madrid: Angel Alcoy, 1917). For Mexican translations, see *Gitanjalí: poemas místicos*, trans. Pedro Requena Legarreta (Mexico City: n.p., 1918); *La luna nueva, Nacionalismo, Personalidad, Sadhana*, trans. Departamento editorial (Mexico City: Universidad Nacional de México, 1924); and *Chitra, un drama en un acto*. See also the adaptation by Pedro Requena Lagarreta, *El jardín de los niños: paráfrasis de 16 poemas de Rabindranath Tagore* (Mexico City: Cultura, 1938). For Camprubí's role in promoting Tagore, see Tomás Sarramía, *Zenobia Camprubí: eslabón hispánico de Rabindranath Tagore* (New Delhi: Indian Council for Cultural Relations, 1981); and Guillermo Sheridan, *Los Contemporáneos ayer* (Mexico City: Fondo de Cultura Económica, 1985), 138. I thank Guillermo Sheridan for his help in tracing these forgotten influences. For an explanation of the Jiménez translation of Tagore, see Graciela Palau de Nemes, "Tagore and Jiménez: Poetic Coincidences," in *A Centenary Volume Rabindranath Tagore* (New Delhi: Sahitya Akademi, 1961), 187–97. To my knowledge, there is no direct translation of Tagore from Bengali to Spanish. Even today's translations of Bengali poetry are done through the intermediacy of English or French. See, for instance, the recent book *Doce poetas bengalíes: Todo es camino*, ed. Sinana Sinha and Lionel Ray, trans. by them to French, and from French to Spanish by F. Torres Monreal (Murcia: Lancelot, 2006).

61. Octavio Paz, "Los manuscritos de Rabindranath Tagore," *Obras Completas*, vol. 2, 377. Curiously, Paz mentions Tagore's paintings and drawings as the Indian poet's greatest contribution, which Paz finds to be close to vanguard Latin American and French trends.

62. *La Antorcha* (January, 1925). The text was "La enseñanza del loro," and was translated, from the English, by Gorostiza.

63. *Revista de Revistas* (September 5, 1920): 19–20.

64. Dipesh Chakrabarty, *Provincializing Europe* (Princeton: Princeton University Press, 2000), chapter 6.

65. Cecilia Mireles, an excellent poet herself, tells the story of Barbosa in "Tagore in Brazil," in *A Centenary Volume*. See also Ketaki Kushari Dyson, *In Your Blossoming Flower-Garden: Rabindranath Tagore and Victoria Ocampo* (New Delhi: Sahitya Akademi, 1988). Tagore as therapy is also a self-created image that Tagore himself put forth with his own English translation of his Bengali poetry.

66. One of the songs was published in *Gaceta musical*, 1 (July–August, 1928), Ponce's Paris gazette. See also "Dos cantos: pour chant et piano" (Paris: M. Senart, 1927), songs with piano, poems by R. Tagore, English, Spanish, and French words, French and Spanish adaptation by Mr. and Mrs. Brull. Curiously, Japan also played a part in this fascination with music; for example, there are Tablada's Haikus for Piano, by Luis Sandi: *Diez haikais* [sic]: *para canto y piano*, created in collaboration with José Juan Tablada and Noel Lindsay (Mexico City: Ediciones Mexicanas de Música, 1947).

67. Diego Rivera's letter to Xavier Icaza, November 2, 1926, Bertram and Ella Wolfe Collection, Hoover Institution, Stanford University.

68. Manuel Gamio, *Forjando Patria (pro nacionalismo)* (Mexico City: Porrúa, 1916), 51, 99.

69. Jesús Urueta, "La danza del vientre: Jardín de París," El Mundo Ilustrado (February 19, 1899). The article includes a drawing of odalisque belly dancers.

70. *Arte y Letras*, segunda epoca, 27 (August 22, 1914).

71. Carlos Pellicer Cámara, "La Bayadera," *San-Ev-Ank: Revista semanaria estudiantil* (July 11, 1918): 5.

72. El Universal Ilustrado (May 29, 1919 and 1921). Valencia's parents died in Oaxaca in the 1890s. His father was Catalan, and she became a nationalistic Catalan republican in the 1930s. On the intriguing personality of Valencia, and her research on Indian and African dances, see Kurt Peters, "Die Legende einer Ballerina: Ausstellung uber Tortola Valencia im Theatermuseum von Barcelona," *Ballett-Journal/Das Tanzarchiv*, 34, 3 (June 1986): 76–78; Irene Peypoch, *Carmen Tórtola Valencia* (Barcelona: Editions de Nou Art Thor, 1984); and Odelot Solrac, *Tortola Valencia and Her Times* (New York: Vantage Press, 1982), though this last book includes very little interesting information. See also: Iris Garland, "Early Modern Dance in Spain: Tortola Valencia, Dancer of Historical Intuition," *Dance Research Journal*, 29, 2 (Fall 1997): 1–22; and Iris Garland, "Masquerade as Exile: Tórtola Valencia, Dancer of the Belle Époque," *Cairon: Revista de Ciencias de la Danza*, 6 (2000): 7–15. I thank Antonio Saborit for referring me to the subject of the Mexican poets' fascination with Tórtola.

73. Carlos Pellicer Cámara, "La Gitana," *San-Ev-Ank: Revista semanaria estudiantil* (July 11, 1918): 4.

74. On this drawing see Oles, *South of the Border*, 18; Karen Cordero, "Para devolver su inocencia a la nación: apuntes sobre el origen y el desarrollo del Método Best Maugard," in *Abraham Ángel y su tiempo* (Monclava: Museo Biblioteca Pape; Toluca: Museo de Bellas Artes; Mexico City: Museo de San Carlos, 1985); and the catalogue of the exhibition *Del istmo y sus mujeres: tehuanas en el arte mexicano: Museo Nacional de Arte, agosto–noviembre 1992* (Mexico City: CONACULTA, 1992).

75. "El arte nacionalista de Best Maugard," *Revista de Revistas* (December 12, 1920). Illustrations are taken from this magazine's reproductions.

76. It is not clear why the "Tehuana" was painted. At the University of California at Riverside, there is a collection of drawings for a Mexican regional folk dance and costume book, which was to be published around 1940 by the Ministry of Education, and illustrated by Mauro Rafael Moya and Alfredo Best Maugard. However, it is not certain whether the figure was drawn for that reason. The figure was photographed by Tina Modotti. But the 1920 essay in *Revista de Revistas* shows that the "Tehuana" was part of a larger series, which was produced by Best Maugard in New York.

77. "El arte nacionalista."

78. *La lámpara de Aladino: Cuento de Las Mil y Una Noches* (Barcelona: Librería de las Galerías Layetanas, 1917); Mexico, Secretaría de Educación Pública, *Lecturas clásicas para niños*, 2 vols. (Mexico City: Secretaría de Educación Pública, 1924). For Montenegro's influences and works, see Julieta Ortiz de Villaseñor, "Auge de las artes aplicadas: Dos figuras en el escritorio de José Vasconcelos," *Anales del Instituto de Investigaciones Estéticas*, no. 71 (1997): 77–86; Rodrigo Gutiérrez Viñueles, "Roberto Montenegro y los artistas americanos de Mallorca (1915–1919)," *Anales del Instituto de Investigaciones Estéticas*, no. 83 (2003): 93–121; and Esperanza Balderas, *Roberto Montenegro: ilustrador (1900–1930)* (Mexico City: CONACULTA, 2000).

79. *María Conesa la gatita blanca* (Mexico City: Documental, 1986), sound recording, 1907, including Conesa in Chin Chun Chan, as Conesa as Geisha; Luis Reyes de la Maza, *El teatro en México durante el porfirismo*, 3 vols. (Mexico City: Impr. Universitaria, 1964–1968); John B. Nomland, *Teatro mexicano contemporáneo: 1900–1950* (Mexico City: Instituto Nacional de Bellas Artes, Dept. de Literatura, 1967); Manuel Mañón, *Historia del Teatro Principal de México* (Mexico City: Editorial Cultura, 1932); Armando de Maria y Campos, *Las tandas del Principal* (Mexico City: Editorial Diana, 1989); and Museo Nacional de Culturas Populares, *El País de las Tandas: teatro de revista, 1900–1940* (Mexico City: Museo Nacional de Culturas Populares, Dirección General de Culturas Populares, 1987). The most insightful contemporary social critic of these shows was Manuel Gutiérrez Nájera; see his *Espectáculos: teatro, conciertos, ópera, opereta y zarzuela, tandas y títeres, circo y acrobacia, deportes y toros, gente de teatro, el público, la prensa, organización y locales*, ed. Elvira López Aparicio and Ana Elena Díaz Alejo (Mexico City: UNAM, 1985).

80. Casey M. Blake, *Beloved Community: The Cultural Criticism of Randolph Bourne, Van Wyck Brooks, Waldo Frank & Lewis Mumford* (Chapel Hill: University of North Carolina Press, 1990); and Warren Susman, "The Culture of the Thirties," in *Culture as History: The Transformation of American Society in the Twentieth Century* (New York: Pantheon, 1983), 150–83.

81. U.S. military intelligence knew of all of Roy's moves; apparently this was due to Allen's reports, as he seems to have been a U.S. informant (as well as a U.S. citizen). In his memoirs Roy claims that Gale asked him for financial support for *Gale's Magazine*, a bizarre "personal" magazine that Gale started in Worcester, Massachusetts, in 1917; Roy declined. Charles Phillips, like Roy, characterized Gale as a combination of a New Age, socialist, and egocentrical character. In his memoirs Roy recalls his given Mexican name to be Roberto Allen y Villa Garcia [sic], and says that it was Carranza himself who furnished him with the passport. In fact it was Allen who provided passports to both Roy and Evelyn. M. N. Roy, *Memoirs* (New Delhi and London: Allied Publishers Private Limited, 1964), 223. Regarding Allen, see Barry Carr, *Marxism and Communism in Twentieth-Century Mexico* (Lincoln: University of Nebraska Press, 1992). About this complicated period in the history of the international left in Mexico, see Carleton Beals, *Glass Houses: Ten Years of Free-Lancing* (Philadelphia: J. B. Lippincott Company, 1938); Héctor Cárdenas and Evgeni Dik, *Historia de las relaciones entre México y Rusia* (Mexico City: Secretaría de Relaciones Exteriores, Fondo de Cultura Económica, 1993); and see chapter 4.

82. Mukherjee was a well-known author and the brother of Dr. Jadugopal Mukherjee, a renowned activist in the era following Lord Curzon's partition of Bengal and organizer of international support for Indian revolutionaries (especially with contacts in Germany). As such, he assisted M. N. Roy in contacting German officers in order to acquire arms. In 1914 in Berlin the Indian Independence Committee was formed.

83. In New York Roy met Basanta Kumar Roy, who was close to the Vivekananda'circle. Roy, *Memoirs*, 32.

84. Shipman, *It Had to Be Revolution*, 73.

85. For Gale's justification of the need for New Thought, see "Do I Believe in New Thought?," *Gale's Magazine* (February 1918): 3, 23.

86. Roy, *Memoirs*, 185–87.

87. Roy, *Memoirs*, 215.

88. M. N. Roy, *La India, su pasado, su presente y su porvenir* (Mexico City: n.p., 1918).

89. Roy, *La India*, xiii.

90. José Carlos Mariátegui, *Siete ensayos de interpretación de la realidad peruana* (1928) (La Habana: Casa de las Américas, 1973), 27–32. Mariátegui uses Luis E. Valcárcel's *Tempestad en los Andes* (Lima: Populibros Peruanos, 1927). I thank the late Charles A. Hale for calling my attention to this.

91. The novel by Agnes Smedley was *The Daughter of Earth*, quoted in Sibnarayan Ray, *In Freedom's Quest*, vol. 1, 93. Beals's and Murphy's opinions as quoted in ibid., 12–13.

92. Ray, *In Freedom's Quest*.

CHAPTER 9

1. Paul Valéry, *Cahiers*, vol. 2 (Paris: Gallimard, Bibliothéque de la Pléiade, 1974), 836.

2. François Choay, *L'Urbanisme: Utopies et realités* (Paris: Éditions du Seuil, 1965); Hall, *Cities of Tomorrow*; Spiro Kostof, *The City Assembled: The Elements of Urban Form Through History* (London: Thames and Hudson, 1992); Giusseppe Dato, curator, *L'urbanistica di Haussmann: un modello impossibile?* (Rome: Officina, 1995).

3. Elías Trabulse, *Ciencia y tecnología en el Nuevo Mundo* (Mexico City: El Colegio de México, Fideicomiso Historia de las Américas, Fondo de Cultura Económica, 1994); and edited by the same author, *Historia de la ciencia en México: estudios y textos*, 3 vols. (Mexico City: Fondo de Cultura Económica, 1983); J. J. Saldaña, "La ciencia y el Leviatán mexicano," *Actas de la Sociedad Mexicana de Historia de la Ciencia y de la Tecnología*, vol. 1 (1989).

4. M. A. Carreño, *Manual de urbanidad y buenas maneras* (Mexico City: Editorial Patria, 1934), 141 ff.

5. Artemio del Valle-Arizpe, *Cuadros de México* (Mcxico City: Editorial Jus, 1943), 165–82. Sedano is quoted by Valle-Arizpe; the reference is very likely the García Icazbalceta reedition: Francisco Sedano, *Noticias de México, recogidas por D. Francisco Sedano . . . desde el año de 1756, coordinadas, escritas de nuevo y puestas por orden alfábetico en 1800. Primera impresión, con un prólogo del Sr. D. Joaquín García Icazbalceta: Y con notas y apéndices del presbitero V. de P. A. Ed. de la "Voz de México"* (Mexico City: Impr. de J. R. Barbedillo y Ca, 1880). See also "Los perros aztecas y el origen de los perros de hoy," *Anales del Museo Nacional de Arqueología, Historia y Etnografía*, 11, quinta época (1937): 90–92.

6. Archivo Histórico del Ayuntamiento, Perros, esp. 12, 1820; Demetrio Medina, "El perro que asesinó a su dueña," *Todo*, 11, 83 (April 12, 1935): 45–50.

7. Liceaga's memoirs, *Mis recuerdos de otros tiempos* (Mexico: n.p., 1949), and his conference in the Hygienic Exposition at the *Centenario*, "Progresos alcanzados por la higiene de 1810 a la fecha," in SSA, Box 9, Exp. 9. See also his paper delivered at the Sociedad Pedro Escovedo in 1911, "Algunas consideraciones acerca de la higiene social en Mexico," SSA, Box 10, Exp. 3. About how the rabies vaccine was brought to Mexico, see *Congreso Médico Panamericano*, vol. 2 (Mexico, 1896),

899–905. About the way the vaccine was developed in Mexico, see N. Ramírez de Arellano, "Higiene: Profilaxis de la rabia," *Gaceta Médica de México*, 24 (June 1, 1889): 206–9.

8. In 1944, Dr. Gerardo Varela reconsidered Mexico's Pasteurian history—the various failed rabies vaccines, the creation of an Anti-Rabies Institute, and finally success in 1900 when the vaccine developed by Fernando López Prieto was used in more than three thousand persons who had been attacked by infected dogs, with 2.2% mortality rate. See "Proyecto de Código Sanitario de los Estados Unidos Mexicanos, sometido a la Secretaría de Gobernación, 30 de Junio de 1889," reproduced in José Álvarez, ed., *Historia de la salubridad y de la asistencia en México*, vol. 3 (Mexico City: Secretaría de Salubridad, 1960), 327–29. Gayol was named general engineer of Mexico City in 1884. Gerardo Varela, "La vacuna antirrábica, su introducción en México," *Gaceta Médica de México*, 76 (1946): 19–22; Ana Cecilia Rodríguez de Romo, "La ciencia pasteuriana a través de la vacuna antirrábica: el caso mexicano," *Dynamis*, 16 (1996): 291–316.

9. Article in *El País* (January 22, 1904).

10. *Memoria del ayuntamiento* (1902): 559.

11. AGN GRBI Box 26, exp. 22, "Contrato para matar animales, José Quesada; reglamento de posesión de perros," in Fondo Plutarco Elías Calles, Archivo Calles-Torreblance, exp. 143, inv. 156618, Dec. 1928.

12. Archivo Histórico del Ayuntamiento, Perros, Suplemento al noticioso general número 736, del viernes 15 de septiembre de 1920.

13. *Memoria General del IV Congreso Médico Nacional Mexicano, efectuado en la ciudad de México del 19 al 25 de septiembre de 1910, bajo los auspicios de la Comisión Nacional del Centenario y el patrocinio de la Secretaría de Instrucción Pública y Bellas Artes* (Mexico City: Tipografía Económica, 1910), 122.

14. Gregorio López y Fuentes, in *Nosotros:Revista de artes y educación* (Dec. 1912): 127; Juan B. Delgado, *El cancionero nómada* (Mexico City: Herrero Hermanos Sucesores, 1925).

15. Ricardo Colt, *Es el amor que pasa . . . La novela de los perros* (Mexico City: Botas, 1907), 9.

16. Short story by Carlos Noriega Hope, in *La inútil curiosidad* (Mexico City: n.p., 1923), 135.

17. Quoted in Manuel Maples Arce, *El paisaje en la literatura mexicana* (Mexico City: Porrúa Hermanos, 1944), 43.

18. Valle-Arizpe, *Cuadros de México*, 399.

19. Reproduced in Valle-Arizpe, *Cuadros de México*, 400. See also Silvia M. Arrom, *Containing the Poor: The Mexico City Poor House, 1774–1871* (Durham: Duke University Press, 2000).

20. Margaret T. Mitchell, "The Porfirian State and Public Beneficence: The Hospicio de Pobres of Mexico City, 1877–1911," Ph.D. diss., Tulane University, 1998; Ann S. Blum, *Domestic Economies: Family, Work, and Welfare in Mexico City, 1884–1943* (Lincoln: University of Nebraska Press, 2009).

21. W. E. Carson, *Mexico, the Wonderland of the South*, revised with new chapters (New York: Macmillan Company, 1914), 66.

22. *Arte y Letras* (June 27, 1914).

23. Cover, *Revista de Revistas* (March 29, 1919); Carlos Roumagnac, *Por los mundos del delito, los criminales en México ensayo de psicología criminal, seguido de dos casos de hemafrodismo observados por los señores doctores Ricardo Egea e Ignacio Ocampo (jefe del servicio médico de la cárcel de Belém)* (Mexico City: Tip. el Fénix, 1904), 40–46.

24. Cover, *Arte y Letras* (February 3, 1910); cover, *Arte y Letras* (April 21, 1912); Machado photo, *Arte y Letras* (October 10, 1914).

25. Petronio, "A través de México," *Arte y Letras* (Sep. 26, 1914).

26. Víctor Manuel Macías-González, "The Mexican Aristocracy and Porfirio Díaz, 1876–1911," Ph.D. diss., Texas Christian University, 1999; *Savia Moderna*, 1 (April 1906): 107–13; Verónica Villarespe, *La solidaridad: beneficencia y programas: pasado y presente del tratamiento de la pobreza en México* (Mexico City: UNAM, 2001); Albert Judson Steelman, *Charities for Children in the City of Mexico* (Joliet, Ill.: E. M. Steelman, 1907).

27. "Informe sobre las instituciones de beneficiencia privada rendindo por el Lic. Manuel Miranda Marrón," AGN GRBI, Box 89, exp. 27. About wealthy Porfirian female charity, see Víctor Manuel Macías-González, "The Mexican Aristocracy and Porfirio Díaz, 1876–1911."

28. *La mendicidad en México*, composed by Ramón Beteta and Eyler N. Simpson (Mexico City: Beneficencia Pública and A. Mijares y Hermanos, 1931).

29. *La mendicidad en México*, 124.

30. *Asistencia*, 1, 4 (November 1934), editorial.

31. Alfonso Millán, "El carácter antisocial de los homosexuales," *Asistencia*, 1, 5 (December 1934): 11–12.

32. Image in *Asistencia*, 2, 6 (January 1935).

33. Luis de Velasco, letter to the Consejo de Indias, September 16, 1555, quoted in José Sala Catalá, *Ciencia y técnica en la metropolización de América* (Madrid: Consejo Superior de Investigaciones Científicas, 1994), 27.

34. J. María Marroquí, *La ciudad de México*, vol. 3 (Mexico City: La Europea, 1903); Sala Catalá, *Ciencia y técnica en la metropolización de América*; Richard M. Morse, "Cities as People," in Jorge Hardoy and R. Morse, eds., *Rethinking the Latin American City* (Baltimore: Johns Hopkins University Press, 1992), 3–19; and Leonardo Mattos-Cárdenas, "Ideología barroca y traza urbanística en la América española (siglos XVII–XVIIII)," *Storia della città*, no. 28 (1984): 59–70.

35. Irving A. Leonard, *Baroque Times in Old Mexico: Seventeenth-Century Persons, Places, and Practices* (Ann Arbor: University of Michigan Press, 1959).

36. Bernardo de Balvuena, *Grandeza mexicana* (1604).

37. Jean-Louis Cohen, "Urban Architecture and the Crisis of the Modern Metropolis," in Richard Koshalek and Elizabeth A. T. Smith, eds., *At the End of the Century: One Hundred Years of Architecture* (Los Angeles: Museum of Contemporary Art, Harry N. Abrams Inc. Publishers, 1998), 229–74; J.-L. Cohen and H. Damisch, *Américanisme et modernité: L'idéal américain dans l'architecture* (Paris: Flamarion, 1993); and Peter Hall, *Cities of Tomorrow: An Intellectual History of Urban Planning and Design in the Twentieth Century* (Oxford: Blackwell Publishers, 1996).

38. Zeynep Çelik, *Displaying the Orient: Architecture of Islam at Nineteenth-Century World's Fairs* (Berkeley: University of California Press, 1992); and Çelik, *The Remaking of Istanbul: Portrait of an Ottoman City in the Nineteenth Century* (Seattle: University of Washington Press, 1986).

39. Eleni Bastéa, *The Creation of Modern Athens: Planning the Myth* (Cambridge: Cambridge University Press, 1999).

CHAPTER 10

1. *Rickettsial Diseases*, ed. Didier Raoult and Philippe Parola (New York: CRC Press, 2007); Hans Zinsser, *Rats, Lice, and History: Being a Study in Biography, Which, after Twelve Preliminary Chapters Indispensable for the Preparation of the Lay Reader, Deals with the Life History of Typhus Fever* (Boston: Printed and Pub. for the Atlantic Monthly Press by Little, Brown, and Company, 1935).

2. Bruno Latour, *The Pasteurization of France*, trans. Alan Sheridan and John Law (Cambridge:

Harvard University Press, 1988); Steven Shapin, *The Scientific Life: A Moral History of a Late Modern Vocation* (Chicago: University of Chicago Press, 2008); Ana Barahona Echeverría and Ismael Ledesma-Mateos, "El positivismo y los orígenes de la biología en México: El entrelazado de los desarrollos filosófico y científico en un contexto histórico particular," *Archives Internationales d'Histoire des Sciences* 52 (2002): 277–305; Juan José Saldaña and Natalia Priego, "Entrenando a los cazadores de microbios de la república: la domesticación de la microbiología en México," *Quipu*, 13 (2000): 225–42; Ana María Carrillo, "Los comienzos de la bacteriología en México," *Elementos*, 32 (2001): 23–27; Natalia Priego, *Science, Culture and Society in Mexico 1860–1940: The Contradictions of the Quest for Modernity* (Saarbrücken: VDM Verlag Dr. Müller, 2009); Antonio Cadeddu, *Dal mito alla storia: biologia e medicina in Pasteur* (Milano: Franco Angeli, 1991); Jean-Pierre Dedet, *Les Instituts Pasteur d'outre-mer: cent vingt ans de microbiologie française dans le monde* (Paris: L'Harmattan, 2000); Diego Armus, "Disease in the Historiography of Modern Latin America," in *Disease in the History of Modern Latin America, from Malaria to AIDS*, ed. Diego Armus (Durham: Duke University Press, 2003), 1–24.

3. Zinsser, *Rats, Lice, and History*, 160; Francisco Guerra, "Origen y efectos demográficos del tifo en el México colonial," *Colonial Latin American Historical Review*, 8, 3 (1999): 273–319.

4. Ricardo Granillo, "La mortalildad en la ciudad de México," *Boletín del Departamento de Salubridad Pública*, no. 1 (Mexico City: Editorial Cultura, 1925), 10; Dolores Morales "La expansión de la ciudad de México (1855–1910)," in G. Garza, *Atlas de la ciudad de México* (Mexico City: El Colegio de México, 1987).

5. Lourdes Márques Morfin, *La desigualdad ante la muerte en la ciudad de México, el tifo y el cólera* (Mexico City: Siglo XXI, 1994); Fernando Ocaranza, "El tifo en el Distrito Federal en el año de 1921," *Memorias y actas del segundo congreso nacional del tabardillo, verificado en la ciudad de México del 25 al 31 de diciembre de 1921, bajo el patronato del Departamento de Salubridad* (Mexico City: Imprenta y Encuadernación de Rosendo Terrazas, 1922).

6. On the 1876 Congress, see *Trabajos emprendidos para mejorar la salubridad del valle y de la ciudad de México, por una asociación de médicos* (Mexico City: Impr. de la Escuela de Artes y Oficios, 1877), quote on p. 15; Max von Pettenkofer, *Boden und Grundwasser in ihren Beziehungen zu Cholera und Typhus* (Munich: Oldenbourg, 1869).

7. These last two paragraphs follow several sources: Luis E. Ruiz, "El tifo de enero de 1889 a junio de 1893 en el Hospital Juárez," *Public Health Papers and Reports*, vol. 12, presented at the 21st meeting of the American Public Health Association, Chicago, 1893; Mexico, Consejo Superior de Salubridad, *Memoria de los trabajos ejecutados por el Consejo Superior de Salubridad, en el año de 1902* (Mexico City: Tip. y Lit. La Europea de J. Aguilar Vera, 1903). The comparison with Washington was found in *La mendicidad en México* (Mexico City: Beneficencia Pública, 1931); Miguel E. Bustamante and Álvaro Aldama, "Principales causas de muerte en México 1922–1937," *Revista del Instituto de Salubridad y Enfermedades Tropicales*, vol. 1 (September 1940); Mexico City, Departamento de Salubridad, *Memoria de los trabajos ejecutados por el Departamento de Salubridad del 1 de diciembre de 1920 al 31 de agosto de 1921* (Mexico City: Talleres Gráficos de la Nación, 1923); Mexico City, Departamento de Salubridad, *Memoria de los trabajos relizados por el Departamento de Salubridad Pública 1925–1928*, vol. 1 (Mexico City: Ediciones del Departamento de Salubridad Pública, 1928); José G. Lobato, "Estudio higiénico sobre el tifo exantemático," *Gaceta Médica de México*, 12, no. 3 (1877); Everardo Landa, "La cooperación de la Academia Nacional de Medicina de México en el estudio del tifo exantemático," *Gaceta Médica de México*, 12, no. 3 (1877); Francisco Javier Meyer Cosío, "Epidemia de tifo exantemático en Guanajuato, México, 1892–1893," *SECOLAS annals*, 29 (1998):

61–69; Celia Maldonado López, *Ciudad de México, 1800–1860: epidemias y población* (Mexico City: INAH, 1995); Claudia Agostini, "Popular Health Education and Propaganda in Times of Peace and War in Mexico City, 1890s–1920s," *American Journal of Public Health*, 96, 1 (January 2006): 52–61. On London, see Anne Hardy, *The Epidemic Streets: Infectious Disease and the Rise of Preventive Medicine, 1856–1900* (Oxford: Clarendon Press, 1993).

8. Ernesto Cervera, "Cómo ha contribuido México al estudio del tifo," *Boletín del Instituto de Higiene*, 3, 1 (May 1947): 5–11; Consuelo Cuevas Cardona, "Ciencia de punta en el Instituto Bacteriológico Nacional, 1905–1921," *Historia Mexicana*, 57, 1 (2007): 53–89; Paul Michael Ross, "From Sanitary Police to Sanitary Dictatorship : Mexico's Nineteenth-Century Public Health Movement," Ph.D. diss., University of Chicago, 2005; Priego, *Science, Culture and Society*, 80–91.

9. Charles Nicolle and Hélène Sparrow, "Le typhus exanthématique méxicain," *Bulletin de l'Institut Pasteur*, 39, 20 (October 31, 1931): 945–59; H. da Rocha Lima, *Estudos sôbre o tifo exantemático*, ed. Edgar de Cerqueria Falção, commentaries by Otto G. Bier (São Paulo: Ed. da Univ. de São Paulo, 1967); Kim Pelis, *Charles Nicolle: Pasteur's Imperial Missionary: Typhus and Tunisia* (Rochester: University of Rochester Press, 2006).

10. Miguel Otero, *Trabajos presentados en el primer congreso médico Mexicano* (San Luis Potosí: M. Esquivel, 1893); Miguel Otero, *Contribución al diagnóstico, pronóstico y tratamiento del tifo petequial basados en la bacteriología: Moralidad de la experimentación sobre seres humanos, con restringidas condiciones: Disertación leída en la sesión general científica, el 23 de septiembre de 1910, ante el IV Congreso Médico Nacional* (Mexico City: Aguilar Vera, 1910); Fernando Quijano Pitman, "La transmisión del tifo por el piojo: Dr. Miguel Otero (1906)," *Gaceta Médico de México*, 136, 2 (March–April 2000): 169–179; Ana Cecilia Rodríguez de Romo, "La ciencia pasteuriana a través de la vacuna antirrábica: el caso mexicano," *Dynamis*, 16 (1996): 291–316; José Terrés, "Informe de la comision central para el estudio del tabardillo," in *Memorias y actas del segundo congreso nacional del tabardillo, verificado en la ciudad de México del 25 al 31 de diciembre de 1921, bajo el patronato del Departamento de Salubridad* (Mexico City: Imprenta y Encuadernación de Rosendo Terrazas, 1922); Landa, "La cooperación de la Academia Nacional de Medicina de México en el estudio del tifo exantemático," 23–36; Francisco Fernández del Castillo, "El tifus en México antes de Zinsser," *Gaceta Médica de Mexico*, 86, 3 (1956): 181–87.

11. Von Pettenkofer, *Boden und Grundwasser*; Landa, "La cooperación"; Priego, *Science, Culture and Society*, 90.

12. On Gaviño's hiring of Girard, see AGN-Instrucción Pública y Bellas Artes, Box 139, Exp. 1. On Girard and his Pasteurian origins, see Priego, *Science, Culture and Society*, 91–92; and Cuevas Cardona, "Ciencia de punta en el Instituto Bacteriológico Nacional, 1905–1921."

13. AGN-Instrucción Pública y Bellas Artes, Box 139, Exp. 1; Nicolle and Sparrow, "Le typhus exanthématique mexicain."

14. AGN-Instrucción Pública y Bellas Artes, Box 140, Exp. 4, and "Informe de labores 1906," Box 140, Exp. 22; Angel Gaviño and Joseph Girard: "Nota preliminar sobre el tifo experimental en los monos inferiores," Publicaciones del Instituto Bacteriológico Nacional, May 1910; "Nota Preliminar sobre ciertos cuerpos encontrados en la sangre de los individuos atacados de tifo (Tabardillo)," Publicaciones del Instituto Bacteriológico Nacional, May 1910; "Tercera Nota sobre el tifo experimental de los monos inferiores," Publicaciones del Instituto Bacteriológico Nacional, August 1910; "Cuarta nota sobre el tifo experimental en los monos inferiores," Publicaciones del Instituto Bacteriológico Nacional, November 9, 1910; "Estudio experimental sobre el tifo exantemático," Publicaciones del Instituto Bacteriológico Nacional, November 12, 1911.

15. A paraphrase of General Álvaro Obregón's well-known expression: "No hay general que aguante un cañonazo de 50,000 pesos."

16. Heriberto Frías, *Crónicas desde la cárcel* (Mexico City: Breve Fondo Editorial, 1997), 52–56; letter from Russell Wilder to Ludwig Hektoon, no date: H. Ricketts Papers, Univerity of Chicago; Carlos Toro, *Horrores del presidio (la cárcel de Belém): Novela de un perseguido* (Mexico City: Biblioteca de El Gráfico, 1931). The text was written in 1909. I thank Antonio Saborit for this reference.

17. Report on experiments and quote in AGN-Instrucción Pública y Bellas Artes, Box 141, Exp. 1; collection of lice and geographical distribution in Box 141, Exp. 9; report on the experiment from May 20, 1910, involving a monkey injected with blood from a typhus patient at the French hospital, ibid.; Gaviño's argument about having succeeded at inoculating monkeys and guinea pigs before (May 1911) Nicolle (June 1911), Box 141, Exp. 17.

18. Dennis J. Pollack, *James Francis Conneffe, M.D., 1877–1910: Assistant Professor of Pathology and Instructor of Bacteriology, the Ohio State University* (Columbus: Ohio State University, 2003); letters from Howard T. Ricketts to Myra Ricketts, December 14 and December 16, 1909, Box 4, Folder 6; letter from E. F. McCampbell to Howard T. Ricketts, November 26, 1909, Box 8, Folder 1: Howard T. Ricketts Papers, University of Chicago.

19. Alan M. Kraut, *Goldberger's War: The Life and Work of a Public Health Crusader* (New York: Hill and Wang, 2003); Goldbeger's opinion of Mexicans from his letters to his wife, p. 54.

20. Kraut, *Goldberger's War*, 76.

21. John F. Anderson and Joseph Goldberger: "On the Relation of Rocky Mountain Spotted Fever to the Typhus Fever of Mexico, Preliminary Note"; "A Note on the Etiology of 'Tabardillo'"; "On the Infectivity of Tabardillo or Mexican Typhus for Monkeys and Studies on Its Mode of Transmission"; "The Relation of So-Called Brill's Disease to Typhus Fever"; "The Transmission of Typhus Fever, with Special Reference to Transmission by the Head Louse (*Pediculus capitis*)"; "Studies on the Virus of Typhus"; "Studies in Immunity and Means of Transmission of Typhus"—all published in 1910 and 1911, all included in Joseph Goldberger and John F. Anderson, *Collected Studies on Typhus* (Washington, D.C.: G.P.O., 1912).

22. E. F. McCampbell, "Observation on Typhus Exanthematicus (Tabardillo) in Mexico," February 7, 1910, a preliminary report to the Academia Nacional de Medicina de México, May 1910; E. F. McCampbell, "Notes of the University Expedition to Mexico," *Ohio State University Quarterly* (1910): 21–31. According to Pollack, McCampbell did not have official backing from Ohio State University. Pollack, *James Francis Conneffe*.

23. Letter from Howard T. Ricketts to Joseph Goldberger, April 14, 1910, Box 8, Folder 1: Howard T. Ricketts Papers, The University of Chicago; Dennis J. Pollack, *James Francis Conneffe*.

24. Letter from Howard T. Ricketts to Myra Ricketts: February 3, April 5, 1910, Box 4, Folder 6, Howard T. Ricketts Papers, University of Chicago. See also anonymous, "Mártir de la microbiología," *MD en Español*, 9 (1971): 12; C. E. Medina de la Garza, "Howard Taylor Ricketts y el tifo epidémico en México," *Medicina Universitaria*, 1, 3, (1999): 149–52; Maximiliano Ruiz Castañeda, "A la memoria de Howard Taylor Ricketts," *Gaceta Médica Mexicana*, 104 (1972): 257–63; E. Weiss and B. S. Strauss, "The Life and Career of Howard Taylor Ricketts," *Review of Infectious Diseases*, 13 (1991): 1241–42.

25. Goldberger and Anderson, "The Transmission of Typhus Fever."

26. About Ricketts's death see Box 5, Folder 1, Howard T. Ricketts Papers, University of Chicago; AGN-Instrucción Pública y Bellas Artes, Box. 141, Exp. 3; *Howard Taylor Ricketts y sus*

trabajos sobre el tabardillo (tifo de México) publicado por la Secretaría de Instrucción Pública y Bellas Artes en cumplimiento del acuerdo relativo del Presidente de la República (Mexico City: Secretaría de Instrucción Pública y Bellas Artes, 1910).

27. Da Rocha Lima, Estudos, 38.

28. Rubén Saucedo Fuentes, Dr. Howard Taylor Ricketts, su vida y obra, novela biografía (Mexico City: n.p., 1953).

29. Francisco Fernández del Castillo, "La Academia y Charles Nicolle," in Francisco Fernández del Castillo, Antología de escritos histórico-médicos del dr. Francisco Fernández del Castillo (Mexico City: UNAM, n.d.), 517–37.

30. Maximiliano Ruiz Castañeda, "Cincuentenario de Ricketts," in Maximiliano Ruiz Castañeda, Escritos y entrevistas (Toluca: Serie José Antonio Alzate y Ramírez, Colección Testimonios del Estados de México, 1978), 11–24; Maximiliano Ruiz Castañeda, "Nicole 1931," in Ruiz Castañeda, Escritos y entrevistas, 39–48; quote in interview with M. Ruiz Castañeda, included in Escritos y entrevistas, 71; Antonio Castillo de Lucas, ed., Refranero médico, refranes de aplicación médica, selecionados de clásicos autores de obras de paremiología y en parte directamente recogidos y anotados, por Antonio Castillo de Lucas (Madrid: Consejo Superior de Investigaciones Científicas, Patronato Menéndez y Pelayo, Instituto "Antonio de Nebrija," 1944); Herón Pérez Martínez, Refranero mexicano (Mexico City: Academia Mexicana, Fondo de Cultura Económica, 2004); Julio Cejador y Frauca, Refranero castellano, 3 vols. (Madrid: Hernando, 1928–1929).

31. Javier Garciadiego, Rudos contra científicos: la Universidad Nacional durante la Revolución mexicana (Mexico City: El Colegio de México, 1996); Manuel Servín Massieu, Microbiología, vacunas y el rezago científico de México a partir del siglo XIX (Mexico City: Instituto Politécnico Nacional, Centro Interdisciplinario de Investigaciones y Estudios sobre Medio Ambiente y Desarrollo, Plaza y Valdés, 2000); Priego, Science, Culture and Society; and Cuevas Cardona, "Ciencia de punta en el Instituto Bacteriológico Nacional."

32. G. Gandara, La destrucción de las ratas (Mexico City: Sec. de Fomento, Imprenta y Fototipia de la Sec. de Fomento, 1912); Hermann Mooser, "Sobre la enfermedad producida por mordedura de rata (Soduku)," Gaceta Médica de México, 58 (1927): 123; Memoria de los trabajos relizados por el Departamento de Salubridad Pública, 1925–1928, 2 vols. (Mexico City: Ediciones del Departamento de Salubridad Públcia, 1928); see also "Instrucciones sobre ratas y disposición de cadáveres por peste bubónica," in Memoria de los trabajos ejecutados por el Departamento de Salubridad del 1 de mayo al 15 de noviembre de 1920 (Mexico City: Talleres Gráficos de la Nación, 1923); Ocaranza, "El tifo en el Distrito Federal en el año de 1921"; Silvino Riquelme, "La profilaxis del tifo," Memorias de la Sociedad Científica Antonio Alzate, 37 (1918): 129–35.

33. Zinsser, Rats, Lice, and History; Hans Zinsser, As I Remember Him: The Biography of R. S. (Boston: Little, Brown, and Company, 1940); about Zinsser, see W. C. Summers, "Hans Zinsser: A Tale of Two Cultures," Yale Journal of Biology and Medicine, 72, 5 (1999): 341–47; Gerald Weissmann, "Rats, Lice, and Zinsser," Emerging Infectious Diseases, 11, 3 (March 2005): 492–96; Pelis, Charles Nicolle: Pasteur's Imperial Missionary; Ruiz Castañeda, "Cincuentenario de Ricketts."

34. Ana María Carrillo, "Los comienzos de la bacteriología en México," Elementos, 8, 42 (2001): 23–27; Cuevas Cardona, "Ciencia de punta en el Instituto Bacteriológico Nacional"; Juan José Saldaña and Luz Fernanda Azuela, "De amateurs a profesionales: las sociedades científicas en México en el siglo XIX," Quipu, 11, 2 (May–August, 1994): 135–72; Juan José Saldaña and Natalia

Priego, "Entrenando a los cazadores de micróbios de la República," *Quipu*, 13, 2 (May–August 2000): 225–42; Luz Fernanda Azuela, *Tres sociedades científicas en el Porfiriato: Las disciplinas, las instituciones y las relaciones entre la ciencia y el poder* (Mexico City: Sociedad Mexicana de Historia de la Ciencia y la Tecnología, UNAM, 1995); Charles A. Hale, *The Transfromation of Liberalism in Late Nineteenth-Century Mexico* (Princeton: Princeton University Press, 1989); Laura Cházaro, ed., *Medicina, ciencia y sociedad en México, siglo XIX* (Zamora: El Colegio de Michoacán, 2002); Marta-Aleksandra Balinska, "Assistance and Not Mere Relief: The Epidemic Commission of the League of Nations, 1920–1923," in Paul Weindling, ed., *Cambridge History of Medicine, International Health Organization and Movements, 1918–1939* (Cambridge: Cambridge University Press, 1995); Paul Weindling, *Epidemics and Genocide in Eastern Europe, 1890–1945* (Oxford, New York: Oxford University Press, 2000).

35. A first congress had taken place in 1919, but its visibility and importance paled vis-à-vis the 1921 congress, which was part both of the *Centenario* and of a more stable political situation. *Memorias y actas del congreso nacional del tabardillo; verificado en la ciudad de México del 14 al 21 de enero de 1919* (Mexico City: Imprenta Franco-Mexicana,1919); and *Memorias y actas del segundo congreso nacional del tabardillo.*

36. Ruiz Castañeda, *Escritos y entrevistas*, 15; letter H. Mooser to Hans Zinsser, September 18, 1928, Hans Zinsser Papers, Harvard University, Box 2, Folder 88.

37. Carrillo, "Los comienzos de la bacteriología en México"; *Historia de la salubridad y de la asistencia en México*, 5 vols., ed. José Álvarez Amézquita (Mexico City: Secretaría de Salubridad y Asistencia, 1960-); *New York Times*, (December 23, 1915); *The Rockefeller Foundation: Annual Report, 1931* (New York: Rockefeller Foundation, 1931), 339; *Rockefeller Philanthropy and Modern Biomedicine: International Initiatives from World War I to the Cold War*, ed. William H. Schneider (Bloomington: Indiana University Press, 2002); John Farley, *To Cast Out Disease: A History of the International Health Division of the Rockefeller Foundation (1913–1951)* (Oxford: Oxford University Press, 2004); Deborah Fitzgerald, "Exporting American Agriculture: The Rockefeller Foundation in Mexico, 1943–1953," and Joseph Cotter, "The Rockefeller Foundation's Mexican Agricultural Project: A Cross-Cultural Encounter, 1943–1949," both in Marcos Cueto, ed., *Missionaries of Science: The Rockefeller Foundation and Latin America* (Bloomington: Indiana University Press, 1994); Anne-Emanuelle Birn, *Marriage of Convenience: Rockefeller International Health and Revolutionary Mexico* (Rochester: University of Rochester Press, 2006); Marcos Cueto, "The Cycles of Eradication: The Rockefeller Foundation and Latin American Public Health, 1918–1940," in *International Health Organisations and Movements, 1918–1939*, ed. Paul Weindling (Cambridge: Cambridge University Press, 1995); Armando Solórzano Ramos, *Fiebre dorada o Fiebre amarilla? La Fundación Rockefeller en México* (Guadalajara: Universidad de Guadalajara, 1997); Anne-Emanuelle Birn, "Wa(i)ves of Influence: Rockefeller Public Health in Mexico, 1920–50," *Studies in the History and Philosophy of Biology and Biomedical Sciences*, 31 (2000): 381–95. On Zinsser's lobbying, see the letter from H. Zinsser to H. Mooser, October 27, 1933, Hans Zinsser Papers, Harvard University, Box 2, Folder 88.

38. Zinsser, *As I Remember Him*, 333. For the origins of the invitation to Ruiz Castañeda, see letters: Hermann Mooser to Hans Zinsser, December 6, 1929; Zinsser to Mooser, December 9, 1929; Maximiliano Ruiz Castañeda to Hans Zinsser, December 5, 1929; Zinsser to Ruiz Castañeda, December 11 and 29, 1929, Hans Zinsser Papers, Harvard University, Box 2, Folders 88 and 70.

39. Hermann Mooser to Hans Zinsser, December 18, 1929, Hans Zinsser Papers, Harvard Uni-

versity, Box 2, Folder 88; G. Varela, Everardo Landa, Francisco de P. Miranda, et.al., "Estudio de suero contra tifo," *Revista Mexicana de Biología*, 14, 5 (1934): 171–79.

40. Zinsser, *As I Remember Him*, 344.

41. Ruiz Castañeda, *Escritos y entrevistas*, 88. For Ruiz Castañeda's "rectal inoculation" abilities see the letter from Hermann Mooser to Hans Zinsser, December 6, 1929, and Hans Zinsser to Hermann Mooser, March 3, 1930, Hans Zinsser Papers, Harvard University, Box 2, Folder 88; Maximiliano Ruiz Castañeda to Hans Zinsser, December 5, 1929, Hans Zinsser Papers, Harvard University, Box 2, Folder 70.

42. Alberto J. Pani, *La higiene en México* (Mexico City: Imprenta de J. Ballescá, 1915).

43. Federico Gómez S., *Escenas de hospital*, segunda serie, segunda edición (Mexico City: Hospital Infantil, 1955); Guadalupe Dueñas, *Las ratas y otros cuentos* (Mexico City: Ábside, 1954), 13.

44. Ruiz Castañeda, *Escritos y entrevistas*, 67; Zinsser, *As I Remember Him*, 332; Hermann Mooser to Maximiliano Ruiz Castañeda, November 12, 1931, Hans Zinsser Papers, Harvard University, Box 2, Folder 88.

45. Zinsser, *As I Remember Him*, 8; Ruiz Castañeda, *Escritos y entrevistas*, 20; Hart Crane, *The Letters of Hart Crane, 1916–1932*, ed. B. Weber (Berkeley: University of California Press, 1965); Paul Mariani, *The Broken Tower: The Life of Hart Crane* (New York: Norton, 1999); George Hendrick, "Hart Crane Aboard the Ship of Fools: Some Speculations," *Twentieth Century Literature*, 9, 1 (August 1963): 3–10. "Ship of Fools" refers to Katherine Anne Porter's novel. Porter was Crane's best friend in Mexico City, until Porter broke with him over scandals involving alcohol, servants, brawls, and sex.

46. Paul Weindling, *Epidemics and Genocide in Eastern Europe, 1890–1945* (Oxford: Oxford University Press, 2000); Robert Sullivan, *Rats: Observations on the History and Habitat of the City's Most Unwanted Inhabitants* (New York: Bloomsbury, 2004); Robert Hendrickson, *More Cunning than Man: A Social History of Rats and Men* (New York: Stein and Day, 1983); Carlos Macías, *La destrucción de las ratas* (Mexico City: Secretaría de Fomento, Dirección General de Agricultura, 1912); Marta-Aleksandra Balinska, "Le typhus: Une maladie idéologisée," *La Revue du Praticien*, 55, 14 (2005): 1619–1621.

47. Gustavo Malo, *Historia de las cárceles en México: Etapa precolonial hasta el México moderno* (Mexico City: INACIPE, 1979); Miguel S. Macedo, "Los establecimientos penales en México," *Criminalia*, 20 (1954): 417–25; Guillermo Mellado, "Belém por dentro y por fuera," *Criminalia*, 25 (1959): 320–28.

48. Gerardo Varela, "Transmisión del tifo exantemático al sigmodon hispidus y al microtus mexicanus," *Medicina*, 17 (March 1934).

49. M. H. Neill, "Experimental Typhus Fever in Guinea Pigs: A Description of Scrotal Lesion in Guinea Pigs Infected with Mexican Typhus," *Public Health Report*, 32 (1917): 1105–1108; Kenneth F. Maxcy, "Clinical Observations on Endemic Typhus (Brill's Disease) in the Southern United States," *Public Health Repport*, 41 (1926): 1213–1220; "An Epidemiological Study of Endemic Typhus (Brill's Disease) in the Southeastern United States, with Special Reference to Its Mode of Transmission, *Public Health Report*, 41 (1926): 2967–95; Kenneth F. Maxcy and Charles Sinclair, "Mild Typhus (Brill's Diseases) in the Lower Rio Grande Valley," *Public Health Report*, 40 (1925): 241–52; "Typhus Fever in the United States," *Public Health Report*, 44 (1929): 1735–42.

50. T. E. Woodward, "Epidemiologic Classics of Carter, Maxcy, Trudeau, and Smith," *Journal of Infectious Diseases*, 165, 2 (Feb. 1992): 235–44; Hermann Mooser, "Contribución al estudio de la etiología del tifo mexicano," *Gaceta Medica de México*, 59, 4 (1928): 261–70; Mooser, "Ein Beitrag

zur Ätiologie des Mexikanischen Fleckfiebers," *Archiv für Schiffs- und Tropen-Hygiene,* 35 (1931): 261–68; Mooser, "Experiments Relating to the Pathology and the Etiology of Mexican Typhus (Tabardillo): 1. Clinical Course and Pathologic Anatomy of Tabardillo in Guinea-Pigs," *Journal of Infectious Diseases,* 43 (1928): 241–50; Mooser, "Experiments Relating to the Pathology and the Etiology of Mexican Typhus (Tabardillo): 2. Diplobacillus from Proliferated Tunica vaginalis of Guinea-Pigs Reacting to Mexican Typhus," *Journal of Infectious Diseases,* 43 (1928): 261–69; H. Mooser, Gerardo Varela, and Hans Pilz, "Experiments on the Conversion of Typhus Strain," *Journal of Experimental Medicine,* 59 (1934): 137–57, 153–54; Mooser, "American Variety of Typhus," *Transactions of the Royal Society of Tropical Medicine and Hygiene,* 22, 2 (August 1928): 310–15; Mooser, "Uber das Gewebsvirus beim Mexikanischen Fleckfieber," *Sonderabdruck aus der Schweizerischen Medizinischen Wochenschrift,* 59, 23 (1929): 599–609; H. Mooser and Clyde Summer, "On the Relation of the Organism in the Tunica Vaginalis of Animals Inoculated with Mexican Typhus to Rickettsia Prowazekii and the Causative Agent of the Disease," *Journal of Experimental Medicine,* 51, 2 (February 1930): 189–99. For a complete bibliography of Mooser's work (up to 1959), see *Pathologia et Microbiologia,* 24, suppl. 1 (1961), a special issue devoted to Mooser. S. Burt Wolbach and John L. Todd, "Note sur l'étiologie et l'anatomie pathologique du typhus exanthématique au Mexique," *Archive de l'Institute Pasteur,* 34 (1920): 153–58; Varela, "Transmisión del tifo exantemático."

51. Letters from Charles Nicolle to Hans Zinsser, March 23 and March 29, 1932, Hans Zinsser Papers, Harvard University, Box 2, Folder 90.

52. Summary of findings in Rodolfo Sánchez Casco, "Tifo exantemático experimental en el hombre: Vacunación preventiva contra el tifo," tésis, UNAM, 1932. The product of Zinsser and Ruiz Castañeda's collaboration went as follows: Hans Zinsser and M. Ruiz Castañeda, "Studies on Typhus Fever II—Studies on the Etiology of Mexican Typhus Fever," *Journal of Experimental Medicine,* 52, 5 (November 1, 1930): 649–60; Hans Zinsser and Albert Batchelder, "Studies on Mexican Typhus Fever 1," *Journal of Experimental Medicine,* 51, 6 (June 1, 1930): 847–58; Hans Zinsser and M. Ruiz Castañeda, "Studies on Tyhus Fever III—Studies of Lice and Bedbugs (Cimex lectularias) with Mexican Typhus Fever Virus," *Journal of Experimental Medicine,* 52, 5 (November 18, 1930): 661–68; Hans Zinsser and M. Ruiz Castañeda, "Studies on Typhus Fever V—Active Immunization against Typhus Fever with Formalized Virus," *Journal of Experimental Medicine,* 53, 3 (March 1, 1931): 325–31; Hans Zinsser and M. Ruiz Castañeda, "Further Experiments in Typhus Fever IV—Infections with Washed Mexican Rickettsiae and Immunity to European Typhus," *Journal of Experimental Medicine,* 53, 6 (December 1, 1931): 865–72; Hans Zinsser and M. Ruiz Castañeda, "Active and Passive Immunization in Typhus Fever," *Proceedings of the National Academy of Sciences of the United States of America,* 20, 1 (Jan. 15, 1934): 9–11. Ruiz Castañeda also published by himself: M. Ruiz Castañeda, "A New Strain for Rickettsia Bodies," *Journal of Infectious Diseases,* 47 (November 1930): 640–46; M. Ruiz Castañeda, "A Study of the Relationship of the Scrotal Swelling and Rickettsia Bodies to Mexican Typhus Fever," *Journal of Experimental Medicine,* 52, 2 (August 1, 1930): 520–23; M. Ruiz Castañeda, "Estudio comparativo de la *Rickettsia prowasekii* y de los cuerpos de Mooser," *Medicina,* 12, 183 (November 10, 1939): 120–25; M. Ruiz Castañeda, "Recent Advances in Research on Typhus in Mexico," *Proceedings of the Institute of Medicine, Chicago,* 13, 7 (October 15, 1940): 170–75. Charles Nicolle, *Naissance, vie et mort des maladies infectieuses,* 19, as quoted in Pelis, *Charles Nicolle: Pasteur's Imperial Missionary,* 191–93; Maurice Huet, *Le pommier et l'olivier : Charles Nicolle : une biographie (1866–1936)* (Montpellier: Sauramps médical, 1995). See his views from his *Naissance, vie et mort des maladies infectieuses* (Paris: Alcan, 1930), to *Biologie de l'invention* (Paris: Alcan, 1932), to

La nature; conception et morale biologiques (Paris: F. Alcan, 1934) and, finally, his last book, *La destinée humaine* (Paris: Presses Universitaires de France, 1941).

53. Letters from Charles Nicolle to Hans Zinsser, March 23 and 29, 1932, Hans Zinsser Papers, Harvard University, Box 2, Folder 90; Hermann Mooser to Hans Zinsser, February 7, 1932, Hans Zinsser to Hermann Mooser, January 28, 1931, Hans Zinsser Papers, Harvard University, Box 2, Folder 88; Zinsser, *As I Remember Him*, 339.

54. Letter H. Zinsser to Ch. Nicolle, February 5, 1934, Hans Zinsser Papers, Harvard University, Box 2, Folder 90; H. Mooser and H. Sparrow, "Immunisations croisées entre un virus du typhus historique (souche tunisienne) et des virus du typhus d'origine mexicaine (souche murine et souche humaine)," *Archives de l'Institut Pasteur du Tunis*, first part, 22, 1 (July 1933): 1–8. In the same volume, see H. Sparrow, "Transmission du typhus murin du Mexique par les puces de rat à rat," 10–12; see also Pelis, *Chares Nicolle: Pasteur's Imperial Missionary*, 202–10.

55. Fernando Ocaranza, "Papel que desempeña el piojo en la transmisión del tifo exantemático," in *Memorias y actas del segundo congreso nacional del tabardillo*, 79.

56. Zinsser, *Rats, Lice, and History*, 166.

57. Ruiz Castañeda, "Cincuentenario de Ricketts," 19–20.

58. Zinsser, *Rats, Lice, and History*, 169.

59. Zinsser, *Rats, Lice, and History*, 170.

60. Letter from Hans Zinsser to Maximiliano Ruiz Castañeda, July 31, 1939, Hans Zinsser Papers, Harvard University, Box 2, Folder 88, 70; Maximiliano Ruiz Castañeda to Hans Zinsser, August 5, 1939; Maximiliano Ruiz Castañeda, "Hans Zinsser en el XXV aniversario de la vacuna contra el tifo," originally in *Gaceta Médica de México* (1956), included in Ruiz Castañeda, *Escritos y entrevistas*.

61. Ruiz Castañeda, "Hans Zinsser en el XXV aniversario de la vacuna contra el tifo," 35; Edmund P. Russell, *War and Nature: Fighting Humans and Insects with Chemicals from World War I to "Silent Spring"* (Cambridge: Cambridge University Press, 2001); John H. Perkins, *Insects, Experts, and the Insecticide Crisis: The Quest for New Pest Management Strategies* (New York: Plenum Press, 1982); Darwin H. Stapleton, "The Dawn of DDT and its Experimental Use by the Rockefeller Foundation in Mexico, 1943–1952," *Parassitologia*, 40 (1998): 149–58; Carlos Ortiz-Mariotte, Felipe Malo-Juvera, and George C. Payne, "Control of Typhus Fever in Mexican Villages and Rural Populations through the use of DDT," *American Journal of Public Health*, 35 (November 1945): 1191–95; Darwin H. Stapleton, "A Lost Chapter in the Early History of DDT: The Development of Anti-Typhus Technologies by the Rockefeller Foundation's Louse Laboratory, 1942–1944," *Technology and Culture*, 46, no. 3 (July 2005): 513–34; Armando Solórzano Ramos, *Fiebre dorada Fiebre amarilla?*; Armando Solorzano, "La influencia de la Fundación Rockefeller en la conformación de la profesión médica mexicana, 1921–1949," *Revista Mexicana de Sociología*, 58, 1 (January–March 1996): 173–203; Anne-Emanuelle Birn, *Marriage of Convenience*. David Dorado Romo documents the anti-lice campaigns implemented against Mexicans on the border in 1917; see D. D. Romo, *Ringside Seat to a Revolution: An Underground Cultural History of El Paso and Juárez, 1893–1923* (El Paso: Cinco Puntos Press, 2005).

62. Zinsser, *Rats, Lice, and History*, 174; Ruiz Castañeda, *Escritos y entrevistas*, 99.

63. Hans Zinsser to Maximiliano Ruiz Castañeda, June 23, 1933, July 19, 1937, and July 19, 1938, Hans Zinsser Papers, Harvard University, Box 2, Folder 88.

64. Hermann Mooser to Maximiliano Ruiz Castañeda, December 2, 1932, Hermann Mooser to Hans Zinsser, December 18, 1929, and Hans Zinsser to Hermann Mooser, no date, Hans Zinsser

Papers, Harvard University, Box 2, Folder 88; Maximiliano Ruiz Castañeda, "Nicolle 1931, capítulo de memorias inéditas," included in Ruiz Castañeda, *Escritos y entrevistas*, 44.

65. Zinsser, *As I Remember Him*, 340 and ff.

66. Hermann Mooser to Hans Zinsser, January 6, 1930, and H. Zinsser to H. Mooser, October 30, 1928, Hans Zinsser Papers, Harvard University, Box 2, Folder 70. Theobald Smith (1859–1934) was the most prominent U.S. entomologist and bacteriologist of the 1920s, proving the role of insects in many diseases. H. Mooser to M. Ruiz Castañeda, August 17, 1931, H. Mooser to M. Ruiz Castañeda, November 13, 1931, and H. Mooser to M. Ruiz Castañeda, February 2, 1931, Hans Zinsser Papers, Harvard University, Box 2, Folder 88, 70. See also A. Grumbacht, "Professor Dr. Dr. h.c. Hermann Mooser zum 80. Geburtstag," *Pathologia et Microbiologia*, 37 (1971): 164. On his seventieth birthday, a special issue of *Pathologia et Microbiologia* was devoted to Mooser; in it Ruiz Castañeda included "On the Evaluation of Diagnostic Tests for Brucellosis," and Varela (in collaboration with R. Fournier) wrote "Presencia de Rickettsia quintana en piojos Pediculus humanus de la ciudad de México. Inoculación experimental." See the entire issue *Pathologia et Microbiologia*, vol. 24, suppl. 1 (1961) (Ruiz Castañeda in 40–44, Varela 149–51); H. Mooser, "El papel que jugó el decubrimiento del tifo murino en el estudio bacteriológco de las rikettsiosis," in *Memoria del congreso científico mexicano (IV Centenario de la Universidad de México, 1551–1951)* (Mexico City: UNAM, 1953).

67. About Sparrow, see Jean Lindernmann, "Women Scientists in Typhus Research During the First Half of the Twentieth Century," *Gesnerus*, 62 (2005): 257–272.

68. Charles Nicolle to Hans Zinsser, March 4, 1931; May 31, 1930; *Atlas General del Distrito Federal: Geográfico, histórico, commercial, estadístico, agrario: Su descripción más completa, profusamente ilustrada con mapas, fotografías y gráficos: Se forma esta . . .*, vol. 1 (Mexico City: Talleres Gráficos de la Nación, 1930); *Entretiens d'humanistes: Correspondance de Charles Nicolle et Georges Duhamel, 1922–1936, présentée et anotée par le docteur J. J. Hueber* (Rouen: Académie des Sciences, Belles-Lettres et Arts de Rouen, 1996); Rodríguez de Romo, "La ciencia pasteuriana a través de la vacuna antirrábica."

69. Zinsser, *As I Remember Him*, 305; Ch. Nicolle to H. Zinsser, April 2, 1934; Georges Duhamel, *Scènes de la vie future* (Paris: Mercure de France, 1930), 115–16.

70. Charles Nicolle, "Comme au souvenir qui ne vieillit point," in Charles Nicolle, *Les feuilles de la sagittaire* (Paris: n.p., 1920).

71. Cfr., Marcos Cueto, *Cold War, Deadly Fevers, Malaria Eradication in Mexico, 1955–1975*, 9. Ignacio Millán, "Necesidad de un nuevo tipo de médico en la república," in *Departamento de Salubridad Pública: Boletín del Instituto de Higiene*, 6, 12 (December 1938): 165–72. Image "Los Médicos Mexicanos en Caricatura," *Revista de Revistas* (October 16, 1921): 31.

CHAPTER 11

1. Fernando Pessoa, *A língua portuguesa*, ed. Luísa Medeiros (Lisbon: Assírio & Alvim, 1997).

2. J. G. A. Pocock, "Languages and Their Interpretations: The Transformation of the Study of Political Thought," in J. G. A. Pocock, *Politics, Language, and Time: Essays on Political Thought and History* (New York: Atheneum, 1971); Quentin Skinner, *Reason and Rhetoric in the Philosophy of Hobbes* (Cambridge: Cambridge University Press, 1996); Peter Burke and Roy Porter, eds., *Languages and Jargons: Contributions to a Social History of Language* (Cambridge: Polity Press, 1995); George Steiner, *After Babel: Aspects of Language and Translation* (New York: Oxford University Press, 1975); Penelope J. Corfield, ed., *Language, History, and Class* (Boston: Basil Blackwell, 1991); Kenneth Cmiel, *Demo-*

cratic Eloquence: The Fight over Popular Speech in Nineteenth-Century America (New York: W. Morrow, 1990); Lawrence Levine, Highbrow/Lowbrow: The Emergence of Cultural Hierarchy in America (Cambridge Harvard University Press, 1988); Peter Burke, ed., The Social History of Language (Cambridge: Cambridge University Press, 1987); Octavio Paz, El arco y la lira: El poema, la revelación poética, poesía e historia (Mexico City: Fondo de Cultura Económica, 1956); Antonio Alatorre, 1001 años de la lengua española (Mexico City: Fondo de Cultura Económica, 1995); José Ángel Valente, Las palabras de la tribu (Madrid: Siglo Veintiuno de España Editores, 1971); María Zambrano, Filosofía y poesía (Madrid: Ediciones de la Universidad, Fondo de Cultura Económica, 1993); Eliseo Vivas, Creation and Discovery: Essays in Criticism and Aesthetics (New York: Noonday Press, 1955); Henri Meschonnic, Critique du rythme: anthropologie historique du langage (Lagrasse: Verdier, 1982).

3. Not much has been written about the history of Mexico City's language. The literature focuses on the post-1960s. For a list of early studies, see C. Carroll Maden, The Phonology of the Spanish Dialect of Mexico City (Baltimore: Modern Language Association of America, 1896).

4. See James Lockhart's explanation of the Nahuatl language in central Mexico, in The Nahuas after the Conquest: A Social and Cultural History of the Indians of Central Mexico, Sixteenth through Eighteenth Centuries (Stanford: Stanford University Press, 1992).

5. Quoted in Octavio Paz, Cuadrivio (Mexico City: Joaquín Mortiz, 1965), 69.

6. The line is by P. B. Shelley, "Stanzas written in dejection, near Naples" (ca. 1810).

7. Salvador Diego Fernández, La ciudad de Méjico a fines del siglo XIX (Mexico City: n.p., 1937), 5.

8. Vicente T. Mendoza, "Pregones y pregoneros," Anuario de la Sociedad Folklórica de México, 1938–1940 (1942): 51–78.

9. Enrique Fernández Ledesma, Viajes al siglo XIX (Mexico City: Talleres Gráficos de la Nación, 1933), 98.

10. Juana G. Campos and Ana Barella, Diccionario de refranes (Madrid: n.p., 1975); Gabriel María Vergara y Martín, Refranes y cantares geográficos de España (Madrid: Librería General de Victoriano Suárez, 1906); José María Sbarbi, El refranero general español: parte recopilado, y parte compuesto (Madrid: Imprenta de A. Gómez Fuentenebro, 1874–1878); José E. Iturriaga, Lo religioso en el refranero mexicano, o, Como decía mi abuelita (Mexico City: Sociedad Cooperativa Publicaciones Mexicanas, 1984); Herón Pérez Martínez, Refranero mexicano (Mexico City: Academia Mexicana, Fondo de Cultura Económica, 2004); Miguel Velasco Valdés, Refranero popular mexicano (Mexico City: B. Costa-Amic, 1967); Domingo Blanco, A poesía popular en Galicia, vol. 2 (Vigo: E. Xerais de Galicia, 1992), 9.

11. Darío Rubio, Estudios paremiológicos: Refranes, proverbios y dichos y dicharachos mexicanos (Mexico City: Editorial A. P. Márquez, 1940), xii; José Trini Laris, Historia de modismos y refranes mexicanos (Guadalajara: Fortino Jaime, 1921).

12. Proverbs included, not without apologies, in Darío Rubio, Estudios paremiológicos; F. J. Altamirano, Provérbios, facsimile ed. (Mexico City: Porrúa, 1997); Vicente T. Mendoza, "Pregones y pregoneros," Anvario de la Sociedad Folklórica de México (1942): 51–78.

13. There are rural versions of the same copla, for instance, among Cristero troops. Ezequiel Mendoza Barragán, Confesiones de un cristero (Mexico City: Breve Fondo Editorial, 2001).

14. All these coplas, collected in Mexico City, come from the most authoritative, complete, and wonderful collection done in the 1960s at El Colegio de México. Margit Frenk Alatorre and Yvette Jiménez de Báez, Coplas de amor del folklore mexicano (Mexico City: El Colegio de México, 1970).

15. Salvador Cordero, *Barbarismos, galicismo y* . . . (Mexico City, Paris: Librería de la Viuda de C. Bouret, 1918).

16. Vicente T. Mendoza, *La canción mexicana, ensayo de clasificación y antología* (Mexico City: UNAM, 1961), 17

17. Jesús Sánchez, "Glosario de voces castellanas derivadas del idioma nahutl," *Anales del Museo Nacional* 3 (1886): 57–67.

18. All these tunes come from personal recollections and from such collections as Higinio Vázquez Santa Ana, *Historia de la canción mexicana*, vol. 3 (Mexico City: Talleres Gráficos de la Nación, 1931); A. Reyes, *Cancionero estrella* (Mexico City: n.p., 1940); Ángel A. Salas, Graciela Amador, and Frances Toor, eds., *Cancionero Mexicano de Mexican Folkways*, illustrated by Rufino Tamayo (Mexico City: Mexican Folkways, 1931); Vicente T. Mendoza, *Panorama de la música tradicional mexicana* (Mexico City: UNAM, 1956); Vicente T. Mendoza, *La canción mexicana, ensayo de clasificación y antología*; Rubén M. Campos, *El folklore musical de las ciudades; investigación acerca de la música mexicana para bailar y cantar, obra integrada con 85 composiciones para piano, cuyas melodías están intactas* (Mexico City: Secretaría de Educación Pública, 1930); J. Frank Dobie, *Puro mexicano* (Austin: Texas Folk-lore Society, 1935); *Melodías mexicanas núm. 2: canciones modernas y antiguas, sección literaria escogida con esmero* (C. Juárez: Central de Publicaciones "Benito Juárez," 1933); Higinio Vázquez Santa Ana, *Canciones, cantares y corridos mexicanos* (Mexico City: Imprenta M. León Sánchez, 1924).

19. Julio Sesto, *La bohemia de la muerte* (Mexico City: El Libro Español, 1929); Ángel Escudero, *El duelo en México: recopilación de los desafíos habidos en nuestra república, precedidos de la historia de la esgrima en México y de los duelos más famosos verificados en el mundo desde los juicios de Dios hasta nuestros días* (Mexico City: Imprenta Mundial, 1936). For an interpretation of the duel in late nineteenth-century Mexico City, see Pablo Piccato, *The Tyranny of Opinion: Honor in the Construction of the Mexican Public Sphere* (Durham: Duke University Press, 2010).

20. Darío Rubio, *Estudios paremiológicos*, xxi.

21. Antonio García Cubas, *El libro de mis recuerdos: narraciones históricas, anecdóticas y de costumbres mexicanas anteriores al actual estado social, ilustradas con más de trescientos fotograbados* (Mexico City: Editorial Patria, 1945); Juan S. Garrido, *Historia de la música popular en México [1896–1973]* (Mexico City: Extemporáneos, 1974); Victoriano Salado Álvarez, *Minucias del lenguaje* (Mexico City: Secretaría de Educación Pública, 1957).

22. Amado Nervo, "Del estilo exuberante," in vol. 23, *Obras Completas*, 49.

23. Ramón Gómez de la Serna, *Don Ramón María del Valle Inclán* (Madrid: Espasa Calpe, 1944), 167.

24. Anecdote told in Alfonso Reyes, *Obras Completas*, vol. 3, 310.

25. Amado Nervo, "El catalán y la supremacía del castellano," in *Obras Completas*, vol. 30, 21; Enrique González Martínez, *La apacible locura: Segunda parte de El hombre del búho, misterio de una vocación* (Mexico City: Ediciones de Cuadernos Americanos, 1951), 49; Rubén N. Campos, *El folklore y la música mexicana: Investigación acerca de la cultura musical en México (1525–1925)* (Mexico City: Talleres Gráficos de la Nación, 1928); Alfonso Reyes's letter to Pedro Henríquez Ureña, May 8, 1914, reproduced in *Alfonso Reyes/Pedro Henríquez Ureña Correspondencia I, 1907–1914*, ed. José Luis Martínez (Mexico City: Fondo de Cultura Económica, 1985), 318–21, quoted on p. 321; Max Leopold Wagner, "Mexikanisches Rotwelsch," *Zeitschrift für romanische Philologie*, 39 (1919): 513–50.

26. In addition to his *Modismos, locuciones y términos mexicanos* (Madrid: M. Minuesa de los Ríos, 1892) José Sánchez Somoano published an insightful account of the U.S., full of cultural com-

mentary à la petit Tocqueville. See his *Costumbres yankees: viajes por la América del Norte* (Mexico City: Tip. de El Correo Español, 1894).

27. Arturo Langle, *Vocabulario, apodos, seudónimos, sobrenombres y hemerografía de la Revolución* (Mexico City: UNAM, 1966), 49.

28. Ramón del Valle Inclán, *Tirano Banderas: novela de tierra caliente* (1926), 6th ed. (Madrid: Austral, 1965), 10, 21, 26; Gómez de la Serna, *Don Ramón María del Valle Inclán*; and Miguel Alberca and Cristóbal González, *Valle Inclán: La fiebre del estilo* (Madrid: Espasa, 2002).

29. *Paraules d'Opoton el vell* (Barcelona: Cadí, 1968).

30. Alfredo M. Saavedra, "El calo de la delicuencia y la expresión sexual," *Anuario del la Sociedad Folklórico de México*, 2 (1942): 23–55; Wagner, "Mexikanisches Rotwelsch"; José Raúl Aguilar, *Los métodos criminales en México*, (Mexico City: Editorial Lux, 1941); Carlos Roumagnac, *Por los mundos del delito, los criminales en México: Ensayo de psicología criminal* (Mexico City: Tipografía el Fenix, 1904); Sommer, "Über die mexikanische Gaunersprache," *Archiv für Kriminologie*, 28 (1907): 209–14; Julio Guerreo, *La génesis del crimen en México*, (Paris: Vda de C. Bouret, 1901); Benjamín Martínez, *Jerga carcelaria* (Mexico City: n.p., 1930).

31. Wagner, "Mexikanisches Rotwelsch," 529, 550.

32. Wagner: "Amerikanisch-Spanisch und Vulgärlatein," *Zeitschrift für romanische Philologie*, 40 (1920): 286–312, 385–404; Wagner, "Los elementos español y catalán en los dialectos sardos," *Revista de Filología Española*, 9 (1922): 255–65; Wagner, "Notes linguistiques sur l'argot barcelonais," *Biblioteca Filològica de l'Institut de la Llengua Catalana*, 6 (1924).

33. "La coprolalia se encuentra típicamente representada en ese vocabulario como exponente de situaciones psicológicas unidas a la inadecuación, a la ignorancia, a la malicia, a la sátira que hinca sobre la nobleza del sexo . . ." Carlos Roumagnac, *Los criminales en México*, 376–80.

34. Renato Rosaldo, "A List of Slang and Colloquial Expressions of Mexico City," *Hispania*, 21, 4 (November 1948): 437–45. Taming my own logophilia, I do not use examples from the following sources: Ignacio Alcocer, *El español que se habla en México* (Washington: Instituto Panamericano, 1936); Francisco Castillo Nájera, "Breves consideraciones sobre el español que se habla en México," RMI (1936): 157–69; R. S. Boggs, "El habla popular," in *Bibliografía del folklore mexicano* (Mexico City: Instituto Panamericano de Geografía y Estadística, 1939), 108–18; A. B. Gaarder, *El hablar popular y la conciencia colectiva* (Mexico City: UNAM, 1954); Frank C. Pierce, *Colloquial and Idiomatic Mexican: The Spanish Language as Pronounced and Used by the Mexican People of the Uneducated Class* (Brownsville, Tex. : n.p., 1916); Benjamín Martínez, *Jerga carcelaria*; Roberto Guerrero de la Rosa, "El slang americano y la jerga mexicana," *Revista Iberoamericana*, 1 (1939): 365–74; R. S. Boggs, "Términos del lenguaje popular y caló de la capital de Méjico," *Boletín de Filología* (Universidad de Chile), 8 (1954–1955): 35–43; Beatrice Griffith, *American Me* (Boston: Houghton Mifflin Co., 1948); Benito Fentanes, *Combatiendo barbarismos, contribución al bien hablar* (Mexico City: Botas, 1937).

35. Saavedra's article in *Anuario del la Sociedad Folklórica de México*, 2 (1941–1942): 23–55.

36. Brenner and Toor were U.S. citizens. Brenner was the only foreigner in Mexico City from the 1910s to the 1950s who was fully bilingual, a Mexican and American, so her logophilia, her command of chilango, is as telling as that of any native of Mexico City. Toor's logophilia clearly followed that of her friends in Mexico City.

37. "Si alguien les hubiera pedido," she wrote about garbage collectors in the city, "una defin-

ición de la vida, hubieran dicho como quien escupe un salivazo amargo: la vida es un basurero." Magdalena Mondragón, *Yo como pobre* (Mexico City: Editorial Ariel, 1944), 34.

38. Guadalupe Marín, *La única* (Mexico City: Editorial Jalisco, 1938), 45.

39. Frida Kahlo to Anita Brenner, September 15, 1924, Anita Brenner Papers, HRC.

40. Frida Kahlo to Ella and Bertram Wolfe, October 18, 1934, Ella and Bertram Wolfe Papers, Hoover Institution, Stanford University.

41. F.K. to Ella and Bertram Wolfe, March 26, 1934, Ella and Bertram Wolfe Papers, Hoover Institution, Stanford University.

42. *Correspondencia de Antonieta Rivas Mercado*, ed. F. Bradu (Jalapa: Universidad de Veracruz, 2005).

43. *Examen* (1932). About the novel, see Guillermo Sheridan, *México en 1932: La polémica nacionalista* (Mexico City: Fondo de Cultura Económica, 1999).

CHAPTER 12

1. Alfonso Reyes, "El hombre desnudo," *Nosotros: Revista de arte y decoración*, 1 (December 12, 1912): 10.

2. Ocatvio Paz, *El arco y la lira* (Mexico City: Fondo de Cultura Económica, 1956), 42.

3. Guillermo Prieto, *Musa callejera* (1883). I use the Porrúa edition (Mexico City: Editorial Porrúa, 1976), 83.

4. Michael P. Kramer, *Imagining Language in America: From the Revolution to the Civil War* (Princeton: Princeton University Press, 1991); Ramón Menéndez Pidal, "La unidad del idioma: Discurso inaugural de la Asamblea del Libro Español, celebrado en Madrid el 31 de mayo de 1944," included in his *Mis páginas preferidas: Estudios lingüísticos y literarios* (Madrid: Editorial Gredos, 1957), 46–83; María Jesús Fuente Pérez, *Diccionario de historia urbana y urbanismo: el lenguaje de la ciudad en el tiempo* (Madrid: Boletín Oficial del Estado, 1999); Emma Sepúlveda-Pulvirenti, *Los límites del lenguaje: un acercamiento a la poética del silencio* (Madrid: Ediciones Torremozas, 1990); Carlos Arniches y Barrera, *Arniches: el alma popular* (Torremolinos: Litoral, 1994).

5. José Joaquín Fernández de Lizardi, *El periquillo sarniento* (1816) (Madrid: Asociación de la Prensa Hispano Americana, 2001), 188–89. See also Albert Donell, *El lenguaje del pensador mexicano* (Mexico City: UNAM, 1950)—this book is printed, but it seems to be an M.A. thesis from UNAM.

6. Penelope J. Corfield, ed., *Language, History, and Class* (Oxford: B. Blackwell, 1991); Michael Shapiro, *The Sense of Change: Language as History* (Bloomington: Indiana University Press, 1991); Roger Chartier, *Culture écrite et socété: l'ordre des livres XIVe–XVIIIe siécle* (Paris: Albin Michel, 1996).

7. Edward Sapir, *Language: An Introduction to the Study of Speech* (New York: Harcourt, Bruce and Company, 1921).

8. Joaquín García Icazbalceta, *Vocabulario de mexicanismos, comprobado con ejemplos y comparado con los de otros países hispano-americanos: Propónense además adiciones y enmiendas a la última edición (12) del Diccionario de la Academia: Por el señor don Joaquín Garcia Icazbalceta . . . Obra póstuma publicada por su hijo Luis García Pimentel* (Mexico City: Tipografía y litografía "La Europea" de J. Aguilar Vera y C., 1899); Manuel Orozco y Berra, *Geografía de las lenguas y carta etnográfica de México; precedidas de un ensayo de clasificación de las mismas lenguas y de apuntes para las inmigraciones de las tribus* (Mexico City: Imprenta de J. M. Andrade y F. Escalante, 1864); Francisco Javier Santamaria, *Diccionario de mejicanismos, razonado; comprobado con citas de autoridades, comparado con el de americanismos y con los*

vocabularios provinciales de los más distinguidos diccionaristas hispanoamericanos (Mexico City: Porrúa, 1959). Another attempt at a Mexican dictionary was coordinated by Emiliano Bustos in the 1880s: Emiliano Bustos, ed., *Diccionario enciclopédico-mejicano del idioma español: Contiene todas las voces usadas en España, Méjico, y las demás naciones de la América española; las de ciencias artes y oficios; las notables de historia, biografía, mitolojía, geografía universal y principalmente de geografía, historia y estadística de la República Mejicana*, 2 vols. (Mexico City: Impr. de F. Mata, 1882). See also Salvador Cordero, *Barbarismos, galicismos y solecismos de uso más frecuente; manera de evitarlos, conforme a los cánones establecidos por los buenos hablistas, con un apéndice de los principales modismos, refranes y provincialismos, de empleo corriente en la República Mexicana, asi como una pequeña relación de las principales reglas ortográficas* (Mexico City, Paris: Vda. de C. Bouret, 1918). The only comparable effort has been taking place for many years at El Colegio de México, with the *Diccionario del español usual de México*, still in progress as I write this. A preliminary version of this dictionary was published in 1996 as *Diccionario del español usual de México* (Mexico City: El Colegio de México, 1996). On Pimentel, see Joseph Albert Ellis, "Francisco Pimentel; His Life and Times," Ph.D. diss., Columbia University, 1961.

9. Féliz Ramos i Duarte, *Diccionario de mejicanismos; colección de locuciones i frases viciosas, con sus correspondientes críticas i correcciones fundadas en autoridades de la lengua; máximas, refranes, provincialismos i remoques populares de todos los estados de la República mejicana* (Mexico City: Impr. de E. Dublán, 1895), 5.

10. Manuel G. Revilla, *El lenguaje popular y el erudito: Réplica a don Julio Cejador y Frauca, autor de la "Gramática de la lengua de Cervantes"* (Mexico City: Casa Unida de Publicaciones, 1921); Ricardo del Castillo (Darío Rubio), *Los llamados mexicanismos de la academia española* (Mexico City: Imp. Franco-Mexicana, 1917).

11. F. J. Santamaria, *Americanismo y barbarismo: Entrenamientos lexicográficos y filológicos* (Mexico City: Editorial Cultura, 1921), 228.

12. Darío Rubio, *Los llamados mexicanismos*, 33–34, 70, 105.

13. Santamaria, *Americanismo y barbarismo*, 126.

14. Amado Alonso, *El problema de la lengua en América* (Madrid: Espasa Calpe, 1935), 87; Manuel G. Revilla, "Provincialismos de fonética en Méjico," in Pedro Henríquez Ureña, ed., *El español en Méjico, los Estados Unidos y la América Central; trabajos de E. C. Hills, F. Semeleder, C. Carroll Marden, M. G. Revilla, A. R. Nykl, K. Lentzner, C. Gagini y R. J. Cuervo: Con anotaciones y estudios de Pedro Henríquez Ureña* (Buenos Aires: Imprenta de la Universidad de Buenos Aires, 1938), 199–206, quotation on 204–5; Menéndez Pidal, "La unidad del idioma," 46–83; José Sánchez Somoano, *Modismos, locuciones y términos mexicanos* (Madrid: Manuel M. de los Ríos, 1892), 115, 83. See also Alberto María Carreño and Enrique Martínez Sobral, *La lengua castellana en Méjico: Discurso de recepción en la Academia Mejicana correspondiente de la Real Española y respuesta al mismo discurso, leídos el día 17 de abril de 1925* (Mexico City: Imprenta Victoria, 1925); and Gastón Maspero, "Sur quelques singularités phonétiques de l'espagnol parlé dans le campagne de Buenos Aires et de Montevideo," *Mémoires de la Société de Linguistique de Paris*, 2 (1875): 51–65.

15. Ramón Menéndez Pidal, *Los romances de América y otros estudios* (Madrid: Espasa Calpe, 1939; first published in 1906).

16. Menéndez Pidal, *Los romances de América*.

17. Menéndez Pidal, *Los romances de América*; E. Asensio, *Política y realidad en el cancionero peninsular de la Edad Media* (Madrid: Gredos, 1970); J. J. Nunes, *Cantigas d'amigo dos trovadores galego-portugueses*, vol. 1 (Lisbon: Centro do Livro Brasileiro, 1973); Aurelio Espinosa, *The Spanish Language*

in *New Mexico and Southern Colorado* (Santa Fe: New Mexican P.C., 1911); Espinosa, *Cuentos populares españoles: Recogidos de la tradición oral de España y publicados con una introducción y notas comparativas,* 3 vols. (Palo Alto: Stanford University Press, 1923–1926); A. Griera, *Atlas lingüístic de Catalunya* (Barcelona: Institut d'Estudis Catalans, 1923); Pedro Benvenutto Murrieta, *El lenguaje peruano* (Lima: Talleres de San Martí, 1936); Lisandro Segovia, *Diccionario de argentinismos, neologismos y barbarismos* (Buenos Aires: Imprenta de Coni Hermanos, 1911); Francisco Rodríguez Marín, *Cantos Populares Españoles,* 5 vols. (Seville: F. Álvarez y cia, 1882–83); Julio Vicuña Cifuentes, *Coa: jerga de los delincuentes chilenos* (Santiago: Imprenta Universitaria, 1910); Joan Amades, *Folklore de Catalunya,* 3 vols. (Barcelona: E. Selecta, 1951–69).

18. Salas, Amador, and Toor, *Cancionero mexicano,* cover.

19. Pedro Henríquez Ureña and Bertram Wolfe, "Romances tradicionales en Méjico," in *Homenaje ofrecido a Menéndez Pidal,* vol. 2 (Madrid: Librería y Casa Editorial Hernando, 1925), 375–90. For different Spanish and American versions of "La Delgadina" and "La adultera," see Menéndez Pidal, *Los romances de América.*

20. Franz Boas, "Cuentos en mexicano de Milpa Alta D. F., recogidos por Franz Boas: traducidos al español por el professor José María Arreola (filólogo de la dirección de Estudios Arqueológicos y Etnográficos de México)," *Journal of American Folk-Lore,* 33 (January–March, 1920): 1–27; Pablo González Casanova, "Un corrido 'macarrónico' hispano-azteca," *Investigaciones Lingüísticas,* 2 (March–April, 1934): 20–23; Charles Caroll Marden, *The Phonology of the Spanish Dialect of Mexico City: Dissertation Presented to the Board of University Studies of the Johns Hopkins University for the Degree of Doctor of Philosophy* (Baltimore: Modern Language Association of America, 1896); E. Mendoza and C. Carillo, "Apuntes para un catálogo de las palabras mexicanas introducidas al castellano," *Boletín de la Sociedad Mexicana de Geografía y Estadística,* segunda época, special supplement (1872), no pagination; Sánchez, "Glosario de voces castellanas derivadas del idioma Nahuatl"; Sánchez Somoano, *Modismos, locuciones y términos mexicanos;* F. Semeleder, "Das Spanische der Mexikaner," *Mittheilungen des deutschen wissenschaftlichen Vereins in Mexiko,* I (1890): 13–17; Wagner, "Mexikanisches Rotwelsch"; and Wagner, "Mexikanisches Rotwelsch und asturische Xíriga," *Zeitschrift für romanische Philologie,* 50 (1930): 738–40, also reprinted in Max Leopold Wagner, *Sondersprachen der Romania I,* (Stuttgart: Franz Steiner Verlag Stuttgart, 1990). See also Sommer, "Über die mexikanische Gaunersprache"; Campos, *El folklore musical de las ciudades;* and Ramos i Duarte, *Diccionario de mejicanismos.*

21. M. Gutiérrez Nájera, "El españo de América," *El partido liberal* (February 4, 1894).

22. The titles of the novels show how much they meant to be an appropriation of *vulgata:* Luis Inclán, *Astucia, el jefe de los hermanos de la hoja, o Los charros contrabandistas de la rama: Novela histórica de costumbres mexicanas, con episodios originales, excrita por Luis Inclán en vista de auténticas apuntaciones del protagonista, amenizada con sus correpondientes litografías . . .* (Mexico City: Imprenta de Inclán, 1865–1866); Manuel Payno, *Los bandidos de Río Frío; novela naturalista, humoristica, de costumbres, de crímenes y de horrores, por Manuel Payno: Única edición autorizada por sus herederos y corregida con vista de los apuntes y borradores facilitados por los mismos, e ilustrada por artistas mexicanos: Prólogo explicativo de la época y los personajes que figuran en la obra con otros nombres . . .* (Mexico City: Impr. M. León Sánchez, 1928); Fernández de Lizardi, *El periquillo sarniento.*

23. Cayetano Rodríguez Beltrán, *Pajarito* (Mexico City: Eusébio Gómez de la Puente Editor, 1908), 11.

24. Prieto, *Memorias de mis tiempos.* Prieto's description of Negrito's importance, and the an-

ecdotes transcribed here, are included in Enrique Fernández Ledesma, *Galería de fantasmas, años y sombras del siglo XIX* (Mexico City: Editorial México Nuevo, 1939); *Calendario del negrito poeta mexicano para el año de 1863 arreglado al meridiano de México* (Mexico City: Simón Blanquel, n.d.); Nicolás León, *El negrito poeta mexicano y sus populares versos: Contribución para el folk-lore nacional* (Mexico City: Impr. del Museo Nacional, 1912); Fernández de Lizardi, *El periquillo sarniento*.

25. We know of all of these anecdotes thanks to the 1920s collection by Rubén M. Campos, *El folklore literario de México: Investigación acerca de la producción literaria popular (1525–1925)* (Mexico City: Secretaría de Educación Pública, 1929),

26. Anecdote recounted in Mario Talavera, *Miguel Lerdo de Tejada, su vida pintoresca y anecdótica* (Mexico City: Editorial Compás, n.d.), 112. Of course this was not published at the time it happened; only after some years had passed could these lines be published.

27. Enrique Aguilar, *Elías Nandino, una vida no/velada* (Mexico City: Grijalbo, 1986), 100. Nandino later published his own version of this biography; see E. Nandino, *Juntando mis pasos* (Mexico City: Editorial Aldus, 2000).

28. *El Chahuiscle* (December 10, 1910), cover.

29. Antonio Machado, *Juan de Mairena, sentencias, donaires, apuntes y recuerdos de un profesor apócrifo, 1936*, ed. José María Valverde (Madrid: Castalia, 1985), 41.

30. *El Valedor* (Nov. 30, 1885): 1.

31. *La Guacamaya* (June 16, 1904).

32. *La Guacamaya* (October 13, 1902).

33. *La Guacamaya* (July 2, 1903).

34. *Multicolor* (January 1, 1914): 2.

35. *Multicolor* (January 29, 1914): 2.

36. *El Microbio* (December 28, 1911).

37. *Boletín del Departamento del Trabajo*, 1, 2 (August 1913).

38. *El mero petatero* (August 25, 1912).

39. Moisés González Navarro, *Historia moderna de México: El porfiriato: La vida social*, vol. 4 (Mexico City: Editorial Hermés, 1957), 25–31.

40. Henríquez Ureña, ed., *El español en Méjico*, xi.

41. Andrés Lira, *Las comunidades indígenas frente a la ciudad de México* (Mexico City: El Colegio de México, 1990).

42. Cecilio Agustín Robelo, *Diccionario de aztequismos, o sea, Jardín de las raíces aztecas, palabras del idioma nahuatl, azteca o mexicano, introducidas al idioma castellano bajo diversas formas: Contribución al Diccionario nacional*, various editions (1st ed. Cuernavaca: Impresión del autor, 1904); see also by the same author an appendix to this dictionary published as *Diccionario de seudoaztequismos; o sea, Catálogo de palabras exóticas al castellano, que se reputan aztequismos o mexicanismos* (Cuernavaca: Impr. del autor, 1906). See also Pablo González Casanova, *Aztequismos: Ensayo etimológico de los mejicanismos de origen azteca* (Mexico City: Secretaría de Educación Pública, 1923); and Luis Cabrera, *Diccionario de aztequismos* (Mexico City: Oasis, 1984).

43. See, for instance, the page-to-page Nahuatl-Spanish text in "Cuentos en mexicano de Milpa Alta DF recogidos por Franz Boas traducidos al español por el profesor José María Arreola," and "Cuento mexicano en mexicano de Milpa Alta por el Dr. Pablo González Casanova," both in *Journal of American Folk-Lore*, 33, 127 (January–March 1920): 11–24, 25–27.

44. Salado Álvarez, *Minucias del lenguaje*, 11.

45. Salvador Quevedo y Zubieta, *México, recuerdos de un emigrado* (Mexico City: Tipográfico de los sucesores de Rivadeneyra, 1983), 158.

46. Ángel del Campo, *Cosas vistas* (Mexico City: Porrúa, 1958), 15.

47. Max Leopold Wagner, "Ein mexikanisch-amerikanischer Argot: das Pachuco," *Romanistisches Jahrbuch*, 6 (1953–1954): 237–66; José Raúl Aguilar, *Los métodos criminales en México* (Mexico City: Editorial Lux, 1941); George C. Baker, "Pachuco: An American-Spanish Argot and Its Social Functions in Tucson Arizona," *University of Arizona Bulletin Series*, 21, 1 (January 1950); Renato Rosaldo, "A List of Slang and Colloquial Expressions in Mexico City," *Hispania*, 31 (1948): 439–45; Beatrice Griffith, *American Me* (Boston: Houghton Mifflin Co., 1948); Beatrice Griffith, "Glosario de caló y pachuco," in *American MLA* (New York: MLA, 1948).

48. Single paper sheet, poem "Ya no lloverán pelonas," by E. Guerrero (n.p., n.d.).

49. Féliz Ramos i Duarte, *Crítica de lenguaje por Féliz Ramos i Duarte: En esta obra se critica a los pincipales literatos de la república mejicana* (Mexico City: Eduardo Dublán, 1897), 49.

50. *Manuel Gutiérrez Nájera* (Mexico City: Cal y Arena), 39.

51. Otilio González, *Incensario* (Mexico City: Talleres Gráficos del Gobierno Nacional, 1919), n.p.

52. Alfonso Reyes, "La lengua universal problema de la posguerra," *Todo* (July 20, 1944): 11.

53. Yaacov (or Jacobo) Glantz, *Trit in di berg; lider un poemes, 1926–1936* (Mexico City: n.p., 1939); in Spanish version in 1997, *Tres caminos: el germen de la literatura judía en México* (Mexico City: Ediciones El Tucán de Virginia, 1997).

54. Alberto Leduc, et al., *Diccionario de geografía, historia y biografías mexicanas* (Paris: Librería de la Viuda de C. Bouret, 1910); Francisco Castillo Nájera, *Breves consideraciones sobre el español que se habla en México* (New York: Instituto de las Españas, 1936); Alatorre, *1001 años*.

55. Alberto María Carreño, *Noticia biográfica del Señor D. Santiago Ballescá* (Mexico City: Impr. Lacaud, 1913); Dolores Pla Brugat, María Magdalena Ordoñez, and Teresa Férriz Roure, *El exilio catalán en México: notas para su estudio* (Zapopan, Jalisco: El Colegio de Jalisco, Generalitat de Catalunya, 1997).

56. Rubén M. Campos, "Del lépero al pelado," included in R. M. Campos, *El folklore literario*, 626, 629.

57. Moisés Sáenz, *Carapan* (Morelia: Dep. de Promoción Cultural del Gobierno de Michoacán, 1970), 128.

58. Rafael Rámirez, *Como dar a todo México un idioma*, (Mexico City: Secretaría de Educación Publica, 1928), 47, 5.

59. Juan León, *El fonetismo de la lengua nasional: Una nueba fase de la revolusión mejicana* [sic] (Mexico City: Linotipografía de J. M. Lemis, 1930), 26.

60. Francisco L. Urquizo, *Tropa vieja*, 2nd ed. (Mexico City: Editorial Yucatense Club del Libro, 192?), 74.

61. Langle, *Vocabulario*.

62. Langle, *Vocabulario*; Ciro R. de la Garza Treviño, *Apodos en la bola: el lenguaje y la Revolución* (Monterrey: Gobierno del Estado de Nuevo León, Secretaría de Administración, Archivo General del Estado, 1987); Justino N. Palomares, *Anecdotario de la Revolución* (Mexico City: Ediciones del autor, 1954).

63. *La palomilla*, no. 8 (August 1937): 3, and "niño el país . . ." in no. 15 (June 1938): 3.

64. *Atlas general del Distrito Federal, geográfico, histórico, comercial, estadístico, agrario*; and "The Mexican Broadcasting Situtaton," *Modern Mexico* (November 1931): 24–27.

65. Jorge Mejía Prieto, *Historia de la radio y la televisión*; Armando de Maria y Campos, *Periodismo en micrófono* (Mexico City: Ediciones Botas, 1938), 8; for the number and names of stations in the late 1920s, see *Atlas general del Distrito Federal, geográfico, histórico, commercial, estadístcico, agrario*. The interesting history of XER/XERA is lucidly told in José Luis Ortiz Garza, *Una radio entre dos reinos: La increíble historia de la radiodifusora mexicana más potente del mundo en los años 30* (Mexico City: Javier Vergara Editor, 1997).

66. See map inserted in *Revista del Ejército y Marina*, tercera época, 6, no. 3 (1921): n.p.

67. "The Mexican Broadcasting Situation," 26; Salvador Novo, *Toda la prosa* (Mexico City: Empresas Editoriales, 1964), 95.

68. Ricardo Pérez Montfort identified this phenomenon; see his *Expresiones populares y estereotipos culturales en México, siglos XIX y XX: diez ensayos* (Mexico City: CIESAS, 2007); and *Cotidianidades, imaginarios y contextos: ensayos de historia y cultura en México, 1850–1950* (Mexico City: CIESAS, 2008).

69. Dromundo, *Mi barrio*, 98.

70. Paco Ignacio Taibo I, *Agustín Lara* (Mexico City: Jucar, 1985).

71. *Cartas de Villaurrutia a Novo, 1935–1936* (Mexico City: Ediciones de Bellas Artes, 1966), 21.

FINAL WORD

1. Jorge Luis Borges, "Las traducciones de las 1001 noches," *Historia de la eternidad* (Buenos Aires: Emecé, 1952), 101.

2. Borges, "Las traducciones," 131.

3. Borges, "Las traducciones," 131.

4. Edward Said, *Culture and Imperialism* (New York: Vintage, 1994), 3–14.

5. Ludwig Wittgenstein, *Philosophical Investigations*, trans. G. E. M. Anscombe (Oxford: Basil Blackwell, 1984), no. 115.

6. This is a spinoff of Carlos Pereda's analysis in "Sur," unpublished paper.

7. Octavio Paz, *The Labyrinth of Solitude: Life and Thought in Mexico*, trans. L. Kemp (New York: Grove Press, 1961).

8. Two English Poems (1939), *Poemas 1923–1958* (Buenos Aires: Emecé, 1960), 125–38.

ARCHIVES CITED

AGN: Archivo General de la Nación, Mexico City
AGN Felipe Teixidor: Felipe Teixidor Collection
AGN GOB: Porfiriato, Gobernación
AGN GRBI: Gobierno Revolucionario, Bienes Intervenidos
AGN Instrucción Pública y Bellas Artes
AGN SCOP: Porfirato, Comunicaciones y Obras Públicas
American Philosophical Society, Philadelphia
Archivo Calles-Torreblanca: Plutarco Elías Calles Archive, Mexico City
Archivo Histórico del Ayuntamiento, Mexico City
Centro de Estudios de Historia de México Carso, Mexico City
Hans Zinsser Papers, Harvard University (Francis A. Countway Library of Medicine, Center for
    the History of Medicine)
Hoover Institution: Hoover Institution on War, Revolution and Peace, Stanford University
Hoover Institution, Ella and Bertram Wolfe Collection
Hoover Institution, Joseph Freeman Collection
Howard T. Ricketts Papers, The University of Chicago
HRC: Harry Ransom Center, The University of Texas, Austin
HRC Idella Purnell Stone Papers
HRC Anita Brenner Papers
Nettie Lee Benson Latin American Collection, The University of Texas, Austin
Genaro García Collection
PHO: Proyecto Historia Oral, Archivo de la Palabra, Instituto Nacional de Antropología e Histo-
    ria and Instituto de Investigaciones Dr. José María Luis Mora, Mexico City
SRE: Archivo Histórico Genaro Estrada, Secretaría de Relaciones Exteriores, Mexico City
SSA: Archivo Histórico de la Secretaría de Salud, Mexico City

INDEX

Duhamel, Georges, 348, 350
Durieux, Caroline, 197–200
Durieux, Pierre, 197

earthquake, of 1919, 95; of 1985, 60, 76
eclecticism, in design, 79, 88
Edison, Thomas Alva, 254, 313
education, 5, 58, 128, 242, 244–46, 363, 402,
    406; bilingual, 407; revolutionary, 410–11
electrification, 12, 59, 102, 202, 204, 367–68
Eliot, T. S., 150, 164
Emerson, Ralph Waldo, 45, 252, 256, 403
English language: author's choice of, xvii, xix;
    influence on Mexican Spanish, 402–4; in
    literature, 372; for science, 323, 329, 339
ensimismamientos (one-in-self-ness), xvi, xix,
    89, 288, 299
epidemics, 17, 370. See also typhus
eroticism, of the East, 261, 269, 272; in im-
    ages, 235–36; in poetry, 232, 234
Escalante, Fernando, 57
Esparza Oteo, Alfonso, 109, 412
Espinosa, Aurelio, 389, 390
essay, as genre and tradition, xvii–xviii, 254,
    350, 416–18
Estrada, Genaro, 163, 456n61
evasion, 148, 165
exile, 121, 184, 226
exoticism, 82–85, 95, 222, 277; of MC (by
    foreigners and natives), xxii–xxiii, 101, 117,
    130, 279
experimentation, 55, 58, 94, 95, 103, 105,
    238, 388, 401, 416

Fabrés, Antonio, 87–88
factories, 72
fakeness, xxii. See also authenticity
federalization, 47, 53
Felipe, Léon (Felipe Camino), 115–16, 127,
    163, 437n14
feminism, 238
Fenollosa, Ernest, 213, 220, 222, 278
Fernández Bustamante, Adolfo, 109, 412
Fernández de Lizardi, José Joaquín, 385, 393

Fernández de Moratín, Nicolás, 371
Fernánez Ledesma, Gabriel, 264, 266
films, 15, 74, 75, 108, 110, 184, 211, 273–74,
    366, 382, 406; of 1910 Centenario, 426n81
folklorists, 106, 356–60, 373, 382, 389, 399
food, 38–39, 80, 131, 263
Foujita, 241, 244–46
Fraina, Louis, 114, 121–22
France, artistic work outsourced to, 33;
    diplomacy with Mexico, 6; parallelisms
    and connections to MC, xx; relationship
    to Spanish Empire, 44–45; residence of
    Mexican expatriates, 22
Frank, Waldo, 129, 151, 163, 197
Freeman, Joseph, 122, 125, 129, 136, 161,
    195; collector of corridos, 389
Frías, Heriberto, 318
Fuentes, Carlos, 370, 418
futurists, 116

Gale, Linn A., 114, 115, 119, 124, 125–26,
    129, 275, 276
Gamboa, Federico, 5, 15, 108, 145,152, 372
Gamio, Manuel, 39, 73, 99–100, 105, 106,
    130, 131, 143, 162, 166, 268, 407
García, Genaro, , 425n67, 455n51
García Cabral, Ernesto, 105, 107, 108, 118,
    169, 199, 270, 350–51
García Cubas, Antonio, 370
García de Polavieja y del Castillo, Camilo, 30
García Icazbalceta, Joaquín, 370, 386, 387, 391
García Lorca, Federico, 126
gardens and parks, 4–6, 11, 13–14, 38–39,
    46, 50, 59–60, 80, 85, 113, 186–87, 224,
    229–30, 238, 324, 361–62. See also Alameda
Gautier, Léon, 151
Gautier, Théophile, 223
Gaviño, Ángel, 312, 316, 317–19, 320, 322,
    323, 324, 326, 330, 339, 346
Gayol, Roberto, 228, 289
Gedovius, Germán, 169
geisha, 238, 246
Geissler, Louise, 115, 122, 124
gender, 57, 58, 66; in language, 374, 392

Genova Hotel, 97, 112, 114

Gériolles, A. de (L. Génu de Régiol), 238–40

ghosts, vii, 140–43, 248

Gide, André, 103

Gillette, Howard, 52

Giner de los Ríos, Francisco, 386

Girard, Joseph, 316, 317–19, 320, 324, 326, 339

Glantz, J., 204–5

Glikowski, M., 204–5

Glintenkamp, Henry (Hendrik), 114, 120, 123, 134, 180–81, 192, 200, 201, 241

global flow of ideas, xix, 416

globalization, 213, 284

Godoy, C., 238–40

Goitia, Francisco, 67, 69, 100, 105, 108, 197

Gold, Michael, 111, 114, 134, 201

Goldberger, Joseph, 317, 318–19, 320, 321–22, 324, 347

Gómez, Manuel. See Phillips, Charles

Gómez de la Serna, Ramón, 76, 89, 372

Goncourt brothers, 213, 223, 224, 232 (Edmund de, 224)

González Casanova, Pablo, 39, 391, 401

González de Mendoza, J. M., 232, 234, 254

González-Macías, Victor, 87

González Martínez, Enrique, 98, 139, 373

González Mello, Renato, 255

González Obregón, Luis, 24

González Peña, Carlos, 50, 67

Gonzalo Sandoval street, Popotla, 317

government of MC. See ayuntamiento

Greece, mythic past, 53, 261, 273, 309

Greene, Graham, 180, 189

green space, 46, 50, 52, 186, 224, 360; in Japan, 229

Gruening, Ernest, 124–25

Guacamaya, La, 65–66, 219, 376, 396–99

Guadalajara, 252

Guanajuato, 149, 252

Guerrero, Julio, 72, 377

guinea pigs, 319, 338, 341, 350–51

Gupta, H., 120, 263

Gutiérrez Cruz, Carlos, 232–33

Gutiérrez Nájera, Manuel: criticizing, 403,

465n79; as part of essayist tradition, xviii; poet and dandy, 392, 412; writing as Negrito Poeta, 394

Guzmán, Juan (Hans Gutman), 168, 204

Haberman, Roberto, 114, 115, 125–26, 182

Haberman, Thorberg. See Brundin, Thorberg

Harvard University, 220, 320, 331

Hearn, Lafcadio, 220, 229

Heijenoort, Jean Van, 128, 442n10

Henle, Fritz, 173

Henríquez Ureña, Pedro, 111, 118, 127, 389, 391, 401, 403

Herbst, Josephine, 131, 242

Heredia, Guillermo, 25, 35, 427n94

heroes, 6, 39, 52, 59, 96, 324, 394; revolutionary, 410

heroin, 137, 301–3

Herrán, Saturnino, 30, 32, 104–5, 108, 121, 204, 295, 296, 298

Hidalgo, Colonia, 64, 69

Hidalgo, Father Miguel, 5, 59

Hinduism, 122, 222, 248, 249, 258, 270, 277

Hiroishi, Yoshiro, 246–47

historicism, in design, 79

history, 103; as presented at 1910 Centenario, 29–31; rhetoric of, 371; scientific, 27–28. See also Desfile Histórico

homosexuality, 304. See also sexuality

horses, 319

Hotel del Prado, 60

housing, model, 73. See also architecture; colonias (housing developments); vecindades

Huerta, Victoriana, 224, 259, 326

Hughes, Langston, 112, 120

Humboldt, Alexander von, 150; honored at 1910 Centenario, 4

Humboldt, Wilhelm von, 386

Huxley, Aldous, 159

hygiene, 17, 52, 59, 286, 340. See also sanitation

Ibargüengoitia, Jorge, 50

idealism, 15 (cities ultimately surpassing the corruption of the modernist city), 31

Morelos, José María, 6, 22, 30
Morones, Luis N., 114, 115, 125, 276
Moses, Jasper T., 173
movies. *See* films
Mukherjee, Dhan Gopal, 275
Müller, J. W. von., 174
Mumford, Lewis, taking city as subject, xix
murals, 235, 244, 255, 267
Murata, Kishio, 457n87
murder, 128–29
music, 106–7, 143, 192, 246–47; 267; 331;
   folk, 111–12, 267, 281, 332–33, 363–68,
   390; popular, 403, 405, 412
Müsil, Robert, as part of essayist tradition,
   xviii
myths, making, 129; national, 52, 53, 159

Nahuatl culture, 222, 264; influence on Mexican Spanish, 366, 401–2, 416; language,
   58, 73, 130, 240, 249, 355, 358, 401, 407,
   478n4; music, 391
Namban art, 216
Nandino, Elías, 394, 395
Nandy, Ashis, 163
Napoleon Bonaparte, 56, 97
national anthem, 31
National Congress of Medicine, 17
nationalism, 24, 43, 60, 93, 103, 140, 219;
   American, 46; Bengali, 123, 212, 275–78;
   expressed in 1910 *Centenario*, 3, 7, 8, 15;
   expressed in 1921 *Centenario*, 42, Indian,
   249, 462n50
National Library, 4
National Palace, 17, 25, 27, 33, 137
National Penitentiary, 5
National Theater, 17
nationhood, epitomized by MC, 1
nativism, 166
Negrito Poeta, 393–95
Neill, M. H., 328, 338
Nervo, Amado, 1, 97–98, 103, 110, 254–58,
   261, 391, 412, 413
Neve, Carlos D., 270, 271
New Thought, 253, 275–77

New York, 11, 36
Nicolle, Charles, 313, 314, 316, 317, 319,
   320, 322, 323, 325, 326, 327, 328–29, 331,
   338–41
Nietzsche, Friedrich, 76, 94, 100, 163, 213,
   262
nihonga, 240
Ninomiya, Zetsuko, 242
Nobel Prize, 311, 322, 326, 348
Noguchi, Isamu, 241
Noriega Hope, Carlos, 292
nostalgia, xv, 15, 60, 96, 100, 102, 109, 122,
   169, 226, 286, 349, 353, 406, 413
novels, 100, 118, 119, 200, 204–5, 235,
   254–55, 316; language of, 370, 382, 409
Novo, Salvador, 64, 77, 98, 112, 120, 140,
   159, 164, 204, 456n61; correspondence,
   413; outing, 395; on radio, 411; taking
   city as subject, xix; vices, 137; writing as
   Negrito Poeta, 394
Nutall, Zelia, 189

Oaxaca, as source of knowledge about indig-
   enous peoples, 27
Obregón Santacilia, Carlos, 33, 41–42, 60, 61
Obregón, Álvaro, xix, 38–39, 233, 331–32
obscenity, 383, 392. See also *palabrotas*
Ocampo, Victoria, 262–65
Ocaranza, Fernando, 326, 341, 351
odalisque (imagery), 237, 418
odalisque-mania, xxiii; defined, 211–13,
   217–18, 220, 224–47, 248–62, 267–79
O'Gorman, Juan, 60–61, 286
Ohio State University, 317, 321
Olaguíbel, Juan, 241
Oles, James, 178
Olivares, Púas, 76
Ollin, Nahui. *See* Mondragón, Carmen
Olympic Games, MC 1968, 10, 422n19
Onís, Federico de, 117, 437n 14
Opera House, Mexican, 17, 19, 32, 33, 35,
   157, 188, 205
opium, 137, 218; metaphorical, 223
optimism, 128, 265

Prévost, Jean, 158–59
Prieto, Guillermo, 67, 383–84, 393
primitivism, 101, 105. See also *indigenismo*
promiscuity, 74, 137; intellectual, 101; linguistic, 405. *See also* sexuality
prostitution, 67, 98–99, 108, 184, 188–89, 190, 203, 236, 237, 412; in literature, 371, 372, 423n38
proverbs, 357–60, 369
provincialism, 101–2
Prowazek, Stanislaus von, 323
public space, 11, 360
Pugibet, Ernesto, 80
pulque, 5, 11, 108, 175, 203, 226, 291, 400; as term, 392
pulquerías, 67, 136, 168, 175, 178–79, 186
purity, 135; racial, xxii, 166
Purnell, Idella, 111

Querétaro, 53
Quevedo, Francisco de, 163, 371
Quevedo, Miguel Ángel de, 14, 50, 51, 96, 97, 228, 289
Quevedo y Zubieta, Salvador, 402

Rabasa, Emilio, 6, 100
rabies, 289, 291, 336, 467n8
race, 41, 56–57, 118, 148–49, 153–61, 165, 176, 340
racial specificity, 155–56, 161, 181
racial theories, 52, 72, 101, 251
racism, 28, 48, 50, 111, 202, 359
Radical Humanism, 122
radicals, 115, 119, 122; attracted to MC, xxii, 101; politicians, 111
radio, 75, 109, 110, 363–64, 366; influence on language, 411–12
railroads, xviii, 153, 188, 202, 225
Ramírez, Fausto, 104, 255
Ramírez de Aguilar, Fernando (Jacobo Delavuelta), 137–38, 440n39
Ramos i Duarte, Féliz, 376, 387, 391, 403
Ramos Martínez, Alfredo, 241
rats, 289, 311, 317, 326, 327, 330, 331–37;

distinctive strains in MC, 331, 336–37; metaphorical, 370; transported by ship, 333–35, 350
Ray, Sibnarayan, 278
Rebolledo, Efrén, 214, 217, 232, 236
Reconstruction, 44, 49, 58
Redfield, Robert, 73, 130, 195, 201, 286
Reed, Alma, 111, 255
Reed, John, 151, 163
reinvention, 56, 119, 127, 137, 138, 163, 195; collective, aided by history, xx
Rejano, Juan, 131, 202
Reko, V. A., 142–43
Republicanism, xix, 46, 55
Requena Legarreta, Pedro, 263–64
Retinger, Joseph, 114, 115
Revilla, Manuel G. , 387, 388, 391
revolution, xviii, 114, 132, 133, 164–65, 174
Revolution, French, 8
Revolution, Mexican, of 1910, xxi, 15, 37, 88, 94, 99, 118, 255, 385; effect on language, 407–10; recovery from, 286; typhus outbreaks during, 325, 326; U.S. views of, 129
Revolution, Russian, 93, 97, 103, 121, 257
Reyes, Alfonso, 98, 116, 373, 391; opposed to Americanization of Spanish, 403
rhetoric, 304
Ricketts, Howard T., 317–25, 339
Rickettsia. *See* typhus
Riis, Jacob, 59
Rio, João do, xviii, 383
Riva Palacio, Vicente, 24
Rivas Mercado, Antonieta, 137, 381, 424n56
Rivas Mercado, Antonio, 15–16, 22, 35, 425n70, 427n91
Rivera, Diego, 30, 32, 41, 59–60, 77, 101, 104, 105, 114–15, 117–19, 124, 127–29, 136, 139, 144, 155, 161, 164, 184, 255, 269; drawn, 200; illustrating others' works, 151, 156–57, 174, 199, 205–6, 244; language of, 381; marriage to Guadalupe Marín, 378; opposition to odalisque-mania, 238, 267; politics, 133, 267
Robelo, Cecilio, 376

Unamuno, Miguel de, 256, 386–87
universal, related to particular, xxi, 286–87
universalism, 122, 253, 260, 262
urban experience, xvi, 287
urbanization, 74, 93
urban planning, xviii; Americanization of, 44, 48; *Centenario* of 1910 as opportunity for 7, 8, 25; influence of foreign, 11; global currents, 43, 286, 308–10
Urbina, Luis G., writing as Negrito Poeta, 394, 395
Urquizo, Francisco, 370, 408
U.S.: funding world's fairs, 9; against Mexican immigrants in, 38, 130; parallelisms and connections to MC, xx, 8
utopia, 1, 95, 248; urban, 48, 55, 284

vaccination, 70, 289
Valadés, José, 114
Valcárel, Luis E., 277
Valdés, Germán (Tin-Tán) 211, 365
Valedor, El, 397
Valencia, Tórtola, 271–73
Valenzuela, Jesús, writing as Negrito Poeta, 394
Valéry, Paul, 103, 163–64
Valle, Rafael Heliodoro, 102, 118, 140, 263
Valle-Arispe, Artemio del, 294
Valle Inclán, Ramón del, 118, 139, 372
Vallejo, Fernando, 139
vampires, 256
Varela, Gerardo, 312, 316, 329, 330, 337, 338, 339, 341, 343, 467n8
Vasconcelos, José (Negrito Poeta), 393–94
Vasconcelos, José, 30, 41, 48, 114–15, 117, 120, 122 , 131, 139, 232, 255, 257, 258, 260–63, 269, 276, 387; lover, 381, 424n56; opposed to Americanization of Spanish, 403; promoted by Camprubí, 463n60
vecindades, 63, 64–76, 99, 197; characterization, 65; in literature, 384; patios of, 65–66
Vela, Arqueles, 118, 140
Velasco, José María, 15
vendors, street, 290

Veríssimo, Érico, 61–62
Versailles, model for Washington, D.C., 46
Vicarino, Regina, 237
Vienna: as cosmopolitan ideal, 7; as typical modernist capital, 7
Villa, Francisco, 96, 99, 164
Villaurrutia, Xavier, 98, 112, 243–44; correspondence, 413; sexuality, 395–96
violence, 129, 166, 259; political 114, 169, 255, 286
Vivekananda, 252, 257, 261–62
vivencias (lived moments), xvi–xvii, 96
Vivero y Velasco, Rodrigo, 216
Viviani, Alessandro, 309
volcanoes, 61, 97, 121. *See also* Popocatepetl
vulgarity, 383. See also *palabrotas*

Wagner, Max Leopold, 373, 376–77, 391
Waite, C. B., 152, 169–70, 192–93
Walbach, Simeon B., 327
Walsh, Thomas F., 131
war, xviii, 7, 45; represented, 22; Russo-Japanese, 218; WWII, 218; and typhus, 313–14, 327
Washington, D.C., African-Americans, 57–59; centenary, 47; contrasted with MC, xxi, 43–62; Europeanization, 43; exceptionality, 53, mockery of, 49; modernization of, 50–52; population, 47, 49; as southern (U.S.) city, 55; as typical modernist capital, 7, 35; unfinished, 46–47, 49, 52
Weber, P. J., 34
welfare: public efforts, 300–301, 303; responsibility of church and private institutions, 300
"Westernization," 158, 212–13, 416
Weston, Edward, 67, 108, 117, 124, 132, 144, 158, 164, 168, 176, 180, 182, 189, 197, 201, 263
Wilde, Oscar, 103, 403
Wilder, Russell, 317, 320, 322, 323, 324
Wilson, Edmund, 134
wine, 141–42, 226
Wolbach, S. B., 339, 341